ESPECIALLY FOR YOU

ESPECIALLY FOR YOU

Finding a New Purpose
after Unspeakable Loss

KEN BRACK

FLOAT
TIDE
PUBLISHING

Composed in 11.5/14.5 Fournier MT Std with Gill Sans display at Hobblebush Design (www.hobblebush.com)

Printed in the United States of America

Cover design by Karen Alves
Front cover illustration by Amanda Brack
Back cover photo by Denise Brack
Author photo by Lou Goodman

Publisher's Cataloging-In-Publication Data
(Prepared by The Donohue Group, Inc.)

Names: Brack, Ken.
Title: Especially for you : finding a new purpose after unspeakable loss / Ken
    Brack.
Description: Kingston, Massachusetts : Float Tide Publishing, [2017]
Identifiers: ISBN 978-0-9992113-0-4 (paperback) | ISBN 978-0-9992113-1-1
    (ebook)
Subjects: LCSH: Loss (Psychology) | Posttraumatic growth. | Bereavement--
    Religious aspects. | Resilience (Personality trait) | Children--Death--
    Psychological aspects. | Consolation. | Brack, Ken--Family.
Classification: LCC BF575.G7 B73 2017 (print) | LCC BF575.G7 (ebook) |
    DDC 155.9/37--dc23

FLOAT TIDE PUBLISHING
8 Elm Street
Kingston, Massachusetts 02364
www.floattide.com

To my mother, Joan,
who left the front door unlocked
and coffee on, for the robbers.

CONTENTS

Preface   1

PART ONE: INTO THE RIP

  1. What Now?   7
  2. The Crash   15

PART TWO: WRENCHED OPEN

  3. The Best Qualities of Both   33
  4. Compelled to Act   49
  5. No More   67
  6. Grinder   93
  7. More to Do   107
  8. An Abundance of Caution   127
  9. If Not for Themselves   147

PART THREE: A WAY FORWARD

  10. Into Harm's Way   167
  11. Affirmation   191
  12. Best Man McGinty   217
  13. Finding Her Voice   247
  14. 9/12   273
  15. A Place of Service   299
  16. Heart Work   315

PART FOUR: THE DEPTHS OF HEALING

  17. Free-falling   341
  18. Podgórze   343
  19. Sounds in the Stones   357
  20. Liberation   375
  21. American Fishing   403
  22. Tattoo in the Mirror   425
  23. Reclaiming the Past   443
  24. Hope for a Broader Day   471

PART FIVE: THE COST

25. Wheels Off 501
26. Warped 515

PART SIX: UNSPEAKABLE GIFTS

27. Say His Name 529
28. Their Gifts 551

Acknowledgments 577
Notes 581
Permissions Acknowledgments 613
About the Author 615

PREFACE

Two a.m. remains our immutable moment. The flip clock radio is long gone, replaced by an iPhone on her nightstand and digital eyes perched above a TV in the cherry armoire. Quite often one of us lies awake on the hour—Denise sometimes half-soaked, loaded down with worry about work, or my brain clanging on some parallel overdrive.

When I look up, we're usually there again. Yanking a piece of the cover from one another, recognizing that despite the passing of time each night, this hour will never budge.

Tanya's call snapped us both awake that morning. There'd been a bad accident, and she told Denise she did not know if our son Mike was okay. He and a few buddies were out celebrating their friend P.J.'s twentieth birthday. She had pleaded with Mike to stay home with her and watch a movie on the couch, but he told Tanya his head would be on the pillow beside hers the next morning.

My wife jumped from our bed first. Always a mom's sixth sense, always the one half-awake waiting for his call. The first to hear tires crunch up our gravel driveway.

I got up right away. We began pacing the kitchen, dialing hospitals, back to Tanya, the police. Denise woke up one of the other boy's parents, the driver's, friends of ours from their soccer teams. "We haven't heard from them yet, but I'm sure they're fine," she told them. Seconds and minutes warped by without answers.

None of the hospitals said they had admitted our son.

They had stopped at P.J.'s house before heading out and his mom offered slices of cake. Cory, who was driving his dad's Jeep Cherokee, told her, "Don't worry, I'll bring him home safe." Yet someone had bought beer. They drank—Bud and Bud Light—on the forty-minute ride down to Providence and in a parking lot. There was a taste of Captain Morgan, and someone brought a little weed. They went into a bar that served underage college students and visiting teenagers at will.

Mike never made it back. Home, where he and I had begun to patch things up, and where his younger sister and brother looked up to him. Where his mom, who once snuggled with him in a cramped fifth-floor apartment, waited for his one-thrust bounce up the front steps, clicking open the door to burst in with no announcement required.

He was Bubaloo first. A little guy with Rag u-smeared cheeks and straw curls with twists at the ends like soft serve vanilla ready to melt on a languid summer evening. Then he was Wee-Dude with his buds. Shadow jumping with Jeff off the highway bridge, facing each other as they made a river plunge. Wise guys thumping to the 8 Mile. Michael Thomas Brack, who received his middle name from his maternal grandfather, Carroll, a restless man who bought his first house for not quite six thousand dollars while he was a supervisor setting foundation forms, and who kept working well into his eighties. He enjoyed boasting how when he was left in charge one time, Mike the toddler pooped his diaper. He took it off and hosed his grandson off outside the house. "And the grass grew really good there too," Carroll Thomas Fonseca would crack.

Mike was the child they invented plug covers for. He gave you the best giggle when you caught him for a belly kiss. Oldest of all the cousins, he did flips into his aunt's pool, horrifying the adults but rarely our nieces. One of them often says he could find trouble inside a cardboard box and still get out. Mike hopped boulders and scaled small crags with his mom and brother Chris near our camp in coastal Maine, one of the Lost Boys with his dog seeking treasure in a sea cave.

He was eighteen, a young man with shining green eyes. He loved his family, even while not always showing that to his parents. He was just starting out.

Perhaps I staggered for a moment across the rug downstairs. But I knew where to find out what happened. Reaching the State Police barracks in Foxborough, a sergeant came on the line. It may have been past 3:30 in the morning, and his voice grated like sleet on pavement. I thought I heard something sympathetic in the din.

He must have realized I was the one. Two passengers were thrown far from the Jeep on I-95, and they had trouble identifying them. There was something about finding a fake ID. One had been airlifted to Boston, one Peter Shaughnessy, Jr. But one of them died on impact, and they weren't sure who he was.

I faced the wall in a corner of our living room, our other children asleep upstairs, my wife about to wail. Something fell down deep inside of me, and I realized that life as we knew it would never be the same.

PART ONE

INTO THE RIP

There it was, the vortex.

—Joan Didion

1

WHAT NOW?

....

W hat do you do when the bottom suddenly drops out?
Whether it is the loss of a child, a partner, a parent, or another loved one, the capriciousness of their unexpected death levels us. We may not have said good night, goodbye, or I love you—and then they're gone. Perhaps a life's promise went unfulfilled. Big chunks of things were left undone or unsaid. We're left flailing about to pick up the pieces.

Most potently, reality is turned inside out following a catastrophic event. It's as if we're thrown into deep water, and finding ourselves in a rip current, shock gives way to despair and anger. Mistakes replay in time-lapse sequences that seem spliced out of sync while our questions smolder with self-blame. We may not have even appreciated all that we had—until his shoulder is no longer there to clasp, or until the momentum of one's life is dashed on the rocks.

You may be looking for answers just as my wife and I did after losing our son. You're staggering from someone's terrible choices or strafed by inexplicable violence. A life-ending disease has ground down your family, or perhaps an unimaginable calamity has claimed a soul mate. Your daughter wonders if she's been forgotten in the wake of her brother's death. You and your spouse suddenly find yourselves on different sides of a divide.

Screaming into the gale, the questions are both archaic and fresh: How could God let this happen? Why her? Why me?

What now?

The answers are complex and paradoxical, in moments pushing us one step ahead and then two back. Yet while winding along this tortuous new path most of us ultimately move forward.

We have to pick ourselves up. We have careers and responsibilities. The bills don't stop coming, and for most, it's simply what we must do. Yet while these things will still exist tomorrow, they also cease to matter in the same way. Why even get out of bed, except to find another reason to live?

How we answer those questions can transform our lives in positive ways. Not by "getting over it," but rather by trying to assemble meaning from our ordeals as we move through them. Like a quilter who stitches together used pieces of cloth (as my wife was able to do many years later in memory of our son), we can recast the fabric and perhaps the very fragments of our trials into something lasting. We recognize that the faint scent of a loved one or even his expression will not always stay with us. At first, we may not grasp how his gifts can continue to inform and sustain us.

This book is about what comes next and how we get there. You will meet a select group of people whose responses to really tough stuff shed light on outcomes that are possible, and palpable, as they step beyond themselves. Among the parents and siblings I meet, along with entrepreneurs, students, and others, many inch forward to reclaim their lives while wrestling with the confirmation of their worst fears.

My goal is that you will be uplifted by the stories woven together here. They offer us hope, which is a wellspring of healing. Climbing with grit, their narratives have an emotional intimacy that is sure to envelop you. Being among those who "get it" opens us to a new family with shared experiences to pass around in a safe setting. Their accounts may not even be what we expect. They are rarely expressions of pure selflessness, in the sense that stepping from one's own agony to affect others is a profound act of self-care and preservation.

In many respects their experiences are singular, yet these individuals and families also share a few common denominators. They primarily make some sense of unspeakable events by finding a new purpose, even striving to prevent strangers from being swept under by the same forces that took their loved ones. Their steps forward often extend beyond healthy coping responses to hardship, or showing resilience or optimism—attributes that are so often noticed in the aftermath of attacks, mass shootings, and other horrific events.

Less celebrated than these strengths is the recognition that people who struggle directly with their experiences often grow in profound ways that may improve the lot for others. Rather than retreating into a shell of bitterness or revenge seeking, they reach out to serve humanity. Instead of sidestepping their pain or numbing themselves, they remain open, expressive, and inquisitive. Rather than shuttering their daughter's room, they take up the causes she pursued, striving to keep her present in their lives.

This is never easy to do, and of course not everyone can. Nor does it minimize one's distress. In fact, growing in this way—which often includes making closer connections with others, finding greater personal strength, or going deeper in one's spiritual or faith journey—often co-exists in a striking synergy alongside continued pain and re-experienced trauma. Grappling with both is our attempt to balance and integrate these seeming opposites, finding small sparks of light even while weighed by grief or depression. Psychologists call this posttraumatic growth. I compare it to hiking switchbacks on steep terrain to reach an extraordinary new vista.

This isn't a book I would have ever chosen to write. Until we lost Michael in 2002, preceded by losing my mother to ovarian cancer almost three years earlier, I mainly observed grief and trauma from a distance. On occasion I marveled at people who reached out to neighbors and strangers following natural calamities; the tenacity of popular movements seeking justice from Chiapas to South Africa; and the intuitive response of many Americans during 9/11. In the years ahead I witnessed how many of my urban students persevered amidst street violence and poverty, some of whom wore buttons in tribute to relatives stolen away by gangs or disease. Yet like many others, as if watching a hockey game from behind plexiglass, I could easily turn away, the sweat and swears and ice sprays never quite reaching me. All that changed on a Friday morning two weeks before Thanksgiving.

As Denise and I wrestled with many of those questions, I became more attuned to how people rise from their ordeals. Not just surviving, but living fully again with a commitment to end an injustice or carry on a legacy to help others. Some became more compassionate; others shed material pursuits and people whose ambitions paled as superfluous before them; while a few struggled to reconcile the glaring paradoxes around them. What became most inspiring to me were those who picked themselves off the ground by giving back.

I wondered how long people could sustain that effort and what toll it exacts. Plunging back into those waters surely must come at a heavy cost.

A friend who runs a foundation in our community supporting residents who fall through the cracks—pretty much a one-stop social services agency—offered a version of this response to trauma. After the Boston Marathon bombings, when first responders and bystanders rushed over to aid innocent victims and fear spread through neighborhoods as the city shut down during the manhunt, another woman expressed to her the one marvel gleaned from the fury.

"After a tragedy, look for the helpers," Mary Rizzo reminded us. Not merely ogling and branding the strong.

When the world goes crazy, just look for the helpers.

On a midsummer night, Sandy Phillips' daughter went with her boyfriend to a midnight premier of *The Dark Knight Rises,* and a shooter killed her in a rampage. Immediately learning of the horror in Aurora, Colorado, Sandy and her husband Lonnie decided they had to do something.

They turned their sights and hearts toward enacting sensible gun control. They pushed for expanding background checks and eliminating exceptions that enable unrestricted gun show sales. Not six months later, they flew to Newtown offering comfort to other families following the Sandy Hook shooting. After the Navy Yard shootings the following fall, Sandy Phillips would not falsely promise anyone that grief gets easier. She and her husband could no longer go to the movies. The smell of popcorn repulsed her. They became advocates for finding meaning.

She advised other families: "Find an outlet that you can pour yourself into to help the process."

"We have a purpose," she told a radio host. "We don't want to see other parents go through what we've had to go through."

We have a purpose.

Several years after Mike's death, while connecting with people whose circumstances seemed to be very different from mine, quite often I found we really weren't that far apart. Our quests as fellow seekers led to new places and fresh questions. While I became fixated for some time on addressing underage drinking and driving, this intersected with adults in distant states who sought meaning and closure for their own tragedies. Each of us at some point had been feeling around in the dark asking, "What the hell do you expect of me now?"

As a longtime journalist, I knew where to look, what to ask. I would follow nearly every lead, every suggested contact, every scrap uncovered or laid out before me. I had already come upon enough bloodstained wrecks, once observing blue bodies being pulled through a hole in the ice.

As a grieving parent, I also recognized what not to ask. When and where not to go. Doors opened because I knew when it was appropriate to reach to the other side. A dad who lost his baby girl would talk to me because he understood that I got it. A mom in Fort Worth who began her life's work just a few years after cancer claimed her son welcomed my wife and I into her home. I listened to many people first. Three hundred or more, often in numerous conversations spanning several years. Gathering their stories and remembrances, and sometimes sharing mine. Striving to attest to their desire, which so often feels crushed, that their loved ones go forward with them.

The catalyst to embark upon this was meeting a Holocaust survivor who spoke at the high school where I taught English in 2008. A native of Kraków, Poland, Nathan Offen had felt abandoned by humanity during the twentieth century's worst atrocity. The Nazis murdered most of his family, more than fifty relatives, and my impression was that Offen retained an impenetrable shell. He explained to and admonished our students that while he did not know exactly why he survived, his hatred of the Germans fed him during months of systemic starvation. Hearing some of Offen's story and contemplating my students' queries ratcheted my own concerns. I wanted to know whether he had been able to heal at all, and how this might work.

I set out to interview Nathan and his two other surviving brothers the following year, relying again on the familiar modes a reporter uses. Yet my anguish as a dad and the few wedges I had yet to reconcile drove me much further.

While attempting to figure out *how* this healing and renewal actually works, the question *why* would not really factor in. The answers to that are both mystical and relatively clear-cut, as faith traditions across many cultures have long held that pain and suffering are prerequisites for the highest levels of spiritual growth and attainment. This resonates in much of our greatest literature and music, in all of the arts. It's what God requires of us. It's the reality you deal with on the ground floor before you can step into the elevator: Naked shall I return.

Regardless of our beliefs, we're all expected to move forward. Whether through avoidance, plunging into new projects, sheltering others, or finding anything to stay somewhat sane. *Keep on keeping on.*

With time, and perhaps traces of grace, most people's feelings of abandonment will abate; synthesis and reclamation are possible.

But that doesn't make it any easier to accomplish. The real question remains *how*.

Edie Lutnick lost her brother Gary during 9/11. Since then she has helped steward a charity that reaches thousands of families devastated by tornadoes, fire, and other disasters. Her life's work became bringing people together through the Cantor Fitzgerald Relief Fund. In one clean stroke, Edie nails what this has meant to her.

"I credit the families for healing me," she says. "Because when you have a purpose greater than yourself, that is when you heal. That is what I live by."

A purpose greater than yourself.

Gail Minger lives on Florida's Gulf coast, seemingly worlds away from the small Kentucky state college where her son died in a dorm fire set by an arsonist in 1998. Minger is able to keep Michael present in her life by advocating for fire safety, and she has become a preeminent proponent of this cause. Gail crosses the country to impress her message—her mission—upon parents and students, lawmakers and administrators.

"There are days I am sad and there are days this is rewarding," she says, "but this is kind of what I do."

Sitting on our couch one day many years later, Denise asked me, "What is it that makes people grab that lifeline when others can't?"

In the decade following our son's loss there would be recurring tumult and wounds ripped open.

We just wanted him back. Our life. Denise came home and sometimes expected to see him in the kitchen. We sought solace, craving signs of Mike's presence.

I bought a woodstove shortly after his memorial service. We had built an addition on our house the previous summer with a cozy rustic room that looks out to perennial gardens and the woods. Out back there's lots of white pine and a stand of beech atop a small ridge, where sometimes I'll go at dusk especially early in a snowfall; the trees' copper leaves shimmer in a light patter that sounds like waves lapping a jasper beach. The room has a vaulted ceiling with mellowing exposed beams, and built-in bookshelves nesting some of our treasured texts along with a sweet stereo system. This space also functions as a small studio for Denise, with her oils on a corner table alongside stacks of canvases, some that she is still too shy to bring out. There's a large old redwood-stained easel we found at a barn sale in Rome, Maine, living up north when the kids were little and money was tight. The handsome DutchWest stove on the hearth is a keeper. It fits twenty-inch logs and nearly heats the entire downstairs, and during frequent power outages has more than earned its way.

This room became our retreat from the get-go. We fell back on the scuffed couch, sagging with its cheap sepia throw cover, uncoiling on Friday nights over drinks. We watched the fire through the stove's window as the day closed in, sometimes clinging to one another as if we might otherwise spiral down. Denise was already the glue holding things together: keeping the house going for our kids and supporting her parents, all while nurturing her first graders. I did whatever I could in the midst of a career transition toward teaching, finishing graduate school, and working part-time. Several years later, she acted on a vision to help other grieving families by creating a nonprofit bereavement center with support groups, counselors, and wellness programs.

We did this together, usually in sync, at other times scrapping with every fiber to make it all work.

In moments I wondered how both of us would make it through the next year. Bits of information and gut-wrenching visits and phone calls with bad advice got tossed into an unkempt filing cabinet. Yet on those nights, after Chris and Amanda went to bed we held on, sometimes playing the music we loved loud on the stereo, dancing to Carlos or Jerry and soloing air guitar chops; other times having to tamp it shut. It was all a blur.

One day her primary care doctor warned us how many couples split after losing a child. Take care of each other, she advised. Be aware of blame, and not giving each other space to grieve differently. Or feeling things the other does not. Watch for the gaps, and try to close what needs to be bridged. Recognize the signs in one another.

We had no inkling of what to do, other than getting up again the next day—though on many mornings she wanted to crawl back under the covers once the kids caught the school bus.

We just wanted him back.

2

THE CRASH

His mom never got to say goodbye to her firstborn. She never saw Michael's wiry face again, his smooth jaw, the few dark hairs pricking from his chin like rebel strays. The medical examiner, or a nurse—someone—wouldn't let us see him. There was no viewing at the hospital or funeral home.

No one really explained why. Perhaps Trooper Suarez tried to in a halting way. He may have intimated how bad it was, since Mike's body had been broken in two. We would not learn this until four months later when I was handed the accident report in a courthouse hallway. I had to shield it from Denise for several days until Friday night, when her week of teaching first graders and parents' conferences had finished. Then I could bring it out as we huddled on the couch near the woodstove and drank ourselves numb.

That was our refuge on many of those nights—taking off our game faces from the week in a space we fell upon to vent and listen and hold each other. With no idea of what we were now doing or facing. Perhaps I should have been able to read between the lines. A friend's wife who worked in the emergency room where one of the boys was rushed mentioned later that some of the EMTs were shaken up at the scene; it was the worst crash they'd ever come upon.

We didn't push for all the details at first. It was enough just to hold on to anything that had ballast. A filter in our gutted brains managed to screen inflows of facts.

Besides, logic was mere flotsam. There was nothing left of it.

We drove up Route 3 to Boston Medical Center in near silence with our kids later that morning, a pit widening in our guts. Mike's girlfriend Tanya and her mother came along, and I found it hard to look back at anyone. Denise and I may have held hands. In a basement room we sat with the Shaughnessys on plastic scoop chairs, and the state troopers told us what they had found.

P.J. did not survive either; he was thrown even further than Michael and had been airlifted to the city. Everyone loved P.J., a talented junior league hockey player who lived the mantra, "Skate hard on every shift." Yet Cory, the driver who had promised P.J.'s mother they would get back safely after celebrating her son's twentieth birthday, was alive upstairs with a broken leg.

A fourth friend, Brendan, crawled out from the front passenger side of the Jeep. I could not process much of what the troopers said; many years later, I still cannot picture my other son and daughter sitting in that dank room. They were beside us. Yet I don't recall the sound of their tears, nor the rise of their chests holding back. Denise saw blood on one of the trooper's boots and almost spoke up. I did not, rising instead to get outside for some air. Somehow we went up to see Cory's parents, who were friends.

We did not see him.

Phones began ringing off the hook as the grey November chill clamped on to us. Two sons' grainy portraits riddled the front pages, confusion swirling over which bar they had gone to. A news crew waited at the end of our driveway. Unthinkable holidays bore down. Denise's sister coming from Florida, mine driving down from Vermont. I saw myself in Filene's buying a suit, heard an answer to a reporter's call, confiding how Mike lit up a room with his smile. Before long Denise would flee into the school bathroom to cry, her friend Deb checking on her young charges.

I underestimated for the first but not the last time how this impacted my wife. I could not get my arms completely around this, and then ten and even fourteen years later, while sifting through and writing yet again, peeling back layers as if tracing each ring of our family tree for the first time, I still didn't get it all.

In the wretched moment no parent ever expects to be in, Denise could not fully release her child. She could never kiss his forehead as if laying him down again, or feel his young man's energy in a hug. Her worst fears—of losing another child, losing her partner, or the one that seemed most real, being deprived of a connection with Mike—these came like hot flashes in the dark. Over time, each of us, his sister and brother and dad, would feel some of this torque.

In the foothills of western Maine there is a small mountain we used to hike with the kids when we lived outside of Augusta. Mike was five or six years old, active and itchy, a little squirt who got into trouble on the school bus when a girl his age asked to see his, and he showed her. One fall day after climbing Tumbledown Mountain, he and I checked out the views near its little pond, the White Mountains rising in the southwest. "Take a look out there," I said to him. "This is your life, there are no limits. You can go as far as you want to go." *You can do it.*

Yet it didn't all come to pass. And I would not get to embrace my first son and make good for my mistakes. To say the words that perhaps he needed to hear. Or convey my belief that, hey, you're going in the right direction, and you are absolutely going to get there.

But I did get to talk with him a few days before the crash. Since he was living with Tanya at her dad's house and working full time, we didn't see him very much. Over the phone I asked if he'd help me run a soccer clinic for Amanda's indoor team, and he agreed to. He told me that he missed the game itself. Mike was an electric player in high school—quick, tough, and prescient in his ability to see the field and thread a ball through. If an opponent beat him to a ball, he roared back, pestering and battling the other guy until he stripped it or disrupted the play.

The weekend before he died, Mike came to Amanda's last outdoor game of the season. I was not there, but he stretched out on the grass in the sun with his mother, a blade of green stuck between his teeth. He'd been working as a grill cook at Friendly's and talked about taking classes that winter at a community college, or moving to Florida with Tanya and starting school.

"Your beautiful smile, you were laughing and telling me stories," his mom wrote to him a few weeks later. "I wish I could remember every detail of that conversation, but I didn't know it would be our last."

Denise read *Goodnight Moon* to him one last time at his funeral. Her voice throbbed, yet she had the presence to stand and finish a story he loved. She would not have forgiven herself otherwise. I stood beside her, unaware of the long struggle facing us. *Goodnight stars.*

Flowing through the church sanctuary, Mike's classmates filled in behind the pulpit where the choir usually sits, and old friends of ours stood by the doors. The scuffed plank floor of the Congregational church groaned with the weight. I looked up into sunlight straining through a window, not yet able to even ask, why us? Wisps of snow drifted outside as Chris helped Mike's friends carry his brother's casket. Chris was only a sophomore and stepping up—who could fathom this sight? At the grave my own brother began singing "Amazing Grace" in his surging bass, the same hymn we'd only recently offered my mother on a bright December morning. Someone handed me a sheet of lyrics. As if I had ever needed them.

There was cold rain and bringing fold-up chairs from the fellowship hall to our house. Raking soggy oak leaves, the last ones to fall, just to get outside again and breathe. To do the one freaking thing I had any measure of control over: pull a cap down, keep my eyes down and rake hard, clearing the spindly, crappy hardening lawn on which leaves were stamped and trampled by hoar-dust.

I remember the sound of her heart rattled by the gusts. "All I want is my son back," she cried. "Is that asking too much?"

I remember not ever letting go.

Chris and Amanda kept us grounded much of the time. Our daughter was in middle school, teaching herself to draw with Corel Painter and beginning to write stories about outcasts and boy wizards moving through contorted Middle Earth-like landscapes. Her brother—always deliberate, so different than Mike as he built K'NEX towers and Lego houses for hours on end—joined the high school business club. His friends were the tennis team guys, those in-between geek types, far from the poker-playing varsity dudes who pulled off parties at their families' summer cottages. If not perhaps for our kids, more than once Denise imagined jumping into her car to get away. She said she might call me from some hotel down south. We held fast to them.

Cory promised Sharon Shaughnessy that he would bring her son and ours home.

Hours later, lying on a grassy shoulder by the guardrail, in between screaming as a bone protruded from his thigh, Cory told two people who stopped to help that he was the driver. Minutes later he told a state trooper that Mike was driving his father's red Jeep Cherokee.

It was a Thursday night, November 14th, P.J.'s twentieth birthday. Mike, Cory, and Brendan Carey had each graduated from high school the previous spring—while Peter Shaughnessy Jr. graduated from Tilton Academy prep school in New Hampshire. They'd known each other since at least freshman year at Silver Lake Regional High School, our home district south of Boston, where the three of them excluding Brendan played soccer together. While P.J. left for Tilton, Mike and Cory continued playing together through high school, with Mike starting on varsity first among his friends as a junior. Cory's dad, Dan, coached their spring league teams and we had spent some memorable weekends with the Scanlons at state tournaments cheering the guys on. The four of them set out for Providence from the Shaughnessys, and their destination was a no-brainer.

For underage teens from greater Boston, Rhode Island, and eastern Connecticut, the city's college bars and clubs were a party magnet. An hour's drive from Cape Cod or north of Worcester was nothing for them. Bring your fake IDs, or try it without one. Eighteen-plus nights were free-for-alls. Being under twenty-one—the legal drinking age—meant squat, and kids everywhere knew it. They drove over thinking, *No way will that happen to me*. Cops made arrests and tried to get the sleaziest and most dangerous places closed. Yet bartenders, managers, and to some extent, city officials looked the other way. The guys went to a place near the Rhode Island School of Design campus that too often was a Wild West scene for hip-hop wannabes.

Mike's girlfriend Tanya had a bad feeling about this, and pleaded with him not to go. She was working that night, while he had it off.

At least two of them had fake IDs, the state police would tell us later, although it was never clear who actually did. We never thought Mike carried one, as Tanya said he did not. Cory admitted he drank two beers and two shots in the bar and I'm sure that Mike, P.J., and Brendan also had their share. A small piece of me would still like to picture him there, undoubtedly laughing and giving his friends shit. It's not a vision I can hold for long.

They may have cracked open more beers in the parking lot before leaving. Providence is a fifty-minute ride from our area at normal speeds, which means they stayed there perhaps past 1:30 a.m. Cory drove back on I-95. He barely made it halfway home.

Cory Scanlon was never charged with operating under the influence. Some hours later he was given a blood alcohol test, which registered 0.07 BAC, just below the legal limit.

Mike and P.J. were in the back, P.J. leaning toward Brendan in the front talking hockey, his passion. He was taking a year before college to play for a junior hockey league team, the Walpole Junior Stars. Cory wasn't paying attention, and both P.J. and Brendan yelled at him to slow down. They didn't ask, they yelled, Brendan told Denise and I at our house maybe a week later. But Cory kept turning around as the Jeep went up to 105 miles an hour. They "became nervous with the very high rate of speed and at times, (Cory) not watching the road ahead," state police said in their incident report. No one wore a seat belt.

It was 2:00 a.m. as the Jeep sped past an exit. Cory came upon a white truck in the center lane and veered left trying to avoid it, then swerved right and lost control, crossing all the lanes and smashing into a guardrail. As the Jeep rolled over, Mike was thrown sixty-two feet. P.J. went 140 feet to the other side of the highway. Cory landed twenty feet away. By some fate, Brendan was able to crawl out of the wreck that landed on its top with only scrapes.

Somehow standing and walking around, Brendan told a trooper he could not find some of his friends. Two motorists were trying to help P.J., who was still barely alive, his body broken. Trooper Suarez went to him on the other side of the highway. Finally, he located Mike beyond the guardrail to the right, calling the medical examiner. Brendan identified Cory as the driver.

Mike died instantly hitting that guardrail. My son's body was severed and no one had the balls to tell us, though perhaps now that my tunnel vision has been eviscerated—like a tree trunk long since split in a thundering crack, and pummeled to the ground—I might consider that was an appropriate thing to do.

Viewing him was out of the question; the opportunity was taken away from us. A mom and dad unable to see their oldest child one last time. A few years later I developed an occasional stammer that I choked back during staff meetings and conversations. Perhaps this was why.

We limped through Michael's service and P.J.'s Mass as winter closed in. Thanksgiving arrived at our house, both our families crushed and fully present, attempting to slog through the dry remnants of tradition. The creamed onions seemed overdone, and I don't recall who cooked the bird. My father led grace, robust in his mid-sixties not three years after losing his companion, his Joan-o, straining to now deal with the death of his oldest grandchild. He paused for both Mike and Nana Joanie as if ushering in a new rite. The holiday I had grown to fully appreciate—once catching glimpses of my grandfather's sprawling clan at the Haskell farm beside the Merrimack River, shooting hoops with rangy cousins after dinner and trying plum pudding baked with suet in a coffee can—it could never be the same again.

A day or two later I was raking leaves once more when some guy I don't even know from down the street stopped his car. He rolled down his window. He had heard about our son and told me he was sorry.

Sorry? What does that even mean? If you tell me *he's in a better place* I'm going to scream.

We lingered a moment but I had nothing to say, turning away to swear under my breath and bear down again.

Mike's unfilled stocking hung by the hearth in the weeks ahead, and we weren't sure what to do with it. Many of his boys showed up on Christmas Eve, crammed into our kitchen as I went downstairs to grab beers. Maybe I wasn't supposed to do this, but locking eyes we raised a toast. Later that night, carols hung like a dirge inside the frostbitten country church as if suspended by ancient shades. Songs that for me had once resonated with other childhood memories, my mother and her good friend leading carols at nursing homes, instead felt suffocating as the air pressed down inside the dim sanctuary. As we left in a crowd of their classmates, we saw that Cory sat in the back with crutches and his parents.

More than a decade later, a couple who had just lost their son asked us how we got through those first holidays. I may have stammered again, for I do not really know. We did it for our other children. Opening gifts early, frying bacon with pancakes, then retreating to another couch likely to watch *The Fellowship of the Ring*, any epic that could take us far away. We stoked that woodstove. We did fill Mike's stocking, and soon began doing other rituals for him.

Soon after those first holidays we received advice from Denise's primary care doctor. Laying out a glimpse of the fractures many couples go through, she gently urged us to allow each other space to grieve differently, while taking great care of one another. I forget the exact statistic she mentioned, but supposedly about half or even a larger percentage of marriages were said to break apart in the wake of such an ordeal. We looked at each other in the closet-sized examination room, trusting one another implicitly. We had already lost so much, and there was no way I would not be there for her. Nor would either of us put Chris and Amanda through that.

Before we knew what had actually happened in November—how fast Cory was driving, his denials, the guys yelling at him to slow down—we began to reach out. Before the gears of the court crushing plant fired up in advance of my own shock giving way to anger, I had an inkling to step beyond myself.

We received this card from him with flowers: "Mike was my best friend and I will miss him so much. No one will be able to replace him. I will never forget him. He will live in my memory forever. Love, Cory."

There was confusion in the days following November 15, 2002 about which club the guys went to. Some of the newspapers and TV stations reported it was a place called The Bar. But Brendan Carey set us straight about this and a few other things.

He came over to our house one afternoon, sitting on an ottoman in a corner of the living room. Like Mike he was mid-sized and athletic, plus square-jawed and intense looking. That Brendan had survived physically intact astounded both of us. Looking into his eyes, Denise formed an impression that he was lost, or perhaps something had been vacated. He seemed dazed to me, and rightly so.

Speaking almost dryly about what happened, Brendan was not without any emotion, but I had to wonder if he had begun erecting a wall to shield his fears from us, or from anyone. When we met occasionally in the years ahead, I caught myself trying to penetrate his hardened eyes and taut face. He apparently argued with the trooper, who was unable to believe that Carey had been in the Jeep. Brendan finally located P.J., who was barely clinging to life. We wondered about the terrible burden he shouldered. Like Mike he was eighteen, and while I had not really known Brendan before the crash, I felt that we were listening to an enigma.

Quietly dismissing some of the rumors, he told us they partied at another place called Bar One.

Located not far from the Rhode Island State House at the foot of College Hill, Bar One was a short walk from the RISD and Brown University campuses. By Thursday night as the weekend revels cranked up it usually morphed into a dance club with a DJ spinning house, hip-hop and R&B, techno and funk. But it wasn't mainly a destination for avant-garde fashionistas and Russian literature majors.

The club was just one of the city's open valves attracting a steady supply of underage drinkers. They bragged about it on My Space: IDs often weren't checked, so you might be just eighteen and find a spot near the bar until you could barely stand. No doors on the bathroom stalls—quite the dive, one guy posted on thisplaceiknow.com—but *there's always going to be a price to pay*. It would be a sweet, sweet time.

The pump sucked them in and spit some out.

It was operated by a well-known nightclub owner whose joints around Providence repeatedly flaunted the law. By the time Mike and his friends arrived there in 2002, the scene was often out of control. Police made repeated arrests for underage drinking and disorderly conduct, while also responding to reports of gunshots, stabbings, and assaults both inside and out. High school girls were served shots; the security staff and bartenders neglected to issue wristbands and stamps to identify underage patrons; doormen stopped using counters during weekends when crowds sometimes doubled its fire code capacity limit. The result was often ugly. Including teens, defiant and jacked, getting behind the wheel.

Yet the city never revoked the club's license. As I would find in my forays to investigate Bar One's record, appraising underage drinking at clubs across the city, it got far worse. Enough to make one retch again a decade later.

Somehow Denise and I kept our heads above water. She returned to her class of first graders after Christmas break, fine-tuning units on penguins and weather. There were daily lessons in reading and math, and she loved circle time with them, especially in the mornings when they did a yoga-like sun salutation with stretched arms, and she asked each child to express something positive about the day. Soon there would be a coveted rainforest unit with students researching an animal in the library, and each one creating a puppet to help introduce facts about that animal to the class.

Her kids had been told about Mike, and as little ones do, they came to her without the stiffness of adults. Sensing when she was sad, a few asked her about him, such as when Denise told a story that involved our son to introduce a unite on bats.

Mike had once found one in a toilet and saved its life. She couldn't resist sharing the tale; it reminded her of him and made her laugh. Then it was back to managing the class and following the curriculum, copying handouts and reorganizing her room in the afternoons. Her charges were heaven sent, helping Denise stay focused during long fogged-in stretches. Walking into her basement-level room in the old brick-covered school, she had to pretend everything was okay. "I just did my job," she reflects. "But they kept me going." Yet by that spring, it was becoming too much and her principal supported her request to teach four days a week, relieved by a substitute teacher.

I was in the midst of a career change from business publishing, having decided a year before Mike's death to go into teaching. Finishing graduate education classes at Northeastern University while cutting back hours at work, I took courses on developing units and lessons along with eclectic literary topics like comparing Greek tragedies.

One night two weeks after the crash I returned to campus. Propped against another hard chair as a professor offered her condolences, I realized that I existed in some new realm. Her words passed through me as if I was watching from the ceiling, untethered and yet unable to leave, like a trapped balloon nudging the wall as it rises. Everyone around me seemed to have heard about it; their eyes were fixed on my back or avoiding the guy who had straggled back to class. Later that winter I got connected with my future school and its visionary principal. Walking out after observing an English class and occasionally tutoring a Korean-born student with her writing, I felt more like a pretender than someone about to be thrown into an urban classroom.

I made the first phone calls by that woodstove, seeking answers about underage drinking and whether anyone was holding sleazy bar owners accountable. My reporter's instincts kicked in, and taking notes on a legal pad provided a wedge of familiar ground. I wasn't exactly aware of why I was doing this—was it an attempt to cope, or was I only stoking the churning in my gut? Warmed by the fire, I just leaned into what I knew.

This was about far more than gathering information though. Everything would be subjective from here on in, filtered through the hole in our life, leading to new and sharper questions.

Wondering about the under-twenty-one scene in Providence, I spoke with a former state attorney general who advocated for the families of drunk-driving victims, and someone from Rhode Island Mothers Against Drunk Driving (MADD). I asked the Providence licensing board for records of Bar One's liquor license violations and received several dozen pages of citations, police reports, and board minutes with the dispositions. Yet it was too soon to wade far into that sludge.

Turning to our home turf, an investigator at the state alcoholic beverages commission described the problems here in the Bay State, and their attempts to suspend licenses of those bad apples. Our local state representative was eager to help in any way. Denise and I visited a local MADD office (actually located just over our town line), meeting a father who had lost two sons. Covering a large wall inside, he showed us a victims' quilt with faded photos and names going back several decades. My senses itched, as the room was dark and the hanging quilt smelled like damp towels. Adding Mike to this felt overwhelming. We excused ourselves.

Yet Denise and I kept talking about other families. What could we do to help another from going through this? At some point, she realized that kids at Mike and Chris's high school needed to see that quilt, to take in how many lives had been lost.

One day I met a grandfather of a thirteen-year-old girl whose family shared too much in common with us. Melanie Powell was with friends crossing the street on the way to a birthday party when a driver who had too many glasses of chardonnay at a local bar struck her. After Melanie's life was stolen, Ron Bersani began advocating for tougher laws and sentences for repeat offenders. Bersani never seemed to give up on this, and we shared a brief cry when we met at his office.

He showed me pictures of dragonflies, which had become a vital symbol of Melanie's spirit to her family. We, too, had been noticing dragonflies everywhere: on Mike's granite bench well after the first hard frost, and swarms of them while hiking a coastal headland. And always out around our house. Crazy translucent green ones, royal blue, even maroon. Perched on his mother's leg in the sunshine, which she interpreted as a brief sign of his presence. Leaving Bersani's office, I felt awakened to the ties binding families like ours.

We got away that winter for a few days in Florida where Denise's sister, Lisa, lives. Our daughter was sick and had to stay indoors for two days, and a pipe bomb went off in a parking lot, unsettling Denise. Beers eventually flowed on the beach while Amanda and Chris hung out with their cousins. Yet looking back at pictures from Naples, most striking is the freshness of grief that hung on our faces. One afternoon, a small sperm whale beached itself in Pelican Bay where my dad had a condo, and Denise and Lisa rushed to it, trying to hydrate and sooth the sick baby. A crowd gathered with many attempting to do the same. I went over as well, and while trying to fathom what illness may have brought the whale ashore, I found myself silently seething at others who stood around yakking in their inaction and trifling ignorance.

Another day we released balloons for Mike alongside the Gulf. We hoped this would help our youngest nieces, and all of us, doing something for him that felt just a little better. Around this time Denise wrote in a journal we had started, "I think you are holding me, giving me one of your awesome hugs. I keep thinking that you will come through that front door and [our dogs] Nikki and Ginger will be so excited. Ginger of course will have to pee on you."

What mattered most was realizing how much Mike was loved. The stories that began rolling out in our kitchen on Christmas Eve, the notes left by gals and guys in a little book at his grave. We learned how helpful he had been around Tanya's house, and all of the people who wouldn't forget: his soccer coach, a friend's mom who steered him through confirmation class, young people he'd touched whom we never knew. When passing through Foxborough on I-95, my uncle blasted the air horn of his flatbed truck, or stopped by the roadside memorial to pay his respects.

Our worst fears eased a few notches, knowing that he had been moving in a positive direction following the family clashes that punctuated his finishing high school. Yet when out alone taking a run or skiing around the cranberry bogs behind our house, I felt something else. The torrent of Mike's unfulfilled life gnawed at me.

We had so far to go.

PART TWO

WRENCHED OPEN

There is only one thing I dread: not to be worthy of my sufferings.
—Fyodor Dostoyevsky

DRIVING TO WORK WITH THE NEWS ON, I heard Connie Clery's voice hush for the first time.

She was talking about every parent's worst nightmare: losing a child. A brief, tortured sigh came over the airwaves as she paused to conjugate a memory of nearly twenty-four years. It was the morning when her daughter Jeanne was discovered strangled in her dormitory bed. What happened, she said, "was so amazingly unreal.

"She didn't have an enemy in the world," Mrs. Clery continued, exhaling again to unknot the next thought. "If it happened to Jeanne, it could certainly happen to someone else, and that's why I decided I had to do something."

Her last statement attached itself to me, and I have been unable to shake it ever since.

Long swept under the rug to preserve the reputations of academia, the alarming number of unreported sexual assaults, and the systemic mishandling of those that are reported, had become a public issue in 2010. Yet for many students, the self-blame, recriminations, and a sense of being betrayed by their college were far from over. And here was a mom from the Philadelphia suburbs, straining and vital, a woman who had stood up to do something about this mess.

Along with her late husband, Howard, Connie Clery was the one chiefly responsible for first bringing this issue into the light. The Clerys forced colleges across the country to disclose campus crimes, and they helped lay the groundwork for better treatment of student sexual assault survivors, a scourge that has not relented.

I just happened to dial up NPR rather than my favorite folk-roots station heading to work that winter morning. Yet hearing Connie Clery's voice did not feel like a sheer coincidence.

This couple had set out to prevent another family from going through the same ordeal they faced. Denise and I had tried to respond to Michael's loss in a similar way, albeit on a much smaller scale. Along with some other parents we brought drunk-driving prevention programs to our school district. I wondered about the enormity and toll of what the Clerys had attempted to accomplish. How the heck did they do this? And what had that road looked like?

Learning about the Clerys' efforts during the next several years, the complexity of their response drilled into me. It involved something more than showing some of those erstwhile attributes we often hold up when people are well equipped to deal with tragedy. Both parents were certainly resilient and hardy, but this was not really about that. Nor was it about being optimistic or having those other skill sets that help one manage or even rise beyond measure in a crisis.

There was something deeper to this, and I was on to it without knowing the name or much about its psychological underpinnings. Each of the parents, and to some extent their two adult sons, had to battle the trauma of their daughter and sister's violent death directly—repeatedly plunging back into the vile details and widespread ramifications that rippled out for other students and families. That very struggle was also the stained, despised ground floor that became crucial for their growth. The parents, at least, never ran away from what they felt they had to do.

This came at some personal cost, but for the rest of us, it brought tangible gains. Connie and Howard were the first to break open a culture of silence and sexual entitlement as they led a drive to hold colleges accountable.

Thinking back to when I was an undergraduate, I remembered a fleeting conversation with a young woman who had also gone to my high school. Seeing me on campus one day, she asked to speak with me alone.

I barely knew her, and feel ashamed that today I cannot even recall her name. She told me she had been raped. I believe it was a guy she knew, as is most often the case. She seemed to have nowhere to turn; speaking about it was obviously brutal, and my blurred memory is that it hadn't been that long since the assault. I must have seemed trustworthy or been sympathetic, and hopefully offered something supportive such as asking if she had spoken to anyone at the women's center. Yet I don't believe I offered to accompany her there. I wonder whether she ever got help, or bottled this up. Being idealistic and naive about these things, I was shocked.

She walked on, and I never saw her again.

3

THE BEST QUALITIES OF BOTH

To approach the marble altar, Howard Clery maneuvered himself exactly as he had every day for the past forty years. He locked his right leg brace and pushed himself to a standing position. Wielding two canes with his thick forearms slipped into a cuff atop each one, he rounded the podium. He looked out at six hundred mourners, each one stunned by his daughter's murder.

His voice quivered for a moment, but the steel penetrating Clery's eyes would soon have to be reckoned with.

Jeanne, his adored youngest child, their only girl, was gone. Unlike her older brothers, she alone would stand up to her father, and he loved her for that especially. Her life had been ripped away four days earlier, apparently by a burglar who entered Jeanne's third-floor dormitory room while she slept, then raped and strangled her. Police arrested a student whose friends turned him in after he bragged about killing a girl in a rage. Her camera and wallet and other items, including her roommate's jewelry, were found in the man's bedroom a few blocks from the Lehigh University campus.

At first, the school offered its support for Jeanne's family in that automatic way people expect when a tragedy occurs. Lehigh's president called with his condolences. He called again two days later saying he was sorry to report that the suspect was another student.

Within a few days both Howard and his wife Connie felt the university circling its wagons. Administrators who talked to the media appeared to duck responsibility for lapses in dorm security. There were no surveillance cameras or electronic devices to swipe ID cards at the time, and no guards were assigned to Stoughton House, Jeanne's residence hall. Students in the co-ed dorm routinely jammed paper towels into the locks of the main entrance and stairwell doors to make way for friends and pizza deliveries. When one Lehigh higher-up insinuated that such crimes were the fault of the students' negligence to keep the doors locked, the Clerys were astonished. *How could the university take this position?* Howard wondered. *How could an intruder walk unobstructed on to an all-girls floor?*

Howard Clery regarded the strained faces filling Saint Thomas of Villanova Church. Jeanne's funeral Mass was held on the Villanova University campus, close to the Clerys' home in Bryn Mawr, one of Philadelphia's exclusive suburbs in what is known as the Main Line. It was less than a two-hour drive to Lehigh in Bethlehem, amidst the hilly steel country north of the city. Connie attended Mass there regularly, while Howard had not been to church in nearly two decades. With its twin spires and fieldstone facade, the church was modeled on a French Gothic masterpiece. Yet no one was admiring its looming stained glass windows on this murky spring morning. The air inside was stilted, a hint of moisture diffusing throughout the nave. Almost everyone was numb.

He did not know them, but Clery certainly took note of Lehigh's president and the student affairs administrator sitting near the front. Their comments had already pierced his shock and drawn his ire. Where was the conciliatory tone? He thought Lehigh had scarcely made an admission that it needed to improve security. This was a great injustice to all of its students.

Then he dropped the hammer, speaking directly to the university's representatives. Clery set the bar, if not the tone, for what was to come during the next quarter of a century. He and his wife were about to set out attempting to prevent other families from enduring the same hell they now faced.

"Have you forgotten to attempt to screen out the rapists, the morally perverted, the drug addicts, the dormitory thieves?" he asked.

A few people squirmed in their pews. But those who knew Howard Clery, who had been crippled by polio as a boy and was articulate and not at all afraid to be combative, were not surprised. His wrath was just beginning its ascent, and he never fully let go.

Fresh from an Easter week break, Jeanne Ann Clery turned in a short essay for her English class on a drizzly Friday. Its title was "Sex Roles and Society," and the nineteen-year-old had formed some strong opinions on the topic.

"It is a fact that our society is not truly androgynous," the freshman began in her paper. "The old prejudices and stereotypes between the sexes do exist. Men are still considered and expected to be macho, tough, unemotional, and in control. Women, although they have made leeway in society, are still considered and expected to be passive, sensitive, nurturing, and emotional." Yet despite these assumed roles, Jeanne declared, "I have not been affected in the least . . . due to my upbringing and scholastic background."

It was April 4, 1986. She was struggling a bit academically, despite having gone to a prestigious private girls' school near her home in Bryn Mawr. Jeanne seemed to know she needed to work harder. Several factors had weighed heavily in her selection of Lehigh, which was known as a solid mid-sized liberal arts college, its chief strength being a highly regarded engineering school. She was a talented tennis player and the university's tennis coach had recruited her.

A high-ranked amateur in the Middle States Tennis Association, Jeanne also played with Connie in mother-daughter tournaments. The duo actually competed in an amateur tournament held alongside the 1984 US Open at Flushing Meadows, and Jeanne mingled with the pros, meeting Martina Navratilova in the locker room. But neither Navratilova nor Chris Evert were her idols. Instead, it was the cantankerous Jimmy Connors. She admired his courage and boldness. Jeanne even imitated Connors' stiff-shouldered walk, and his home-schooled, two-handed backhand. She adopted a similar hard-hitting style from the baseline, and seemed most comfortable with her unruly curly blonde mane draped over her sweatshirt.

Her first college choice had actually been Tulane, where both Ben and Howard III had gone. But her parents ruled out New Orleans as too dangerous. During Jeanne's senior year, a girl at Tulane was murdered in an off-campus apartment, discovered naked with a telephone cord wrapped around her neck. Ben was a senior at Tulane then, and he sounded the alarm. His parents became convinced that a city was not the right place for their daughter to attend school. They insisted she go somewhere safer, and closer to home.

Jeanne had been a tomboy until nearly entering college, and that was one of the qualities that endeared her to so many. Despite having cherubic features—a deep cleft in her chin, her father's sky-blue eyes, and her mother's elegant broad tipped nose—she had a rough and tumble nature. At an early age, she wanted to do the same things her brothers did. Her dad would come home from work to find her wearing her brother's Little League cap and glove, repeatedly throwing a tennis ball against the side of the house. Playing third base for the Radnor Cubs in Little League as a fifteen-year-old, she had a strong arm and hit for a higher average than all but two of her teammates, all guys. As a kid she imitated a television wrestler named "Beautiful Bobby," giving knee-drops to the stomachs of her compliant siblings. Feisty as any of the boys on the playground, in seventh grade Jeanne got into a fistfight, which one teacher called "not at all lady-like." Seeing a reflection of himself, her dad feigned concern, admiring her spunk in stealth.

Often smiling, Jeanne almost always accommodated others. "Even when she was upset, she had a way of making you feel the world is a happy place," says Shannon Wood, who became Jeanne's friend in ninth grade, where they attended the Agnes Irwin School, only minutes from the Clerys' home and just down the street from Villanova. Wood, too, enjoyed tennis, and both girls practiced at the same club—on clay outdoors, or on the hard court inside.

Still, Jeanne was no angel. Growing up in the rambunctious eighties, she couldn't help but slip into a little mischief. While continuing to sleep with a frayed gray Snoopy doll as a senior, from time to time Clery defied her parents. On the rare occasion it was grabbing vegetables from a neighbor's garden. Another old friend, Mary Swanson, recalls once asking Jeanne's brother Hal to buy beer for them. He did, and the girls hid it behind some thorn bushes. When they retrieved it a few days later, Jeanne got so many cuts on her arm that her mom noticed and immediately grew suspicious. Her favorite band was the Police, and there were also the Stones, even George Thorogood and the Destroyers, whose mashed-up bar tunes echoing Bo Diddley riffs had caught fire. The sight of Jeannie rocking to rough slide guitar gems like "Bad to the Bone" struck Wood as funny. Shannon says, "She would look like the last person to listen to that."

The night of her senior prom, Jeanne and Mary thought they pulled off the big switcheroo. Jeanne had been dating a guy named Bob, whom her parents did not approve of. Her father warned Jeanne not to go with him. Another date showed up at her house, but Bob met them at a country club, taking the other guy's place. The second corsage gave her away.

When she arrived home later, Howard noticed something was a little off. The flowers he had spotted earlier were not the same ones now pinned to his daughter's dress. The next day Mary got a telephone call from Jeanne, who told her, "My mom wants to see you—now." Sitting in the living room, Connie Clery let Swanson have it in a grim, rock-steady fashion. As Mary took her verbal thrashing, Jeanne sat across from her friend, "making faces at me, making me laugh, and kind of looking at her mother rolling her eyes." Her parents reprimanded their daughter as well, but inside Howard may have been tickled by her derring-do.

Jeanne thrived academically and socially at Agnes Irwin, while her parents' expectations were high and crystal clear. Her father was a graduate of Dartmouth's Tuck School of Business, her mother fluent in romance languages and a Barnard College standout. Both had been the first to attend college in their families.

As they graduated, Wood, who was about to enter art school, saw her friend heave a sigh of relief. "As she left, I think it was like, 'Wow, I survived high school,'" Wood says. "It was, 'Phew.' I think it was the freedom. She really was looking forward to that."

The following spring at Lehigh, tennis was beginning to take a back seat. Even her mother had recognized that success on the court was not the end-all goal, more of a character-builder. Driving to a tournament before Jeanne entered college, Connie once asked Jeanne what she wanted to be when she grew up. "Happy" was her reply. New worlds and friendships were opening up on campus. Her roommate Sarah Bean was from Staten Island, and Susan Kwon, a New Jersey resident of Korean descent, fascinated Jeanne. She'd also met some decent guys at their favorite fraternity, but there was nothing serious, and no one-night hookups. That wasn't

Jeanne. She also was transitioning away from her old boyfriend. Loyalty and respect for her parents' wishes continued to reign.

"I have never felt inadequate or inferior in comparison to men," she declared in that English essay. "Instead, I am confident, independent, and proud . . . I have never been set back or disadvantaged from the sexist stereotypes of our society." She expected there would be "sexist prejudgments and stereotypes" to overcome in the future, and "as a businesswoman, I will have to prove myself as a competent and qualified individual."

Late that afternoon, Jeanne's friends began preparing for a circuit of Friday night parties. The young women prepped themselves on the third floor at Stoughton House, home to about forty students, their blow dyers bleating inside the cinder block walls, while Jeanne read at her desk in Room 301. It was a typically cramped space with separate alcove beds. A large poster of James Dean dominated her side, while Sarah hung a poster of a basset hound on her wall along with photos of high school friends and their new ones. Jeanne turned down Sarah's offer to go out with her for an early drink. She seemed quiet and preoccupied, still reading when her roommate returned around 7:30 p.m.

A few hours later, Jeanne decided to go along with Susan up "the Hill," as the cluster of fraternities above the main campus buildings are known. Leaving their dorm they scarcely noticed the paper towels stuffed into the locks of three safety doors—in their hallway, the stairwell, and a dorm entrance.

They went to one party and got a ride to another at Phi Sigma Kappa, where Jeanne's boyfriend, Andy Cagnetta, a junior marketing major with a good sense of humor, would be returning late. He and some friends were off at a Dire Straits concert in New Jersey. Not an athlete or wannabe stud, Cagnetta was president of Phi Sigma Kappa, one of "the kind of nondescript guys" of the house, as he says. He was the one Jeanne felt most comfortable with.

When Cagnetta returned close to midnight, Jeanne was at the house bar nursing a beer, and they had a few over the next two hours.

It was a social, low-key night, yet Jeanne's girlfriends sensed something was different. Jeanne had been unusually moody studying alone. Then, at the fraternity, she became markedly emotional, embracing Sara and Susan repeatedly. She told them how much she loved them as if saying good-bye.

Around 2:00 a.m. she said she was going home, and Andy knew that meant goodnight. She was not one who would stay over at the house. They never did that.

Jeanne stayed true to herself, in part the product of living with two older brothers, and embracing something that began to approach her mother's vehement faith. Plus, Cagnetta recalls, "She definitely was not going to put up with any guy crap. Maybe that's why I didn't lay it on thick with her. I knew I wasn't going to get away with it."

Andy kissed her outside, and she walked back down to her dorm alone. It was the last time he saw Jeannie alive.

It took just one look from a lanky stranger to unsettle Desiree Coe.

It was her sophomore year at Lehigh, and Coe was up on the Hill at a party with some girlfriends. One of about seventy African-American students on campus, she saw a thin guy dancing around. She said to herself, "There's a black guy. I want to dance with a black guy." She walked over and noticed his unusual hairstyle. It was a box cut fashioned after the brawny singer Grace Jones. But that's not what drove her immediately away.

"When he asked me [to dance], when he looked at me, I just froze. Looking up at him—he was tall—he asked me a second time, and shook me out of my position. And I said, 'No,' and backed away. I went back to my friends and said 'Don't dance with him. There's something wrong with him.'"

One of the other girls looked at Coe and said, "You're crazy." But Desiree felt something was terribly off. In that instant appraisal she saw a shadow. "It was a darkness that came directly out of him," she says. "And it slapped me in the face."

Josoph Martin Henry was about to erupt.

Chock full of self-hatred, the struggling Lehigh student was a deeply troubled young man. Henry harbored an ego that had been fractured in childhood and burst open by repeated romantic failures. The academic and social pressures applied on the highly competitive campus further stressed his low self-esteem. But there was something else fractured deeper below the surface.

His friends saw him urinate in a punch bowl at a party. He masturbated in public. At six foot three inches, he could fly off into a twisted, vengeful rage, and friends came to expect Henry's outbursts. He lit a student lounge on fire. Another time he uprooted a small tree and dragged it into his apartment in a drunken stupor.

He grew up a child of dysfunction in Newark. His mother Marie raised Josoph in a second-floor apartment after his father, a Vietnam veteran who battled schizophrenia and alcoholism, left when he was three. In Clinton Hills, a working class area on the city's south side, the neighborhood kids knew him as Jo-Jo, or Joe. Heavy as a child, Jo-Jo wore glasses and was protected by his younger brother from bullies. Classmates regarded him as curious and studious.

Marie Henry held a job as a school security guard and found other side work. "We were just trying, trying to make it in this world," she would later plead to a jury on the day her son was sentenced to the death penalty.

Although an honors student in high school, Henry's SAT scores were mediocre. Lehigh recruited him through its fledgling affirmative action program, which offered little tutoring, mentors, or other scaffolding for minority students. He flunked out of the engineering program his first spring, took a year off, and was admitted into Lehigh's business program in 1985. The next spring, as Jeanne Clery put more effort into her second semester, the pressures Josoph felt both on and off campus had not abated. He had already let down his mother and his neighborhood. He dropped an economics theory course and carried only nine credits, which jeopardized his eligibility for financial aid.

The overweight child was long gone, and a toxic mix of self-loathing and alcohol abuse had taken over. Even small amounts of beer or liquor triggered what his lawyer would call "an insanity state." Henry may have suffered from a pathological disorder tied to alcohol abuse, which his defense claimed impaired his ability to understand right from wrong. Whatever the merits of this claim, booze's effect on Josoph was clear to his friends and co-workers. He looked for fights at fraternities, and his buddies knew the drill, keeping an eye on him at parties. As weekends revved up on Thursday nights, Josoph would get high and often stay on a bender through Sunday.

Even when sober, if his urban Ichabod Crane-like appearance did not repulse women immediately, Henry was rejected when he attempted to date his roommates' girlfriends, and friends of other black students.

Living off campus with three other guys, a disturbing pattern of violence tied to substance abuse was emerging. Henry allegedly flipped over and damaged a motorcycle while drunk. After following a young woman into her dorm and throwing a large rock through a glass window, his punishment was to make a video on the dangers of drinking. Yet he never completed the video. While not all of these incidents were known to campus police or administrators, both Henry's lawyer and the Clerys' attorney later blamed the university for not interceding.

Meanwhile, he was allowed to retain a job in the financial aid department of the university's housing office.

A clash of events further ripped apart the twenty-year-old's self-image, spurring him to carry out a wretched assault that ended an innocent woman's life. To Jeanne's father and brothers, it was an act of pure evil.

For Henry, a gleaming prize, a lunging shot at redemption, came in sight that April. He had joined the Black Student Union, a campus social club whose roots went back to the mid-seventies as minority students began to organize at Lehigh. Often articulate and active in the group, Joe wanted to become its president. So did Desiree Coe.

The election was held that first Friday in April. Sometime before the votes were counted, Desiree found Henry inside the Black Student Union Room. Other than a forced "Hi" in passing, she had not spoken to him since the night of the dance. Doubting her intuition, Coe convinced herself to speak with Henry. "I turned to him and said, 'Joe, what is it that you intend to do if you become president?' And he answered then to my satisfaction. He answered that with some constructive thoughts that seemed intelligent. I thought perhaps then it was silly to consider him to be so dark."

She beat him by a single ballot, and Henry cried foul. He wanted another try but was denied. Henry thought being elected to the office would assure that he remained in school. And then the bottom fell out.

The weekend kicked off early for Joe and his crew. Lehigh was holding a minority students' recruiting drive, and his brother Jason was coming up among the throng of prospects. After a student-alumni basketball game and several cocktail parties, a good buzz was underway. Later that night, Josoph would be seen drinking malt liquor, rum, and vodka.

Henry's friend Ken Copeland and his roommates threw a party a few blocks away from Henry's off-campus apartment close to the university in South Bethlehem. While those guys seemed to always have a girl in their pocket or be working a fresh angle, Joe's most recent endeavor was going nowhere. He was keen on a girl named Toni Perry, who attended college in nearby Allentown. He had met her the previous fall and overreached again. Josoph wrote her letters spilling out his frustrations, his loneliness—even his intimate fantasies—and she backed away.

Drunk and wounded from losing the election, shortly after midnight on April 5, 1986, Joe saw Toni walk in. She rebuffed an attempted kiss and he followed her around the apartment. When she slipped outside with another guy, he watched from the shadows as the other kissed her on the cheek. She left, and Henry raged. He walked upstairs, punched a hole through a door, and kicked it off its hinges.

His friends knew what to do. Sometime after 3:00 a.m., Copeland gave Joe and his brother a ride to Henry's apartment where, along with a few housemates, they sat around the kitchen table waiting for Henry to calm down. After perhaps more than an hour he seemed to be mellowing. Jason and a few others went to bed. Copeland went home. It was close to daybreak and the last remaining housemate awake, Roger Faison, heard birds stirring outside of the kitchen. At some point, Joe got up and announced he was "going to go back on campus and steal some things," Faison told state police later. Henry mumbled as he left, slamming the door. Faison peered outside the door, but Joe was gone.

He headed toward campus. Three blocks away was a cluster of dorms called the Lower Centennial complex, or the lower quad. He picked up a beer bottle on the ground and holding its neck, smashed the lower part on a curb. Cursing, his hand cut, he had a weapon. Somewhere up there he would give testimony to his anger. He set to steal anything—a watch, a ring, maybe a credit card—or do worse. Henry mounted a hill heading toward the quad and entered Jeanne's dorm. Through his university job, he knew the layout of the dorms well, even how they were furnished. He knew damn well that Stoughton House was co-ed.

On the first floor lounge he passed a student sleeping on a chair, a freshman guy who'd fallen asleep watching a basketball game. Henry thought about slashing his throat, but passed him by, cutting a swath of fabric from a curtain instead, wrapping it around the bottleneck. He had a weapon, and there were possibilities. He might deliver a message to the Toni Perrys of the world. A second-level door to the boys' hall was locked, so he went upstairs. The third-floor girls' hallway door was jammed with paper, similar to the entrance and stairwell doors. He opened it easily, taking a few steps in, turning to the first door on his left. It was Room 301. He turned the knob as Jeanne slept in her usual fetal position facing the wall.

Her roommate was still out, and Clery had left the door unlocked for her. He closed the door and began going through their things. Jeanne stirred on her pillow, apparently alerted to a presence, squinting over her right shoulder toward him. Perhaps she saw a guy in the half darkness. Henry wasn't sure, and he approached her, holding the broken bottle in his bleeding hand. It was close to 6:00 a.m.

What he did next is just as vicious in what seems a lifetime later: He grabbed a pillow and tried to suffocate Jeanne, scratching her neck with the bottle in small cuts. She fought back, grabbing his wrists and gasping for air. He was too strong, and smashed his elbow into her larynx. Then Henry began strangling Jeanne. He pulled off her shorts, finding himself strangely aroused. He forced himself into her and then sodomized her. She kept fighting as two hands choked her. At some point he picked up a Slinky toy by the bed and wrapped the coil around her neck. When he was done, and Jeanne's soul went with God, he kicked and struck her in the face.

Josoph Henry then collected the young woman's camera and wallet, her silver radio, and some of her roommate's jewelry. He stuffed them inside a laundry bag after emptying its contents. He found a hair pick that had fallen from his back pocket. He rushed out of the room as day was breaking, panicked that he'd lost his wallet.

Within an hour he would brag about his crime to a friend, feigning to laugh it off. To the Clerys, Henry remained unrepentant up until the very last moment of his trial.

After returning from Jeanne's dorm, Henry dropped the laundry bag in a trashcan outside his apartment. He couldn't find his wallet inside his room. He scrambled to the apartment where his friends had held the party. He woke up Ken Copeland, who looked over at his night table, and there it was. Expelling the air that had been pent up in his lungs, Henry threw himself on to the bed. He needed to tell someone what he had just done. If not, who would know? His futility was still burning, his objection to being rejected, as if he was the one who had been mistreated.

"I killed a girl in the Lower Centennials tonight." Henry said that he kicked her in the crotch.

Kenny looked at Joe for a sign, some body language that would indicate this was a bad joke. "Stop fooling around. Tell me this is a joke," Copeland said.

Joe caught a look of terror in his friend's face. He decided this was not the time. "Yeah, it is a joke," he said, but his laughter was forced, ready to unreel itself. Copeland did not catch this.

"I knew it was a joke, I was just waiting, you sounded so serious," his friend said. "I'm going to kick your ass."

They both chuckled, and soon fell asleep. Later that day, Copeland told two roommates what Henry had confided, believing it was a joke. When news of the murder broke, the three reconvened and decided to go to the police.

They arrested Henry in his underwear and a bathrobe at 2:20 on Monday morning.

The Clerys' trip to Bermuda had been a nagging disappointment. Despite staying at the stately Hamilton Princess, where spring blooms of sprawling bougainvillea and white trumpet-shaded Easter lily usually wrap guests in a fragrant embrace, this time the island's weather had been rainy and dismal. Service at the resort had been not been up to snuff, though Howard's meetings at the Direct Mail Association convention had gone well enough. They both got in some golf between the business sessions and dinners.

Yet something didn't feel right. Howard was unsettled. As they finished packing that Saturday morning, he noticed the sun was gone again, *disparu*. The sky had shut like a gray steel grate.

Connie knelt down to pray in the bedroom unseen as a horrible feeling washed over her. She could not place it, and they did not discuss their unease. As the flight took off she looked down grimly at Castle Harbour, where they had spent their honeymoon.

They landed in Philadelphia early in the afternoon. A porter brought their bags to the curb, and Howard hailed a cab. Cruising past the city, it wasn't long before they were winding through the former Welsh Quaker country, past mature trees and what had been old estates and subsistence farms, many long since carved up into lanes and subdivisions. They came to a private drive leading up to their beige stucco house, past a small pond that was a perennial home to ducks and geese. They had it built with a master bedroom on the first floor to make it easy for Howard to get around. Jeanne's room was on that floor as well, while the sons' bedrooms were upstairs.

The Clerys' housekeeper, Katherine, stood in the driveway holding the arm of a police officer, wavering in tears. A squad car was parked nearby. Connie's first thought was that there had been a burglary, but that didn't make sense with Katherine there. Then she thought of Howard's mother, who lived nearby.

She called out, "Is it Grandma?"

Katherine Bridges shook her head. Connie didn't hear another word, and headed inside as Howard lifted himself out. She began reciting Psalm 23 and entered her home.

Yea, though I walk through the valley of the shadow of death, I will fear no evil.

She sat down in a dining room chair, and turned to the cop: "Now tell me."

One of their first phone calls went to a nun who led Bible study at Saint Thomas of Villanova. Both of the Clerys had attended Sister Miriam Najimy's Tuesday night sessions for several years. For Connie, it was a straight-up extension of her steady embrace of conventional liturgy and doctrine. For Howard, who at first resisted joining the class, it was something else.

Slightly more than five feet tall, Sister Miriam was both demure and assertive in a learned way, skilled at listening closely and then interjecting to challenge her group at a critical juncture. Her style suited Howard especially well, since he had long spurned the trappings and rituals of Roman Catholicism. Najimy's approach to sacred texts was more revolutionary than traditionally academic. She engaged the adults to grapple with the same primordial struggles the people of Palestine had faced in the first century—on the ground and in real life. She offered that one's struggles with the Father reflected the Son's struggles; the slashing questions, doubts and rejection, these were not things to condemn.

Howard, too, had been venting about what he saw as God's injustices and prejudices, questions that to Najimy were not sacrilege. If anything, she saw him probing deeper than many did even before his anguish commenced.

That first day, as friends and neighbors arrived at the Clerys' house, Sister Miriam stayed on. Howard told her, "We're going to need you."

Toward the end of Jeanne's Mass, her mother found the will to speak. Connie read a prayer written by a friend for her daughter.

"May you take some comfort in this saddest of times that Jeanne has chosen not to give up her high principles and deep sense of religion and love of God, to become a modern day martyr," Mrs. Clery read.

"She chose to suffer untold pain and total violation to pass her test in life and be with God today.

"Books have been written about such martyrs as these, and their example will live forever and will serve as a model for youth in the mixed up world of morals and standards."

She added, "May her death help you to live as she would have wanted you to live."

But there would be little such comfort for her husband, and perhaps even less for their sons. Howard could never quite reconcile Jeanne's death. His eyes flashed with anger, in terror, at the nightmarish vision of a man—a black bugger, no less—raping Jeanne. Family routines and traditions were trashed, and to some extent, both parents ceased being parents. The younger son Ben's anger seethed, molded most in his father's makeup, as he stayed close to home and began a career in real estate. Seven years older than his sister, Howard III muddled through. Carrying his mother's sweet, emotive temperament, Howie sought refuge far from Bryn Mawr.

Their father called out: "If you were a loving God, where were you for Jeanne? If, as we were told, Jeanne was your child, where the hell were you?"

4

COMPELLED TO ACT

. . . .

The Clerys' first confrontation with Jeanne's killer came three weeks later in court. As an assistant district attorney explained what was about to take place at a preliminary hearing, the parents sat in the first row with their sons not far from the defense table, likely unaware of just how close they would be to him.

With little warning, two large sheriff's deputies brought Josoph Henry in. His presence in and of itself was an affront: angular in a tan suit, with his alien, flattop hair and oversized glasses. He walked by both parents without looking up. Howard jumped up and locked in his leg brace. He moved quickly, catching the Clerys' attorney off guard. Joseph Fioravanti had been asked by his law partner to guide the family through the criminal case, and as a father of two young girls himself, he wasn't sure he even wanted to be there. For the Clerys, it was the first of endless courtroom machinations that bored into their guts.

Howard moved toward the defendant. *Good God*, Fioravanti thought, *is he going to pull a gun on this kid?* There were no metal detectors in the Northampton County Courthouse in Easton, the county seat, although the sheriff had patted everyone down. Standing to Clery's left, Fioravanti grabbed his arm as Howard's face went beet red. He stared at Henry, cursing under his breath. "Then we sat down and he looked at me and said, 'Everything is going to be okay.'"

Henry sat with his head bowed and shoulders slumped forward, nearly within reach of the Clery sons. Connie's whole body shook. Her eyes filled with tears, her chin quivered, and for a long time she made no sound. Howard continued to grimace as he gripped the railing. The veins on his forehead and neck pulsated, and he ground his teeth together. Deputies sat behind the defendant, and two state troopers stood nearby.

Susan Kwon had discovered Jeanne's body that Saturday morning. She returned from the party after her friend did, and looked in on her sleeping sometime after 4:00 a.m. A phone ringing woke Kwon up around eleven, and as she passed Jeanne's room, Susan noticed a door ajar. Jeanne lay in bed with only a nightshirt pulled around her shoulders, facing the wall partly exposed. Covering her up, Susan saw dried blood on the pillow. Her face was blue.

As Kwon mounted the witness stand, both Connie and Howard agonized for her. She had barely made it through final exams. Howard shifted in his seat and frowned at Fioravanti as Kwon described how students often propped open the doors with pizza boxes. Had the university known of this practice before? Susan's voice soon left her, and she could only nod or shake her head as tears came.

Two of Henry's friends described his eruption at the party and Henry's sudden departure from his apartment into the pre-dawn darkness. Ken Copeland also recalled how Henry woke him up later that morning. His testimony cut further: "He said he beat her bad." Jeanne's roommate then had the awful task of identifying items that were hers and Jeanne's, recovered during a search of Henry's room.

The Clerys left the room when the coroner and a forensic pathologist were called in to testify. One of them said it took up to four minutes for Jeanne to die of strangulation. Bruises and cuts were found on her neck, along with indications that Jeanne had fought back. The pathologist noted that marks of the wire Slinky toy found in the room were around her neck. And bite marks on both of her cheeks revealed a large gap that matched the one between Henry's two top front teeth.

Having read the autopsy report already, Howard still felt as if he would vomit upon returning to his seat. He fought back bile rising up his esophagus. The sordid cruelty floored both parents, and they also felt that the insensitivity of disclosing intimate details in public was unconscionable. Taking in more testimony from a male student who had spent the night in a girl's room on the same floor and noticed Jeanne's half-naked body as he was leaving around 8:00 a.m., Howard couldn't fathom the violation of her privacy—even in death. As the hearing ended, Connie stood and turned to the back of the courtroom, unable to face Henry and the lawyers.

Henry rose and Howard stood up, reaching down for his leg brace. A state trooper grabbed Clery's arm, mistaking the movement as reaching for a weapon. Howard merely smiled to reassure the officer. But as Henry took a step, he turned and got off a round: "You slimy son of a bitch. I'm going to get you."

The collateral damage to Jeanne's college and longtime friends was instantaneous. Some lives were altered with a blunt force, while rumors and misinformation spread on campus. Desiree Coe was in a theatre group and before Saturday's performance she heard stories of a suicide in the lower quads. By that evening, news broke that someone had been murdered, "and the kids were saying it had to be a townie." Following Henry's arrest, Coe felt updrafts of ignorance—derogatory sexual remarks and racially tinged recriminations began. "A life had been taken, not a color, and so many people couldn't see beyond that," she says.

Lehigh administrators expressed their sympathy to Jeanne's friends, yet few supports were in place for a traumatized student community. An offer came to move the dorm residents elsewhere, while the university tried to placate rattled parents, even assuring some who were nervous about off-campus safety to place their sons and daughters on lists for campus housing. Patrols by campus police doubled that Saturday.

The outreach only went so far. With final exams a few weeks away, administrators told Jeanne's friends they were expected to take them. Their concession was offering that a failing grade could be overcome at summer school. This rankled Howard, yet Connie had bigger things to contend with. "I had a family I had to keep alive, and there was so much anger," she says. Beyond receiving a reinforced message that they should keep their doors locked, Jeanne's friends were largely on their own.

What students heard was: We're sorry, but now you must move on.

Some suffered silently, and not just those closest to Jeanne. Details of her murder were sparse apart from newspaper accounts of Henry's arrest and trial coverage a year later. Most of the young adults on campus were kept on the outside; they didn't know the Clerys, nor Jeanne's high school friends whom her mother coveted. Upon leaving the funeral, Andy Cagnetta and his fraternity brothers chose not to go to her interment. "No one knew us there," he recalled. Instead, he and the guys had some beers and remembered Jeanne in their own way. Her parents did not know that Andy existed until he tracked them down years later.

Cagnetta saw others around him falling apart. One pledge was drinking out of control. The guy looked to the university for help, and his father called Cagnetta, blaming the fraternity for providing alcohol. But this was about far more than free-flowing beer. The pledge's father scalded Andy, demanding, "'Where the hell were you that night?' I remember being crushed by that. I said, 'You don't get what I'm saying. This is your son I'm talking about, not myself.'" There were other casualties. Another pledge who had felt close to Jeanne struggled to straighten up. A young woman with a background of depression, a close friend of Andy's, "never got over it," he says.

In the months ahead, Cagnetta sometimes dreamed of choking Henry himself. The thought of Jeanne's death sent his heart racing, and he could not reconcile it. He and friends discussed the merits of the death penalty and seeking retribution, whether a society can justify taking another life.

"I still don't know," he told me twenty-five years later. "Still, even if I had the ability to pull the switch on him, I'd probably do it just out of anger."

As he talked to Josoph's friends and investigated his father's mental health troubles, Henry's defense attorney saw a disturbing pattern that he thought might be genetically based.

Small amounts of alcohol, even two beers, brought marked changes in his client's behavior. It had been similar for his dad. Joseph Henry had been institutionalized for schizophrenia and pathological intoxication, or going crazy when he drank. Marie Henry apparently tried to shield her sons from this, and J. Michael Farrell was forced to pry open the father's history.

Farrell, who a year earlier had made it his mission to defend folks that the state wanted to kill, made a novel bid to build Henry's defense. He needed demonstrative evidence that Henry suffered from a disorder similar to his father's. The trial judge granted him permission to conduct a test—called a sleep deprived alcohol provocative brain scan—meant to simulate the conditions in Henry's brain leading into his entering Jeanne's room. This involved videotaping Henry as he drank beer in a hospital, guided by a neurologist, to show that his decision-making abilities had shut down. But the court barred showing the videotape at the trial since it didn't accurately simulate what happened that night. The "intoxication blackout defense" failed.

Still, Farrell believed there were other mitigating factors. Henry's abhorrent conduct had been documented by Lehigh yet little help was offered. There were inadequate supports for a rigorous academic load and he had been isolated on campus due to his race. Henry also stuck to his claim of having little recollection of that morning. Farrell saw a chain forming, what he called "tragic events that were part of the calculus ultimately of his breakdown."

His breakdown? What about *her* murder?

Had he known all this, Howard Clery would have issued a succession of expletives, perhaps ending with: *Liberal apologist, go fuck yourself. Shove your sleep-deprived alcohol rage theories where the sun don't shine.*

The trial lasted for nearly three weeks the following April. Each day, Howard and Connie made the grueling climb up the courthouse steps with Ben and Howie in Easton, a handful of miles from the Lehigh campus. They stayed at a local hotel and several friends accompanied them in court, as did Howard's business partner and his wife. Josoph's mother Marie and his grandmother also attended.

Seeing Henry in court sickened those close to Jeanne and her parents. To her high school friend Shannon Wood, the trial was overwhelming, long, and boring at times with blips of legalese and other formalities. It was a double whammy for her—she had felt unable to read or watch the news about the murder and was sitting on a hard bench to hear exactly what happened for the first time. At one point Shannon caught the defendant taking a nap. *How dare you? How dare you fall asleep!* she thought. "I really wanted to get up and flip him out of his chair."

She had called Jeanne the morning of the murder and felt a strange sensation. Shannon was in Baltimore, and spring break at her school was just about over. Often she would call around eight thirty in the morning on weekends, figuring Jeannie would still be in her room.

There was no answer that Saturday. Yet Wood sensed Jeanne was there somewhere on the other end. "Then two hours later my dad called and told me what had happened. From that point on it was kind of a supernatural moment," she says. "I felt it—for some reason I made the call at that moment. To this day it blows my mind."

Howard got on the witness stand to identify items belonging to his daughter, including a Konica thirty five-millimeter camera he had given her. Clery's face reddened as he looked down, his voice halting. On the second day, one of the couple's friends offered support in the form of seat cushions. Anne Simpson realized that Howard, whose right buttock was paralyzed, had been sitting almost bone-to-wood all day. "To be in the same room as that monster" was bad enough, she says. Along with her husband, Simpson and other friends rallied to the family's side.

Farrell urged jurors to consider the documented mental illness histories of Henry's father, and uncle, and two suicide notes Josoph had written after flunking out his first year at Lehigh. Rejecting the alcohol-related insanity defense, the prosecution's psychiatrist countered that Henry was in full control and knew exactly what he was doing. Jurors refused to believe that he had made a break with reality after drinking. Henry had squirreled away the stolen goods, after all, and retrieved them.

The prosecution brought in a snitch, a state prison inmate who had shared a cell with Henry after his arrest. Marvin Brunson testified that Henry explained to him that he hated white people.

He recalled asking Henry, "How do you feel, you know, that you got a body?"

"'It ain't nothin'," was his response.

In his summation, the assistant district attorney placed photos of Jeanne's body on an easel facing the jury. He reminded them that the pathologist had said it took two to four minutes for Henry to strangle her. He placed a clock on the table and stood silently as four minutes passed. Birds sang outside the window.

When the guilty verdict came back, Hal and Ben held on to their parents.

Convicted of first-degree murder, three days later Henry was sentenced to death by electrocution.

The jury took less than two and a half hours to decide. They agreed with the key aggravating factors brought by the prosecution, mainly that he killed Jeanne to prevent her from testifying against him, and that torture was part of her death.

Farrell used every means of an impassioned appeal he could muster. After criticizing the jury's racial makeup, he threw history at them, noting there had been 152 legal executions in their state "by the cold, cold hand of vengeance." He called upon Saint Paul, who admonished, "Be not conquered by evil; conquer evil with good." All to no avail.

Henry's mother and two friends pleaded for his life. Marie Henry described raising Josoph alone since he was three. She insisted that both boys needed to work really hard and to be persistent, "because if we couldn't get it this week we had to take our time and save up a little longer and try again another time. I tried to teach him that being poor and being black you have to try so hard, you just can't accept everything because nobody is going to give you a chance."

Marie Henry then tried to reach out to the Clerys. She said, "When I sent my son to school, I sent him to school so that he could survive and I could be proud of him. I'm sure the Clerys did the same thing. I'm sure they loved Jeanne Ann as much as I love Josoph. And if I had the power I would try to raise her like Jesus raised Lazarus. But I don't have that power. I wish I could just change things."

Finally, her son stood in the witness stand for the first time. He didn't take ownership, and he didn't apologize. "I wish I could give you an answer to what happened, but I can't," he said in a gravelly voice. "I have searched my soul for an answer as to why this horrible tragedy occurred. I can't give you an answer as to why."

The district attorney tore into him.

"Where were you after you killed her?"

He was reinforcing what jurors already knew: Henry stuffed the laundry bag with Jeanne's possessions after taking her life. Farrell objected to this, and the judge sustained his motion. The photographs were again on the easel, pointed toward Henry.

"Look at these pictures, Mr. Henry. You say now you're sorry. *Were you sorry the day after?*"

Farrell again objected, but he was overruled. Henry looked at the photos and gave no response.

After a long silence, it was over.

When the defense asked that each juror be polled individually about the sentencing, each one firmly responded, "Death."

As the Clerys held each other—Connie wearing an outfit of her daughter's, a black skirt and white top that Jeanne had selected for Easter—Marie Henry was inconsolable.

Grieving the loss of our son, months streamed by ushering in a cold, hard reality. Mike's anniversary meshed with holidays and other signature days of our family life. Not a day went by when Denise and I did not think of what he would be doing—starting school, or working.

We took breaks as a family and as a couple. Even vacations were bound around grabbing any connection to Mike that felt right. We followed a trail that he and five buddies made on a graduation trip through the British Virgin Islands, close to St. John, where we had once gone together. We stopped at the Baths, exquisite volcanic grottoes on Virgin Gorda, where a great swarm of dragonflies funneled up toward us on a path. We snorkeled on reefs where he, Travis, John, Kevin, Griffin and John likely dove in, and made it to the Willy T, a floating bar on a lumber barge where they imbibed, for a raucous afternoon set in motion when two guys mooned our boat.

Mostly we just tried to hold on.

"I feel you in the gentle breezes," his mom wrote. "I feel your warmth on my face. I know you are here close to us all, our spirit guide."

After the Red Sox finally won the World Series in 2004, ending eighty-six years of futility, we brought the kids in for the parade and bought a pennant for Mike. Watching the team approach in the Duck boats along Tremont Street, I thought of how my grandfathers would have relished the championship. And I wondered if Mike was grinning above.

Just a few weeks before this, his sister played soccer for the first and only time on the varsity field where he had thrived. By then a freshman, Amanda got called up for a junior varsity game. The field was just below the high school, flanked by grandstands on both sidelines. She flew down the right wing, not far from where her brother had crossed a stage during commencement.

I stepped back to another afternoon only five years earlier when he battled and streaked across the field. My mom, their Nana Joanie, came to her last game to see Mike play. Ovarian cancer would soon claim her life, and there she was, wrapped in a maroon-grey wool shawl and her hat in the chill. It began to hail, portending snow, and my dad and my uncle and all of us huddled around her, and stayed. Just as the match ended the deluge broke and the day's last light reflected luminously against the departing clouds. "What a beautiful night," she told me.

Denise and I held hands watching our daughter play. Later I tried to tell Amanda what this moment meant: how I felt a deep loss for her, that her brother could not be there to congratulate her, and maybe kid her about a missed ball or two.

How proud he would be.

Manifest to us was not only that nothing could ever be the same again. We also were not going to get over it.

Nor would we drown in grief. To keep going, we needed to find some meaning from Mike's death.

That second winter she and I began to reach out. We wanted to do something proactive about drunk driving, desperate to make even a small difference, as crazy at it seemed heading into that fire. A friend who co-chaired the high school PTO in the regional school district became our champion. Having three sons of her own, Karen deOgburn embraced our desire to address the risks and irreversible damage it caused. Karen was a go-getter, meticulous if not over-achieving in planning and executing the details. With her help we put the word out through the PTO.

While many people had rallied in the aftermath, with some suggesting "call me if you need anything"—truly an absurd half-gesture—much more difficult was engaging parents to address those behaviors that actually made their own families vulnerable. We knew that some parents looked the other way as their teens held parties when they were out of town. Kids flocked to the basements of friends' homes where an adult winked at the rave going on below, and whoever was driving home. Graduation bashes, canoe trips on the Saco River, late night drives to the Cape—each of these things could backfire.

For other adults, the fears just cut too close. Temporarily shaken after someone who considered himself invincible demonstrated that he actually was not, adults offered sympathy, and might even get in their son's face, while expecting him to make a better decision.

Yet it would happen to some of them as well. A small group of us, including P.J.'s oldest sister, along with a neighborhood friend and several other dedicated moms, vetted speakers and performances to offer the high school. We called ourselves Safe Teen OUI Prevention, or S.T.O.P., adopting the acronym for operating under the influence.

It's only early May, but the strong glare of late afternoon sun through a school cafeteria window is doubling down on my nerves. A bead of sweat slides down my back. For some reason, I am unable to close the blinds or remember what I intend to say. My hands are clammy. I cannot find my wife.

Our group is capping off its first "S.T.O.P. Week" with a pasta night and speakers. A day or so earlier, Denise managed to address an assembly of juniors and seniors.

We find ourselves applying last-minute touches in the cafeteria: putting feedback forms on tables, filling baskets with pens and our group's buttons, taping posters, and stacking literature handouts. A chef has donated pasta and meatballs, while parents drop off salads and plates of brownies and cookies. Many of them do not stay—I figure, there must be a Thursday ball game to get to, or supper on the fly. After setting up my school projector with a PowerPoint ready to go, I wander around the room as others finish up.

Denise is in a hallway alone with our son, Chris, who wants to speak. "Are you sure, do you really want to do this?"

He's going to talk about losing his brother. This is enormous. No one's asking him to do it.

By then a junior, Chris had pretty much landed on his feet. Having joined the school's DECA business club, he would soon be competing at conventions in Dallas and Anaheim. He had stocked shelves at the local Walmart and worked at a hat store in the mall, and for a short stint drove Mike's old Golf delivering Dominos pizza. No one could ever fault him for struggling a bit in a few classes while forming enduring relationships with a group of other well-rounded, bright guys.

He kept his black hair in a buzz cut like his brother's occasional style, accentuating a lean face and the olive skin tone he inherited from both of us. Wounded and determinedly emergent, there was still something of a kid about Buds—a nickname bestowed by his sister. His arms remained rail-thin, and the way he held them at times with his elbows angled down and fingers bent at the knuckles reminded me for some reason of a mini-T Rex stalking prey. We hadn't been sure that Chris was actually going through with this. He's going to speak.

In the cafeteria, our friend Karen looks ashen, the crescent folds under her eyes even more pronounced tonight. One of the speakers is late, a man who was driving drunk and paralyzed another guy by slamming into him. The survivor's mother is also coming to speak. Somehow, she has apparently forgiven him.

As more than one hundred people finish eating, our local state representative gets things started—an eager, sure-handed emcee. He introduces a mom who speaks about her son's drunk driving death soon after he had received a college scholarship. I open my slideshow to introduce student-parent driving contracts, asking those gathered to make a commitment that might include adults agreeing to pick teens up anywhere, anytime. Another mom we know who had recently lost her son in a crash just up the street from their house stands up. Remarkably, she offers to retrieve teens at any hour. Then Chris comes forward.

He tells them about Mike, somehow voicing how his death has impacted him. "No fifteen-year-old should ever have to bury his brother," he says, looking out to his classmates and some seniors. "Many kids still do not get the point. Please make the right choices about drinking and speeding. No one deserves to go through what me and my family have gone through." His mom is sobbing, flanked by his sister and cousins and aunts. Our best friends and a son of theirs about the same age as Chris are fully present; my father is also here, and my sister has driven down to be with us yet again.

He does not talk long; the impact is immediate. I'm not sure I even process it all watching from another plane again. What he says will reside forever in my gut but I'll never access it exactly the same way. I see Chris Bean coming out of the church; I watch him with those curled arms ascending a Cretaceous era-layered switchback in the Grand Canyon, his sister keeping up in a cowboy hat, his brother bounding forward in a tie dye

Steal Your Face shirt; never, never, never. I'm ashamed of the few times he witnessed Mike and I fighting, what his brother never deserved. I cannot speak of this yet. I cannot fathom how he's able to do it.

Some of his classmates don't really know. We have to believe they will begin to see.

We do this for four years. Not with Chris out front again, but trying to hammer home the message in different ways.

Another spring, students take advanced driver training on the runway of an old Navy air station, speeding and then trying to brake before hitting the cones and experiencing the distances you actually need to be safe. We bring in a troupe of actors to portray the consequences of drug choices; a drunk-driving simulator; a series of disturbing crash photos from the sheriff's department; and most keenly, testimonials. A mom whose son died after wandering into the woods leaving a party, and the grandfather I had met who is devoted to monitoring repeat drunk-driving offenders and exposing the defense attorney industry-abetted loopholes. A lawyer warns parents about social hosting liability, our collective responsibility to not look the other way. There's empathetic support: from Marty's GMC, a chef at the Radisson Hotel, the police and local newspaper.

Denise and I hit the wall often. Attendance should be bigger for the evening events: where are all the parents?

In this suburb forty miles south of the city, perhaps like anywhere else, we still feel like outsiders. It's so great what you're doing, people tell us. Such an important message. But no one thinks it can happen to their own. Don't go there. So you sing to the choir. They rarely admit it, but many students still feel invincible. There's no buy-in from athletic coaches, nor does the administration push them to make this stick with student athletes. During another pasta night, a group of football players barge in from the weight room scavenging our desserts, and exit.

That same spring I guess, a dad who once coached Chris in soccer hosts his son's graduation party. A keg flows, and teens gulp whiskey soaring down an ice luge. People we know sit around outside drinking and apparently do nothing. Our mouths drop learning of this a few days later. Mom takes their keys away, but some of the partygoers retrieve them anyway. I go to the police station to ask about this, not to rant, but trying to confirm. A sergeant tells me he was heading up the driveway when dad came out, squaring himself up enough to promise that no one was leaving. There were no arrests. Thankfully, no funerals either.

"Does this even make a difference?" I write in my journal. "Are we preaching? And why should we be?"

My retort against drunk driving turns into something else. We get busier. Denise continues teaching; I plunge into it, with so far to go toward anything like mastery. Maybe my wrath is hypocritical at best, for I once cruised through my hometown center slumped on a buddy's shoulder. Hell, I had even been arrested for OUI in college—I wasn't supposed to make the mile-long return from a party, but the intended driver puked on some pills. After being sentenced and losing my license, I walked defiantly out of the court in Bangor and drove off in my pickup.

But Mike's life was squandered: there can be no denying that.

Soon after losing their daughter, the Clerys made a number of alarming discoveries that propelled them to act. The university's disclosure of its security and crime records and the recognition that it had long had a serious problem with propped doors sickened and enraged them.

Within two months a hastily-assembled group of Lehigh administrators, faculty and student leaders pieced together a review of its residential life policies, including reporting on pizza boxes wedged in doors. Howard was astonished that they did not redact the raw data in a copy of the report that was sent to him, facts which the school had dutifully gathered but apparently not acted on. The committee chairman, a board of trustee's member, concluded that he took "comfort" in the findings. Howard began gathering ammunition. He'd hoped that Lehigh would be self-critical and honest; instead, he read self-exonerating comments contradicted by their own statistics. In the margin he scribbled "Bullshit."

One month prior to Jeanne's murder, in her dorm alone there were twenty-one reports of doors propped open. And during the previous seven months, Lehigh counted 2,178 such reports across campus. The college had even conducted a ten-year study on the problem, yet the preventive measure taken was largely assigning two students with flashlights to check twenty-four dorms each night. As Lehigh's student newspaper later reported, that Friday night in April, the duo in charge of checking the doors fudged their report and went out partying instead. To his dismay, Howard also learned that while campus police patrolled in two or three cars, they did not regularly go inside dorms or go out on foot.

Scouring through the report he discovered there had been an alarming number of violent crimes. A six-year summary listed eight reported rapes and seven other sexual assaults, plus forcible robberies and 169 burglaries on campus. Despite this internal accounting of rampant crime, the university had only twelve campus police officers protecting 5,400 students. Something else Howard saw was equally agonizing: Lehigh students had been sounding alarms about their own safety. In a survey done about eighteen months before Jeanne's death, a majority of women reported feeling "conscious of danger" on the supposedly bucolic campus. They also made suggestions that went unheeded: assigning more campus police near the lower campus dorms and having desk security in dorms "to prevent people from getting in."

"Lehigh was a dangerous place, and no one in the family knew it," Howard concluded, as Joseph Fioravanti recorded. Clery scribbled another margin note that precipitated part of his higher purpose: "This is the evidence that they knew."

Festering details of Jeanne's murder became infected by Lehigh's response, rattling his brain. Some nights he barely slept, imagining a sequence of how she was killed, which made him vomit. His vitriol at the killer—and at Henry's family, and the excuses spewed in his defense, and then toward Lehigh's initial intransigence and perceived callousness—was about to spill over.

One day he called Fioravanti asking him to drive over pronto. Newspapers were on the table and Howard had flagged comments by the university president that he felt amounted to, "These kids don't look after themselves." The university's liability exposure was clear. He told Joe, "'I want to know how the hell that guy got into her room, and I want to do it because these people are insular . . . I want those dorms safe for Jeanne's friends." All Jeanne had done was return from a party and fall asleep, believing she was fine.

Perhaps Howard returned to work a bit early, but that's exactly what many grieving parents are driven to do. Clery co-owned a mail-order business forms company that was growing steadily, and they were planning to move into a new facility. He was already wealthy, thanks to no one's hand but his own. He had entered the burgeoning business systems industry in the early sixties, at first selling typewriters and systems for Royal McBee Co. A decade later he was the one-third owner of a company doing $2 million in sales. Revenue and profits continued to increase at the firm through the mid-eighties. No one could tell Clery not to go back to the office, and Connie agreed. "Otherwise, what are you going to do, dig a hole and cry?" she reflected.

One day Howard was confronted by the terror of trying to retain normalcy and avert the growing wound in his soul. After making the drive into New Jersey, he maintained focus for a two-hour meeting, satisfied he had functioned at his usual high level. Upon leaving the conference room, reality checked in. Seeing Jeanne's portrait in his office, he said aloud, "My God, my daughter [was] raped and murdered." Having overcome polio as a teenager, he knew full well about life's crucibles. Yet this was something else.

There was also the torment of looking in the rear view mirror. He and Connie had quashed Jeanne's first college choice as Ben in particular argued that Tulane was not safe in the wake of sophomore Karin Minkin's murder. Howard agreed, steering his daughter closer to home. She also was interested in the University of Miami, but her father ruled that out as being too far away. When Lehigh's tennis coach called to recruit Jeanne, her dad could not have known the cover-ups occurring in Bethlehem. He also could not have known that Minkin's parents, like he and his wife, would also soon be speaking out about the lack of safety at Tulane, and elsewhere. The Minkins would face painful delays in the arrest of a suspect and the prosecution of his crime. Little could Howard have known about all this.

Yet if only his daughter had.

The more the Clerys learned, "he became more enraged, and she became more quietly determined," Fioravanti says. Howard's instinct was to go for the jugular. A well-connected colleague urged him not to sue, and while he disagreed, Clery waited to see what Lehigh's response would be. By ducking any responsibility, through its arrogance, the university roused the pit bull in him.

"We are not the type of people who are going to go home and not say anything about it," he told a reporter.

Neither of her parents collapsed, yet their grief rippled out. Connie kept Jeanne's room untouched. She often went in alone, clothes folded in the drawers, sweaters and skirts hanging in the closet. Her daughter's tennis trophies rested on a shelf above her bed, a framed Prayer of St. Francis of Assisi hung nearby. No more would fresh portraits of Jeannie be placed on the mantel or atop a desk.

In those first weeks especially, and a generation later, Yvonne Ameche Davis had Connie's back. She was that first phone call. Her son Paul had died in a car crash a few years earlier, and Yvonne and her husband offered to help make the arrangements for Jeanne. She remembers the coroner asking permission to cut Jeanne's cheek where Henry's bite marks were to preserve the evidence. Yvonne was in the kitchen when Ben and Howie returned from viewing her body. "I recall thinking, are they ever going to be all right again?" she says.

It was enough to get lost in the pain. The puzzle pieces lay scattered, and who knew if they could ever be made whole again?

Davis already grasped a few things. "The grief experience zaps our ability to do everything as a parent," she laments. "We figure out that nothing we do is going to make a difference." She sat with Connie. She urged her to continue playing tennis. After one match Connie broke down, telling Davis that Jeanne's possessions at school, which police had impounded, were being released. Yvonne got dressed to help retrieve those clothes and personal items, putting on a skirt with oversized deep pockets. When her husband noticed the skirt, she explained that, "If I see one thing in there that I believe Jeanne would not want Connie to see, I will take it. He said, 'Are you playing God?'" She could not disagree.

Not only did the Clerys become members of a club for which there is no apt name. Who come home one afternoon to find the tree of life uprooted, its gnarled limbs pounded into the ground, snapped in jagged angles. Cast from daily routines, they had instantly matriculated as outsiders. Stuck in their own time, even as the years moved swiftly like skiffs of reed flowing in a brook.

Not only did they face their own grief in part by giving it away. Thrust into the public eye, they set out in a very non-plebeian way to do the one thing that made any sense: Jeanne's life could not be in vain.

While starting a movement, to varying degrees, they inched toward reconciliation, recognizing the gift Jeanne left for them. While never forgiving her killer.

Bob Malin, another of the couple's many old friends, shakes his head in wonder. "I kept thinking if that had happened to me, would I be able to rise above it? No. I never would have been able to," Malin says. "Because all that energy, the public speaking, the speeches, that must have just seared at their souls. That wasn't just courage, that was fantastic dedication. You can say, 'Well I was just doing this for my daughter.' But that doesn't even begin to tell the story."

5

NO MORE

. . . .

Weighing their response to Lehigh University in 1986, Howard and Connie would soon join people from other walks of life in a rising tide.

Survivors of violent crime and their relatives were opening the public's consciousness of just how poorly crime victims were too often treated. Demanding that the scales of justice be rebalanced, they sought greater recognition and protections, compensation through the courts, and an end to institutional cover-ups. Perhaps most decisively, as spotlights trained on long-hidden abuses, more victims began to end their own silence and isolation. A generation of advocates and practitioners grew around them, and victims increasingly viewed themselves instead as survivors—one by one, and in clumps, empowering others to fight through their own blistering trials.

As the Clerys attempted to scrape their life back together, the victims' rights movement was gaining traction across the United States. While far from complete, the early gains were already significant as awareness and outrage grew about crimes including domestic abuse, child abuse, and sexual assault. It would take many more years to get at the root causes and enact meaningful interventions and preventive measures. Combatting the scourge of violence against women, for one, would require overcoming systemic denials and ripping open entrenched cultural norms.

Still, during the Clerys' era more survivors and families like themselves were at least finally being heard. The movement's roots were deep and wide, some being laid early in the 1970s as the first victim assistance programs emerged in St. Louis and Washington, D.C., and by women gathering in San Francisco to oppose rape. Shelters and hotlines for battered women soon opened in the upper Midwest, while Oregon became the first state to enact mandatory arrests in domestic violence cases. In the following decade, state legislatures and Congress passed laws establishing victims' compensation in criminal cases and codifying other rights for survivors. National coalitions formed to give voice to the parents of murdered children, to rape victims, and to battered women.

In 1980, Candy Lightner started Mothers Against Drunk Driving from her den. A drunk driver who had passed out struck Lightner's thirteen-year-old daughter, Cari, as she walked through her neighborhood to a church carnival. On that same day, Lightner promised herself to fight and make something positive out of Cari's senseless death. Far from an original idea, her response is perhaps wired in our DNA, getting off one's scarred knees to try and protect a neighbor from the same threat. But whereas Lightner and Karin Minkin's parents and untold others had initially tilted alone, straining to make any sense of the debris at their feet, other victims' relatives were emerging from the shadows.

Desperate to be heard and to do something, they found one another. So-called little things that Lightner and others initiated began steamrolling into something bigger: speaking out in local newspaper columns, presenting at school committee meetings, raising money at bake sales and memorial walks. To a growing audience, they called out: No more.

They began to be heard. Key statutes and other shifts elevating crime victims were enacted during Ronald Reagan's presidency. With Reagan himself and his administration often its chief stalwarts, more sensitive and timely laws and policies were enacted, implementing many recommendations from the President's Task Force on Victims of Crime. Among the highlights, the Federal Victim and Witness Protection Act of 1982 improved treatment standards for victims and witnesses; and two years later, the Victims Of Crime Act established a fund for state victim compensation and victim service programs. An office for crime victims was created within the Justice Department, and bipartisan support sent funding to state and local governments for expanded victims' services. Even the motto, "Take a bite out of crime" by the animated crime-fighting mascot McGruff seemed to be everywhere one looked.

Very soon, a man known as the "father of the victims' rights movement" would help the Clerys mount the first national campaign to secure every student's right to know about crimes and security measures on the campus he or she wanted to attend. It would be a big leap toward making colleges accountable to not sweep violent crimes under the rug. Extending further, during the next two decades the couple wrenched open one of America's dirtiest secrets. On college campuses that are often idealized as places where society levels the field for our daughters, many young women are preyed upon, far more than we have ever faced up to. The façade of secure campuses and affording assault survivors justice remained intact until the Clerys clawed back.

While no one apparently heard Jeanne call out, her parents would actually help crack the guilt and silence that survivors often impose on themselves—and the nasty recriminations often dealt by the very institutions they paid to attend. But first there was much heavy lifting to do.

Bill Bagnell had to read the story three or four times to believe it.

Scanning newspapers at his internship, a front-page article about Jeanne's murder screamed out at him. He knew her, not very well, but their moms played tennis together and his family moved in the same social circles back on the Main Line. Bagnell was a senior at Texas Christian University in Fort Worth, a pre-law Horned Frog, although not destined for that career track.

His internship was in a downtown office for crime victims. A few TCU co-eds had recently been assaulted and another student was missing, which galvanized coverage in the city's leading newspaper. Bagnell couldn't fathom Jeanne being a victim, and he was hit hard. He called a friend who worked for a television station in Philadelphia. Yes, his contact confirmed, it was the same Jeanne Clery from Bryn Mawr.

Bagnell rushed in to see his boss. While only a half-dozen or so years older than Bill, Anne Seymour was already a rising force in victims' rights advocacy, and he was beginning to appreciate her tenacity and vision. Just three months before, Seymour helped start the fledgling Sunny von Bülow

National Victim Advocacy Center. "We have a situation, a family friend," Bagnell told Seymour. "'I knew her. She was strangled at Lehigh.' She looked at me and said this is something we have to bite into."

He called the Clerys and Connie picked up. "God, I'm so sorry," he told her. Explaining who he was working for, Bagnell said, "We think we can do something for you." Just a few days later, he and Seymour flew east.

Before starting the von Bülow victims' center, Seymour helped Candy Lightner catapult MADD into the spotlight as its public affairs coordinator. She went to Capitol Hill pressing for the twenty-one drinking age bill and within two months it passed and was signed into law by Reagan. In Fort Worth, Sunny von Bülow's children had created the victims' center after her husband, Claus, was acquitted on appeal for trying to kill her with insulin injections. His two trials became a media circus of titillating bits about the heiress and her Fifth Avenue-Newport socialite orbit. But after Claus von Bülow walked, and as his wife lay comatose (for twenty-eight years), her family put something bigger in motion. Determined, as her son Alex said, "to lessen the tragedy for other people, to take our frustration and channel it positively." He approached Seymour about creating the center. On the same gut-spilling morning the Challenger space shuttle exploded in 1986, she was opening its new office.

The Clerys' trajectory intersected with Seymour's. Her mission was getting the future National Center for Victims of Crime up to speed. While her office at the old Tandy Center was still littered with unpacked boxes, Seymour scouted for cases to help the nonprofit go national.

She and Bill Bagnell sat with the Clerys in their living room. Anne held Connie's hand, and acting in part on the fly, sketched out how she wanted to help. She told them how the criminal case would proceed, how to work with the prosecutor, and some of the hazards they would face now that they were *that family*. Seymour suggested they might carry their personal story beyond themselves to make a difference. She fell in love with them.

Being an only daughter herself, Seymour understood the acuteness of their loss. They struck her as fearless and savvy. "Howard looked like he was kind of an elf and then his eyes would fire up and I'd say, 'Okay, get out of his way,'" she says. "Very powerful. And Connie was the most effective advocate, and she's got a little Zen going on, always has. Howard was always on, and she was the anchor."

Seymour visited for two days. "It was a lot of tears, and comforting," Bagnell recalls. "Howard, he wanted to hang somebody, that was his personality. But he also knew he had to do something to make this right. Connie was devastated, and it rocked their sons. She saw the logic. She saw this could become something. It became her crusade."

They formed strategic and emotional bonds. Both sides had mutual and separate interests that were understood in a natural way, and the Clerys soon agreed to lend their story to the victims' center. But as Bagnell says, "they weren't there to toot their own horn." Anne's immediate role was looking out for the family's needs, including Ben's and Howie's, sometimes accompanying them to navigate new waters. Within a few years, Seymour was often the Clerys' liaison to key people in the justice and education departments as they explored ways to mandate crime reporting and improve security at colleges across the country. "Their personal story was such a driving force," she says.

An enduring friendship developed, especially between the two women. In some respects, Connie saw a younger version of herself in Anne: compassionate and wise, "electric," and an attractive brunette to boot. "She had wonderful ideas, she was highly respected," Connie says. "I was amazed at how young she was, and how much she had achieved." Many times the two just sat and cried together, often with Howard as well. "And the fact that it should've been and could've been prevented added a little bit of oil on the fire," Seymour says.

In the months and years that followed, she watched the couple become mentors to others undergoing similar trials. It was all happening so fast. "It's very difficult to heal others when you yourself are traumatized," Seymour reflected. "When you go from victims to advocates so quickly, you do lose a sense of your own grief so quickly helping others." Yet they pressed on.

Seymour introduced the Clerys to another key ally, Frank Carrington, who is held up as a pillar in advancing victims' rights law. A gentleman from the Virginia Tidewater, Carrington was a former Marine who had worked in federal law enforcement. He earned a law degree with a goal to help victims, and as early as the end of the sixties, he was bringing attention to this neglected part of the criminal justice system. As most law students can attest to, Carrington's legacy advancing victims' law is prolific. He wrote books and law journal articles, lectured widely, and perhaps of the most practical value, built an early database of case law used by attorneys in defense of victims. In the late seventies he founded a national nonprofit to further rights in the civil, criminal, and juvenile justice systems.

Plainspoken and humble, perhaps more than anything else Carrington lent a humane streak to this work. With warm eyes that reflected the lighter colors in a thick, greying mustache, he helped set the tone for victims' advocacy. "The numbers are just astronomical," he once said, describing campus sexual assaults in the early nineties. "Probably for every one that we get, there are ten, or probably more than ten that are not reported. The more that are reported, the more other girls are going to listen." Student surveys continued to confirm his estimation twenty-five years later.

As one eulogizer remarked after his death in 1992, Carrington was "never too busy. He never turned down a call for help, from anyone." He also contributed to writing many of the core procedures and rights afforded victims' families in criminal cases today. When victims' impact statements scrawled by relatives are read aloud or considered by a judge—which has become an unimpeachable right in most jurisdictions, no matter how draining and even perverse this may feel—we owe him a nod of gratitude. Strapped on to what can feel like a conveyor belt passing through the criminal justice system, heading into the crushing plant of the courtroom, in that moment at least, our shaking voices are heard.

When he and the Clerys were introduced, despite being well informed and politically attuned, even Howard and Connie did not fully realize what a nugget they had come upon.

Driving with his wife to meet the Clerys at their home, Carrington did not discourage Howard's idea to sue Lehigh. He knew precedents where institutions had been held accountable for their negligence and believed a lawsuit would fully expose the university's flawed security. The media attention this brought would force other colleges to examine their own practices.

Carrington offered to help the couple with the lawsuit free of charge. He also had a larger design that dovetailed with Anne Seymour's advocacy strategy. The Clerys' story was so powerful, and they were both eloquent and attractive, that he thought they would be impressive spokesmen for victims' rights on a larger platform. While it would be Connie in particular who pushed her way into the offices of senators and congressmen in the years ahead, Carrington helped plant those seeds.

Joe Fioravanti called Frank's office in Virginia Beach one day, and to his surprise, Carrington answered the phone himself: "How may I help you?" The case was underway.

With Connie or Howard often at his side, Fioravanti prepared a complaint against the university as the discovery process for Henry's trial ground on. She frequently drove up to Lehigh Valley with him to take depositions, covering some twenty or more trips. They were road warriors, and she was his co-pilot. It was draining work. She asked good questions, and with her large brown eyes focused on her target, usually got answers. In moments Connie "cried a lot and prayed a lot," he says. Fioravanti found her elegant and warm.

Howard became a consummate consumer advocate. He often framed the issue this way: like many universities, Lehigh had failed to provide truthful information to the consumers of a college education, whose parents would invest tens of thousands of dollars there. It wasn't complicated; he saw it as an act of fraud. A violation of every student's and parent's right to know. "He would bang on the table with his finger," says S. Daniel Carter, who worked beside the Clerys for many years as a campus security advocate and policy liaison. Carter channeled Howard, who became one of his mentors: "And you're paying, you're paying for the tuition. You have a right, not a courtesy."

Fioravanti became friends with the couple, who began inviting him to dinners at their country club, sometimes after playing eighteen holes with Howard. Clery's determination was never more apparent than on the course. Howard usually drove the cart, and using crutches and locking his heavy leg brace, set himself over his ball. He'd then drop a crutch and hit, using all of his upper body—"a vicious swing," Fioravanti says. While never a scratch golfer, Howard had a ten or twelve handicap. He was a sturdy driver, hitting straight down the middle, and terrific on the green.

Over meals and drinks in the ballroom, Fioravanti began to see that the two could not put aside the case against Lehigh, or the emerging cause.

"You'd sit down with them socially during an evening designed to be relaxing, and you'd have a knot in your stomach from all the stuff you talked about," he says. "Jeanne would always come up. There was never a time with Connie when tears didn't come to her eyes. I hoped that changed during the years, but they were never free from that."

While struggling at times to focus on his job, in the months before Henry's trial Howard stayed true to his purpose. Determined to shine a light on the university's failures as an example for others, he instructed Fioravanti to leave no stone unturned.

Early in 1987 they made Lehigh a proposal. In addition to insisting that the university rework its security system, the Clerys wanted Lehigh to acknowledge its errors and take leadership by hosting a symposium for other colleges on improving dormitory safety. They sought an offer before the end of Henry's trial. The university declined.

Minutes after Josoph Henry was sentenced to death, Howard and Connie briefly stepped away from their pain. Outside the courtroom they announced the formation of a campus security advocacy group. At the very least, Howard told the media, their nonprofit organization would fight for safer conditions elsewhere.

A day later, the Clerys filed a $25 million suit against Lehigh. They named eighteen defendants, including Lehigh's president and trustees, the student affairs chief whose remarks had amounted to igniting petrol, the campus police chief, and Henry. They claimed the university had breached terms of its room contract by failing to provide security. If needed, Howard would go to the mat before another jury.

Connie told a reporter, "When Lehigh is forced to do something about security, other schools will also."

A few relatives and friends did not get the point. Why pursue this? Going after Lehigh seemed like a long shot. Why prolong their suffering? Even Connie's sister, who attended Henry's sentencing in support, voiced doubts years later.

But not everyone did. Howard's closet cousin, Jack Boyle, understood firsthand what motivated Clery. Boyle was Howard's frequent companion playing pond hockey and other sports until polio struck Clery as a high school sophomore. Howard endured a demanding rehabilitation while he transformed himself into a top student.

"Really tough," Boyle says. "This is where Security On Campus [the Clerys' nonprofit] comes from. Those assholes that run that goddamned place? You think he's impressed with the president of Lehigh? Are you kidding? An *extremely* competent, confident man."

Bob Malin, a friend of Clery's since college, saw both parents' resolve a little differently. "They had to pursue the hell out of Lehigh," he says. "That was painful, really painful." As they expanded their mission in the years ahead, "Every single day they were almost rubbing themselves raw with the whole anguish and anger while trying to help others. They went at it hammer and tongs."

The day Cory Scanlon changed his plea we felt ambushed again.

It was a grim, rainy early spring morning some sixteen months after the car crash. Denise had continued teaching and was considering taking a leave of absence the following fall in 2004. I had stepped into a classroom for the first time the previous year, struggling to complete lessons and manage noisy groups of ninth-graders to absorb Poe, Lorraine Hansberry, and Shakespeare. While our shock had lifted, that second winter had been a blur for both of us. It just happened to be my forty-first birthday.

Coming up the stairs into the main courtroom we passed through a gauntlet of Cory's friends and relatives. We felt suddenly outnumbered, as if many of the guys' mutual friends had switched sides; or more likely, I was just unable to process anything in their blank looks. Many sat near the Scanlon family behind the defendant's table where there was ample room. We sat with the Shaughnessys along with our kids, Mike's aunt and grandparents.

The Scanlons had hired a heavyweight defense lawyer whom we grew to despise, probably naturally and predictably so. I had actually observed and spoken with him while covering a trial some years before as a reporter when he defended a cop who killed a guy while driving shitfaced. Even in defense-rich greater Boston, Kevin Reddington was notorious. He once convinced a jury that former Red Sox first baseman Mo Vaughn failed a sobriety test because of a bad knee. He defended a child-raping priest and much later, Whitey Bulger's girlfriend. And cutting closest to us and families in the town next door, he represented the killer Gary Sampson.

Only fifteen months before our son's death this evil piece of rejected rat scat murdered three people during an interstate spree, including Jonathan Rizzo, the beautiful, idealistic son of friends from youth soccer. As the Rizzos pushed for the death penalty during the next fifteen years—enduring a retrial for Sampson's sentencing—the returning specter of Cory's so-called affable attorney churned my stomach.

Everyone else except for us in Norfolk Superior Court seemed to know Scanlon was going to plead guilty to vehicular homicide and negligent driving. No one had given us a heads up about this. Not the assistant DA, the victims' advocate, nor the phalanx of faces we knew. Weeping in a dark tie and blue button-down shirt as some of us addressed the judge, Cory admitted his recklessness. He was never charged with operating under the influence.

P.J.'s dad Peter told Cory he forgave him, and that he was abiding by what his son would want him to do. Denise and I were close to feeling the same way, though we did not say so at this juncture. Stopping for lunch on the way home with my dad and Denise's family, it felt that at least some weight had been lifted. Cory had spared all of us the ordeal of a trial.

Around this time we decided to go after the owners of Bar One and found a well-connected law firm in Providence. Initiating the case meant digging out the official documents we had tried to seal out of sight in a small safe that might as well have been a stone crypt. Fumbling with the keys in my office, I retrieved and made copies of the state trooper's report, the accident report and Michael's death certificate. The worst was a section of the report reconstructing the crash with technical calculations based on tire marks and wreckage strewn, the hideous distances our sons had been thrown. The numbers were a fresh assault: how could they both have been launched that far? *How could he?*

Driving down to meet one of the law partners was like a bad job interview. I felt nauseous and vaguely incompetent, as if realizing that I'd worn a tie conspicuously out of style. Although the partner was sympathetic in that momentary way, telling us about his own fears for his son, we both sensed this was strictly business. We told our story as he took notes behind an oversized desk. Advising us that the chances of success were limited and it would be a very long haul given Rhode Island's liquor liability statute, the firm filed a wrongful death complaint for the Shaughnessys and ourselves. We each did it for accountability. Not for the money.

Ultimately, neither of those things would amount to squat.

In a twisted way, filing the lawsuit opened my personal rabbit hole. It fed a compulsion that I would be unable to blame on anyone but myself.

The Clerys went to work in a very public fashion. In the months following Henry's trial they took two tacks: developing a campus crime questionnaire for high school students to send to their prospective colleges and pushing the country's first campus crime disclosure bill in their home state. To do this, Connie had to reinvent herself.

Like Howard, she was articulate and well read. While he once impressed his business school buddies with a sweeping grasp of world affairs and an uncanny ability to recall facts, Connie was more than his match. Urbane and worldly, she had lived in Greenwich Village while attending trilingual secretarial school after graduating from Barnard. Her old roommates moved to places like Paris and Copenhagen. She had talked her daughter's elementary school principal into introducing French to the children, and Connie tutored kindergarteners through third graders as Jeanne moved up. On other days, she volunteered at a home for children with disabilities in neighboring Rosemont, serving on its board.

As Howard's career soared, she was a dutiful mom and wife. There was no need to work, and when she wasn't volunteering, Connie chauffeured the kids. Each of them took swimming lessons—young Howie had been a top swimmer at his private high school—and there had always been Little League too. Yet while both parents' skill sets and affluence afforded them the means to branch out into bigger things, the driving force in starting the nonprofit was always the nature of their response. Advocating for other parents' children, they grabbed whatever bullhorns they could find.

Parents from all over the country reached out to the Clerys. More than three thousand notes of condolences arrived as Henry's trial began, and a group of Connie's friends helped her write thank-you notes. They became her "choir of angels," converging in the dining room to answer and organize more correspondence. College guidance counselors and security authorities also began contacting them. Connie knew she needed to do more than work out of the house, which was already becoming a repository for grim news clippings of other victims' accounts.

While not one to bring attention to herself, she agreed with Howard to do media interviews. At first, this was just in the moment, meeting reporters or answering their phone calls. Then they got strategic, at Howard's lead initially, as he began using the media for his purpose. The couple did radio and television interviews, starting in the Philadelphia market and then with national hosts like Sally Jesse Raphael and Larry King. Producers began calling them, and it was rarely easy to pull off. "Never would you have imagined Connie doing anything like that," says Dodie Boyle, one of Mrs. Clery's confidants. Whereas Connie was once a little "ditzy," Boyle says, "she got up and that little giggly voice was gone. She stood up and there before you was that motivated voice, to safeguard those kids. She is amazing."

As Connie retold Jeanne's story during those charged broadcasts, viewers might have expected to see her mom well up, and she often did. No one but Howard could really gauge how tough it was on her. Those appearances were a double-edged blade that resisted dulling with time: trying to advance their cause, while having to revisit the pain. Putting themselves through it again and again.

Somehow this felt right. Connie believed in stepping outside herself, especially as more parents suffering their own tragedies wrote and called for advice. Increasingly, she considered this work and the new relationships they were forming to be her calling. While Jeanne's death had torn her apart, Connie offered, "In one sense it's been good, because we're helping so many others. And it deadens you. Nothing can hurt me now, and I have no fear. In a way, Jeanne's death has freed me."

She got the notion to create a directory listing the types of security systems campuses provide. Connie figured that since schools told publishers like Barrons how many dorms they had and what their facilities were, they could also describe their security infrastructure. Jeanne had poured through a guide listing colleges with tennis teams, after all, so why shouldn't there be one for colleges with automatic locking doors and cameras? Before compiling such a guide, however, the Clerys attempted to help students obtain the information themselves. The couple sent out more than two thousand questionnaires within a year, mostly to high school guidance counselors, whom they figured would distribute the forms to students. The requests for colleges were pointblank: During the past three years, how many assaults, burglaries, rapes and homicides were committed on school grounds? Were these statistics disseminated to parents and students each year? Are campus security trained professionals? On it went.

Instead of being seen a tool to gather information, the questionnaires raised the defensive guard of many college admissions officials. Parents reported that their queries about security stirred intimidating remarks, and in some cases, a rationale for rejecting their son's or daughter's application. Although more than ten thousand eventually went out with help from Connie's volunteers.

They were also skewered in Bethlehem. As classes resumed at Lehigh in the fall of 1987—not quite eighteen months after Jeanne's death—an editorial in the campus newspaper called her parents' mission to make campus security a national issue "noble but futile." Safety would continue to place far lower than "academic quality and social atmosphere" on an applicant's priority list. Others assailed the family's motives in suing the university, asserting the Clerys showed "bigotry, arrogance and greed."

Still, a few students urged others try walking in the family's shoes. "If one student is spared from death and the students' parents don't have to go through the agony and grief that the Clerys endure, then isn't their campaign worth it?" senior John Amorison asked.

While irritated by some of the students' potshots, Howard and Connie shook those off. They decided that if questionnaires were not the best route, they would try to mandate campus crime disclosures by getting a law passed. One day after church, Connie approached a local state representative she recognized as being a member at their country club. It took two meetings to warm him to the idea, but the lawmaker rose to the occasion. In time for the second anniversary of Jeanne's death the next spring, a bill requiring all Pennsylvania public and private colleges to publish an annual brochure on campus security was closing in on passage. The couple's inaugural legislation for "truth in advertising" was about to take hold.

The bill passed the Pennsylvania legislature in May of 1988. As Connie explained, it was a two-pronged approach. First, informing not only students, but the faculty and campus employees, about crime and security measures so they could take precautions. "It will not be effective unless the campus families act to protect themselves," she said. A second prong was holding university officials responsible to implement better security policies and techniques. The Clerys had to give up a few things in order to secure its passage. Originally she and Howard wanted schools to send a campus crime brochure to every applicant. But this was amended to ensuring that students were made aware the reports were readily available.

News of the law spread, and soon a handful of states from Washington to Florida considered enacting similar measures dubbed "Clery bills." Howard and Connie came to testify and lobby alongside other parents who had their own difficult stories.

A couple from Laguna Beach, California, John and Genelle Reilley, were among those who found the Clerys. Their daughter Robbin was murdered outside a campus concert in 1986. While the crime was never solved, over the next few years her parents learned of two abductions and several rapes that had occurred at her community college. Questioning the security lapses, they pushed for a Clery-style bill in Sacramento. Connie and another mom whose son was stabbed at a college party flew in to help, pressing a powerful legislator to get it passed. While forming a long-distance relationship with the couple, the Reilleys later joined the Clerys' nonprofit as board members, and remained friends for many years. They weren't the last.

There were other newfound allies: the Getzingers, whose daughter Dana survived a knife attack to the heart in her University of Georgia dorm; the Niewswands, one of two families whose daughters were taken hostage at Cornell University and killed by a man armed with a .22 caliber rifle; and the Hawelkas, who lost their daughter in an attack outside a campus building at Clarkson University. To Connie and Howard, these people were not just names tossed over the airwaves. On top of everything else, these parents wrestled with guilt, questioning "how stupid we were," blaming themselves. Why did we not check? Their contacts with the Clerys—their shared experiences, and sometimes, activism—often helped both sides inch forward.

It would be difficult even for some of the couple's many longtime friends, whose own careers set a torrid pace in fields like investment banking and international management consulting, to keep up with all this. They were all impressed, if not in awe at many junctures. "They had a mission and they were going to succeed," says Bob Simpson, who met Howard in college.

Still, each success came at a cost, which grew over time. As the couple advanced their cause, at times they had little left for their sons.

Both parents focused on what they saw as the greatest need, and Connie believed that pouring herself into the nonprofit actually saved her life. She saw no alternative to moving beyond her suffering, which transformed her own self-preservation into a selfless act.

At times this displaced sons Ben and Howie. Yet each of them supported their parents' mission in various ways. Ben played a big role as the nonprofit's president, helping with daily operations and doing public events such as testifying before a House of Representatives committee in the nineties. He continued as the group's treasurer for many years.

His brother made short forays into the office and briefly served as the nonprofit's executive director after Ben left for a new job. Howard III soon withdrew, perhaps having enough to contend with without noticing the ever-present portrait of his sister in a pink Izod sweater, which became emblematic on the center's brochures and website. Besides, his parents were a force. "Howard was the brains, and I was the brawn," Connie says. "I did the work in Congress, ran the office, paid the bills. Howard wrote the wording for the Clery brochures and prepared testimony. We were a good team."

While different in temperament, both sons shared much of their father's anger toward Henry. Ben inherited his dad's square-jawed, "don't screw with me attitude," while Howie was quiet and reserved. In moments they shouldered undeserved guilt that they had not taught Jeanne how to protect herself. Ben reluctantly returned to graduate school at Loyola University after her funeral, and while he didn't complete his MBA there, he built a career appraising real estate near home. Howie drove back to his sales job at a business forms company in New Hampshire. Family friends caught only glimpses of him in the years ahead.

Having paved his own way through life, their father demanded a similar grit from both. Connie understood that her husband had inherited a streak of severity from his mother, who had raised Howard alone under difficult circumstances. Yet Connie rarely upbraided him for being harsh on their sons.

Many years later, Howie, who had gone through a busted relationship and other battles, told a relative, "I'm doing the best I can. Don't judge me."

No one is ever in a position to do that, and Connie's dear friend Yvonne Ameche Davis is no exception. Years after her own son's death, Davis received a wakeup call from her younger daughter, Beth, who was the only sibling at home when the word of a car crash reached them. When she returned to school a week or so later, a nun scolded Beth for not completing her homework. "After Paul died," Davis says her daughter reprimanded her, "You just looked at me and said, 'Handle it.'"

Her mother reflected that in the aftermath of such a loss, parents often cannot find the right tools—even if they know what to look for. "I just don't think we're capable of doing everything. For a while, we just sit back. I think we just get numb."

"You know they say that when you lose a child, a part of you dies," she says.

Yet the Clerys got even busier. In effect they erected a giant, perpetual memorial to Jeanne as their mission went national. Renting a small office five miles from their home, three years after starting the nonprofit they had three paid staffers along with a handful of full-time volunteers. With the staff fielding many of the incoming calls, Connie, on at least a weekly basis, went through stacks of letters from parents. They took short breaks, but the work was never far behind. Friends who had bought into a new golf course development near Port St. Lucie offered their unit to Howard and Connie for a respite in the sunshine state. The two spent a couple of months there, enjoying Harbour Ridge so much they soon bought a place themselves, as it also attracted many other Dartmouth alums and spouses whom they knew, including Jack and Dodie Boyle. The Clerys kept a room for Jeanne that was sealed off like a shrine.

Even in Florida, it was impossible to stay insulated for long. In later years their friends saw how difficult it was for Connie to remove herself from breaking cases of on-campus violence or reports of official wrongdoing. She took many incidents personally. "It was very hard for her to back away," Bob Simpson observed, "and even difficult for the Clerys' nonprofit staff."

"Any time there was a rape or murder, there was a reliving of it," Simpson's wife Anne agrees. "But at the same time, she was tough. She would really give it to some of those people in Washington."

Back home, Howard's focus and participation at work dwindled. By 1985, Rapidforms, the company he and a partner had acquired in 1972, had been bought out. Clery made out very well in the deal and continued to run it as chairman while becoming a director in the new ownership. He had also invested in real estate which, with its leases, yielded additional income for many years.

Still, Howard was miserable. He told Fioravanti his mind was so cluttered with nightmares "and these feelings that I just can't do this anymore." He wanted to sell his share to help Connie and commit himself to their cause. Clery's former laser-like business focus waned, and by late in 1988 he was sometimes a divisive influence, arguing with other managers. Plus, things in his field were also changing. At fifty-seven, Howard agreed to take early retirement, selling back his stock.

He and Connie had all the money they'd ever need for a comfortable retirement. But that wasn't even close to being important.

In the summer of 1988, Lehigh agreed to an out of court settlement for an amount north of $4 million. After paying their legal fees, the Clerys put all of it into their baby, the nonprofit they called Security On Campus. The university agreed to begin a three-part security program, at least in the Lower Centennial dorm complex where Jeanne had lived. This involved placing electronically monitored locks on dorm entrances, increasing security staff, and limiting access to each dorm to one well-lit main entrance.

The couple attained each of their three goals: forcing Lehigh to make changes; spreading awareness of the issue; and supporting their nonprofit's mission. Howard, who also demanded that he advise Lehigh in implementing the security improvements, said the program would set an example. Too often, he said, universities' consideration of campus security was built "on the premise that the reputation of the school is more important than the safety of any individual." They pushed the pendulum the other way.

As his friends had long experienced, Howard was not a guy to be trifled with. And Connie was just beginning to hone her own skills. Before long she would take the lead in training the spotlight on colleges' obligations.

We were back in court just after Mike's twentieth birthday, Cory Scanlon entering handcuffed and in leg shackles.

While some pressure had been relieved with his change of plea, it brought us little rest. Most of our family members had submitted statements for the judge to consider along with ours in announcing his sentencing. Sitting on the benches with P.J.'s family again, my expectations were somewhat ambivalent. More forgiving than myself, Denise privately was not calling for the maximum possible sentence, as her father and others did. I was somewhere in the middle. While ultimately agreeing with my wife to support the DA's recommendation of two-year terms for each count of motor vehicle homicide, my gut said that was not enough.

Lisa, Mike's closest aunt, got up and reflected on the totality of his life, from his christening to the morning when her family was in Disney World and she learned of the crash. She sometimes would embarrass him as a teenager, asking, "So who's the lucky girl?" noting that he would blush but still try maintain a certain cool, "and I knew that someday I would get to meet someone special." In her statement, my other sister-in-law, Jessica, said she had no good answer when my youngest niece, who was only three, asked why Michael had died.

Denise went up again alone beside the bench holding on to the words she had cobbled together. She couldn't remember if she had told Mike she loved him the last time they were alone watching his sister's game. Yet she recognized that somehow he still knew this. She knew that for the rest of our lives we'd be asking, "What if he was here right now?" Their risky decisions had brought suffering to so many.

She addressed Cory, who seemed to be seated closer than the actual distance to the witness stand, acknowledging that he, too, carried untold pain. "But there has to be consequences for our actions and you did the right thing by taking responsibility . . . Mike and P.J. should be with us here today, making their plans." Following my wife, I also spoke directly to him, telling Cory that he had avoided dragging two families through a trial of agony. Taking that step was a decision I thought would benefit him years ahead. I urged him to carry his friends with him every day of his life, and never give up—not on himself, and also for them.

He stood facing the judge, who apparently had received nearly one hundred letters supporting Cory's character. He apologized through muffled tears. "They would have done anything for me, and I would have done anything for them," he said. Earlier, his counsel, Kevin Reddington, tried to remind the judge that "any one of them could have been driving."

Judge Cratsley was having none of it. He issued the maximum sentence, saying he intended to send a message of deterrence to other young drivers. Technically this meant four years, but it resulted in Cory serving only two.

Before we left, Reddington strode calmly over, telling us he felt badly for our loss.

It didn't matter whether the question came from Joan Lunden or Geraldo Rivera.

"Would you tell us how your daughter died, Mrs. Clery?" In those brief moments Connie could not continue.

Yet she and Howard kept amplifying Jeanne's story in other venues, in countless newspaper and radio interviews, even on other talk shows. This roused interest from other alarmed parents. Armed with their validation, the Main Line couple set their sights higher.

Their initial success had spread beyond Pennsylvania, but the Clerys were frustrated that some states had passed watered down versions of the campus crime bill. The gains for students' safety were still hodgepodge. Inside their nonprofit's office a United States map hung on the wall. It would soon be marked with twelve red flags, each pinned to a state that had enacted a law inspired by theirs, and eventually, with twenty-two. Still, they knew that a national mandate with more teeth was needed. To make sure students were armed with information, they wanted colleges to publish annual reports containing their security policies and crime statistics, and to provide campus crime logs to the public. On what would have been Jeanne's twenty-third birthday in 1989, a bill was introduced in the House.

The couple drew maps of their own, deciding which lawmakers to pigeonhole and how to energize constituents to help push open doors. During this stretch, with Frank Carrington serving as their nonprofit's counsel and chief guide, Anne Simpson traveled with the Clerys to meet congressional aides and their bosses in the capital. Besides being longtime friends, Anne and her husband were early board members. Howard and Connie would review their talking points a bit on the ride, but not in a last-minute way. "Mostly, I think they were just very controlled," Anne says.

Howard especially could look anyone in the eye and distill what true intentions resided there. Simpson found him to be unfailingly articulate. Inevitably, Connie continued taking the difficult lead in telling Jeanne's story, but it was easier for her to do that in person than in the glare of those broadcast interviews. She also began driving much of their campaign. Those who had worked alongside her already marveled at her analytical skills. Besides being a good listener, Connie often asked questions that otherwise would slip through the cracks. And she became a tough advocate.

The Clerys then stepped up to a larger platform, a carousel with many of the country's most powerful law enforcement and education authorities. Carrington arranged for an invitation to a White House reception soon after President George H.W. Bush's election, and that evening they pressed the flesh with senior senators and other heavyweights. In a triumphant foreshadowing of their success, by the spring of 1990, Bush recognized the Clerys at a Rose Garden ceremony highlighting National Crime Victims' Rights Week. The president said the couple "embodies the power of volunteerism, the power of the physically challenged, the power of a just cause, a campaign to build an America where every victim of every crime is treated with the dignity and compassion they deserve."

By the fall of 1990, what was first called the Students Right-to-Know and Campus Security Act was moving through Congress. It extended what the couple had achieved in other states, requiring colleges to automatically provide basic campus crime statistics and security policies to students and staff. Nine categories of crimes were covered, from murder and burglary to arrests for drug and alcohol violations. The data and security details were to be easily available for prospective students, although another mandate they sought to provide public access to campus police crime logs was dropped—for the time being.

A letter-writing campaign organized by Connie's angels ensued, plus more talk show appearances drummed up by their publicist, and extensive articles in *Family Circle* and *USA Today*. Even the Clerys' housekeeper, Katherine Bridges, urged her congressman's support. "I'm Jeanne's other mother, who has helped care for her for most of her life," Bridges wrote. If lawmakers had any lingering doubts, those evaporated that August after a series of grisly murders at the University of Florida in Gainesville, where a man with a hunting knife butchered five students and terrorized the community. While tormenting the Clerys, the students' deaths galvanized the politicians.

Stella Goldberg sat beside Connie one day inside the Rayburn House Office Building, a stone's throw from the Capitol, ready to testify on the bill. Not a year after the Clerys' tragedy, Goldberg lost her own daughter. She, too, was twenty, and her name also was Jeanne.

She had been stabbed after attending a party on the Carnegie Mellon University campus in Pittsburgh, their hometown. An honor student and talented pianist, Jeanne Goldberg undoubtedly was in the wrong place and not in full control of herself at the time. Another student who borrowed Goldberg's car with her in it to find his drug dealer attacked Jeanne and left her beside a tree in a park.

Her mother was managing a store when Connie called some months later. Perhaps not by coincidence, they were on the same path.

"I won't take no for an answer, you're going to help me," Connie insisted. A draftsman by trade, Stella jumped right in, sending letters and buying extra toner and ink at the store to help the campaign.

"Here is the miracle," she says looking back. "A lot of us don't ask the kids, 'Where are you going?' I didn't ask her. [That night] I was getting ready to watch *Dallas*."

The Clerys' purpose was crystal clear to her, and alongside Connie, she needed to act in her daughter's memory. She saw Connie stand up to speak, maintaining her poise as though an earthquake had not ripped through her family. Then Stella Goldberg put away her own prepared remarks.

Connie had told Jeanne's story once again. And Goldberg wondered if the initial sympathy they heard from the congressmen would bear any fruit. "A lot of people have other tragedies," she thought to herself. *You wonder where the hand of God is.*

So she took another tack. Speaking to members of the House panel,

Goldberg announced that she came to talk about *their* children, not her own daughter. She told them, to the effect, "Do you ever stop to think about how they've been living at home for eighteen years, you tuck them into bed . . . do you ever stop to think about that security door that's not locked at night? Do you ever stop to think about what could happen to your kid?"

"My idea was to knock the crap out of them," she says.

In early fall of 1990, Howard and Connie were up in Bethlehem visiting some state troopers when word came that the president had signed what would become known as the Jeanne Clery Act.

After her daughter was taken, "a seed was planted almost immediately," Connie reflected later. She knew that what had happened to Jeanne was occurring elsewhere, muzzled from earshot, far from the spotlight. Finally, some tools were being put in place to rectify this.

The Clerys' lives resumed in Bryn Mawr, but not in any routine way. Manifestations of Jeanne's loss surrounded them. Her portraits hung throughout the house and they built a memorial in their small courtyard. They commissioned a bronze sculpture that Connie wanted to symbolize life resurrected. The sculptor, an Italian priest, created a slaughtered lamb with a coat strafed by cuts—not exactly the paschal lamb that often symbolizes Jesus.

The image unnerved both her and Howard at first. Yet they came to accept the sacrificed lamb, which had its legs folded and eyes half closed. Howard had told the priest, "Look, I didn't want some kind of happy-talk symbol, because we have personal memories, and those are happy. But her death, our memories of her death, will never be happy."

"We have our martyrs," he continued, speaking collectively for other families like the Baers and Reilleys. "Those kids are our martyrs, and there are many more, and they're growing every day."

He and Connie also did a lot to preserve Jeanne's memory at her high school, donating a pointed fieldstone fountain and landscaping with English garden benches. They established a scholarship for students in financial need and furnished new bleachers for the tennis courts beside a memorial stone that reads, "Her laughter will always live in our hearts." There were other plaques, a memory garden, and a class night award.

Each of these things would auger deep into their conception of what is bittersweet. Each would inevitably gather dust and even hint at feeling perversely ubiquitous, blending over time with other families' attempts to preserve another loved one's legacy.

At some point, the Clerys would need to skip the lengthening scholarship ceremonies. In the best case, their daughter's closest friends and others who mattered most would retain their connections with Jeanne, distilled from what once was the clarity of her presence. Even as the sharpness faded, her essence remained: "Truly a fighter and a hard worker, just a nice solid athlete, and a good kid," her tennis coach summed up. Memory continued to believe, even if holding on to threads.

Back home, Howard's father developed a routine with Sister Miriam, a Lebanese-American nun who conducted their Bible study group. He invited her to their house, and during those first six months or so, five and even six times a week Miriam drove over during the afternoons.

Both parents greeted her at the door, and after offering her a cold drink Connie left Miriam and her husband alone. He vented, often for two hours, and she cried along with him. But mostly she listened. Each disclosure stabbed at him: Lehigh's knowledge of doors propped open; the access to dormitories Henry had through his university job; the denials of responsibility. "For Connie and Howard it was like throwing acid on raw skin," she says. Howard often repeated himself in their sessions together, which she found to be so necessary.

He needed to know it was all right to hurt. He needed to know it was all right to sob his heart out. He needed to know it was perfectly normal and justified that he would feel so much anger, so much confusion and desire such ravenous revenge. "He needed to know," she recalls, "it was okay to feel that. Because some people believe you can't feel that way, it's a sin."

You only feel pain because you love.

Miriam and Howard already had an indelible connection. She was a member of the Daughters of the Heart of Mary, a religious order founded in secrecy during the French Revolution. To avoid persecution under Robespierre's Reign of Terror, its members avoided external identifications of their faith, and they continue this practice today. They do not wear habits, assume titles, or live in a convent. They often work as doctors, teachers, or social workers, and conduct retreats around the world and missions in places including the Bronx and Atlantic City.

Miriam Najimy believes Divine Providence led her to make her vows after what she describes as years of devastating lows. She struggled growing up with a severe speech impediment and teachers told Miriam's parents that she was borderline retarded but should stay in school—just in case. "I believed it and they believed it, and I never saw much of a future for myself," she says. Howard marveled at how this petite woman overcame her disability and embraced a theology that was so grounded, and unvarnished by ritual.

At age eighty-two she was vigorous and spry, a member of an assisted living residence for retirees of her order. Her brown eyes were warm and she relished learning new things. She offered a clarity of redemptive wisdom, an affirmation of what she called "how to live as authentic human beings." People of great faith doubted they even had it, she told me. They railed, they drove loved ones away. They even numbed themselves.

But mostly, they searched.

Howard, she said, was constantly searching and learning. Even before losing Jeanne he argued that God was unjust, or absent, during genocide, wars, and famine—not uncommon questions, which she found perfectly valid. As he prepared to challenge their study group, eyes would roll again throughout the room. "Will we ever get the answer? I don't know that we ever will, on this side of eternity," she says. "And when we reach the other side of eternity, will it matter? I don't know."

Over those months and the seasons ahead, Sister Miriam affirmed Howard Clery's questions and pain. She observed how he and Connie were living among that full canopy. "This thing they call Catholic guilt— you're not supposed to feel this way—that's a bunch of nonsense," she says. "When you hurt you need to cry out."

The specter of Josoph Henry hovered close by, snapping the family back in a whiplash with each of his court appeals.

Some fourteen months after sentencing the trial judge denied his first attempt, rebuffing the claim that an all-white jury did not give Henry a fair trial. In a forty-page opinion, the judge said jurors were correct both in finding that the crime was committed as a means of torture, and that

Henry murdered Jeanne to "silence a witness," realizing she would easily identify him as the burglar. The Pennsylvania Supreme Court then upheld the death sentence as proportional. Henry was transferred from the county jail to death row at the Huntingdon State Prison. Once there, as the state switched its execution method from electrocution to lethal injection, his belated attempts at redemption got serious.

He found religion. He admitted to having emotional wounds. Targeting the first woman he saw. He flip-flopped to taking responsibility, writing to his trial lawyer that whatever "mental state I was in I don't think it could be considered insanity."

In the midst of appealing to the US Supreme Court, Henry wrote a note to Jeanne's family:

"I have sinned against you. I am and always will be filled with sorrow. I beg you, please forgive me. Sincerely, Josoph M. Henry."

Farrell knew he could not pass this on. Not while he represented Henry. Years later, after Henry hired another attorney, the letter made its way through Fioravanti to the Clerys. Connie kept it in a vault; there was no need to open it again.

She did not believe Henry was genuine. His writing fell short of demonstrating a true baring of his soul, and seemed more part of his calculation to get off. Yet unlike her husband, Connie didn't care if he died by injection or in the chair or rotted for life. She knew his ultimate judgment would come later.

Howard scoffed at the very notion of forgiveness. Those attempts by the killer to save his neck only drove Clery's anger harder. Vowing to be at Huntingdon for the final scene, he offered to throw the switch himself. *The sonofabitch should be burned and I want to go see him burn.* This grew stronger with time, despite the steps he was making with Sister Miriam.

Jack Boyle knew that his husky cousin could take just about any shot. But these appeals went on for fifteen years. There were four major attempts, endless filings and motions, even a four-day evidentiary hearing in 1996. Both sons were often back in court with their parents as the crushing plant churned and fumed around them.

Jack's brother, Ed Boyle, was a Jesuit priest who also grew up playing hockey and baseball with Clery, and he kept urging Howard to take another path. He, too, had been near the altar at Jeanne's Mass. During her interment, the Reverend Edward Boyle's message was to practice unconditional love, and accept that there could be no earthly explanation.

"Look beyond this trauma and move forward," Jack recalled his late brother's advice. "And appreciate the joy that Jeanne brought to her community, and thank God for that."

None of which was so easy to do.

6

GRINDER

A s the late summer sunshine poured over Peirce Field, Howard squared himself to receive a practice punt. His Arlington High Raiders' opening game was less than a week away, and the varsity squad looked promising. Three starters had been held over in school from the previous year, and a solid offense was led by a "triple-threater" back named George Faulkner.

His friends called Clery a speed demon, and Howard was a sturdy and dependable athlete. He went hard in every sport, sometimes playing hockey for five straight hours with few breaks, which built up his legs and stamina. Entering his sophomore year, he made starting halfback on the third team and played both sides of the ball. He'd already caught the attention of his coaches and seemed destined for greater things.

It was a glorious day to be alive.

Just a few weeks earlier, the Japanese had surrendered aboard the USS *Missouri*. The people of Arlington, as in other towns surrounding Boston and all over the nation, celebrated the long war's end in spontaneous jubilation. It began on a Tuesday afternoon with an impromptu parade along the main avenue, neighbors banging tin cans and pails as children rode bicycles adorned with flags. Marchers carried large placards proclaiming "V-J Day," while the manager of the Ben Franklin Store in Arlington Heights gave out 1,200 flags, some as large as three by five feet.

Just as the previous May when war had ended in Europe, services of thanksgiving soon followed in the town's Catholic churches and the stalwart First Parish Church. Solemn calls went out to focus on the hard work of rebuilding, and to honor the sacrifices of so many. In one sense it was nothing new for the town, which had played a role secondary only to nearby Lexington and Concord back in 1775. Later on during that infamous April day, as a column of British regulars retreated, fighting with the converging militia was heaviest in Arlington, and half of the Minutemen killed in the battle fell there. Once again, the town had made a hefty sacrifice during the Second World War. More than one in every ten of its 43,500 residents had entered into wartime service, and 109 local men died.

The fighting was finally over. In September of 1945, for Clery and his cousins in the neighboring towns, there was a cloudless sky. The only limit to what they might accomplish would be determined by their own spit and grit.

Howard squinted upwards to track the ball. Stretching his arms to receive the punt, he took a step back as his legs fell out from him. His senses and balance quit, and he found himself on the ground. Thinking it was due to the lingering heat, he asked to sit out for a few minutes. After taking a drink, he went back on the field to take another punt.

As the ball reached the peak of its arc, Howard steadied himself again, looked skyward, and "collapsed into a seated position, his legs folding beneath him. Once again, he experienced a feeling of involuntary collapse. And now he was frightened," Joe Fioravanti wrote years later.

After the coach brought Howard to the locker room, it quickly got worse. A sharp pain knifed through the back of his head and neck, and his body went into disequilibrium. He had suffered bad heat cramps before, but never anything like this. A massive headache ensued and his legs convulsed in spasms. He made it home and his mother Margaret put him to bed. The stiffness and convulsions continued, and the headaches made him delirious. Several doctors were called in, and the diagnosis was poliomyelitis.

Polio brought panic. Young children were often the targets of the mysterious virus widely called "infantile paralysis." The immediate fear was death, or a lifetime of being unable to move one's arms and legs. Polio epidemics had swept the world since the 1840s, and the worst epidemic in the United States would arrive relatively soon in 1952, causing more than three thousand deaths that year before the first vaccines were developed.

Some fears were irrational. Don't get too close, you may catch it. Didn't you shower with him after practice?

"Howard has polio. What the hell is polio?" his cousin Jack Boyle recalls. "Of course, no one knows why you get polio. There was nothing we could do about it. He could not walk. Well, how do you *not* walk?"

The high school canceled its first two football games. Howard was baffled. And furious, pounding his legs in frustration. Why him? How did it happen? *No idea. No idea.*

More than a week after Clery was stricken, the *Arlington Advocate* sought to quell rumors of a polio epidemic. "Only Two Infantile Paralysis Cases Here," a front-page headline advised. Besides identifying Howard, the newspaper reported that a young woman had also been diagnosed, while the quarantine had been lifted for a third suspected victim, a toddler. The games had been called off "not because of the danger of contagion, but because of the probable repercussions should polio develop in Medford following the [opening away] game," the *Advocate* reported. Finally, on October 6, the Raiders opened their season against Lynn.

Howard was admitted to Massachusetts General Hospital and stayed until after Thanksgiving. Polio was confirmed. The hospital had an artificial respirator called an iron lung, a long airtight tank resembling a coffin, or maybe a space capsule that set designers would have cooked up for an early sci-fi movie. The iron lung was used to treat children in polio's acute phase, when the diaphragm is paralyzed so that breathing becomes very difficult. While dreaded, and making a noise similar to a modern dishwasher, the metal cylinder was the best-known method for rebuilding a patient's chest muscles. As Howard lay prone with his head protruding from the chamber, nurses and doctors looked through a porthole to monitor his chest rising and falling with the huffing of vacuum pumps.

While despondent at first, Howard learned that he was relatively fortunate. Some polio victims had to rely on the iron lung for the rest of their lives. The virus had invaded his lumbar spine, which meant he would lose all or some of the function of his legs, but his upper body functions were okay. He would not be paralyzed from the neck down, and would be able to use the bathroom on his own, and have children. Yet as his wife would recall later, there was no place nearby yet where he could get intensive physical therapy and learn to live with his sudden disability. "That wasn't enough," Connie says of the iron lung. "They didn't have the water treatments."

His mother worked at the American Red Cross chapter in Cambridge. Despite not having much money, Margaret Clery somehow pulled enough strings to get Howard into the one place renowned for rehabilitating polio patients with its therapeutic waters: Warm Springs, Georgia. President Franklin D. Roosevelt had made the healing spas of the West Georgia mountainside community popular in his quest to find a cure for polio and provide therapy for those afflicted like himself. It was there that Roosevelt had spent his final days the previous April, and it became Clery's destination.

The spa was already legendary for its healing qualities when FDR established a polio hospital and research center there in the mid-1920s, as water with average temperature of 86 degrees flowed from the nearby foothills. Creek Indian warriors had first bathed in the thermal springs to heal their wounds and spirits. Roosevelt visited dozens of times as president at the "Little White House," as he dubbed his retreat, a cottage with a back porch overlooking a ravine. He exercised in the pool while attempting to rebuild his muscles, and in later years renewed his health with swims, by sunning himself and with country drives in a specially fitted open coupe. Although interrupted during the war, his spring and autumn visits throughout the Depression restored Roosevelt's vigor when the country needed it most.

Almost a decade before Howard was stricken, the president decided to take on polio full-bore. Roosevelt created an advocacy group called the National Foundation for Infantile Paralysis to research and publicize polio. Soon the March of Dimes campaign kicked off for the foundation, and millions of Americans responded in kind. As the public spotlight focused on combatting the disease, hope began to rise—even if not for Clery, at least for another generation.

Howard carried a deep respect for FDR the rest of his life. Years later, even as he became a staunch Republican and railed at liberals for what he believed were overreaching government policies, Howard's admiration for the man never waned. "Of course, he knew firsthand what Roosevelt had to face," old friend Bob Malin recalls. "The loss of a dream to which he was somehow able to surmount. I think it was inspiring to Howard. It had to be."

One morning late in 1945, Jack Boyle's dad lifted Howard up inside

South Station. They placed him on a stretcher, passing him through the window onto a train. He was southbound for Warm Springs.

"I will overcome this too," Boyle says, scrunching his face into a fist. "High discipline." *Don't you worry about me fella. You might worry about yourself.*

In his unpublished manuscript about the Clerys, Fioravanti described Howard's early months in Georgia this way:

Life in Warm Springs provided no time for self-pity or self-doubt. This was a place for arduous work, for special exploration. This was a place where Howard would learn where and what he could still move, and what might be useful to him. He came to understand that hours would be spent with dreaded hot packs, and with being submerged, weightless, in a pool lying on top of therapeutic tables sunken beneath the water. There were therapists who spent hours experimenting to determine with Howard whether a spasm in a muscle might indicate a sign of capability, something to be developed and enhanced.

Howard learned how to dress himself again. He learned how to use the wheelchair. He learned to groom himself, and to make himself ready for the dining room. The Warm Springs youngster who could dress and groom himself, and wheel himself into the dining room for a meal, felt a special sense of accomplishment. When it happened to Howard Clery, the smile came back to his face. It was a grand smile. As he sat there, receiving and passing food to and from his "classmates" at Warm Springs, his yellow hair seemed to shine again, the twinkle returned to his blue eyes, and the firm, sure broad smile came back to Howard's face.

While the muscles on his right leg atrophied and that side was useless, Howard retained some movement in his left leg. A brace was fitted for his right leg, and using that and what was known as an "Everett cane," which had cuffs around his arms, he used his upper body strength to walk. Having learned to do this, he was discharged in April of 1946, and returned home.

He hadn't really focused on school before, but Howard began grinding away, climbing three flights of stairs at school and raising his grades.

Although he didn't regularly make the honor roll or join clubs like the student council, he became popular. By his senior year he was voted vice president in a class of 582 students. For his yearbook blurb, Clery remarked that his sophomore year was memorable "because of the fine friends made then."

Yet something became knotted inside him, a shade instilled by his mother. Life had embittered Margaret Clery, and her son learned to be a requisite hard ass. Boys were meant to grow up quickly and become men.

One day she told Howard, "The world is made up of people who are strong and weak. Which do you choose to be?"

One Mother's Day, Howard pushed himself down Massachusetts Avenue to buy her some flowers. She demanded to know why.

"I'm bringing this to you because I love you."

"Take this back to the florist and demand the money back," she responded. "I do not want the flowers."

She asked how much they cost. He returned to the store, retrieving the full five dollars.

If Howard wanted more than to merely survive, he would have to pick himself up. His resilience and self-propelled drive, anchored in the sweep of his mother's family making their way up among Boston's Irish clans, infused what he and Connie accomplished later.

His father died when he was nine. They were living in New Jersey, but Margaret moved back to her native Massachusetts, where her only child had been born in 1930. Although her in-laws were well off, and despite it being the depth of the Depression, they cut her off. They'd always felt that Margaret Clery and her kind weren't good enough for their son. They did, however, provide for their grandson's college education later. Margaret moved back with her mother, a sister, and an unmarried brother. She found work, as all the Fenton women did, as a secretary and clerk.

In a sense Howard was far from an only child. His extended Fenton family in Arlington and neighboring Belmont included five boy cousins who were close in age. They played pond hockey and loved football, any sport that didn't require much equipment or a ticket. Walking four or five miles to a ball field across town with their gloves and cleats was no big deal.

Back then they didn't much follow pro teams like the Braves, Red Sox, or Bruins; those clubs were distant for working-class kids, and nobody ever dreamed of going to a game. High school rivalries were far more relevant, and they also followed the local college teams. Along with several of his cousins, Howard caddied on local courses and learned to play golf. A few were gifted athletes. Each was bright, highly competitive, and destined for big things.

The Fentons had something else going for them.

Margaret and her sister, Marie (Jack Boyle's mom), were among six siblings who grew up in a three-decker in Somerville. As with many Irish families, whether cloistered in Southie or Charlestown, or patrolling Dorchester Avenue and later fanning out to the suburbs, they spat out life's ironies like broken teeth. Their father, who had emigrated from County Cork in the 1870s, worked on railroads and was killed in an accident. His first son, Thomas, also lost his life at work in a transit accident. Along with Margaret, two of her sisters became widows within a few years of marrying, each with a single child, as if strapped to their mother's fate. This didn't break them. Some of the men were workers; the women, who were competent and attractive, found jobs as secretaries, several in high-level, coveted positions at the city's blueblood law firms. "They all grew up supporting each other," Boyle says. To compete with Boston's Brahmins and quit the second-story apartments or public housing, it would take education, discipline, and leadership.

A trace of a workingman's Kennedys coursed through their tribe, but there was something more definitive than this going for them. In Boston's often-parochial social circles and business networks, many of the Fenton men of Howard's generation were more akin to a Jack Connors, who is legendary in the Hub, at least, as founder of the Hill Holliday advertising agency. Raised in a two-family home in Roslindale, Connors put himself through Boston College driving a cab and hawking hotdogs at Fenway Park. He stayed a homeboy even as he later advised the governor on health care reform and helped revamp the archdiocese's parochial schools. While becoming one of the city's true powerbrokers, Connors resisted forgetting who he was: the grandson of a cop who'd lost his job in a labor dispute.

A similar fusion of obligatory duty, Catholic morality, and competitive fire spiked through the veins of these Fenton sons and cousins. The Boyles, O'Donnells, Thorntons, Fentons, and Howard Clery—they all had it. Jack Boyle's younger brother Ed became a track captain at Belmont High and started each year in football and basketball. Jack captained his football team at Saint Sebastian and was a hockey and baseball standout. David Fenton would captain football at Saint Columbkille and again at Tufts. On it went. They climbed up to successful careers and bought vacation homes, unapologetic to townies who sneered at the "two-toilet Irish."

Howard and Jack were nearly identical twins. Born just three months apart, both were compact and broad-shouldered, five-foot-nine or -ten inches of muscle. Each a scrapper, Howard a grinder in the best sense on skates, and in other ways.

While not exceptional on any playing field, Howard was still a standout. When he was younger, his Tigers were playing Leo Clancy's Yankees in a ballgame. Clancy, who lived in a nicer side of town near the Winchester line, doesn't remember the score. "But I do recall the speed merchant who flashed around the bases. Everybody called him 'Howie,'" he says. "From what I saw he was very competent, as a kid more slender, but he could run well. When he ran his hair would sort of flow a little bit and it was an interesting sort of look."

Leo's buddies were guys nicknamed Brownie, Red, Shadow, and Swede. By the time he reached high school, Howie was another. Clery made a splash with the football coaches too. In addition to running the ball as a halfback, on the defensive side his job was to tackle bigger and faster running backs. "And every tackle hurt," Bob Malin says.

Expectations for the male Fenton cousins ratcheted even higher. As teenagers, they might dig ditches to lay granite curbing or run wheelbarrows for the parks department. But they sought those jobs in part to build themselves up physically for the coming sports season, as athletic scholarships were the stamped ticket out. Boyle's father, John, had worked running orders at the Boston Stock Exchange, and was hired as a broker only when the brokerage house wanted him to play third base on its semipro baseball team. When Ed and Jack approached college age, Jack recalls his dad asking, "Which Ivy school will you guys grace with your presence with a full scholarship? Because I have no money." He threw the challenge down only once or twice.

Beyond his extended family, Howard lived in a community that went all-out in the war effort. His neighbors' eagerness knew no bounds as they mobilized in every conceivable way. They joined requisite collections for aluminum, rubber, and junk; the rationing of gasoline and commodities like sugar, ground beef, or bananas; and complied with air raid drills, brownouts, calls to make coupons for ration books, blood drives, Victory Bonds, war loans, and draft registration. High school woodshop students built chests to hold medical supplies for evacuees in case of an emergency, while both guys and gals took civil defense communications classes.

Howard and his mom were right in the thick of it. Their second-story apartment was just off bustling Massachusetts Avenue in East Arlington near the Cambridge line, amidst an aspiring middle class. Downstairs from them were the Youngs—a fireman and his sister, a bookkeeper, living with their mother. A carpenter and salesman lived next door near an electrical engineer and his housewife. Scores of professionals lived beside meat packers, artists, and a postmaster in a large brick complex nearby. Margaret didn't own a car, but few people they knew drove anyway.

Howie and his friends undoubtedly saw many of the twice-weekly war newsreels shown before feature films at the Capitol Theatre just a few blocks away. Like the rival Regent theatre in the town center, the Capitol became a vital source for wartime news. It also ran special children's features on Saturday afternoons and when the shows were done, "if you had any talent you would go on stage and perform" for cash prizes, one resident recalled. For other diversions, they might take the train to the Boston Garden or a subway to Revere Beach in the summer, but there were also recreation dances at the town hall, bowling, and swimming at Spy Pond.

The boys had a champion in their Uncle Jack. A bachelor most of his life, Jack Fenton was a father figure to the children of his three widowed sisters and each of his nephews. He worked at the United States Customs office, a plum job, and earned a law degree at night. Only of medium height and barely 140 pounds, Uncle Jack was a fitness nut. A sharp dresser, he bought his clothes at Filene's Basement and took good care of himself. The formula he showed his nephews was straightforward. "Do pushups, run sprints, get strong and look good, and study," Boyle says. "A very simple program."

Fenton occasionally found the boys work. Young Jack got an internship at the customs office, and worked for a while as a longshoreman unloading six-foot-tall bales of wool with a hook and a two-wheel dolly. This initiation started his career as an entrepreneur in the material handling industry. Their uncle also attended many of their games, finding ways to leave work early. Most keenly though, along with the Boyles' dad, Fenton delivered the family ethos, the same refrains from the Book of Luke that compelled a Jack Connors, or a Tom Flatley, the Boston commercial real estate guru from County Mayo.

Where much is given—good health, brains, physical strength—much is expected!

If they worked hard enough, each of the cousins realized a bright future was within reach. They also knew full well it was the fighting and war factories and Navy Yard jobs that had finally brought about economic recovery. It was about sacrifice. Someday their wives would need Frigidaires and ask for a new Chrysler or Packard. They dreamed of moving farther out from the city.

By the fall of 1945, anything below half A's and half B's was unacceptable. The pressure was real, but surmountable. They mostly got it. Except for Howard, who didn't give it his all until he turned sixteen.

One day two generations later, Jack Boyle articulated those values as if dealing from a deck. We met at his condominium at Flagship Wharf in Charlestown on a bright autumn day. From the fourth floor Jack and Dodie held a sweeping view of the harbor and Boston skyline. He motioned beside us to the large cranes and sheds of the Navy Yard, where a British destroyer, the HMS *Dauntless*, was docked for a few days. The yard is not far from his dad's old neighborhood, the "Irish ghetto" up on Bunker Hill, John Boyle Sr. being a third-generation townie whose grandfather fought in the Civil War. When young Jack Boyle was discharged from the navy after Korea, he stepped on to Dry Dock Number 2 just outside his window.

At eighty-two, Boyle still carried the phrasings and intonations of his father, and Uncle Jack, and Howard. The pure blue of his eyes, once mirroring his cousin's, had long been diluted and filtered by metallic clouds. He picked up mental snapshots like faded Polaroids spread out on a table.

Life passes. "No time wasted, nothing left unsaid," he began, raising Howard's voice again. The memory of his closest brother, Ed, who lived this next value in full, and who delivered a homily for Jeanne, this brought him to tears. "Very strong," he said.

Give back, Jack. Howard, give back. Ed, David Fenton, give back.

Howard's hard work began to pay off at Arlington High. He had learned to get around, climbing the stairwells with his leg brace and carrying his books. Although he'd been set back a year, friends don't remember him complaining. A growing self-reliance impressed them. Clery's grades shot up, and as Boyle puts it, "he became a very, very talented student."

As a senior both Howard and Leo Clancy were representatives at Boy's State, learning about government firsthand as they participated in a student debate at the State House. While Leo joined the school's Gilbert & Sullivan musical theatre club, Howard became a class officer. His high school yearbook blurb—apparently written by an advisor—says the "prospects of a bright teaching career loom for Howie."

In their entry for the yearbook's "Last Will and Testament," Clery and two pals announced they were leaving "to find some parties to crash."

Howard's cousins and his Uncle Jack had a hand in getting him to apply to Dartmouth College, where he was accepted. As Boyle tells it, two men, including a neighbor of his maybe ten years older who had captained the Big Green hockey team, were impressed with his own hockey talent. They pushed Boyle to go to Dartmouth. A year later, a similar press was put upon Howard. "He was a student of interest," Boyle says. "Because of being an athlete and with polio, and now a good student."

Entering in the fall of 1949, Howard had to drive himself harder in a competitive new world. Everyone in his class of seven hundred-plus had something going for him. Whether as intellectuals, prospective engineers, actors, football or hockey players, or those singing bass and tenor in the glee club, each seemed to be bright or gifted. Like others of their generation, many were on overdrive to succeed. Whereas before the war admission to Dartmouth and other Ivy League schools was often a matter of pedigree, a meritocracy was on the rise. Generally, "nobody cared who your family was, what your name was," Boyle says. Right away, Howard and Jack, Leo Clancy, too, and Ed Boyle—who came to Hanover a year after Clery— they all knew: "You better study. These guys are smart."

Opportunities were rife for those who stepped up. Several of Howard's new friends and relatives, including Jack Boyle, took advantage of the peacetime Naval Reserve Officer Training Corps program, which paid tuition and books in exchange for a three-year commitment after graduation. Howard's disability made him ineligible. But he made the first-year transition, bearing down on his studies while rooming with Clancy. He continued grinding. "He was not a scholar, he was a hardworking student," says Clancy. "Nothing came easy. He was smart enough to do the work, and he worked hard on top of it. That's a good combination."

Clancy called the initial load that year "compelling." A professor would easily assign one hundred pages of reading overnight, regardless of the bulk from other classes. Howard never vented about it or seemed unduly frustrated. "I just think he went out and did—or didn't—do it," Leo laughs. "If you didn't, the next day you were cooked."

Personable and instantly recognizable with his leg braces, Howard quickly became well known and liked. He talked up his chief interests, current events and history. Classmates twice elected him as their president, starting in his freshmen year, and he ran a time or two against a readily identifiable Irishman named Red Brady. "It was just name recognition and popularity," Clancy says, "more an honorific title." He also served on a student judicial panel that meted out punishment for minor infractions.

Howard had other things going for him. Not having something extra to prove, his longtime roommate and friend Fred Whittemore explains, "but something to be active in." Clery had an opinion on everything, and didn't shirk from giving it. He sought out all types among his classmates. "It was getting to know people, their names and information, Howard was very good at that," says Whittemore, who roomed with Howard as an upperclassman. "That got him elected on a repeated basis, and he did that after Jeanne died, and in business."

"At Dartmouth you make good friends," says Whittemore, who went on to a long career at Morgan Stanley. "That's the activity the needs to be done, really socializing."

Along with Whittemore, Howard joined Sigma Alpha Epsilon. The requisite drinking flowed at the basement bar, and Whittemore recalls hazing initiations that would be condemned today. But it was more about camaraderie. From playing ping-pong to telling stories to getting to know each other, he says, "the whole question was how accommodating to the group you could be. Howard fit in." Later Howard joined the Cask & Gauntlet, one of Dartmouth's coveted senior societies. Girls were imported—often nurses from the nearby hospital, or up from Smith or schools in Boston, and Howard was often a hit with them. While sharply opinionated, he usually also displayed a good sense of humor. By their senior year, Howard and Fred had devised a signal if either was entertaining a member of the opposite sex in their room: A necktie would be hung around the doorknob. "I don't know if there were many romances," laughs Bob Malin—who met Howard about the same time—when I asked him about those alleged necktie glory nights. "That was mostly a myth."

Capable of a fiery temper, Howard could take as well as give. One time when Clery was away from the dorm, Malin and some others moved Howard's bed to the basement where there was a squash court. He returned to an empty room. "To think a guy like that we could play a practical joke on, shows what a guy he was," Malin says. "We all jumped in there and took everything back."

He majored in history, completing a bachelor's degree as his interests turned to business. Along with most of his pack, he entered Dartmouth's Tuck School of Business during his senior year, earning an MBA in 1954.

Looking back, some of his old friends have a lasting vision of him crunching across the snowpack to get around campus. Dorms were located as close as possible to many classroom buildings, but it often still required a half-mile trek. Howard was virtually alone shouldering a backpack with his books in order to keep his hands free. "The quality of being," Clancy expressed many years later during Clery's memorial service. "On occasion if he fell or slipped he would brush off all attempts to help pick him up, except perhaps for a brusque request to pick up his books. But he had to get back on his feet by himself. He had the courage to stand by his convictions. He might say, 'Hurry up Leo. We're late for class.'"

It wasn't just the long auburn hair falling across her shoulders that immediately attracted him. Howard noticed a sticker on her briefcase, "Barnard," the all-women's college that's long been Columbia University's sister school. Connie had graduated the same year as him, majoring in French with a minor in Spanish. She could take shorthand in the three romance languages. This Constance Benjamin was erudite and lived on Commonwealth Avenue. He was impressed.

Connie grew up in New Bedford, the eldest daughter of a grocer who looked after his customers in lean times. A child of salt air and open-water swimming, from early on she seemed destined for pursuits beyond the hard-shelled former whaling capital. Both of her parents were French-Canadian, whose families had joined a late wave of immigrants coming to work primarily in the city's textile mills. Many of her neighbors on Clark's Point spent much of their lives replacing spindles and running the looms to produce fine wools, silk, and tire fabrics. She adored being alongside her dad in his neighborhood store, and it was there Connie first began to appreciate working with people. Its potbelly stove helped stave off the winter chill from Buzzards Bay and there was a large brass cash register, wondrous to a young girl's eyes with heavy numeric keys and mysterious receipts bundled under the metal tabs.

She and Howard both worked at the Gillette Company in South Boston—Howard in the finance department through a management-training program, Connie as a secretary in its international office. A few times in the cafeteria they eyed each other. He was cute enough, but what really attracted Connie was seeing him get around with his brace and cane. She thought, he's got to have real courage.

Still, no one had introduced them. One day he walked into her office and said, "I'm Howard Clery. Who are you?"

7

MORE TO DO

Steven Daniel Carter is not one to linger. A large man with great bushy eyebrows just shy of Leonid Brezhnev, he sizes you up as if weighing how much time you're worth before he returns to tweet an update. He moves from one thing to the next like a consummate businessman, dispatching three items and planning five steps ahead.

He flies into Logan on a warm June day to help part the clouds. For commanders in the Boston Police Department's sexual assault unit, there's confusion over jurisdiction among the city's many campus police units and themselves. If there's a rape along Huntington Avenue, do the Northeastern or Wentworth police investigate along with city cops? Occasional tensions flare between town and gown as universities continue to sprawl into the neighborhoods. And several recent reported college rapes have city councilors squawking about how Boston police handle sexual violence cases on campuses.

By now, two decades after his college days, Carter is a steady hand walking this terrain. He has brought along a primer on a subject that is second nature to him but gray matter to most people, and even to many in law enforcement: what colleges should do when sexual assaults are reported, and how municipal police should coordinate efforts with their campus counterparts. Both sides should have clear communication of their respective roles. Yet the lines in Beantown remain murky.

John Doherty, a close relative of Howard Clery's, picks up Carter at the airport. Doherty has invited me along to meet Daniel—as Carter prefers to be called—and observe the Clerys' nonprofit, Security on Campus, in the field. Stepping into the back seat of a cluttered minivan crossover, Carter shifts some boxes and papers to make room. Doherty, whose mom is a cousin of Howard's, is a marketing consultant who yaks like a true Bostonian, his nasal assonant windup just shy of the counter guy's rasp at Kelly's Roast Beef in Revere. John considers Connie to be as close as any of his aunts. Behind the scenes he has supported the legislative goals of the Clerys' nonprofit for many years.

Two minutes into the ride Carter is on the phone. He dials an Associated Press reporter to squeeze in an interview, then checks his voicemail before we reach an appointment. Later he emails an undersecretary at the US Department of Education to set up a briefing about a sex discrimination case. It's an unfolding college scandal, a Title IX investigation, which refers to the federal statute prohibiting discrimination on the basis of sex in schools. A few weeks earlier, students had lodged a complaint against an iconic university for failing to protect women from harassment in an environment of open sexual intimidation. Apparently administrators opted to not handle students' claims in a way that most grade school janitors know would be humane and meet the letter of the law. All of which is on Carter's oscillating radar.

For several years, Carter has been public policy director at the Clerys' nonprofit. His title sounds a tad grandiose, since Security On Campus has just four full-time paid employees in a small office, but Daniel has earned his stripes. As a longtime campus safety advocate, he knows how to navigate many state houses and prominent politicians' offices. He's a regular visitor to the Department of Education in the capital, where he's sometimes called in to help write federal guidance for colleges on how to handle sexual assault complaints or issue timely notifications during an emergency.

While he's a policy wonk who can recite the page numbers and sections of bills encyclopedically, Carter is not completely wedded to the arcane world of legislative sausage making and regulations. On first impression he has a gruff look and dishes out criticism to every side, yet Carter rarely does this in a personal way. He's had a soft spot for campus police officers since his college days. He's bothered by the mixed results of the Clery Act, rules that are sometimes unclear and burdensome to colleges, as well as by slack enforcement by federal authorities. He's also held many college administrators' feet to the fire, filing complaints with the feds himself after scouring through reports of the worst cover-ups of rape and even murder. "People who know me have said I really want them to succeed," Carter offers, referring to both administrators and police. "When I filed a complaint it was because I wanted to make them better, not to hurt them, and to be better equipped to serve their community."

Daniel can be a gentle bear. His best days are spent alongside others who are similarly driven to improve campus safety and empower an incoming generation of students and assault survivors—sometimes, even lifting themselves. What keeps him going, he tells me later over lunch, is "helping out one person knowing that they're not alone."

Which all sounds very noble. Except Doherty can't find a parking space and they're running ten minutes late for a date at police headquarters. The HQ is a palatial box in Roxbury with too much reflective glass. The parking snafu doesn't ruffle Carter, who calmly suggests they call their contact, Deputy Superintendent Kelly Nee, for help. Nee secures a reserved spot, and when we finally get inside, eleven supervisors crammed in the department's command post are waiting with long faces.

Carter's at ease waiting for his PowerPoint to load. Joining Nee are lieutenants and sergeants, and Carter credits the officers for being the largest group of cops he's ever spoken to, his chirpy accent starting to percolate. He introduces the organization and shows them Jeanne Clery's portrait. "The largest function of Security On Campus was to foster improvements in campus safety and protect victims of violence," he begins. He hits highlights of the Clery Act and does not attempt the granular details, sensing their practicality and time limits. Pointing out that while Clery is widely known for requiring colleges to furnish annual campus crime reports—which most colleges post on their web sites—there's other vital stuff schools should be doing.

After the inaugural law passed in 1990, a handful of amendments followed to extend and strengthen Clery, along with the passage of sister statutes. The Buckley Amendment of 1992 clarified that campus police and security records were not confidential "education records" and must be made public. The same year, in part due to heavy lifting by the Clerys and many others like Frank Carrington, the Campus Sexual Assault Victims'

Bill of Rights sailed through Congress, requiring colleges to give survivors certain basic protections including assistance notifying the police.

Schools must have policies in place to address these assaults, including assuring equal treatment of both the accuser and accused during their disciplinary hearings, a subject that would be hotly contested in the years ahead. Also included were provisions for survivors to be told of their options to contact municipal police, change their academic and living situations, and to receive counseling support. Later amendments addressed other safeguards such as public disclosure of the final adjudication of school disciplinary hearings, eliminating loopholes in campus crime reporting, and disclosing registered sex offenders on campus.

One of the first things the Clerys did, Carter tells the group, was getting colleges to print statements of their security policies rather than making parents hunt for them. Real basic stuff like how dorm keys are distributed.

Several officers explain that they see a mishmash of responses to sex crimes. Lieutenant Detective George Juliano is the most talkative. He tells Carter and Doherty that smaller schools like Fisher College call them to help with such crimes, while a few larger ones like Boston College handle it with their own campus police. "Some of the major colleges are very good. If there's a major attack, they call us too," Juliano says. Yet often, while campus police "wants us to help them out, administration does not," he says.

There's more to every school's obligations, Carter tells them. Assault survivors—whether students or university employees—for example, have a right to contact either a municipal or campus police officer to press charges. They have a choice. "That's important," he says, urging the supervisors to check with colleges to confirm this is in place. "If they don't they [colleges] can get in a lot of trouble."

Less than half of the officers are taking notes. A few seem inert and excuse themselves before the meeting ends, yet most are clearly aware of the problem's depth, and their comments are etched in experience. Campus assaults have also become a hot-button issue this spring, in 2011, as several news agencies have spotlighted the vast underreporting of campus sexual violence and mishandling of cases by many colleges.

Carter keeps going and brings in the dilemma of timely reporting. First, communicating an attack or threat, whether on or off-campus, quickly to students. And later in the university's annual crime reports. Among the reasons universities resist reporting sexual assault cases is when the two students know each other, versus an outsider attack. Juliano submits, "It's a hot-button issue at rape crisis centers." Turf battles also come into play again. "BU owns half of Kenmore Square," another officer complains. "We have problems getting reports from a business owner" who is in fact a BU tenant. "If there's a video store robbery, who's going to investigate that?"

Daniel seizes his opening. He cuts to the advice he wants to impart while whisking through other key changes to the law. His pace is break-neck, but he uses straightforward language, prompting nods. He recommends that police reach agreements with every college in the city on how sexual assaults and other crimes get handled: who takes the lead, formalizing supports between departments, imminent threat notifications, and assuring transparency. A 2008 amendment to the Clery Act required such memos of understanding to cover a plethora of crimes, Carter says, and while colleges can be held accountable if they haven't done this, the bottom line is better communication to improve students' safety. He encourages Nee and the others to get going on this, "so that when something goes down everyone knows what they're supposed to do, and who they can call on."

Then he brings up the tragic poster child of when this coordination did not occur in an extreme context: the Virginia Tech shootings in 2007. His main critique, which is shared by other security experts, is that the school failed to notify local police and the community during a two-hour gap after the shooter killed the first two students. "These schools don't necessarily have to tell their local PD," Carter stresses. Yet, "If there is an ongoing threat, they're not supposed to wait a couple of days. That was the crux of the Virginia Tech case."

"We have some work to do," Juliano comments as the meeting wraps up. "We didn't know the law is on our side."

Another officer adds, "If I'm a vice president at BU, wouldn't I side with giving the Boston PD more of a role?"

After leaving police headquarters we head to the South Boston waterfront, and Doherty suggests the Legal Harborside restaurant for lunch. Seated in the open air, Carter announces he's never had clam chowder before. John and I look at each other aghast as he orders a cup of Legal Seafood's signature dish.

Carter begins filling me in on the timeline of his work with the Clerys and some of the nuances providing useful guidance to colleges on handling sexual assault cases. One is that education authorities muddied their advice on what evidence standard schools should adopt in their disciplinary hearings. For years colleges were told that the standard should be beyond a reasonable doubt, the same used to obtain criminal convictions. When the Department of Education changed the benchmark to a less stringent preponderance of evidence standard in 2011, meaning more likely than not to be true, catcalls of "travesty" and "trampling the rights of the accused" came from conservatives and civil libertarians. Advocates, however, contended only that standard afforded complainants a level playing field where their voices would be heard. Meanwhile, more assault survivors, women being the vast majority, continued to come forward to report and challenge institutional denials.

Internal grievance proceedings at colleges are separate from and unlike the criminal process. Hearings are held to weigh complaints of violating the student handbook, and there is less due process afforded defendants. Critics argue that these cases should be meted out to the criminal courts rather than through a separate judicial system. Advocates like Carter contend that duality and separation is correct and necessary, and point to circuit court rulings in their favor. The two goals of the campus hearing process are "education and protecting the community, as opposed to the punitive nature of the criminal justice system," he says.

In addition, Carter says applying the tougher evidence standard in campus proceedings saddled assault victims with an additional burden of proof, another disincentive to come forward. Over lunch, he tells us that federal education officials confused the matter by not informing all universities of the new evidence standard. "So it was actually unfair to the schools being held to a standard they were not being advised of," he says. The waitress returns and inquires about his chowder. Carter is noncommittal and a tad obtuse, saying, "At least now I know that I don't dislike it."

I perk up from engulfing a fish sandwich as he shifts to describe his entry into the world of campus safety and the Clerys' early achievements.

Like many people who become victims' advocates or activists, Daniel knows harassment firsthand. Growing up in Knoxville, he was pudgy and considered by some classmates to be a bit of a dork. He stood up to bullies in middle school who taunted and physically harmed him. The worst part of it, he recalls, "was the name calling, the derogatory stuff. It left an impression." His parents went to the principal, the school department, and they told a police officer. Yet, those authorities "didn't have the tools or resources to know what to do," he says. "That was the hardest part."

This was a primer for life. An introduction, he says, "to the fact that our educational systems have a lot of challenges dealing with safety, and didn't always deal with it as best they could. Often times they didn't have the tools."

Carter didn't blame the police or school administrators. And he never forgot those feelings.

While starting his senior year of high school in 1988, the murder of a student attending the nearby University of Tennessee vaulted Carter into the emerging field of improving student safety. Idealistic enough to believe that public policy can right society's wrongs, he continued making this his life's work going on three decades later.

A friend of his was dating a sophomore named Tom Baer, who was stabbed in the heart by a guy who pulled a knife during a back-to-school bash at his fraternity house. Baer's murder drew national attention, and UT was excoriated for bungling the investigation amidst a rowdy, look-the-other-way campus culture.

Entering the same university, Carter soon joined a student campus safety committee. They raised awareness about unsafe off-campus areas where most UT students lived, posting billboards and doing weekend community patrols with flashlights and two-way radios. Yet most students still had no handle on how often serious crimes occurred; no one compiled and published those statistics.

Other issues came to the fore: police handling of armed and sexual assaults—including a series of rapes that allegedly involved student athletes—and a lack of public access to police reports. His group focused on providing campus cops training and materials. As critiques lingered about their handling of Tom Baer's case, Carter thought the officers lacked adequate resources and protocols.

Staying in contact with Baer's parents, the political science major went statewide. Carter was a driving force behind another Clery-fashioned state law requiring colleges in Tennessee to share crime data for incidents both on and off-campus. Armed with information about the most dangerous areas, the argument went, students could protect themselves better. More broadly, their parents would be able to monitor which schools were doing a better job at security and prevention.

His zeal caught the Clerys' attention. Connie offered him a job and kept calling when he resisted moving north. By the mid-'90s, the twenty-four-year-old relented on the condition that he largely telecommute. Yet soon Carter became a road warrior, visiting colleges and making the rounds of congressional and federal education offices. While he and others on Connie's staff identified flaws in the law and set out to improve them, Carter never relinquished his personal touch, extending a hand to survivors of assaults and other campus violence. Life experience continued to inform him: *This must not stand.*

Back at our table, Carter is leapfrogging through the signature years when laws protecting students were strengthened. "We always do bipartisan," he says, noting that both Newt Gingrich and Barney Frank co-sponsored the landmark campus sexual assault victims' bill in 1992. "We don't do Republican or Democratic—that's not in our DNA. We do gradations of it." Connie spearheaded the recruiting of almost two hundred co-sponsors for that bill, along with a massive student letter-writing campaign, a precursor of sorts to fast-tracking online petitions. "Mrs. Clery went after Ted Kennedy morning, noon, and night," Doherty jumps in, "and she would go after Gingrich."

Daniel breaks into an adoring, high-pitched snicker and puts down his fork. "She just doesn't care," he agrees. "She knew she was right and she knew if she could get in front of them, that's all that matters."

By 1998, Carter was playing a leading role pushing amendments to the Clery Act, which he says were needed once they identified "ways the law wasn't working out of the gate." They closed loopholes such as one that allowed the non-disclosure of crimes that occurred in certain off-campus areas, and mandated that colleges with security departments maintain a daily crime log. Another shortfall was that education authorities weren't enforcing the law until Security On Campus and its allies prompted Congress to conduct an oversight hearing, which brought more compliance.

Other gaps would need to be filled during the next two decades, such as confusion as to which campus employees must report assault complaints to police. By 2013 this responsibility became clear, covering most staff who have direct contacts with students or oversee student activities—from resident assistants to athletics coaches. Those complaints were also supposed to make their way into a college's published crime reports.

Such distinctions may feel inscrutable to an outsider. Yet the bottom line for Carter was that while more tweaking and protections were needed, there'd been real progress. "My career has all been based on making something good from something bad," he told me on another occasion.

Finishing lunch, I sense that he feels indebted to Howard, and I am eager to learn more about this man and their relationship. Howard had stepped back from an active role as the new millennium began, and he remained relatively healthy until a heart attack ended his life at seventy-seven in 2008. While often intense, Clery had been a coveted mentor to Carter. One time Carter was preparing testimony for a hearing chaired by Senator Arlen Specter, and Howard made sure he culled it down to two pages. "I darn well ran it by him," Daniel says. "He was right. There was no way I was going to read through that. I had to highlight it. That's what he was most about, hitting the relevant points concisely."

I raise the subject of the Clerys' legacy and how they each responded to their daughter's death. Not asking so much to pry, yet, for better or worse, I must attempt to step lightly and go there. This is really the question driving me forward.

Meeting people like Carter and Mrs. Clery feels like assembling a challenging jigsaw puzzle. Sometimes their stories and experiences form interlocking patterns that fit. Other times my attempts to arrange them are a clumsy barrage of queries and answers. While spending some time with Carter and Doherty, I realize that I have quite a ways to go. More than a few crazy-shaped outlier pieces still need a home.

Beside the waterfront, the two men continue reminiscing about Howard Clery. They segue to Josoph Henry's atrocity and its long-smoldering aftermath. They saw how Lehigh's deception lit a forge inside Howard. Seething, he identified the gaps to rectify, and refused to take no for an answer.

Then Carter pauses thoughtfully as he considers Connie. He's been streaming granular details all morning, yet there's another voice that catches my ear, a gregarious tenor seemingly at odds with a Beltway policy wonk. It's not unlike the well-developed touch of a dobro player whose fills and soaring solos complete the music that's being made around him. Perhaps Daniel never got to join the school band as a child. Into his mid-forties he continued showing up at protests with college activists outside the Education Department.

"It wasn't mad," he slows, reflecting on Mrs. Clery. "It was almost more love, love for what needed to be done in memory of her daughter. I mean, she keeps coming back to that plaque" outside Jeanne's old dormitory. "The essence of it is, her death must not have been in vain."

I knew where Bar One was.

Spilling into an alley near one of the city's canals. Ironically, the club was just a block away from the office of the lawyers we had hired to go after its owners.

I couldn't let it go.

The principal owner, a plumber's son from North Providence, was a prolific entrepreneur regarded as one of the city's nightclub impresarios. He was able to open six clubs in Providence starting in 1994 staggered over fourteen years, plus another club and some pizza restaurants in nearby cities. Around this time, Mayor Vincent "Buddy" Cianci, Jr. was credited for restoring the downtown, yet there was a sordid underside to the city's so-called renaissance. Cianci and some portion of Providence City Hall were as crooked as they come. The mayor almost survived two FBI stings, one during his third term, when twenty-two city workers including his chief of staff went down on corruption charges along with some contractors; yet he was spared that time. Then came "Operation Plunder Dome"—so-named by an FBI agent investigating what went on under the copper-fringed city hall dome—and in 2002 Cianci was convicted of racketeering and conspiracy, serving a five-year sentence.

This mire continued to stir well after the mayor's demise. One thick wedge of this—the co-ownership of bars and the city's numerous strip clubs by shadowy businessmen and politicians—was often obscured and ethically contorted, at minimum. Regulation of these establishments and the sanctioning of violations resembled a murky game of musical chairs, as players took multiple roles with conflicting angles. During licensing board meetings held in a small side room at city hall, state representatives getting paid as attorneys represented owners charged with violations like underage drinking and filling clubs beyond capacity.

Some of these same lawmakers also served as registered agents representing other bar owners, or were owners themselves, while occasionally cops also co-owned bars that came under scrutiny. And unlike many other states, Rhode Island did not require bar and club owners to have liquor liability insurance. Having it was *recommended*. If something went wrong, if an owner's failure to abide by the law resulted in harm, this could mean no one was held accountable.

Unaccountable. For teens getting sloshed. For cue stick assaults. For bloody chaos in the streets and alongside highways.

In my private rants I began dubbing this swamp "SumpPumpville." Mike and his buddies were sucked in by the promise of easy alcohol mixed in a slick, rampant stew. For sure, each of them was responsible for his share of the poor decisions made that night. They weren't alone in that, and the pump would continue to spit others out.

The further I dug into this a few years after we lost him, the more it began to drill into me.

The proprietor of Bar One owned other larger troubled nightclubs whose excesses were well known in the city. A patron at one was shot and killed in a parking lot during a fight after a rap concert, with no detail officers present because the club was behind on its payments to police, the *Providence Journal* reported. Officials also finally revoked the license of another slurring haunt following police warnings and life-threatening incidents, including juveniles overdosing on liquid Ecstasy. Its owner was fined for failing to curb violence inside, and the shooting of a man near the dance floor was the last straw. A similar record spiked for years at Bar One. Police made repeated arrests for underage drinking—bringing twenty-two counts—and disorderly conduct between 2001 and 2007. During that span the owner came before the city's Board of Licenses nine times, resulting in more than $10,000 in fines and half a dozen days of closure. Yet there was never a serious threat of shutting him down for good.

It took me a while gathering the nerve to dig this stuff up. Even though

Providence was an easy drive from our home—and Chris attended Johnson & Wales University there, studying business before transferring to Suffolk University—I was aware that wading into this cesspool might cross a point of no return. Certainly Denise would object to me doing this. Yet I got sucked in.

It wasn't so hard finding a trail of records about Bar One and its owner. I'd done investigative reporting before and had been able to get around most every obstacle thrown my way. Pursuing public records—police reports, licensing board hearings, court cases, secretary of state records—and gumshoeing around to meet some of the principals came naturally enough. Except that the pursuit now involved my son hitting that guardrail.

Following every possible lead, any random name and tangentially related mishap I came across became a seething impulse. I let it lie for weeks at a time, only for this to rear up again. Then I hit it hard, tilting alone against the pump.

One morning I found myself reading old notes about the bar in a folder along with faded news clippings about Mike's crash. Why was I taking a break from school prep on a Sunday to go there again? Too many questions kept boring down.

I pushed back an urge to stop at the club for a beer while driving through Rhode Island another day. Maybe wear one of Mike's T-shirts from the soccer tournament we ran for his memorial scholarship as a piece of battle armor. Confront the manager with "Brack 3"—three was his varsity number—on the backside. Maybe tell him who I was.

A far cry from love for what needed to be done.

That was ego chatter combusting in an oily sludge. Still, I wanted an update on the club and its owner. So I contacted the licensing board again and asked for eight years of records.

A few weeks later a woman called from city hall. She had 322 pages on Tomasso Bar and Grill, the corporate entity that had owned Bar One and now a new club at the same place called State Ultra Lounge. There'd been a makeover. The board had allowed the owner to transfer the license to a so-called upscale club catering to thirty-somethings. The packet included copies of police citations and transcripts of show cause hearings. At 15 cents a page and a $5 fee, she needed $53.30.

I thanked her and felt a thud in my chest. *Not again.* This cannot happen to anyone else again.

Three hundred-plus pages. I let out a straggled cry at my desk.

A quarter century after Jeanne's death, Connie Clery and her small staff felt encouraged by the improvements in campus safety taking hold across America. Violent crime at colleges had dropped by nine percent in a decade. Most schools had finally got past admitting they had problems to do something about them. There was a time when even the most disturbing campus crimes weren't talked about, like a death in the family. But that was then.

Most colleges eagerly moved ahead: instituting swipe cards, texting and tweeting safety alerts to students, repeating messages about date rape, explaining what constitutes consent, bullying, stalking, and ways to protect oneself from harm. Advocates and resource officers, rape crisis counselors and police increasingly worked together. Guys became more sensitized to intervene as bystanders rather than being passive observers; some stepped up as mentors calling attention to men's obligations, poking holes in pervasive male stereotypes—the alpha male stud and belt-notching hustler. Schools rewrote grievance procedures so that both sides knew their rights and were treated more equally.

While imperfect perhaps on every score, much had changed.

The Clery Act is not something one typically brings up at supper. Despite the law's sometimes-dank details, the security and crime record at any university being considered by your daughter or son became a topic meriting an open-table discussion.

Yet even with these gains, far too many college-age women continue to be threatened. At least one in five experiences an attempted or completed sexual assault—ranging from nonconsensual touching to penetration—during her college career. More likely it is one in four, as successive studies that encourage anonymous reporting have shown. For those few who choose to report sexual assaults, too often what follows is a betrayal by school authorities, and victim-blaming by society.

Many universities still do not fully get it. At best, many colleges' handling of sexual assaults continued to be a work in progress through 2017.

Some fail to inform students of their rights and reporting options, such as going to a health center to report confidentially, or making a complaint to a dean or someone else with the authority to act. Too often, rape investigations are flawed while institutional self-preservation reigns. Complainants feel that the university's disciplinary hearings are skewed against them: they face a power disparity up against the schools' lawyers while many perpetrators receive a slap on the wrist, rather than expulsion, or even suspension. Elemental steps like allowing survivors to drop courses or change living quarters are denied.

For those willing to look deeper, a culture of rape flows like untreated polluted groundwater. When so many young women are threatened, call it what it is: an epidemic.

It's little wonder that only the tip of this plume is visible. You need not be the parent of a daughter like I am to be outraged.

The vast majority of these attacks—an estimated eight or nine of every ten—go unreported. In part this is because victims on a campus almost always know the perpetrators or do not consider the offense to be "serious enough." As few as 7 percent of campus rapes get formally reported to any school authority, and less than half that amount to law enforcement, one sweeping study found, while survivors confide in family and friends about two-thirds of the time. In addition, research suggests that repeat perpetrators account for up to 90 percent of campus sexual assaults.

Pinned down by self-blame and fears of public disclosure, it's too agonizing for many students to come forward. "Victims in these cases often feel they bear some responsibility for the rape, and fail to report it, fearing they'll be treated poorly by the police or other parts of the system," wrote Mary Lou Leary, former Acting Assistant Attorney General for the Office of Justice Programs, who addressed a conference hosted by the Clerys' nonprofit in 2012. "As long as this fear of reporting prevails, we have more to do."

More to do. This mantle would be taken up largely by young women themselves, and their supporters networking across the country. Not only breaking through walls to reveal what's often unspeakable, but laying out a charge for us to clean up this toxic pool.

The closer one looks, the scope of this scourge worsens. Sexual assault is widely considered the most underreported crime in America, affecting an estimated nearly twenty-two million women during their lifetime. A variety of factors on college campuses compound the picture: mainly, along with involving acquaintances, alcohol is almost always involved. In many cases, gurgling underground are our stubborn double standards regarding a girl's drinking habits and her so-called promiscuity, versus a guy's slurring rites and a Hooters'-leering sense of entitlement. Most campus assaults also occur in a woman's living quarters, where usually no weapon is used; and most times there are no signs of physical injury. Half of all student victims do not label the incident "rape."

Then there's the issue of informed consent. Despite the efforts of many colleges to educate students about what constitutes consent to have sex when drinking is involved, a minority of guys—often those who are most aggressive, and skilled at coercion—blame the booze. They claim to have received a signal that's different than what she may have actually issued. Their crutch consists of: there must have been a misunderstanding; we were both pretty trashed. Dubbed "gray rape," advocates contend this defense amounts to a decrepit attempt at manipulation.

It roils Alison Kiss, executive director of the renamed Clery Center for Security on Campus, for one. "Alcohol use is never an excuse," she says. "An individual who is incapacitated cannot consent to sexual activity." Kiss, who began leading the Clery's nonprofit in 2011, has long advised colleges to define precisely what consent means and reinforce that message via peers, resident assistants, and on up.

By 2015, states including California and New York began taking this a step further by enacting affirmative consent laws for private and public campuses. Opponents argued that those measures overreached, were out of step with the reality of many students' sexual encounters, and would lead to discriminatory enforcement. While "yes means yes" sounds straightforward enough, critics countered that those laws tilt against a student trying to demonstrate that he obtained consent. Regardless of this dispute, Kiss contends that every institution should clearly draw the lines for students: for example, the differences between being intoxicated and incapacitated.

The well-established connection between alcohol abuse and sexual assault remained perhaps the most disturbing and intractable aspect of this threat. A high proportion of rapes occur when a girl and guy are drunk— or when she is, at least. Nearly three-quarters of victims experienced rape while they were intoxicated, one far-reaching study found. These violations immobilize and drive victims to self-medicate, drop out, or worse.

As if this wasn't daunting enough for our daughters, they risk being re-victimized even when they find the courage to come forward. Time and again, young women report being denied justice by their universities. In some cases, hearings that drag on through multiple semesters prolong their ordeal, despite guidelines that call for their resolution in less than sixty days. Carter, for one, says many campus crime victims have told him that "the more lasting impression was the inability of their school to do something about it. That's what stuck with them."

The other main option survivors have—pursuing criminal charges—carries it own hazards: inadequate rape kit testing, backlogs at crime labs, miscommunications, and cops and prosecutors not trained to interview traumatized victims with full sensitivity.

As the number of reported campus assaults continued to increase, more students confronted their schools for inaction, duplicity, and betrayal. In complaints filed with the federal government, they charged colleges with botching investigations of harassment and rape, attempting to intimidate them, and showing alleged assailants leniency. These are the Title IX cases that have proliferated through the media and blogosphere since 2013, filed under the federal law that's supposed to protect our kids from gender inequity in schools—including how students are treated after reporting sexual harassment, and worse. With growing urgency, young adults have taken on Ivies to small state colleges, declaring for themselves what victims' families including the Clerys had issued a generation earlier: No more.

The inevitable pushback against the Title IX complaints became a tempest of its own. It had been building for years, led at times by professors and students in prestigious climes like Harvard Law School, whose main critique was that the campus hearings violated civil liberties with the less stringent evidence standard and due process limits. Critics argued that universities were simply unequipped to adjudicate sexual assault claims and prejudged alleged perpetrators. Encouraged by free speech advocates, more accused college men fired back, even appropriating the language of victims' advocacy with cunning as they called foul.

As more assault complaints and countercharges went viral, voices from every angle piled in.

Predictable neocons lambasted the women's rights movement for going too far. Jezebel.com slammed those who deny the existence of a "rape culture." Feminist and postfeminist writers debated suggestions that women tone down their own drinking. King media misogynist Rush Limbaugh attacked the Violence Against Women Act as an Obama ploy against the GOP that assumed "women are being beat to a pulp in this country." A bill was introduced to bar colleges from investigating sexual assault claims unless the victim went to police first—decried by many as adding another barrier to reporting.

The parting on the right kept tacking to the right. Stir in the perception of untouchable student athletes and this scaled up even higher. The idolization of celebrity jocks, who occasionally get their kinks on the rink, or refuse to yield off the field. On it went: from Montana Grizzlies to Boston University hockey players, Fightin' Irish and Florida State Seminoles. It was unclear who would have the last word.

We may have been alarmed, or more likely, just annoyed by all the static while gripping a Coors Light in front of another busty blonde on the tube. Some waited for a prosecutor to get past his "we just couldn't prove it" stance; others questioned the unnamed woman's motives; discussions ensued about entitlement and perks and Heisman Trophy adoration. The issue fell aside for bowl games. We refilled on chips and salsa as warnings were issued not to paint everyone with too broad a brush.

Ultimately, most of us shrugged. As long as it hadn't happened on our watch or involved the star running back. Or your daughter or son.

Then came Angie Epifano, an Amherst College student who had to drop out.

"Silence has the rusty taste of shame," she wrote.

"Are you *sure* it was rape? It might have just been a bad hookup," she was advised, "You should forgive and forget."

How are you supposed to forget the worst night of your life?

Sophomore Andrea Pino suffered a concussion when she was assaulted at an off-campus party at the University of North Carolina at Chapel Hill. She had not been drinking. She had just been hired as an RA, and had walked a friend to a party.

For a time, silence became her language as well.

"Every night, my head felt as if it was slammed again, and I began to want to get away," she wrote. "I was keeping in a big secret, and it was eating me up inside.

"I 'left' my body during classes, and on many days had to physically rush out—dropping my books sometimes—wondering how many could see that the girl who was once valedictorian could no longer read or write."

At the University of Connecticut, Kylie Angell was re-traumatized by indignities that defy common sense, if not the law as well.

Upon appeal of his suspension, her attacker was allowed back on campus a few weeks later.

UConn failed to tell her this. The man came up to her in a dining hall his first day back.

Someone who made such decisions thought there would be no conflict. Since the two students would not be "in the same building at the same time."

Disgusted, Kylie finally went to campus police and filed a report.

An officer told Angell, "Women need to stop spreading their legs like peanut butter or rape is going to keep on happening 'til the cows come home."

How are you supposed to forget the worst night of your life?

The issue, a blight on the nation's soul, finally began to garner mass attention after a probe by the Center for Public Integrity, a nonprofit investigative news agency, in conjunction with National Public Radio and other news outlets in 2010. Reviewing ten years of complaints filed with federal education authorities against institutions, and meeting dozens of young women, the CPI found that the students deemed responsible for assaults often faced little or no consequences. In addition, education officials were often lax in their oversight and enforcement of whether schools met their Title IX obligations handling assault reports. The bottom line was that while college administrators believed sanctions commonly issued in their judicial system were "an effective way to hold culpable students accountable, victims and advocates said the punishment rarely fits the crime."

Public awareness spread. Yet the signals coming from many schools still did not square with what students self-report. For example, by one official accounting, reported forcible sex offenses jumped 34 percent to 4,850 complaints on campuses between 2010 and 2012. However, of about 11,000 colleges disclosing their crime data under the Clery Act two years later, 91 percent said they had not received a single report of rape. Not one.

Underreporting by survivors was systemic. A 2016 review of 23,000 student responses to surveys at nine schools found that only sixty of 2,380 named completed rapes—relayed anonymously—had been reported to campus authorities.

As usual, further context is required to make sense of the statistics. Carmen Hotvedt, a violence prevention specialist who assists students at the University of Wisconsin-Madison, says, "Reporting doesn't tell us the story of victimization. It tells us the story of who feels comfortable coming forward and who knows about us. It actually rounds out that we're looking at a substantially very bigger problem. I think some people say it's so underreported that if victims just report it more, it will be understood more. No, it's a person's choice to report sexual assault, and we shouldn't put the onus on victims."

Just like Angie Epifano, Andrea Pino and Kylie Angells felt the blame had been placed on them.

Meeting assault survivors where they are—shutting off our noisemaking to actually listen—was denied them.

Shame on us.

8

AN ABUNDANCE OF CAUTION

For five years, she waited until she had the strength to call Connie. Cradling her first child, a son, in her arms, Desiree Michael was taken back to Lehigh University. She found herself shaken at the very thought of losing him. The inconceivable, the unspeakable, gnawed at her. *El árbol de la vida*, the tree of life, toppled—a sodden mass of busted roots encased in clay and stones. It weighed on her thin frame.

She saw the split felled trunk, its limbs rotting away. Where was the eternal cord for Jeanne's parents? Where had God been for them?

Desiree was about to move out of the country. Her husband, Michalakis Michael, a Greek Cypriot whom she met in college, was taking a job in Nigeria. Soon, their son Melese would have a sister.

She had stayed in the background after Jeanne's murder. Desiree didn't think the Clerys wanted to meet the woman who beat Josoph Henry in the Black Student Union election, sparking his rage, albeit without a scrap of just cause. She wanted to send them flowers on behalf of the student group. But the others rejected her idea. "We're not responsible for his actions," they said, "so why should we send them flowers?" Taken back by this response, Desiree attempted to instill empathy—but in that moment, she lost.

Having doubted her intuition that something was wrong with Henry, and over time Michael piled blame on herself. She believed that she had somehow failed to protect Jeanne. She was the one.

Michael dialed the Clerys from her Santa Clara home late in the afternoon on April 5, 1991. Howard and Connie sat cloistered together in Bryn Mawr attempting to get through the grim anniversary. It was five years to the day.

For many of us, straining to hold on to one another, stumbling perhaps toward some understanding of how we cope differently as parents, or already splintered apart, some of the worst days marking the loss of a child are those weeks in advance. You feel it coming on, irreversible, a leaden fog cloying to your skin and penetrating your clothes. Knots twine in your gut as an acid reflex serves up coughing fits. Thoughts immobilize like fingers stuck to a frozen steel railing as you muddle through nights. And then you must relive that day again.

For Howard, perhaps, the worst was the din of grey rain, foreboding just as on the morning of Jeanne's death, when a blank discomfort unsettled him. He and Connie had both felt this as their Bermuda trip ended, yet neither spoke of it. When they came up the drive and saw the police waiting, the world they had carefully constructed lay in ruins.

Howard answered the phone. The voice on the other end of the line was unfamiliar, and wavering. But he recalled the name. His face sagged as he handed the receiver to his wife. Connie repeated the name to herself.

"Hello, Mrs. Clery, this is Desiree Coe."

Desiree was crying, unable at first to express what she needed to say. "I don't know if you will want to talk to me."

It still didn't register with Connie. She didn't know Desiree existed. She knew that an African-American girl had beaten Henry in the student election, but that was all. As Desiree explained who she was, Connie's face flushed. Her mouth dropped open.

"I have lived with such terrible guilt for the last five years, Mrs. Clery." There was no hesitation.

"It is not your fault," Connie told her, unwilling to turn the young woman away. She felt amazed that Michael had reached out to her.

They began corresponding with letters and cards, with Desiree occasionally sending her small gifts of crystal and other items. She told Connie how haunted she still felt. She and other students had noticed there was something very wrong with Henry. Yet he was never exposed as being violent toward women. Henry had been alienated from most of the Lehigh community, and there was no useful interface to help him, no accountability—until it was too late.

Desiree Michael shouldered another load, one in a mounting pile of bitter ironies. Earlier in the year that Jeanne was killed, Michael had moved out of one of the Lehigh quads into a more secure hall, where rules against propping open doors were strictly enforced. She had actually yelled at girls who inserted pizza boxes in the doors before moving. Yet pondering the night after the student election, Desiree knew she easily could have been Henry's target. "And since I had excused him earlier that day, I probably would have opened the door," she says.

She had no idea what to expect from the Clerys. She wondered if they would hate every black person they saw, but Connie, for one, certainly did not. The family had limited contacts with people of color, mainly their relationship with their housekeeper. They all loved Katherine and knew her family. Yet while she was an adoring, observant second mother to Jeanne, she was still their housekeeper. Howard, while outwardly welcoming Desiree later, had many miles to go along the road of race relations and tolerance. When they met Desiree, sons Ben and Howie were also friendly, yet she sensed, only to a point.

Being able to connect mother-to-mother was paramount for Desiree Michael. She felt that Connie was able to transcend hatred, which in turn helped Desiree overcome her own anger toward Henry and her disgust over the hostile climate she had felt on the campus.

Soon Desiree learned she was pregnant again. She called Mrs. Clery to ask if she would be willing to become the baby's godmother if she had a daughter, and Connie agreed. Yet it wasn't such a simple thing to do. The next spring, Connie flew out to Stanford to attend the medical school graduation of one of Jeanne's old tennis friends. The occasion seemed perfect because Desiree had just come home from the hospital with her new baby girl, so Connie was able to meet her. As Connie held the newborn, Desiree again brought up her wish. She was thrilled, but this came with a sharp twist, and Connie felt she had to say yes. As much as she tried to resist the thought, there it was high among a stack of ruminations: Jeanne would never be able to have children.

Some months later, the couple came east to have their daughter baptized in Bryn Mawr. Following Greek tradition, their children were named after the paternal grandparents, and Michalakis's mother's given name is Anastassia. So they adopted that name, dropping the first letter when Nastassia arrived. Connie asked what the name means, learning that Anastassia signifies "resurrection." While embracing this connection, on the day of the baptism at a local Episcopal church, to her surprise Connie felt herself teetering on the verge of a breakdown. Howard pulled her through the sacramental ceremony. It all cut too close.

Michael hoped that the gift of her daughter's life would somehow help the Clerys heal. "It felt like a full circle," she reflects, "although I couldn't have given her anything to replace her daughter."

Howard continued wrestling with the questions. What had they done to deserve this? *Why should the wicked worry? They are not punished. Why?*

A man of action and not emotion, Howard nonetheless was a voracious reader. In Sister Miriam's Bible class he delved further into Job. Having already engaged this text as a younger man, he found himself living there. The faithful servant's livestock were destroyed, his children taken, his eyes shut until he uttered what he could not understand. Howard groaned under a comparable weight.

He believed he had committed no wrongs, but still the pain gnashed; he felt broken down on every side, yet friends counseled him to be humble; his faith was untethered, yet he looked hard into the whirlwind. He still wanted the guy fried.

At times this surged and he drove friends away. Rants against fags, niggers, sluts. Dinners were declined, Connie looked away, golf partners scattered, their friend Dodie Boyle said, "I'm not going to sit at this table with you if you're going to continue with that."

So Howard began to change.

Both he and Connie felt a deep satisfaction as well. As the Clery Act was sharpened, with loopholes filled and breakthrough protections added, they saw progress. Each amendment was a retooled engine cylinder, every student and family or survivor they reached adding fuel, as their nonprofit fastened on new spark plugs that fired up change. Many schools were warming up to them. College security became more professional and officers sought out the training. There were challenges with fundraising and looking for new blood on their board, suitable leadership, stuff that all charities face. He wanted Connie to step back from the day-to-day and not react so much to each new revelation, each new case on a campus they had never even set foot on.

When it came to Josoph Henry, Howard's wrath still gave no quarter. But gradually he yielded to the prospect that Henry might live, and even outlive him. While still torqued, he was less pissed off as time went by. Eventually the legal process wore him out, the rattling din of ceaseless motions and appeals as new loads were hauled to the conveyor belt.

He also knew that Jeanne was secure with God. Sister Miriam had helped him gather this in as she guided their Old Testament readings. Clery may also have appreciated that he wasn't walking this journey alone. Job fell in a sudden reversal of fortune, lying prostate for nights until he began cursing the day he was born. Howard's situation differed markedly—he still had his sons, an indoor pool and a winter home, after all—but he, too, had been pummeled in the time-honored tragic sense. Gradually he shifted from anger to living again.

Still, it wasn't quite over.

In the spring of 2002, a federal judge overturned Henry's death sentence. She ruled that a trial judge had issued ambiguous jury instructions during the sentencing fifteen years earlier. Essentially the trial judge had failed to clearly explain how the jury should consider mitigating factors—which called for life imprisonment—versus weighing aggravating factors that led to the death penalty. Henry's lawyers, who had appealed more than one hundred capital cases across the state with some success, got one of their fourteen challenges to stick. The facts of Jeanne's murder were never challenged, and Henry's first-degree murder conviction was upheld.

The Clerys were momentarily shaken, but Howard was not surprised by the reversal. He read the writing before it dried. The same federal court had recently overturned other death sentences on the same principle, including that of Mumia Abu-Jamal, the former Black Panther and radio reporter whose appeals had received international attention. The couple would have to decide whether to seek the death penalty again. That would mean retrying the case with its excruciating evidence at a new sentencing hearing. Heading into the gravel crusher again. Or they could drop the case with Henry sentenced to life in prison.

Soon after the court ruling, Yvonne Ameche Davis and her husband were having dinner with the Clerys. She remembers how resigned Howard was to the news. He could have persisted, but Connie asked him not to, and, after all, they believed life in prison might even be worse for Henry. Connie had grown weary of Howard's anger and could not continue to operate the nonprofit amidst that festering bile. He acquiesced.

"It was an amazing act of love for Howard," one family member confided. "It was brave. It never left him." As they dined together that night, Davis did not recognize Howard's anger any more. "He said, 'This is how it's going to be.'"

That August, Henry agreed to end all appeals in exchange for a life sentence. He was thirty-seven by then, and he finally attempted to apologize to the Clerys. "If the bereaved family [wants to] shout at me, kick me, whatever, I'm willing to do anything to help them feel at all better," he said in court, while looking only at the judge. Howard, Connie, and Howie sat unmoved, though Connie bowed her head, crying softly throughout the hearing. Afterwards she said, "This is justice for Jeanne. He will never get out to hurt anyone else."

Howard mellowed a bit with time. He could still complain about the hapless Eagles during football season. At Harbour Ridge, he and old pal Leo Clancy formed a Wednesday lunch group dubbed "the Romeos," an acronym for "Retired Old Men Eating Out." Lively conversations ensued about sports, politics, and the world, often spurred on by Clery. He continued drumming away at religion, its rites and over-hawked messiahs, and Clancy felt Howard's rage return when the Catholic priest sex abuse scandal broke. Yet in moments he was also able to simply offer, "I'm looking forward to dinner tonight."

Some years earlier, he and his business partner were vacationing with their wives at a resort in Puerto Rico. Jack Farber had seen Howard astonish people by winning golf tournaments, and on that morning Clery wore a canary yellow shirt and pants on the course, clenching a huge cigar between his teeth as he moved around with his leg brace and cane. He hit a ball that stopped on a downhill lie inches from a lake, which put Howard in a difficult position. He could not bend his knees. The green was reachable, and Howard wouldn't back down, so he tried to hit the ball. He topped it and fell face first into the water. "We were afraid he might drown," Farber wrote. "I pulled him out by his ankles, his outfit wet and muddy, but the cigar still clenched in his mouth. He did not win the hole, but continued the game."

Another time he made a point of returning to Warm Springs with his wife, where Clery had spent five months healing as a teenager.

Howard was about to give a talk on FDR at their Florida community. He had regularly donated to what became the Roosevelt Warm Springs Institute for Rehabilitation, but he actually idolized FDR for being his own man and doing what he felt was right. During Clery's months of isolation, there had been plenty of time for him to think. He was finally ready to share it all with Connie. They drove up to see Roosevelt's house in Hyde Park before making the trip to the Georgia countryside.

As he showed her the pools, and how they were taught to fall and deal with life, she glimpsed a side he had not revealed before. "I think that's what made him so capable. Of course, he had the strength of character," she told me. "He loved Warm Springs. I think it made him."

As dementia enveloped her waning life at age ninety-four, Katherine Bridges kept three 10-by-12-inch photos on a dresser. One was of Jeanne. She continued to gaze at the young girl she had loved like her own daughter.

Bridges, who began working for the Clerys when Jeanne was seven or eight, had been more like a grandmother to her than a housekeeper. She took young Jeannie shopping, to the post office, and later brought her along when Bridges was cleaning other people's homes. After school, Jeanne would often go over to a neighbor's house that was a five-minute walk away. If Mrs. Clery wasn't home, Katherine would make sure Jeanne called her upon reaching the Lindgrens, and then call her again just before leaving her friend Lauri to come home. Standing in the backyard, Katherine watched Jeanne come over the hill, awaiting a big hug and a thank you for letting her go play.

Katherine was a basket case for months following the murder. "Just disbelief about it and sadness, as a child she had helped raise," her daughter-in-law says. Like Howard and his son Ben, Katherine saw a counselor. Sometimes she paused in Jeanne's bedroom to regard the fading birthday cards made out to Mrs. Clery, which had been matted and framed.

Despite the venom the men spit at Henry, not always out of her earshot, Katherine didn't express her own anger. It didn't matter so much that she was of the same race as Jeanne's murderer. "Her being a part of it, not an employee's part," says her son, Roscoe Jones. Bridges owned a single-family home in West Philadelphia's Wynnefield section, a well-kept neighborhood. She occasionally brought Jeanne there, and years later Connie or her sons would visit. Katherine became the young men's confidant as well, and when Ben and Howie had problems they sometimes drove to her house. Katherine would cook tacos or another of their favorite meals, talking things over at the table.

As her health declined, Bridges cut back her hours, though for many years the Clerys continued to compensate her generously. Even at seventy-four, she still worked once a week in Bryn Mawr, ironing especially for Howard, who insisted that Katherine's pressed shirts were the best, doing laundry, and seeing to other things around the house. While Bridges's relatives at times felt she showed too much loyalty to the Main Line family—in earlier years Katherine spent holidays with the Clerys, rather than with her own children—appreciation flowed on both sides.

On a Valentine's Day after Jeanne died, Katherine shared a card with Connie that Jeanne had given her. It read, "To my other mother."

On a mid-April morning in 2007, a spiteful, heavily armed Virginia Tech senior chained shut three exit doors of an engineering classroom building. Walking methodically from room to room, Seung-Hui Cho massacred thirty people before killing himself.

Not only had no one on the campus connected multiple warning signs— Cho's frightening pattern of stalking female students, threatening suicide, and outright menacing expressions in class—the deadliest school shooting in United States history quickly revealed an agonizing gap in campus security protocols. There was no immediate notification system for such emergency threats.

Connie Clery and her staff knew full well that the Virginia Polytechnic Institute and State University was not alone in this shortcoming.

Hours later, after driving from Tennessee to the Blacksburg campus, S. Daniel Carter sat with CBS Evening News anchor Katie Couric in another building. By then, the death toll had reached thirty-three. To Carter, the scene outside was surreal. He had come upon students on their cell phones assuring relatives they were safe; others, including adults he thought must have been the victims' parents or friends, huddled together crying profusely. Every branch of law enforcement imaginable swarmed the campus. He stopped counting the number of satellite news trucks and interviews he gave. Meanwhile, the university president was defending his decision to wait nearly two hours to alert students by email after an initial shooting of two students in a dorm.

"How do you think the students could have been better protected today?" Couric asked Carter during the broadcast.

"Well, two key things," he said, motioning with his arms. "Better use of technology—get text messages out to their cell phones. When you've got a time-critical situation like this, that's the quickest way to reach them. Email is good, but text messages are better. When you have an unknown shooter at large, you've got to be sure you have security in your campus buildings, and lock down the buildings as best you can."

Couric continued: "Ideally, as a campus security expert, what should they have done?"

Carter didn't flinch, selecting his language carefully. "Ideally they should have locked down their campus. They needed to get everyone protected," he says. "The problem is they did not know for sure who was doing this, and until you know for sure you've got to use an abundance of caution."

While condemnation of top university officials came swiftly, Connie and her staff pushed to make Virginia Tech an example. The goal was to force other colleges to beef up their own threat assessment and community emergency notification protocols. "We had to make sure that campuses are alerted much more quickly, because that was ridiculous that it would take two hours," she told me. "Ridiculous."

Investigators would discover that had the university notified the first victim's parents immediately after her identity became known, they might have been able to call her in the ambulance and hear their daughter's voice for the last time.

Other tough lessons were learned. Shaken, and knowing it could happen to them, schools nationwide followed suit as Virginia Tech implemented a text-alert system. Upgrades included having an array of notification methods such as texts, tweets, and an outdoor siren system alerting people to check their e-mail, cell phones, or emergency information centers; tailoring their alert broadcasts in advance to different types of threats; and adding locks on doors and camera systems in academic buildings where they hadn't been placed before. Many hurdles remained, like closing holes in the mental health system. Even getting students to sign up for the messaging networks was never a sure thing.

To mandate some of these measures, the Clery Act was amended a year after the Virginia Tech massacre. Fuzzy language was clarified. For Connie, the bottom line was a new thirty-minute notification window. Within that time, a campus community must be notified of a significant emergency or immediate threat.

"Has to be totally informed," she emphasized. "To me, it was the main accomplishment. To me it's one of the most important pieces of legislation we've accomplished."

How universities assess potential threats from hateful or mentally unstable students continues to be a thorny challenge. While imperfect, more colleges began training staff to monitor and intervene in at least the more basic, ongoing "red-flag" behaviors: stalking; distributing disturbing content in writing, social media, or through the arts; and issuing threats. Hollis Stambaugh, a security consultant who interviewed Cho's parents, said that despite plenty of warning signs, apparently no one at Virginia Tech put it all together. Nor did they inform Cho's parents about his history. "If you looked at everything Cho had written from his sophomore year, the pattern was frightening," Stambaugh said in 2011. "Whether his poetry, short stories, historical research, he never followed the professor's directions, and he scared others in class. It was a recipe for disaster."

Only ten months after Virginia Tech, another campus tragedy erupted approaching the same scale. A former Northern Illinois University student with a history of mental illness walked into a large classroom and opened fire, killing five students and injuring twenty-one others on Valentine's Day. The shooter, who wore a T-shirt with "Terrorist" across the front, might have inflicted even greater damage because police found fifty-five unused rounds of ammunition after he killed himself.

Yet multiple police agencies arrived quickly, and NIU was credited for having recently updated its campus notification process, which resulted in no delay getting the word out. In another bright spot, which was also among the few highlights of Virginia Tech's response, the performance of emergency medical service teams doing triage and the coordination between hospitals and the campus was heralded. Local law enforcement officials in DeKalb, Illinois, also acknowledged the response could be improved with clearer guidelines for establishing a staging area for personnel and assets. Overall though, NIU's rapid response and its treatment of victims suggested that the tide had turned—which continued to be borne out when tragedies were averted in places like Ohio State University in 2016.

The Virginia Tech massacre forced open the country's consciousness. As Carter says, "for the first time the whole world realized that college campuses were not immune from safety threats."

Stepping back for a moment at least, if feels callous and uncaring to suggest that following these hideous murders a victory of sorts came within reach.

On one hand, this feels like a violation. As if someone standing in another universe is calling to me in a perky voice, "Well, dad, telling your son's story again is bound to get the message across to these kids."

A statement that shoots a sliver of copper liquid up my throat. Please tell me, who the hell are you?

Is it upside down, is it wrong, to suggest that some good may arise from this carnage? Does spring-boarding from such a mess disregard the memories of those who were killed? Or does it honor their lives in full?

Pouring a foundation in the very ruins. As Carter explained years after Virginia Tech, his immediate impulse, his full intention, was to *take this tragedy and make sure that it has meaning.*

But he didn't lose any children there. Those who did may ask: Where is this place of understanding?

When will it come? What did I do wrong?

My skin turns black and falls from me, and my bones burn with heat, Job told Elihu. *My lyre is tuned to mourning, and my pipe to the voice of those who weep.* An ageless story with its ultimate forward arc. The possibilities of transformation from the ashes. Which may even sound illustrious from a distance.

Until you can't bring yourself to attend any more graduations. Wafts of lilac generate a clammy chill, your forehead pounding with the glare of sunshine. Until his friends' weddings become too much to bear. Grooms strutting their entrance on the dance floor, shades drawn in a revel that's raised forever—minus one. Until her voice is distant, rasp-threads straggling to get through, and you almost recognize her singing, but are no longer quite sure. Until you fail to hear him thump across the threshold.

Until you just can't do this any longer. Stepping inside again. Knowing that what should have been will never be.

Outcry and numbness as vast as the crust of your life's winters. Loss as a whipsaw cutting the trunk from both sides. Who says you work through this?

Building from these ruins? The questions reverberate, sometimes steering me into the ditch: At what cost?

For some, perhaps for many, it's easier to melt away. You really should move on. I worry about what you're doing to yourself. Avoidance. Denial. Acceptance. Keepin' on.

Fucking complicated grief.

I wanted to ask Connie about this. Since she had stayed in the trenches all these years, Mrs. Clery had something extra to offer us. Yet I worried about my timing.

We had spoken together probably ten times over several years, and I had met her once back in 2011. She had become accustomed to my phone calls, graciously willing to dig deep to discuss a few pivotal cases on campuses and moments in her family's life, while most often abruptly ending a conversation as long-percolating feelings threatened to spill over again. I carried Connie's remark to heart about setting out trying to prevent another family from undergoing the same ordeal. While I might not have articulated this to her, it continued to be a touchstone for my own response.

When I contacted Mrs. Clery again in 2013, Holy Week was just underway, punctuating the Ides of March. It's what Connie calls her "week from hell."

Howard's birthday was March 29, followed by Jeanne's anniversary the next week. Her son Ben's birthday comes two days later. It's often been an excruciating day for him, Connie says, because back in 1986 he went out to celebrate two nights early with a girlfriend. Sitting in a restaurant, he learned of his sister's death on the TV news. "I always try to make his birthday important because he's always faced this," Connie says. He never married.

I'd heard this strain in her voice before. An understanding at once stretched close to its limits, because *no one needed to tell her* what this was like. She took it so hard. The news of almost any school shooting, or of a student who dies in the freezing cold, choking on vomit after another careening, drunken marathon, or hazing, or the exposé of another wretched assault cover-up, and even a school leveling the assault victim who dares to speak out—each of these was another arrow to her heart.

You could see her flinch, eyes darting. You felt the chirpy tone of her voice drop out. Yet Connie's ability to rise and step from herself never fully drained away. She always reclaimed empathy, far above sympathy, replenishing her cup. Able to reach out once again as she rounded eighty-two years of a life. Even after Newtown she went out, preferring, this time, not to say exactly how she was helping.

"The three landmark cases I think of are Virginia Tech, Eastern Michigan, and Notre Dame," she told me. "Those three case have affected me tremendously."

In 2006, Eastern Michigan University administrators lied to the parents of a young woman who was found dead in her room just days before Christmas. For the next ten weeks, the university told Laura Dickinson's family there was no reason to suspect foul play, even as campus police investigated her death as a homicide. Laura, who was twenty-two, had a history of heart arrhythmia, and her parents buried her believing she had died of natural causes, including stress over final exams.

EMU also misled its student body and the entire community as a suspected rapist and murderer lived in their midst. Dickinson was found half-naked with a pillow covering her face, and a male student who had been high on pot was seen on videotape entering her room around the time of her death and leaving with one of her Christmas gifts. A medical examiner concluded it was suspicious, yet one administrator ordered a report on the slaying to be shredded even as the suspect continued to live on campus.

As the truth came to light and went national, to many observers it was by far the most blatant, boneheaded attempt yet to hide such a campus crime. "EMU's cover-up and complacency put every student at risk," one newspaper admonished. "And why? To avoid a few bad headlines?" In 2008 a twenty-one-year-old student was convicted—after his first trial ended in a mistrial—of first-degree murder and sentenced to life, but the damage went much further.

A tremor rippled through Connie like a long-delayed aftershock. There were indisputable parallels between Laura and Jeanne; both young women lying in their own beds, and both perversely assaulted by men they had never met. Yet her disgust was far greater than even this relived terror. So many colleges were ignoring Clery Act protections at students' peril. There were hollow promises by federal watchdogs to hold schools accountable. "How could they never have told the student body—all those kids— they had a murderer in their midst?" she asked a reporter. "What is more important to these administrators? Is it money or the kids' lives?"

She contacted Laura's father, Bob Dickinson, who had been measured in his response. He did not go ballistic, buoyed largely by his faith, although it surely had been tested. His daughter was studying nutrition, enjoyed rowing, and had a budding talent for photography. To her mother, Laura was a compassionate ray of sunshine in their lives. "You totally destroyed my family," her dad wrote in a letter that was read at the sentencing. "You tore it limb from limb. Not only did you kill Laura, you killed a very big part of me."

They never met in person, but Connie stayed in touch mainly with Bob in the following years. She took up the mantle yet again, sounding off against EMU in the media as the Dickinsons began to find vindication on several fronts. A law firm's independent report confirmed the cover-up.

Abandoning their ethics, a trio of administrators including the college president had formed what Daniel Carter would later call a mutual firing squad, pointing fingers at one another. With students and faculty justifiably outraged, the three were canned. Then came the feds. They found that the university also failed to report the crime as mandated under Clery, and probing further, uncovered a history of systemic violations in the school's reporting, resulting in a $357,500 fine, the largest ever issued. In another irony, the university contacted Security On Campus to schedule a Clery Act training seminar a week after being blown apart by the law firm's review. "It's better than nothing," Connie remarked. Including a civil settlement with the Dickinsons, the total monetary cost to EMU was close to $4 million.

But of course, that was not the true cost.

"EMU made mistakes," Bob Dickinson told an interviewer in 2007. "None of that matters to us. What we want to see is that parents and students make sure they know where they're going and what they're doing. It's important to ask all the questions before you decide on a school."

Over the years Connie connected with other parents, continuing what she and Howard had started doing soon after losing Jeanne. Craving a safe haven from the heaviness in Bryn Mawr, the two bought a winter home in Florida, and when they moved in along the St. Lucie River there was only one other couple in their building.

Retirees from the Midwest, Elly and Bob Campbell asked the Clerys to have dinner and play golf. As they ate together one night, Connie sensed something was wrong concerning the couple's daughter, whom they called Bun. She asked Elly, thinking they were out of earshot of Bob, and learned that her daughter had been killed at the University of Illinois at Urbana-Champaign in the mid-seventies. The university never gave an official explanation for the cause of death. Allison Campbell fell to her death in a stairwell in the psychology building. From what little evidence her parents could gather, they believe she was sexually assaulted and pushed. Her top had been ripped off and put in a trashcan. Yet Mrs. Campbell says the university claimed that Bun had killed herself.

Their conversation was cut short, and Connie was floored. The next day Bob Campbell came to the Clerys' condominium and asked Howard not to mention it again, and for Connie not to ask his wife about Bun. He was terrified that Elly would consider taking her own life. For many years following, Connie never spoke about the Campbells' daughter.

Connie and Elly remained friends after their husbands died. Before leaving Florida one spring to return north, Mrs. Clery wanted to apply at her bank for a grant to help the nonprofit. Knowing she would have to tell Jeanne's story once again, Connie asked Elly Campbell to go with her. She was shocked when her friend agreed. As they got to the bank, Connie was surprised—and then grateful—to hear Elly sharing her daughter's story with a receptionist.

Approaching forty years later, Elly Campbell still thought she might never know what caused her daughter's death. She hesitated to say whether things had changed for the better.

When Bun was a toddler, Allison's grandmother called her, "my little sunny bunny," and the nickname stuck. She became a terrific golfer whose dream was to turn pro. Teenage summers were spent practicing, and Campbell won quite a few driving contests. She often played with her dad, a World War II veteran, and they thrived in many father-daughter tournaments. Allison was on the college women's team and preparing to go home for the weekend to celebrate her brother's birthday. There were no signs of depression, and her parents never bought the suggestion that it was suicide.

"They could tell she had been attacked," Elly Campbell said, "but we never knew if she fell down the stairs trying to get away from him or if he pushed her. We never found out who did it."

"The university would not let us speak to any of the kids who knew her," she says, although with the help of some friends they did reach one boy. Campus police handled the case themselves, rather than turning it over to city detectives. When her husband talked to a lieutenant at the Urbana Police Department, "he told [Bob] it was the worst case in how it was mishandled," she says. "They were just covering up."

Forging these ties with other victims' families threatened to reopen old wounds. Yet Connie remained lifted by them: the Campbells and Reilleys, the Dickinsons, Baers and Goldbergs, among others. Just before another Easter, her voice creaked momentarily again considering this. "So many connections, that I just know it's God's design," she said. "Somehow, we're helping one another."

When Connie hired Deb Shelley as her part-time assistant in 2006, Shelley joined a staff of four occupying the second-floor of a house near the King of Prussia Mall. She was quickly impressed at how much they had accomplished. Yet as she took over handling the donations and writing checks out of a black ledger the nonprofit had been using for years, Shelley also saw things needing an upgrade. After the staff conducted Clery Act training sessions, she was amazed to find that occasionally participants failed to pay their registration even months later, and follow through had not been formalized. During the next year the office finally bought QuickBooks, which became her forte.

Having a daughter of her own who was a college freshman, Shelley immediately embraced the Clerys' mission. Interviewing Shelley in a restaurant one morning, Connie couldn't help but relay some of the stories, and both women found themselves crying. Deb realized that while she, too, had considered the topic of campus safety in an abstract way, she had never really focused on it. "I took it as a given, but it's not a given," she says. "It just isn't." She wanted to help get the word out to other parents, and eight years later her role had expanded to executive director of finance and operations.

The group evolved in other ways. It became less of a watchdog of campus abuses, while continuing to inform students about their rights and advocate for workable national policies targeting campus sexual violence. Although still called in after egregious errors by colleges, the nonprofit's approach became decidedly proactive. The change was reflected in rebranding Security On Campus as the Clery Center for Campus Security, complete with a new logo in 2012 to crystallize its identification with the family and the Clery Act. This transformation, Shelley says, "was way overdue, I thought, but we got it done in a fast and furious hurry."

This segue was led in large part by Alison Kiss, a Connecticut native whose skill sets include her experiences counseling crime victims and ties with academia. Previously a Spanish and Latin teacher, Kiss began working at SOC in 2005 as its programs director, moving up to executive director six years later after a stint working nearby at Saint Joseph's University. While a few Clery staff members had life experience with assaults, Kiss did not, and the absence of this plus her academic orientation were refreshing to Connie. With her blessing and also that of board members who included several of the Clerys' longtime friends, Kiss steered the group to work more closely with the higher education community. "We saw colleges and universities really taking note of the Clery Act, so we made a shift to training and technical support, and collaboration," she says. "Compliance truly needs to be institutionalized, top down and bottom up."

To accomplish this, Kiss and a staff that would soon nearly double in size scaled up their seminars, covering not only the nuts and bolts of crime reporting but also demonstrating protocols for schools to adopt in sexual assault cases. They held training workshops around the country drawing campus officers and other university employees, growing to a dozen or so sessions each year, while adding inventive online courses and team-based programs for schools to customize their own training. Their annual conferences became go-to events offering the latest tools to empower students and advice for colleges on complying with sex discrimination laws and other measures.

The Clery Center reached more students, including assisting young filmmakers who produced a provocative series that encourages their peers to lead sexual violence prevention on campus. As classes resume each fall, its staff promotes National Campus Safety Awareness Month to refresh the dialogue, including raising awareness of the "red zone," the stretch into Thanksgiving break when many freshmen women are most susceptible to assaults. They worked alongside other advocacy groups and a new generation of student activists—some connected to Carter, or Kiss—and who coalesced with names like "Know Your IX" and "End Rape On Campus." A new tone emerged: We're here to help.

Meanwhile, the center took off financially, growing its operations from about $500,000 annually to nearly $800,000 by 2013. It attracted corporate sponsors like security providers Siemens and Allied Barton while landing several large government grants, including one from the Justice Department. Individual contributions remained vital, providing almost thirty cents of every dollar brought in, while fees for training programs became the largest income producer. The nonprofit also connected with law firms specializing in victims' rights and institutional responses to sexual misconduct.

Mainly though, the group embedded itself with colleges across the country, providing training and best practices to help them go beyond minimal compliance with new regulations. With Kiss's ameliorative approach to academia setting the tone, at times she disagreed with hardline activists. Rather than seeking hefty fines to penalize colleges that failed to address harassment under Title IX, for example, Kiss argued that most institutions benefitted more from program reviews by federal education officials. "From my viewpoint the effort is there," she told me in 2014. "In order to be proactive, they need more guidance from OCR [the DOE's Office for Civil Rights] first. In all fairness, before enforcing something you need guidance. Or it's issuing a speeding ticket before the sign is posted."

Others joined the nonprofit with their own gouged experiences as if renewing a bitter rite. Newcomers to its board of directors included a California couple who lost their son because of apparent fraternity hazing, and a mom whose son died in a dorm fire.

Gail Minger began a quest to educate college students and parents about fire safety for students with disabilities in 1998. The reach of the Michael H. Minger Foundation named for her son expands because of her persistence, since Gail tries just about everything. She'll speak to handfuls of students, advocate before fire marshals and administrators, or confer with survivors and victims' parents.

Minger hears the doubts, the hardened voices saying, "You'll never get through to them." Her response is declaring that, *even if a few kids are saved, it's worth it.*

Before collaborating with the Clery Center to film a new fire safety video, she produced a sobering documentary called *9 Fires*. The film depicts the impact of blazes at nine campuses that occurred within a three-week stretch, how families and communities were affected long after news crews had moved on. Minger also pursued a dream to build a model dorm incorporating the latest technology and safety equipment to largely benefit disabled students. A gifted musician studying broadcast journalism, Michael also had an autism spectrum disorder. His mom sought to create a place at his college, the University of the Cumberlands in Kentucky, for students with hearing, sight, and mobility impairments, and for those with conditions such as Asperger's Syndrome.

Like many of us, Vicky Tornetta, a former board member and neighbor of Connie's, has seen people crumble in a vice grip that once held Gail Minger and the Clerys. She continues to admire those who extricate themselves from their own pain to help others, knowing this can be messy.

"What does it take? I don't know," she says. In Connie's case, "there is a lot of faith in her, and a belief that there is a greater purpose. And even in something as horrific as what happened, you wrestle through that. It doesn't happen cleanly, but wrestling through that, [the question becomes], 'What do you do with this now?'"

9

IF NOT FOR THEMSELVES

Mary Swanson can still pinpoint the Continental Divide of her life, separating those years before and after Jeanne Clery's death.

Close friends in high school, her last days with Jeanne were a weekend of skiing in Boulder, near where Swanson had moved with her mom when her parents split up. Mary doesn't recall those last conversations, as there are large gaps with certain things blocked out. In college on the West Coast the following months, she walked around campus glancing behind her shoulder, trying to discern hidden intentions. Rattled, she was consumed by anger "and a lot of not understanding."

Swanson kept her distance from the Clerys for a time. Suing Jeanne's school didn't make any sense to her. Being idealistic, she did not initially see the correlation between taking on Lehigh with their larger purpose.

As a mom with three adopted children, she does today. When bullying became a concern at one daughter's school, Swanson, an English teacher who has taught abroad in China and the Congo, chafed when the principal attempted to sweep the behavior under the rug.

One day Connie called seeking her help with an important task. Swanson flew east only somewhat prepared to assist cleaning out Jeanne's bedroom. Mrs. Clery wanted to go through her clothes and donate them to charity. It had been nearly twenty-five years.

They found her prom dress, the one with the telltale corsage once pinned on it. There were stories for other outfits: *I remember buying this for*

Jeanne before she was a freshman. Nearly two hours of thumbing through her skirts and blouses, sweaters and dresses, many threaded to a creation narrative, exhausted Mary. "But I knew there was nobody else who cared enough to listen," she says. Although the Clerys had built an addition on to their stucco home, she noticed that Jeanne's room had scarcely changed.

Swanson had just endured a major ordeal of her own. About a year earlier, she experienced problems breathing and a tumor appeared in her trachea. It was Stage Four cancer, and she underwent twenty-seven weeks of chemo and radiation. She beat it, yet Swanson felt that she had become an enigma to others around her. She saw their body language, the unspoken whispers and self-denials: "How did she get this?" *This can't happen to me.* Soon afterwards, Swanson lost a close friend to throat cancer, a woman who herself was mourning the death of a child. She saw that when friends lose a spouse or child, "so many people are here initially for them, but are not when you need them later. It's tough. They don't know what to say."

She sends Mrs. Clery flowers on Jeanne's birthday every November 23. When Connie asked her to join the nonprofit as a board member, Mary agreed to come again a handful of times each year for meetings, even after she and her husband relocated to Hawaii. She became one of two members who were Jeanne's peers. Some years earlier, Andy Cagnetta, Jeanne's boyfriend at Lehigh, stunned the Clerys by reaching out to them—they hadn't known he existed—and he later joined the board.

Before finally going through Jeanne's clothes, Connie had some other housekeeping in mind. She had long agonized over returning to Lehigh. As hard as it was considering a return, and impossible for both her sons, Clery wanted to reach out to the school. Returning to Jeanne's memorial gazebo, the one built next to her old dorm, was one thing, probably way too much. Offering an olive branch was another.

The time felt right.

Howard likely would have rejected this, but she did not care. They had never discussed reconciliation. "He would've thought I was crazy," she says. "But it had to be done."

Long the strategist, Connie selected Lehigh with a high purpose. She wanted to hold a campus security conference at the university. While her nonprofit was committed to partnering with colleges, this was more visceral, the release of another twining knot. "I wanted to show that I did not hold Lehigh responsible for Jeanne's death, and Jeanne loved Lehigh," she says. "I saw her grow into such a mature young lady in such a short time."

At Connie's request, Swanson drove up to Bethlehem with Carter and the group's executive director who preceded Kiss. They met two men who played very different roles after Jeanne's murder in 1986. To Swanson at least, both appeared to be very nervous.

One was the campus police chief, Ed Shupp, who as a young detective had worked the case every day for nine months assisting the state police investigation, his first homicide. Shupp had to comb through Jeanne's room, a scene that brought on many sleepless nights. Years later he had four daughters himself. Beside him was John Smeaton, the dean of students when Jeanne was there and by then a vice provost of student affairs. He, too, had witnessed the breadth of change in safety awareness over two-plus decades. Smeaton had long since commended the Clerys for their determination, acknowledging the devastation that drove their lawsuit against the university. Swanson told both men that holding the conference would help Connie build a bridge that had once been inconceivable. "She's ready to move forward."

The organization had also largely shed its role of clamping onto someone's pant legs, as if shedding the memory of Howard's venom. "Back ten years ago people were scared of the Clerys," Swanson said. "I can't imagine there's anyone still saying the Clerys are a bitter family still out for vengeance.

"She [Connie] knew you can't really be driven by anger," Mary continued. "You have to be driven by the right vision, and that was Jeanne. Everything has been to save lives on campus, and through Jeanne she has been able to do that."

The table was set. Shortly after turning eighty, in the spring of 2011 Connie stepped back as chairwoman of her board, handing the reins to Swanson in advance of the conference. She joked that Ben had told her, "You've got emeritus, Mom. You know it's time."

Soon after Lehigh agreed with her proposal, the university sent Connie a Moravian Star representing the star of Bethlehem and the beginning of Advent. She hung it outside her home.

Edward Shupp gave Connie a one-armed hug. Drawing his bulk down in deference, he patted her gently on the back. So many years earlier they had met in the worst imaginable crisis after he was called to Room 301. Yet this moment transcended the past.

What mattered most were the improvements for students Shupp had seen since then: upgraded surveillance, swipe-card access to dorms and buildings, security screens on first-floor windows, and nearly two hundred emergency callboxes. State-certified campus officers coordinated their patrols, sharing information and doing community policing alongside their Bethlehem brethren. And lots of education. Helping students learn about sexual assaults, caring for their personal safety, and drinking hazards—some 140 events each year. Spinning off their Lehigh Mountain Hawks mascot, police organized student volunteers in a "Hawk Watch" to report crimes and even replace burned-out porch lights. Referring to other campuses, Chief Shupp said, "These are changes that should not be balked at."

Shupp's demeanor is pleasant if not sympathetic. Below a broad forehead, his eyes seem to emit a pale blue light from the telltale squint of a veteran cop. He regards student safety and victims' rights as paramount and agrees that sexual assaults are vastly underreported, even on his campus. "Of course I do," he says. Often it's due to guilt, a student feeling that "maybe I had too much to drink and that played a part in it. We try to tell them that's not the case."

He holds up the Clerys for the work they've done, and carries no grudge. "They lost their pride and joy," he says. "What they did, the positive things they did as a result of this tragedy are just tremendous."

On a humid early fall morning, he introduced Mrs. Clery as a friend to about 120 guests gathered atop the campus.

She wore a forest green suit with a butterfly brooch, her once natural auburn hair refreshed in color. Connie's brown eyes opened wide, regarding her audience in an adoring way, unlike fifteen or twenty years before, when she and her husband were out stumping for legislation they hoped would change the times. Before her were other police supervisors and chiefs, frontline college staffers who work with students on binge drinking and preventing sexual violence, professors, student affairs administrators, security technology providers, and several longtime victims' advocates. An assistant US attorney general would brief them about upcoming legislation, warning that more than half of all colleges still lacked written policies on how to follow up on reported assaults. The panel sessions would include robust discussions on emergency response assessments and addressing high-risk behaviors.

As Connie looked out of the conference hall, full-length windows provided a view over the valley. Thin clouds carried a wisp of rain. She felt a weight lifting as Jeanne, too, was smiling down.

It was time, finally, for her mother to go. To step away and be home with her sons.

For Connie there was nothing to hide, no shred of pretense.

"I am overwhelmed," she began. "This is a day of celebration for me, and it's hard to be here. But we're here all together." She invoked Jeanne, her voice choking once more in a brief uptick. Regarding her audience, it was almost a dream come true. As the plaque beside Stoughton House read, Jeanne would be remembered. If her life had not continued as a beacon for some other student, that abyss might have swallowed her mother, and perhaps her entire family.

Constance Benjamin Clery righted herself one more time. Every phoneme of her diction signaling intention, Connie asserted her vision again. She laid down this charge: "We can and must continue to change the culture of high-risk drinking and sexual assault. These institutions, leaders, and you can't do it all. We must engage the students. We have to reach them. Respect and responsibility need to come back into style and *stay* in style.

"Young people today live in a different world where there is a lot of fear and terror. Students can feel empowered by helping one another to take ownership of their campus's safety. This summit gives me hope that we will have people working on solutions all over the country. I expect you to infect everybody else."

She moved rapidly to finish, beginning to tighten up. "This summit is a gift to my family and me. It shows me that Jeanne's life wasn't in vain."

There were only one or two more things more to do. One of her heroes, the president emeritus at the University of Rhode Island, presented about taking on a college community's denial of its party culture—a challenge that Connie agreed must be addressed annually. The linkage between excessive drinking and sexual assaults had never eluded her. Still, even after leaving Lehigh before lunch, clearly spent, squired home by Swanson after giving an interview to a TV station, eager to embrace her sons and having officially signed off, Mrs. Clery wasn't finished.

Not two months after her emotional rapprochement with Lehigh, Connie was brought to tears again. This time while reading reports out of State College, home of Penn State University's flagship campus.

Three years after a high school freshman's mom first reported a sexual assault, Jerry Sandusky was arrested on charges of abusing eight boys. Penn State's athletic director and a vice president were charged with perjury and failure to report the allegations to police.

The charges against Sandusky, the team's longtime defensive coordinator, were vile enough. And while the worst was yet to come for the Nittany Lions' vaunted football program and legendary head coach—the university's moneymaking brand—also at stake was Penn State's possible violation of a key responsibility universities have to protect their campus community. Under the Clery Act, complaints of sexual harassment or assault must be passed along to appropriate authorities. After a graduate assistant reported witnessing the assault of a ten-year-old child in the showers, rather than forwarding the claim to law enforcement or a state child welfare agency, the university president and other top administrators did nothing.

Before the case blew open, in a self-serving lament, President Graham Spanier had feared that should Sandusky continue as a predator, "we then become vulnerable for not having reported it."

Vulnerable for not having reported it.

As Louis Freeh, the former FBI director, concluded in his investigation of Penn State, perhaps the most damning finding was that senior leaders showed a "total and consistent disregard for the safety and welfare of Sandusky's child victims." Protecting reputations trumped. No one really wanted to believe that head coach Joe Paterno may have been flawed. Yet for Mrs. Clery, who was in contact with at least one university trustee, the writing was already on the wall.

A few days after Sandusky's arrest, she told Carter, "A few heads are going to roll." Paterno and Spanier were fired that week.

Connie and her staff knew full well that many university employees who have direct contacts with students share a duty to report such allegations. It's not just up to the campus police. She quickly saw that, in some ways similar to the lack of timely threat notifications at Virginia Tech, Penn State's debacle could pave the way for other schools to do the right thing.

By law, if not by moral obligation, an array of college staffers must relay threats and other incidents up the chain. This includes those who oversee student clubs or work in offices that receive reports, resident advisers and housing directors, the dean of students, vice presidents. "And yes, team coaches," Carter says. Among the few exceptions to this are privileged communications between students and mental health practitioners or pastoral counselors—if those employees are acting in that capacity when a student approaches them.

As the scandal went viral, an old friend of the Clerys posted on Facebook to the effect that, "the Clery Act has come into its own with this."

This was a game changer. Every school's obligation to disclose crimes and report claims to police was beginning to stick in the public's consciousness. A few years before, the Department of Justice had found that only a third of colleges and universities were even sharing their sexual assault statistics with the public. The challenge was laid bare. "How can we get out in front of this?" Alison Kiss, director of the Clery's nonprofit, asked around this time. "How can we make some institutions be more proactive in this?"

Meeting the reporting mandate is a sizeable undertaking, and Penn State soon stepped up to the plate. Among its twenty thousand employees on twenty-three campuses, the system identified three thousand staffers having that reporting authority. As the criminal case against Sandusky went to trial in 2012, the university selected the Clery Center to train its staff. That summer, Kiss led a team for two days with sixty or more department heads and other administrators. Any expectation of not being welcomed was turned on its head.

"They wanted to learn, they talked about their frustrations," Kiss said.

The focus was handing off tools so they could build compliance among their peers. A few hours into the first day, Kiss and her colleagues got the full group involved. Armed with some slides and materials, participants at each table were given five minutes to develop talking points—to address the public safety staff, resident directors, or student orientation, rotating around the room. "We opened it right up, what went well, and what doesn't work well," said Kiersten White, a student life administrator at Saint Joseph's University who assisted in the training.

Driving home together, she and Kiss were on cloud nine. They hadn't anticipated feeling so proud of the team they had just worked with. Many staffers in the room understood the law and seemed committed to implementing it.

Still, reaching all the university employees with reporting responsibilities would be a tireless task. Gabriel Gates, Penn State's Clery compliance manager, who came on after the scandal, anticipated ongoing vigilance would be needed to protect students and assure compliance. "We've walked through a lot of deep snow," he told me. "A lot of smaller and bigger universities can use some of our footprints to make it easier on themselves."

Laura Dunn stepped into a taxi on a raw, wet March afternoon. Heavy snow was falling west of the city, but the capital itself had been spared. She told the cabbie she was heading to the Department of the Interior, not a routine stop for a second-year law student.

Dunn was about to attend a bill signing. After several years of inane infighting, Congress had finally reauthorized the Violence Against Women Act (VAWA) to expand protections against domestic and sexual violence. Despite being only twenty-seven, Laura had actually helped write some changes into the law in an area she knew firsthand: making campus disciplinary hearings fairer and more transparent.

An activist since her days at the University of Wisconsin at Madison, Dunn shared too much in common with other survivors, some of whom were also taking on their universities even if that meant stepping into a public spotlight. The spring of her freshmen year in 2004, two men assaulted Dunn in an apartment, fellow athletes from the crew team whom Dunn had trusted to walk her to a party. Once she was able to stop blaming herself, since she had been drinking heavily—as both men were—Dunn was outraged that the university took nine months to investigate and then declined to pursue disciplinary action. An assistant dean said there were no witnesses and the men claimed to be "not clear on what happened"— although Dunn insists she told them, "No," and to stop.

Over time, Dunn vowed to help other survivors obtain the justice that had eluded her. She made the perilous leap to share her story, refusing to accept her own silence and shame. Resolving, as she said, "to share my experience using my name and face so that the nation could have a personalized view of the people who are affected by campus sexual violence." This put her on a new path. Dunn got connected with the Clerys' nonprofit as an advocate and trainer presenting to college staffers. She was among a group that pushed the Department of Education to get tougher on schools, delivering more than 100,000 student signatures that got the attention of the Obama Administration. Meanwhile, often working alongside Carter and a growing student network, Dunn contributed to new measures that attempt to help make victims whole.

Included in VAWA was the Campus Sexual Violence Elimination Act, known better as the Campus SaVE Act, all of which is folded into what is often called the Jeanne Clery Act. Amendments to VAWA in 2013 spelled out more clearly not only what institutions must do when students report claims of assault, stalking, or dating violence, but also the breadth of proactive efforts they should already have in place: student-centered prevention and education; defining what sexual violence and informed consent means; and modeling strategies for bystander intervention. Taking a cue from some of the Title IX guidance to colleges announced two years earlier, Laura suggested adding assurances that a victim, not just the accused, could appeal the outcome of a campus grievance hearing. She also suggested that each party receive timely notice of the findings—addressing two points that were persistent thorns during her ordeal in Madison.

Just a week or so before, many advocates had fumed as another political stalemate made the passage of VAWA seem unlikely. That was solved despite objections to so-called controversial measures benefitting gays and lesbians, immigrants, and native peoples. Big concessions were needed to get it done. While the outcome was still in doubt, Dunn stood off the floor of the US Capitol with House minority leaders, wearing a black jacket and a pink blouse. Another assault survivor from Dunn's home state, Representative Gwen Moore, a lead sponsor of the bill, was incensed by the House's inaction.

"How can we *fathom* turning women away because of their sexual orientation, and being so cavalier?" Moore asked, her pitch rising like the scraping on a classroom board. "*How* could they strip away protecting against rape of our college students?" Soon she introduced Laura to speak to the media and a throng of advocates in the briefing room.

"I am humbled, because I am a victim," Dunn began. "But I am speaking for many more."

"Justice delayed is justice denied."

Many advocates hailed the reauthorized law for making huge strides on behalf of campus victims. Among them was codifying institutions' responsibilities after reported assaults, such as issuing protective and no-contact orders against alleged campus perpetrators, or to seek restraining orders depending on the severity of the case. Survivors would receive timely information about health and counseling services, legal aid, and written notification about their options to change academic, living, or work situations, regardless of whether or not they reported an alleged crime to campus or local police. Bringing an advisor of their choice to disciplinary hearings became the law of the land; before then, universities had control whether to provide that option. For Carter and other many others, these were the most sweeping changes to address campus sexual violence in twenty years.

Others contended that upon closer examination, provisions of Campus SaVE actually gutted vital measures seeking justice for gender-based violence. The new law, contended Wendy Murphy, a former sex crimes prosecutor and leading critic, was "a wolf in sheep's clothing." Among the changes was dropping the preponderance of evidence standard that the Department of Education had recommended colleges use in their disciplinary hearings. This standard of proof—which amounts to 51 percent, compared to the criminal law burden of proof "beyond a reasonable doubt," which is about 95 percent—"is the only option that treats the word of a victim as equal in weight to that of her assailant," wrote Murphy, an adjunct professor of sexual violence law at New England School of Law.

Other changes watered down protections for women compared to other victims of violence based on race and national origin, Murphy said, while also overrunning the "prompt and equitable" standard education officials had set for colleges' responses to sexual violence complaints. Schools could again run out the clock, as Dunn believed her alma mater did, by delaying a "final determination" of a complaint until the eve of the complainant's graduation.

Carter, who by then had left the Clerys' group to work for a campus safety foundation formed by families of Virginia Tech victims and survivors, countered that new protections outweighed the law's flaws. Provisions were added to address hate crimes against gay, bisexual, and transgender students, plus hate crimes against foreign-born students. Public consensus to address campus assaults seemed to be rising, although by 2017, advocates feared those gains might be reversed. To Daniel, a key breakthrough was the turnaround of colleges recognizing that their policies can re-victimize assault survivors. They need to be believed and afforded privacy, not retaliated against. "That one-to-one contact with them is one of the most important things that they have," he stressed during a webinar. "So understand both their trauma and also how your interaction can double back" on it.

Naturally, Connie kept close tabs on much of this. She continued reading news accounts and called Kiss at the office for updates. While she had truly stepped back—no longer pushing board members in a certain direction—Mrs. Clery could still delineate key points in the new law. "When we started, there was never any update on domestic violence on campuses that we knew of, but stalking has always been a very, very serious situation, and this bullying goes along with that," she told me a week after Campus SaVE passed. "It's all kind of the same family, there's just so much to it.

"It's amazing how the law has expanded and expanded. It's hard for me to believe we've accomplished so much," she said. "Until recently it went so fast—I didn't have time—but now I have time to think. I'm amazed. The one thing we wanted that I thought was a pipe dream, attempting to change the culture. At least we're attempting to."

Connie let out another long sigh. "It seems to be getting worse than getting better. But at least we're getting out into society, and that will affect campuses."

Her mother pauses again, her voice draining from a remote cranny only those of us who have lost a child can access.

"She is not just a name, you know," Connie says. "I wish people would realize that."

Facing her high school speech class, Jeanne Ann Clery stands erect with feet shoulder-width apart as if bolted to the floor. Her thick hair is loosely layered, nearly covering eyes that look up from her notes. One arm pats and cajoles her pet shitzu, which is on a table beside Jeanne and resisting face time with the audience. The dog's name is Mei Ling. Clery will hesitate only long enough to enunciate a few words like "profuse" and "eunuch." Otherwise she's in full control.

Wearing a blazing yellow T-shirt and dark plaid mini-skirt, a spinoff of, or perhaps a minor retort against the requisite school uniform, Jeanne begins.

"Today I'm here to inform you of the profuse history of the shitzu and how you groom and care for it." Her formal presenting voice is deep and confident, sparkling in short riffs after dispensing with the drier material. "The legend was born in the mid-seventeenth century when dogs were brought from Tibet to the Imperial Court . . ." She explains that shitzu means "lion," or a chrysanthemum-flowered face, and turns Mei Ling around to show off her long wisps of facial hair.

The dog's floppy brown ears redirect toward her caregiver. Jeanne serves up a few more facts and introduces the grooming tools. A wire bristle brush, which she advises her listeners use first, then a long-stemmed comb, eyebrow pluckers, and nail trimmers.

"You might be saying to yourself, 'What a pain!'" she grins at her audience, her voice lightening. "I just don't want to brush my dog today, there's just no way. Well, it takes about five minutes, and the shitzu likes to be groomed, and Mei Ling often falls asleep in the process, which I guess is *not* very normal." She grins again and gives another pat. "They love it, so why not? They don't give you any problems!"

Demonstrating the tools—she runs her hand along Mei Ling's back showing how to make a part and pony tail—Jeanne relaxes. A consistent schedule is necessary, she advises, brushing the coat every day to "get the snarls out" and retain a glossy sheen, and bathing her at least every two weeks. Human shampoo works fine. "And I'm not going to lie. They hate that," she smirks. "They get so scared they hyperventilate." This happened the very first time she washed the puppy. "She started snorting, she couldn't breathe," Jeanne says, patting her own stomach as a few girls giggle. "I thought she was going to die. I was pretty young."

Her other tips mostly cut right to the point: plucking excess hairs from inside the ears to forestall wax buildup, and how to use clippers to prevent ingrown nails. Then she lets out what amounts to a rebel yell regarding hair grooming. "You're not supposed to, but I trim the top because it's cuter. It's supposed to be a lot longer." And another thing that's not recommended: trimming the back hair short. But Jeanne explains, prompting outright laughter among the other girls, "If she gets sick, or a little messy, it gets caught, and dingle berries are everywhere. So I just cut it off."

She scoops up Mei Ling to give her a hug.

Andy Cagnetta looked back on this many times. Seized by guilt, as if walking Jeanne to her dorm would have spared her, he fought depression and anxiety attacks. He saw a psychiatrist for two years, and when he turned forty, stunned the man by calling and thanking him.

Cagnetta is married with two daughters and hugely successful beyond his home near Fort Lauderdale. He owns and runs one of the country's largest business brokers specializing in mergers and acquisitions, and franchises. He gives back to his community, including organizing a big pasta dinner fundraiser to support families who struggle to put food on the table. For three or four years he thought of Jeanne everyday, and he's thankful he can speak of it. "I don't feel cured, but that is my salvation that I am able to talk about it," he says.

He still pictures Jeanne at Lehigh beside Phi Sig's tiny bar playing Whales Tales, a favorite drinking game. Other friends like Susan Kwon could spot her "a mile away" in her blue sweatshirt, green pants, pink winter coat and boots. Among the so-called "freshmen fifteen" victims,

Jeanne had put on a few extra pounds her first year, "dieting" on French fries and pizza. One time she single-handedly offered to protect the guys in her dorm by beating up the football players in a nearby hall.

Her portrait still hangs in the fraternity house, which Cagnetta made sure of the last time he stopped by. The Clerys had it made, with Jeanne wearing her Izod sweater, and gave it to the house. Walking in, Cagnetta saw they were repainting the walls and it wasn't there. "I said, 'I'm going to take it if you don't put it back up.'"

When Andy returned to Lehigh for the conference twenty-five years later, he purposefully stopped on the lawn where he and Jeanne said good night. "We were making it a point to get to know each other and testing the waters," he recalls.

He hears her throaty laugh as it almost turns into a primal scream. He can just about feel her playful whack on the arm, which actually hurt. They played a little doubles together, and once when he challenged her to a singles match, she kicked his butt.

Laura Dunn glimpsed a path forward, for herself, and legions of others.

During her final year of law school at the University of Maryland, Laura sowed seeds at a dizzying pace. Working in the Justice Department's Office of Violence Against Women, she was impressed by a staff she saw holding universities accountable for the grants they received. She got a clerkship at a Baltimore-based law firm working with a victims' rights attorney, meeting other women from varied backgrounds and ages. Most keenly, before graduating she formed a nonprofit called SurvJustice to support survivors, advocating for criminal prosecution and representing them in civil and campus cases—a huge risk rather than joining a firm. Dunn also soon began training institutions to meet their obligations addressing sexual violence, consulting with the State University of New York system to help it create a uniform policy on violence prevention and response for its campuses.

Early in 2014, she participated with Carter and Kiss on a rulemaking committee negotiating more specific mandates for colleges under the new law, petitioning federal education officials to let her lend the voice of a student survivor and advocate to the committee. Akin to engineers taking input from hydrologists and geologists to understand an underground plume's migration, the group wrote specs for the equivalent of groundwater pumps, filters, and monitoring wells. Dunn felt some validation. Her perseverance had caught the attention of the White House and played a small role in it also forming a task force to fast-forward recommendations to end campus assaults. Yet ever practical, she remained guarded. "There's no final result yet," Dunn told me that winter. "I'm still in this mode of push for more. This isn't a victory, this is the time to fight hardest."

Her vigilance, and that of scores of younger women and men just making their way through college, would be needed to combat those forces seeking to reverse gains for campus victims' rights. Dunn, for one, rebutted a *Wall Street Journal* columnist who decried the so-called "war on men," undressing the writer's starched euphemisms, including his framing an alleged forcible sodomy that began when the victim was asleep as an "intimate encounter." Meanwhile, she took on the nuts-and-bolts work of building a nonprofit, wrestling with grant writing and wearing too many hats. Carter joined Dunn's board along with an authority on victim's rights at the National Crime Victim Law Institute. By 2017—not three years after starting—SurvJustice had assisted on about 120 federal complaints and fielded more than five hundred requests to help students, which sometimes meant filing Title IX and Clery complaints. The group's focus, she told *Forbes*, included assisting campus survivors to prevent repeat perpetrators long not held accountable from committing similar acts.

More broadly, Laura was building on a commitment that people like Candi Lightner, Frank Carrington and the Clerys had made many years earlier. Her goal was "to change the national legal landscape to recognize victims' rights hand in hand with defendants' rights." From life experience and observations as a litigator, Dunn saw this was not practiced often in courtrooms or outside in society. Too often in sexual assault cases, she saw the law trained on a victim's behavior rather than the accused.

There would be many setbacks in the years ahead: a fabricated gang rape narrative published in *Rolling Stone*; the short sentence that Stanford swimmer Brock Turner received following his assault of a comatose woman; an alleged culture of systemic sexual violence embedded in Baylor

University's football program. On and on. Pushback came from those worried about eroding defendants' rights, including the university lawyers who construct policies—their schools' responses to rape accusations—built upon the fear of lawsuits by the parents of the accused.

In spite of all this, cracks were spreading across those legacy foundations—and beyond. The scales were recalibrated on campuses as expectations for colleges and universities became clear as day. The public's disgust with sexual harassment and assaults seemed to puncture a point of no return, despite the election of a self-professed groper-in-chief.

Along with other student activists turning to advocacy and practicing law, Laura continued to field late night texts and calls. She offered advice and resources, learning to set limits like not taking a case with less than a week's notice or traveling at crazy hours to make a campus hearing. While draining, some of these exchanges brought relative victories. "Sometimes they just need a community that's outraged like they are, and wants change," Laura told me. "Almost every survivor amazes me because they want justice beyond themselves, so it's really about helping them figure out how they can maintain a life and take on an advocate's role."

Finding balance would not be easy. Over long stretches it might not even be attainable. Yet for the others, if not for herself, she vowed to never stop trying.

PART THREE

A WAY FORWARD

Giving and receiving are one
This is called,
    "The great wonder"
    "The essential mystery"
    "The very heart of all that is true"
            —Lao Tzu

THE QUESTION, "WHO SAYS YOU WORK THROUGH THIS?" had largely been answered by the Clerys.

Yet I still had a ways to go before answering, "What do you *do* with this?"

Some years after the 9/11 terrorist attacks, I was introduced to several families who had managed to step through an excruciating and very public pain. I had read of victims' relatives "paying it forward," adopting the popular idiom about doing altruistic acts. I wanted to know more about this response. How do you actually get there? What does it take when the life you've built has been pulverized?

I met a mom in a nearby town who lost her husband on the first plane that hijackers crashed into one of the Twin Towers. Christie Coombs had become a well-known advocate for military families' needs and honoring the fallen in Massachusetts. A journalist herself, Christie had recently interviewed my wife for an article in *The Boston Globe* about creating bereavement supports for families. Our experience with the local drunk-driving prevention group was leading to something more far-reaching. We had recently opened a nonprofit center with support groups for grieving parents, figuring out how to do this on the fly.

I contacted Coombs in hopes of understanding how her family had held up after the crush of attention and sympathy had largely moved on. How did they try to keep their memories of him close?

Poised and engaging, Christie welcomed me into her home to share some family stories of her husband Jeff and what she and her children were doing. She pointed out the fireplace mantle that he had built upon which a prominent portrait stood vigil, similar to a few displays in our living room. It was a picture of her family on a beach, washed in the clean, bittersweet light of Labor Day weekend just a week before the bottom fell out.

One of the things that Christie and her children had done was to start a foundation helping people all over the state going through their own hardships. When they initiated an annual road race in Jeff's memory to support this, she insisted it benefit families whose needs differed from theirs, "to cover something that somebody else won't cover." This meant paying for a wheelchair or someone's funeral expenses, filling small holiday wishes for strapped parents, guitar lessons for a boy who lost his father, or funding school enrichment programs and scholarships. Coombs was part of a network of 9/11 widows and parents who were moving forward into a new role.

I hoped that it didn't seem I was approaching Christie merely as a late voyeur to her family's trauma. This was not the case, and like nearly everyone else I would contact in my reporting and conversations for this book, she seemed to get where I was coming from.

What did we really know of what transpired over the next decade—and beyond—for those who had been left sorting through their grief?

Meeting Christie was another springboard. She introduced me to some of the organizations that continued to support the financial and mental health needs of 9/11 families, as well as groups helping relatives create meaningful tributes. On the anniversary weekend in 2010, she oversaw her husband's memorial 5K road race in their hometown. I came to run and for my writing hoped to casually meet some family members. But I also went just to be there. As their friends and neighbors filled the blacktop behind an elementary school, it absolutely felt like the right place.

Approaching the whirlwind of the tenth anniversary, I found myself on a new path. I met a group of people who not only observed or were recipients of random acts of kindness that terrible September—they picked up the ball and took off with it.

The first was a New Yorker whose younger brother's sacrifice inspired him to help create the September 11th National Day of Service and Remembrance.

10

INTO HARM'S WAY

Andy Sausmer wouldn't forget that Glenn owed him one.

Sausmer had hoped to catch up with his best friend for the Giants-Broncos game on Monday Night Football the previous evening. It didn't happen. Glenn Winuk was tired, and they both had full days coming up.

Either way, Sausmer figured he'd see his longtime pal soon. They talked nearly every day, sometimes four or five times. Bachelors who grew up in the same Long Island town, they had a tradition of celebrating each other's birthdays over dinner. Glenn's fortieth had come in May, while Andy's swept by in August when Glenn was out of town. Always considerate and deliberate even when responding to a crisis, Winuk needed to redeem his rain check.

Sausmer heard about a plane crash on the radio that morning, at first thinking it was a sick joke. He switched on the television and called Glenn, the first of three attempts. Winuk worked at a law firm in the financial district, where he had become a partner. He wasn't answering.

Winuk could have stayed in his midtown apartment and missed the whole damn thing. Yet Sausmer and the rest of Glenn's buddies knew right where he'd be.

Andy figured that Winuk had gone down to the World Trade Center a block and a half from his office. That would be typical. Glenn, who was selfless especially in a pinch, had a penchant for being in the wrong place at the right time, taking off-duty risks to save lives.

For many years, Glenn had volunteered as a firefighter and emergency medical technician on weekends in their hometown. Winuk and Sausmer had joined the Jericho Fire Department together back in high school, and many in their core group of friends were also volunteer firemen. While both Andy and Glenn were on a hiatus—Winuk had not been an active member of the department for more than two years—Sausmer knew how Glenn had run into danger before. During the WTC garage bombing in 1993, he hoofed over to do rescue, and he had been on a platform pulling people out during the subway chemical bomb scare.

Sausmer hurried to work. He managed Cafe Baci, a popular Italian restaurant in Westbury, next to Jericho in the heart of Nassau County. As two TVs blared images and reports of the attacks, he had waiters write down numbers being broadcast of where to call for information. Lunchtime was unusually slow and yet panicked, the staff running around, patrons vying for the restaurant's two phone lines. The rumors escalated: someone's father was missing, a friend who used to work for the fire department, a wife screaming into the receiver. Sausmer took calls as he checked on others. An off-duty city firefighter, one of his and Glenn's buddies, called asking Andy to gather numbers for him. He was heading in.

By dinner a crush of people had come in, many desperate to talk with others. Looking west from the dining room Sausmer saw smoke billowing. More were feared missing and eventually he heard from all of his close friends except Glenn. By the second attempted call that morning, Andy knew what had happened. With his gut advising him to expect the worst, he told others to keep Glenn in their prayers. He formed a picture of his pal wearing a suit with his trench coat and brief case, running into harm's way.

John Navaretta also figured Glenn had headed into the thick of it. To John, he was non-stop. They, too, went back many years, and Navaretta doubled as an attorney and a Jericho fireman. Glenn could be driving with his girlfriend on the Meadowbrook Parkway, and coming upon a car accident, the next thing you know he'd be giving mouth-to-mouth resuscitation to someone on the roadside.

Navaretta had been a full-time firefighter with a city engine company for a decade, retiring after an injury. But now he was due in court on Long Island. His brother, a FDNY captain, called him minutes after the North Tower was hit. Like Sausmer, John could only get Glenn's voice mail.

"The last message I left was, 'I know you're down there. Be careful,'" he says. "There was a lot of shit going on. My brother called me back and said, 'I think we're under attack, another plane hit,' and the FDNY had a total recall—all members had to come in. At that point no one really knew if it was an accident, or what was going on." Navaretta thought about meeting up with his brother to get downtown. But he was forty minutes away on a good day, and perhaps it was not meant to be.

Joe Mlynarczyk saw distant smoke as he drove to his part-time job in Queens teaching CPR to other firefighters. Mlynarczyk was with Squad Co. 1 in Brooklyn's Park Slope neighborhood. He was actually on vacation—for once, Joe had taken his weeks together because he and his wife were fixing up their house and planning a big first birthday for their twin boys. Otherwise, he would have been at the station house.

He usually listened to the traffic report to plot his route coming in. Yet on September 11, 2001, Mlynarczyk broke his routine, playing a rock station instead. Seeing the smoke, he figured there was a really bad brush fire in New Jersey. Between songs the DJ announced that one of the Twin Towers had been hit, possibly by a sightseeing plane. But when the second jet struck there was no mistake. Reaching his class, Mlynarczyk and the guys teaching the course scrambled to figure out if they should go to the nearest firehouse or what. A lieutenant at a nearby station told them he didn't have any more gear. They had to try and make it to their own stations.

Mlynarczyk's chest heaved with spiking adrenaline. He knew his mates had left, and he became stuck bumper to bumper on the Jackie Robinson Parkway trying to get to the west side of Brooklyn. Hearing that the first tower had collapsed, he thought to himself: the reporter must have been wrong. *The whole tower did not collapse.* It could not possibly be this bad.

He swerved onto the grass median and into the emergency lane, veering between traffic as if in a chase scene, and got off at the first exit. His car flew into an intersection as a bus came through, and he hit the brakes hard enough to stall it, missing the bus. Reaching the station, Mlynarczyk found its two rigs had already left along with most of the crew.

The 1060 signal had gone out, which meant that Squad 1 would go to any major emergency such as a terrorist attack, anywhere, citywide. Checking the chalkboard to see who was still on, Mlynarczyk thought something didn't add up. Guys on the night crew whom he expected to be on the rig had answered the call, along with the day crew. Tallying up their names, "I think we came up with two sets of gear [gone] not on the night shift and not on the day shift." Others who had been off duty had already arrived and gone in. Joe grabbed a ride with a small group who had also been off duty and was just over the Brooklyn Bridge when the second tower came down.

He wasn't thinking about Glenn right away, believing they had a deal in place.

Mlynarczyk figured they each had set roles to play. His job was to be a fireman, Glenn was the attorney. Joe knew that as a partner at Holland & Knight, one of the largest commercial law firms in the country, Winuk was on the rise in the legal world. He'd gained a little weight working long hours, his broad face accentuated by receding brown hair. Yet he remained grounded, looking out for the little guy as much as his eagle colleagues. Rather than stepping on people, Winuk chose to pick them up. Before leaving a restaurant he might go to the front desk and drop a nice word about the busboy or waiter. Besides that, Glenn had been Joe's best man and was godfather of two of the Mlynarczyks' four children. He was Uncle Glenn to each of them, making sure they did what they were supposed to.

Dan King, another friend who was a cop, was getting ready for work. A detective sergeant in a vice unit, King was hoping for an early day in and out because it was his son Ryan's tenth birthday. His radio was on. As a witness was interviewed about the first plane, someone close to the microphone screamed, "Oh my God, my God, it's another one!" King charged toward his precinct station in Brooklyn, coming across a Jamaican guy in a beat-up van who rolled down his window to exclaim: "They're trying to kill us, man! We are all going to die!"

As he pulled on his uniform, King began making rapid attempts to reach Glenn.

At 8:46 a.m., Bill Honan, the man in charge of Winuk's law office at 195 Broadway, was taking the lid off his coffee and about to make a call when the first plane hit. He heard sort of "a round sound," which seemed dull and strangely distant. "None of us really thought of it anything untoward,"

Honan says. "Then we saw a lot of paper flying from west to east—our building is directly east of the World Trade Center—which was extraordinary." He couldn't yet see flames or smoke. The executive partner at Holland & Knight switched on the radio to hear a report suggesting that a private plane had tried to fly between the towers. He thought it had been a terrible accident.

Then at 9:03 there was a second explosion, "a jagged sound like lightning, far more menacing," he says, as the terrorists breached the South Tower with United Airlines Flight 175.

They began evacuating right away, with Honan checking each of the three floors where about two hundred people worked at the firm. Broadway was in complete disarray outside. There was little traffic, but he saw people overcome with emotion lying everywhere amidst a deafening blitz of sirens and circling helicopters. Looking back he saw the top of the South Tower in flames.

Glenn's girlfriend, Bessie, called Winuk at his apartment on 35th Street and Park Avenue.

"Have you seen the news?" she asked.

Glenn's brother Jay believes his younger sibling left in a hurry after her call, perhaps minutes before or just after the second plane struck. It was routine for him to arrive at the office sometime after 9:00 or 9:30 a.m. and work well into the evening. "He must have been really ready to get to work and dashed out," Jay Winuk says.

The doorman got Glenn a cab but warned him against going down there. Nevertheless, as Honan swept through checking the floors he was responsible for, Glenn was on his way.

Holland & Knight's office was located on the corner of Dey Street, just behind the Hilton Millenium Hotel and beside Saint Paul's Chapel, perhaps a thousand feet away from the South Tower as the crow flies. Upon arriving, Winuk helped evacuate his office building, guiding a woman in respiratory distress down the stairs and waiting for an EMT to arrive, unbeknownst to Honan. He borrowed a first response medical kit from some guys who were also evacuating the building, grabbing a mask and gloves, and rushed down to the South Tower, moving against the flow trying to escape the World Trade Center complex.

Honan told everyone to go home and come back tomorrow. Yet he went to another office a bit farther away where a friend of his worked, staying there until the South Tower collapsed. As each floor crashed upon the next, he heard a sound like giant snapping matchsticks coming down—which to people on the ground was a massive, screeching roar. It took only eight or ten seconds to fall. Following the collapse, a black cloud overtook those in the streets trying to find cover, a wall of dust and debris and inscrutable toxins. Honan grabbed a woman he knew in the building and said, 'Let's get out of here.'" They missed being swarmed by the cloud.

Fifty-six minutes after it was struck, as the tower fell, Glenn Jonathan Winuk was in the lobby doing triage.

When his partial remains were uncovered the following March, Winuk was wearing surgical gloves and a stethoscope, and the medical kit was beside him. Also found were his volunteer firefighter's and EMT's credentials from Jericho. Since police were already trying to keep anyone but first responders out of the WTC minutes after the attacks, it is likely that Winuk produced his firefighter's photo ID and EMT card to get in. The priority needs were triage and evacuation, and during those frantic minutes the tower lobby became a staging area to treat cuts and burns and supply oxygen.

As his friends expected, Glenn had raced right to where he was needed.

Jay Winuk was working from home that day about an hour north of the city. His wife Carolyn had dropped their four-year-old son off for his first day at a new preschool, and she was in line at a department store when she heard a commotion of cries. Rushing home, Carolyn found Jay on the sofa with the TV on. Regarding each other in shock, they both said, "'He's there.'"

Glenn didn't pick up his cell or office phone or the phone at his apartment. Jay knew that he was in town. On occasion Glenn and some of the guys would take off to Mohegan Sun or Foxwoods for a weekend, and Glenn had recently been traveling a lot for work—but he was home. No return call came, which was unlike him. Then they learned that there was no cell service downtown, but they still didn't panic.

Jay and Carolyn sat and watched the news for hours. She picked up Justin early from school, fearing that another attack was imminent after the

Pentagon was hit. They stayed at their house, continuously calling Jay's parents, his older brother in South Carolina and each of Glenn's numbers. Friends in the city began contacting the police and hospitals for them. As the hours went by, they figured that, at best, he was still doing triage.

Glenn had called Jay the night before to get directions to a family friend's house in New Jersey since their friend's father had passed. Both the Winuks and the other family are Jewish, and Jay had already made the traditional shiva call at the home of Marty Schwartz's daughter. Schwartz had served in the fire department with Glenn, and Jay had grown up with his son. Expecting to pay his respects the next day, Glenn ordered flowers that arrived on Tuesday.

In those first few days, the Winuks clung to the same thread grasped by thousands of others: that Glenn might be hospitalized, or even wandering somewhere with a head injury. As Jay and their friends continued calling around, Glenn's parents did not immediately think the worst. Seymour Winuk, a bright man who had owned an auto repair shop and dabbled in inventing, knew along with his ex-wife, Elaine, that their youngest son had been in close calls before. He'd been a volunteer fireman for two decades. They figured that Glenn, like his oldest brother Jeff, who had also been a Jericho firefighter, had the requisite training to give him a shot at survival. While he had not been lifting weights and working out as much lately, Glenn was still a muscular five foot ten. He had a black belt in Shotokan karate and had done stuff like an Outward Bound course.

A remote possibility was being trapped in an air pocket under the rubble. Down there, after all, was the concourse, a huge underground shopping mall. God or some other entity had at least delivered a few miracles, such as those fourteen people who were somehow shielded from the North Tower collapse in stairwell B—all but one first responders. "And to have that glimmer of hope for several weeks, that question of life hanging over you, is also very unusual," Jay said.

Yet unlike Glenn's buddies, none of the Winuks were down at the pile.

Andy Sausmer plotted how to get in and assist at Ground Zero. He wanted to help out at all costs, especially to find Glenn.

Although no longer active in the Jericho Fire Department because of his work schedule, Sausmer still had his firefighter's photo ID, and he coordinated what their group of friends could bring over. John Navaretta went in that morning with a friend from Rescue 4 and continued for more than a week. Both Dan King and Joe Mlynarczyk were also on the scene.

On Thursday, September 13, Sausmer went to the local firehouse with Mlynarczyk and loaded gear into his SUV: boxes of dust masks, flashlights, shovels, bandages and bottled water. He also bought a few dozen miniature American flags at a store. They dropped much of the gear off with Rescue 1 near the Brooklyn Bridge.

They met King in a police van, and flashing their city credentials, Mlynarczyk, King, and a fourth friend got below 14th Street along with a couple of cops. The street was blocked off to anyone other than to residents and rescue workers. Sausmer threw on one of Joe's FDNY work shirts and brought his outdated credentials anyway.

They parked south of the towers and joined a bucket brigade. "What we saw," King says, "was amazing, how many crushed fire trucks and police cars, and just the amount of dust. It was sunny and bright but a pile of steel and dust and dirt and the amount of people working hand by hand, bucket lines and passing them." King compared it to the destruction in a grainy Godzilla movie, amplified a hundred times as sirens wailed trying to move workers away from buildings suspected of nearing collapse. Emotions spiked among firefighters desperate to find their three hundred-plus missing brethren and police trying to back them off the pile. Some firemen refused to back down; King was ordered to get the men with him out.

One slice of good fortune came Sausmer's way as he headed to the smoldering pile. He looked up just in time to bump into a friend, an elite firefighter named Dave Marmann, who also happened to be a Jericho volunteer. His family is among the many in the FDNY with intricate firefighting bloodlines—his father Gene was a retired battalion chief, his grandfather had been a fireman, one of Marmann's brothers was an FDNY lieutenant, and another brother was both a city cop and a Jericho volunteer. The senior Marmann had been a surrogate father to Andy and Glenn's generation coming up through the ranks in their hometown. Dave Marmann was in Rescue Company 1, which lost eleven men. But none of the FDNY Marmanns were on duty September 11. Dave and Andy hugged on the ramp.

To Winuk's friends, the financial district had been gouged out in a heinous inversion of itself. Mlynarczyk worked there six weeks, and in some places he saw perhaps twenty stories of a building compacted into a five-foot height, while close by was a wasteland with no one around.

Joe and his squad members crunched into the lobby of the Marriott Hotel. Wine glasses still hung on racks, bar drinks sat half full; other stemware lay untouched by an unbroken mirror. Utter madness lurked just outside. A solid steel roof hook had been crumpled like an accordion. "Things that just shouldn't happen happened, and things that didn't happen should've happened," he says. Still, even though twelve members of his own company were unaccounted for and hope was tenuous, early on he felt that it hung in the fibrous air. "With anyone who you were looking for who was personal to you, your hope was they were in a hospital or trapped in an air pocket," he says. "There were vast areas where there was no destruction."

The enormity of it slammed each of them, feelings that have never quite gone away. Picking through smoldering wreckage, they entered a zone most people will never know, as if crossing into Hades itself past patrols of shell-shocked reservists. "You realized at that point that anyone in there was not coming out," Sausmer says. He handed the American flags on sticks to hardhats and cops, giving them over to someone else to distribute when the clamor of people asking for one became too much. They made it over to Glenn's office, tracking what they thought would have been his path down to the tower. Sausmer etched a note in dust on the lobby desk. Something like, "Glenn Winuk, we miss you and love you."

That Thursday night, most of their group met up at Joshua Tree on Third Avenue. It was Glenn's favorite haunt, a choice spot for many of them to accompany Winuk as his wingman. He was a regular and had befriended the owner and a manager years earlier. One of his Jericho friends had just gone to get Winuk's dental records, and another contacted the city's temporary morgue. Seeing their FDNY shirts, restaurant patrons offered to buy the guys drinks and meals. Accolades flowed, and while appreciated, this made Sausmer and the others a bit uneasy. They tried to explain that they were just helping out, and they had a friend who might still be found. Perhaps Glenn was in a hospital in New Jersey or on Staten Island, or stuck somewhere without cell service.

Navaretta recalls the reality unfolding this way. Driving into Ground

Zero for the first time, "We were all thinking, we've all been through some sort of building collapse at one time or another. But when we got down there it became obvious there weren't going to be too many survivors. It was beyond anyone's comprehension." Around the tenth day Navaretta realized he couldn't do much more, and he needed to get back to his practice.

Firefighters from as far away as Detroit also came to help, and what they mostly found was death. Lieutenant George Orzech drove in with his brother Mark, initially because they were consumed with finding some relatives who lived near the Trade Center. Their cousins were located, and a battalion chief who noticed Orzech's helmet stopped him at the pile that first Friday. He asked the out-of-towner if he knew the smell, and Orzech had to nod, yes.

One of five brothers who had followed their father's footsteps into the profession, Orzech looked for caverns where bodies might be, pointing when he caught a whiff. It kept snowing debris day and night and their mask filters clogged up, quickly becoming useless. He saw body-sniffing dogs sidelined by the dust, their paws scorched by the heat. "There was nothing but hope," Orzech says. "Everyone was hoping they'd find something." He carried spray cans, painting orange dots for body parts, green for aircraft parts. Along with his brother, they located parts of 953 people in three days.

Dan King worked twelve- to fifteen-hour days for two weeks. For a while he, too, held out that they might locate Glenn. While his police unit technically wasn't supposed to be there, King convinced his lieutenant and continued working eight hours or so on the pile before returning to his precinct. Soon he was assigned the midnight shift at the Fresh Kills landfill that had been reopened for demolition debris, which to him was worse than being at Ground Zero. He sifted through rubble for body parts, looking for bits of identification. The stench was almost overwhelming. The strain grew; he'd barely seen his kids or wife for days. "The visions I saw, my brain started playing tricks on me," he says. "It was very weird, emotional stress." His oldest son—who had watched adults burst into tears that Tuesday while gathering their children at his school—was beginning to show signs of his own trauma.

Mlynarczyk crunched through distorted scenes that became commonplace during the following weeks. He didn't get used to it: piles so hot that the soles of his heavy leather and rubber boots stuck to metal; on some days firefighters changed boots every half hour at a nearby school. People gave foot massages and chiropractors worked inside Saint Paul's sanctuary across the street, transforming the church into a respite center in a mission of mercy. Yet he found little relief.

One night a desperate relative called in a psychic, who thought she had located a loved one below a subway line. Mlynarczyk and his crew went in. They didn't find a human, but there was something else. Piercing more than forty feet below ground was an I-beam from one of the towers. "It looked like a giant took it and threw a dagger into the ground and it went down through the ground level, the train station and through the rail line," he said. "As we're looking at that we're hearing something that doesn't sound like water dripping, it sounds like something plopping. We crawled up into a crevice, and a buddy and myself went into it and it was molten steel, like lava."

About two weeks in, the finality struck him. One of his supervisor's remains had been identified. Lieutenant Edward D'atri was a force to be reckoned with. "This guy was one of the absolute toughest, strongest," Mlynarczyk says. "As a fireman, you went as far as you could and as hard as you could because there were guys like this who would come and get you. When we found him that's when I thought, 'We're done.' If he couldn't live through it, no one could."

Mlynarczyk had also lost his one phone call: Glenn.

When Joe was in high school, a few grades behind Glenn, four guys once threatened to beat him up at a party. Both Winuk and Sausmer were also there—Mlynarczyk had looked up to Sausmer because he was a good football player—and the two had his back. "I was willing but there was no way I would win," Joe says. "They barely knew me, but they saw a mismatch and didn't like the odds and jumped in on my side." Years later, once imagining himself blindfolded in front of a firing squad, Mlynarczyk envisioned calling Glenn to extract him again.

Joe Mlynarczyk's roller coaster ride was just beginning, a travail that would force him into self-exile in Florida with his wife and children. Sometimes, but not always, he can step back to a day when Glenn would come over and they'd sip Wild Turkey with cigars out behind his house. "Life would slow down a little bit, sometimes you don't even have to talk, when things are good," he says. He still has one bottle untouched, and Mlynarczyk promises, "I'll keep it for something."

One day Jay Winuk retrieved his brother's maroon Honda Accord from a parking lot and drove it to his house. Opening the trunk, he found a Xeroxed certificate for a building collapse training course Glenn had completed, just the kind of preparation he would have needed to save lives. There it was, for no good reason his brother could think of.

He also later noticed that the car's inspection expiration date was September 11.

The *Daily News* began its top story: "On a day of unspeakable horror for New York and the nation . . ." and we know the rest.

Yet what do we actually remember?

We think we know the narrative of September 11, having either spilled out onto city streets or seen the iconic images looping. We partake in the histories and anniversary specials, and perhaps the findings of the 9/11 Commission or the conspiracy theories. We hear about what surviving relatives have done, or the health issues that dog many first responders. We take note of the lingering agony, if not reliving a piece of it, each year.

That newspaper's lead sentence on September 12 might well have ended with ". . . America's first impulse was compassion." Equal in measure to the heroism, the shared resolve and retribution seeking, acts of kindness began immediately. They did not stop, and they continue to inspire us.

A city employee emerging from the subway near the Trade Center was blinded by a wall of soot and then pulled back down into a tiny room by a man, her angel, who then went out to get others.

In a suburb near the Pentagon, friends and coworkers of a flight attendant killed there remembered her volunteer work at a local infants and maternity home. The next spring they donated a video library with a DVD player, a television, and hundreds of videotapes in her memory.

Manufacturers and distributors of steel cutting blades, power tools, respirators and safety gear loaded pallets and sent their trucks to supply rescuers.

A poet began writing tributes in verse for scores of victims she never met, relying on articles and items sent by relatives.

A couple from Idaho invited a Long Island widow and her three children for a therapeutic week of horseback riding and life at their ranch.

Four golden dogs—Jake, Jessie, Mattie, and Macie—walked by a Staten Island couple began arriving at the pile to comfort relatives and workers. They were soon dubbed the Smile Retrievers.

Such acts moved the spirit of David Paine, another Long Islander who had transplanted himself to southern California. Eventually Paine and Jay Winuk would orchestrate the biggest day of charitable service in the nation's history.

It began with two brothers who went in opposite directions.

David Paine's half-brother, Andrew Schmertz, was working at World Financial Center just west of the Twin Towers on a project for Merrill Lynch. A former reporter with the news station NY1, Schmertz had gone into video production and was doing a corporate video for Merrill. His office overlooked the North Tower, and given the buildings' heights they appeared to be almost up against one another. He remembers the windows shaking violently seconds before he saw the tower explode, but he didn't see the first plane. Amidst the confusion at his office, they decided to stay, thinking it was an isolated event. Until they saw a second jet.

"We were told to evacuate down the stairs toward the back of the building toward the waterfront side. That was the correct procedure, away from towers," he says. They walked north as a group and were just outside of the debris field when the buildings fell. Schmertz continued toward his apartment on West Sixty Sixth Street. "By the time I got back to the Upper West Side there was an eerie sense of normalcy for a short time," he says. "I think it was far enough away, that the scope of what had happened hadn't quite reached there. People weren't reacting yet."

Schmertz reached his parents and talked with David later that day. While relieved that his younger brother was fine, what Paine heard and saw on the broadcasts shook and ignited him. New York was David's hometown as well. He and Jay Winuk both worked in public relations; the two had met at the same firm while starting out in the early eighties but were not close friends.

David soon moved west to follow his future bride. On September 11 he was up early, about to leave his house in Newport Beach for San Diego for the launch of a big client, XM Satellite Radio, when the president of his company called and told Paine to turn on the TV. Watching with his wife, Laney, Paine remembers seeing a huge wall of smoke billowing. He turned to her and said, "Did that entire building just come down?" The ads that were set to air the next day featured musicians like David Bowie and BB King falling through the sky, so they quickly pulled the $100 million campaign.

Some days later a mutual friend told Paine that Jay's brother was missing. They hadn't talked in years, but he gave Winuk a call. Their intersecting points were chilling. "I took it for granted that he would get out, but I still had moments of anxiety," Paine recalls of his brother's orderly escape. "I was the juxtaposition to Jay."

About a week later, Paine flew in and tried to get to Ground Zero. "When I got within three or four blocks of it, I smelled something I've never smelled before and I couldn't go any farther. It was horrifying, because you knew what it was. It literally made me nauseous. It didn't look real, it was like something that Universal Studios would have created, like someone made it," he says. "It was unbelievable."

He desperately wanted to help. While up close only briefly, he observed Manhattan's heroes and victims, with armies of volunteers pouring in. Paine read about Mets players donating a day's pay to police and firefighters' widows and children's families. The collective response gave him pause. "We experienced for a brief moment what the world would be like if we worked together and put aside all of our differences," he told me. "It's possible. It's just a question of how. It starts one person at a time." Amidst the destruction, seedlings were being planted.

Returning home, Paine went to work addressing a residual effect that he noticed after the attacks. He had business contacts with many large United Ways across the country, and they were soon reporting that on top of a sluggish economy, local charities were hurting as more donations went to 9/11 relief. He didn't want to duplicate the efforts that 9/11 groups were starting. So in Orange County and elsewhere, he organized promotions encouraging people to give to local charities that were not responding to the terrorist attacks.

Paine emailed and called Jay a few weeks later with his condolences about Glenn, whom he had never met. David held off on offering another idea he had: giving up a day's pay to support charities helping 9/11 victims, modeled on the Mets' initiative. It was too soon anyways for Winuk to consider this. Glenn's body had not been recovered, and Jay and Carolyn had their hands full taking care of his brother's affairs. Jay had offered to be the point of contact on almost every front: with the police and fire department, Glenn's law firm, and the media, and dealing with insurance and other parts of his estate.

Paine persisted with his idea to dedicate a day to honor and support families of the fallen. He created a charity called One Day's Pay, starting small-scale with word spreading mostly through colleagues in the PR industry. He grabbed a domain name and invited people to register their intentions to help charities on a web site. Some months into 2002, Winuk was able to climb aboard. Before encouraging acts of kindness on the first anniversary, they both knew they should first win over the leading 9/11 groups representing families.

David contacted Alice Hoagland, the mother of Mark Bingham, one of the four passengers on United Airlines Flight 93 who stormed the cockpit above western Pennsylvania and prevented terrorists from possibly crashing the jet into the US Capitol. Hoagland is a former flight attendant who, in the wake of her only son's death, became an activist for aviation security and eradicating terrorism. Pulling her aside at a reception honoring Bingham and other 9/11 heroes in San Francisco, Paine learned she was thrilled to jump in. "Their effort was peaceful and not political," says Hoagland, "so I threw my weight behind it."

David and Winuk also invited the principals of several major groups to meet in New York, igniting a chain reaction. They met with Mary Fetchet, who along with her husband started Voices of September 11, which honors their son, Bradley; Sally Regenhard, who co-founded the Skyscraper Safety Campaign; and others who started Families of September 11th and WTC United Family Group, which fought to preserve the footprints of the towers. They met early with the founder of Tuesday's Children, and the nonprofit's executive director became a longtime ally as well. "We felt if we didn't have buy-in from the 9/11 community, then we were not on the right road," Jay recalls. Support came from nearly every corner.

Jay also tracked down an old family acquaintance from Jericho, Edie

Lutnick, the sister of Cantor Fitzgerald CEO Howard Lutnick. Howard and Glenn had been friends and were about the same age, and Edie's post-9/11 life was beginning to parallel Jay's in many respects. Cantor, the international brokerage firm and Wall Street giant that operated essentially as "the New York Stock Exchange for bonds," lost 658 employees in the North Tower, by far the largest loss of life within any company. Gary Lutnick, Edie and Howard's younger brother, was one of them. Edie had begun to steward a massive relief fund for the Cantor families that became legendary.

When Winuk met her at the temporary Cantor offices, they renewed a friendship, talking about shared loss and their responses to it. Edie Lutnick joined the board of Paine and Winuk's charity several years later, insisting that they focus on fostering remembrance along with volunteerism. Edie warned she might not always offer what they wanted to hear. That was precisely what they needed, as Jay says, a voice "to tell it like it is and speak for so many families."

Jay and David later also tapped some leaders in the growing service field and newcomers arrived as well, including a housewife from Massachusetts whose husband had been at a meeting just below Cantor's offices, a friend of Christie Coombs who sought healing for herself and her sons. As Jay began to tell Glenn's story, and with other family members in the forefront, their group One Day's Pay began to take off.

It was purely grassroots, with Paine and Winuk sending tight versions of their promotional spiel to business contacts, winging it without a budget. Nearly fifty thousand people posted their good faith intentions to help charities, and their web site received three hundred thousand hits in the final month before the second anniversary in 2003. A fifth-grade teacher in Graham, Texas caught the wave and wanted to help her students turn the tragedy into something good. Challenged to choose a good deed to do for someone else, one girl pet sat and babysat her brother; another donated a bike to a kid who didn't have one. In Tampa, a couple that owned a florist shop planned to give out twelve thousand red roses.

While hoping that such participation would become infectious, Paine saw more of it occurring in heartland communities like Graham than in New York itself. The city and many family members simply weren't ready. "I mean, you know, they talk about the country moving on," Paine told

CNN in 2003. "Maybe that's somewhat true, but family members are not moving on." Despite a quick blush of media coverage, he and Winuk were already concerned about how to sustain a mini-movement.

Making some changes the following year, they began going nationwide for the third anniversary. The name One Day's Pay had confused people who thought the nonprofit wanted their money, so Paine and Winuk adopted "MyGoodDeed," which was more in line with their mission. Both wanted to facilitate something much bigger than dedicating part of a week's paycheck: establishing a national day of service to commemorate both the fallen and the spirit of giving back. Paine sold his PR firm of about sixty-five employees to a Canadian marketing company, and despite being under contract to the new owner for four more years, he could increasingly devote more energy to the day of service.

To Carolyn Winuk, the Californian was a natural complement to her meticulous, overloaded husband. Thin-boned and barely filling his suit at times, Jay was often wrapped up managing the paperwork for Glenn's affairs or his own business alongside building the new enterprise with Paine. While similarly driven in his professional life, David is a contrast in styles. He comes off as a modern transcendentalist who might have pitched a tent beside Walden Pond during a college break. His dark, Brillo-like hair stays in place on a windy day, compared to Jay's thinning wisps of silver brown. While Jay covers logistics and dots all the I's, David concerns himself with acoustics, noting diffused ambient light penetrating the fog.

Paine describes himself as someone who, while devastated by 9/11, "wanted to bottle that feeling that so many people had. So many barriers seemed to drop afterwards, people helping each other who wouldn't normally have." He approached Winuk knowing that while Jay had seasoned public relations skills, he was also "someone who was living it." In Carolyn's eyes, their connection came at exactly the right moment.

It's worth taking stock of how much Americans gave following the 2001 attacks. In one accounting, the Associated Press found that more than three hundred charities were formed to assist 9/11 families, distributing $1.5 billion to affected communities over the following decade. The greatest share, $722 million, went to victims' families. When one counts the local memorial scholarships up to large nongovernmental organizations, the number of groups actually totaled more than 1,800—almost half of those outside of New York.

Although many charities closed shop after funds were distributed to the families, and a few scandalously never fulfilled their stated goals, others expanded their reach years later. Chefs raised money for families of the workers killed at Windows on the World and others in the hospitality industry. A few relatives trained their anger on specific issues like pursuing the proper burial of victims' remains. Quilters stitched to help teenagers who'd lost a parent pay for college. Two parents in Vermont, Sally and Don Goodrich, built a school for girls in Afghanistan in memory of their son Peter, extending his passion to appreciate other cultures.

Americans contributed a record-breaking $2.8 billion to 9/11 charities over the decade, an amount surpassed only by the $5.3 billion to help those displaced by Hurricane Katrina. Years later, we gave $1.45 billion to assist survivors of the Haiti earthquakes. Meanwhile, during that same stretch most 9/11 nonprofits fizzled out. By 2006, less than one in five that had filed for expedited tax-exempt status remained, and only thirty-eight charities filed returns in the years leading up to the tenth anniversary. Those that endured, like the well-known groups Tuesday's Children and Voices of September 11, evolved to meet the changing developmental needs of teenagers, and offered adults practical supports like help with their taxes, job retraining, or responded to the surge in first responders' health claims— without shedding their core principles.

David and Jay believed they had a winner. Tracking more polls of Americans' charitable giving and from their own surveys, they realized that their growth was not guaranteed. But there was something organic to all this, and they turned over a compost pile that would generate unexpected seedlings and replenish perennials. Their goal was to engage people to do service in their own comfort zone, not necessarily directed by a large organization, reflecting how people actually responded in 2001.

"Even just helping an elderly neighbor get groceries for the day, or donating your time at the local library or school," Winuk says. "Because it didn't matter who you were in this country, your age, ethnic background, geographic area, or how much money you had. Millions of people found ways to pitch in and contribute in whatever way made sense to them because the need was so great."

They were about to embark on a campaign inspiring the nation to pay tribute in new ways each year. Nurturing MyGoodDeed was exactly the catalyst Jay Winuk needed.

There is a certain relentless quality to Winuk that is incongruous at first. He has a runner's thin frame, a scratchy voice and a patchy, graying beard. He's a button-down detail person who emits hints of mischievous charm, and in the weeks and months following Glenn's death he gathered small bits to cherish and retell the full story. Jay amassed file after file of his brother's records in his home office along with boxes of Glenn's stuff and hundreds of his CDs. As he and Carolyn were making important discoveries, organizing all this became part of his daily schema. Handling the agonizing details of his brother's affairs, they both tried to minimize the burden on his parents.

The couple went to Glenn's closed-down law office on the edge of what to Jay was a war zone, the buildings covered in a wretched white dust and military personnel everywhere in sight. They took a utility elevator and searched for clues, finding his suit jacket, his laptop and car keys still there. Carolyn felt terribly invasive sorting through his things for much of the day, but they had no choice.

Meeting some of his brother's colleagues, Jay asked what Glenn was last wearing and for any details they could add to the police report. Later on, someone reported having seen him don a mask and gloves outside the building at about 9:30 a.m. Navaretta suggested that Glenn may have gone to the nearest station, Ten House, Ladder Company 10, before heading in. Jay figured his brother must have been carrying his firefighter's credentials.

A few days later the Winuks went to Pier 94, a vast, hangar-like building on the West Side flooded with relatives filing missing person's reports and scrounging for their own shards of information. Jay described a Swiss watch with a black face and stainless steel and gold band that he knew Glenn was wearing, which would become vital to the family in the years ahead. Outside, the "Have you seen?" posters seemed to be everywhere.

Carolyn was overwhelmed by walls pockmarked with images of their faces, signposts screaming in pain, and people in tears. She felt herself beginning to shut down, and for a while things became a blur.

There were other revelations to come. Glenn had been dating for several years, and while the Winuks knew about Bessie, the family had never actually met her.

His friends all had, and when out together for drinks or dinner, they knew that Bessie and Glenn shared a lot in common. The two had met through work and both put in very long hours. She also seemed to understand that for Glenn, service came first: to his profession, to the firehouse, and to others. Buddy Kenney, another friend of Winuk's from Jericho who had worked in restaurants and became a sommelier, saw the couple regularly, as they seemed to follow him over a few years from place to place, sometimes hanging out while he was on the job. Bessie had gone through a failed marriage, Kenney says, and "here she was, here's this super guy, and he treated her well, and with dignity."

Glenn's friends thought he had kept the relationship at arms length from his parents and siblings in part because she'd been a coworker when they met. He also was modest and just kept things private. While Bessie was able to share details of her last conversation with Glenn, pointing Jay to Glenn's office, she was largely an enigma.

For Jay, the confluence of knowing that his brother must have died helping out and not having his remains was magnified by the enormity around them. He quickly did the math. "You go home and find out it's three thousand people [believed dead], and how many people are within your close circle, directly, directly affected by this?" he asked. "And then take the people you work with, and the family members. So take the three thousand and multiply it by maybe one hundred."

While his parents delegated much of the work contacting authorities to Jay, they did not shrink from making pivotal decisions. Divorced and in their early seventies, both continued living in Jericho, his mother in an apartment attended by a home health aide, his dad at home. Each wanted to stay informed and made it up to Jay's home in Mahopac for family meetings, including painful discussions on how to navigate religious customs. In that first month, the Winuks were among more than 2,500 families waiting for any word about recovered remains. Even fifteen years later, the remains of about 1,100 victims had not been identified as the city's medical examiner continued sifting through DNA fragments.

"Complications," Jay recalls. "There's no body, do you sit shiva or not sit shiva? Do you have a funeral or not?" One of his uncles, an Orthodox rabbi, suggested that without a body a proper funeral was impossible and as such there should also be no shiva. But the Winuks decided to share grief in their home in the traditional way, gathering at Jay and Carolyn's. That uncle chose to stay away, which Jay respected. Another uncle who was a retired cop urged him to plan the funeral. Seymour Winuk went with his middle son to the Jericho Jewish Center to do that.

On October 14, just days after the mayor and fire chief said no one was coming out any more—declaring Ground Zero to be a recovery rather than rescue site—the Winuks held a memorial service at the center beside the old fire station. Friends and fire department colleagues lined the inside walls of the temple where Glenn and his brothers had held their bar mitzvahs, while other firefighters unable to get in stood in honor outside. People from all walks of life paid tribute: doormen and guys he had trained as recruits at the station, along with colleagues from the firm, competing lawyers, and CEOs.

They gave testimony to what Glenn's pals had long felt. Never pretentious, he had gone to the same dry cleaner and barber for many years when he could afford better. He knew the first names of a janitor's children at the office, and chose to drive cars like a beat-up Acura he had bought at a gas station rather than an Audi that might become a target in the city. A good listener, Glenn had preferred to focus on other people. He entered conversations with purpose. To them, he was a giant. Many considered him as their best friend.

Buddy Kenney, who met Glenn in a karate class when he was fourteen, saw Winuk become an effective teacher as he moved up the ranks. "His time," Kenney says, "was better spent helping out others. He never forgot the people who struggled, and I think he related to them more."

Kenney and other friends made a promise to honor Glenn by keeping that spirit alive.

Taking a cue from what relatives of Holocaust victims did when they had no remains to bury, the Winuks collected about two dozen possessions representing Glenn's life and put them in a pine box: Cub Scout badges, a toy fire truck, his karate belts, some law books, and memorabilia from his bar mitzvah. A counselor advised Jay and Carolyn that they should explain to Justin what happened, even at age four. So when he drew pictures showing his understanding of it, those were added to the box as well.

Both Jay and Carolyn struggled to get through their eulogies, with Jay holding up the certificate for the building collapse training course in front of more than six hundred mourners. Carolyn temporarily broke the tension with an anecdote recounting her brother-in-law's conservative political views.

As mourners finally exhaled in laughter, Carolyn knew she would get through the rest. Sausmer told everyone, "This love and virtue of compassion that brought so many people into his life also led to his death. If you'd like to know the essence of Glenn, just look around. What mattered most was you were a good person."

Often stoic during the preceding weeks, his parents held up through much of the service. Yet when a family friend presented Glenn's mom with a framed American flag, Elaine Winuk could no longer hold back.

It wasn't so much the condolences and sweeping oratory from managers at Glenn's firm that made a difference to his older brother.

Glenn had made partner at Holland & Knight's litigation group during his mid-thirties as he built up clients with his sharp analytical and interpersonal skills. Energetic if not obsessed, Winuk was often first in and last to leave. Colleagues with Harvard and Princeton pedigrees who had once sniffed at a Hofstra Law School graduate were eventually politely knocking on his door with questions. A colleague in Atlanta recalls that when discussing strategy for a case that Winuk was local counsel on in New York, he offered, "just do the Glenn thing," knowing Winuk would win.

He had something else going for him that is perhaps rare in his profession: a very accepting personality. Brian Starer, a managing partner, saw that by having this ability, Winuk could concentrate on the matter at hand rather the person delivering the message. "That's a good asset as a litigator. That was one of his strongest traits," Starer says. "He didn't see good and bad in people, he saw people as human beings."

Other expressions lifted the family, if even momentarily. His colleague Lisa Miller was across the river in Hoboken when the second plane struck and she, too, just felt it. "I knew you'd be racing there to help," she posted in an online tribute. "The world is a better place because you were here."

Less than two weeks after the funeral in Jericho, Holland & Knight held a second memorial service at an old synagogue on the Upper East Side. Both Jay and Sausmer eulogized Glenn once again, and there was a new fiery speaker, future US Attorney General Michael Mukasey, then chief of the US District Court in Manhattan. Mukasey railed against terrorists and supported taking the fight to them, sentiments all of Glenn's friends knew he would have agreed with. Honan, for one, recalls that Mukasey's remarks were well received. "People were surprised, thinking the chief judge of the circuit would be more circumspect, but he wasn't," Honan says. "He was very tough." The firm continued to stay in touch with Jay and his parents and helped them sort out Glenn's affairs, which would soon lead to greater things.

Years later, another attorney who had worked with Glenn arrived one day at the firm's office in Portland, Oregon, feeling unsettled that he didn't really know anyone there. Alan Reitzfeld came upon a portrait of Winuk in a conference room. It reminded him not only of Glenn's exceptional warmth and sincerity, but also how he had since strived to be a better person, and more humane.

Reitzfeld told himself: "Alan, you're home."

Despite such pronouncements, Jay learned the most about his brother from the notes and cards sent by secretaries and legal assistants in offices across the country. After having stopped by their desks to say hello, or sending someone a note in recognition that they'd done a good job on a case, Glenn was appreciated in full.

Around this time a friend working at Ground Zero collected some dirt and brought it to Winuk as a way to symbolically retain something linked to Glenn. Jay tucked that gesture with others into his burgeoning mental scrapbook. He and Carolyn thought the salvaged dirt was as close as they might come to safeguarding his remains.

11

AFFIRMATION

John Navaretta and Tom Casey were busting Glenn's chops.

Sipping drinks poolside at the Mirage in Vegas, near their suite at Treasure Island, Glenn was finally releasing into vacation mode. All morning he'd been on the phone with clients and the office. Until Navaretta chided him, "Let's go relax."

It's not like Winuk didn't live it up at times. On two other occasions, his pal Casey bought tickets to Paradise Island in the Bahamas and instructed Glenn, "We're going." This time John flew with Glenn to Nevada for Casey's bachelor party.

On that weekend in 1994, not everything that happened in Vegas stayed there.

Casey, another former volunteer firefighter who became a banker, arrived at the end of a business trip after his two friends. Things picked up when he was greeted in their hotel suite by a spread of cheese and crackers, champagne and strawberries. Glenn and John had been at the pool for four hours by that time, imbibing the libation foundations for a night that became a scaled-down version of *Hangover*, sans Mike Tyson's tiger and other excesses.

They went for dinner—somewhere. More champagne arrived in the suite—who ordered this? Amidst the whirlwind of the next twenty-four hours Casey had to leave on a red-eye, his fiancée insisting that he stay one day only.

Stranded for an encore night, John and Glenn kept the party rolling at Caesar's Palace. They went to eat at the Palm.

Navaretta takes it from here: "We're having a grand old time, laughing how Tom came and went. We are hammered now, we're walking out of the Palm and Glenn says, 'I got to buy something. I got to buy something to remember this.' That's the type of weekend it was. Right next to Palm is this jewelry store. He goes inside and comes out with a piece of paper and says, 'I bought a watch.'

"I say, 'Where is it?'

"He said, 'They're going to mail it to me.'

"So I'm young and foolish—and the watch, it's ridiculously expensive—and I said, 'You just bought a four thousand dollar watch, like you're ever going to see it!'

"So we're like rolling on the floor laughing outside of Caesar's—and that's it, we came home. And we'd always talk about it as he wore the watch. We'd be out and he'd have that watch on and he'd tell a story."

Even on that excitable weekend, Casey recalls that Glenn's calm side prevailed. Technically they weren't supposed to use the Mirage pool, and on the second day someone told them so. But Glenn remained polite and asked to speak to the manager. "He told him, 'This is what the ad said, that we could get in,'" Casey recalls. "And after five minutes the guy said, 'Okay, go ahead.'"

The Swiss wristwatch grew in value to Glenn's family, and not only because of its bachelorhood lore. It helped the Winuks close a loop of his legacy when it was finally recovered at Ground Zero.

Everything in Glenn's hometown on Long Island's north shore feels condensed. Jericho is a hamlet of 13,500 people occupying only four square miles, and technically it's mostly part of the town of Oyster Bay. There are a handful of famous residents: an actress from the *The Sopranos*, a keyboardist who's played with Pink Floyd, and Billy Joel who grew up next door in Hicksville. The high school and the Winuks' old elementary school are within a mile of one another, and their temple, too, is close to the modest spilt-level home where the family lived.

Every year there's a Turkey Bowl touch football game on Thanksgiving morning, which Jay's son Justin used to call his favorite day of the year. It used to draw back many of Glenn and Jay's old classmates from the mid- and late seventies.

Glenn's parents moved to Jericho from Brooklyn in 1961, the year he was born. He shared a room with Jay, who is three years older, while Jeff, eight years ahead of Glenn, had his own bedroom. Their dad sold electronics components and became a manager at his company, but he gave up that career to buy a King Bear auto repair shop, doing well as a franchise owner. Also a part-time inventor, Seymour Winuk patented a battery-operated burglar alarm device you could hang on a door and a device to water hanging plants. Their mother Elaine took care of the house.

Glenn's adoration of firefighters started early. The station's beeping alarm sounded frequently from up the street, and he would chase the trucks on his Stingray along with his pals. Around the corner from his house was a service road where the firemen trained, and on those days Glenn was always easy to find. His buddies caught the bug early too—Andy Sausmer tried hard never to miss an open house at the station. He also lived nearby, and one time when he heard the firemen were giving rides, Andy rushed over and was told he was too late. But "two firemen larger than life let me sit in the front and play with the bell. From that point on, that did it," he says.

Their uncle was a city firefighter, and when the boys were young Harold Einhorn occasionally took them to the firehouse and carried them down the pole. Glenn caught the bug, and as Jay saw it, once his brother locked into something, he went at it full bore. Even starting Cub Scouts, "there was nothing else he would think about," Jay says. Emergency medical technicians fascinated him in a similar way. His dad helped him build an oversized wooden first aid kit, and Glenn wrote to companies for free samples of bandages, wraps, and other supplies. Enamored of the military, police and the FBI, as an adolescent he watched Jeff join as a volunteer firefighter and dispatcher in Jericho. During their senior year Glenn and Andy Sausmer signed up together, entering what became a rite of passage for many of their crew.

After high school Glenn followed Jay to the State University of New York at Oneonta, majoring in communications. Active in student government, he was popular with his professors and for a while worked as a bartender. Winuk's law school entrance involved a twist of fate that Jay later discovered while sorting through his brother's papers. David Paine's father, a noted labor law expert and arbitrator, was the dean at Hofstra who signed Glenn's letter of acceptance.

Upon finishing law school, Glenn began his career as a shipping lawyer at a firm that later became a part of Holland & Knight. He moved into the city and began a routine that would go on for twelve years, usually returning to Jericho on weekends to fight fires, hang out with friends, and see his parents. Work was never far from his mind; on Sunday afternoons Glenn often drove to the Hofstra law library in Hempstead to prepare for the week. Over time he took on more commercial litigation cases, cutting a bigger swath as he brought in his own clients. Winuk wasn't often in on the splashy cases like marine disasters that made the news; his caseload was more nuts and bolts stuff. But his boss, Brian Starer, and other senior partners recognized Glenn's other assets. While thoroughly analytical, he also retained a humanism in reserve until the moment it was needed most.

While devoting himself increasingly to the firm, Glenn's friends found that his loyalties did not shift. He still did his own laundry at his parents, and other relationships remained paramount.

Among his closest was with the sometimes-feisty Navaretta. A few years older than Winuk, Navaretta was a Jericho volunteer and took Glenn under his wing in Guardian Engine Company 2 when Winuk joined. "He taught me a lot about life, and I taught him a lot about firefighting," Navaretta recalls. "Me being the Italian hothead, he could always calm me down." Navaretta had dreamed of becoming a lawyer and when he got hurt and retired from the FDNY, Glenn urged him to enroll in law school. Starting out as a small town real estate lawyer a few years later, he and Glenn hung out more often as Navaretta went through a divorce. During the summers they relaxed on the water aboard John's powerboat, and other excitable times followed.

Carolyn had Jay's back. As other amazing women so often do during severe trials, she held the family together.

They had met when she moved into an apartment just above his on

Madison Avenue at Ninety-Seventh Street. He worked at a PR firm; she was a physical therapist at nearby Metropolitan Hospital. Jay had just relocated downstairs, vacating the unit that became her studio, and she called him to check it out. "He was lovely on the phone and lovely in person," she says. They soon dated and were married two years later, moving into a townhouse and continuing a city lifestyle for several years, going out after work, and sometimes renting a summerhouse in the Hamptons. Justin arrived in 1997, and a new phase began.

In the months following September 11, their home became an epicenter of calls and faxes, open to Glenn's friends and extended family, dealing with detectives, attorneys, on and on. Jay knew that he enjoyed the relative good fortune of running his own business; otherwise he would have had to take a leave of absence from work. Like his parents, Winuk also had a vein of stoicism helping him deal with the onslaught. There was little doubt, and perhaps no alternative, to he and Carolyn being frontline filters for them. "We just did what had to be done and at the same time live[d] our life," Jay says. His wife saw something else as well. He was not one to stay depressed for long, and he savoured his time with his son and taking short breaks from all of the hubbub, such as getting occasional exercise. Soon they both realized that they needed to do a few things for themselves.

Glenn and Jay shared common musical tastes, and among those was the breezy pop group America. Jay had bought tickets over the summer, and early in October the couple saw the band perform at a nearby college, taking in sun-streaked hits like "Ventura Highway" from their teenage years. Within a few weeks they went out again to hear U2 at Madison Square Garden, just one night after the memorial service for Glenn organized by his company. For two hours, Jay found himself juggling something else: joining in with the soaring songs that his brother loved, and sitting to enjoy them for himself.

He and Carolyn went out again early that winter to hear another of Jay's favorites, the folk-rock duo Aztec Two-Step. Carolyn jumped on an idea as Jay used the men's room in between sets, approaching guitarist Rex Fowler to ask if he would play a private house party in March. Fowler and his partner agreed, and Jay's forty-fourth birthday celebration became a turning point. Fowler and Neal Shulman performed in the living room for more than fifty of Jay's friends and colleagues. "I had to bring him something that was not Glenn-related," Carolyn recalls. After debating with herself if this was right, she decided they had to move forward—but not rush—while also doing things in her brother-in-law's memory.

She pulled Jay aside as the celebration surged around them, telling him, "'Glenn would have wanted you to have this party. You did not betray him.'"

Fowler felt honored to be there. In the years since the singer-songwriter has been moved by how the Winuks and others rallied around Glenn's memory. He and Jay continued as friends, enough so that Fowler and another writing partner invited Winuk and his family to sing backup when he recorded a song about 9/11 called "Towers of Love." "The first person I thought of was Jay," he says. "Symbolically they were the ones. They added a real poignancy to the project."

Jay does not hesitate answering how he got through it all. "As devastated as Carolyn was, and she was, I don't know what I could've really done without her," he says. "She showed and continues to show enormous strength and love. Time and time again she steered us to safe waters."

A week after that birthday jam, Glenn's partial remains were found.

As the recovery and cleanup continued at Ground Zero, firefighters with Jericho connections put the word out to look for a Jericho Fire Department identification. On March 20, 2002, crews discovered a number of rescuers' remains as they excavated a truck ramp down to the site that was being replaced by a more permanent one. Winuk's partial remains were among those in two lots. His gloves and stethoscope were in one, while his watch and other remains were found in the other. His fire department ID card was in a wallet, and within twenty-four hours dental records confirmed that it was Glenn.

As the remains of Winuk and others including Moira Smith, the lone female officer among twenty-three NYPD casualties, were brought out, firefighters and police lined up on the ramp and saluted.

Glenn's parents felt a relief that twined tightly with renewed loss. However minute, the possibility had still lingered in their minds that he might have somehow survived. "That's the only hope parents can have after a loss of a child in this way," Jay says. "It's not the normal way of losing someone; you're not sick, no heart attack, it's not a car accident, and you still don't have his body."

Being able to bury Glenn properly was crucial, Jay reminded me, emphasizing the tenor of this with a hard look and near growl one of the times we met. They held another funeral and went back to the cemetery, placing his remains above the pine box that stored his belongings. They had been spared the added ordeal imposed on many other families, including the relatives of more than one hundred firefighters, who continued to suffer without any remains.

The Winuks also received another pick-me-up around this time. Carolyn was pregnant with their second child, and Melanie would arrive in November 2002. Along with Melanie's parents and grandparents, the extended family allowed itself to feel joy again. The couple had not told anyone they were trying.

Although Glenn's watch had been recovered, it took almost four years before his family could present the proof of ownership required to claim it from the police, who were holding on to thousands of pieces of jewelry and artifacts. The Winuks knew he had been wearing it, and Jay especially wanted it back. But the NYPD was strict about requiring a receipt, a serial number, or other proof. An old girlfriend gave the family a photo of Glenn wearing the watch, but that wasn't enough evidence for the property clerk. Jay haggled with the clerk for months on end, to no avail.

A serendipitous breach in the form of frozen pipes finally gave Jay the proof he needed. His neighborhood lost electricity and the pipes burst, damaging a home office where he kept some of Glenn's files. He moved boxes around, and even though he'd already looked through everything before, something made him do it again. This time he found a photocopy of the watch warranty with a serial number. He faxed a copy to the property clerk, and it was a match. The city returned it with a bit of fanfare early in February of 2006. Jay was invited to a press conference at police headquarters held to deflect criticism from 9/11 families over the pace and manner of returning such items. City officials showed off Glenn's watch before the news cameras as a shining example of their efforts.

"I have been chasing this watch," Winuk told reporters. "There are so many open ends and this is now a closed one." The manufacturer offered to refurbish the piece for his family, but they wanted it as it was. Jay told the company no one was ever going to wear it.

The timepiece resides in a display case in his office in Carmel, New York.

The crystal over the face is intact and there's a tiny smudge of soot near the band's clip. It frozen hands point to 12:55, and the date is September 12.

When our kids were young, a big, juicy slice of summertime meant sailing on our boat. We bought a fiberglass sloop when Mike was in the eighth grade, naming her *Cinnamon Girl*—a long story, unless you're an old Neil fan. And absolutely, Denise is the one.

I grew up sailing the Wareham River and Buzzards Bay, a wedge of water that abuts the west side of Cape Cod. The shallow bay is known to be cranky, since the prevailing southwest winds inevitably stiffen in the afternoon as the heated land draws cooler air up its funnel-shape, lending a bit of skirmish to both an uninformed and practiced crew. With good access to the Elizabeth Islands and Martha's Vineyard, it's a day sailor's crystal ballroom complete with a rollicking finish.

Several times each season we instructed our brood to pack a few things for a weekend—or longer—on the boat. Spring soccer had wilted along with scorched clumps of lawn, and the kids didn't do regular camps other than a theatre camp that Amanda and Chris sometimes attended. In retrospect, gearing up to sail seems almost easy to pull off: gathering a change of clothes, mostly shorts, T-shirts and swimsuits; stuffing a cooler; Denise collecting clean linens and usually a few blankets and pillows; listening to the marine forecast the night before and first thing that morning; picking up blocks of ice; and double-checking on propane, sunscreen, agua, and beer. Our dog Nikki, a gentle Black Labrador mix, usually came unless we planned to be away three or four days and anticipated spending a fair amount of time ashore. The only difficult thing was getting everyone in motion and ferrying supplies in the dinghy.

The first summer after Mike's death we felt adventurous enough to meet friends in Provincetown, motoring through the canal triumphantly and raising sail. The early morning was clear and still, with barely enough wind to make headway entering Cape Cod Bay. Yet just enough.

Noticing few other boats around, the subtle sounds and salty tang of the bay began to eclipse my thoughts. The hull nudged ahead lightly clipping along, the sail toying with us good-naturedly in a slight luff. The kids giggled below in the cabin, lying on the cushions with the dog. Aware that we were entering waters frequented by minke whales, porpoises, and an occasional sea ray, Denise and I kept a casual watch. She sipped water and opened a book as I stretched feeling the wheel, my senses unencumbered as land-rooted aggravations lifted. Excessive conversation slipped away along with internal chatter, and time began to drift from its rending as if inhaling the coolness of a long rolling swell itself.

We had our bearings from a course I had charted by hand. Guided by wind and current, we settled into the soft peel of a nearby bell.

After a few hours of variable winds, a quirk of weather emerged in front of us. A sort of travel lane opened up defined by two parallel lines of wind edged on the water, filing toward our destination. Once we slipped into this lane, the wind picked up comfortably and I brought in slack on the main and jib sheets. It wasn't long before we could make out Race Point, the tip of P-town. Rounding the deep approach to the harbor close to the beach, I felt goose bumps exploring a new place.

We met our friends Matt and Cindy with their sons in their power-boat, enjoying two spirited days together on adjacent guest moorings. Commercial Street was in its full glory and we ambled through as tourists, taking in a flow of humanity in this outpost of ribald identity and lunar-like dunes. Some of the kids stumbled into a sex shop and a man said, no, they could not go upstairs. We went around the point in Matt's boat the next day, his Luhrs equipped with outriggers for tuna fishing, and Denise caught two stripers. Watching the day close down back in the harbor, we relished the break.

On the trip back we felt Mike's spirit join us in the form of a seal.

The wind was comfortably light again and a pup poked up his head just behind the boat. He proceeded to swim beside us, diving under the keel to reappear on the other side, showing himself, regarding us with dark, soulful eyes.

We called the kids and everyone locked in with him. Amanda recorded the pup on a video camera; he was not shy at all, as if exhorting us on. *My family. You are my family and I am here.*

Play, dive, cracking up. Burrp that herring lunch. Snort. *You are my family. I want to be with you. I'm happy for you.*

Denise and I just looked at each other and believed. He stayed with us perhaps ten minutes, a lingering presence so familiar as we continued crossing the bay. We've kept a photo of the pup on our refrigerator ever since. *I'm here with you.*

It was painful enough that Seymour and Elaine Winuk had lost their forty-year-old son. A bunch of butt-headed bureaucrats added insult to their injuries.

When the Winuks asked that Glenn be recognized along with other fallen first responders, the US Department of Justice tried to steamroll them on a technicality. The family fought the law for nearly five years, and with the aid of another volunteer weekend warrior, they won.

Jay filed a claim for his brother's recognition as a volunteer rescue worker killed in the line of duty, which came with a $250,000 benefit for the next of kin. The DOJ balked, saying Glenn technically was not on duty when he went into the South Tower. It thanked him for being a brave civilian. Officials refused to acknowledge him as a public safety officer because Glenn had changed from active status as a volunteer firefighter to associate status when he became a law firm partner in 1998. The government also claimed that Glenn had let his emergency medical services certification lapse.

In their eyes, Winuk did not represent the Jericho Fire Department in an official capacity. His family also could not prove that he actually had identified himself as a rescue worker offering mutual aid to a FDNY officer during the calamity. To Jay and everyone else, this flew in the face of everything they had learned: the recovery of his remains beside those of other FDNY rescue workers and physical evidence of his involvement, including a stethoscope around his neck. It seemed clear that he'd been allowed in. During an administrative hearing, former FDNY Commissioner Tom Von Essen testified that Glenn would not have been permitted to enter the lobby at the time he arrived unless he had shown his credentials and was authorized to assist. Yet those officers who would have let him in had also perished. And while Glenn was applauded posthumously by the FDNY for helping, the DOJ said he was not directly authorized by either Jericho or the FDNY.

Making matters worse, an official reviewing their application told Jay early on that the government formally recognized his sacrifice. "I can go ahead and tell my parents, yes?" Jay asked. Affirming his question, the official said Winuk's parents would soon be notified and the benefit wired to their bank. They waited for weeks. Calling back, Jay learned that his brother had been denied. The snag was documentation sent by the Jericho Fire Department showing he had no longer been an active member. Jay was incensed, an emotion Carolyn rarely witnessed in him, but he didn't blame the fire department. He had asked the question point-blank, and felt that the DOJ's retraction was not only callous but also unfair. Still early in their grief, this initiated a painstaking battle to get Glenn his full due.

The DOJ's narrow view of the law—the Public Safety Officers Benefits Act—which had actually been broadened to favor families of 9/11 responders, also infuriated New York's political leaders in Congress, who would long support the Winuks and other 9/11 family members. In 2005, Governor George Pataki signed a bill stating that Winuk "was an active member of the Jericho Fire Department" and had died in the line of duty, but justice officials discounted this. National fallen EMS' and firefighters' groups, the FDNY's Honor Legion and others honored Glenn, but that didn't mean squat to the higher-ups. When President Bush returned to New York to award the Medal of Valor to the families of fallen rescue workers on 9/11, Glenn was ignored.

The tide began to turn after Jay met another volunteer firefighter who also doubled as an attorney. Andrew "Duke" Maloney's firm was a client of Jay's, and visiting his office one day Winuk spotted some firefighters' memorabilia on Maloney's desk. He brought up Glenn's case. By then the Winuks had successfully gone through the September 11 Victims Compensation Fund, but the DOJ was in denial.

Their plight immediately grabbed Maloney, who lived in Greenwich, Connecticut, and had helped dig bodies out of the pile a week after the attacks. His empathy for the Winuks ignited his anger. "Glenn was more than a Good Samaritan," Maloney insists. "He was someone who had trained for more than twenty years and his passion was to regularly put himself in harm's way to rescue strangers in dire need. It was painful for me to hear and I said, 'That's not right. What can we do?'" Already renowned as a sharp litigator, Maloney had represented 9/11 families in the compensation fund and was a former prosecutor in the US Attorney's Office. He took the case for free and didn't track his hours.

He thought the appeal would be straightforward. Jay jumped in and helped find witnesses at Glenn's firm and among the FDNY brass while digging through mounds of documents and rallying lawmakers' support. Jay arranged a meeting between Maloney and Jericho's fire commissioners, whose support and even testimony they would need. At first, local officials were skittish about the case. Some worried that the town might be exposed to paying death benefits if the commissioners agreed that Glenn had represented the fire department at the WTC. Maloney found a creative solution, keying in on the EMT angle, and he was able to convince the fire commissioners it was the right thing to do.

This was the essence of Glenn Winuk in those catastrophic minutes: he was last seen with an EMT kit heading toward the South Tower, not running away. He needed to show his credentials to get through the police cordon. As Von Essen testified, in those frantic minutes the FDNY needed all the qualified help it could get. "There was no time, nor the inclination, to differentiate whether firefighters and rescuers were on or off duty, active or inactive," he said.

The family scored the first points. A DOJ-appointed hearing officer agreed with the Winuks a day before the anniversary in 2005. But higher-ups said, "Not so fast. We need a review," Maloney recalls, and took a year to issue a twenty-six-page decision overruling their own judge. The cruel blow came ten days before the next anniversary when the Bureau of Justice Assistance—Jay and Duke still chafe at the Orwellian irony—said that under the law, Glenn wasn't in the "line of duty," because as an associate Jericho fireman he was not authorized to respond to an emergency outside of his hamlet. "It was just a bureaucratic screw job basically," Maloney says.

He told Jay that this was only round one, but Winuk found it atrocious nonetheless. With Von Essen's testimony, with newspaper editorials reaming the DOJ, and despite three retired FDNY members automatically and promptly receiving similar recognition, "in the face of this, the DOJ's treatment of Glenn was completely unfair and completely contrary to the spirit of the PSOB" law, Jay says.

Justice had another maneuver up its sleeve, saying that under a New

York mutual aid statute, a firefighter helping outside his district needed to report to an officer who accepted his aid. "The DOJ said you must show us the officer," Maloney complained. "I said, 'They're all dead.'" No one disputed that along with Glenn's remains were the tools an EMT would need. So Maloney sued the Justice Department itself in US Federal Claims Court.

In the summer of 2007, a federal judge rejected the DOJ's decision as arbitrary and slammed it for wasting everyone's time. The department's earlier denial went against the intent of 9/11 amendments to the original statute "designed to resolve doubts in favor of the applicant for benefits," the ruling stated. Glenn's EMT tools and bag showed his active participation, and the special legislation enacted in New York acknowledging Glenn as an active member at the time of his death overruled the emergency worker qualification provisions. "That should have been the end of it," wrote Federal Court of Claims Justice Marian Blank Horn. Glenn's parents were entitled to a modest award in light of his tremendous sacrifice.

But the case still wasn't over. Justice appealed for the second time, this time to the US Circuit Court, and by then Maloney believed it had turned into a personal vendetta by a few people at the department. Months later, following a chance encounter Maloney had with the solicitor general and formal meetings with high-level DOJ officials, the department finally dropped its appeal.

Maloney and his wife attended a friend's wedding in Washington, D.C. during the summer of 2007 along with a star-studded guest list of legal elites. Three Supreme Court Justices—Ginsburg, Kennedy and Scalia—were on hand along with court clerks and senior DOJ attorneys. During the reception Maloney nursed a mojito as he chatted with Justice Antonin Scalia for fifteen minutes about a case Duke had argued before the high court. His side lost, five to four, but Scalia had supported him. "We were right and Ginsburg was wrong," Scalia railed.

"I was like, 'Justice Scalia, not so loud, she's right over there.'" Maloney then spotted the Justice Department's Solicitor General Paul Clement and a deputy, and got up the nerve after another drink to introduce himself. He described the Winuk case and told them, "This one's going to give you a black eye." A few weeks later he followed up with another assistant and went over the case details, but did not receive a definitive answer.

The DOJ dropped its appeal that winter. Jay got a call at his desk from

Chuck Schumer the following September. New York's senior senator told him that Glenn would posthumously receive the 9/11 Heroes Medal of Valor which Schumer, along with then-Senator Hillary Clinton and Representative Peter King, had continued seeking.

"'It's over, Jay,'" Schumer told him. "It was the greatest phone call of my life."

The Winuks cherish gaining that recognition for Glenn, but it can still amount to a stomach churning mix. Days before the anniversary in 2009, there was a big moment when Glenn was recognized with the heroes medal in Jericho. Schumer and King and other politicians came to present a certificate to the Winuks signed by President Obama. Glenn's dad was seventy-eight by then, and his mom a year younger. "We're sorry we lost him," Seymour Winuk told a reporter. "But he's getting an award that's well deserved for many reasons. He was always running to help people."

"Justice at last," one editorial saluted, while urging the government to also finally do the right thing for survivors' health benefits.

A year before, Andrew Maloney stood in front of a thousand people in Philadelphia, looking directly at his seven-year-old son. Duke was being recognized by the American Association for Justice as its Pro Bono Attorney of the Year for his work on Glenn's case.

His son, Dylan, like most kids his age, was taken by superheroes and video games featuring characters with illustrious powers. "For them, that's what a hero is, somebody who fights," Maloney says. "I told him in the real world, you didn't need superpowers or a cape or a mask. There are real heroes like Glenn who walk among us every day."

Jay and David Paine realized they needed to adopt a marathoner's approach to establish a national day of service.

Winuk had long known he was walking in his brother's shoes, yet until 2004, he and David had really only done a few laps themselves. Paine called it "an episodic thing that I didn't start to think about until July, and then sprinted toward it." The currency of their profession is communication, so they'd push out the message stirring up what was still a relatively small wave. To reach their goal of making 9/11 ubiquitous with service, they needed more support in the business world and engaging people on social networks. To go national they needed a sharper campaign that grabbed people's imaginations.

With support from other 9/11 groups, they initiated a congressional resolution proclaiming September 11 as a national day of voluntary service. By 2006, about two hundred thousand people registered their charitable ideas on a revamped website, which Paine and Winuk estimated reflected one of every ten who actually participated. More than five hundred groups posted community service projects for the fifth anniversary, spotlighted by volunteers cleaning up the visitors' areas on Governors Island in New York Bay. Late that summer, networks began running MyGoodDeed's PSAs with actor Gary Sinise of *CSI: NY* and other stars promoting service. It was by far their largest effort, but they still had a long way to go. Corporate America's involvement was still nascent, and despite a push from lawmakers and their own lobbying, the Bush administration didn't make the formal authorization of a national day of service its priority.

Nothing was ever expressed directly by the White House—nor would Paine or Winuk have expected that. The administration was busy with the wars on terrorism and Iraq. But Paine says, "By extrapolating, they were concerned that making it a day of service would be construed that the nation was soft on crime or we had forgotten the horror of the moment. Since Bush had been there, they felt that was his place; he was the keeper of 9/11. To some degree, President Obama was able to become the keeper of 9/12." That doesn't mean President George W. Bush opposed the idea. "Bush supported us," Paine says, "but didn't think it was the right message at the time." David and Jay understood the distinctions, and they added their own.

"You don't want to convert the tragedy and suddenly transform it into something warm and fuzzy," Paine would say later. "That's not our goal at all. We wanted to see something good come from it, and honor those who were lost." Jay put it this way the first time we spoke in depth: "This is a way forward out of the ashes at Ground Zero, the Pentagon, and Shanksville. This is not about wallowing in the past and tragedy, but at once provides a look back to honor those who died and offers an active and meaningful way forward, doing for those in need."

Jay never doubted Paine's original vision. It was mostly uphill sledding, but they continued to push for a national day of service codified into the law, frequently traveling to Washington to meet up with a board member and lobbyist to make their case on Capitol Hill, at the White House, or with others. It took some sleight of hand during and after the 2008 election cycle to reach full status. They worked every side of the political aisle.

Things really took off at a national summit on volunteerism and service at Columbia University during the 9/11 anniversary weekend in 2008. The first night, Senators Orrin Hatch and Edward Kennedy announced that they were introducing a bill authorizing the greatest expansion of national service since the Great Depression. It had the fingerprints of Jay, David, and groups driving the summit like City Year and the Points of Light Institute all over it. Yet despite strong bipartisan support, after the election, the authorization for a national day of service and remembrance still wasn't included in the Senate version of the bill. It took a late prod from an unlikely source to get it done.

At the eleventh hour, while Kennedy was in Florida recovering from brain tumor surgery, Paine called Cindy McGinty, a 9/11 widow from Massachusetts whose family Kennedy had assisted. McGinty also served on MyGoodDeed's board. After Paine explained the situation, Cindy called her contacts on the senator's staff. Within fifteen minutes she got a call back saying they would place the language in.

In April 2009, September 11 was formally declared a National Day of Service and Remembrance when President Obama signed the Edward M. Kennedy Service America Act. David and Jay attended the signing ceremony. The Act's 9/11 service provision added to President Bush's Patriot Day proclamation first set forth for September 14, 2001. Bush's urging of citizens to attend noontime services and pause for the ringing of bells was augmented by a new call.

Andy Sausmer kept asking Jay, "What do you need?"

When they were kids, Andy and Glenn and others in the neighborhood would climb and hang from a rusting metal gym set, a spider with bars pitched at crazy angles. It was the centerpiece of a scruffy playground up the street from the Winuks' house. One day the idea just came to Sausmer to improve Spider Park and dedicate it to Glenn.

He talked to a friend who was a former town supervisor to get the ball rolling, and the idea passed unanimously at a town meeting. Sausmer lined up some guys who do construction and excavating to help, and he drove Glenn's dad to a jobsite to pick out the perfect boulder on which to embed a plaque. Two other friends landscaped the area, adding shrubs in a bed centered by a crimson Japanese maple. The project came to fruition in less than six months.

When it was dedicated in 2002, Sausmer asked townspeople to stop by often. He spoke about longevity, and how after people put their flags away, the park would still be there. In Jay's mind, Glenn would have relished having the revamped space named after him more than seeing his name displayed in Times Square.

Sometimes John Navaretta goes to the Glenn J. Winuk Memorial Park with a sandwich to sit and think. Like Sausmer and some of the other guys, he prefers going alone. On the anniversaries small groups gather and politicians make speeches. But that can feel like noise tromping on hallowed ground that's shared among a few tested comrades.

I had a chance to meet Navaretta and several of Glenn's other close friends prior to and during the tenth anniversary. One early winter day, John joined Jay and I for lunch at a diner not far from the park. Recalling their friendship and exploits, Navaretta grew animated at points, his formidable eyebrows raised over dark eyes, summoning expressions that cannot always be seamlessly retrieved. When John's daughter was about seven, Glenn would tease her at the table about her prospective first date, saying, "That's okay, we'll be right with you."

Around the time of his daughter's sweet sixteen, John caught himself wondering about her Uncle Glenn and all the laughs they'd had. Even in his wildest thoughts he could not have imagined this.

"I still have trouble dealing with it," he said with a short laugh. "He's a brother. Basically that's what it's all about."

One time floating around in his Sea Ray off Oyster Bay they came across some kids in a boat whose engine was smoking. Glenn gathered the fire extinguishers, jumping aboard as they tied up, and lifted up the engine cover and put the fire out. There were crazy Saturday nights at Frank's Steakhouse, then back to Navaretta's place. "Two lawyers, we're trying to solve the problems of the world, watching the late night news," he said. Glenn slept on the couch and would get up early to go see his dad. "It's just incredible," he told me. "It's an emptiness that I don't think will ever go away."

Jay jumped in to spell him momentarily as we sat over our half-finished plates. "These guys were together all the time," he said. "Every Monday or Tuesday I'd hear about what they had gotten themselves into the weekend before. Someone like that, you just assume you're going to spend the rest of your lives together."

They never made it to Block Island, something John had always wanted to do.

I felt an instant affinity for their bond, and for that gaping hole as well. My thoughts flicked inward to my close friend Matt, and how for years we'd done similar things, not so much as bachelors, but rafting up in boats with our families. We'd meet wherever made sense, and for Denise and I, where the winds would reasonably take us: anchored in Quick's Hole or picking up a mooring in Oak Bluffs. There were morning swims before strong coffee; taking in a Cuttyhunk sunset with a beach fire; and assembling a makeshift grill for those fresh stripers. Our kids experienced Cher rollerblading down Commercial Street that time in Provincetown; we hooted over too much wine and visions of men in kilts and bleating sheep, breaking out dark rum in the galley.

Irreplaceable.

Back in the diner, Navaretta wiped his eyes once or twice. His kids had missed out on knowing Glenn. John realized how proud of them he would be.

Jay briefly told him about my story, introducing what had brought me to ask about Glenn.

I felt a bit unprepared to discuss it. Yet I wanted to remain open because that felt natural, and preparation had never been part of this equation either way.

"How do *you* get by?" John asked me.

I paused for a moment. "We take what we can," I offered. "We take what's positive."

The past weekend several of my son's close friends had stopped by for a holiday open house, including the first of his crew engaged to get married the following summer. Just those guys and their girlfriends making that time meant the world to us. For them to hold up Mike even intermittently, making that effort to connect. I put on the brakes.

We didn't linger too long, and Jay wrapped things up. "Your son wants you to move ahead for your other children, he'd want that," he told me. "And we agree, you do what you can do to honor him, in your own way."

There's an accompanying story to Glenn Winuk's life and how his brother forged ahead along with David Paine. It can be summed up as "ice to bronze."

In the spring of 2006, the first large-scale monument at Ground Zero was consecrated, a memorial wall erected in honor of 343 FDNY members and EMTs who died. The cast bas-relief bronze memorial, fifty-six feet long, is an epic tribute that can halt one's overloaded consciousness.

It represents a final resting place for about one hundred firemen whose families have no remains to properly bury. Its design follows a classical tradition of Rome's marble columns that wordlessly retell the emperors' battles. The wall is intended to be a one hundred-year monument, telling the story to the unknowing, and when one finally stops there on the corner of Liberty Street, you're drawn into its colossal center. Scenes depict the second jet hitting the South Tower with firemen laying hose lines and working at command posts, washing their faces and carrying gear. A tired firefighter reaches skyward, and engraved are the names of the fallen.

The wall is a gift from Holland & Knight and it is dedicated to Glenn Winuk.

Many acts of generosity led to its construction, their narratives sequestered over the years and some yet to be told. Here is one.

A few days after the attacks, Cheryl Roy Starer was four blocks north of Ground Zero helping to treat workers in a makeshift triage center at Public School 234. Firemen and others were coming off the pile and they needed new heavy boots. Their eyes were a mess from all the dust and toxic crap in the air. Many had beet red pupils because of all the eye drops they were using, which wasn't cutting it. So Cheryl and others improvised, making pads with gauze and crushed ice to sooth them. Her husband, Brian Starer, executive partner at Glenn's office, was walking on a street in midtown when she called. He was looking for space where his lawyers and staff could get back to work.

She told him to stop whatever he was doing and listen. "I need ice. I'm not asking you, I'm telling you," she said. He asked how much, and she responded, "All you can get."

He called the owners of some ice companies upstate and on Long Island, and three of them began delivering it for free to five locations, some hauling in twenty tons every day. The ice was a godsend because the heat coming off the pile was intense in addition to the warm early fall weather. After a month the ice company owners said they needed to get paid. Starer started an ice fund, calling friends and clients, including three international shipping executives, who raised nearly $300,000. By the ninth week, as the days cooled and the Ground Zero mission changed to a recovery effort, the deliveries stopped. "The last four weeks we paid for the ice, and that's it. We thought that was all it's going to be," Starer says. "I had a little bit left, sixty or seventy thousand [dollars], I called the individuals and said, 'I'll send it back to you.' They said, 'Keep it.'"

One day he walked over to Ten House on the edge of Ground Zero and asked a captain what they might like as a gesture. He put Starer in touch with Harry Meyers, the Manhattan borough commander, who at first laughed at his idea to help buy a truck. Those cost upwards of a half-million dollars, and the government was going to replace their apparatus anyway. But when they met in person, Meyers told him what he would appreciate: a memorial. Those who had perished amounted to one-third of all the department's firefighters lost since the 1800s. "He said, these widows, these families, need some place to direct their attention and mourn, and if you can help us do that, we'd appreciate it," Starer recalls.

Starer had watched both planes fly into the towers on the morning of September 11 as he sat on Runway 12 at JFK aboard an American Airlines jet bound for London. He had a clear view downtown, and "I knew exactly what had happened. We were listening to radio and a commentator said a small plane, but we could see it was a big plane clearly. I knew it was a terrorist attack." His plane was next in line for takeoff, but after air traffic was shut down they evacuated. He paid someone one hundred dollars to drive him to the home of his priest on Long Island. Later he reunited with Cheryl and his family. For much of the day his wife thought he'd been on one of the crashed planes. Pointedly, Starer acknowledges a morose truth that after the 1993 bombing at the WTC, "it was kind of unspoken, you knew that the Trade Center would be a target."

He didn't consider Glenn's whereabouts until the next morning when Bill Honan told him everyone was accounted for—except Winuk. Then it all made sense.

Starer later won the backing of Holland & Knight's charitable foundation to build the memorial, but only to a point, as he was told most of the money had to be raised independently. He began a campaign within the company, which had about 3,800 employees at the time, and nearly a third of them contributed for a total of $600,000. He'd need a few million more to get it done.

He understood why colleagues in places like Miami or Atlanta might only give so much; after all, they didn't go through the siege of their city. "We did it almost as a way to work our way through the grief of the event, and it was very helpful," he says. There was also initial resistance within the fire department to a memorial being anchored by the death of a non-FDNY member, but that was the deal Holland & Knight's foundation struck, and a compromise was reached to have Winuk's name on a plaque separate from the main listing. Meanwhile, Starer approached the Rambusch Company in New Jersey, renowned for its decorative metalwork, and a preliminary design was sketched out during a meeting with firefighters who relayed details of the day. Models in plaster and full-scale panels in clay were made as the composition became set: large figures on the outside moving in toward the Twin Towers.

Nearing the end of its design and production, Jay went to see a clay model of the wall. Its magnificence hit him even then. While he didn't play a significant role in the project apart from speaking occasionally to a few of the partners and employees at the firm about the wall's progress, he later learned what it truly meant to other families. "How terribly sad that, for many, Ground Zero's their cemetery. The firefighters' wall is the place for them to go, a fitting place to remember, pay tribute and reflect on true heroism," Winuk told me. Holding together his thumb and index finger to show a thimble's volume, he added, "I know families that have no remains at all, and for them the experience seems completely different. It's unbelievable."

Over the years Starer estimates he's literally touched hands with all three hundred-plus families. It's a solemn feeling. There's pride, but something much more. "This means so much for these families," he said. "You can't imagine, you just can't imagine, how comforted they are by this memorial. It makes all the nights when you couldn't sleep, when you said, 'You're a cheap bastard, you've got to give me more money,' it makes it all worthwhile."

Of course, there's even more to this. Starer won't say how much it ultimately cost—just that it probably could not be done for under $5.5 million a few years later. The majority of the donations did not come from Americans, and those sources don't want recognition. But that's not even what really gets to him. "Remove yourself to another country five thousand miles away and think about why do you want to get involved?" he says. "And that's where this story gets very interesting."

"You can do things in life that really register," he continues. "I'll never forget this . . . these people who had not one dog in the fight in any way, and they did this. It gives me great faith not only in humanity, but also in the world community who felt your pain. That's encouraging."

On the night the six-foot-tall murals were installed, firemen from Ten House were permitted to write messages on the back to their fallen brothers. Experiencing all this, Chief Harry Meyers told *The New York Times*, "I'm not a misty guy, but I have to tell you, I had a misty moment."

On May 29, 2002, a construction worker who had struggled to believe in God stood in the sanctuary at Saint Paul's Chapel, across from Ground Zero.

Tom Geraghty lost his sister-in-law in the attacks, and for months afterward, like scores of others, he found refuge in the colonial-era church. George Washington prayed there after his inauguration, and Saint Paul's somehow escaped damage on 9/11, even when a steel beam from the North Tower toppled a massive sycamore in its yard, the graves at the edge not thirty feet away from rubble. By one account the church was spared destruction from the blasts by the innocence of some homeless men who spent the night on cots in the organ loft shelter. They cracked open a window to get some air, forgetting to close it as they left early Tuesday morning, and that opening provided a pathway to relieve some of the thundering pressure.

Within a few days something remarkable started to happen. The chapel was transformed into a rescue center and stayed open continuously 260 days for rescue and recovery workers desperate for food, sleep, even a momentary slice of grace. Volunteers provided water and coffee, more cots, foot massages and counselors, while some of the same men from the shelter grilled burgers. Firefighters grabbed a couple of hours in a pew. Some half million meals were served.

It took a few days to actually open up since the building had to be declared safe by city inspectors. On September 12 the associate minister, the Reverend Lyndon Harris, walked down from Greenwich Village, not expecting to see the church spire. "The place so eerie, yet so filled with spiritual energy, was covered with soot, but it was almost as if sparks were flying off my boots as I walked in," Harris recalled. "It was clear to me that we were spared, not because we were holier than anybody who died across the street, but because we had a big job to do."

By September 13 people were digging out paper and dust in the cemetery, and the next day at noon, workers at the pile stood up, astonished, when the church bell rang out twelve times. Saint Paul's became a restorative enclave with daily celebrations of the Eucharist reserved for rescuers. By the next spring nearly every surface in the sanctuary was covered in banners and well wishes from around the world. Geraghty and others—EMTs, port authority workers, and city police and firemen—thanked the church, which was officially closing its mission that morning.

Reverend Harris noted in his homily that through three seasons of trying to restore order from chaos and reclaim their humanity, what emerged was "a season of renewal." He continued, "Ultimately, what began in hatred has evolved into, in the words from that great song in the musical *Rent*, a season of love." Drawing from Matthew 25, he urged the crowd "to be a community that exists, not for itself, but for the sake of others." Thanking the more than five thousand volunteers, he then offered: "Emerging here is a dynamic I like to refer to as a 'reciprocity of gratitude'—a circle of thanksgiving—in which people have risen to the scriptural challenge . . . 'to try and outdo one another in showing love.' Both giver and receiver have been changed by it. This circle of gratitude is infectious. And I hope it spreads. I hope it turns into an epidemic."

That reciprocity is the baton that David Paine and Jay Winuk grabbed hold of.

Glenn's friend Dan King felt it too. In those first weeks he worked at Ground Zero even on his days off. The flood of volunteers, their compassion for rescuers and officers, and for each other, almost overwhelmed him. "I'd go down there, all these people who were volunteering and handing things out, food, and they're thanking us. I'm looking at them and saying, 'Thank you, look at what you're doing.' I spent a lot of time crying in my car on the way in and on the way home. For a long time I just couldn't sit still."

Neither was it easy for King's family. His son Ryan struggled to understand what had happened. He'd been given a birthday cake in class that Tuesday, but the adults around him were in tears, parents pulling his friends out of school. Ryan even wrote a letter that his dad kept hanging on his office wall for at least a decade. His fifth-grade class made an American flag out of handprints, and King and another parent, a city firefighter, had an idea. Rather than hang it at the firehouse in their hometown of North Merrick, they brought it to Ten House.

In the years ahead, King tried to instill those values that Glenn lived by in each of his three sons. "I tell them, 'Lead by example.' I try to keep his memory alive by trying to do the right thing—by being true and honest."

One morning I walked Glenn's possible routes from his office to the Trade Center. If he had gone one way he'd have passed Saint Paul's to his right and come down beside its gently sloping burial ground. To me, the church stood like a defiant sentinel amidst the crimes of humanity, pressed against the crucible of those draining months, and resuming its watch over the swells of people who press forward and aft through the financial district every working day. But Glenn's co-workers and friends insist he took another, more direct way, exiting his building to Dey Street. I continued in that direction and then toward the firefighters' memorial wall.

It was five days after Christmas, and reaching the corner of Greenwich and Liberty streets shortly after daybreak I came upon a small balsam fir, not seven feet tall, decorated with men's photos and prayer cards. I took another step and there was Glenn Winuk's memorial affixed to a large marble slab. I took a while there and offered a prayer to the Winuks, and to all the families who lost loved ones and continue to suffer from the attacks.

A cluster of small candles remained burning on the sidewalk. The air was still, strangely hushed, other than the beeping of a loader and other heavy equipment across the street.

Beside Glenn's plaque begins the FDNY Memorial Wall. I followed the mural slowly from left to right, panning the expressions on the etched faces, their language silent, evocative. I read the dedication and felt complete accord: "To those who fell and to those who carry on. May we never forget."

A worker on the corner, a large man hooded against the cold, saw me as I came back to the Christmas tree and struck up a conversation.

I told him I came down mainly for Glenn. This guy hadn't been there that day—by the grace of God. He immediately got it. "It could have been me, man. You just never know."

On a June morning in 2006 Jay helped dedicate the memorial wall. He called it "nothing short of a statement to the world that in this city and country we value life. We value courage. We value honor and we honor those who sacrifice for others. We are at once compassionate and resilient. We are principled. We survive adversity and then we flourish."

12

BEST MAN MCGINTY

....

Within a few hours, as the world around her collapsed, Cindy McGinty saw the change in her oldest boy.

Lithe and perceptive, he reacted immediately to the looming sense that his father was dead. The night of September 11, all she could tell him and his younger brother was that their dad was in New York and some very bad men had flown planes into some buildings. She didn't know if he had made it out of his office. Cindy would not have certainty for about a month when some of his remains were identified. Yet deep inside she already knew, and so did her son. He gestured wildly, squirming and raising his voice.

A switch went off. The happy boy she put on the bus that morning became aggressive. He went from getting all A's to being asked to do the impossible: sit in a chair all day when you've been traumatized. The person who meant everything to him had been murdered.

He began building the Twin Towers out of Legos and crashing objects into them. As his mother became more sure, he posed questions beyond the realm of most third-graders. *Do you think Dad knew he was going to die? Do you think he was scared?* At Sunday school they were learning about a loving God, and he tried to puzzle it out. *How could he be a loving God and let this happen to my dad?* It made no sense. In the months ahead he concocted ways to kill Osama bin Laden like trapping him in a tank and sucking out the oxygen.

Pondering how someone so young could ask those questions, McGinty thought, "His mind went to a place where eight-year-olds don't go. His was older and wiser." In her eyes, her son and his dad were so inextricably linked that his whole being changed overnight. Neither could she have predicted the transformation soon to take place in herself.

McGinty was a dutiful housewife, a bit shy and doe eyed, though less deferential than centered in a true partnership. A few years earlier she had a no-frills career doing systems documentation for an insurance company. But Cindy had always wanted "to be Beaver Cleaver's mom." In Michael McGinty she found an energetic and devoted spouse. He was a highly mobile businessman who, if not entirely the antithesis of Ward Cleaver's suburban archetype, was a modern version distilled from a dysfunctional childhood. McGinty was determined to do better for his family than what he'd known growing up.

When Mike died Cindy found herself on a road that was at once terrifying and already climbing. Rather than burrowing under the covers, she had no choice but to set both feet on the bedroom floor and put on a smile for her sons—though on some days she crept back into bed until the school bus returned. Yet something else happened in those early days. Neighbors rushed to help, showing up with meals and rides. One sat with the young widow to help figure out her family's finances. Such small gestures gave her pause, and hope.

In the years following 9/11, Cindy recognized the one gift that almost superseded the attacks themselves. She discovered a passion to support others going through hard times. Like many other widows, family members and partners, though perhaps not a majority of them, McGinty rebuilt her life by stepping outside of her pain, which complimented honoring her husband without being overshadowed by his memorialization. "I like to be doing something positive for people who have suffered the same trauma in a lot of ways," she said. "It gives me a chance to help others in a way like people helped me." She modeled this for her sons, especially aiding active duty military families whose service she respects, like her husband's, and whom she believes deserve much better for their sacrifices. That is how McGinty made her own peace.

Her husband hadn't intended to, but he left an indelible legacy for his wife and sons. To not be forever defined by 9/11, they had to emerge from it, releasing themselves from being stuck in anger.

A strapping bear of a man, Michael Gregory McGinty was a dad who wanted to be around his kids every possible minute. He willed the boys to come out in the yard with him. A typical weekend meant grilling on Sunday, watching movies and playing board games. Vacations to Block Island or the Outer Banks, and of course Disney World, were for the kids. "It's not so much what he did with them but being with them," his sister-in-law says.

Stern looking and six feet three inches tall, the former naval officer was really a child trapped in a forty-two-year-old body. He wanted more for his kids than he'd had, which also meant Cub Scouts, teaching strategy games like Risk, and reading together on the couch. He always competed as a model to give them the best.

McGinty worked for Marsh Inc., a large insurance brokerage and risk analyst firm, overseeing its power and utilities practice as a senior vice president. He had been a nuclear power specialist on a submarine tender in the navy, discharged with well-rounded skill sets that also included docking his ship, teaching young officers, and cooking a Middle Eastern-style chicken with a yogurt marinade. Later on, McGinty leveraged his engineer's intellect and near photographic memory for clients in the corporate world. While impressive, none of that mattered as much to him as the drive home, when he might bop into a Strawberries store and buy the boys a CD.

Mike had a nightly ritual when he wasn't traveling. Bounding through a side door into the kitchen from the garage, he slid his briefcase across the linoleum floor, roaring, "Where's my dinner?" The boys came running, often from their toy room on the first floor, squealing with laughter as he hoisted them up. Sometimes throwing a new disc on and cranking it up, he soared around the house leaving work far behind. He adored his wife of ten years, on occasion flying Cindy out to extend a business trip for a few days together. Completely committed to their marriage, family meant everything. As one of Mike's colleagues says, "He wanted to do this right."

An Air Force brat, he was born in 1959 in Wichita Falls, Texas, and grew up in eleven different states with combative parents. John and Sandy McGinty married at seventeen and weren't great parents, McGinty's younger sister, Erin James, recalls. Their father became a raging alcoholic and the two eventually split up. Mike and his dad were never close, and when he visited John for the last time, his father barely knew him. John McGinty died a month later. Mike paid for his father's cremation and burial plot but didn't have enough money to fly out again for the funeral.

Along with a competitive streak, McGinty had a natural ability in math and largely flourished at Bellevue High School near Omaha, where his father was stationed at Offutt Air Force Base, home of the Fightin' 55th Wing. In the mid-seventies Bellevue had one really big high school, and McGinty graduated eighteenth in a class of just over seven hundred. He also received a perfect math score on the ACT and was on the National Honor Society and chess club. He joined the Naval JROTC and its drill team, known as the "Zoomies," a small group largely set apart from the jocks and other cliques. They'd twirl rifles and march at basketball games, setting out afterwards for hot fudge sundaes and fries at a local Big Boy restaurant. His chief entertainment was listening to classic rock, and Mike showered his sister Erin, eleven years younger, with eight-track cassettes and albums by bands like The Who and Aerosmith.

His parents moved again during junior year and he lived with a friend in Bellevue for his final year. McGinty received an appointment to the Naval Academy and a JROTC scholarship, which was his second choice. Erin recalls that he wanted an Air Force career but was disqualified because of sinus polyps. At the last minute his parents told Mike they couldn't afford college.

As he headed to Annapolis Mike largely severed ties with his family. Once there, McGinty survived by driving himself to higher academic levels and overcoming his social deficits and unhappy teen years. He also became unusually close with a Navy brat named Dan McGarvey.

They met in a plebe physics class where Mike sat quietly in the rear. He didn't often volunteer, but when the professor called on him, he usually had the right answer. Mike was a studious physics major, but McGarvey noticed a few other things. This McGinty guy was far from colorless; he didn't always say the right thing, and he had some special skills.

"He didn't take the easy way out, that's for sure, with anything," Dan says. Mike played percussion in the drum and bugle corps, but not because he had any rhythm. "He'd do anything to escape the hazards of plebe year," Dan says. Similarly by marching with a flag. "It wasn't his proudest moment doing flag stuff, but he said, 'I need to do something to escape.'" As they became friends, Mike regaled McGarvey with an expansive musicology library he kept in his head—mostly more of his classic rock bent—and an arch sense of humor. "You weren't really sure if he was joking or not," McGarvey says, "but of course as you got to know him, he was a riot."

Mike's uncanny musical memory helped him survive an occasionally brutal environment. Upperclassmen would routinely challenge plebes to a trivia game called "Stop the Music," setting up a quaking midshipman for a verbal terrorizing in the hallway. As McGinty ran down the corridors and was halted, he didn't often fail to name the song, group, and album that an upperclassman was playing. Years later, when Cindy took her sons to see the Eagles, like his dad, her older son seemed to know the words to each song.

McGarvey grew to know Mike as well as anyone, and the two lived remarkably intertwined if not parallel lives. Dan was born at Camp Lejeune, where his father was a supply officer, and he, too, was rootless. They talked about that challenge, and the opportunities it presented: often on the move, always having to re-establish oneself and make new connections. Strengths, stress cracks, and fast food. They each studied at the Navy's Nuclear Power School and became instructors at Department Head School for surface warfare officers. Both entered civilian life almost simultaneously, even joining the same firm, and McGinty was hired for a job that McGarvey thought was meant for him. They got married back-to-back. Even their oldest children, both sons, would enter college the same year.

Both also had early jobs scraping by at fast food restaurants. Mike told hilarious tales of working as a short order cook at a Denny's in Omaha, while Dan plied a McDonald's in Alexandria and later was on the night shift at a Howard Johnson's as a side job. McGarvey struggled with math and physics at the academy, which were Mike's strengths, but both graduated high in their class. "I was very challenged and Mike not so challenged," he says.

They both wanted to work on surface ships supporting submarines, which required another eighteen months at nuclear school in Orlando. After that they were assigned to different cruisers—Mike on the USS *Mississippi*, a nuclear-powered guided missile cruiser, and McGarvey on a sister cruiser, the USS *Bainbridge*—for three-year tours. "We sort of joined the Navy to see the world and we certainly wanted to see it, so we went on the surface side." Mike sailed mainly in the Mediterranean and Indian Ocean.

McGinty's second sea tour in the mid-eighties was aboard the USS *Shenandoah*, a submarine tender where he won plaudits as a senior nuclear-trained officer. He qualified as chief engineer and his expertise included radiological controls, handling radioactive material, plus "lots of record keeping and preparing for repair jobs," McGarvey says. "He went on a unique tour. He was one of a handful of nuclear people in that role. He was pretty proud of that. They scored pretty highly on a nuclear inspection, and I think when he went aboard things weren't in that great of shape and he turned it around." In 1986, after Libyan agents bombed a West Berlin nightclub and the United States retaliated with a bombing raid, McGinty's tender was in the region while the *Bainbridge* was off Libya with an aircraft carrier group in the disputed Gulf of Sidra. Although Moammar Khadafy warned the United States not to cross the gulf, the group did so with impunity. "For all the bluster coming out of Tripoli I never felt any danger," McGarvey recalls.

Mike wasn't easily rattled by belligerent threats or tight quarters. His old friend envisions him on the bridge as the *Shenandoah* edged into a port, guiding the beamy, 642-foot-long ship as officer of the day. "He'd be at the helm, he'd earned that on the cruiser," he says. "I guess he was viewed as a very good ship handler."

It was never all dull, and Mike's predisposition for high jinx sometimes included the high seas. As Cindy tells it, he once got caught speeding the *Shenandoah* in the Mediterranean. His commanding officer was below napping and McGinty wanted to see how fast it would go opened up. Unfortunately the CO woke up.

His shipmates later wrote this tribute on a card: "You're a nuclear man and that's no jive, but put you on the bridge and forty knots you'll drive."

Because they did consecutive sea tours, both McGinty and McGarvey received plum shore duty: teaching engineering in Newport, Rhode Island. The curricula included thermodynamics, materials science, and fluid dynamics. Mike used creative approaches that made him a popular instructor, including making a card on each student with his photo, college major and current job—and memorizing it. "He'd call out, 'Didn't they teach you this at MIT?'" McGarvey says.

McGinty naturally devised techniques that good teachers use, making up clever mnemonics to help memorize technical stuff, or throwing out candy bars when someone did well. It broke up eight-hour-a-day courses that went for eight months. He continued that strategy making out note cards in his business life, emailing birthday greetings to clients and prospects. "I think it was actually a coping mechanism," McGarvey reflects, "something he latched on to in some way to exude a little warmth, and connect."

While pursuing their MBAs at the University of Rhode Island, they glimpsed the next step: civilian life. They met high-powered managers, watching their interactions, and were not cowed. Meanwhile, as Mike met Cindy and Dan met his future bride, Maria, McGarvey realized, "maybe not going to sea isn't the worst thing in the world." He was first to resign his commission with an honorable discharge in 1989, and McGinty followed a few months later. Both would stay on active duty long enough—McGarvey in the Navy Reserves for another eleven years—to retire as lieutenant commanders. McGinty joined an insurance brokerage firm called Johnson & Higgins four months after McGarvey did, entering a pipeline of navy officers going into the insurance business. He jumped right into the work of assessing nuclear power plants and risk management consulting. Since McGinty was fluent in nuclear engineering, "the fact that he didn't know a word of insurance was a minor issue," McGarvey says. "He connected with clients right away because he spoke their language."

Posted on the back door of his office in Charlotte, McGarvey keeps a magazine advertisement that McGinty gave him when they were both pursuing their MBAs. Both men were attending night school courtesy of the GI Bill and teaching younger officers by day. One morning after each of them had presented in class, Mike left a glossy ad for an overhead projector on Dan's desk. It reads, "There's only one thing worse than sitting through a bad presentation—giving one."

"It was a reminder to me to not be cocky," laughs McGarvey, who later became chairman of the US Power Facilities Practice at Marsh, Inc.

Their blind date may have easily gone askew.

Quiet and thin, Cindy Sheffs lived a fairly straightforward life. The middle of three girls who grew up in a blue-collar town near Hartford, she worked as a business systems analyst and was also taking night school courses. After dinner, Mike took her to an unlikely movie, a black comedy, *The War of the Roses*. In the film, a sparring couple with a superficially golden marriage splits into an outrageous divorce fed by mammon worship. Cindy began to intuit his sense of humor. He told her straight up that he wanted a serious and committed relationship, and she was impressed. They dated about fifteen months and married in 1991—she was thirty-three, and Mike a year younger.

For their reception Cindy wanted to spare expenses on flowers and accoutrements to focus on three things: great food, an open bar, and a good DJ. Dancing and drinks flowed all night while Mike went table-to-table thanking everyone. Erin flew in—the one representative of Mike's family—as did McGarvey and his new bride. It was a small reception of about seventy-five at a nearby Marriott, mostly Cindy's friends and some of Mike's work colleagues, as several of his other friends were still in the Navy. They had a blast. Instead of clinking glasses, each table sang part of a love song to prompt the couple into another smooch. "It became an icebreaker and all the tables got to know each other," she recalls. One group made up a rap song. Mike's toast was a Shakespeare sonnet, which McGarvey half-kidded he'd screw up. But of course, he recalled it verbatim. The couple celebrated their honeymoon in California wine country.

There was a moment at Dan and Maria's wedding a few months earlier that always draws a laugh. As the ushers approached the altar, they paused, genuflecting as they made the sign of the cross. Having grown up Baptist, best man McGinty didn't know how to do this, and someone shooting video recorded him faking it. The camera captures Mike turning to see how the others did it, improvising with his hands in the air. "It looks like he's paying homage to some heathen god or something," Dan says. "He pulled it off sort of calmly and no one behind him saw it. He was not afraid to wing it."

The couple weathered a few crazy years. This started with Mike's mammoth commute from central Connecticut to Manhattan, usually two and three-quarters hours each way. On top of the drive, train, and subway, he had to walk three or four blocks, "so on a rainy or snow day, after that commute he'd show up wet," McGarvey says. Then came a deluge of moves and two babies. Around the same time their first child was born, Mike got a job offer at another brokerage firm in Boston, Sedgwick, so they found an apartment nearby. Within a few months Cindy was pregnant again and they bought a house in the suburbs. They picked Foxborough in part because it just felt right to her. Driving around the town green, they spotted a homey-looking Congregational church across the street and Cindy told Mike, "I could live here." They stopped into a realtor's office, and the second house they looked at became theirs.

Their second son arrived in a rush, as Cindy's water broke at ten weeks and he was eight weeks premature. Mike was her rock through this cascade of change. While teaching Cindy how to trust, he never quite succeeded in teaching his wife not to worry. For her part, Cindy settled him down and gave Mike a softer edge.

From there on it was always about the boys. On their frequent business trips, he often told McGarvey or another friend and colleague, Charlie Moore, about his sons' accomplishments. He'd do extra things like fly halfway around the country to get home for a half day and then fly out again on the next leg when he might have stayed at a hotel. Moore, who met McGinty at Sedgwick, recalls how connected to home Mike was: the frequent calls, and his boys' photos were always handy. He was not the type of guy who morphed into someone different on a business trip, rarely taking a drink other than a glass of wine. Moore and others knew that family meant everything.

In the summer of 2001 Mike wanted to spend extra time with Cindy and his sons. Looking back, she wonders if he sensed something coming.

Work was stressful. He had moved over to Marsh, which had acquired his old firm and was cutting back staff and adding to his load. He'd resumed humming in his sleep, which to her signaled fresh strain. He had negotiated working the first two days of the week in New York and the rest in Boston, but Marsh was pressuring Mike to move back closer to its base. Yet the roots the couple had planted in Foxborough were spreading. There was scouting and developing their gardens, and his role as a deacon at the Bethany Congregational Church, which he had jumped into headfirst. Cindy had stopped working but was also busy volunteering at school, with church groups and Cub Scouts. Neither of them normally took a lot of time off.

That season they drove to Chicago with the kids for a conference. Each year he arranged for Cindy to join him on a get-away dovetailing with a business trip, and she felt a little peeved that it wasn't going to be just the two of them. But he said he really wanted to spend time with the boys. Next they went to New Jersey to visit friends, who remarked that Mike hadn't brought his laptop. He even rejected a cellphone that Marsh wanted him to have; he never carried one. Mike always worked on the train to and from work, but "his thing was, he wanted to ride home in peace," she says. They went to Cape Cod visiting friends and were even the last ones to leave the beach one day. The couple also got away to Maine for two nights by themselves.

"It was really kind of bizarre how much time we spent together that summer. Like he knew something was up," she says. Recalling this almost ten years later, Cindy sat back on her couch, at once relaxed and reflective with her arms folded in a self-hug. Plainspoken with a mild country lilt in her voice, she beamed momentarily. I had driven out to meet her for the first time at Cindy's home in a new development outside of Hartford, where she'd moved back about two years earlier. She chuckled at the memory of Mike's nocturnal noisemaking.

On McGinty's last night home, Sunday, September 9, he and Cindy had good conversation, among those that spouses need to seal tiny cracks forming in their marriage patio. They'd been leading a couple's group at church and sometimes the participants skipped doing the readings. At times they questioned why they stuck with it, but that night's session had actually clicked. The two reflected on their marriage and the kids. As a bonus, both boys had enjoyed a really good day. The subject ending the weekend could have been calling the plumber, but it wasn't. "We went to bed and Mike said, 'I'm going to get up early Monday. I'll try and get home really early Tuesday. We'll hit the ground running.'"

He called her Monday night from New York. "And this was weird. Mike never said 'I love you' on the phone," Cindy says. "It was always our joke. I'd say, 'I love you,' he'd say, 'You too,' or 'Have a nice day,' or he'd say something funny.

"But Monday night, he said, 'I'll be home Tuesday. I love you.' That's the first time he ever said that on the phone."

He never got the chance to see it through. McGinty was starting a business meeting on the 99th floor of the North Tower when American Airlines Flight 11 struck just below.

Cindy was at the church that morning with a staple gun re-covering chairs with a group who called themselves the "Sprucers." By 8:30 a.m., Mike's meeting with Marsh's global power group was underway. Up to thirty people were in a conference room, an airy location coveted for its views north to the Hudson. Visitors from Oracle were presenting a large financial package systems implementation, and McGinty and other managers were there to learn. A radio station that's often on in the church office broke in with news of a plane crash, and someone's cell phone rang with word of it. Cindy wasn't concerned. Then her sister Sue called, but Cindy didn't think it was a big deal. "She was very, 'I'm sure he's fine' and 'You know Mike,' very low key," Sue Quinlan recalls.

Quinlan was torn about whether to drive to her sister's from Connecticut because she had a big meeting at work herself. Her husband, Ed, urged her to leave. After the second jet crashed, Sue called Cindy again. Ed had just reached her, insisting, "We're going."

Cindy still wasn't outwardly worried. Mike had been a senior officer dealing with radioactive material, after all. She figured he knew what to do. By the time she got home people were in her driveway and someone had gone to school to pick up her boys. One friend went to the grocery store and was making food. Soon a TV crew was at the edge of her lawn with their trucks parked down the street. "Already my life was out of control," she recalls. She still has no idea how the media located her so quickly.

Her sister was driving home when one of the towers collapsed, and the entirety of it hit Quinlan. Sue and Ed took their son Connor out of school. Ed Quinlan insisted over the principal's objections that he be with his family. They drove north to Foxborough. Cindy got on the phone, but lines into Manhattan were dead and she didn't know where to call. Someone at Marsh's Boston office gave her numbers for the New York hospitals, and she and Sue began making those calls that evening.

Despite what her gut was telling her, Cindy resisted surrendering to her worst fear. In the weeks ahead she'd demand a floor plan to know exactly where Mike was, but not yet. Even as it became likely that everything was not going to be fine, she told her sister, "We're just not going there." Sue was much more emotional, sensing the worst, and worried that she wasn't really helping.

Chipped away bit by bit, her sister's slim hopes dissolved when they went down to Ground Zero.

Ending its agonizing path, the first hijacked plane breached nearly all of Marsh & McLennan Companies' North Tower offices upon impact.

On that morning the insurance giant had 845 employees with offices and workstations on the 93rd through 100th floors. The Boeing 767 cut through the 93rd and 99th floors, sending a fireball of jet fuel through at least one bank of elevators and making three stairwells impassable above the 91st. Another 934 people at three Marsh sister companies worked in the South Tower, with offices between the 48th and 54th floors that were below the impact area of the second jet. Most of those employees survived. Mike McGinty was one of the 295 MMC employees and sixty-three consultants who died in the Twin Towers. One of them was aboard Flight 11.

While many were killed instantly, most of the casualties in the North Tower were trapped on or above the 99th floor—an estimated 1,360 of 1,432 people believed to have died in the strike and collapse of 1 WTC. Just above Marsh was the international brokerage firm Cantor Fitzgerald, which lost two-thirds of its New York employees on the 101st through 105th floors, and above that, the Windows on the World Restaurant. The 9/11 Commission Report recalls:

> Hundreds of civilians trapped on or above the 92nd floor gathered in large and small groups, primarily between the 103rd and 106th floors. A large group was reported on the 92nd floor, technically below impact but unable to descend. Civilians were also trapped in elevators. Others below the impact zone—mostly on floors in the 70s and 80s, but also on at least the 47th and 22nd floors—were either trapped or waiting for assistance.

Before the debilitating heat and smoke came, some were able to reach a loved one in their last moments, or leave a message that even the passage of time seems incapable of scrubbing away. When a desk officer at the Port

Authority Police Department picked up the phone, he learned that more than one hundred people were stuck inside the restaurant.

Mike didn't get to make a last call.

Sue Quinlan imagines him in those final moments staying within himself, remaining logical. "I always have this image of him coolly checking exits and deducing, 'This is it, there's no getting to the roof, there's no getting down,' where other people would be frantically thinking things." He'd shown those qualities many times before. When Cindy had gone into premature labor, Sue called frantically in the middle of the night asking if she should come up. Mike "was just so, 'Whatever works for you.' He kept his composure. He really had a belief that whatever it is, we're going to work it out."

Cindy had long known that her husband was a horrible winner. Playing Stratego with the family, he'd be in their face egging them on after winning a round. But whenever he lost, Mike was supremely gracious.

Dan McGarvey would have been at the same meeting on September 11th had he not been presenting a project for clients in San Antonio. That was the only day he could make it work. He found three voice mails from colleagues who died, including Mike's discussing some routine work, which he's never erased. "I played those over and over again and it was very haunting," McGarvey told me. He believes Mike was killed instantly, but it took nearly a week to be certain that his old friend was gone. Despite the confusion at Marsh and conflicting reports coming out of New York, as McGarvey drove cross country in a rental car to his North Carolina home a few days later, he knew the chances were slim.

The breadth of an unfolding disaster shook McGinty's colleagues and others working four dozen blocks away at Marsh & McLennan Companies' headquarters. From her office window on Avenue of the Americas, Kathryn Komsa saw flames pouring out of the first tower. Soon she was on the phone with her boss in London, Marsh Inc.'s head of human resources, who told her to do whatever it would take to respond.

Around midday a colleague who'd escaped the Trade Center walked in, the first Marsh survivor. Komsa found that the man could barely speak, and she put her arms around him. She and others were setting up phones, not yet watching the news. "'You have no idea what's happening down there,'" he told Komsa. "'Nobody knows.'"

The number of lives lost and the complexity of sorting this out remained staggering. With the exception of Cantor Fitzgerald, nowhere was this more true than within the network of Marsh & McLennan Companies' firms. With its four operating units including the flagship insurance brokerage, Marsh Inc., MMC had nearly two thousand employees at the World Trade Center, including 129 Marsh-affiliated colleagues visiting from other offices. More than 169 consultants were also in that morning. Overall, the Marsh entities were the second largest tenant in the Twin Towers after Morgan Stanley.

"One of the big things we had to deal with was, who was actually in the buildings?" says Reginald McQuay, then a human resources manager at Marsh. "It was a terrible process." A decade later, MMC did not know exactly how many of its employees perished in each building.

Komsa, McQuay, and Laurie Ledford, another senior HR manager, helped cobble together Marsh and McLennan's immediate response. Ledford's husband worked for Citibank at 7 WTC, the forty-seven-story tower that apparently caught fire from debris and collapsed late in the afternoon. She actually called him first, finding out that he was okay, and he made it uptown later. Ledford rushed over to headquarters from her office a block away. As details began filtering in, the cafeteria and meeting rooms on MMC's 35th floor became a communications post with tables and more than sixty phones—ultimately staffed by four hundred employees. Four task forces were created focused on identifying where people were, communications, operational issues, and analyzing the attacks' financial blow.

The immediate challenge was massive. Since the Port Authority system that scanned and recorded employees and visitors was lost, MMC's technology team scrambled to retrieve backups of HR data. Sheets of names went up on the walls and were checked off as confirmations were made. Members of the HR team began collecting the recorded final conversations of missing employees.

Desperate voices of girlfriends, spouses, and parents were routed through. "We realized there needed to be outreach for families," Ledford says. "They didn't know where to call. And we didn't really know what was going on." A Marsh business partner sent its airline disaster consultants over and suggested creating a space just for the families—with clergy, counselors, and information on benefits—and fast. Ledford called over to an outplacement counseling firm, but they were not as equipped as crisis therapists. Komsa took a call from a woman asking about her son. She checked the logs and said she was sorry, but he wasn't on the list yet. Komsa realized she had probably just told this woman that her son had died. The surge was underway.

Relatives arrived at MMC headquarters, a few dozen by that first evening. Informal wakes started: a mother, father, and brother sat together "and they were just going to wait until they heard," Komsa says. Like their counterparts at the other decimated firms, Marsh & McLennan Companies' executives knew frustratingly little, and they sensed the colossal scope unfolding. They had no idea how many had perished. Their first estimate was seven hundred.

While dwarfed by the long-term commitment that Cantor Fitzgerald made to support its 658 victims' families—plus sixty-one employees at an affiliated company and forty-nine contractors—by Friday Marsh & McLennan Companies took considerable steps that many view as remarkable for the breadth of a company's crisis response. The first was opening a family assistance center at the Millennium Broadway Hotel in Times Square. Securing ballrooms, beds, and explaining benefits was one thing. The company also desperately needed people who knew how to sit with a spouse or parents entering shock. Demand for experienced therapists was spiking citywide, but CEO Jeffrey Greenberg and his wife, Kim Greenberg, had connections at New York Presbyterian Hospital Burn Center, where burn survivors were being treated. Through the center's liaison at Weill Cornell University Medical College, experienced counselors and faculty members were soon snapped up and put to the test. The company began offering resources that many families would need just as much as financial aid in the years ahead.

On Thursday, September 13, John C. Smith, the head of Marsh's Boston office, parked his car in a cul de sac just beyond the McGinty driveway.

He didn't know what to say to Mrs. McGinty, whom he'd never met. He saw the boys' swing set and toys scattered on the lawn—"remnants of a family," he reflected. A recently transplanted New Yorker, Smith had a close friend who worked in the South Tower and was missing. He hadn't added all of them up yet, but nearly two dozen other friends and colleagues in the insurance industry were believed to be dead: a neighbor, a former secretary, and people whose names he was finding on faxed lists. He sat in the car for maybe thirty minutes and it felt like an hour. He pulled into the driveway and got out with a platter of brownies and cookies.

Mike McGinty was the only person unaccounted for in Boston. "I decided the right thing to do was to drive down and let her know we were going to do everything we can as a company and to support her," Smith recalls.

He'll never forget opening the front door. Right there in the hallway two young boys had constructed the Twin Towers out of Legos.

They asked, "Do you know my daddy? Do you work with my daddy?" Smith made it out to a closed-in porch where Cindy sat with her sister. He really didn't know much more than they did but offered his help, staying about forty-five minutes, never mentioning the weight he carried. To Cindy and his sister, this large man was calm and solemn. He urged them to stay put for a few days rather than go to New York.

Smith had worked in Manhattan for more than a decade until Marsh asked him to oversee its New England operations that July. His old office was at MMC headquarters with a view downtown from the 42nd floor. He would have seen it all too. Bitter ironies mounted from there.

After meetings in New York that Monday, on September 11 he hopped a 6:00 a.m. Delta shuttle back to Boston in time to host a marketing seminar for clients and prospects on disaster planning. As his flight landed at Logan, Flight 11 with its five terrorists was about to board for a 7:59 takeoff. Smith grabbed a cab and gathered with other managers and clients at the renowned Bull and Finch Pub, the "Cheers" bar from the television series, when his executive assistant called.

In her office at Hancock Tower, Jacqueline Ferreira's computer went down as the first plane took out Marsh's servers. She heard about it and tried to reach Smith, but whoever answered at first thought her call was a fake. After the second jet struck, Smith and the others raced back to the

Hancock, the city's tallest building. Assembling the managers who over-saw about two hundred employees on the 34th through 38th floors, they considered Hancock to be another potential target.

The phone rang on Ferreira's desk. On the other end was a tiny, frail voice that she'll never forget.

"My name is Cindy McGinty, my husband is Mike McGinty, and he's in the World Trade Center and somebody has to find him and let me know that he is safe." Jacqueline saw that the call came from Foxborough—it was her hometown as well—and Cindy was at the Bethany church. Ferreira jotted down the number. A few minutes later the third jet crashed into the Pentagon, and Smith told Ferreira to make the announcement to evacuate.

He checked every bathroom on the way out, then asked for three things: a flip chart, markers, and phone numbers. On Ferreira's way out, "I handed him this crumpled piece of paper and said this woman just called." Smith listed the names of his staff as "missing," and by day's end only one name remained.

Two nights earlier Smith had dinner in New York with a longtime friend. John Niven grew up with Smith in Oyster Bay and was an insur-ance executive with Aon in the South Tower. Niven and his wife had just returned from a vacation with their eighteen-month-old son. Over dinner Niven told Smith he couldn't wait to teach young Jack how to fish. On Tuesday morning, Niven was about to leave his office for a business trip. Like many workers there who saw disaster unfolding next door or smelled smoke, he started down to the sky lobby to leave with a colleague. Not everyone tried to exit, as many stayed at their posts—electricians, traders, janitors, and analysts alike.

In one of the cruel vagaries of the day, despite instructions from FDNY chiefs who gathered in the North Tower lobby to evacuate all buildings in the complex at 8:57 a.m., fire safety directors in the South Tower did not do the same. Instead, just eight minutes before United Airlines Flight 175 crashed through floors 77–85, a Port Authority official went on the public address system saying an incident had occurred next door, but their building was safe and workers should remain or return to their offices. In retrospect, the 9/11 Commission Report noted, "The prospect of another plane hitting the second building was beyond the contemplation of anyone giving advice." One of the first fire chiefs to arrive called such a scenario "beyond our consciousness." Niven went back up the elevator to Aon's offices, which began on the 92nd floor, above the impact area.

Niven told someone, "'Everything's fine,' and went back up to get his briefcase," Smith says. "And we never saw him again."

In Boston, Smith began receiving lists of Marsh & McLennan Companies' employees thought to be dead. Later he made charts of which memorial services he could attend. That first week a grief counselor came to the office and advised managers what to expect with so many of their colleagues traumatized. While a session went on downstairs, Ferreira noticed Smith alone in his office, his door ajar. "I went in and opened the door and he was looking out the window and I think he was crying. I stood there and didn't know what to do and called the counselor to go see him. I just think he was looking out the window and realizing the enormity of what was ahead of him and not knowing quite how to deal with it."

Smith didn't mention any of this to Cindy and her sister, which they regard as an act of grace. It wasn't his place to unload his anguish. "I had in front of me a spouse with children and real toys and a real dog and it was all about them," he says. "To try and make them feel not completely alone."

A few days later, Cindy McGinty entered the truly surreal: Manhattan incapacitated. Marsh sent a car for her and the boys and her sister. Mike's boss and some friends who had first introduced the couple met them and went over to the Millennium in Times Square.

The airy old hotel with floor-to-ceiling windows and its landmark theatre had transformed into a crisis center. As MMC took over three floors, priests and rabbis began showing up to counsel the families, and food was served 'round the clock while technicians helped relatives make contacts in rooms stuffed with phone banks and computers. Adults were consoled in nooks and wherever a quiet space could be found. A conference room became a meditative area, a kind of chapel reserved for the stricken bringing in photos, children's drawings and their own writing. Rides were arranged to hospitals and morgues, and for some, as close as they could get to Ground Zero. McGinty and others were told to bring in hairbrushes and toothbrushes that could be used for DNA identification.

In a contorted way, the scene resembled a business conference with photo IDs taken at registration and sign-up sheets for sessions with therapists and benefits advisors. Marsh employees and the Millennium staff seemed to do headstands providing service. "Even if you needed toothpaste, they would get it for you," says Cindy. "If you had a thought, they would appear." Arriving at the hotel, Ellen Clarke, the chief of Marsh Inc.'s global technology group, found a mishmash of attempted normalcy overwhelmed by duress. Spouses broke down in the hallways while people picked away at roasted pork with blueberry sauce at supper. Sitting with family members while someone from HR gave them a folder and explained their salary and health benefits, Clarke sensed how acutely they needed an ally. As relatives got hysterical, "we'd take them out somewhere to calm them down," she says. "We were a true definition of a crisis."

John Smith came to the hotel helping to usher other families to places they needed to be. Amidst the frenzy he felt an accompanying vacuity. "You'd sit and all these round tables in a ballroom kind of thing, and at each table were families—and one piece was missing, whether a father, mother, grandparent or child, one piece was missing." He found it very upsetting.

Twice a day families gathered in the Millennium's gilded Hudson Theatre for updates on the city's response, even though there usually wasn't much encouraging news to share. The playhouse itself was steeped in disaster, built in 1903 by an up-and-coming producer who perished on the doomed RMS *Titanic*. Dan McGarvey, who flew in to meet Cindy at the hotel, felt that his firm did really well surrounding the families and providing them information. Relatives also found a few strands of comfort in sharing common concerns. Yet he became more certain that most of the missing weren't going to be found.

Meanwhile, the Greenbergs' contacts came through. Grief counselors arrived at the hotel, led by an expert on post traumatic stress disorder, Dr. JoAnn Difede. Her immediate mission was to assemble a team, initially mostly faculty volunteers from the psychiatry department at Weill Medical College of Cornell University, where she directed the Program for Anxiety and Traumatic Stress Studies. For two weeks they met families into the mid-evenings as she began training Marsh managers on how to help their grief-stricken colleagues. "A lot of it was managing logistics and getting people there," Difede recalls. "At the end of the day there was a shortage of general crisis counselors, but we were able to get enough people." Attempting to impose order on chaos was an intense, drawn-out experience. Difede and others would also spend years treating firefighters, police officers, and implementing new therapies for other disaster relief workers who experienced the painful reliving of sharp memories from the attacks.

A psychiatrist met several times with Cindy and the boys. "Everybody had PTSD, she could tell right away," Cindy says. "And it was going to be a long road. And she was worried about my sons."

While the prospects for those at Ground Zero were grim from the start, fifteen days later only three hundred bodies had been recovered and 6,400 people were still thought to be missing. Only a handful of survivors had been pulled from the rubble, each on the first day.

In this setting, Marsh & McLennan Companies' managers and staffers were thrust into new roles. McQuay, then a global talent management vice president, oversaw thirty employees on the phones and took many calls himself. "Especially in the early days, the first week," he says, "there were a lot of calls that would rip your heart out." He spoke with an Asian woman new to America who didn't speak English well and whose husband was missing. She seemed to be holed up in a closet in her apartment, desperate for information, a child screaming in the background. McQuay met many families with orphaned children, a role that grew as the company organized long-term supports during the next two years.

One day Cindy and her sister left the hotel to file Mike's missing person's report at an armory on Twenty-Sixth Street. A taxi driver refused to charge them once he learned where they were headed. They joined a line of dazed and overwhelmed relatives teeming on the sidewalk outside the vast brick building. McGinty noticed the missing persons fliers and posters taped on anything with a fixed face—on lampposts, walls, and mailboxes. Inside, the armory felt over-populated with stuffed animals and water bottles. There were tables upon tables with detectives and veteran police officers, many of who looked frazzled even to her. Someone took her DNA mouth swab, and a nurse later stopped by McGinty's home to swab each of the boys. She hesitated trying to picture what Mike was wearing, attempting to hold herself together as she gave a description. Talking to a detective slid from confounding into feeling punch-drunk silly: she figured Mike had his signature khakis on, but the rest was speculation—how much he would want to weigh, and how tall he wanted to be.

Finally reaching Ground Zero, Cindy knew it was time to go home.

Some friends from New Jersey had taken the boys to the Central Park Zoo, and the two sisters walked down. They reached a police blockade some blocks away from the pile, and after some wrangling a cop finally let them through.

Seeing the destruction, McGinty concluded, *There's no way*. She and Sue walked back to the hotel and had dinner with the kids at another round table. She heard someone's relative say, "'We're going to find her,' and Susan and I looked at each other because I wasn't feeling that way, and I didn't want the boys to hear that."

Cindy told her sister, "I've got to get out of here."

The city's psyche, and that of the tri-state region of nearly fifteen million people, was battered, yet in no way beaten. How could the fate of so many turn in such an arbitrary wind on a perfectly clear morning?

JoAnn Difede remembers a woman who came to the Marsh & McLennan family center accompanied by a male friend of her missing husband's. Both men had worked at the World Trade Center. The second man lived near the couple, and both usually left their homes at about the same time. Yet they took different routes to office that day. The friend got stuck in traffic while the woman's husband "had clear sailing and thought he was getting to work early," Difede says. "Capricious things like that. Just details like oversleeping saved people's lives."

The traumatic impact multiplied far beyond downtown. New York City did a sweeping study of more than eight thousand children in grades four through twelve, following those who indirectly witnessed the attacks through a family member such as a first responder or a transit worker, along with kids who experienced it firsthand. Six months later, the rise in various psychiatric disorders was triple what investigators had expected: 15 percent of children showed symptoms of disorders. The most common ones were a fear of crowds, bridges, of being alone, and separation anxieties. Their exposure often came from relationships with adults who were at the Trade Center, while a bombardment of media images added to the toll.

Yet perseverance still carried the day. As bystanders, journalists, and researchers chronicled, so many New Yorkers took action to help themselves and their neighbors. They formed human hand chains in the debris cloud and evacuated as many as three hundred thousand by boat. Scores of people descending a stairway were determined not to overrun an overweight, slower woman. If anything, author Rebecca Solnit found, "the mainstream narrative crafted from the ruins . . . also tended to portray everyone remotely connected to the calamity as a traumatized victim." Volumes of research later bore out that while the emotional collateral was visceral, and the challenge to reach so many who were impacted was steep, resilience usually trumped. Many people responded by drawing on their strengths, their personal makeup, family supports, or the social conditioning of their jobs.

Difede and some colleagues at Weill Cornell tracked more than eight hundred Con Edison workers who were called to Ground Zero during the following weeks. Their twelve- to sixteen-hour shifts were physically and mentally taxing. Many workers described their disbelief, similar to Glenn Winuk's friends, staring at a six-story pile of rubble absent of desks and computers, and "walking by medical units set up to help the survivors, only to see the cots were empty." Adding to this was a multiplier effect for those who grew up or lived in communities that suffered heavy losses. Topping this off, they worried about the very air they breathed.

Yet the number of utility workers who showed substantial PTSD symptoms later was on the low end compared to other studies of the general population, and consistent with other rescue and recovery workers—about 12 percent. One reason for this identified by researchers was that these people as a group were typically involved in high-risk duties and expected to show extra resolve following a disaster. "Resilience may be related to working toward a common goal that contributes to a sense of personal meaning and value," the study's authors said, while noting that utility crews, like other relief workers, might "react intensely afterwards." To others who study this phenomenon, resilience and recovery emerge as the most common responses to disaster and other sources of trauma. "What is perhaps most intriguing about resilience is not how prevalent it is; rather, it is that we are consistently surprised by it," writes George Bonanno, an expert at Columbia University.

Despite this tenacity, complications like survivor's guilt also took root, especially for first responders like Joe Mlynarcyk, and for the many others who lost multiple brothers. "We don't think of this as an act of war, no one was shot at," Difede told me, "but in terms of the effect on someone's wider social network it's sometimes as bad. It's not unusual to talk to a firefighter who knew twenty people and knew them well—at Little League, he went to their weddings. One guy told me that if you took out a photo of his wedding, not one of his party survived. But he's alive."

It would take years for mental health practitioners to help the survivors and victims' families sort through the debris. And those widows like Cindy McGinty somehow had to keep moving. Trying to not bounce checks while getting the kids to school. Dealing with an accountant about her taxes, or sucking it up to see the lawyer about victims' compensation. Each of these grainy tasks, mundane in their fine print, bit into her like marauding horseflies.

Just before Mike died, he and the boys were reading a Patrick O'Brian sea novel, one in a series of Royal Navy adventures during the Napoleonic Wars. As he dubbed in an occasional British accent of naval officer Jack Aubrey with his physician friend, Cindy noticed the slight curl of her sons' mouths at their dad's feigning. "You never say no to a book, never," she recalled with an instant smile. Those days had been stolen from her, but McGinty couldn't split open in front of her sons.

While operating in a glaze, she tried to be strong for others in her family. "I remember being on the phone thinking, 'Mike would not want me to fall apart.' If my kids see me fall apart, they're going to know how bad this really is.

"All of us, all the widows, we fell apart in the shower—that's where we cried. That's when I did. I couldn't let the kids see me fall apart. I was determined—not that they couldn't see me sad, but at that point if they saw me fall apart they'd know how bad it was, and there was plenty of time for that."

When she and Mike were dating, on a lark she had her palm read at a psychic fair. A woman began to read her and suddenly closed Cindy's hand. She told Cindy, "'This has never happened to me, but I can't read your palm.' We looked at each other like, 'What?' and she said, 'Something very bad is going to happen to you. But I have to tell you that it will be okay.'"

For Cindy and some of the others, something beyond resilience eventually emerged. While continuing to mourn their loved ones and dread that day, they grew from it.

Mike McGinty's company attempted to inflate life rafts for the families as it closed the relief center at the hotel. Working alongside Difede's team of counselors, Reg McQuay began to see daunting long-term needs. His team had become the main point of contact for the stricken relatives of 295 victims, some of whom seemed to be in denial and were just cashing their checks. As the holidays approached a suicide watch was formed. McQuay's group needed debriefing and pauses themselves.

Marsh & McLennan created a specialized unit of HR managers each responsible to help up to forty families. They became advocates, overseeing unlimited counseling that was extended to many for nearly three years and distributing information from the city. The managers sometimes tried to settle benefits issues while MMC established a charitable fund and helped each family apply for federal 9/11 compensation, hooking up relatives with volunteer attorneys. The family supports were never intended to last more than a few years.

At its core, McQuay and the others wrestled with: how do people pick up and go on?

Therapists and specialists advised the company not to let the families view Marsh as a crutch for all their needs. Rather, to help survivors grieve in a healthy way after a phase of compassionate intervention, they were told to let the families go. Cindy remains forever grateful to McQuay and Sally Bott, who was then Marsh Inc.'s top human resources officer, for their persistence, although she was never provided a designated advocate. "She [Bott] looked at me once and said, 'You can call at any time,'" she says. "I didn't call with minutia like some of the other families, but I called with big stuff.'"

Meanwhile, Marsh paid Cindy her husband's salary through the end of the year, plus a one-time payment from its victims' relief fund, which totaled $24 million. She didn't publicly complain about it, but she asserts that covering Mike's pay did not net all that much since he preferred getting bonuses over straight salary increases. "It kept him under the radar, based on performance, rather than a large base," she says. "That was his play money."

Providing ongoing health benefits soon became a thorny issue. Toward the end of 2001, Marsh & McLennan Companies was roundly criticized for doing something none of the other large firms decimated by the attacks had done: it planned to pay for three years of ongoing health coverage out of its victims' relief fund. That amounted to taking $2 million for health insurance premiums out of a $13 million pool, which the company says later grew to $25 million, shrinking the cash payments and infuriating family members and donors. Other firms including several much smaller than Marsh were providing spouses health coverage for five or more years. One woman whose husband had been a senior Marsh vice president told a reporter, "If my husband had a body and I had buried it, he would be rolling over in his grave right now."

Cindy doesn't recall much of that criticism, but her experience with Marsh was decidedly mixed. On one hand, she continued purchasing health insurance through the company for at least a decade at a group rate that cost her about $1,900 a month by 2011. After the third year, Marsh contributed nil toward her health premiums. "You'd think I could at least get a discount," she said. "It's not like they're mean or anything, but they went back to business as usual." On the other hand, she lauds the company's immediate response, crediting Marsh for extending its payment of her family's counseling and other mental health services an additional two years, which was vital. Occasionally, however, McGinty lamented the company's ethical decisions.

"I'm not saying they have to take care of us, but I think that Mike worked really hard for them. It's a hard thing to come out and say, but when you pour your blood, sweat, and tears for someone, and you give them your life, isn't there an obligation there? Not to make me rich, but look what I'm pouring out for healthcare. Maybe help with scholarships and internships." And for someone to occasionally ask, *How are you doing?*

Marsh & McLennan Companies took the complaints over how it extended health coverage in stride, insisting the focus of its response was the families, not on the firm. While not a panacea for the bitterness some families felt about this, a few years later MMC built a memorial in the plaza below its midtown headquarters. The firm collected signatures of every lost colleague, elegantly inscribed in a glass plate to portray that person's uniqueness. Beginning in 2012, it offered a paid day on September 11th for employees who volunteer in honor of their colleagues.

Dan McGarvey stops at the plaza when he's in town, and on a sunny or warm day he takes comfort in seeing others sitting there enjoying the outdoors. "Mike's signature is so recognizable," he says.

Cindy stepped away from this whorl of pain and controversy. How can you keep breathing in all of that?

She had more than enough to deal with at home. Her oldest son was in crisis: he knew exactly what he had lost, the person who was best equipped to help him. They were two peas in a pod, and his anger spilled over.

His brother, eleven months younger, became a frequent target and Cindy couldn't always be the referee. Where they had once played on the swing set together without mishaps, she felt she needed to be there every minute. Therapy wasn't cutting it and she felt like the professionals weren't really listening. Her sister was the only one who did, and a mother's instinct told McGinty that something more disturbing was going on. An outburst next summer at an overnight camp for 9/11 families blew things open. Cindy tried to restrain her son during a flare-up and got a black eye; the camp called his doctor and put him on medication. When they got home, McGinty realized he needed acute care.

At this juncture someone reached out to Cindy in a booming, unmistakable voice. She had spoken with him before during one of the senator's 177 phone calls to families in Massachusetts who had lost a loved one during 9/11.

"Hi, this is Ted Kennedy from Washington. I'm sorry. I heard about what happened. What can we do to get him the best help possible?"

She was desperate, and had no idea how he even found out. Yet here was Kennedy on the phone again. He spared no resource, connecting McGinty to the head of a psychology unit who teamed her son up successfully—she was expecting a social worker at best. Kennedy then introduced her to a longtime mental health expert in Congress, who helped Cindy access more care and find appropriate schools for her son.

Earlier, during that first month, while preparing her husband's funeral she had to fight to get a navy honor guard. Mike had been in Admiral Rickover's nuclear navy, for Christ's sake, and was honorably discharged, but they couldn't find his discharge papers. McGarvey intervened, but Cindy says no one from the navy would help them locate the records. She had a Naval Academy alumni yearbook showing that Mike had graduated from Annapolis, "and they sent me a freaking flag," she railed. She got hold of a Kennedy aide and in less than twenty-four hours a commitment for an honor guard came through. It turned out that Mike had been discharged from a different port than usual and that had complicated his record.

The McGinty's pastor suggested the boys be involved in the service by drawing the outside of the program. One drew some pretty clouds and an image of his dad in heaven; the eldest drew the towers. On September 22 the first of two services was held at their church, even though their mom had no remains to bury. Not only had their father been taken away, the boys endured an overflow of strangers and distraught relatives. Television cameras were allowed inside the church as a crowd gathered outside. But the Reverend Paul Sangree did not say that this was God's will. Instead, he suggested, "We don't know why it happened, I don't believe God wanted it to happen, and God is grieving with you."

After the service Cindy asked everyone to leave. Resisting her mother's wish for them to move back to Connecticut, McGinty knew that she and the boys needed to figure out how to live again.

New realities set in. A swarm of issues emerged at school, along with doctor's appointments, getting medications, and loads of paperwork. Each task was tough to fight off, each resulting welt unexpected.

Her husband lived with what Cindy believes was Asperger's syndrome. Mike had developed ways to overcome shortfalls such as recognizing social cues, relying on his engineer's skill sets while compartmentalizing his emotions. Even when stressed at work, he would rush home and put it aside. Shortly after the disaster Cindy went to his office in Boston, finding a box with files of all his clients. He made notes of their spouses' names and children, anniversaries and birthdays, the names of schools, their hobbies and passions outside of work. It was another of his successful strategies. Cindy knew that her oldest child was smart enough to learn some of those coping mechanisms his dad had discovered. Both sons also carried Mike's keen intelligence, which was legend to friends and co-workers. Traveling with his insurance colleague Charlie Moore, the two did puzzle races to kill time on a flight. Mike would often finish his Delta puzzle so fast that Moore half wondered if he'd done it earlier.

Only seven and eight, the boys were especially vulnerable. The youngest was on the cusp of processing it all, and his family worried about the impact on him. Just before a second memorial service when some of McGinty's remains were recovered, Cindy's sister took him to get a card that he could place in his father's casket. As the totality of it smacked her, Susan bawled in the aisle at CVS, then tried to break it off in front of him: "'What do you think of this Snoopy card? Your dad liked Snoopy.' And I remember him looking at me and feeling how surreal it was."

Cindy found a counselor for both boys, and one for herself, plus a social worker for all of them. During the first winter they also joined a support group for 9/11 families, one of the supports Senator Kennedy had a hand in offering. The next spring, Cindy got a new dog for the kids, a bijon they named Zoe.

Before his dad's birthday in July, the youngest son wrote a note for his tribute page:

Dear Beloved Daddy

I miss you, I miss you, I miss you!!! I hope you got my balloon that I sent up to you with my wish. If you got it do you like it, it was silver. You were the best dad ever. I wish you could take me to one more football game. I miss doing all the fun things we used to do and I will think about you on father's day. I will send some more stuff to you with balloons. I cry for you sometimes. Sob, Sob, Cry, Cry.

I love you.

After a year had passed, Cindy brought them both to the recovery site, and her second born seemed to grasp it for the first time. They walked down a ramp into what looked like a crater, laying flowers and cards. At times, she admitted that day, she still felt as if Mike might walk in the back door and say, "Boys, I'm home." But it was real, and she hoped this was the worst it would ever get.

"Now I feel like I can move forward," she told a reporter. "We'll never get over this, but in Mike's honor and memory, I'll raise the boys the way we chose. I'll do that for him."

They went across the street into a building overlooking the World Trade Center, up to a space known as the Family Room reserved for 9/11 relatives. The room became an unofficial shrine where untold hundreds brought their photos and prayer cards, along with homemade posters and fading, rain-smeared missing person's fliers. They taped these to walls and windows, some with spattered streaks of magic markers, others blooming in florid colors, unyielding in a collective cry above a mass grave.

She asked her younger son if he wanted to write something in the family log book. "He was like, 'I-Miss-My-Dad,' as if graduating to some new understanding. Cindy helped him get it out while steadying herself, knowing this could not be about her. Susan Quinlan stood beside her nephews and sister.

"Cindy just held him and said, 'I know, it's so hard,' 'It's not fair,' and 'He was a good dad, and he loves you very much.'"

13

FINDING HER VOICE

. . . .

The moment Cindy McGinty found her voice Ted Kennedy's face went white.

Five weeks after the terrorist attacks, McGinty and several hundred relatives of 9/11 victims packed a room at Boston's Park Plaza Hotel. The goal of the meeting was to get help for 9/11 families and answer their questions. Things like filing for survivors' benefits, transferring mortgages into their names, or getting free in-state tuition for their children. Dozens of thunderstruck widows and widowers surrounded her.

Aides had kept the session private and hidden from the media—"classic Kennedy," one crooned. One side of the stately, high-ceiled Georgian Room was a meet-and-greet with families over coffee and muffins. On another side mini kiosks were readied with forms and pamphlets. One victim's sister played a song on an acoustic guitar before Kennedy offered his condolences. He urged the families to try to get back on their feet, saying that's what their loved ones would want. He introduced representatives of more than two dozen agencies, from a bankers group to the IRS and the United Way, a phalanx of suits touting their services. They took questions on a big stage.

Cindy felt like a zombie. She knew that her husband of ten years was gone, but Mike's body had not been recovered. Still, the insurance carrier wanted a death certificate before benefits would start, and the bills were already mounting. Worst of all, her oldest son was not yet receiving the help he needed. She was frustrated from filling out endless forms. Cindy shifted uncomfortably in her seat.

She'd heard too much talk. She raised her hand and stood up.

"My name is Cindy McGinty and I just have to say I can barely get out of bed in the morning and I have a seven and an eight-year-old boy. I'm totally traumatized and I can barely put one foot in front of the other. And I know you all say you're helping us, but you're not—you're getting in our way." Applause broke out around her. She addressed Kennedy: "This is great that you have all these people here, but what happens tomorrow, when I have to call this agency, and I have to call them ten times?"

Kennedy listened and thanked her. He turned around on the dais and told the officials that if they had to receive a second call from any of the families, the next call would be from him. A lot of people looked at their shoes, but they got the message.

Up to that day McGinty thought of herself as a "little mouse" who'd never so much as taken a high school speech class. She'd never even ridden the train into Boston, so the night before she memorized the number of stops to the subway station near the hotel. Yet as she rose from her seat in the conference room, she recalled, "Right then and there I realized I have this job to do. That's the day I realized it was bigger than just me." She has no regrets.

Leaving the room, Kennedy closed in on his constituent outreach director in what Steve Kerrigan calls "my almost-broken-elbow moment." The senator told Kerrigan that what he had heard was intolerable. He emphasized the point to two other aides as they walked toward his car before he caught a flight to Washington. Turning, Kennedy stopped and looked the three of them in the eyes. "I don't ever want to hear again that Mrs. McGinty or any of the people in this room ever have another problem like this. Fix it, and fix it fast."

Before returning to work, Kerrigan and his colleagues, Scott Fay and Tom Crohan, huddled with members of the state's victims assistance unit from the attorney general's office. Their boss had also instructed them to "get these people helpers," by which they knew Kennedy meant counselors and social workers. The advocates hesitated at the first mention of creating a program, but the three pressed and inserted their mission into a training session that was scheduled for grief counselors. The goal was clear: recruit experts to pair with the families, and provide resources to address all the issues they faced. As they brought this vision to workers at the state Department of Mental Health, Crohan, who was fresh out of college, says Kennedy instructed them to provide "true service, not red-tape service, streamline, and make one phone call." They went to work coordinating a prototype of advocates—therapists, and later, lawyers and others—assigned to 206 grieving Massachusetts families, the eventual number of those in the Bay State connected to 9/11 victims.

This meant cross-training social workers in the mechanisms of other agencies to better assist the families' complex needs, and extending that approach so that a financial planner who heard a widower break down on the phone would know how to talk him through. "One thing when Cindy stood up," says Kerrigan, "it showed us we clearly weren't done. That moment was the ultimate reminder of how vulnerable people can be, how strong they could be, and from our end of the table, what service should be about. What they needed was a clearinghouse, a resource of information." From that point on, when a 9/11 family had an urgent matter, one of the three often took the call.

Kennedy's staff later helped connect the McGintys and other families to a support group just for the children of 9/11 victims and surviving spouses. Drawing upon the experience of grief "circle" groups facilitated by the Good Grief Program at Boston Medical Center, groups were organized around family relationships—gathering younger children together, older siblings, and parents, with a goal of bridging their isolation and helping them build coping skills.

Like McGinty's sons, most of the other kids were the only ones in their school suffering in such a way. The biweekly sessions began with each of the families gathering to express a memory of a loved one: lighting a candle, placing flowers, or a rock, and often saying his or her name. Young children did activities to build memory bonds and demonstrate their competency in grasping and recalling what had happened. Older ones were encouraged to write acrostic poems and construct scream boxes, even filling "power boxes" with their solutions to, "What do I do when I'm feeling bad?" Cindy learned strategies to help her kids rebound, how to anticipate the expressions of grief as each reached a new stage, and prepare for the inevitable triggers: hanging Christmas ornaments, the anniversaries, or a bombardment of images of war.

The sessions often ended with children expressing a memory, perhaps recalling their dad's favorite snack, or thinking of a different way to connect. It might be attaching notes to a balloon and setting it free at a ball field where Dad pitched batting practice, or walking a beach during the winter to vent into the gusts. The groups met this way for three years, scaling back to once a month through 2006, with some families continuing to gather for holiday parties and commemorations during the following years.

While Kennedy's personal touch and unflagging empathy affected her, Cindy was deeply moved by something else that felt more powerful and vast, yet instantly familiar. It had begun with her neighbors and total strangers stepping in to help. Looking at other communities, she observed people giving service, including young adults saying they had joined the military because of the 9/11 attacks. She wanted to give back. Along with other widows and parents, she adopted the "pay it forward" mantra, determined to instill this ethic in her sons.

Over a few years McGinty became a voice for frustrated and depressed families. She started by advising the Massachusetts 9/11 Fund, a group that developed from a network of advocates to assist survivors with their financial struggles and other needs. Besides needing cash, many relatives asked for one-on-one help with emotionally charged and technical matters like doing taxes and estate planning. In 2002, family members, led by an attorney who had represented scores of molestation survivors in the clergy sex abuse scandal, suggested creating one entity to provide those services.

During a decade the 9/11 fund would reach about 350 families, filling in many gaps and helping relatives to also focus on legacy, education, and proper oversight of commemorative events. Their needs pressed on: federal funding lapsed for community mental health supports, charities like the Red Cross had distributed money and withdrawn, and families who felt disconnected to other 9/11 groups sought a champion. "They were still in a crisis or shock mode, even a few years after, because of the horrific nature of the attacks," says Diane Nealon, a licensed social worker who became the group's executive director in 2004. For some, the reminders and thorny logistical issues had protracted their grieving.

A few times when Cindy's oldest son returned home from a private school, the group arranged for a social worker to give her some hours of respite. In return, meeting other widows and expressing their grievances before the 9/11 fund's board, McGinty sensed that the lessons being learned could be applied elsewhere.

Something much bigger was at work. Cindy met Christie Coombs, who had dropped her husband off at the commuter rail station that late summer morning to leave for a business conference in California. Jeffrey Coombs was aboard Flight 11, and an outpouring of support followed in their hometown, similar to what coursed through Long Island's hamlets, on the narrow Rockaway peninsula in Queens, across the tri-states and into the countryside beyond the capital's beltway. Chords and gestures that will never be severed, invisible to the unknowing, connecting Coombs to Cindy McGinty and Jay Winuk and thousands of others.

Along with Christie, Cindy met people taking steps to find meaning amidst their pain. A retired teacher honored her daughter in part by supporting a local YMCA's efforts to include more special needs children in its youth programs. A nurse who lost her brother began speaking to eighth graders on the anniversary. A selectwoman in a nearby town attempted to bring Palestinian and Israeli children together for a dialogue, while two wives met with Afghan women to support microbusinesses in that region.

Like Coombs, McGinty pivoted to support military families as well. As the wars in Iraq and Afghanistan ground on, awareness in the Bay State grew about the needs of active duty families and children and spouses of the fallen. Both women and several others hooked up again with Kerrigan, whose thinking about helping soldiers' families aligned with theirs. They were joined by the parents of an Army private who died in Iraq when his convoy was ambushed while on patrol.

Knowing their burden all too well, Senator Kennedy again worked behind the scenes to make it happen. He and his staffers spent nine months asking veterans groups where the gaps were, as no one wanted to duplicate services. They created a sort of catchall for the families' needs in 2009, the Massachusetts Military Heroes Fund, starting with money left over from a collection for the upkeep of a 9/11 memorial in the Boston Public Garden.

To Coombs, the fund would become a gift of guidance, as she wanted those families to receive what hers had after the attacks.

Renewal came in sudden bursts. One big idea sprang from Christie's oldest daughter, Meaghan, who experienced something terrific as she entered college. On 9/11, students planted a sea of flags outside the student union at Roger Williams University, one for each victim. Meaghan told her mom, "I now know this is the right school for me." Over the phone Christie tried to hold herself together, thinking, "I know she's okay now." They held on to that moment, and when the military heroes group was planning its first Memorial Day event the following year, it dawned on Coombs to include all Massachusetts veterans who had died since World War I—nearly twenty thousand. As people flocked to the Boston Common, helping plant and remove thousands of flags that weekend, a news helicopter shot video, and they were off.

Cindy had another notion around the same time. Why not put together soldiers' care packages on the 9/11 anniversary? She had recently met Paine and Winuk, and her project fit the spirit of what they were trying to spread. A year or so later, scores of volunteers gathered on Boston's Rose Fitzgerald Kennedy Greenway during a similarly brilliant late summer day.

One of them, Beth Stone, might have gone to her nine-year-old's soccer practice or lingered at the beach that September 11. Instead, both she and her son, Cam, helped with the soldiers' packages. Her husband had a friend, a municipal bond broker, who died in one of the towers. And while honoring his life, Stone also wanted those serving abroad to know that people at home remember and value them. "I think events like this are turning it into something more, something positive," she told me. "To send lip balms and sunscreen, that seems like a no-brainer." After she and Cam each filled about a dozen Priority Mail boxes, she wrote a few short notes to update soldiers on the weather and the demise of the Red Sox.

Nearby, a father watching his son dash through a water fountain told me that he had seen the Pentagon burning from his office, a sight he could not forget. Helping out alongside City Year volunteers and office workers, Angel Roque, a twenty-something from Florida, said his stepfather had served in the first Gulf War. "It's my way of showing respect for him and also showing it for the people in Iraq right now," he said.

Christie Coombs came through the packing line with the governor and the attorney general, but seemed to relish most finding some down time to fill boxes on her own. Kerrigan told the crowd, "This is our way of taking back 9/11 with a day of service."

If Chris Mitchell ever doubts why he volunteers, all he needs to do is head uptown to Spoodles Soup Factory for coffee. Undoubtedly he'll run into somebody in Foxborough who will remind him.

Mitchell owned a landscaping company for many years, and his work ran the gambit from lawns to patios. He's got an eye for design and managed to keep two or three guys working for him when the economy stalled. His wife, Paula, worked evenings waitressing at a nearby 99 Restaurant, a job she had held for two decades as they raised four children.

Chris had long been a scoutmaster of Pack 70 and had known Mike and the McGinty boys for less than a year when the hijackers struck. He was putting in a lawn, and the next day was working five houses away from theirs. One of the sons' den leaders called to tell him Mike McGinty was in one of the towers. Mitchell felt compelled to act.

Cindy looked out her window and saw Mitchell cutting the lawn with a helper. He continued mowing it for eight years, and when she offered to pay, he'd say, "It's just something I do." The following spring he reseeded her yard and planted new nursery stock, even bringing in a tree service to prune limbs that were threatening the house. He grabbed her sons, telling them, "Go tell your mother, happy Mother's Day." Like a mini home makeover crew, Chris showed up one Saturday morning and built her a concrete walk.

This, too, was just the start of something bigger. As years went by, Chris and Paula got stirred up enough to organize cleanups and other service projects around town. They created a group called Foxboro Never Forgets, spearheading a drive to construct a granite memorial in time for the tenth anniversary. Located beside the public safety building, the small park has obelisk replicas of the Twin Towers and thought-provoking inscriptions that describe the day and pay respect to the many first responders. It is a first-class tribute, surpassing what might be considered an earnest effort by a town of about seventeen thousand. Along the way it transformed Mitchell's gift to the McGintys into one town's active and lasting remembrance.

For all this to happen, the burly contractor first had to get really ticked off.

Before the eighth anniversary of September 11, Cindy invited Chris to New York with her. Along with the two Massachusetts' groups she was involved with, McGinty was also helping out MyGoodDeed, the nonprofit Jay Winuk had cofounded. When Jay and David contributed to a high-profile event promoting community service, they asked Cindy to speak about homegrown volunteerism. One of the Mitchell's sons, Patrick, was just starting as a cadet at West Point that fall, and his parents were driving down to see a football game that weekend. "The speech is going to be about you," McGinty told them. Chris would rather avoid any spotlight, but he deferred and agreed to go.

On the morning of the anniversary he went out for coffee. What he didn't see bothered him. "It was 9/11 and no flags were flying in Foxborough. I told Paula, 'This is wrong.'" As a scoutmaster, he vowed that next year his troop would at least hold flags on the town common just across the way from Spoodles. It was the same in Manhattan; he didn't see flags there either, except for a few blocks around Ground Zero. "It was just like any other day, and that was strange," he says.

Inside the Beacon Theatre that evening, McGinty lauded Mitchell for his simple, unflinching response to her husband's loss, which she said had inspired her to do more. He received a standing ovation from celebrities and a very tall man approached Chris calling him a hero. When Mitchell later read the business card handed to him, he found it was the mayor of Sacramento, former NBA star Kevin Johnson.

This was all a bit much. Chris is a guy in a fading West Point T-shirt who'd rather just go do stuff and then relax with a Lite beer. "As we were there I was thinking about plans in Foxborough," he smirked. But he learned to promote his cause and play the media as needed. He already had a healthy habit of making stealth donations—including maintaining a lawn for an active duty National Guardsman—and Chris half-kids that he hid some of this from Paula. A few years earlier he helped plant a memorial garden in memory of a young girl who was hit by a truck on her bike, getting a tree and materials donated at cost.

Chris and Paula wanted to encourage people to remember, a feeling reinforced by their son's military commitment. He recalled the sweeping patriotism in town and going to 9:00 a.m. Mass each day that week noticing that the pews were filled. He met with the police and fire chiefs and school superintendent, telling them he wanted to do something in town, but he didn't know exactly what.

Perhaps call it java serendipity, but his urgings were soon boosted by connections made at Spoodles. One idea was bringing back the McGinty Family Fun Day, which Cindy and her friends had established to benefit a memorial scholarship in Mike's memory. It awards up to $5,000 for graduates pursuing a career with a public service component, and it was pure Mike: a dunk tank, kids' face painting, balloon animals and a bouncy tent. The event had lapsed when Cindy moved back to Connecticut. Mitchell happened to come in for coffee and met the treasurer of the family fun day, who was about to close the bank account. He suggested re-establishing it as a community day with service projects, and she agreed. But he didn't want to try running something like a town-wide cleanup himself.

The Mitchells began writing one of their many yellow legal pad lists. They noted all the organizations and nonprofits in town, from the Knights of Columbus to the PTOs. Out for coffee once again, he ran into two women who had helped with the fun day, and they quickly embraced the idea of expanding its scope. "That's what kind of made me feel like this is fate. This is what I'm meant to do," Chris says. He gathered the groups, forty or fifty people, together in a room to make his pitch. Support grew, and in their first year more than 130 people did morning projects before games resumed on the town common.

Chris also got going on the memorial itself. A selectman who is a tax attorney helped the Mitchells form a nonprofit, and high school students designed a logo. Someone created a web site, someone else took care of Facebook, and by 2010 Foxborough Never Forgets was officially underway. Paula, not normally a computer person, learned how to do mail merge and spreadsheets. A friend who owns a monument company took Mitchell's design ideas and ran with them. The couple's main thought was to educate and inspire. "We didn't want it to be about Mike," Chris says, "but about all that happened on 9/11."

They both chuckle looking back on it—"How did we spend the holidays?"—but heading up the project exacted a toll at times. When bids came in, the initial estimates doubled to as much as $150,000, and Chris had to use less solid granite and a stamped concrete walkway. The core design would endure: a walkway the family saw at West Point with pillars depicting famous battles; bronze medallions bearing the emblems of all the first responders; and three granite benches flanking the two towers, seven feet by two feet, lighted by beacons only on the anniversary. "Not a walk through," Paula says. "A tranquil, reflective place where you can stop."

"I want it so when my granddaughter walks through there with her kindergarten class she can understand what happened," Chris says.

Since Foxborough is home to the New England Patriots, a few locals suggested that Chris's group should turn to a familiar deep pocket, Patriots' owner Robert Kraft. But while the team donated a package including executive suite seats to be raffled off, that was a nonstarter for Mitchell. He wanted to get more of his neighbors involved, like a guy driving behind him who beeps and beeps until Chris stops to sell him a bumper sticker, or the custodian at Saint Mary's. A July Fourth road race raised five hundred dollars. Their first donation came anonymously in the mail, a ten-dollar bill with a note: "God bless you." Using his contacts and business suppliers, Chris arranged many in-kind donations. Still, he says, "I'd much rather just go do it than tell anyone about it. That's why this is killing me."

While she's still blown away by their kindness, Cindy always makes it a point to express with a broader brush what the Mitchells did. "What Chris got was, he got the importance of teaching and remembering. He got the importance of service and a call to action," she says.

She circles back: "I think I had to move to get him to stop cutting the grass."

When the former naval officer introduced himself to Paul Sangree, the pastoral candidate at Bethany Congregational Church sensed an intimidating presence. But as a member of his church's search committee, Mike McGinty asked good questions and his warmth soon came through. Reverend Sangree joined the parish early in 2001 and recalls McGinty being very supportive during the transition. Mike voted for him, Sangree recalled Cindy confiding to him, because "he sensed that I loved God, and he also did—not in a fake or surreal way, but it was real. Apart from all his theology or other projects in church, that's what it was all about."

Faith was essential, and despite his workload Mike made no excuses. He found time to exercise it. He became a confirmation mentor, deploying his organizational skills to prepare retreats and pair confirmands with the proper adults. He and Cindy stewarded the couples group, five pairs who became close. Even there, Sangree recalls, one of Mike's objectives was to prepare the next round of leaders. After being in the military, his passion was "building up people on a small stage like this. That's just where his heart was." He soared as a deacon, decisive in a way that could temporarily overwhelm some, but soon he'd establish their trust and friendship. He brought his sons with him to serve communion to shut-ins in their homes.

During the interim before a new minister was called, McGinty had a quandary when he was penciled in to pitch-preach. He called Dan McGarvey for some advice on how to connect with his audience. Dan did not envy the task, thinking this might be Mike's toughest public speaking assignment ever. He assured Mike that everyone probably wanted to see him do well, and while they wanted to be moved, they'd be rooting for him.

"You don't understand," Mike shot back, suggesting that he was perceived as having played a role in an apparent rift with the former minister.

"Maybe open with humor that will support your message, but don't try to shoehorn it in," McGarvey advised.

What came out was a sermon on the power of prayer, which he opened with a joke that goes something like this: A minister walking through a forest comes across a clearing and a huge bear starts chasing him. The bear catches up with him and as the minister falls to the ground, he says, "Please, Lord, let this bear be a Christian." The bear slides in beside him. Slapping a big paw on the minister's shoulder, he says, "Lord, thank you for the food I'm about to eat."

"It went over well," McGinty reported back.

In the years ahead, although Cindy felt Mike's embrace of faith lingering beside her like a warm ember, some of that feeling eluded her. When they joined the church she was pregnant with her second child, and she and Mike decided to attend a Bible class. This entailed not only doing scripture readings but journeying through the ancient history and geography as well. "We kind of made it our date night, and it really got us on our path," she says. The church was family friendly and Mike plugged in, which was supplemented by long talks with his friend Charlie Moore on their business trips. "He could tap into that intellectual side because the answers aren't always there, you have to dig deeper for it," Cindy recalls. "It just really did a lot for him. I think he found a lot of peace there."

She hasn't quite found the same thing for herself since his death. Cindy comes across as something of a minimalist, moderate in her expressions, having learned to cut right to the chase in much of what she perceives, and in most everything she does. She may have once appeared slight, but her eyes are steady and bore in with a verve that grabbed Senator Kennedy.

"My faith, I still carry it but it's evolved a little more. I'm struggling a little more," she told me a decade after losing Mike. "I'm more lazy in my faith, I think—I'm a little madder at God." Saying this, her voice strained in a high, self-critical pitch. "I wish I wasn't, but I haven't quite found the church home here that I had in Foxborough. I haven't found that same peace anywhere else."

One Saturday on the cusp of summer Denise and I began doing something for our son, hosting a co-ed soccer tournament behind the high school. We had established a memorial scholarship from which we give grants to both a guy and a girl who played varsity and shared Mike's passion for the game. We lean toward helping seniors who have struggled a bit academically like he had or face other challenges. While supporting the endowment, the tournament also gave players of both genders a chance to battle together, which is unusual at their age.

Although truly bittersweet, starting a scholarship seemed to be one of the few things that made any sense to us.

I began to almost relish the morning of the tourney, anticipating what quickly became a day of reunion. By mid-June we could expect sweltering humidity. My strawberries had usually just peaked and a succulent fragrance of viburnum flooding our yard was being replaced by a waft of drying white pines. The night before, I met Mike's former coach as he prepared to line the shortened field for our six-on-six matches, often with his oldest son—another future player—tagging along.

Jeff Doyle ran a business installing wood floors, and he organized the tournament brackets and gave the players instructions. He always seemed eager to help us, and as if sensing the load on my shoulders, told me he was fine to finish the preparations himself before I left him rolling a field striper in the gathering dusk. When I returned with a first load of coolers and gear the next day, the field was just as still with the dew beginning to burn off. I paused for a moment, scanning empty playing fields that were about to be transformed.

Within an hour or two our friends and family members were unloading tables, cases of water, soda, and raffle gifts as some of us dragged the goal frames over, hung nets, or relearned how to set up our tents. We had T-shirts printed with Mike's varsity number, "Brack 3," in a vibrant span of colors: lime green and hot pink to brown and gold. Soon Grampa Carroll was cooking burgers and dogs over a rusted oil drum grill with his friend, Merritt, a shellfish warden in Bourne who had welded the grill with his son. Another committee with other moms did the heavy logistical lifting, and they gathered in the shade with green tournament aprons and wearing large buttons with our son's image.

Regardless of the forecast, the rain always held off for Mike.

His buddies and many of the girls they hung out with and dated were all there, forming teams with names like "2 Legit to Quit," "Aches and Pains," and "Buccaneer's Pride." At least one year, Mike's cadre all joined his pal Jeff Walsh's team. Others were formed by guys like the Teich brothers, who had lost both their parents as teen-agers, and a group of Denise's colleagues from her elementary school in a neighboring town. Soon our son Chris formed his own "Brack Attack" squad, who met my "Over the Hill Gang" in a feisty match one year—my team often included my dad and Mike's uncles, an aunt, and nieces and nephews—Chris and I entangling as he drove to the net in a highlight-frame set. Most of us worked off some rust, and Mike's old teammates rekindled glory days with their volleys and chips and feints. Others dug out balls, cursing and laughing simultaneously with their mates as if in testimony to him.

As his mom and I greeted his friends along with newcomers and parents we had met alongside other fields, we felt something else at work. There were good-natured skirmishes in competitive matches, especially into the final sets. But as these young adults and teens stretched together on the grass in between games, their conversations and cajoling settling down with the day's heat, more than once I caught myself wondering, *what had we initiated here?*

They stepped out of busy routines to catch up. They paused to remember. They kept showing up. For Mike, for us, and for each other.

We saw his friends growing up, hearing about new jobs and a few exploits, and meeting female friends whose names we had missed. Catching each other alone beside a tent, she and I restrained the brief tear in our voices.

That first Saturday was overcast and warm. It felt good running the field to clear my nerves after lacing up. I think I misplayed two opportunities to score with my head on nice crosses—but none of that mattered. We felt moved by everyone who came out: many of his classmates and graduating seniors, including four varsity players whom we gave the initial scholarships to—two guys and two girls. Our close friends' youngest son, Patrick, took over emceeing and was an instant hit. While I can't recall exactly what we both said during opening remarks, standing close enough to catch one another if needed, we knew this was the start of an extraordinary day.

Connections flowed. Some years there were seventeen or eighteen teams. P.J.'s mom and his sister Mary often stopped by, soon with Mary's young sons. By 2008, while technically underage, our niece McKenzie and nephew Sam both jumped in for my team and did really well, each carrying a piece of their oldest cousin's spirit. Twice a group of students from my school in Dorchester formed teams, and I felt a surge of joy including them. One year Joey Walsh, Jeff's older brother, made it back from Afghanistan to play. An Army Ranger, he had been emailing home to make sure his brother put him on the team when he returned on leave. Mike's girlfriend Tanya usually came by, and Brendan Carey played several times.

"A celebration of indelible moments," I journaled.

The Teich Brothers team won that first year, with siblings Greg and Ben hosting the trophy late in the mellowing late afternoon light. Before loading the last gear into my truck, I gave the school janitor a tip and looked back at fields that had hummed just a few hours earlier, now matted down, the dust settled again on a baseball infield. A supple breeze swished the tops of some tall pines.

I considered whether some of Mike's energy lingered, and how we might tap into it.

Early in 2011, as if defying a succession of snowstorms that had besieged central Connecticut, the McGintys were upbeat.

Cindy's oldest son had been accepted by his first choice, St. John's College in Santa Fe, where he hoped to study sociology and linguistics. First he anticipated delving into the classics in their original forms, starting with Homer's *The Iliad* the next fall. His brother, who loved photography, was accepted for a service learning trip to Cambodia for three weeks in June, part of a global studies program at his prep school. He had done something similar the previous summer, spending a few weeks in Europe that combined service projects with sightseeing. Topping it off, Mike's sister, Erin, had moved to Santa Fe and would soon be seeing her nephew regularly.

In Cindy's eyes, her oldest had clearly turned the corner and begun to reconcile his sometimes remote, close-to-the-vest manner. Bringing him home from school one day, Cindy felt that she was driving with a young man. She glowed when another adult there told her, "Thanks for sharing him with me." Of course, raising teenagers is a seesaw, and new challenges would soon arise.

Thrust into parenting completely on her own, Cindy had learned a ton about raising sons into young men. Like many of us, she rebounded from her missteps. One was "to get out of his way and accept him for who he is," and let him grow from his own mistakes. "I used to think if I did everything perfectly I could fix him," she told me that winter. "That was just impossible. Every kid has issues, and they have to learn there are consequences for them. Once I was able to do that and allow him to accept consequences, that turned him around. And things changed for me, taking away some of my anxiety." Earlier, her oldest son's school had threatened to suspend him for not getting up in time for class. Once Cindy stopped intervening and he got suspended, he stopped sleeping late.

She did all the right things to nurture the boys. Two keys for her first-born were finding him a Big Brother mentor when he first attended boarding school, and a male counselor he clicked with. His younger brother dealt with it differently, and did not get connected with a strong male mentor. Cindy says he sometimes coped as if trying to backfill a trench. In a basement bathroom, he lined up a variety of Axe body sprays, and one time his mom surmised he must have bought every scent in the brand. "I tried to explain to him, 'That stuff is never going to fill that hole.' It's not big things, it's little things. So we talk about that, and it's kind of our joke. Okay, what are you going to fill the hole with this week?'"

For Deborah Rivlin, what Cindy and her sons went through reinforces a metaphor she expresses in her work helping children and families who cope with loss: a braid of remembrance and renewal that's woven together. Rivlin is an educator and counselor—not a licensed therapist—who led a support group for 9/11 families including the McGintys, helping them especially to develop key coping skills: understanding, grieving, commemorating, and going on.

Not forgetting, not necessarily "moving on," but piecing together their loss with everything else.

"How do you remember your loved one as you go on?" Rivlin asks. "It's not, are you grieving? Or are you okay? It's a braid. It's integrating your grief with your life. There is no closure, since loss is forever."

Rivlin recalls another widow grappling with the what-ifs in that elusive chase to change what happened. Her husband might have traveled a week before September 11, but their son was starting kindergarten seven days earlier, so dad stayed home. "'What if I had told him to go on the fourth— he'd still be here,'" the woman told Rivlin. Many kids the same age and makeup as Cindy's older son did some magical thinking of their own. Being early abstract thinkers, they knew that death was final, and might see it as a punishment for bad behavior. They worried how their world would change. A few even plotted revenge.

Rivlin, who through 2017 assisted families at The Children's Room, a bereavement center in Arlington, Massachusetts, continued with her 9/11 group for many years. While the sibling groups kept meeting, the adults got together occasionally over lunch or dinner for what she calls "stealth therapy." She's still warmed by how many widows emerged as role models to make the world a better place. "When your assumptive world is shattered, you can either crawl up in a ball and say, 'Why did this happen?' or you can reframe it into an opportunity," she offers. "There is incredible opportunity in crisis. That is the posttraumatic growth."

Not everyone can unfurl that ball, at least not for a long while, perhaps over many years. Cindy continued getting up for everyone else. Like some of the other spouses, she often felt she was doing what was expected of her. Allowing herself a moment to peer into her soul, Cindy knew *that's what he'd want for me.*

She had her down moments. Routine ones like taking out the trash, which she knew was *his job,* and catching glimpses of when Mike's absence hurt the boys so much. *He should have been there* while they learned to shave. Beaming at their oldest son's graduation. Their final Saturday night together with him, camped out in the sunroom, "No girls allowed." Mouths agape as he read of Gandolf and Sauron's tower on the couch. "I feel bad for them because I can't be a dad for them," she says. "I feel they will never be the people they should have been, and that was taken from them."

Yet within minutes in the same conversation, Cindy is able to light up at the memory of their marriage, transmitting a palpable joy that has not dimmed. "I had it for ten years," she says. "I feel like I had this great gift." And there are times when she senses Mike's presence.

One really hard day back in Foxborough, Cindy called to Mike: *I can't find you right now!* She went out on the front porch and received what she, like many of us whose lives have been uprooted by loss, consider to be a sign from her loved one: Dragonflies.

Zigzagging by in translucent blues and greens. She often sees them solo or in a pair. In that moment, perhaps one hundred of them showed up.

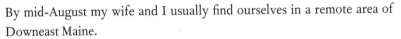

By mid-August my wife and I usually find ourselves in a remote area of Downeast Maine.

Our family has a cottage overlooking Machias Bay, where there's plenty of hiking, rolling fog banks, and large birds of prey around. In this part of hardscrabble Washington County, many locals get by with a rotation of lobstering, digging clams, raking blueberries or working other on-and-off-again jobs like processing salmon and wreath-making. Visitors like us gain an appreciation for their gritty self-reliance while sharing in the solitude the bay provides. There is early first light and a convergence with tide time.

It is also one of those thin places with luminous boundaries between the earth and spirit world, where communication with the divine is possible when one is centered and still beside the fast-flowing tide. On a calm day, pliant clouds inch along as if reflecting a line of canoes paddled by ancestors of the Passamaquoddy tribe, who made their summer camps in fields beside abundant mudflats.

My parents first discovered a healing energy here when I was a teenager. This is where they recharged, both from work and their commitment to each other. On her frequent sojourns to Machiasport with friends, my mom went further to develop her own spirituality, later gathering in those who loved her to face the disease that cut short her life. She named the camp "Little Respite," and Denise and I have been drawn back there since we first met, setting Mike in his car seat aboard my Chevy stepside truck in those earliest trips. It's an ongoing connection that I hope to appreciate in full someday.

Our kids have always loved coming up, and still do. We took long beach walks, the dog following them over steep ledges, which I imagined glaciers once scarring and compressing. We hiked upland trails dense with a cool wash of balsam firs, noticing clusters of scarlet Bunchberry along the sides and the scat of porcupine and deer. Occasionally someone waded in with me over a stretch of smoothened gravel for a quick swim in the cold water. We read for hours out on the little deck, fooling around while the kids napped, and the girls took showers outside as the boys dug clams or cut a trail. Around the fire, I made up stories about a Captain John Holmes and his brother, Asa, who lived just down the coast, with ghosts in caves and small whales leading them back during storms.

When Mike was probably three, I showed him how to safely scale the rocks, finding handholds and positioning his weight so as not to slip on the rockweed at low tide. Finding a tough driftwood stick, he batted small stones into the water until we told him to stop.

Late one night he woke up to pee and saw something moving in the toilet bowl. He came upstairs to Denise, shaking her awake.

"Mom, there's a bat in the toilet," he said.

"Go back to sleep, Mike."

"There really is."

They fished the little guy out, sliding him into a box and washing him off. Mike placed the bat outside to dry. Later that morning our kids saw him take off.

His mother recalled the tale many times with her children in class starting their unit on bats. Doing so became a blend of longing and relief, relief that the memory reminded her to smile. She gave herself permission to pass it on in a new way.

Our stories were both countless and numbered, many routed in our sense of this place.

Two summers after Mike's death he contacted the four of us at Little Respite. After finishing our usual round of gin rummy one night at the kitchen table—Amanda may have won, since like her oldest brother, she's kind of an unflinching card shark—I was the last one up. Blowing out a candle, I headed upstairs to the loft.

Denise woke up sometime just after 2:00 a.m. in the pitch-dark loft as a glare reflected from downstairs off a skylight. Looking down she saw that the candle was lit. At first, we reacted rationally: Was there any way it didn't go out when I thought it had? Could the wick have retained just enough spark to re-ignite? Did I have one too many?

We came downstairs and accepted the possibility that this didn't have to make sense. We checked the clock above the refrigerator, which I usually turn facing away from the room when we arrive; it was the time of the car crash.

What was rational anyway, what good had that thinking and living brought us? Was it logical that a fifteen-year-old should help carry his older brother's casket? What was the point in a guy who thought of himself as Mike's best friend not to slow down when others yelled at him to do just that? All of that had been obliterated.

Mike clearly spoke to us, directly for the first time: *I'm here. I'm so glad you're in Machias together! I am here with you.*

We realized that it was the 15th of August, exactly twenty-one months out. She and I began to embrace the reality of staying connected with him.

A few months before the tenth anniversary of 9/11, the world threatened to steamroll Cindy again.

Helping to plan service events and family supports for the approaching remembrances, McGinty felt the pieces congealing. MyGoodDeed and other large charities were coordinating projects across the country. She flew to Washington twice for meetings along with Winuk and Paine, finding support from politicians of every stripe. She met a freshman congressman from Minnesota who'd been in the same Plebe brigade as Mike at the Naval Academy, and the lawmaker threw in his support for a 9/11 day.

At home she dealt with more tough stuff that had been festering largely out of view. She had surgery for a bad knee and began grueling physical therapy in March. Her youngest was acting fully as a self-absorbed seventeen-year-old, which, while not a surprise, came with a flurry of troubling signs: she didn't trust the guys he hung out with, risky driving, plummeting grades—and she suspected something else. Then in April, the Justice Department announced it would prosecute accused 9/11 mastermind Khalid Shaikh Mohammed before a military commission rather than in criminal court. The reversal stunned many families who had felt strafed by the arduous process. It was only the first bombshell of the season.

The Obama Administration's switch threw her for a loop. Compared to the previous spring, "this year I feel like I'm in a really crappy place," she said one morning sitting on her living room couch. The prospect of having to relive those events during a trial amounted to an approaching tempest, imperceptible to most people on the outside. "I really didn't care one way or another" whether to use a civilian or military trial, she told me. "I just want it done with. Why couldn't we have done something eight years ago and be done with him? I'm ticked off about that, and I feel like people do not understand what that means." Cindy paused and let go a few tears that had welled up. "I feel like my whole family does not understand what that means."

"Even some people look at you and they say, 'It's been ten years, get on with your life.' But we're going to have to relive it again. People ask why, but you say if it was your loved one and the person who killed them went to trial, would you go?"

Her therapist suggested that at some point Cindy would be unable to talk about this anymore. She knew all the issues by heart, and most of them had not changed. Many years later, as the charade of justice at Guantánamo Bay slogged on with Khalid Shaikh Mohammed still awaiting trial in 2016, the black cloud hadn't quite dispersed. "How can you get ready for that?" she asked about the trial. "I don't know if you can. I just get tired walking around and pretending I'm normal."

For anyone still wondering why the teenage sons and daughters of 9/11 victims could be markedly caustic and remote, consider their seething resentment as well: By 2011, her sons were eighteen and seventeen, on the cusp of starting their lives as young men. "That's how long they had to wait for justice?" their mom asked. "That to me is unconscionable."

Then late on a Sunday night that May, President Obama announced that a Navy SEALs team had killed Osama bin Laden in Pakistan. Sue Quinlan called her sister again after learning about it from her son who'd been on Facebook. Cindy's oldest was away at school and his brother was asleep at home. But by seven thirty the next morning he'd already been tweeted. Cindy went numb as she switched on the news. "Then I felt okay, they got him." During the next twenty-four hours she veered from tears to a despair that justice still felt elusive, answering phones and emails, calling both boys' schools, and huddling with her youngest when he got home.

She felt empty.

Bin Laden's demise didn't bring any peace. "Nothing changes for us," she offered two days later. "Mike still doesn't come home, he still doesn't have a dad. Even though you expect something to be different, nothing is different.

"It made me let my guard down a little bit, and I didn't understand how exhausted I am. You want it to go away and it can't."

Both sons seemed to dismiss the breakthrough being celebrated in New York and many other cities. Her youngest told her, "I'm fine. I'm going to school." A couple of classmates reached out and said something supportive that he was grateful for. And while he didn't need a hug then, at least he'd let her in on that. She reached his brother at school in New Mexico the next day. He told her he was good, and went back to class.

The media was relentless. A reporter called McGinty at 1:30 a.m., and the next day, both Piers Morgan and Nancy Grace of CNN wanted to send a car and drive Cindy to Gotham for a live appearance. She declined, telling them she had a teenager to take care of.

"I'm tired of people saying I'm strong. I don't want to be strong," she told me. "I'm tired of being a strong woman after a while. I want someone to come in and take it all away, and I know that's not going to happen. So you've got to get up the next morning and be strong." She went back to routines: bringing the dog to the groomer and resuming her work.

She wasn't alone. Bin Laden's death triggered a mix of emotions for other 9/11 families, bringing some relief, but not closure.

One day after the news broke, Celeste Pollicino sat in her history of photography class at Towson University outside of Baltimore. Her hometown is Plainview, New York, and Celeste was twelve when she lost her dad, Steve Pollicino, a bond broker at Cantor Fitzgerald.

Pollicino was a spur-of-the moment guy who might change the ordinary by declaring, "Let's eat out." His gift was making people feel comfortable. He was also a dad who didn't miss many things that mattered to his children, big or small. When Celeste was in middle school, he memorized the school schedule and would call a pay phone near the office between a class, so if she heard that ringing in the hallway, she never second-guessed who it was. Her photography class topic, long on the course syllabus, was the appropriateness of photos showing the "falling man" on 9/11, the restaurant worker who apparently jumped from the tower where her father died. Many of her classmates were living in Maryland then and, like her, were not yet in high school. As their 9/11 stories gushed out, Celeste hung back. "A fly on the wall," she was struck by their responses.

"It was sort of interesting to hear people ten years later who you would think weren't interested at all and hearing how they were attached to it," she said. "When the opportunity was there people just opened up." She didn't speak about her dad, realizing that doing so might alter the mood in the lecture hall. She felt knocked back emotionally, but only briefly, having seen the spotlight on the terrorist leader fading a bit. "It doesn't really change anything for me," she said several days later.

While her own identity growing up was tied to tragedy, Pollicino had learned to deal with it. Through high school she often felt known as "the girl who lost her dad on 9/11," and entering college Celeste began to select whom she would mention this to. She didn't hide it either, continuing to wear a bracelet with her father's name. The anniversary was another mixed bag.

"It feels like it happened yesterday, but when I look back and see how much I've done, it feels like I've lived a totally different life," she told me.

"I just try to keep taking steps in my life and keep moving forward—and then it's there."

Her mom, Jane Pollicino, had been set adrift looking for answers. Like Cindy McGinty, she, too, occasionally glimpsed the ups. Trying to process exactly what had happened, Pollicino was drawn time and again to the official and sometimes conspicuous 9/11 remembrances. Jane read victims' names at the ceremonies and was among the first to compile a living memorial page for her husband. She went on sunset cruises and swapped stories with other widows at luncheons. "I try to never miss an opportunity to honor or give my voice on Steve's behalf," she said. Soon after bin Laden's comeuppance, Pollicino met Obama when he came to lower Manhattan seeking out 9/11 family members.

On the subway in, Jane asked her daughter what she should say to the president. Celeste texted back: Tell him we don't need to see the pictures of the body.

Pollicino told Obama, "I don't know if I agree with her but that's my message for you." She appreciated how comfortable he seemed and his expression about arriving that week "to honor and respect the victims, and to show that we haven't forgotten." She asked Barack Obama one favor and dug into her purse for notepaper—she also has an adult son named after his father—and he wrote: "To Celeste and Steve, We will never forget."

When Cindy McGinty's oldest son was only eight, his feelings about bin Laden were sharp and prescient. He asked his mother, "If Osama bin Laden accepted Jesus Christ as his savior, would he go to heaven?"

That was a tough one, but it did not stump her. Cindy told him that yes, that's what a Christian believes. "And then I told him that because he was so evil I didn't think he had room for God in his heart, and even if he did he'd have to account for what he did."

His dad's friend Charlie Moore remembers this query with great clarity. Moore is a religious man who lives in Nashville, and how to exercise forgiveness came up during his many conversations with Mike about spiritual principles. He considers the question tough and crucial. And he's not sure he's even found the answer. "When you've had friends killed, it's easy to say, I know what I think I'm supposed to do by scripture," he said, "but it's one of those areas I try to leave it in God's hands as much as I can."

Jay Winuk had a chance to address some of those blistering questions publicly that May. He wrote an op-ed piece for CNN and addressed the prospect of finding closure after bin Laden's death:

> It's an understandable question, but the word doesn't apply. Not for me. There is no closure when we cannot ever know what my brother's last minutes on earth were like. Was he in pain? Was he scared? Was he alone? Was he suffering? Anyone who could speak to this, everyone around Glenn that September morning, anyone he tried to save or perhaps had reached out to for help, was murdered along with him.
>
> There is no closure when you get to bury only parts of a lost loved one. Or when the effects of the tragedy permanently ripple through the world our children are inheriting. And there is no closure, it seems clear, for the more than 40 percent of September 11 families who retrieved no remains at all to properly bury. There is gratitude that bin Laden can no longer harm and was brought to justice and for the end of this chapter—but no closure to be found.
>
> I do have hope for a better world. Perhaps we have turned the tide, even just a little. No one knows for sure whether the elimination of this figure of death will result in more or less safety for the innocent people of the world. But I do have hope.

Things came undone for Cindy and her youngest son that June. He cried out for help: speeding around town, lying to her, and outwardly self-medicating. She took away his car.

She'd seen him spiraling out of control for months. Fearing the worst, she took an agonizing step, removing him from the house and sending him to a wilderness therapeutic program. "I was afraid he would hurt someone or hurt himself if he was in charge, and I had to take it back," she told me. "I wanted to stop it before he crashed and burned." She would not see him again for more than two months, until the summer's end, their contact restricted to one letter he wrote her each week. A therapist called her every

Friday, and after an hour-long discussion she wrote a letter back to him. With the anniversary fast approaching by mid-August, Cindy had found a new prep school and was negotiating a start date.

It would have been easy to blame herself, but Cindy knew this was not due to a lack of good parenting. "There's something extra going on," she said. And her son was far from alone among teens who had lost a parent during 9/11 and were acting out. Dr. JoAnn Difede, who saw many families during the following years, noted that children about the same age as Cindy's sons were especially vulnerable. To Difede and others who supported these young people, the torment emerging years later was understandable—and workable.

"A lot of times people assume younger kids are not affected because they don't understand loss, but they actually have more trouble because they didn't and it comes out later," she said. Compounding all this for Cindy was the public perception of 9/11 families' resiliency. Television specials, celebrity-studded galas, and the media onslaught amounted to a hall of mirrors she saw growing more distorted as the months barreled along.

"Everyone paints such a rosy picture, but it's not," McGinty said, the pitch of her voice rising again. "It just kills me because you're not hearing about all the families that are still struggling."

14

9/12

In the months leading up to the tenth anniversary of the terrorist attacks, David Paine and Jay Winuk tended humanity's best organic garden. From the get-go, Paine observed that the notion of honoring the fallen with service had been planted in the nation's soul. "And all we did was water it."

The seedlings they planted for a record day of public service sent out fresh shoots. They partnered with huge umbrella charities like the HandsOn Network to coordinate service projects across the country, and enticed new corporate sponsors to sign on. Firms such as Target and GlaxoSmithKline had chipped in more than $2 million by the spring, American Express gave a lead $1 million gift, and they lined up major media partners. Companies including Viacom—which would create ads for its gigantic window in Times Square—plus Clear Channel and AOL would soon pump in $15 million worth of space for public service announcements. Signature events were planned in California, Washington, D.C., New York, and Boston, along with smaller ones in nearly two dozen local markets.

Most potently, the pair spaded over their promotional campaign with a new brand that emphasized giving tribute. Their revamped social media strategy drew in everyday Joes and hipsters, movie stars and musicians. Paine's youngest son, Eric, jumped aboard, leaving behind his college business classes to help implement the platforms synonymous with his generation. He would play a key role sparking a global buzz on the big weekend via two of MyGoodDeed's primary engines, Facebook and Twitter.

His father also connected with an A-list creative team that included an Oscar-winning film editor, Angus Wall, and Kirk Souder, executive creative director at GOOD Corps. The Los Angeles-based media consulting firm focused on developing sustainable brands and helping companies tie their financial success to social progress. Souder had helped build presidential candidate Obama's social media plan in 2008 and knew a thing or two about why people do altruistic deeds.

Souder's marching orders were to "take all the negative energy that surrounds this day and convert that into positive action. That's about as good as it gets in my perspective," he says. Souder had learned to transform negativity as a teenager after being diagnosed with a rare bone cancer and told he likely had less than three years to live. It spread to his lungs and he underwent treatments for five years, yet he was among the 0.001 percent of those who survive that form of sarcoma. "It shifted the lens of how I looked at my life for more purpose and meaning," he told me. "I wanted to use my craft to improve the planet and other people—having seen my mortality face to face was a blessing—getting through it and make a positive impact while I'm here."

Plunging in, he asked Paine what success on 9/11 would look like. David responded that it would be a million people posting their intentions online to do good deeds, plus perhaps ten million others rolling up their sleeves. To surpass that goal, Souder suggested they shift from focusing on "service" and "volunteering" to "tribute." "People admire those things," he says, "but at same time, there is a part of them that may say, 'That may just be too much for me,' especially when people are so busy." Eric Paine, for one, agreed. "The words 'community service' were always holding us back," he says. "It was more about joining the 9/11 tribute movement."

Two guys on the team boiled the campaign down to two words: "I will . . ." They were rolling again, and everything would flow from that one pronoun and verb.

Edie Lutnick, Jay's former Jericho neighbor, brought another decisive perspective to this framing. During years of slashing through thickets of issues on behalf of the Cantor Fitzgerald families, remembrance had always been the hilt of Lutnick's brush axe. And she wouldn't let David or Jay or any newcomers forget it. Edie, after all, might have been in her North Tower office that morning as well—on the 101st floor.

Her brother Howard had been among the first to initiate a "charity day" for his employees on the first anniversary, analogous to the "one day's pay" concept. All of the firm's revenue on 9/11 continued to replenish the Cantor relief fund, and fifteen years later, its staff was still encouraged to take the day and do service. Joining Winuk's nonprofit, Edie broadened her role as a conscience for the Cantor families to embrace a national day of service. "We were always on the same page," she says.

Lutnick offered suggestions to make sure the remembrance piece remained paramount. Taking a lead from Yad Vashem, the central archive and database of Holocaust victims that encourages visitors to locate intimate portraits, Lutnick felt that people registering their 9/11 service intentions should be able to write about who they were dedicating them to. Or express another motivation. "If you go and paint a house on 9/11, that's great that you're painting a house, but why?" she asks. "Just engaging in charity, there's nothing wrong with that, but as a family member of a victim I want you to know why you are doing that.

"When people ask me what they can do," Lutnick continues, "I always say, pick the name of a 9/11 person, learn something about them, and do an act of kindness that day."

As all of this developed, I caught up with David and Jay one afternoon outside the World Trade Center, their frenetic schedules in step with the urgent pace of construction in 2011. We stood in front of the 9/11 Memorial Preview Site, a storefront with a bookshop and displays of the coming national memorial and museum across the way. A thunderstorm had passed through, and by late afternoon sunshine returned, the early spring air freshening. Paine remarked upon the flowering trees in the Saint Paul's Chapel burial grounds, a sharp contrast to the images of them covered in soot.

"It's an avalanche of activity," he said of his own preparations. "The irony of all this is the press, the intensity of the project is now, and to have it ready between now and really July 15th. It doesn't bother or trouble me."

Paine had endured a horrid nine-and-a half-hour flight from California the previous night and after landing got diverted to a different hotel because his first choice lost power. Having gone to bed around 2:30 a.m., he still appeared no worse for the wear. Talking rapidly, water-smooth, he looked relaxed in a crisp blue jacket and designer jeans. While midsized and physically unimposing, Paine's self-assurance almost seemed to add a few more inches to his stature. "The moral of the story was I didn't really care," he added to finish his travel narrative. "I feel like this is a good thing. It's par for the course. There's so many things worse that could happen than that—it's kind of an adventure."

This typifies Paine's sense of perspective. He'd worked full time almost three years on this, plugging in with big players like the US Chamber of Commerce and the Corporation for National and Community Service. Congressmen made time to meet with him and 9/11 family members.

Yet this was not really about grand gestures, and all the largesse and namedropping didn't seem to faze him. Paine still gravitated to small things: an eight-year-old girl who decides to help her mom clean the house. Such unscripted acts were exactly what he and Jay had hoped Americans would continue doing, equated almost subconsciously with how we remember 9/11, which to them is no different than associating Valentine's Day with an expression of love. "I think the interesting thing about this will be sort of redefining what we mean by paying tribute and doing service," Paine continued as we looked across where steel was being placed at sixty-plus floors in the new 1WTC, no longer called the "Freedom Tower." "It's a day of helping one another and being kind to each other as human beings, where volunteering could be one thing that you do but there are thousands of things you can do."

Many people's distillations of what we learned over the decade would soon be uploaded and consumed: essays and penetrating journalism, documentaries, exhibitions and albums, people gathering to hold hands at Battery Park, commentaries by religious leaders, and ad nauseam. Paine offered his take. One lesson "is the importance of human beings and human life, understanding our most important priorities as people—our family members, friends. You've got to give room for people to decide in a way that they would like to pay tribute in that type of fashion."

As David spoke Jay kept checking his BlackBerry and suggested they break off and get a cab. They were due at a documentary film screening at the Tribeca Film Festival, an event that had been started to help revive the depleted downtown. The film was about city firefighters and volun-teers who help communities across the country impacted by disasters. It featured Jeff Parness, a legend not only in the Upper West Side where he lived but also in places like Harbison Canyon, California, where his charity, New York Says Thank You—also the film's title—conducted good works. Inspired by his son, Evan, who told his father he wanted to send toys to children displaced by wildfires, Parness's group sent volunteers out every September 11 to help rebuild somewhere. It was his way of returning in kind what people did for New Yorkers. Naturally, he had become a friend of Jay's, who showed me a clip looping in the museum preview center with both he and Parness.

The threads connecting people like Parness and Souder to McGinty, Winuk, and Paine continued to resonate with me. One might consider them second responders striving to rekindle our collective good side, whose intentions infuse one another. That summer, MyGoodDeed helped orga-nize a ceremony in Washington for the National 9/11 Flag, the iconic, tat-tered flag that hung from scaffolding and became a focal point for recovery crews. Parness played a role in its recovery. He brought the flag to a Kansas town that had been struck by a tornado, and women at the senior cen-ter began reinforcing it with local flags that had been salvaged from the damage. Later it traveled to all fifty states and would fly in the National September 11 Memorial & Museum.

Earlier that afternoon, Jay brought me to a delicate if not unwieldy place known as the Family Room. This is where Cindy and her sons went on the first anniversary, a space reserved for relatives of the victims over-looking the WTC from the twentieth floor of One Liberty Plaza.

The room served as a shrine sealing in memories and associations. Roughly the size of a large living room, the view outside was mostly obscured, with nearly every inch of wall space covered by photos, notes, and fliers, typed poems and fading newsprint, poster boards with recol-lections scrawled both shakily and with sweeping flourishes. A small play area for kids still had a Little Tykes picnic bench and Pooh Bear table. I found two books left on one of the vinyl couches—a collection of Haiku left by a dad from Japan, and a book of remembrance dedicated to sixty-seven colleagues who died at the investment banking firm Keefe, Bruyette and Woods.

Jay and I were alone, and he pointed to Glenn's black and white missing person's flier on one of the windows. A second color picture of him had fallen to the carpet, and he taped it back up. "This room is something that has organically grown over the years, especially the early years," he told me. "There's probably not another room quite like it anywhere in the world."

One task of a committee of family members working with the National September 11 Memorial & Museum was to replicate the family room at the museum. Jay, a member of the committee helping to steer this transition, didn't quite yet know how they would accomplish that. Ultimately the museum encouraged victims' families to bring in new photos and artifacts for a new space rather than transferring the mementos. Original items were archived at a museum in Albany.

As Jay ushered me through, I caught another glimpse of this man. He is a gentle soul with a trimmed russet beard. Somehow he seemed equipped to carry such a large burden with a grace that no doubt had been tested, but appeared to be untainted. I felt an immense privacy in this moment, beside him in such a torqued and sacred place. "There's stuff here that stretches back nine-plus years," he said in a voice that was scratchy and pious, and orderly. "At some point it has to go to its appropriate home."

Three people entered as we were about to leave, an older couple and a woman perhaps in her forties. Winuk introduced himself. The older woman said they hadn't come up in years—her son had worked at Cantor Fitzgerald. They quickly found his photo, and we made our leave.

The idea was hers from the get-go. Where could families go for help after losing a child that was not in a clinical setting, surrounded by those who understand?

Could we create such a place?

Though laden with the weight of missing Mike, my wife remained alert to the possibilities as we began looking. Denise envisioned providing a resource center and a space where grieving families could get together.

Facing what felt like an unscalable wall following the car crash, we had not come across any such place. We had no clue what to even look for.

She considered attending a Compassionate Friends meeting, where a few dozen people in a room rotate telling their stories, but the location was too far from home. We brought our kids to a few family sessions with a therapist. They continued meeting separately with one for a while, with Chris seeing a gifted counselor who later became one of my wife's colleagues. Amanda also checked in with a school guidance counselor and for a while saw the same therapist as Denise, but her main release came from drawing portraits up in her room for hours on end. What emerged were angular, wild-haired teens in fantastical scenes.

Having counselors was one option Denise wanted to offer parents. Perhaps most vitally for others, she considered starting peer-led support groups where adults would benefit from being with others walking a similar road. For some, it might be a place to find help with logistical issues before figuring out bigger stuff: What will those first months be like? How do I get through the holidays? How do I react when people expect me to move on? What can I do if my husband shuts down, or my son starts acting out?

What did you do?

Or in the absence of answers, at least a space to vent, and hear what others have tried.

She knew it was crucial to establish a safe, confidential setting. A room without judgment where you can tear up, or pass from speaking. A retreat from acquaintances who are unequipped to understand or express empathy, and a sanctuary from public places you suddenly dread—the supermarket or post office—for fear of running into another soccer mom or a neighbor.

It would house the god-awful club that no adult ever applies for. Among those who need to know—led by others who recognize—that their feelings and setbacks are normal.

While Denise had long worked with six- and seven-year-olds, her dealings with their parents had been among the most demanding, and alternately, deeply rewarding, tasks of teaching. Now she focused on helping the adults first. She realized that parents could not adequately help their children without taking care of themselves—a void both of us had somewhat glossed over early on as we jumped back into work, with me heading into a new career. Meaningful resources for parents were scarce.

Starting support groups was a natural extension of her skills as a teacher.

After all, the best teachers *are* facilitators. They set the stage, the structure and tone, scaffold the lesson, and get kids to engage. As things start humming, they get out of the way.

When Denise sat in IEP meetings alongside parents with a special-needs child, she learned to scan others' reactions when someone was speaking. If mom's eyes were rolling and her fists clenched, Denise knew it was time for the team to let her speak. She bristled inside when a specialist monopolized their session, or others yakked on too long. In the classroom she scanned her charges as well, aware of who was speaking while paying attention to the whole group. Facilitating a cluster of parents who've lost a child, a partner, or spouse would mean being a familiar conductor in a new setting. The nuances of each group and its chemistry, and whether those facing distinctive losses such as from suicide would benefit most by having their own groups, soon came into play.

She had always done what was expected of her. As the oldest daughter she followed her father into the Air Force National Guard rather than attend art school as she had dreamed. With my encouragement—abetted by my mother's early blessing—Denise completed her degrees while waitressing and running our house. Structure and discipline came naturally. She had often managed an inclusion classroom, pegged by administrators as one who could handle it. Like our children and nieces, her school charges must have quickly figured out when not to enter the sights of her pinpoint crosshairs.

Once a skinny peanut with long dirty blonde braids that streaked in the summer sun, she decided to pursue what felt right. Denise had loved teaching, juggling the demands to meet reformulated curricula dictates while nurturing children for thirteen years. It was time.

Starting on this path, my wife would soon be taking care of others in ways that had been unimaginable before. With a different purpose in mind, but in some respects parallel to what Jay, David, and Cindy were doing, we set out as second responders offering grief supports for local families.

She came upon a suitable place early in 2008, five years after losing Michael. We had examined a few locations together—charming old homes in commercial districts, and walked secluded properties including a dilapidated farm that was mired in bankruptcy. I perused tax maps to find owners of retreat lots and wrote a few unanswered letters of inquiry. We resisted renting office space or a storefront, which would have been the top choices if we did not have the means to do something more. Those options seemed imperfect at best.

One spring day she drove up a hill after crossing a small tidal river in neighboring Kingston, a coastal town embedded with the history of the Plymouth Bay Colony. There on the lawn of a Greek Revival-style home was a for-sale sign—by the owner. Soon after its construction, the house had been bought by a shipbuilder who furnished his fireplace mantles with Italian marble brought back as ballast in ships plying Mediterranean fruit trade routes in the 1840s. Close to the corner of Main Street in the town's center, five generations of the same crusty family had resided there, with an addition built on the back some years earlier.

The current occupant, David Holmes, was a Marlboro-inhaling gadfly whom I had seen years earlier lurking around selectmen's meetings and the like when I was a local reporter. He, too, had been a journalist at one time in Washington D.C.—and a bookie, as the local gossip went—where his father worked at the Federal Highway Administration helping plan the country's interstate system. Apparently as David grew up in Maryland, the family house was more like a summer home, which he later retreated to. Gruff in a sort of Tommy Lee Jones way yet alternately giddy like a beardless southern smurf, David introduced us to the old homestead.

We hit it off with Holmes and his wife, Martine, who tended expansive perennial gardens and beds of bold Russian sage and lavender amidst granite benches and flat stonewalls. Something about the land and house immediately felt right to Denise. A cart path ran down to the little river, passing by a grove of towering beech trees with smooth grey trunks that created a quiet alcove in an exposed bank. As she fingered the spiny leafs of an unusual dawn redwood tree he had planted, David seemed to sense how connected Denise already felt to the property.

We went ahead and put it together that summer, retaining some original furnishings including a dark sideboard and parlor chairs. Holmes asked us to care for a large portrait of the family patriarch that hung below a winding staircase, along with one of Edward Holmes, the original homeowner. A carriage house on the grounds contained some vintage shipwright's tools and implements of gardening destruction for me, but we focused most on starting the services in the main house.

One afternoon she found herself painting alone in the kitchen. Denise and her parents had scraped off the fading seventies paisley-patterned wallpaper, and the ceiling in between original exposed beams also needed fresh coats. The radio unexpectedly played one of her favorite songs, "Box of Rain." Phil Lesh's throaty vocals chortled beside Jerry Garcia's adroit pedal steel weave.

What do you want me to do
to do for you to see you through?

Holding a roller, she danced across the crackling linoleum floor. The energy was keen; she felt peace here. The old house with its high ceilings and lingering spirits would support our newfound mission.

By late August some of Glenn Winuk's buddies tried to prepare themselves for what was coming. They knew it would be nearly impossible to filter out the coverage saturating their 4G networks and the airwaves, especially in New York. Even the voracious news cycle spitting out fresh victims and disasters twenty-four-seven was inundated by the tenth anniversary.

Andy Sausmer finds himself getting antsy during this stretch. His birthday is August 11, and he recalls never having that belated dinner with his best friend. He is sensitive to the weather at this time: gorgeous bright days with a dry, lingering heat and a slight premonition of cool nights, as if dappled with the bitters of a prolonged hangover. The media barrage irritates him, a drone of horrific images replaying. "You'd hope that these people are in their thoughts more than just one day," he says. Sausmer also gets reflexively self-critical. "You often reflect on what could have been. Have I done enough? Could I have done any more?"

He could still grin about the good times. Back in Jericho, in the days when they kept Plectron pagers the size of small radios on their nightstands, he and Glenn were gung-ho and inseparable. Cold January mornings running to the station with freezing hair. "Holidays, and even sex, interrupted by a fire," he laughs. "You know, a dispatcher's voice: 'This is it. You can't miss this one.'" Tight for twenty-five years.

Tom Casey's twelfth-floor office overlooked the World Trade Center. He'd watched the painstakingly slow progress there, a continuous reminder of the damage that was protracted by the warring parties in charge of redeveloping the site. In his eyes, the dragged-out affair made people working nearby uneasy: Why couldn't they get this done? Early in the summer the trees showed up for the memorial, and finally a lawn went in.

Casey, who worked as an investment bank executive, had been one of Glenn's chief wingmen back in the day. Often they started at Glenn's studio apartment and headed out to eat, sometimes even on a Monday, but those were not usually late nights. A decade or so later, once in a while he and Sausmer and Dan King gathered and someone ordered a glass of Glenfiddich, Glenn's favorite single-malt scotch. Those occasions had thinned down.

Casey understood how his friends grieved differently, and that they had grown to respect the varied ways people handled this day. Some found comfort in being together for the collective remembrances. Others, including Glenn's girlfriend, had needed to do this her own way and move on, distancing herself from the Winuk family and public memorials. Everyone close to Casey seemed to have figured out what they were going to do—perhaps attend a ceremony or go to the Trade Center site. Or not.

Joe Mlynarckyk could not bring himself back from Florida this time of year. Instead, he might find the energy to open the website of one of his missing brothers, such as a picture of Steve Siller. Doing so refreshed Joe's memory of Siller: his constant energy, renovating the house for his five kids and taking on any challenge—roofing, digging a trench, or running the wrong way like Glenn.

Siller had worked the night shift September 10th and was on his way to play golf with his brothers that morning when his scanner erupted. After returning to Squad 1 to get his gear, he drove his truck to the Brooklyn Battery Tunnel, which had been closed. Strapping sixty pounds of gear to his back, Stephen G. Siller went on foot about 1.7 miles through the tunnel to the towers, where he died. When Mlynarckyk first heard the story, a couple of guys near him were in doubt. How can you physically do that?

His thought was, *How could you expect him* not *to do that?* "There was nothing that was going to stop him," Joe says.

His mind was still boggled by it all. Mlynarckyk didn't expect the tenth anniversary to be any different than the ninth. "It's a crappy day every year," he told me. "I used to hate the saying, 'It is what it is,' but I've become a fan of that."

Jay and David seemed to be everywhere. Their "I will . . ." campaign was set to launch with seventy celebrities from Selena Gomez and Samuel L. Jackson to the Yankees' Mark Teixeira pledging how they would pay tribute on September 11. Their media pitch would soon crest as the duo conducted interviews almost daily and prepared for a session with more than thirty satellite TV and radio stations after Labor Day.

As part of their social media strategy, vendors created two custom Facebook apps—one generating a signature "I will" stamp on the Friends' wall for those who posted a 9/11 pledge, and another connecting users to volunteer opportunities. Facebook fans rocketed and in the final week, more than 100,000 people posted "I will" pledges on 911day.org, the group's website. An estimated thirty million Americans planned to observe 9/11 by doing charitable acts.

Wherever you tuned in or logged on, the pair's miles and meetings were paying dividends. The NFL drove fans to a special auction of game-worn jerseys and other items benefitting Tuesday's Children and MyGoodDeed. Longtime partner Scholastic sent project ideas to a million teachers including 9/11 lesson plans and suggested talking points for students. An "I will" interactive sculpture went up on MTV's studio balcony in New York, while the Mets gave Paine and Winuk two nights to do fundraising and hand out "I will" pledge cards at Citi Field.

One of their goals for a big Friday night concert idea fell through, but a musician friend of Winuk's who had recorded a slew of songs about 9/11 played with his band at a club. Jay gave a speech and a group of Broadway stars sang "New York, New York" in Times Square on the eve of the weekend. They even squeezed in the nonprofit's board meeting.

I wondered how Jay was managing to balance all this. Demurring at first, he waxed in glossy PR speak, although I felt he meant it genuinely.

He had a terrific team working tons of hours, along with great partners and some equally terrific funders. "They're not only writing substantial checks but getting employees and companies involved," he said. Those corporations came from a variety of sectors: retail, law, banking, technology, aerospace, and logistics. Throughout all of this he had tried to fulfill two jobs, while his dad had just been hospitalized with pneumonia and would soon need surgery. When Hurricane Irene blew through, the Winuks lost electricity at home, but the family had a generator and Jay's neighbor helped them out with a chainsaw.

He and Carolyn often talked about the nature of people's limits. She was so proud and supportive of what he helped build, and as a pair—as a family—they saw themselves continuing to bind remembrance and service together. It would have felt wrong not to give back on Glenn's behalf and for others. Yet "the reality is, people move on. People don't dedicate as much of the year and time as we do as a family," she said that September. "With my kids' friends, many were barely alive or don't remember." Like her husband, Carolyn glimpsed the challenge of keeping the movement growing during the coming decade.

Jay and David were able to go almost everywhere spreading the word, virtually and physically. It remained to be seen how far their goal to grow 9/11 tributes would penetrate.

For Jane Pollicino and her growing family, the weeks leading into the anniversary were a jumble of life-changing events and averted disaster.

She became a grandmother the last week of August, when her son Steve's wife delivered a baby boy, Nicholas Michael. He arrived soon after an earthquake shook the East Coast, and just before Irene knocked out power to his grandmother's house. Although Nicholas was discharged from the hospital the same day their Monmouth, New Jersey, neighborhood was evacuated, Steve and Jenna Pollicino returned home with their baby the next day. Shortly afterwards it was Jane's daughter Celeste's turn for a near-seismic move. She landed a graphic designer's job near her apartment, which started on September 12, a big first career step after college.

"I'm taking a deep breath," Jane said heading into the September 11 weekend. As if by pluck and constancy, she finally fit an obstinate piece into a jigsaw puzzle from bits that were once colorless scattered shards, obstreperous in their nothingness. For years she'd kept a stack of unread *Newsdays* from 2001 in her laundry room, and she wondered if it was finally time to go through them. At fifty-seven, even while her face was etched with deep lines, Pollicino kept a brisk and full pace. Somehow she felt re-energized.

That Thursday she had three commemorative events to choose from and did two. She went to a reunion with a group of widows who had met five years earlier. One in particular had shared a story of struggling to set up her Christmas tree for her kids—and the anecdote continued to inspire Pollicino, who thought of it every holiday—and she got to express that to an old friend. "I walked into the same buildings, but it's not in darkness," she told me. "I can see improvement." Another meeting was at a counseling center where she and Celeste once went. She was the only family member there but didn't mind being alone.

Pollicino did other things, some big and airy and very public. She conducted tours at the Tribute WTC Visitors Center, which began next to the Ten House station. Interacting with tourists and walking the paces helped her reassemble those bits. Once the tourists knew her story, they often asked about Steve. "I needed to learn what chaos there was that day, the firefighters, what they went through," she said. "I hear new stories each time, and you think no one wants to hear about it anymore and then you see people lining up. I see people appreciating me telling them about Steve, and it's a win-win."

Months after the attacks, Jane, Celeste and six other sets of mothers and daughters did something else. Barbara Walters' producer contacted them to do a segment about their lives on *20/20*, including their participation in therapy sessions. They received another call in the spring of 2011, and after huddling together, four of the families decided they'd do it again. The show, which aired two nights before the anniversary, focused on how the girls were growing up—without a dad at their sweet sixteen parties and graduations—and asking how they had coped. When Pollicino's hometown dedicated a memorial with a piece of steel from one tower, *20/20's* cameras were there, and Jane was okay with that.

"You want to know what I've been doing for ten years? This is what I've been doing," she said without grousing. The television piece also featured the birth of little Nicholas with video that the Pollicinos took in the hospital, closing with Celeste kissing the baby. "He ended up stealing the show," his grandmother crowed. "In my mind, thirty years from now Celeste's nephew can watch this and what an amazing piece it will be."

Her son was picky about the public memorial events. Knowing his limits, he usually would not spend the whole day there. One year he went to Ground Zero and told her, "I don't know how you do this." Yet she kept going and asked to read the names. Pollicino also continued to follow the controversies in the aftermath: fights over the interment of unidentified remains within the 9/11 museum, the plight of recovery workers, the last families still in court. "I'm choosing to stay on top of it, and I guess it's my way of moving forward," she declared.

Meanwhile, Jane managed to do a few things just for herself. Tuesday's Children offered self-empowerment training, and she improved her fledgling computer skills. She also did yoga and weight training. "I have some envy for women who focused on other things—redoing their house, going back to school," she said. But enrolling in courses or indulging in something like tennis lessons wasn't for her. Pollicino made new friends, but her two sisters and their families remained her greatest supports. When her niece Michelle did a triathlon to support a medical clinic in El Salvador, her uncle's picture was on her back. During the competition and later on the trip, she felt Steve's big hands pushing the hardest.

There was much that felt unfinished. An estimated three thousand children lost a parent on September 11, and the Pollicinos' needs, like those of Cindy McGinty's sons, could not be pigeonholed. As an influx of teenagers neared college age and more first responders' families sought financial aid and help with health benefits, Jane Pollicino and others felt misunderstood. Cranky outsiders acted as if they had won the lottery and should just get on with it.

One day that spring she offered, "My kid are doing exactly what I hoped they would do, but I say that with baited breath. I'm waiting for the other shoe to drop. We never really said to each other—I never had that time with my kids—dad's not coming home, this is it. I don't know if that's positive or negative. We never sat down and cried it out. We never had a funeral, never had remains. I just walk a little bit on edge with all of this; you don't know what they're really thinking." She kept a burial plot in case Steve's remains were someday identified. "When someone asks me how I'm doing I say, 'Okay. Okay is good.' I'm ready for okay the rest of my life. I had great, and my kids somehow think they had great too."

Back when Celeste was brainstorming her college essay, she found her brother's writing in his high school yearbook. The younger Steven Pollicino forecasted: "Life is not a matter of having a good hand. It's playing a bad hand well."

Like the downpours gripping much of the Northeast in a headlock early that September, controversies once again threatened to wash out a chunk of remembrance. The previous year, uproar over the mosque a few blocks from Ground Zero and a Florida pastor's threat to burn the Koran had triggered an absurd din. As all context became unglued, I wondered whether attempts to pitch reconciliation alongside respect for the fallen would backfire.

We were moving my daughter Amanda to a college apartment in Savannah, Georgia, and driving a U-Haul I soaked in news and commentary anywhere I could dial it up: evangelicals, the Glenn Beck show, public radio, Stephen Colbert in the hotel—some of them overwrought with an agenda. A Christian radio guru named Dr. James Dobson vilified the imam in Manhattan. Sarah Palin called on peaceful Muslims "to refudiate" the mosque, and then compared herself to Shakespeare. The *Times* parsed the record of Imam Rauf to set us dumb mortals straight.

A former firefighter named Tim Brown who had lost ninety-three colleagues called the Islamic center a slap in the face to the families. Terry Jones finally called off the holy torching, but claimed falsely that he'd struck a deal with the imam. My Achilles tendon had recently begun deteriorating so it throbbed a bit braking the rental truck in the Beltway traffic slog. I wondered what the hell had happened to unity. The bottom line for me was that while I agreed with Tim Brown, ultimately I could not find solace in that. There had to be some way to honor victims and the responders' sacrifices while taking a fresh step forward.

The angst ratcheted even higher a year later. Tenth anniversaries, I suppose in ways similar to twenty-fives and fifties, have a way of doing that. These numbers carry an extra punch. A clash of heartbreak and hatred. Guilt and denial. Reflection and vitriol. Whiskey and wine. The buildup is often worse than the day itself.

It wasn't enough for some that more than 1,100 families still had no identifiable remains. Not enough, either, that responders' cancers were still not considered a coverable health problem. Not even that a probe began into phone hacking of families by Rupert Murdoch's media muckrake-monster. The mayor's ban against clergy and political speakers at official 9/11 services. Some widows continued to be labeled as whiners and opportunists. One responded by blogging that she was "quitting 9/11." Drained of being seen as victim, or moral beacon, resilience symbol, a dentist's spitting cup for the country's anger and fears, and indeed, confusion, or even defined by any of this. Really telling everyone, piss off.

Not everyone's blood boiled. Some shut out the drama.

Rena Speisman, for one, takes no measure, no credence, in any mere date.

She didn't give a fuck—except for her wedding anniversary. Bob, her soul mate and rock 'n roll man, was on Flight 77 that crashed into the Pentagon. Rena didn't even think 9/11. Not so much even two days before the anniversary as we sat on her deck.

"I lost my husband," she told me.

They have three daughters, young adults who had struggled in their own ways along with their mom. Speisman continued living along the Hudson in Irvington, New York, close to a basketball court that Bob's friends built and named for him. Sundays at 6:00 a.m. was game-on for his over-forty group.

She grew up a city girl and worked in the music business, running wild as a hippie before she met Bobby. Limber at fifty-eight, bronze and twisting her braided hair, Speisman was into crystal energy healing and spoke fluently of aromatherapy and the healing properties of lavender oils—in fact, lavender grew prominently outside her Tudor-style home. Her main work, perhaps her most essential salve, was sitting with four-to-six-year-olds who had lost a parent or sibling. "Littles," she called them.

For nine years she had volunteered at a bereavement center called the Tree House in Mount Kisko, helping kids find their path sometimes just by getting out of their way. Rena embraced the tools for coping that kids already have, encouraging them to grab hold and share those. She demonstrated yoga techniques to take long breaths, rising slowly to stretch and release; she guided rambunctious boys to create memory boxes with superhero stickers, and filled bags with Skittles and M&Ms and color-coded queries to get them talking. If a wee one only wanted to push around the chairs, she learned that he was likely taking it all in his own way. Hugs, coloring, and crafts became her chief implements; her favorite part was the questions that pop up as they formed a group to begin talking. "Someone will say, what's a heart attack? And we'll teach them."

"People look for big moments but I see the little moments turn into big moments," she told me. When a pre-school girl is able to say, "'I miss holding my mother's hand,' that's huge."

Speisman and her husband were fortunate in that they did not leave crucial things unsaid. "I'm guilt free," she offered. "But still, is there a good way?"

Two days later, Rena and her youngest daughter planned on maybe doing yoga and going shopping to keep things light on the anniversary. She pictured her husband downing a roll of Neccos, his favorite food indulgence, because "Bob was all smiles and fun, and he wasn't sad at all."

Neither would Cindy McGinty, Jay, or David allow the 9/11 noise to jam them. For McGinty, things were already a little crazed with her sons, and she stayed focused on them. One was about to fly to New Mexico and begin college, while her youngest remained away at the wilderness program.

She teetered near ambivalence: intense feelings one day, not thinking about it the next, her thoughts creeping back in the closer it got. Anticipating her sons' responses to the anniversary, Cindy thought that her oldest would be fine, being an in-the-moment guy, and especially settling into a new place with young people like himself. He was attending America's Camp for the last year as a counselor and had to finish the prerequisite seven books to begin St. John's College. She was less sure what to expect from her youngest but figured they'd at least be together. Her sadness at being the lone parent preparing for such an event lingered, but it no longer felt like the prevailing force. "They have to make themselves feel better," she said. "You can't give them a hug any more. Now it's how you tell your story and what you choose to do with your story that matters."

Like McGinty, Jay and David knew exactly what they needed to save their best energy for. Occasionally they had to fend off backlash about promoting service on a day of infamy. One of their critics, publisher Pamela Geller, called it "deeply offensive" and sacrilegious. "September 11th is a national day of mourning," Geller wrote. "Is Pearl Harbor a day of service? D Day?"

Paine wasn't flustered by this type of slam, insisting that he didn't hear it often. He and Jay had never taken a dime of federal money, and Paine calls himself politically conservative on many issues. Rather than somehow diluting remembrance, he believed that what they were doing had the opposite effect: in addition to observing the day by perhaps visiting a memorial, volunteerism ensured that another generation would remember. He argued that doing so recognized the victors of 9/11, not only honoring victims. "Those who rose in service," he says. "If we say it's only a day of remembrance we exclude the first responders, the iron workers, all members of the military."

Finally, Paine believed the 9/11 community did not want bin Laden "to define what it is and means to us. If every year we define ourselves as victims, then he wins. Year after year a lot of family members don't want to be victims. They want some triumph over tragedy."

On a Wednesday just before the big weekend, Carolyn Winuk joined a warehouse assembly line of about two dozen volunteers packing fresh apples, onions, beans and other produce for families in need. It wasn't the first time, as one Thursday each month she was often joined by her son and one of his friends.

Winuk helped coordinate a 9/11 community food pack at the Food Bank for Westchester, which distributed a few hundred bags to local soup kitchens, food pantries, and shelters. Complementing her work as a physical therapist, Carolyn was keen on improving nutrition to combat hunger. She found the organization's operations impressive, and also saw it inspiring Justin, Melanie, and their peers to address hunger in their area. "I think this will be a really socially-aware generation," she said. Mahopac, a commuter stop almost fifty miles north of the city, supported those hopes. As part of their freshman year orientation, Justin and the others began to pick through a host of nonprofits—an initiation to a sixty-hour community service requirement for graduation. Besides volunteering at the food bank, Justin would begin training as a junior juror for the Putnam County Youth Court, and his mother saw him maturing at fourteen, developing a sense of giving back. His uncle Glenn's sensibilities and acumen were never far away.

On Long Island, Jericho students brought their own ideas for service projects and tributes to a new level. Nearly three thousand kids from every grade played a role, creating cards for 9/11 family members and organizing service pledges. Many joined a remembrance walk on the anniversary itself raising funds for five charities. Like other schools across the region, the district also integrated 9/11 lessons across age groups—the youngest reading stories of courage and service, upper elementary kids researching how the events changed America and the world, to high school students analyzing how government policies changed in the aftermath. Sophomores explored the new novel, *Extremely Loud and Incredibly Close*.

The previous June, Jay Winuk and leaders of other 9/11 charities keynoted an unusual town hall meeting at Jericho High School. The topic was how the tragedy could be taught in schools, and while the event also kicked off MyGoodDeed's offer of teachers' lesson plans—filmed for a DVD available on its website—the event marked a true homecoming for Jay. Teens embraced the cause, several standing up to announce that they would help build houses for Habitat for Humanity or clean up trash. The next day, guidance counselor Mary Jo Moriarty found her mission for the summer. "We said, what can we do as a community?" she recalls. "That's how I came up with the walkathon, and then every student pledged a good deed for September." Some business students created a website and parents suggested the pledge cards be displayed on boards at each school. A group resumed work before Labor Day, preparing packets for teachers in all disciplines.

Some of Jericho's 1,200 high school students also connected with teens in other countries who expressed their own feelings about the attacks. Moriarty took a small group of National Honor Society students to the 9/11 Tribute Museum, where Japanese children sent three thousand origami cranes they had made in a symbolic wish for world peace. She and her students learned origami, fashioning their own. Some students in France also spotted Jericho's website and sent over their own cards. Moriarty felt the town needed a unifying goal, and it took many hands to accomplish that. "Everyone came together for a cause and put their differences aside for a day," she says, "and that was wonderful for this community."

Setting up an office in the rear of the house behind what had been a master bedroom, in moments Denise felt supremely alone.

After forming a nonprofit she'd begun placing brochures and fliers around nearby towns. Letters and calls went out introducing our bereavement and wellness center to local hospice and other community groups. We called it "Hope Floats," and she was asked about the name.

It came to her during a visit to Mike's grave. Someone had left a plaque with "Hope" inscribed in stone and Denise supplied the verb. While I had to pause for a moment considering the two words together, I liked their combined effusive, radiating quality.

Skeptics might consider "hope" to be an illusory, wishy-washy ideal akin to the overuse of "faith" or "grace." Yet hope requires backbone. A definitive leap. In scripture it signifies a confident expectation in salvation. In our lives this deserved frequent reflection and rededication to inch forward, if only for a day.

Hope is real. It is a path souls travel on, circulating when we least expect it. It exudes from our pores. When stirring in the tall grass, we try to be receptive to it.

We knew this from our early response to Mike's death, trying to reach those teens and parents about safe driving. If even only a handful showed up for a talk, we had to accept that they were meant to be there. Like the Clerys when they first connected to other parents whose children had been harmed on campuses, we ached to believe again.

She added "Floats" because that expectation rises to the surface, lifting you from a dark place. Ebb and flow seeking balance.

Denise felt Mike's approval while sitting on his bench. We built a website, and a freshly painted sign incorporating dragonflies that Amanda had drawn for our logo and hung it under a lamppost in front of the house. Still, Denise sat her desk looking at the phone, wondering when it would ring.

Other people doing this work began gravitating her way. One of the first was a hairdresser and massage therapist who worked up the street and also had a degree in thanatology. A gravelly-voiced ex-smoker, Pat Tessier had lost a son in a motorcycle accident. She wanted to run a support group. Meeting one night in the living room during a performance by a psychic medium doing readings—which was one of the offerings we began to embrace, and while not meant for everyone, provides comfort for some—Pat and Denise hit it off.

After advertising in local newspapers, the two started an adults group early in 2009. It grew to ten or twelve women, a mix mostly of moms along with those who had lost a husband, a brother, or a parent themselves. Being a startup necessitated doing it that way, and during two years they became a close-knit bunch, supporting one another when one of their own members passed suddenly. Pat was a true mentor, but her time with my wife was cut short. Diagnosed with a fast-spreading lung cancer, she also died way too soon. Both of these women's losses brought their group closer together.

Denise soldiered on, making other contacts as we added wellness classes to complement the fledgling supports. A bereavement coordinator at a local hospice agency reached her, and they sat in the kitchen with the hospice director brainstorming what they could do together. The coordinator, an affable, no-nonsense veteran of working with distraught families, confirmed Denise's hunch to organize separate adult support groups for varied types of loss. The hospice already offered groups for partner-spouse and suicide loss. It made little sense, for example, that a widower desperate to connect with another wife who, like her, might be afraid of going to bed alone at night, would be mixed in with couples suffering the loss of a child. This quickly changed.

The second component of our mission, offering programs for mind, body, and spiritual wellness, also took off. In those first months after losing Mike, Denise felt as if someone had beaten her up—her arms, shoulders, and stomach ached. Her therapist recommended trying a body treatment, and she did polarity therapy, lying backside on a table as a woman combined soft and deep touches to help rebalance her energy. As her muscles relaxed Denise felt momentarily restored. Finishing up, the practitioner told Denise that occasionally she picked up things while giving a treatment. "I have to tell you, I felt something about a yellow bike and a little boy," she said. As a pre-teen, our son tore it up bicycling with a neighborhood friend along a woods road out back, on which he built jumps. There was little doubt—this was Mike on his old Mongoose.

The woman had never met my wife; neither did Denise know that the practitioner received messages. Six years later, this first experience became a springboard to offer others a buffet of wellness options. "At that time I was looking for anything that would help us heal," she reflects. "This is the whole premise."

She opened the house to yoga classes in the living room, and the next summer we built a wellness barn on the edge of the woods. Besides housing a true office for her and small treatment rooms, the barn features a great room with a wood floor plus decorative posts and beams. It is a natural space for yoga and Tai chai, for healing workshops, speaking events, or just listening to music on a near-surround sound system. We added doors and transom windows modeled after a roadside barn in her hometown on Cape Cod, sighting the building in line with a row of maples facing the First Parish Church. For myself, whether working around the building or cutting wood nearby, it became one of my favorite places to be in almost any season, as if burnishing a rough gem in the town's historic center.

Which is all great and idyllic. Except for the matter of paying taxes, bills, and clearing piled-up plates.

Not to mention when her phone started ringing.

Chris Mitchell finished typing his speech as a downpour hammered his house.

He'd spent two weeks getting his thoughts down, and that wasn't the only weight off his mind. The 9/11 memorial he spearheaded in Foxborough was 95 percent complete. All he had to do was plant some mums and kale, spread a little mulch, and watch someone else install a few final granite pieces and plaques. What began nearly two years before when he got steamed over the absence of patriotism had grown way beyond one couple's mission.

He got sick in August from a hernia, underwent surgery, and was hospitalized with pneumonia. So others stepped up. Townspeople worked two thousand hours digging and pouring concrete slabs and fitting granite pieces into place. A selectman who remodels homes became the general contractor, bringing the project to life, and sixty volunteers did the bull work from June through Labor Day weekend. Fundraising remained truly grassroots, lots of tens and twenties coming from people who in their hearts would give a hundred times as much. They raised about $70,000 in cash and in-kind donations for things like the irrigation system and plants accomplished the rest. "It's not about Chris Mitchell," said Fire Chief Roger Hatfield, who relished his jackhammer duty. "It's about the community. Chris orchestrated it. Chris's connection to the McGintys gave him energy, and that energy poured out of him to a lot of people to make this happen."

Early that summer Chris and his friend Joe Lally took a road trip in Mitchell's F-350. He'd waited fourteen months for approval from the Port Authority to go down to Hangar 17 at JFK International Airport, where artifacts such as twisted hunks of metal and chunks of fire trucks from the World Trade Center were stored. Their purpose was to transport a dented, 360-pound I-beam from one of the towers back to town as the centerpiece for the memorial.

"I never prepared myself for walking in that hangar," Mitchell explained. He nearly threw up after entering the gigantic, mangled scene. Even Lally, a sixty-five-year-old retired Boston cop, wasn't quite ready. He'd seen his share of horrors—two tours in Vietnam, women and children shot in front of him, and loading bodies into slings on Hamburger Hill. Still, huge steel slabs twisted like taffy were unthinkable—like Dali sculptures on bad acid. "That put the fear of God into me that day," he confessed.

Before leaving, they ran into some Ohio firefighters picking up steel for their own memorial. Their town had waited two and a half years. The ride home was somber for Chris and Joe. They thought of people in the wreckage, and Lally knew a half-dozen people gone including a customs detective he'd worked with. "We talked about loss and the impact we hoped this will have on future generations," Lally told me. "What we are and who we are."

Something enduring was on the move in Foxborough. After 9/11, two of the town manager's sons enlisted in the armed forces, one deployed in Iraq with a National Guard military police unit and another as a National Guard infantryman in Afghanistan. During a Founder's Day parade, a fire truck pulled the steel beam through town on a flatbed. "I think that got the word out and people pumped up that this is great," Paula Mitchell said. Both she and her husband saw their town galvanized by an irresistible energy, symbolized by two three-ton replica towers cut from Pennsylvania granite. "This project changed my whole outlook on a lot of things," Chris reflected. "The best thing that ever happened was not being able to raise enough money and relying on volunteers." Paula, who documented each step with her camera, relished those Saturday mornings when people showed up unannounced.

When he had nearly finished his dedication speech, Mitchell sent it to his son, Patrick, who was beginning his third year at West Point. Unlike his father, Patrick Mitchell is a gifted public speaker. "He called home and said, 'Wow, who wrote that for you?' I said I did, and he said, 'That's pretty damn good.'" Chris tweaked a few more things but stayed focused on his message, which was not the terrorist attacks themselves, but about volunteering and paying tribute. That night he went to a final planning meeting and a walk-through for the dedication, and the forecast was for the weather to break by Saturday's ceremony. Patrick would come home for the weekend.

A few more things were meant to be. Two nights before the dedication, a friend who teaches at the Berklee College of Music messaged Mitchell on Facebook. Chris had an event planner handling these last-minute requests to join the ceremony, which usually rankled him. The professor sent him a clip of a classical guitarist playing "My Country 'Tis of Thee." At first he thought, there's no way to fit this in.

Until he listened to the recording—and then he found a way.

When the time came midway through the ceremony, the guitarist's careful syncopation seemed to stretch everyone out. His playing released a long-coiled pain with its simple melody, a promise at once delicate and resonant enough to halt the day. All chatter suspended, enough so that one could just make out the light fluttering of the flag.

Chris Mitchell immediately knew this would make the moment whole.

15

A PLACE OF SERVICE

A thin veil of clouds linger overhead as morning breaks, but everyone knows bright sunshine is in store for the tenth anniversary. Whole Foods Market is already open in Jericho, a handful of people gather pastries and order at the deli. Starbucks is serving free coffee in a gesture of tribute until ten, while a few joggers get in their early Sunday runs through the sleepy hamlet. Just as Jay said, the old brick firehouse is on the main strip across from the new one, and there I spot a guy who must be Andy Sausmer in his navy blue best.

Sausmer is outside with another firefighter by the flagpole reviewing a few things before the service, mainly the audio equipment. He wears aviator sunglasses and has a copy of the program with his remarks folded inside his jacket. Speaking together a few times before on the phone, I've sensed that Andrew is punctual and purposeful. Meeting in this moment I begin to fully appreciate his connection to Glenn, realizing that I dare not gloss over any aspect of what he's doing today.

Andrew is mid-sized and trim, gesturing a lot with his hands and occasionally pausing in search of the right words. He tells me his speech is about friendship at two levels: when they first form, and how they persevere. All week the movie *Saving Private Ryan* has been popping into his head and he wants to refer to it in his remarks—near the end when the elder Ryan asks his wife if he's lived a good life. Sausmer seeks confirmation that the actor in that sequence is Jason Robards. I tell him I'm not 100 percent, but I think he's got it. We both turn out to be wrong; it's actually Harrison Young.

After checking on a few more things the two men lower and fold the American flag, and we cross the street to the new station where people are gathering in the kitchen over boxes of donuts and coffee. There's the momentary jazz of reunion as older men entering a side door find one another. Many of the smiles are short-lived, their faces weighed by the day at hand. A television mounted in a corner shows the memorial service just underway at Ground Zero, with two people reading surnames in a blistering alphabetical lineup. Several men tell me about Glenn, starting with Arthur Kroll, a former Jericho chief who lived next door to the Winuks around the corner from the old station. When Glenn was an adolescent, he'd often beat Kroll to his car when the alarm sounded, anxious to get a ride to the scene.

Bob Herr, a member of the department for twenty-six years, recalls Glenn's total commitment and thoughtfulness. Years ago a group of two dozen or so from their Guardian Engine Company 2 vacationed together in the Bahamas. As some of the men began drinking at the airport before departure, he asked Glenn what they should do in case any trouble broke out at the all-inclusive resort they would be staying at. He already had it covered. Glenn was only going for three days, and since Holland & Knight had an office in the Bahamas, he had contacted a colleague there. "If I'm not with you, if there's any trouble, call this guy," he told Herr, handing him a card. It turned out that Herr was the guy who called Jay one early morning in March 2002 with the news that Glenn's partial remains had been found.

The group lines up inside one of the bays and then walks over to the old station, maybe sixty firefighters in dress flanked by a nearly equal number of friends and townspeople. As the ceremony begins, a stout man plays the bagpipes, momentarily quieting the traffic behind us on Route 107. A color guard stands at attention, and a firefighter with the same name and interest in fine wines as a rabbi who gives the invocation rings a ceremonial bell.

Sausmer has taken off his glasses. He tells everyone it's okay to be emotional. "Don't try to be a tough guy," he says. "If you feel like crying, if you feel like laughing, if you feel like telling a joke, just go ahead." He mentions that Jericho's class of 1979, his and Glenn's, was rated the most popular high school class of all time—in an exclusive poll he alone conducted. For

Andy, the anniversary marks people coming together. "Today is about friendships," he continues. "Friendships that have been assumed, friendships that have been strengthened, friendships that have been discovered, and friendships that just happened."

He had worked on four different speeches but says he wants to mainly share a story, one I've heard before, from September 13, 2001, when Sausmer and three friends brought those supplies in for Squad 1. Upon arriving at Ground Zero, "one of the best things that happened to me was running into Dave Marmann," an FDNY member who also lived in Jericho, he says. "At least some people were making it through this." Marmann's father, Gene, a retired city battalion chief who can scarcely hide how torn he is today, is among the group listening. He and his two firefighter sons were off work that Tuesday. One look when we're introduced back in the kitchen conveys how thankful, and yet still burdened and perhaps weary, Gene Marmann is of all this.

Then Andy mentions *Private Ryan* and what sticks with him. "At the end of the movie, Ryan says, 'What have I done? How will I be remembered? Was it worth all this?'" Sausmer says. "I thought that to myself, and I think the best thing I can do is ten years from now be here." He encourages others to continue observing the legacies, "not just for Glenn," but also for a host of others, "and the stories from that day."

Soon after the flag is lowered to half-mast everyone takes the short walk rounding the corner to Glenn's park, once known as Spider Park. I find another of Glenn's friends here next to a multi-level playground set, which has replaced·the rusting metal bars of the old climbing set. After guiding his three-year-old daughter up wooden steps, Tom Casey follows her as she hangs from the ladder bars. He and several other men who were closest to Glenn soon meet up. They pose for pictures, including Dan King, with his wife and two of their sons. Rings of this circle fan outward—someone introduces me to Jay's college roommate and other guys who worked with Glenn, joined by a few of their dads—but this feels like Sausmer's moment with his core group. I step back.

A remembrance walk will soon take off at the high school, and Deputy Fire Chief John Lottes closes the ceremony, thanking "those who traded their tomorrows for our todays." Another speaker has extolled Glenn's virtues, and one that jumps out is how he would remind a junior member to tuck in his dress shirt, without being sarcastic about it. The speaker implores everyone, as Winuk did, to "never forget where they came from, and stay united." Lottes finishes: "What we do every day, and when we do things right every day, we give honor to men like Glenn and all his others who have paid the extreme price for our freedom."

By 8:30 a.m. Jay and Carolyn arrive at the National September 11 Memorial with Justin and Melanie, which opens for the first time this morning just for the families. Jay is familiar with the layout of the sixteen-acre site, having walked it a few times during construction. Using the family members' entrance by West Street, they go through security to the plaza, where Presidents Obama and Bush and their wives are meeting a small delegation of other relatives.

A citywide minute of silence at 8:46 ushers in the ceremony. Obama reads from Psalm 46: "God is our refuge and strength, a very present help in trouble. Therefore, we will not fear." Bush then reads a letter that President Abraham Lincoln wrote to a mother whose five sons had died in the Civil War. As victims' names are read, the Winuks move out of the crowd and head for the reflecting pool built in the South Tower's footprint. Jay has a printout showing the location of Glenn's name: on panel S-27 facing Liberty Street.

Approaching the edge of the massive fountain, the sound arrests one's senses. Cascading thirty feet over black granite walls, the waterfalls are a downpour without thunder, a tropical storm that spares trampling mottled leaves, sans rancor and rage. Jay and his family find an inscription in the dark bronze parapet. It identifies Glenn as a member of the Jericho Fire Department.

Perhaps it's the lack of chatter, or the drone of passing cars muffled by the falls. The two fountains representing both towers are called "Reflecting Absence." Reading his brother's name beside the pool, Jay's pulse begins to still.

Years earlier he and Carolyn had learned to take each day as it comes. Each shouldered an inordinate load to minimize the burden on Jay's parents, and on others around them. He admitted *there was no science to it.* Winuk took stewardship of his brother's vast CD collection, discovering more of what Glenn enjoyed and savoring the unexpected crossover with his own musical tastes. Jay occasionally downloads stuff Glenn had, and when a song pops up on his iCloud, "I know which one is his."

Beside the pool, he feels some of the buildup release over its spillways. They take a few pictures and introduce themselves to families around them.

Seeing his brother's name "so very close to where he breathed his last breaths was very important to us and distinctive in my memory," Jay says later. "It was almost like crossing a threshold, crossing a barrier to finally get to see his name and others' where they should be."

There's more to do. The Winuks head toward the Millennium Hilton that's on the same block as Glenn's old law office, where Jay has a series of radio interviews pressing. But first he wants to stop by his brother's plaque at the firefighters' wall, where on this day alone an honor guard stands vigil. He takes comfort seeing uniformed people around the wall. Unknowingly, his timing is perfect.

Someone taps his shoulder as they regard the plaque. A Brooklyn firefighter in dress uniform offers a warm, teary smile. His name is Michael Bernstein, and he takes a minute to compose himself.

Jay is at a momentary loss to understand, but the acuity of their connection is soon revealed. Bernstein was among the guys who found Glenn's remains. He has just spotted "Winuk" on the back of an old blue Holland & Knight T-shirt that Jay is wearing. He has a gift to offer. What he shares can never be forfeited, since Winuk intuited this before he could ever be sure. Bernstein confirms how Glenn was brought out of the pit with full fire department honors, a flag draped over him and rescuers standing at attention. The credentials in his wallet made it clear that Glenn was there in a rescue capacity. Another blank fills in, a new sprig of sage or lavender poking through the soil, refreshed by rain that will clear every May 5th on his brother's birthday. Jay had never believed much in fate before.

He continues to the hotel for his radio interviews, dazzled.

Eric Paine rises from his bed at the Tribeca Hilton and resumes working on his iPad. He has a plan for making a final push, tweeting a message that will ripple out and become a tribute chain.

Paine types, "#WeWill RT @911day: #IWill 9/11/11—Please retweet, and help start a 9/11 Tribute chain."

A deluge begins.

On the fly he contacts several of MyGoodDeed's key partners such as Viacom and Clear Channel, who agree to support the late push. For Viacom this means activating millions of fans on their networks, including MTV, BET and CMT. Once stirred awake, celebrities on those shows begin re-tweeting their "I will" pledges as well. Snooki resends her pledge to shake a firefighter's hand, while fellow cast members of "Jersey Shore" and other MTV shows like "The Real World" also jump in. Soon Eric sees that his message is trending quickly, and his contacts at American Express and Best Buy agree to re-tweet it. He reaches Tim McGraw's rep, who says, no problem. The elusive one is Lady Gaga, who has done a tribute on You Tube that drew eighty thousand visitors, but nothing else. The 9/11 traffic on Viacom's properties alone will reach forty million impressions. It all unfolds in front of him, gaining traction, and it's a rush.

There's work to be done at P.S. 140, a middle school on the Lower East Side. Touching up murals in the schoolyard and painting the basketball court, cleaning gardens and packing student first aid kits with bandages and lip balm. Maybe five hundred people arrive by mid-day, students and retirees and young professionals, and there's a ten-year-old, Victoria, here with her grandmother, Vivienne, from Bedford-Stuyvesant. They came in part because Victoria's mom works at New York Cares, which organizes volunteers doing everything from SAT tutoring to music lessons for mentally disabled people, and her mom is here.

At one table Vivienne folds cards that will become thank-you notes for soldiers. As Denise and I get started making our own, she tells us the school is just a good place for her to be on this day. She was in Brooklyn in 2001 and remembers the smoke and chaos vividly. She asks what brought us to Manhattan. I mention that we wanted to join in the remembrance and that I know one of the event's organizers.

Her granddaughter's got skills; Victoria peppers her cards with stickers—picking through small piles of patriotic symbols, iconic stickies of the Statue of Liberty and Empire State Building and holiday kitsch—with four or five suggested model salutations to work from. Her cards swish with vibrant colors and she displays a creative touch, enjoying the praise of people stopping by to tell her, "I wish I could make cards like that."

The school is both equalizer and host for its charges today: brown, black, and white, twenty-something employees from bulbous financial services firms, and grizzled veterans of nonprofits from the city's boroughs. It's a bit of a media circus, staged in part by Paine and Winuk. Four former NBA players are here and the school principal says it's the fifth year he's partnered with New York Cares, so this is not a one-off thing. When Senator Kirsten Gillibrand cruises the cafeteria tables flanked by cameras and reporters, three women painting silhouettes on the outside walls scarcely flinch. Across the table from us is Miss Teen USA, who hails from Harlingen, Texas. A BBC reporter cuts in to interview her, and Danielle Doty does her best to fashion a few cards aside from the commotion.

Throughout the country, students at many schools do their own tributes on or around this weekend. Elementary-aged kids in Spokane write pledges for service projects on strips of white fabric tied together in a display. Kids pick up trash around schoolyards. In St. Louis, kids ages six to eight create welcome boxes for Bosnian and Serb-Croatian families who are learning English. To help them settle in the area, students were expected to distribute translation dictionaries, maps, handbooks, and school supplies. Students draw "I will" posters in Phoenix, and police and firefighters come to the Arrowhead Elementary School to read to them.

David Paine is standing beside Jay looking over the P.S. 140 auditorium. Fanning out in front of them are volunteers: red tees are Target employees, blues are American Express, a variety of others are in white. "There's something special going on in this country," David tells everyone. "This is a remarkable way to pay our respects and pay tribute, and a way to fight back against evil by doing wonderful things." Jay offers up a little bit about his brother and the spirit that led to all this. "I thought the best thing I could do in his honor was to give back," he says. He's able to tell the story of the firefighter he just met—having begun to process this a few times in those radio interviews. Winuk's belief is that while some 9/11 families were recipients of so much goodwill over the decade, the raw beauty is how Americans reciprocated collectively. "That's what this is all about," he says. "It's what we can do for others in need."

One of the day's big sponsors is JPMorgan Chase, a very, very fortunate son. CEO Jamie Dimon remembers 9/11 with clarity. In this moment, before the public learns of the bank's shady dealings in mortgage-backed securities and massive foreclosure fraud, Dimon's reflections are weatherworn. He seems less the aggressive executive and more like a longtime coach whose team was vanquished in the tournament finals yet fought hard. "It's strange to say, 'We only lost six,'" he tells the volunteers. "It's strange to hear those words roll out of my mouth." He draws a straight line between the work that began evacuating people from the financial district, and recovery, to rebuilding community through service. "On that day, as I was standing on Greenwich Street moving ten thousand of our people, someone pulled on my arm and said, 'I'm with Oppenheimer, can I go with you?' I said, 'We're all human.' Ten years later we're doing that same work."

Outside, Eric Paine sits again with his iPad—there's no service in the building, and fortunately, no rain. Continuing to monitor both Twitter and Facebook, he's amazed by the scale of activity. The tribute chain he started will be the number one globally trending hashtag on Twitter with fifty million impressions. The demographics he'll soon comb through from 9/11 Day's Facebook fans will also yield clues on how to keep growing this day: seven of ten fans are women, and the largest active age group is thirty-five to fifty-four. They pinpoint hubs of activity and cities that may need more attention, as a few suburbs outside of places like Newark and Seattle show more traffic than Houston or Philadelphia.

By any measure, during these three hours on Ridge Street, and by attempting to tally up the people who show up elsewhere, it's a go.

David and Jay dipped a big toe in the water, and across the country an estimated thirty-three million people join them. It may be even more, because most people don't announce when they're about to plunge in; as Chris and Paula Mitchell observe, many neighbors just come on by. No one can know for certain, but Paine and Winuk will soon dice up their alchemy of inputs: online pledges and Twitter traffic, reports from sponsors, other charities, and chamber of commerce affiliates. And research conducted for their nonprofit heading into September combined with the social media surge will point to future pathways. A few years later, some fifty million people will participate in 9/11 tributes.

An estimated one-third of Americans over twenty-one expected to mark the day in some fashion, many through prayer or attending observances. As the duo combed through the data a few months later, this looked even more promising. While another third of the country said they didn't plan to do anything around 9/11, when asked if they would participate if they found something meaningful to do, about half of those said that would be pretty likely. And nearly a quarter of those said helping someone in need would be just the thing to energize them. "So we'll build on this," Paine offered. "It's clear to me there's a lot of room to grow here."

Then another head-turner: the top five motivating factors. Here's why people observed 9/11, at least in 2011, in descending order: to pay tribute to victims and first responders; to show terrorists that America will prevail; for the importance of doing something special on the tenth year; to recapture a feeling of national unity; and because they wanted to make a difference in the world.

Paine points excitedly to number four: the hope for cohesion. "So when it comes to 9/11 . . . they think about honoring the experience of unity. It's a very important distinction and a subtlety that allows for empowering millions of people."

It certainly feels like we're part of something much bigger at P.S. 140. During a break outside near the basketball courts, I ask David if he's really overwhelmed by the response. And what's next? He acknowledges there's a plateau of diminishing returns for the dollars spent on promotion, and like Jay, he realizes that the enthusiasm may tail off. Eventually, he says, "a certain segment of the population won't get involved, and at some point we'll reach a place where that's it."

Perhaps, in the end, something bigger will transform the numbers themselves. By the time people stop counting, what Kirk Souder calls "one giant evolutionary impulse" will have arrived on its own. "Just how far we've come," Jay reflects a few days later, "and however big this gets, and it's gotten big—it's still very personal."

Souder clarifies this further for me a few weeks later. It's about bringing a whole culture out of the box. "The negativity created by 9/11 perpetrators converted into something positive for the planet," he says. Somewhere, truck farmers who've finished a day turning over spoilage before sowing their winter cover crops are gathering at the Grange Hall of Reciprocity. "We are at a real fulcrum," he continues. "Hopefully people see that negativity does not really change things. It just doesn't work. It's time to take personal responsibility for ourselves and take positive action."

"People are ready for a change, they're longing for the world to be different," Paine agrees. "If people don't have a sense of purpose, or your life has no broader meaning, life can become remote."

Back in southeastern Massachusetts, we belonged to a small church stocked with warmth and volunteers wearing multiple hats. Plympton is smack dab in cranberry-growing country, a place populated largely by wetlands and riding stables and where on many mornings the usual suspects gather at its lone coffee and sandwich shop. The town was once a precinct of pilgrim-bred Plymouth and our first minister, Isaac Cushman, was ordained in 1698. The big news of the decade was construction of a Sysco distribution center in a long-empty industrial park. Halfway through this morning's service, the Reverend Mary Donnellan, pastor of the First Congregational Church, delivers a timely sermon challenging how the moderately conservative parish marks this day.

She centers on offering unconditional forgiveness after a great wrong. She posits, in wonderment, how some people do this. She anchors this epochal theme in a scripture reading from Genesis 50:15–21, when Joseph forgives his brothers' transgression after their father's death. "All of us have been hurt during our lives and the human reaction is to stay angry and get even," Donnellan says, "and that may be an honest and even healthy first reaction, but ultimately God asks of all of us a different way, a path that is only possible with God's help."

She connects this directly to the tenth anniversary underway. Over the previous year, she and I have had some remarkable conversations on these things. I sought a dialogue with her about the limits of forgiveness and reconciliation, and when she asked me about my writing, I told her a bit about Jay and Glenn Winuk and the drive for a national day of service. Drawing from a thumbnail sketch I had given her, Mary introduces Glenn and what his brother and David Paine set out to do.

From the pulpit she asks: "How it is that some are able to climb out of that great pit of darkness and find the light—and experience the healing—that leads them into more generous and life-giving ways than before the tragedy? And why [do] some come out of that pit and grab on only to hate and the need for revenge and lead lives stuck in their sorrow?" While the almighty continually urges us on, "many can respond and some cannot. It is one of the great mysteries of life and faith."

Finally, as she often does, Mary Donnellan brings everyone home, asking people to ponder, "How can good work flourish in our personal lives? Might we think of the stuck places in our own lives where we are imprisoned still in a cycle of hurt and anger? And let go . . . as Joseph did?"

The service also includes a candle lighting liturgy, and the readings for the last two candles are:

Lighting of the ninth candle.

While we cannot imagine what would cause persons
to commit such violent acts of terrorism,
we know you call us to forgive.
Move in our hearts to lead us to that place of radical generosity
and love.
Teach us to remember the words of Jesus.
"Forgive them for they know not what they do."

Lighting of the tenth candle.

Most of all, dear God, move us from despair to hope,
from isolation to community, from war to peace, from death to life,
grounded in our relationship with you and your people in every
tribe and nation,
every kindred and tongue
so that together we might build your beloved community on earth
as it is in heaven.

It's a long weekend for Cindy McGinty, one filled with joy and support. On each anniversary she tries to find the right place that will bring her meaning and purpose. This time it's to a place of service.

She opts out of the big official commemorative events. But nothing will keep her away from Foxborough.

Her youngest son just came home—she picked him up from the wilderness therapeutic program Aug. 31, after spending almost three months in the woods. He slept under tarps on the ground, hiked every day and ate crappy food. "I think he was angry he was there eighty days, but he got a lot out of it and now knows that," she says. "It's not a cure-all. There are still a lot of issues now, but I think he knows what he did wasn't doing it for him." He's about to start at a new prep school and she sees him engage during the weekend, taping boxes for hours, and getting in line to load trucks.

Cindy has help arriving, as her sister Sue drives up with other relatives, while McGinty does her part to rally others to attend service events. Facebook friends contact her about doing soldiers' care packages in Boston and she hooks them up. A few days earlier she blogs in *The Huffington Post*, asking, "What will you do to remember and pay tribute?" wondering if that even helps drive a few pledges. On Friday she speaks to a large student group starting community service at Wheaton College.

Saturday begins with Family Fun Day in Foxborough, which draws 130 volunteers, including many scouts, and about four times as many children and teens. The big enchilada is the 9/11 memorial dedication that afternoon. The memorial is a journey unto itself, as three pedestals with plaques describing the day's main events line a path to the centerpiece. It ends at the replica towers, each a steely gray with a fine polish at the top tapering down to a rough flame finish, symbolic of the once-gleaming buildings falling. A large American flag drapes the background hanging from a ladder truck, amplifying the moment along with the unadorned presence of a few once unexpected guests. One is a mother who raised her family in a neighboring town and whose son was working just a few floors above Mike McGinty's meeting. She came up from Florida to privately thank Chris and Paula for creating a place to remember him.

Another is Patrick Mitchell, looking fresh in a green button-down shirt, back from West Point. He's been asked to read the contents of the first plaque. "From the ashes of that day rose a phoenix, a renown dedication to the ideals that have made this country great," he says. "Citizens of the world were reminded that while a building may fall, freedom is forever."

His father Chris isn't smothered in glory. That's because Mitchell sees his job as educating younger generations about the days that followed, and there is much more to be done. He walks up to the microphone slightly stooped, still a little sore from surgery, and thanks everyone en masse, joking about his treasurer "who was foolish enough to answer the phone that day." He mostly speaks about the joy of working together. "This town runs on volunteerism, and the best part of volunteering is the people you meet." His hope is that the organization they built will inspire others to test the waters.

Cindy McGinty follows him right in step. She wears a somber earthy leisure suit, and her voice no longer trembles. Her speaking is declarative, grounded. Her son has been sitting beside her and she senses he's gaining something vital from this. While his phone beeps all day, he seems to be mostly present, appreciating that 1,500 people turn out for the dedication. She recalls the heroic passengers rising up on Flight 93, and workers guiding each other toward safety down stairwells. Any distinction between large and small acts has become moot. "It doesn't really matter. It just matters that we help each other," she says. McGinty ends emphatically with something she's said many times before, and it continues to resound. "The terrorists thought they were going to destroy us, and what they really did was band us together."

On Sunday she and her son head to Boston where volunteers again prepare soldiers' care packages. As they gather everything from boot laces to playing cards in more than one thousand boxes, Cindy mostly goes around thanking people among the lines of tables. As a co-founder of the two groups organizing the effort, she also finds herself explaining what it's all about to newcomers. She's most impressed by parents who bring young children in, teaching their kids to understand why they are packing those items.

During the weekend she emails Jay and David to say: "Nothing will bring back our loved ones but for the first time in a long time I have meaning and purpose on 9/11." It's been a long haul, but she no longer feels mired in pain.

"With all the media attention especially this year I think people almost force you into a place of sadness, where maybe that's not where you should be," she explains later. "It felt good to be in a place of service and I felt Mike's presence, but in a positive way. I didn't feel like I got stuck in the sadness." At another time that's not flagged, she'll go down to Lower Manhattan or the Boston Common, "but I had a place to be that day. I felt that I would have been stuck in my grief, and I had a place outside of that."

If Mike was peeking down, or maybe sending another dragonfly zigging by, there's little doubt he'd have been pleased.

Late that Sunday afternoon Denise and I go down toward the National September 11 Memorial. As we step out of a cab on Broadway, it's a world apart from the feel-good vibe at the middle school.

A long line of demonstrators are slicing through the intersection and filing down beside Saint Paul's. It's crush and cacophony, led by 9/11 conspiracy "Truthers" who believe the government brought down WTC 7 with pre-positioned explosives and fed us other lies. They argue that large pools of molten metal observed under both towers and WTC 7, along with the sulfidation corrosion of structural steel, point to high-temperature reactions that defy the official explanations. Some of these claims were dismissed as junk science. Water lines were broken and there was no way to put out flames in the forty-seven-story building, for one. But here they come—chanting, headstrong, some in rabid costumes—here for the show. For all we know there's some validity underneath this frenzy. Yet our first, even naive reaction is, why today?

The energy is lethal. One guy rotates a sign to the backside, declaring: Legalize pot. A thin young woman in a ponytail leans into bystanders, shrill, squirrely, demanding, "I just want you to know the truth." She withdraws, slides on, ready to pounce again.

They're about to clash with a supporter of pastor Terry Jones, who's here this year with a Koran in his hands saying he wants to respect the fallen. Everyone else seems either pissed off or is snapping pictures of the main tower still under construction. My head is clogged with Slavic accents and whiplash French. The cops look agitated, hundreds of them standing still, often in groups of fifteen and twenty, snarling their most menacing snarls, gnarled in gnawed waiting. They must really hate this day. It's just a shot away. Scruffy smirking guys skateboard past them and I believe that's really why those dudes came down here. "America only knows about two towers!" a man is yelling.

Nearby someone holds a sidewalk seminar, and he rips, "Giuliani is a criminal!" This must be America, this must be what soldiers fight to protect. Everyone's got a freaking angle. That's what I love here—every point on humanity's compass rose crisscrosses the avenue, the needle spinning crazily; but that's also what I hate today—the variation from true seems so distorted, in this place that really is sacred ground where we should only be paying tribute—period—this deviation feels way beyond bounds.

There's the chapel again. A sanctuary on the edge of this whorl. As always.

Its spire and yard should be a glimmering jewel. The church is surrounded with thousands of white ribbons emblazoned with the words, "Remember to Love" attached to its wrought-iron fence, intended to echo the makeshift memorials once erected there as an invitation to build a better world. Their presence is startling, like the appearance of winter moths blinding your headlights during a sudden January thaw. Yet with the marchers and vengeance swirling around the church, that message feels subverted.

We won't get in and view the memorial's waterfalls and pools on this day. The public opening is in another fourteen hours, but we came anyway. There will be another time for this. We go over to the firefighters' memorial wall, set off by sawhorses, and finally, thankfully, there's a glimpse of respect, even camaraderie. Five firemen conduct a change in the honor guard in front of the wall. Most of us hush.

It's time to go, and we start uptown.

Later that evening everything comes full circle.

We stop for a nightcap around the corner from our hotel in Tribeca, at the Nancy Whiskey Pub off Canal Street. A tough blonde bartender looks spent stacking cases of bar bottles and a guy who seems to be the bookkeeper of this dank establishment squawks on an end stool. A couple is playing shuffleboard. They've had a few drinks, so have we, and we get to talking.

Greg is a retired battalion chief from Detroit with a white dress shirt on and his jacket on a chair. He's got one of those quintessential walrus mustaches you might associate with firemen; he seems polite and low-key. He's also attentive to his wife.

"Husband, come here and play," she intones sweetly when he strays from the table, and Denise is immediately attuned to her. He tells me how he and some colleagues came to New York in 2001 to do whatever they could. He wanted to return, this time joining thousands at the Firemen's Memorial remembrance on 100th Street.

A decade before, the most he could do, the only job they had for him, was to be a pallbearer at funerals during his five-day stay.

Greg Best did that without ego or resentment. He offered himself with kindness, and he does not forget.

16

HEART WORK

. . . .

Joe Lally bled when one of the granite pavers slipped.

It nearly crushed his finger. The six-foot-three retired detective sergeant couldn't have cared less. He had worked like an animal the last few days at Foxborough's 9/11 memorial, a true shovel and broom guy. Sweat moons soaked his T-shirt.

His life had seemed to evolve to this day and he was proud to be a part of it. At twenty-one Lally had become an alcoholic in the Air Force, a Roxbury kid from Mission Church High School who had lost his mom—his best friend—at seventeen. His credo became love things and use people. Until he bottomed out in a hospital.

He stayed sober the next three decades. As a cop he befriended two women, a rape victim and another forced into prostitution, and helped them both survive. That still meant a lot, as they both kept in touch with him.

And here was something else. When Joe introduced his friend Chris Mitchell at the memorial dedication, he dipped back to a familiar AA mantra, paraphrasing it along these lines:

Everybody gets ideas, but not all of us entertain them or has the balls to follow up on them. We need one person to make a stand.

"Thirty-five years ago," Lally said one day after downing a bowl of cream of broccoli at Spoodles, "If someone said, 'You're going to do this great thing,' I would've said, 'Yeah. Right.'"

Andy Sausmer asks the question many times, one of only a handful that ultimately matter.

"How can I fill the void in my soul that is Glenn? How can I make a difference, some type of tribute?"

He nailed it once when Glenn Winuk's park was dedicated, and continues to probe. "It's just a question of, okay you do a park, and that can be considered a one-shot deal, and when you look at a tunnel-to-tower run, that's a continuing event, so sometimes I find myself doubting, do I just make noise one day a year? Do I do enough?"

He offers Jay Winuk ideas and occasionally raises money for Glenn's memorial foundation. One time he got an automated external defibrillator donated to a local athletic foundation. He sees possibilities, even unformed ones, to fill gaps. Several old Jericho classmates run small charities, and maybe they'll get together to do a mass fundraiser and divvy up the proceeds. On occasion he hosts mini-alumni reunions at his restaurant. He understands that it's difficult for some of Glenn's other friends—juggling married life, their kids' schedules—while he's single. He's grown to accept, "Gee, has it been that long?"

He doesn't press. At a fire department event, he might offer a toast at the table *Let's not forget those who couldn't be with us tonight.* Other times he won't. Either way, his friends know.

There are times he's sure Glenn's around. Many years ago, perhaps before the memorial service was held without any of Winuk's remains, he was working out and placed a barbell on the ground. "The weights moved and I said, 'Oh, Glenn's there.'" Another time he was driving without really paying attention when his car swerved to avoid something and seemed to correct itself. "I said, 'Thanks, Bud.' I said it automatically."

He visualizes Glenn with a glass of scotch saying, "Buddy, what are you making such a fuss for?"

Once in a while, there's another kind of presence. A few people mention to him that whenever they're in Jericho, they'll stop by and sit in the park. "It brings great joy whenever I see a grandfather or father with their kids," Sausmer says. "Recently I went there to take a look at things and saw a bicyclist there. I invited him to the service, and as I left he was sitting reading the plaque."

Was Ellen Clarke meant to be on the other end?

It wasn't as if she had a cushy load to begin with. Clarke was responsible for global technology at Marsh Inc., the $5.2 billion insurance brokerage. This meant the firm's servers and routers, its applications, laptops, all of it. Three phone clicks on a conference call spun her world around.

She might have been at her office, a plush conference room with a coveted view north to the Hudson from the ninety-seventh floor of the North Tower. Two floors above, Mike McGinty sat with twenty-five or thirty analysts and managers for their presentation. But Clarke was in London, where she'd decided to fly at the last minute. On the morning call CIOs and technology directors from all over the world began reviewing procedures for their annual budget, including three of her managers in New York.

"Three are on the one call and all of a sudden we hear *click click click* and the fellow who ran my governmental management functions said, 'Wow.' We didn't know what happened. We tried to call back but all lines were down. Then we got a call from Australia and he said, 'I'm sorry to tell you, a 747 hit the World Trade Center.' He was a joker and I said, 'This is really not something to laugh about,' and he said, 'I'm not kidding.'"

Over the next hour we watched. I said to everybody, "'I think we just lost our technology staff.'"

Clarke oversaw about 550 people in Manhattan, and she lost one hundred employees and thirty Marsh consultants. The body of Flight 11 plowed into her office. She and colleagues had long known the tower was a leading target. In fact, in moments of futile chatter *we had joked about planes coming down the Hudson and banking left and going into our office.* She'd cancelled a London trip three times before, and on Monday afternoon felt that she needed to go.

I believe in my heart I was meant to be there because I'm a very calm person, especially in a crisis situation. I said it to myself: you cannot afford yourself to be too emotional even though they've had a tremendous impact in your life.

"Then I said, this is a horrific experience we've had, and we really need to start planning the recovery. We had means to recover it and didn't know how long it would take, and we certainly needed a network. Once the lines came back, heads of major technology providers called me personally—it's worth mentioning—they took it upon themselves to pay attention to major clients. Cisco, Verizon, AT&T."

Marsh's networks and servers for its worldwide operations were gutted. Fortunately, applications and databases had been backed up in New Jersey. But the people with long-term knowledge, their IT brain trust, were also dead—the three executives who reported to her, and fifteen next-level managers.

"So we really had to build it all from scratch. We actually got the firm back in business," she says. "The offices in the United States had no computers, no ability to do business. We had to get the network up quickly and an e-mail system up quickly."

Clarke and her remaining group made a recovery plan with an A, B, and C list of priorities. Over the past fifteen months she'd focused on building a team culture and sharing information; technology people knew the business people. It paid off. Networks went up first within twenty-four hours. They built servers, and gradually brought back some 150 applications. "We recovered the firm completely in three days," she says. "The staff was incredible."

On the fourth day flights resumed out of Heathrow and she was one of three passengers aboard British Airways with some marshals. Ellen felt shaky; they landed at night and she couldn't see downtown.

The next day she sat with spouses, parents, uncles, and aunts in support groups Marsh gathered at its family assistance center in the Millenium Hotel. As a human resources person explained benefits, *they kept looking at me throughout the conversation. They felt I was the trusted advisor. Of all the things I had to do, this was the most difficult.*

Their sons and daughters had made last-ditch calls. "We got calls, apparently, on cell phones where people were hiding under desks, the planes had hit. Parents asked me where they physically were on the floor. I had many calls reported to me: Can you help me? Can you call my wife and tell her I love her? I don't read them any more. They're too upsetting."

Holy cow, these were people who knew they were going to die. They knew they were going to die, or said send us some help before we all burn to death.

Clarke attended thirty or more funerals. Meetings were held to determine who would go to which one. She knew the staff well. At one funeral in southern New Jersey *the mom came over to me and held me close like a chokehold on to my neck. She appreciated the effort.*

I loved these people. I really did. They were tremendous individuals, so I felt I had to do everything I could.

She soldiered on. Clarke left Marsh in 2003 and started a consulting firm, discovering later that she'd been twice saved. Around the time she joined the firm in 1999, Ellen was diagnosed with autoimmune hepatitis, and the prognosis was that even with medications, her liver would last only ten years. Almost a decade later to the day, her liver collapsed and she was unconscious. "I was two days away from dying when I got a liver. I did die twice during that time, I'm told, and they brought me back to life."

God saved me twice, at least. That's why I think I was meant to be there to help. Those are real feelings. It helps me all the time. I really believe it. God wanted to keep me around for a while. I'm still trying to figure it out; it gives me great comfort to know if (he) had to choose somebody to go through this process. I think I'm the right person. In various families—we don't know why—some people end up being very strong, some do not, and I ended up being one of the strong ones.

Her questions, as if clinging to a battered, jettisoned life raft, would not abate.

When Jane Pollicino was asked to write a letter to her late husband for a book being compiled by the nonprofit organization Tuesday's Children, she agreed. The group did so much to support Pollicino and her kids over the years, hooking them up with counselors, helping Jane get in touch with her own needs, offering a mom's self-empowerment class, and just being there when things spiked. In time for the decade's observance, Tuesday's Children gathered one hundred offerings for *The Legacy Letters.* Jane sat down and wrote to Steve, and these paragraphs are among those that did not make it in.

You see, you just went to work one day and never came home. You literally disappeared without a trace. It is still so very hard to process. How can anyone begin to deal with or try to understand a death, almost 3,000 murders, involving such outrageous circumstances? I keep going over it in my mind. Wondering so much about how you spent your last hours on earth. It haunts me and there just aren't any answers.

However, it is a comfort for me knowing that you made the most of every moment of your life and you appreciated what you had. I have no doubts about that. I believe that you have no regrets for how you spent all of your days. You know I don't think that many people would feel that way if their lives were to suddenly end tomorrow. Do we all feel cheated? Of course we do, but we all feel blessed with the time we had. I trust in God's plan. My faith is all that I can count on because nothing else makes sense.

I had to learn to share your death with the entire world. The attack was experienced globally and every single person who witnessed the event was changed in some way. So although my loss might be more personal than most, I share the loss nonetheless. The whole world has a piece of what happened to me and our family, and this has made the grieving process tricky if not impossible. I have to admit there are times when I take comfort in sharing my loss but the result is I have no control of what surprises me on a daily basis.

I often feel like I am outside my body looking at myself functioning, or more than likely dysfunctioning. In nine years I have never been able to deal with any of this on my own terms and as a result this continues to be impossible to process.

Not two years later, Jane passed suddenly after a stroke. She was in Mexico vacationing with her family, including her daughter and grandson, her son, and her twin sister, Lorraine. That Sunday was an exceptional day, and they stayed up playing Bananagrams, laughing, "until our sides hurt," her sister says. Everyone jelled. The next morning Jane fed little Nicholas as others took a yoga class. Four days later they were numb.

Lorraine Angeline recalls Jane's signature email sign off, perhaps stretching her toes in the sand, humming a slice of her own redemption song: "Be well."

At times Jeff Winuk feels like the anti-Glenn.

Eight years older, the "rotten brother," born to be having a good time and flipping the bird at tomorrow. Ditched New York early for Florida, where his first marriage went bust. Ten numbers away from being drafted during Vietnam, he lost some friends there; others came back unknown to themselves. His ride was often about sex, drugs, and rock 'n roll.

Yet other things prevail. Once Jeff's role was protecting Glenn and Jay. As kids he'd knock on the neighbor's door and get in a larger guy's face. He, too, joined Jericho's fire department as soon as he could, jumping from their kitchen table when the alarm sounded at the station up the street. Jeff drove an ambulance, and he's sure that's partly why his brother followed suit. "It was the excitement of it all," he says. "I guess at that age we're invincible. We think we are, anyway."

After he moved south he didn't see Glenn often, but they were always there for one another in a pinch. Before remarrying in 1997, Jeff needed a favor. His fiancée, Diane, had asked him about the color scheme, and Jeff blurted out, "Purple!"—for everything, including hats for the guests. He got Glenn on it—his best man, this second time around—and his brother scoured the stores, finding enough to accessorize the groom's party. Jeff and Diane still keep two of the caps.

That Tuesday he was in a doctor's office and someone pointed at the TV. Like all of Glenn's friends, Jeff's gut told him it was so. "I just had a feeling he was involved," he says. "I called all the cops and firefighters I knew." He screamed at one Jericho firefighter to go find him.

He still feels somehow at fault. He was living in South Carolina, and regrets not being home. *I didn't do my job. I wish it were me, not him. He was my baby brother, and I wasn't there for him.* As we spoke another switch was thrown, things he hadn't talked about before. He turned on terrorists—real and imagined. "The hate I have for those people is unbelievable. They walk by me and I walk by the other way. I hate them so much."

Diane made him a collage with newspaper articles and photos of Glenn, which he's looked at once. The only thing he puts out in the open regarding September 11 is an American flag given to him after it was pulled out of the rubble. On the anniversary, "I just sit and vegetate, I don't watch anything." They spend the day together.

Sometimes Jeff Winuk is still furious. But his wife and Jay both tell him that even if he had been up there, Glenn would have done the exact same thing.

"It took me back," he says. "I thought, I would be there also. So I wasn't pissed off at him anymore. I was pissed off at me."

Howard gave his sister heart work, and this became Edie Lutnick's life.

They both knew that their brother Gary was dead. He had called Edie from the 103d floor as the toxic smoke poured in, about to consume his life, careening the course of history. Yet incapable of breaching their love.

Gary Lutnick called Edie to say goodbye. He also left messages on his brother's cell. He reached an ex-girlfriend, calmly telling her he was sorry about how things ended badly between them.

Howard Lutnick, the CEO of Cantor Fitzgerald, could not yet get his arms around the full scope, maybe never. But two nights later he sensed what to do. These people were his family. And he was going to care for his extended family, no matter what the cost. On September 12 Cantor Fitzgerald had found only 127 of its 960 employees. Lutnick told his older sister he needed her to run a charity for the Cantor families. She hesitated only for a few minutes.

"As it turns out, heart work was something I'm pretty good at," Edie Lutnick says.

The Lutnicks had grown into young adulthood as orphans. Their parents both died of cancer within a year and a half of each other, far too young at ages forty-two and fifty-one. Gary was only fourteen, and Edie raised him as she went to law school. When their dad died leaving the three alone, an uncle called inviting them to have Thanksgiving dinner together—something like two months away. Howard asked, "What about tonight?" They stopped speaking with that relative.

Cutting through some of the fog of 9/12 and 9/13, Edie says her brother made it immediately clear he wouldn't let his families go through what we had. *He had seen hell.* "We were going to be the ones who invited people over to dinner," she says.

Edie writes just as she speaks. It pops out and rolls, there's repetition but nothing redundant because she builds from a foundation, gathering from streams and rivulets that brim in a flood, firing and recasting, until suddenly a river pierces through and forms the great falls in front of me. She and I are having a conversation that matters more than I could have hoped. For some reason, I'm brought to a place thundering and immaculate after a light snowfall. Edie connects it all, and through this she found her greatest strength: bringing people together.

Her book, *An Unbroken Bond,* came out shortly before the tenth anniversary. It chronicles not only how the Cantor Fitzgerald families faced tragedy but also how a corporate family struggled in the aftermath and stayed connected. She shined a vital perspective on some ugly post-9/11 debacles—including the duplicity behind redeveloping the World Trade Center site, where families' views were often steamrolled, and the families' desires to have remains returned and be properly interred. While those issues were unsettling, what truly grabbed me is what she did next.

The Cantor Fitzgerald Relief Fund that Edie stewards fulfilled a commitment to support its families. Then it reached out to thousands of other people impacted by war, natural disasters, and terrorism, supporting other charities and distributing aid directly. The fund gave parents prepaid debit cards after a tornado hit Oklahoma and following · Superstorm Sandy. It sent relief to Haiti, assisted wounded veterans, and helped another group build prefabricated homes in Ecuador after a 2016 earthquake. Sometimes the aid enables victims' relatives to do good work locally, such as a family that built a shelter for battered women. What does the tenth or fifteenth year mean to her? "It's a milestone," Lutnick says. "It's not an ending."

In a review of her book, Edie told *USA Today* that she credits the families "for healing me. Because when you have a purpose greater than yourself, that is when you heal. That is what I live by."

I ask her to continue on this. She laughs heartily, thinking back at how her thoughts tend to flow out. She tells me I've identified one of the two things she lives by.

"Howard has a saying all the time after this happened: 'It takes a broken heart to heal a broken heart—and my sister Edie wears a broken heart.'" She does this literally as well. She has a necklace, a large rose gold heart that is divided in three parts, but not severed. One part is for her to give as she will; one is for Howard; and one is for Gary. Her partner Lewis made the necklace, and it never comes off. "As much as we like to think of it otherwise, there is a big difference between sympathy and empathy," she says. "When you see someone in pain and you want to help them, that's what ultimately helps you come back and heal, even though that's not what you're thinking of doing."

So what comes out is if you can find a mission larger than yourself, you can heal spectacularly if you take part in some larger things.

She's learned that this involves crucial responsibilities. Lutnick wants to ensure that a new generation makes a connection to victims' lives as a way to honor them. "I know what we were robbed of," she says, "and just those are enough to make you cry forever." She tells me that conveying a piece of their stories, and hooking someone else up to them, has a multiplier effect. She suggests that if someone like myself feels in awe, humbled by a life I'm sharing, "think what others will take from it." I stop taking notes. My book is now writing itself.

While continuing to run the Cantor fund, she is replenished by meeting people who do extraordinary things—at home in her city, and across other continents. Edie offers this advice to others who want to make a positive impact: listen closely and "make sure the aid you are rendering is what the person wants and needs," rather than making yourself feel better.

Very early on, a reporter was interviewing her in a makeshift office. The phones were going berserk and Edie was doing the equivalent of talking people off the ledge. After several hours, and constant interruptions, the journalist finally looked at Lutnick and said, "'Edie, you do realize you can go home?'

"I looked at her, and it never occurred to me there was a choice— never—not for one split second, at any time of my actions, did it ever occur to me there was choice, because people were in pain. And when people are in pain, you help them. And I never expected that by helping them, they would turn out to be my lifeline."

Chris Mitchell's phone went nuts.

As the Patriots played their home opener against the Chargers, friends at Gillette shouted, "Hey, you look good on the Jumbotron!"

The team's media people had interviewed him at the Foxborough memorial, and then showed it in mid-September. But by then, the buzz from the previous week was fading, and he and Paula were already looking ahead.

He was a reluctant town celebrity again for a short while. Even when his younger son did an Eagle project the following weekend, the local newspaper spotlighted that too. After the memorial dedication, Chris and Paula both felt great and went over to an Irish pub with some cousins who'd come down from Vermont. "The bartender said beers were on him for what I've done—that was cool—then someone else in another room bought a round, and the next day I bought a breakfast sandwich and a cup of coffee, and they paid," he said. "But that wore off real quick. Now I have to reach into my pocket again."

Other changes were already under way. Mitchell sold his landscaping business to a nephew. His back injuries from digging trenches and lugging plants had run their course, and a year before he'd enrolled in a facility management certificate program. He wouldn't have snow plowing on his mind round the clock next winter, and he landed a custodian's job at a local school. As the fall rolled out he and Paula saw their enthusiasm to encourage more teaching about 9/11 expand into instilling a service ethic, a partnership with Foxborough's schools. "In past years it's been community service, like picking up trash," she says. "We'd rather call it 'Doing the right thing,' or 'Helping your neighbor.' We kind of want to get that into the schools, because the need is there and it makes you feel good."

A few finishing touches remained. An electrician installed the lighting for the memorial's walkway and towers, and Chris thought about adding one more plaque the following year listing both the volunteers and donors, and every Massachusetts resident killed in the attacks. It would have to be super-sized. He figured he could find all the names at a memorial that's on the Boston Common.

"I'll check with Cindy," he said, "and even if I have to go in some weekend and write them all down, I will."

Joe Mlynarczyk has a routine with his daughter, Rebecca. If they're having a glass of chocolate milk together, they race to see who can gulp it down the fastest.

He used to do the same thing with his buddy Steve Siller at the Squad Co. 1 firehouse in Park Slope, Brooklyn.

"You think of all the times you laughed, all the times you worked, just spending time," Mlynarczyk says. *That was our nightly race.*

Since 2003, Joe and his wife, Rachel, have been raising their four children in St. Augustine, Florida. Five years into their married life together, the couple was refurbishing some rooms to prepare for their twin sons' first birthdays when life was upended by the terrorist attacks. He tore up a knee, suffered three herniated discs, and, worst of all, damaged his lungs while breathing in the pulverized glass during six weeks at the site. Mlynarczyk retired on a medical disability almost eighteen months later, and the family moved away. He rarely returns.

It had always been their dream to relocate near palm trees, but they anticipated doing that much later, not a dozen years into his career.

Those are not the only reasons he left.

I pretty much severed all contacts. All the guys who are gone I have them in my head every day, and I lost the ability to speak to their families, only because I can't get the words out—not that I wouldn't want to.

I went to wake after wake until I just couldn't go anymore. You were like a zombie. Just trying to find a part of someone so you could have a funeral service.

Mlynarczyk lost an inordinate share of brothers for any generation—twelve of the twenty-seven men in his company. Guys he trained with, sitting at their kitchen tables cracking up for minutes on end, then realizing *Oh, we're just firemen. We're just happy to have the job.*

A jack-of-all-trades, Siller, always on his feet. *I always said he would never lay down to sleep. He would just pass out somewhere.* Tom Butler, always saw eye to eye with him, *Just us man,* arguing with the rest of their crew. Eddie D'atri, a sometimes-menacing lieutenant, a bodybuilder who'd cut up anyone who fucked up. But you knew that in a crunch *he'd be the one coming to get you.*

I only got jammed up a couple of times when it didn't look too good—we always found our way out of it—but I always knew they were there. You might know the fire was getting real bad and you might not want to go any farther but you knew you could because they were there.

These connections went far beyond the station house. Mlynarczyk was one of thirty emergency medical instructors who taught CPR and other courses for thousands. Of the 343 FDNY members who perished, Joe estimates he knew or had worked with nearly half of them.

His dad, Stanley, had lived through D-Day. He was a medic who landed on Omaha Beach with the 2nd Ranger Battalion and scaled the one hundred-foot cliffs of Pointe-du-Hoc by rope ladders to take out enemy gunners. Two weeks after 9/11, feeling himself beginning to crash and burn, Joe called up his father. One of the wives was pleading with him to find her husband in the pile. Joe knew that his father had experienced such things, even though Stanley Mlynarczyk rarely spoke of it.

I asked him, Dad, can you tell me, when do you forget these guys when they're gone? He said, You don't. You don't ever forget them. The memories may fade, you may not dream about them every night, but the memories will always be there. You'll never forget.

In the rubble they located one of his captains, James Amato. It was tough to identify him. Captain Amato was wearing Lieutenant D'atri's coat. He also carried a radio that belonged with a special rig used in building collapses, which gave them a clue. Amato was going to a part-time job on Staten Island that day, but he stopped by the station for coffee first. He must have rushed in and grabbed D'atri's gear, which was next to his.

I don't know if I've really moved on. We certainly seem to occupy more of our time doing other things. But if there is an unoccupied moment of my day, I am thinking about my friends: were there hours or minutes before? What were they doing in the final minutes? One good thing is that of anybody we found, I don't think they suffered, I think they went quick. If there's any justice in it I think they went quick.

Squad Company 1 responded to any major emergency like a building collapse across the city. Its two rigs were a special operations engine with pumps, hose stretchers, and heavy rescue tools, and a technical response vehicle for collapses and water rescue. At 8:47 a.m. Engine 10 came on the radio: "World Trade Center 10-60. Send every available ambulance, everything you've got to the World Trade Center now."

My biggest regret is not being there with my friends that day—they all got on a rig and left without me. Except the outcome: one more dead guy and my kids wouldn't have me. I kind of regret not being there, maybe seeing Glenn and telling him to get out of the building.

Mlynarczyk narrowly escaped calamity later that first day. A captain in a marine unit who was hurt was trying to give his location over the radio. Commanders were expecting another plane, so a battalion chief at first ordered Joe's group not to leave a command post. He then agreed to the search but told them to stay clear of any buildings. They didn't find the injured captain, but outside WTC Buildings 4 and 5—relatively small ones at nine stories—they heard another call about a civilian trapped inside.

Joe broke his promise and found a large elderly man, maybe 330 pounds, pinned under a beam. Many of their tools had been crushed inside the trucks. As they tried to get the man out, an air conditioning unit came crashing down, a piece of rebar at its base slamming into Joe's helmet. Ammonia exploded in his face and he couldn't breathe. Fearing a terrorist gas attack, not knowing what it was, he barked at the others to get out. The man had two broken legs and cried for Joe to stay. Joe wasn't leaving. He thought if he could just lift the I-beam a half-inch the man could get out. One guy came back and they lifted the beam—Mlynarczyk wrenching his back and knee—but it was just enough. The others returned, and they brought the man out.

My little miracle. The guys came back. They came back because that's just what the guys do.

There are guys who were there six to eight months. I don't know how they did it.

Brought up Catholic, Joe's faith imploded as anger prevailed: *Why did you let this happen? And sit through hearing it's part of God's plan and everything happened for a reason.*

"I wasn't a very good person. I found it almost impossible to speak without having my own little breakdown all over again. I got assigned to a counseling unit in the city once my injuries were too much. We'd drive counselors to support groups, and I monopolized their time, I didn't let them rest. I would drive them an hour or two and I was their patient. Sitting in these group meetings I felt better, knowing they were worse off than me."

In St. Augustine he found a new community. There were good schools and endless road construction. He and other guys built a little bar area near his house. Sometimes when he's there he thinks of Tommy Butler and Key West, where they had dreamed of opening a business together. "I said, 'I'll run the bar and you run the charter boat.'"

One of his new neighbors tells Joe, "You're doing your part."

Sometimes he wished his father would fill in some of the blanks about the war. "He doesn't want to rehash it," he said. "I wish I could get a little more out of him just to pass his story down to my kids. I think I'd be more open with my kids about what happened at 9/11." In part to help them understand more, he planned to bring them to the memorial during a rare trip to New York around the holidays.

His lung therapy continues to be tough, yet there are no signs for the worse. Having lost about 70 percent of his capacity, even climbing thirteen stairs to the kids' bedrooms taxes his breathing. The smell of ammonia drives him away. After applying a cleaning agent in the shower, he closes it quickly and bolts. Joe rides a stationary bike, and some days it feels uphill the entire time, forcing him to reach for his inhaler. Other times he leans on his old friends.

When Mlynarcyk played center on the fire department's football team, his left guard wore number 67, and his right tackle wore number 71. Neither of them made it home that Tuesday.

On those days when he's up to it, pushing himself with the bike set at a reasonable intensity, he'll call out their jersey numbers. Reaching sixty-seven, he knows there's only four minutes left to go. "They're always with me," he says, "I use them to get me a little bit farther."

"I look for my friends in crowds all the time. I always have this inner hope that Glenn just wanted to leave and be somewhere on an island with a cold drink."

My friends are with me every day.

While motoring ahead, whether driving the "9/11 day" movement, his next start-up, or a life beyond the reach of those things, on occasion David Paine must check under the hood.

He finds goodness emerging from tragedy where others see dispiriting intransigence. He embraces silver linings in a toxic haze. David feeds off the apparent paradox that in the grand scheme of things, events that are perceived to be punishing crises become transformational opportunities.

"Great beauty and compassion live side by side with some of the worst things imaginable," he chuckles. "It's odd that good and evil are so closely intertwined, and sometimes you can't tell the difference between the two."

The scorching string of mass shootings across the country tested this perpetual optimism. Tucson, Fort Hood, and Aurora. Sandy Hook. The Emanuel African Methodist Episcopal Church. San Bernardino and Orlando. Plus the crude bombs on Boylston Street.

Yet Paine took note of the initial responses: A school principal lunging at the shooter, screaming at him to stay back. Bystanders hurdling barriers to reach the sidewalk. A writing student racing to block a closed door, giving his classmates more time to flee a gunman.

Perhaps we have grown too accustomed to seeing such instinctive reactions to gun violence and other attacks. While uplifting at first, those gut-driven gestures somehow turn into heroic clichés. Some of us actually become inured to get at the root causes. Resistance to expanding background checks for gun sales was emboldened after these killings, after all, even as parents fighting through their grief pleaded for sanity.

No one is really talking about honoring the spirit of unity. Paine wonders, how do we sustain that first response?

In 2015, he and Jay found themselves being led by children—fourteen-year-olds who were born on September 11, 2001.

Participation had continued to grow marking the anniversary with acts of service and kindness, yet they realized that one-quarter of the country had no memory of the attacks. To connect with younger generations and sustain the movement, they would need to tap into something larger. "The motivation has to be deeper and broader than paying tribute to those who lost their lives," David told me as he and Jay sowed new seeds for the fifteenth-year commemoration.

More than thirteen thousand babies arrived across the United States on 9/11, and Paine wondered whether some of those adolescents found the day important. After reaching out to them in the summer of 2015, nearly two dozen teens shared their idealism in interviews. Hillary O'Neill, a middle school student in Norwalk, Connecticut knew families who lost relatives. O'Neill's hope was that her birthday would become a day when people observe how much the world has changed. "How it transformed," she anticipated, speaking in a video done for 911day.org. "If we all do good deeds on 9/11, it will all add up." She set up a lemonade stand to raise money for a charity.

Such enthusiasm helped Paine and Winuk rebrand their campaign as "Hope was born on 9/11."

"They want the world to be better," David said, "and they agree with the day as a concept in itself. The day is about making things better."

On the anniversary, some of the teens helped package meals at a City Harvest food bank alongside adults in New York who had experienced the attacks. The kids fit right in, and David found it was less their physical involvement than how they touched others around them. "They so perfectly communicated the message that there is goodness that came out of 9/11," he said.

Every few years, Paine found himself tweaking the 9/11 day's engine, perhaps cleaning a dirty carburetor to stop the rough idling. He and Jay considered handing it off to O'Neill's generation—and the next.

The anniversary could become a moment to express their hopes. "A moment when they can stop and ask their friends to support them," David said. "Whatever the cause is—it could be about peace, or poverty, or hunger—all those things. They just a need a day that can be theirs."

Paine stands on Vesey Street again, this time within view of the gleaming new One World Trade Center, soon to be the tallest building in the Western Hemisphere. On this chilly April morning he is back downtown with Jay at a 5K tribute run for 9/11 families. Just six days earlier, the attacks at the Boston Marathon finish scared the bejesus out of many of us.

"I think we're all kindred spirits," Paine is saying. "We want to find ways to express our remorse in a constructive fashion, and that whenever we see something, we link to it somehow. It seems to be an emerging movement that is sparked by hate.

"This response, this defiance for peace, is really interesting," he continues. "The fact that we're dealing with it showing sensitivity and compassion, and caring for one another . . ."

He trails off momentarily. Reaction to the bombing in Beantown surrounds us. Many runners carry expressions of solidarity for their usual division rivals. A band performs "Sweet Caroline," the emblematic seventh-inning stretch sing-along of the Red Sox. Paine finishes with, ". . . what Boston just did—they learned that from the 9/11 tragedy."

Perhaps. But where will everyone be six or sixteen years out?

The previous December, Paine was on a treadmill in Newport Beach when CNN reported the Newtown shootings. Running into the bedroom to find his wife, David was crying again. He started an online sympathy card, wanting to reach out in an offer of psychic healing, something, anything, starting with MyGoodDeed's mailing list. He went out for lunch and came back and there were seventy thousand signatures in about two hours. *Which is ridiculous.* It became the fastest-growing petition ever on the Causes.com platform, and within a week he gathered 2.5 million signatures from 140 countries.

David flew east and drove out with his sister. They presented a facsimile of the card with the first twenty thousand signatures the following Friday to Newtown's selectmen, gathering at a soccer field for a vigil attended by two thousand people. Jay jumped in as well. Meeting neighbors who rallied to support the victims' families, both Winuk and Paine helped them organize a nonprofit and prepare their message to kickoff a campaign, advocating for common sense, anything, to address the complex forces that enable the Adam Lanzas to do such incalculable harm.

One of those neighbors, Lee Shull, a software consultant who lives down the street from two of Lanza's victims, finishes running with his son along the Hudson River during the 9/11 family event. His wife and twin daughter have also walked the route, now squeezing down the closed-off road between a kids' play area and food vendors alongside firemen doing a recruiting drive. The group Shull helped start, Sandy Hook Promise, seeks middle ground to address gun violence and improve mental health supports and school safety. *It really just stemmed out of a need, a need to do something, and a feeling that this could happen anywhere.*

A need to do something.

We have a purpose.

There's a solidarity binding Lee Shull with David and Jay and so many others that transcends how we often define empathy. An infectious leap, a roar, to right a wrong. "We came to the realization that we can't live our lives in fear," Shull says. "It's just not a sustainable way for us to live. We're not going to shrink."

Winuk has the marathon response on his mind, in addition to Newtown. "It just seems to bring out the best of people," Jay says. "People rise to the occasion, and that is very promising and empowering, and soothing, and healing."

He and David have a book to write, a modern epic. If they can ever sequester themselves long enough.

PART FOUR

THE DEPTHS OF HEALING

The salvation of man is through love and in love.
—Viktor Frankl

Jeanne Ann Clery

(CLERY FAMILY)

President George H. W. Bush greets Connie and Howard Clery at a 1990 Rose Garden ceremony for crime victims' rights.

Howard and Connie Clery in front of a likeness of their daughter in 1987.

(*THE MORNING CALL*)

Connie Clery, far right, and Howard Clery with three staff members inside the office of their newly-formed nonprofit, Security On Campus, in 1990.

Laura Dunn with S. Daniel Carter on a US Department of Education "Negotiated Rulemaking" committee, helping to draft implementing regulations for the Campus Sexual Violence Elimination Act in 2014.

Glenn Winuk in his Jericho Fire
Department dress uniform in 1992.

(ELAINE WINUK)

Jay Winuk with his brother's missing
person poster in the fall of 2001.

(*THE JOURNAL NEWS*)

A young girl reaches toward the FDNY Memorial Wall
across from the World Trade Center site, dedicated to
343 fallen FDNY members and Glenn J. Winuk.

(9/11 DAY)

David Paine with a resolute Jay Winuk during a 9/11
anniversary service event in 2013 in New York.

(9/11 DAY)

The 9/11 Day co-founders at Citi Field on
the tenth anniversary weekend.

(DAVI SING, 9/11 DAY)

David Paine at the New York Stock Exchange in 2015.

(GARY HE, 9/11 DAY)

Volunteers prepare food packs in New York on the fifteen anniversary of 9/11.

(9/11 DAY)

President Barack Obama meets Jay and Carolyn Winuk near Ground Zero three days after U.S. troops killed Osama Bin Laden.

(JAY WINUK)

Mike and Cindy McGinty

(CINDY MCGINTY)

Being a dad meant everything to Mike McGinty.

(CINDY MCGINTY)

Chris Mitchell speaks at the dedication of a 9/11
memorial in Foxborough, MA in 2011.

(FRANK MORTIMER, *FOXBORO REPORTER*)

Cindy McGinty and her son greet well-wishers
in Foxborough during the tenth anniversary.

(FRANK MORTIMER, *FOXBORO REPORTER*)

Volunteers at a food
pack event sign a
tribute board during
9/11 observances.

(9/11 DAY)

Rochme and Jacob Offen on
their wedding day in 1920.

Prisoners near the Mauthausen Concentration Camp
in Austria transporting stones on the "stairs of death"
in a quarry where Nathan and Sam Offen worked.

(MAUTHAUSEN MEMORIAL)

Recreated scene of American soldiers entering Mauthausen,
probably taken two days after the liberation of about 40,000
prisoners there and at a nearby concentration camp on May 5, 1945.

(US NATIONAL ARCHIVES AND RECORDS ADMINISTRATION)

Nathan Offen and Helen Goldberg celebrating their engagement in London, 1950. Bernard Offen is fourth from left in the back row with an arm on his brother Sam's shoulder, third from left. Their host, Miriam Freedman, sits third from left in the first row.

(STEPHEN FREEDMAN)

Nathan Offen in the 1970s.

(NATHAN OFFEN)

Sam Offen at the Holocaust Memorial Center Zekelman
Family Campus, Farmington Hills, Mich.
(*THE DETROIT NEWS*)

Almost five decades later,
Sam Offen finally meets one
of his liberators, Donald
Montgomery, who arrived at
Mauthausen in May of 1945.

(DIANE WEISS, *THE DETROIT
NEWS*. COURTESY OF *THE
DETROIT NEWS* COLLECTION AT
THE ARCHIVES OF MICHIGAN.)

Sam Offen and his clan visit Kraków together for the first time in 1985. From left, Randy Samuels with his wife, Sam's daughter, Gail Offen, Sam and Hyla, and their son, Jerry.

(GAIL OFFEN)

Bernard Offen gestures during a 2015 broadcast interview.

(THINKTECH HAWAII)

Clockwise from lower center, Sam, Nathan, and Bernard
Offen meet visitors and sign their books at the United States
Holocaust Memorial Museum in Washington, D.C. in 2012.

(KEN BRACK)

Mike, Amanda, and Chris Brack in the Grand Canyon circa 1996.

(KEN BRACK)

Michael Brack, second from left, with pals Travis Dupuis,
Tom Layman (in back), Griffin Benelli (back row with
cap), Jay Gordon, Jeff Walsh, and Cory Scanlon.

Michael Thomas Brack on an Outward Bound trip
in the Maryland mountains in 2001.

Denise and Ken Brack during a tenth anniversary celebration
for Mike and P.J. Shaughnessy hosted by both families.

(LISA PEARSON)

Michael Brack and his
dad in Machiasport.

(DENISE BRACK)

I KNEW THAT CONSECRATING A LOVED ONE'S LEGACY as Jay Winuk had done was not a sure thing. Despite such dedication, paying tribute demanded frequent recharging and balancing of one's energy.

Returning inward to reconcile one's anger and fears in order to heal was quite another task. Six years after our son's death, a trip to Europe with high school seniors studying genocide ushered in a deeper understanding of our capacity to transpose pain into something new, even when the losses of loved ones cut a nearly unimaginable swath.

In April 2009, Denise and I were chaperones aboard a chartered bus crossing Poland with twenty-one students and some of my colleagues at TechBoston Academy. We had just left Kraków, one of the key stops during a journey from Munich to Prague, through Poland and then to Berlin, stepping through scenes of monstrosity and the consequences of indifference.

We had already visited Dachau and Auschwitz, and the bus ground away from the ancient Polish capital heading toward a third concentration camp near the Poland-Ukraine border. Much of the countryside felt ragged even with daffodils and silky magnolias brightening villagers' yards. Clusters of farmers were planting their grey fields, and lines of bare orchards undulated coarsely into the hills. An overcast sky closed over the earth like a worn lid. Even with the emerging verdant cover of spring, I wondered how much of this land might have remained insulated from the memories of war.

As the bus rumbled along, I talked with a student whom I considered exceptional in his intellect and will, gathering his reflections about the trip with a tape recorder. While Ellery Kirkconnell shared his processing of man's cruelty and how he had felt intolerance in his own life, a seed that had been planted in me a year earlier seemed to burst through the surface. It dawned on me to contact a Holocaust survivor who had visited our school, telling the entire student body that he survived because of blind luck and his hatred of the Nazis. Following Nathan Offen's talk, some of my students' questions intersected with my own concerns about overcoming trauma and the possibilities of reconciliation. Kraków was Offen's hometown, the center of his earliest bloody trials as a young man. From there about fifty of his relatives were sent off to die.

Nathan's two brothers had also endured the Holocaust and were still living, both marvels in and of themselves. I yearned to learn more about each of them. What had their paths back been like? Beyond surviving, had they been able to face their trauma?

Were they able to heal at all?

While seemingly so vastly different from Offen, I began wondering whether some of my questions actually sprang from a similar source.

Over the next few years I would learn that neither of the brothers were free to confront their nightmares until decades later. Some people would consider their survival a miracle. Yet something far more complex had actually taken place.

Returning to my seat after speaking with Ellery, I resumed what I had been reading on the long drive to Lublin. *Man's Search for Meaning* is an illuminating book written by another survivor, Viktor Frankl. It was not exactly light fare to spell one's mind from all the heaviness. While struggling to stay alive in Auschwitz, Frankl was able to accept and counteract his suffering by keeping his love for his wife alive. Physically separated, with little chance of ever seeing her again, he did not relent. He realized that doing so represented a monumental achievement, since even a man with nothing can know bliss. This dwarfed his physical pain because no perpetrator could touch his soul and no one would ever be able to take that knowledge from him.

A combination of this wisdom and Ellery's sensibilities and promise awakened me, along with the notion of finding Nathan Offen. I became aware that I should reach beyond what had seemed evident before. Perhaps I needed to fully embrace the possibility of staying connected with our son, which had felt like a sliver of hope that was susceptible to being washed away.

Majdanek, the third concentration camp we visited, felt the most desolate and unearthly. The wind itself was a forceful presence, pummeling wooden barracks across an open plain as our group walked on a self-guided tour. Inside one room with bins of shoes to touch, a lingering swell of musty sweat pushed some of us back. My wife and I placed flowers beside a huge outdoor urn where ashes and bone fragments stirred in the gusts, as if still unable to rest.

Despite the grainy scenes outside the bus window and an emotional weight that had seemed to cloak much of the trip, I felt a faint spark, a lift.

I had no idea whether Nathan or his brothers would agree to speak with me. But I knew right then that I needed to try.

17

FREE-FALLING

A s the plane door opens, Nathan's feet go wobbly like wet noodles on a knife.

He can't quite reach the narrow jumping platform against the rush of air. An untied sneaker lace whips about as the instructor helps place one leg down. Then he gets it, bug-eyed behind goggles that seem clamped to his creased face. One of his daughters warned him not to do this. His other two, who rarely speak to him, have no idea.

Yet he's free-falling from ten thousand feet, strands of grey hair straining against their roots, his hand riveted to his chest.

Offen is strapped to the front of a young guy named Hugh Funk, who drops like a crazed stork with his arms extended out above Nathan's head. Hugh's rock-god locks stream in a frenzy, he's grinning and sticks out his tongue for a camera that's recording the jump. They fall away from a teardrop of swamp hooking into the vast Florida Everglades somewhere below.

Nathan sees specks of housing developments and deep blue water a ways off. Finally, he can just about catch his breath. His difficulties of getting out of the plane are over. This is exactly where he wants to be.

"Heyyyy, Nathan," Hugh yells after the parachute has opened. "Congratulations!"

"Thank you, thank you. You did it!"

His mouth is agape in wonder. Just three days before his ninetieth birthday, Nathan has made good on a promise and treated himself. He's dropping so fast there's barely enough time to take it in, yet he knows this moment will be affixed permanently to his view of the flat panorama below. They drop about five thousand feet before opening the chute, and overdubbed on the video capturing this, an electric guitar begins slashing a four-chord power chop. Few would have thought this moment was plausible for him.

He's like a teenager, maybe even a kid again, always good with his hands and smart mechanically. He used to build crystal radio sets and wanted to become an electrical engineer. When once asked about that he instantly withdrew, a man's vitality tucked inside a shell of his promise.

Yet not now.

Offen saw that former President George H. W. Bush went skydiving at eighty-five, so he planned to mark this pinnacle of his life with a similar punctuation. "And he had ten other guys with him," Nathan declares.

Minutes after landing safely, his face is flush, tight and weathered, his eyes set firm and sparkling. Hugh interviews him for the camera one last time. "What was your favorite part?"

"Coming down, coming down. And steering the parachute to the right and left."

"Now you know why the birds sing," Funk wraps up, flashing his teeth.

Offen can still growl about other stuff, but not so much on his birthday three days later. A torn rotator cuff that's aggravated his shoulder for years impacts his tennis game, weakening his volleys and serves, so he takes cortisone shots and does physical therapy. Sometimes he must even take a few weeks off. But fifty-three guests come to his dinner, including two grandchildren and his daughter, Ruth, from Seattle, plus a niece from Michigan. A friend of his agrees to be the emcee, and there are rounds of speeches and pinochle.

Marveling at his jump a few days later, Nathan says, "You're coming down like a bullet, like lightning. The rest is, as they say, a piece of cake."

18

PODGÓRZE

O n Friday mornings their mother rose early, lighting the coal stove with straw to usher in her daylong preparations. To make the traditional slow-cooked Shabbat meal called cholent, she combined lima beans that had soaked overnight with potatoes in a clay or iron pot. To this, Rochme often added a half-cup of barley and some derma, a beef casing stuffed with chicken fat and matzah, and, if they had it, she laid in buckwheat kasha and a piece of flanken. For Nat and his siblings, the beef would be the simmering crown jewel of their mother's concoction when the family gathered the next day.

When he was tall enough to be eye level with the kitchen table, Nathan's younger brother Bernie no longer required a chair to watch his mother work her other magic. She spread flour on the wood surface, one hand swirling open a hole that became a reservoir for water and eggs. She mixed all of this vigorously until it became dough, the pure gold of so much sustenance, placing it aside in a bowl to rise.

Then she rolled the dough into long pieces for her challah and smaller strips to make noodles for soup that evening. At first it was a mystery how she twisted the flakes together, but like his older brothers and sister, Bernie learned by watching. Soon he, too, braided the strands in anticipation of the soft eggy bread tufts they all adored.

The children shared one room with their parents in a ground-floor apartment at Krakusa 9. Bernie and Miriam slept beside their father and mother while the two oldest, Salman and Nat, doubled up on a straw mattress on an iron cot, folding up the frame and placing the bedding in the hallway each morning, which served as a pantry where preserves, potato sacks and other staples were stored.

With no running water inside, the boys carried it in from a well, and the family used a backyard outhouse shared with neighbors. Their mother did laundry once a week, scrubbing the sheets and clothes on a washboard as the children brought in cold water for rinsing, and wringing the sheets by hand. During the winter, clothes were hung to dry in the attic above the building's fourth floor.

The Offen household was in full motion by early Friday afternoon. Before the cholent could be cooked there were also cakes to make. Their mother usually made both a poppy seed and a chocolate cake, and after spreading more rolled dough Rochme sprinkled on spices and dished in the filling before rolling them to set in two narrow trays. Since their stove lacked a proper oven, and because the family was observant—after sundown Friday there was no work done in their home, and no fire lit on Saturday—it was the children's task sometime that afternoon to bring the bread, cake trays, and their main meal to a bakery a few blocks away.

Rochme entrusted one of the older boys to cover the cholent pot with brown paper secured by string, while Miriam or Bernie carried the cakes and challah. Walking toward the oven in the rear of the baker's house, they were embraced by pungent wafts of breads and sweet cakes. The business wasn't large enough to have a storefront, but the Offen children approached the brick oven in wonder, the assistant wielding his long-handled baker's paddle like a sorcerer to slide the pots and loaves around. Inside it was like a deep cavern, about ten feet wide and extending deeper than most modern pizza shop ovens. The cholent pot would simmer there overnight in the lingering heat, and one of the boys was charged with safeguarding a stub with their pickup number for the next day. Breaking off a piece from the rim of the cake trays as they were carried home was a coveted reward for each errand runner.

Their father, Jacob, was chief provider. A peddler dealing mostly in billiard table supplies, he also branched into selling other goods. Late in the week he took his children to the nearby market square to do the major food shopping. Rynek Podgórski was a bustling place across from a small hill where children went sledding, and on other days they accompanied their mother there to buy eggs, butter, milk, and fresh vegetables. When Jacob had earned enough, he bought carp and a chicken or a goose. His sons noted how he checked under the gills to see how fresh the catch was, inevitably jawing with the vendor to negotiate a better price. Being responsible for his family's health was paramount. Nathan recalls, "You had to be an expert not to buy diseased food, and my father knew about good food."

On a good week, the boys brought a chicken to a kosher slaughterhouse on the other end of their street. They paid a ritual slaughterer the equivalent of a nickel. After the bird's throat had been slit, he handed it over for one of them to grab by the wings and hang on a hook as it flicked about, blood spattering into a drain. Once inert, they brought the bird to an old woman for plucking before carrying it home.

Home provided everything that truly mattered. Though malleable, their father was still a disciplinarian, and he did not hesitate to spank an errant son who came home late for supper—but never to hurt any of them. Even in those brief moments when he was cross, each child knew how to melt his anger.

Bernie in particular knew how ticklish his dad was. After committing some misdeed during the week when his father was traveling, his mother might threaten him with "Wait until your father gets home." Yet being so gentle at the core, upon Jacob's return, all his youngest son had to do was point a finger and his dad would go all jiggly. When Bernie succeeded in poking under the ramparts of his dad's arms for a quick tickle, Jacob forgot what he had intended to do.

Their mother had a bottomless well of love. Petite and dark-eyed, Rochme often worked late into the night sewing dresses, retaining warmth for her children like a corner of their building's courtyard that peeked open to the sun. Unlike their father, they never heard her yell. When he was perhaps five, Nathan contracted scarlet fever and an ambulance came for him, his first ride in a motorcar. As his mother came to see him off he asked her, "'Am I going to live?' And then I saw two big tears coming down her cheeks."

Much later, in the beginning of their confinement to the ghetto, Nathan anticipated not having new clothing for Rosh Hashanah. She told him not to worry, that she would make him a new suit. To do this she used one of her black skirts, bringing it to a tailor to be joined together, though the skirt was only long enough to reach the trousers' knees. Scouring himself for a reminder of her as an adult, Nathan could still feel the clumped edge of the skirt's seam on his pant knees.

After being on the road for much of the week, Jacob Offen always tried to return from work by Friday evening while his wife finished her preparations, and on the rare weekends when he remained away there was less to eat and the children eagerly awaited his return. In earlier years he made and repaired shoes in a corner of the kitchen, having apprenticed with his father-in-law, who told Jacob he would not grant him permission to marry his daughter until Offen acquired a trade.

Nathan's dad yearned to travel. Midsized and of a sturdy build, he was used to making the most out of little. He had lost both parents as a child and grew up in the countryside east of Kraków before twice serving in the army. Selling supplies to bars and inns, Jacob ferried pool balls, cue sticks, and chalk in two suitcases while donning a backpack. Reaching outlying areas by train, he sometimes walked the twenty or thirty miles back home, lacking enough money for a return ticket. He also sold boxes of toothpicks to upscale restaurants, including a famous one favored by diplomats and royalty in Rynek Glowny, the main market square in the city's Old Town.

When the pending sale of a pool table went bust he stored the table in their apartment, to the delight of his children. They each learned how to play and treated their friends to games, with Sam likening himself as the "Fats Domino" of the clan. He and Nathan got to sleep on top of it as well. Yet for their father, life was often mundane and severe.

The children anticipated the candies or little gifts he might bring after a long trip. But mostly, the boys relished their time together with him, including accompanying their father to the ritual baths where they cleansed before sundown on Fridays. The main chamber of the mikveh had steep steps ascending into the searing heat, and Jacob taught his sons to brush themselves with a ritual broom consisting of oak leaves. This felt like a pounding to young Nat, and after showering they went into a steam room where the sight of older men, some of them with bulging hernias, unsettled him. They refreshed by pouring cold water over their heads, their weekend as a family unfolding—augmented by sneaking out sometimes to play soccer with friends after dinner. After attending Friday services there was chicken soup and often several other courses, while the star attractions like sweet, jellied gefilte fish and warm cholent were saved for the day of rest. No matter how thin the past week had been, they counted on being replenished as their parents lit candles, gave blessings and sang *zemirot*, the Shabbat songs.

While materially poor, the Offens were no worse off than many of their neighbors in Podgórze, a close suburb of Kraków. They lived among shopkeepers, tradesmen, and small manufacturers in apartments and modest homes, encircled by orchards and fields planted with wheat and potatoes. Many people kept cows, chickens, and geese, but these were not simple country folk. Democratic and progressive, the community was proud of its gymnasium and a mining school, and there was a well-kept park by the market square.

Their building neighbors included Blonski the butcher, a grocery store owner, an umbrella repairman, and the Katzses and Hofsteters. One of the moms made delicious bean soup and a man who owned a horse carriage gave the children rides. The only Catholic among them was the building's caretaker. Podgórze was widely regarded as honest and safe. There were occasional incidents—drunks fighting, or someone beating a woman with a belt—but robberies and bigger crimes were unheard of.

The Offens' neighborhood was a sister to the larger, wealthier Jewish district of Kazimierz across the river. That was home to more established entrepreneurs such as a family who operated a soda water factory in their cellar, a pioneering Orthodox girls school, Yiddish theaters, and numerous synagogues. Among this mix were many of the city's professionals and intelligentsia: left-wing Bundists representing workers and advocating Yiddish as a national language, ardent Zionists promoting a return to Palestine and moving to the collective farms, teachers, scientists, writers, actors, and musicians.

Only a few miles farther away, Poland's ancient cultural center was nested in the city proper, the place where Polish kings had been crowned and laid to rest. It was also home of historic Jagiellonian University, one of the world's oldest colleges. Jews had lived in Kraków for more than nine hundred years, their first conflicts with its burghers being noted in the fourteenth century. They comprised a quarter of its 250,000 population, and together some 3.3 million in a country of thirty-six million.

Diverse strains of Judaism and Yiddish culture flourished. While Kraków had grown as a center for Hassidic, Haskalah, and Orthodox traditions, other Jews were influenced by a religious reform movement that encouraged limited assimilation while safeguarding their ethnic identity. Jacob was in the latter group, carrying himself as a modern man but moderately so. The Offens kept a kosher home, and Jacob taught his children to observe the kashrut laws, while he refrained from smoking during Shabbat. Rather than wearing a long beard with the peyot side locks, he wore a trim mustache that would brush their cheek in a close hug.

Walking to services at the nearby Lorya shul on Fridays and Saturdays, Nathan and Sam were struck by the differences between their family and Hassidic Jews they encountered. In addition to the men's physical appearance, other children carried their bearded fathers' and uncles' fringed tallits—their ritual shawls—in the practice of men not carrying items into the shul, while the Offen males carried their own. Drawing from their neighborhood's mix, congregants dressed in their best suits and dresses but generally lacked the styles of Jews in Kraków's upscale districts, such as long gabardine coats and hats hemmed with fox fur.

One of more than a half-dozen synagogues in Podgórze, theirs was a modest single gallery in which women sat apart from the men. Invariably, Nathan especially found it hard to get through the typical two-hour service, and feigning to use the bathroom, he ducked out to kick a ball with the other boys. Outside was a courtyard with sheds where tradesmen gathered with their horse-drawn wagons, a scene that also enamored young Bernie. He sat on the wagons imagining he was a champion driver, and while his father occasionally allowed him to skip some of the service, he instructed his son to be back for a certain prayer. If Bernie forgot, his father came out to retrieve him.

Their father also kept up to date on politics and other current affairs. Both parents read Polish newspapers at night, and Jacob hosted friends for spirited conversations in their kitchen and out beside his building in the summer months, debating what the new government was going to do. Offen had served in the Austro-Hungarian Army during the First World War and again with a reconstituted Polish Army in the 1920s under then-Marshal Joseph Pilsudski, the Polish patriot widely revered as the father of his nation's independence.

As a reward for his valor in battle in a campaign to reclaim territory from the Russians, Offen was given a silver cigarette case with an inscription signed by a general, though his sons weren't sure if it actually had Pilsudski's signature. Evidence of having fulfilled his patriotic duty, Jacob showed the case off to friends over the years. Yet its value changed irreversibly when Podgórze was enclosed as a ghetto and the family had to barter it for food.

Because he was a veteran, Jacob was able to obtain a license to sell tobacco and newspapers at a concession that he and his wife operated from a window facing the street. To get permission, Offen hand delivered a letter to Pilsudski while the president was en route to his residence at Wawel Castle. Bursting through a police cordon into a caravan of open cars, he threw the letter into the Pilsudski's lap. Police detailed him for one night, but he returned unharmed.

During his reign, some felt that the de facto dictator tried to hold back rising anti-Semitism across Poland. Yet the venom spread, fed by generations of jealousies and ignorance that ratcheted up with self-preservation and blame during Europe's Depression. By 1935, the same year Pilsudski died, an empowered right-wing party openly embraced targeting Jews, enacting restrictions against work on Sundays and ritual slaughters, and imposing quotas on Jewish students entering universities. Soon they would be falsely labeled as Communists who supported the Bolshevik takeover of eastern Poland.

While not knowing what this rising tide would bring, Nathan and his siblings could sense that history was being made when the Polish leader died. Jacob took them by streetcar into the city to observe Pilsudski's funeral procession, in which dignitaries followed a silver casket with a glass top, the embalmed body visible to those up close. The excitement of the crowds and long lines made a lasting impression on Nathan, and Sam went inside the castle to view the enshrined president.

In their animated discussions, Offen and his friends surely debated how far the repressive forces would go. Having read about the oppression that was sweeping through Germany, Jacob asserted to his family the same thing would not be brought against them. He knew some Christian Poles, after all, and Podgórze itself felt secure. Even when some students began vandalizing Jewish shops in Kazimierz and other parts of the city, that was almost unheard of in their neighborhood.

Perhaps Jacob did not yet know the extent of what his sons were already experiencing. Nathan, physically the strongest and most like his father, sometimes protected Sam, whom classmates teased as a *myszka*, or "little mouse," from being bullied. On their way to Hebrew school in the afternoons, the boys passed a hill where Christian kids launched stones and chased them with sticks. Most ominous was Saint Joseph's Church facing Rynek Podgórski. A handsome yet daunting neo-Gothic structure, it had a polygonal tower and stained glass windows replete with images of Christ suffering at the hands of vindictive Jews.

Each of the Offen children learned to stay clear of the church, especially around Easter, when some priests preached libelous accusations such as Jews preparing their Passover matzah from the blood of Christian children. A classmate of Sam's who played with him on the fields would invite him home, but the boy declined to enter the Offens' apartment because of his mother's fears. Other Jewish parents protested to Gentiles whom they thought would listen, but their message didn't get through; the priests had said it was so. During the Easter holiday, Jacob and Rochme instructed their youngest children to stay indoors.

Their mother's family enveloped the Offen children in Podgórze, most vitally, their maternal grandmother, Ciwie Schiffer-Zwirn, who lived upstairs in the same building. She ran a little store selling candy, fruit, and ice cream, leaving at dawn during the growing season to walk two miles to the peasants' market to buy fresh produce and fruits. On the rare Friday that her son-in-law was unable to return from work, she sent over food to help out her oldest daughter's clan. Her late husband, whose surname Zwirn means "sewing thread," had come from a long line of rabbis and took a different path, becoming a shoemaker instead. Ciwie's older brother also lived close by until he was 104, sometimes tending his gardens with a grandnephew or a grandniece in tow.

Several of Rochme's sisters were nearby along with her brother, Joel, who lived with his mother when the Offen siblings were young. Uncle Joel was sophisticated, a talented singer and dedicated Zionist, well educated in Hebrew and Yiddish. He had completed his training to resettle in Palestine but would not leave his mother and sisters, and during the high holidays he served as an assistant cantor at their shul. Working as a shoemaker, he sometimes struggled to make ends meet. Joel was not above having some fun and accommodating his nephews and nieces. He enjoyed playing soccer with Nathan and Sam, and a few times when the two were going to be late for afternoon religious classes at Talmud Torah, he wrote their teacher an excuse note. This worked well until their father found out, his voice rising in anger. Preparing to receive a few whacks to the backside, Nathan would shut his eyes attempting to screen out the pain.

While most of their teachers in both the public school and the cheder were very strict, with some brandishing a belt to strap the palms of errant boys, the Offen sons matured early enough to realize that it was their parents who actually endured a life of hard knocks. Sam's formal education ended after eighth grade at fourteen. He had excelled in school, becoming adept in three languages including learning German by fourth grade as required. With its similarity to Yiddish, Sam acquired it easily, sometimes helping struggling Christian boys who only knew Polish. He dreamed of becoming a dentist but his parents could not afford to send him to the university. One of his father's friends secured Sam an apprenticeship with a furrier located in Kraków, a viable trade. Working in the morning and attending vocational school in the afternoon, he learned about the varieties of fur and their durability, tanning methods, and how to sew fur coats.

Once Nathan finished school at about the same age, he started on a course similar to his older brother, seeking an apprenticeship with a plumber. Yet, perhaps because he was a little more rebellious, and mostly because he refused to be treated like a mule, the job lasted about a week. Openly anti-Semitic, the master plumber didn't take to Nathan and made him put on a harness to pull a small wagon loaded with toilets and pipes uphill along the cobblestone streets. The work was grueling, and Nathan felt that his boss wanted to break his back. "They didn't have a car or a horse, or a horse-driven wagon or anything," he says. "I was the horse." A few weeks later he found a job in a dry goods store that sold fabrics, continuing there for the next few years.

Delicate and thin, their sister Miriam shared her mother's dark features and often stayed nearby as she worked inside. Nearly four years younger than Nathan and two years older than Bernard, Miriam was named for a paternal grandmother they never knew. Their mother worried that Miriam was too fussy an eater and she was sometimes on the short end of her brothers' light teasing. But they each adored her. She and Bernie played together, often within the apartment complex courtyard, their chief playground, where neighborhood children engaged in hide-and-seek amidst a rich, sweet wash that drifted in from a chocolate factory next door.

Inside the apartment, in addition to making dresses and stitching clothes for neighbors and other clients with her sewing machine, and with everything else mothers do to sustain four children, Rochme found a creative outlet embroidering tapestries. One particular project took an inordinate amount of time, and working late into the evening by a single kerosene lamp she created a family treasure. It was a silk needlepoint of the infant Moses being rescued in a reed basket amongst the bulrushes of the Nile.

Little by little, the children noted the progress as she moved the needle in and out of the weave, creating patterns with striking blues and other bright colors. The stiff canvas was large, measuring nearly three by five feet. When it was done, their parents mounted Moses in a gold frame and hung the picture prominently.

A year before the Nazi invasion, local poet and songwriter Mordechai Gebirtig sounded an alarm against the gathering threats to his people. Reacting to a pogrom against Polish Jews in a small town north of his native Kraków, Gebirtig envisioned the burning of his shtetl, his community, which was defined not only by its close families and their religious adherence, but also by their collective struggle to rise from poverty. Posthumously, "It Burns" became Gebirtig's most recognized poem, far different in its tone and reach from his earlier celebrations of prewar life. "If we don't help ourselves, our fate is dire," he warned. "If you love your poor little town, please don't let them burn it down." The full portent of those lines apparently was not realized until well after the fact.

Like Jacob Offen, despite having served his country in the Great War, Gebirtig was not considered to be a full Pole. His people were alone, increasingly viewed across the continent as the "other" race as long-entrenched superstitions and Christian antipathy stiffened.

Ominous signs hovered like flat-topped thunderhead anvils above Podgórze the following summer.

An uncle of Jacob's knocked on their apartment door with his wife and children, holding suitcases. They had been forced to leave Germany, where he had lived for many years and raised his family. For the first time, the Offens heard direct accounts of persecution, while news of other pogroms continued to circulate in the Jewish newspapers. Eligible friends and relatives were being called up for the Polish Army—being in his mid-forties, Jacob was too old to serve, while Sam, who had just turned eighteen early that August, was still too young. One day a cousin of Rochme's, a tinsmith, Ignac Traubman, came over in his army uniform to say good-bye.

Life's norms waned with its minor joys. The brothers' few experiences attending summer day camp as kids or landing roles in some of the holiday plays at their cheder faded, as did working out at the sports club and riding bikes to the soccer fields. Even taking in Yiddish movies became out of reach.

Nathan went out one afternoon to see a Hollywood film, a rare treat. He feasted on American movies, carrying the tune of the lead song in his head, viewing women dressed in nylon stockings for the first time. Here was Deanna Durbin, a former childhood star and fully blossomed brunette, starring as a girls' school student in Switzerland who writes herself letters from an imaginary explorer-father and gets herself into a pickle. Nathan didn't retain the film title (*Mad About Music*) for too long, but he continued to hear Durbin's sweet soprano singing "I Love to Whistle" for many years. It was the last film he saw before the war.

Late in August they heard planes overhead and antiaircraft artillery. Sam and Nathan joined the civil defense and were stationed beside their building during the evenings. "I don't know what we were looking for," Nathan recalled, "but it was in darkness, and we heard artillery fire from a distance. We found a piece of shrapnel and our father identified that this was real. This wasn't maneuvers or anything, it was a real war." On another night Nathan was again outside on Krakusa Street when he noticed a silhouette, a man emerging from the shadows with his hands in his pockets.

The figure began to ask him questions: "Where was this and that, where was the military operation? I was so petrified. I didn't answer him anything, I told him I didn't know, and he walked away." Nathan guessed that he was a spy.

His father still thought the family would come through unharmed, even if Kraków became occupied. Jacob had fought in the Austrian Army, after all. *If they want I should work for them, I shall*, his middle son channeled. *But nobody is going to touch me. This is my home.*

Fear and propaganda spread amidst denials of what was coming. As the *Wehrmacht* pushed through Poland during the first days of September, and with the Red Army just weeks away from occupying the country's eastern provinces, a plea for patriotic resistance came on the radio. Listeners were asked to place their radios in an open window so that neighbors could hear, and Jacob abided. Holding out a last glimmer of hope, an announcer read an epic ballad by a nineteenth-century Polish poet who had invoked the Athenian hero Miltiades repulsing the invading Persians at Marathon. That feat was not to be repeated. Allied forces were not coming to help either, and soon after the broadcast aired, a bomb destroyed the radio station.

Chaos broke out in anticipation of Kraków's fall. Stores were looted as criminals roamed free from opened jails. The government ordered warehouses emptied, so Nathan and his brothers went out filling a baby carriage with sacks of flour, chocolate, cigarettes—anything they might use or trade in the months ahead. Along the Vistula River, Nathan detected heady wafts of alcohol as workers dumped out liquor and beer kegs to deny the invaders. A day or two later the brothers watched returning soldiers head east toward the Russian front.

They persuaded their father to try joining the army, as if that would give them a better chance. Jacob packed a few belongings and returned a few hours later. "I'm sorry. Whatever will happen, will happen," he told them. "I cannot leave you. I want to be with my family."

The new governor-general of the occupied territory, Hitler's former lawyer, set up in Wawel Castle overlooking the river. As curfews, food rationing, and the issuing of armbands and other restrictions ensued, Nathan and Sam joined work gangs clearing debris from the bombardment of Kraków. They cleaned homes emptied for SS officers' families. Bernie and Miriam were expelled from public school, and by the end of the year Kraków's Jews had registered. As house searches began in the Kazimierz quarter, Hebrew schools closed and nearly two hundred university professors were rounded up and deported. Each of the brothers witnessed the early taunts and attacks; patrols targeted Hassidic and Orthodox men with side locks and long beards.

To oversee Jewish affairs, maintain statistics, and prepare identity cards and work papers, a council called the *Judenrat* was formed, answering to the Gestapo while also tending to the sick and poor.

The barrage progressed: registration of property and assets; prohibitions against using public transport and walking in a greenbelt around the city's main market square; loudspeakers mounted on car roofs announced the collection of furs and fur trimmings; a "Jewish newspaper" began circulating fresh Nazi propaganda. Shops were closed and other small enterprises shut down. By early 1941 the Germans expelled at least fifty-five thousand people from the city, forcing them to join relatives in outlying towns or to find some other roof to live under.

The Offens stayed in Podgórze as their building and the surrounding streets were sequestered into a ghetto. A fifty-acre area of 320 buildings occupied by 3,500 people became designated for 15,000 to 17,000 Jews, while the Kazimierz quarter was closed. Apartments facing out were bricked or boarded up, and a wall three meters high was built along the perimeter using cemetery monuments, topped with arches resembling Jewish tombstones. Each of the Offens received a *Kennkarte* identity card required to live in the ghetto, which enabled them—except for Bernard— to find work. Even Miriam at fourteen was old enough to get a job. Other families were given ten days to move.

A local pharmacist, Tadeusz Pankiewicz, whose shop faced a square where one of the ghetto gates was built, regarded the movements over several days that March. By horse, farm wagons, furniture vans, pushcarts, and packs on their backs, "the rush was incredible," he noted, "because the time was short and the desire to obtain suitable apartments was urgent."

It would be impossible for Jacob's sons to keep everything straight. Most of the facts held up in the decades ahead, and impressions of scenes and faces would not budge, for those were set like thick bluestone packed in stone dust by hard rainfalls. Sequences began to be shuffled; years merged in truncated time, partially chewed, and thrown up.

Waiting in line for a loaf of bread one day with her children, Rochme was bit by a soldier's dog. A young grunt may have snapped, *Jude*, directing the canine toward her, or the animal may have lunged at her arm for no reason, causing their mother to drop her ration card. Bernard seemed to forget this, while Sam remembered it point blank.

At some point Moses had to go.

Rochme's needlepoint, a handmade form of worship intended as an heirloom, was not quite as vital as bread and flour. Like other women, she also made her own tallit and talis bags, which would be among the final things left in her grasp. Her husband knew a Polish Gentile who managed another chocolate factory nearby, a good man who was known to help Jews.

Wladislaw Cieslik promised to keep the needlepoint safe, and he gave them food in exchange for it. Sam, at least, recalled some details of his mother's art, the reed basket, the Pharaoh's daughter, set within a gold frame.

They vowed that whoever survived would try to recover her tapestry.

19

SOUNDS IN THE STONES

The breaking day was cloudless, and by 6:00 a.m., orders to leave their apartments echoed off the stone and brick facades in Podgórze. As cars arrived carrying dignitaries of the SS and Gestapo, family members straggled with bundles and packs toward the labor office two blocks from Plac Zgody. The very name of the place, which means "Concord" or "Agreement Square," cut with a cruel irony.

Anticipating the worst, Jacob sent his youngest out early on October 28, 1942 to get food. Thirteen years old, and skinny like his sister, Bernie knew the few places where one could still crawl under the ghetto wall. Moving in and out had been easier earlier. He had actually carried a small pack during those first smuggling missions and later wore oversized trousers to fill up. One of his parents or brothers would watch for the Polish police outside, lifting up a length of barbed wire when the coast was clear.

Heading to the nearby hills, Bernie rummaged through garbage dumps and bartered clothes or other possessions for anything—potatoes, bread, or scraps. Now he especially needed those childhood skills developed playing in the courtyard or scaling the wall beside the chocolate factory and begging a worker in the yard for a handout: recognizing an unwanted approach, and scrunching down almost breathless. He was completely on his own, with no one around to warn him about a watchman or soldier.

Sam had already left for a job in the city. Seeing an unusual number of patrols just outside the walls with their machine guns, extra trucks, and dogs, he knew something terrible was stirring. Particularly unnerving was a lethal paramilitary unit known as the *Sonderdienst*, grey-jacketed ethnic Germans who formed an unflinching, unforgiving cordon. Sam and his brothers had seen this before during the first week of June, the first time panic seized Podgórze, when seven thousand people were rounded up and deported on freight cars. Many of those targeted—the sick and elderly—lacked special stamps on their work papers that signified a useful trade. Culminating in what became known as "Bloody Thursday," about six hundred others were gunned down in and around Plac Zgody. Among them, the beloved poet, Mordechai Gebirtig, was killed alongside a painter friend. As news of his murder spread, parents wept in front of their children.

Four months later, Sam would not learn the worst until he returned in the evening.

That summer, the Offens had moved in with Rochme's youngest sister and her new husband when the ghetto was cut in half. The new apartment at 5 Limanowskiego Street was close to the labor office where throngs lined up each morning for work details. For a time, Jacob and his youngest son made boots for Julius Madritsch, a sympathizer who, like the pharmacist Pankiewicz and his assistants, helped hundreds of Jewish families. Madristch did this while overseeing several factories as a trustee for German authorities, including the former Optima chocolate works. Both Rochme and her daughter had temporary jobs in the old Optima factory on a floor converted to manufacture uniforms, but they weren't fortunate enough to stay on the rolls for long. They were not among the nearly eight hundred employees Madritsch was able to save from deportations at his main textiles factory nearby in a fashion similar to Oskar Schindler.

Nathan was returning from the nightshift in a rail yard. He noticed an unusual number of police cordoned outside the ghetto walls. Hearing bursts of gunfire inside, he broke into a run toward the corner building where his family lived, finding bodies in the yard and their apartment ransacked. Continuing out to Jozefinska Street, he saw soldiers marching a line of people toward the square and rail station. He kept looking and looking. Both his mother and sister were in the line.

Their eyes met. "I walked over, I was walking over, going to hug her and give her a kiss, and the German guard came over and slapped me over the head with the butt of the rifle and opened up my head," Nathan recalled, revealing the moment nearly forty years later.

The next blow struck his mouth, knocking out some teeth. He started to get up to continue forward, but his mother waved him off, "'Get away, get away, get away.' She was afraid they were going to pick me up too." Miriam, sweet and dutiful like her mother, had turned sixteen just six weeks earlier. She clutched her mother's skirt.

He had one last look at them.

The day turned hot, too much like the previous June. Miriam and her mother were ordered to sit with other deportees in the square. There was no water, and unlike during earlier selections, no doctors were allowed to offer help. "Standing was forbidden; even the need to perform biological functions was not allowed," Pankiewicz described. "The crowds were unbelievable."

The SS invaded the main hospital on Jozefinska Street around noon, targeting patients with infectious diseases and anyone who did not run away, including doctors and nurses who had been warned to leave but stayed anyway. Anticipating the attack, just as some ghetto occupants had passed poison to their next of kin, one doctor gave cyanide to some of her aged patients. Soldiers stormed a shelter for the elderly and took invalids from nursing homes. That afternoon, work crews with young Jews were sent to an orphanage and were ordered to bring babies outside, setting the infants against a wall before each was shot in the head.

Returning from work, Sam came across bodies strewn on the streets. He recognized one of his uncles among them. He went home and waited for his father and brothers to show up, finally learning from Nathan about their mother and sister. The aunt they were living with was missing too. "And, of course, we just didn't know what to make out of it," he said. "We were just hugging and kissing each other, we were glad whoever was here that we're together. But we had the worst fears about what was going to happen to them."

Rumors began to spread, replacing the earlier propaganda that ghetto residents had been transported to farm cooperatives in the east. Rochme, Miriam and others may have gone to Majdanek, or Treblinka. Their family surmised that these were death camps—beyond slave labor. "And, of course, we feared the worst," Sam continued. "I mean, we didn't have concrete evidence that that's where they went. But that's what happened to them." It turned out that Bełżec was their destination.

Bernard slipped back into the ghetto under darkness when the commotion had settled down. From his hiding place, he had heard some of the shooting and screams. But he missed the wetness soaking the gutter along Jozefinska.

Their father was broken.

The thin veneer of hope Jacob had tried to retain in front of his family stripped away. He stopped shaving, and his once robust frame slumped. He ceased communicating at his usual spitfire pace as words became a bankrupt currency. His sons easily read the despair in his eyes. Kraków was to be cleansed of Jews for the first time in six hundred years. The governor-general had privately declared this goal back in the spring of 1940: skilled workers only. Now it was official.

Intolerance had been overrun by savagery. Where once there had been just insults and stones chucked at Nat and his friends, Krakóvians now eschewed the implications of their ancient hatreds, fully awakened and running loose, the aristocracy positioned to make money off slave labor. Where once there had been a glimmer, however false or bought by trading possessions for favors, few illusions remained. As a child, Sam had read signs in Polish stores—which his father avoided—stating, "You only buy from your own kind." He began to know the scorched recesses of immoral impunity.

Nathan, who was turning twenty that December, watched his father wither with a gnawing helplessness. It was over, and Jacob recognized this. He hardly spoke.

He thought he might be able to find enough work to get them through the war. But after the October deportation, "it was a hopeless situation," Nathan said, "out of control." He, too, felt impotent—he was always the protective son, an enforcer. He had never feared facing the boys who launched those rocks, and now he could do nothing.

As winter approached, the ghetto police continued hauling men off the streets to construct a labor camp in a nearby suburb, Płaszów. Nathan and Sam had been commandeered many times for details. In those first months of the occupation, on-call labor was voluntary—in the same sense that herring attempting to spawn must use a fish ladder to go up a river. A soldier or member of the ghetto police—known as the *Ordnungsdienst*, or OD—would come to the Offens' street saying, "I need twenty people," which might be for a day of clearing snow, scrubbing floors, or cleaning streets. Young men were paid a zloty or two or a loaf of bread, and they needed the money even more as routine jobs were denied. Because they remained hardy enough, the two brothers were perhaps a tad less afraid, and they had almost become used to being marched to work, which usually included a midday meal of hot soup as an incentive.

When they still lived on Krakusa Street, Nathan was getting food one day when he was ordered onto a truck. He was sent to a stone quarry about twenty-five kilometers away with a group of other teenagers, away from home alone for the first time in his life, his parents unknowing. He cried himself to sleep. By day, they broke granite into chips with hammers. It was very hard work, continuing for several days.

During the next two or three years, both he and Sam found many jobs around the city. Although he had no such technical experience, Sam fudged his work card application to state he was a mechanic's helper. For a while he helped fix military equipment or found day labor unloading coal and cement from railroad cars.

One of Nathan's jobs was at a brick factory—dull, brutish work loading heavy wet clay. He cut blocks weighing sixty or seventy pounds with a spade and lifted them onto a rail car, topping it off with lime, or sometimes loading a wagon with clay and pushing it down to be mixed. This was done under the watch of ruthless men who took out their wrath on the laborers to prove their worth to the SS. With a friend's help, Nathan was able to get away from this drudgery, taking a job at the blacksmith's shop that forged machine parts to repair equipment. As the master held an iron piece over the anvil with a big set of pliers, Nathan and two coworkers took turns hitting it with their sledgehammers in a precise cadence: one, two, three. If one of them didn't strike it just right, the master threatened to throw a piece of white-hot steel in his face.

The rigorous work suited Nathan's natural vigor, and on occasion there was a bonus. He felt lucky because the Polish master treated him decently, and the other men occasionally gave him some extra food. He could also trade clothing or other items to bring home extra food for his father and brothers, sometimes baking a potato in the fire for himself. Returning to the ghetto and passing the frequent strip search was just another hurdle.

Talk of a labor camp being built just a few kilometers away rattled the ghetto further. The new *Judenrat* president explained that the camp was intended mostly for Poles or Jews from Hungary and other occupied countries. Supposedly, in addition to useful work, it would provide them with shops and a community center.

Surely, Jacob and most of his neighbors weren't buying it.

The camp's very location was insidious, extending the final logic for all of Kraków in a lurid mixture of geographic and economic expediency. Both the ghetto and camp site were located close to the main rail line, with a left fork in the tracks leaving Płaszów station leading directly to Auschwitz. Two Jewish cemeteries were desecrated to make way for the *Arbeitslager* compound, their gravestones broken and crushed into road material, while a Catholic cemetery on a nearby hill was untouched. A digging machine unearthed decomposed bodies wrapped in rotting prayer shawls, which workers brought by wheelbarrow and litters to be burned. The surrounding area was mainly a rocky hillside that crews planed down by hand, and beyond those lay malaria-filled swamps that were drained and filled. Still, while depleted by this, many of the Offens' neighbors realized that their best chances for survival would be among the new wooden barracks.

Amon Goeth, the butcher who would soon take charge of Płaszów, was an aide to the commandant. Both men pushed the Jewish and Christian slave laborers hard that fall and winter. While initially designed to hold perhaps four thousand people, at its peak Płaszów would hold about 24,000. The estimates of inmates vary, but upwards of 35,000 to 50,000 people, to triple that, were held there through the fall of 1944, the vast majority being Jews, who were quickly separated from Poles and others.

The older Offen brothers were put on camp work crews, with Sam doing an especially grueling detail at one of the cemeteries. Forced to knock down monuments and markers that were then broken up, much of it used to pave in front of new SS officers' residences and buildings, he found his grandfather's grave. It was his namesake, Schlomo Zalman Schiffer Zwirn, and he was astonished to see the monument still standing.

Sam had never viewed a skeleton before. Many that were not dumped into a mass grave lay exposed in the ravaged soil or were smashed upon the future sites of the camp's delousing hut, kitchen, and latrine pits. One of the cemeteries was soon blasted apart for a quarry. Perhaps he didn't yet have the means to take this in. Or maybe the "little mouse" did not yet recognize that he had shed his soft coat for a tougher hide. Many years later, as if attempting to resist retrieving the memory that reappeared in stubborn bits, Sam sputtered, "They, they were just treated like, like they were stones."

The ghetto was further reduced into three crammed streets and divided into two sections, even as more Jews from neighboring villages were brought in. Many arrived in rags and without belongings, some lice-infested and lacking shoes. Those deemed fit to work—about ten thousand skilled workers and technicians with their families—moved to section A, including the four Offen males and their uncle Joel. Section B restricted the elderly, sick, children under fourteen, and the unemployed. More than four thousand of these people were starved and not allowed out of their area.

Preparation for the liquidation of the Krakow ghetto was odious. Opening a children's home in January, the Germans rounded up six hundred youths ages thirteen and younger—not including Bernard, who stayed hidden each day and curtailed his wandering. Rationing and escape attempts increased, and people stopped buying household products; the *Judenrat* tried to postpone the last deportation, while towing the official line that all would be kept together and fed at the labor camp.

On March 13 Plac Zgody began filling up at dawn again. Ghetto A was emptied first, with most of its inhabitants lined up with their one allotted pack for a march to Płaszów, including Sam and Bernard, their father and uncle. The pharmacist Pankiewicz again observed the lineup: gaunt figures, unshaven and unwashed, muttering to themselves, rife with terror and resignation; women carried children and pushed carriages; old men shuffled with prayer books and ritual shawls in satin bags under their arms; children held hands with no adults nearby. Next to many were piles of bundles and packages, pots and pans, even dishes, as if "prepared for a long trip," Pankiewicz wrote.

Amon Goeth, tall and paunchy above thin legs, wore a black leather coat and held a short automatic rifle in one hand, a riding crop in the other. His two Great Danes, Rolf and Ralf, moved beside him down the street as the OD men snapped to attention.

What happened next was a blur.

Shooting erupted inside the main hospital. A doctor, a beautiful woman with sapphire blue eyes, stood beside a friend who had broken her leg trying to escape underground. The doctor refused to leave her side, even when confronted by a technical sergeant who burst in targeting patients "with a jeering grin on his bloated face." He ordered the Dr. Katia Blau to turn around.

She didn't budge, saying her last words: "Shoot, I am not afraid of dying."

Soldiers emptied the *Kinderheim*, the children's home, loading babies into wicker baskets for the wagons. Older children were brought around a street corner to meet their end. Yet not all of the *kinders* perished, mostly because of a nighttime smuggling operation organized by Madritsch, the textile factory owner, and an assistant commander of the German police in Podgórze.

Nine thousand Jews were driven to the Płaszów camp while several hundred were murdered. Those stuck in ghetto B hid inside their apartments; faces seen in doorways and windows were shot. The next day, two thousand people were transported to Auschwitz and into the gas chamber. Soldiers, led by Goeth manning a submachine gun, cut down perhaps another 1,500 others in the streets and buildings.

Sent to the hospital on a work crew, Nathan picked up the dead to load on wagons. The bodies went by horses and trucks to a mass grave at Plaszów. "I saw the German SS man picking up the baby," Offen said, casting down his eyes, his face hardening. "One threw it through the window, a little baby—maybe two months old, or just born, I don't know. He just picked it up by the feet and hit it against the curb."

Sons and daughters had to undress and handle the bodies of their parents, or of a sibling. "To weep for them, to allow even a momentary flicker of grief to pass across their faces, meant certain and instantaneous death," survivor Malvina Graf learned. Dogs roamed freely, some fed by soldiers before scampering to their homes in wait for masters who would never return.

Nathan did cleanup duty for at least two days. Perhaps it went on longer, for three or five. Or maybe not.

The count of time ceased to matter, along with all schemas of quantification and order.

The blackened sun beheld a March massacre fallen back on October fastened to June death. A toppled copper beech had grown into the space of a diseased elm in a stand of cleared white oaks.

Perhaps chronology and numbers actually lied. They were yet another construct, which at the end of the day lay shattered, and unverifiable. Perhaps.

Nathan, half a lifetime later, declared again, "The time is immaterial." Yes. Nine months fell back on five months fallen on to June death.

Despite their zeal for recordkeeping, the Nazis never solved Bernard, after all. His dates were never correct. He went to places they never recorded, he forged "schlosser," or machinist, on a work card, his soul vanishing from their clutch like the song of a dove that drops out of range. They would never quite catch him—not knowing himself until a lifetime later that April 17, 1929 was the actual day of his birth.

So perhaps time matters not. No. Fragments still do, to the surviving relatives who uncovered bits of their heirlooms in warehouses or on Craigslist, or sealed in salt mine chambers. To families who can scarcely dream of those they missed out on loving.

After the ghetto's liquidation, soldiers shuttled wagons and trucks back and forth to Płaszów, stopping at the side near the rips in the old cemeteries. Nathan and the other young men threw bodies into trenches mixed with more lime.

They stood at the edge of the pit late in the afternoon, probably finishing the last load, as the shooting resumed.

"I fell down in the grave, into the hole, and heard the screaming of thousands," Nathan said. "I saw what was going on, then I pretended I was dead when they started to machine gun thousands of people . . . they were shooting people in the head." He stayed motionless for a few hours, "and at night I crawled out, and managed to wash myself up and got into the camp . . . some people helped me and gave me something to eat. I washed myself up and changed my clothes."

He acquired the pants and shirt of a dead man.

From his workplace in Barracks 82, Bernard Offen saw lorries loaded with people cresting a hill. They disappeared below, machine guns fired, and the trucks came back empty.

He worked alongside his father in a shoe factory making boots for the German army. This was a good job at the camp. Any shot at survival demanded production, and there were legitimate industries in Płaszów. Cooperatives making army uniforms, machinists, cobblers, carpenters and painters, papermaking and glassmakers, tailors, locksmiths and watchmakers, a cable factory. A print shop prepared secret documents at night for the SS, and there was a brick works and foundry, every trade imaginable, each one under the lash.

Jacob protected his youngest son, filling their quotas with his nimble hands and instructing him before roll call on the nearby *appelplatz*. His father showed him something else: how to slice deep cuts inside the heel of every odd pair of boots, a subtle act of sabotage that made the footwear useless when a soldier ran. They fashioned the hidden defect while workers hauled wood for pyres over the hill, the wind carrying an acrid stench of burning bodies over barbed wire to the barracks. When he was finished and they rested at their bunk, Jacob reassured his son that this would pass, that everything was going to work out.

Yet Bernard was curious.

The prisoners called it "Prick Hill." The name was an acerbic swipe at a sadistic sergeant who had gone wild at the ghetto hospital and continued his fury in the camp. The sergeant, Albert Huyar, entertained himself with a horsewhip that had a little lead ball at the end and bit into the flesh. One time he caught up with Nathan, bending him against a chair in the plaza to take turns with another officer whipping Offen until he passed out.

As a child Bernard once wandered off with a sugar bowl in his family's apartment, squirreling up under the table. After falling asleep no one could find him, prompting his desperate parents to contact the police. He had performed a somewhat similar feat just days after being marched to Płaszów as the ghetto was liquidated. He jumped from a wagon that was hauling children away from the camp to be shot, and hid at a construction site before sneaking into a satellite labor camp. Months later, after being sheltered by an uncle who managed to scrounge up medicine when Bernard contracted typhus, he reunited with his father at the main camp.

Late one afternoon when the shooting ended he crept up Prick Hill. He found piles of corpses stacked up with wood, which would burn for days on end. There were bodies with their heads blown off, and he learned later that the soldiers used modified dumdum bullets to increase the carnage. Two mass graves were being filled nearby. He understood what was happening for the first time. Bernard tucked the vision away and withdrew.

If he could just keep his eyes closed, he started to believe that no bullets would penetrate him. That became his reality: seeing, but not really, "a blindish sight," he says.

He did not know that the unfortunates were ordered to disrobe and lay down over logs in a trench. He did not recognize that plaster was poured into their mouths to prevent screams. After they were shot, the next group had to disrobe, place more logs on, and lie down. The final group poured the benzyene themselves. He could not know all of this.

He didn't talk about it with his father, who remained warm and reassuring. The two of them celebrated Bernard's bar mitzvah while Nathan and Sam lived apart in other barracks. The older brothers usually did heavy menial work such as breaking and moving rocks in the camp quarries. Sam was able to secure a relatively plum job inside the furriers' barracks, as he knew the man who ran it from his years as an apprentice. Fur-lined coats and hats were needed for the Russian front and he knew how to sew skins and bolts of lining together by hand.

He and Nathan also endured more encounters with vicious guards and officers, including the notorious Goeth, who became camp commandant. One morning while at work grading a road close to Goeth's villa, Sam refused to be pulled down by his dogs. During his routine stroll around the camp following breakfast, Goeth often sicced Rolf and Ralph on a prisoner and administered the coup de grace with the same casual flick with which he discarded a spent cigarette.

His heart pounding, Sam figured his time was up as the commandant approached. Pointing the dogs toward him, Goeth commanded, *Jude*, and they began tearing at his side. But Sam stayed erect, keeping his balance and continued working with a pick or shovel. He refused to be pulled down. "And he stays there, stays there and for—I don't know what happened then—and then he sort of like snatched his whip, he says in German, 'Go away!' to the dogs . . . And he starts walking away."

"Something about my resistance must have appealed to Goeth," Sam wrote.

Nathan and Sam remained in Płaszów for about a year. The following spring, while Bernard continued working with their father in the shoe shop, the two were sent to a nearby sub-camp, the Wieliczka salt mine. The transfer ultimately helped prolong their lives in an unlikely way.

The Germans brought in close to two thousand prisoners to build an underground munitions factory. Along with other miners, the brothers enlarged the existing salt-encrusted chambers for warehouses and dug out airshafts. Immediately upon arriving they were tattooed on the back of the wrist with "KL" for *Konzentrationslager*, or concentration camp. The procedure was grueling enough, and Sam wondered if he was up to the task of grinding away twelve hours a day underground. He had no choice. Working hundreds of feet below—some of the deepest chambers descend more than a thousand feet—they spent several early weeks loading wagons of salt rock with their bare hands, which brought on blisters and festering sores. Yet Polish miners befriended them and sometimes provided extra food. Perhaps just as vitally, they began hearing word of the Red Army's approach from the east. For the first time in years, there was a faint glimmer of light.

Despite the often dangerous work, Poles marveled at the splendor in their midst. One of the country's natural and cultural treasures, the Wieliczka mine dated back to the thirteenth century and featured repositories of religious sculptures and chapels carved throughout three main levels. Legend had it that before King Boleslaus V of Poland married around 1250, he offered his Hungarian princess bride a dowry of gold and jewels. Princess Kinga declined, insisting on a gift that would benefit the Polish people and provide them a livelihood. Then she happened upon the salt deposits while traveling to Kraków, which became the dowry of Poland's future patron saint. The mine grew over the centuries with dozens of chambers and chapels created to honor national heroes. Sculptures of gnomes, Polish kings, and Christ and the Apostles abounded with galleries of tiled mosaic floors. While the Nazis exterminated most of the Jews from Wieliczka and its surrounding area, the *Wehrmacht* barely dented the legacy of the mines.

As Nathan and Sam worked underground alongside some of their boyhood friends, someone carved a Star of David deep into a wall. Covered by a wooden structure, it was discovered many years later during renovation and excavation work. As summer commenced, machinery and equipment stopped arriving for the munitions plant, which was never completed.

The two felt something changing in the air. "At night we could hear guns, artillery guns, whatever, in the far distance," Nathan said. "I couldn't sleep but we could hear them. We knew that the Russians were advancing." They made an escape plan with several friends, hiding extra food in a remote section. When guards came down to evacuate the workers ahead of the Red Army, they were to hide in the caves. But that day didn't go as imagined. It all happened too quickly; guards appeared at midday rushing Nathan and his brother into the caged elevator before they could slip away.

Soldiers counted heads out on the *appelplatz*. Their two friends—Zenek Fuchs, whose father had run a tannery and lived in the Offens' building, and Roman Spielman, whose parents owned a bakery—were missing. Some miners betrayed them, and search dogs were sent below. As the Offens rode away on a truck, an SS man sat near Nathan. He huffed to the prisoners that they were deliberately allowing the Russians in, hinting about having a devastating secret weapon to retaliate with. "He said, 'Then we're going to come back with the Jews too,'" Nathan recalled, adding, "I knew they were in trouble then."

Returning to Płaszów, Nathan and Sam did not immediately see their brother or father. There was no time to look. Prisoners were assembled for "a hanging party" in the July heat. Many had endured this before—ordered to stand for hours, beaten or shot if they fainted, urinated, or even defecated on themselves. On another occasion, as night fell and they continued to stand by the thousands, a man leaned into Nathan, seeming to be on the verge of passing out. Nathan opened the man's shirt and massaged his chest, which restored some color and revived him, and no one noticed. On this day it would be his friends Fuchs and Spielman up on the gallows.

Before he was killed, Spielman threw himself at his executioners, cursing and spitting in their faces.

Nathan saw himself on the opposite side of a divide.

One evening outside the ghetto before its liquidation, he was at work transferring wounded soldiers at a railroad station across the river. It was winter, and the Red Cross trains had returned from the front. Many soldiers were frostbitten, to him as if nearly frozen to death. They had lice "about this size of my thumb," he said. "The Germans didn't want to touch them."

At a substation they carried men toward the delousing hut, down the stairs from the platform, usually two guys per soldier. Even in the dark, he could tell these men were relatively young—eighteen or nineteen, just about his age—many six feet tall or larger. One began complaining about his feet to Offen in broken Polish. "He said his feet—that those Russians can stay for two or three days in the snow, nothing happens. He was out for just a few hours in the snow and his legs froze on him. And he called me 'Friend,' that I should help him."

Because he was in pain, Nathan thought to himself. *I want to hurt that son of a bitch.* He took the guy on his back and dragged him out, banging the soldier's legs on each step "and his feet hurt like hell." Nathan didn't flinch, continuing to jerk the man across the rails and timber ties through the dark. No one heard the cries amidst the bleating engines and commotion. Nathan felt a rush of satisfaction, his wrath uncoiled amidst the turbid coal fumes.

Approaching the ghetto that morning after work Nathan was searched. He hadn't resorted to theft. Yet Offen had allowed something to die inside. Even if doing so toughened his callouses and spurred him further on.

He took ownership of this: *I am an animal just like him.* Returning home, Nathan broke down in tears.

The dismantling of Płaszów began in earnest as the summer of 1944 peaked.

The crush of transports, the camp's demise, and Amon Goeth's arrest have long been revealed to the world, chronicled by Polish and American tribunals and other inquiries. The still-smoldering scenes, personalized by witnesses' testimonies and memoirs, in expressions of poems, sculptures, and paintings, held together like fragments melded into a mosaic, trigger a nearly apoplectic reaction. Steven Spielberg's reconstruction continues to confront us: nearly three hundred children gathered to be sent away to die, cynical lullabies playing on the camp loudspeaker—*Gute Nacht Mutti*, ("Goodnight Mummy") and *Nad kolyska matka cʒuwa* ("Over the child's cot, mother stands guard"); naked men and women running during the "health review" of May 7, after which 1,400 were shipped to Auschwitz; and the final deportations that August and October, stocked heavily with women.

As locksmiths installed barbed wire grills blocking the doorways to freight wagons and cattle cars waiting on a spur, a confluence of events swept up the Offens like a clash of great rivers.

In a hurry to leave, the SS sought to remove traces of mass executions. The graves behind Prick Hill were uncovered and exhumed by prisoners wearing masks, replacing the teams with hammers that had gone through knocking out gold teeth, the living dead gathering more logs to stack the dead. Lit pyres spread a gritty dust that settled on the officers' uniforms, the air "filled with the stench of burning flesh and clouds of choking smoke." Another young boy watching from a window saw people, "like ghosts, coming out of the smoke." This final desecration overwhelmed the camp, prompting the most caustic Jews to circulate even more macabre jokes involving soap and lampshades. Eventually prisoners counted the removal of at least seventeen wagonloads of ash. Many thousands more lay buried unmarked in the nearby forest.

Bernard kept closing his eyes. While his father continued his shop work, rendering more boots deficient with subtle slices, he went into hiding within himself. Around them bonfires burned for days without end.

In the infirmary, a German doctor gave typhoid fever patients one last shot: injections of gasoline into their bloodstream. Fearing each new wave of deportations—to death camps including Ravensbrück, Auschwitz, and Flossenbürg—prisoners continued their age-defying deceits. Old men blackened greying hair with pieces of burned cork; others reddened their sunken cheeks with wrappers of chicory.

Following the Warsaw ghetto uprising on August 1, paranoia overtook the SS ranks. Six days later, in a final *aktion*, some seven thousand Polish civilians were rounded up in Kraków and brought to Płaszów to do hard labor. Yet unlike previous political prisoners, most of their lives were spared.

The boundaries separating corruption and treachery had been eroding since the occupation began. They collapsed like ditch walls in the eighth circle of hell.

A procession of shades moved along the remaining bank, their weasel eyes and nocturnal faces reflected in the glowing coals. Through the acrid smog came a menacing column of black-shirted Ukrainian guards, POWs who had volunteered for the camps. Puffed-up block leaders followed them through the gray zone: a tall, chunky Italian Jew who advertised himself with superfluous snarls; Mrs. Webber, scalding hot, afraid for her own life and willing to divide rations and appoint cleanups without a crumb of mercy; and Fehringer, a blue-eyed *kapo* who punched men in the stomach to sort a work crew, marched with other barracks' heads who had just done what they were told, meting out punishment when no work was evident. Dr. Max Blanke emerged in a fur-lined overcoat with its collar turned out, appearing just as when he supervised the May selection, except his bullwhip had finally gone slack.

Goeth slipped away from the line to recheck his stolen booty. Even as Julius Madritsch and other industrialists had plied him with thick stacks of marks to provide them free labor, he shipped valuables home to Vienna or to storage in Czechoslovakia. Several leading OD men who had felt privileged, and even protected, as they ruled over Płaszów prisoners became potential incriminating witnesses to Goeth's fraud. In one stroke they were publicly executed along with their families after the commandant orchestrated a ruse, pretending the leaders had plotted an armed rebellion. One in particular named Chilowicz, the head of the Jewish police, still carrying his thirty pieces of silver, knew all about Goeth's personal stockpiles while skimming goods for himself. Others working as camp clerks were spared as they papered over another scheme that delivered furniture, paintings, and pianos to German dignitaries rather than to Berlin.

The inversion fell onto itself.

Usurpers clung to the money changers of Judaica as the looters were looted. Rations sold on the black market while meat and noodle soup went to Rolf. A prisoner discovered the beauty of Verdi's *Rigoletto* for the first time whistled by a German inmate, while Goeth maintained two acclaimed musicians, Herman and Leon Rosner, to perform at his orgiastic villa parties. Corruption drained in an intravenous drip from flattery, leaking through seduction suspended in a hypocrite's spittle death brine. Officers' quarters built with cheap materials collapsed into Dante's ditches, ravaged by Pharoah's orders to make bricks without straw.

A footbridge into treachery remained open as the dykes flooded. *To where the shades were covered wholly by ice, showing like straw in a glass.*

The commandant's own crates were packed with carpets and furs. He had stashed underwear and jewelry, wines, spirits, and tobacco, some opened by the SS as his mistress watched. The deconstruction of Goeth's private garage was underway when they came for him.

Joseph Bau heard the stones weeping. Picking one up from the road, he felt its smooth marble. He noted bits of Hebraic inscriptions.

He had met his wife Rebecca in the camp, and they married in front of his mother beside her bunk. He traded four loaves of bread for a silver spoon, which a jeweler made into two rings. They were able to work for Schindler at the Emalia enamel works, making the final trip to Brinnlitz with 1,100 others before Płaszów closed down. A graphic artist, Bau had worked in the camp's construction office as a draftsman. He drew maps with precise lines and subtle flourishes. He didn't forget the sounds in the stones. Later he advised visitors to do the same: to pick one up and place it to your ear.

Nathan's sinewy shell was tough as leather. Working the mine had at least provided a respite from some of the worst bludgeoning at Płaszów. Yet he and Sam, whose buoyancy could not be pummeled back, began to keep each other moving when the other wanted to lie down.

Bernard, having endured typhus and separation, would soon need to rely again on the protection and charity of other adults. And much like Nathan, he was starting to learn something else.

In order to survive, he was going to have to feed himself on hate. Along with their father they remained somewhat alive, hanging on to broken luck.

20

LIBERATION

Wheels scraped metal on metal as the door to the cattle car slammed shut, closing out the light. Nathan and Sam stood shoulder-to-shoulder with more than a hundred other prisoners. No water or bread was provided, and while some of the other linked freight cars had a wooden bucket for a toilet, theirs did not.

It was early August. Within minutes anything they might recognize of Płaszów—perhaps one of the guard towers, or Prick Hill—began to fade from view through a small window at the top of the car, their lone source of ventilation. Their home at Krakusa 9 was an elusive dream, their former life next door to the grocer and butcher scarcely a whiff of frayed recollection. Even the warm delicacy of dark chocolate that each of the boys had loved felt like a drowned smudge.

The opening in the car roof was laced with barbed wire, the heat inside already stifling. Soldiers pushed Bernard and their father onto another car, or perhaps they were crammed into a far corner of the same one. No one knew for sure. Sam thought that they were all together; Nathan believed they had been separated. They tried looking among the bodies and called out—to no avail. Bernard sensed he was alone with his dad.

They had no idea where they were going. But soon the cars headed south and southwest, rather than the short distance toward Auschwitz-Birkenau. For no reason they could conceive of, and with no sign from

Yahweh, even as the train pitched gradually toward the foothills it felt as if they were somehow descending.

We were not praying or anything. Just starving, starving to death. You were hungry, you couldn't sing. "You heard the whole car was groaning and moaning, everyone was sick," Nathan said. "People dying, people gasping for air and water. They wouldn't even give us water. People calling out."

The cars moved slowly, stopping every now and then, sometimes languishing for hours on a siding. On rare occasions, villagers tossed loaves and bits of food to them. Sam, at least, recalled this, but not either of his brothers. At each stop soldiers mounted the tops with submachine guns. Bodies of the dead were thrown out, making a little more room.

All around Nathan and Sam people relieved themselves where they stood. The smell was putrid—watery stools of dysentery, and scorched piss. They tried to make room so elders could sit. Some drank their own urine. Others called to loved ones as life drained away. A few bodies slumped on the floor beside the two.

Wherever they were headed, the brothers feared being ordered to strip once they got out. There had been rumors of what the so-called delousing showers really meant. But there were few hard clues, and they lacked tools to pry their way out.

Jacob kept his youngest son close at his side in another attempt to shield him. "My father was standing, I was behind him and he saved me from being crushed," Bernard said, his voice drifting in a wisp nearly seventy years later. "He leaned against a wall and gave me space not to be crushed. He was strong enough, I guess he had a mission to save his offspring."

Two or three years younger than Bernard, Fred Ferber squeezed into another space on one of the boxcars. Near where the door closed, he found a piece of metal flashing or some other part along the bed, and this helped him survive. He bent down and saw water vapor forming in the humidity. Being small enough, he was able to lick it off the metal plate. "As stupid as it is," Ferber recalled, "as much as I didn't realize even at that time, it was such a tremendous benefit and I kept quiet. I didn't want anyone else to [know]."

On August 7, 1944, Sam noted the passing of his twenty-third birthday as he stood in the cell.

The four had a brief moment huddled together to mourn the loss of their family. This most likely occurred in Płaszów just before the transport, but again, they could not be sure. Memories condensed, overlapping in warped lines like tree rings that become difficult to divine after seasons of drought and disease. Jacob was merely forty-nine but appeared to be seventy. "We all looked bedraggled and emaciated, but we could hardly recognize our father," Sam wrote. He suggested their reunion came a few days later; Nathan insisted it was shortly before they boarded; while Bernard could scarcely conjure even an image of his brothers at Płaszów.

It took three and a half days to reach the granite highlands of Upper Austria, where humanity was shredded and spit out at a rate more furious than anything Nathan and his brothers could have ever imagined.

The cars finally stopped for good at a small train station close to a swift-moving river—the Danube. They were in a village beside mountains, and the Offens were rushed out with big dogs snapping at them. Their physical exhaustion convulsed with fear, their confusion ratcheted to yet another level. Where now? Was this the end? They began trudging up a narrow, winding path that quickly grew steep.

"Even then, we had no respite," Sam recalled. Survivors were forced to carry bodies from the cattle cars through the village while townspeople clustered along the roadside. He saw little reaction to the straggling mass in tattered striped gray uniforms. "[They were] sort of, not exactly greeting us, but like waving to us, like almost if they didn't know what was going on," he said. Three miles ahead, a fortress-like gray building overlooked the river and valley, enclosed on three sides with quarry stone and barbed-wire fence on the other.

This was Mauthausen, a full-blown beast.

One of the most feared death camps, its appetite and reach far exceeded Płaszów, consuming a rancid melting pot of POWs and detainees from nearly every country overrun by the Nazis. There were large numbers of Soviet troops, Czech, French, Polish, and Italian civilians, people from the former Yugoslavia, and thousands of anti-fascist Spanish prisoners who had fought against Franco. War objectors including Jehovah's Witnesses were kept separate from homosexuals, gypsies, and others branded as "aso-cial" and of an "alien race."

A significant population of Polish and Hungarian Jews—whose num-bers began to spike only by 1944 as the Offens arrived—were at the bot-tom of the camp's social hierarchy. Whittled down as they arrived, Jews were routinely made to stand naked outside for hours during admission, freezing in the snow wearing only wooden clogs, or executed nearby, with survivors separated in their own block and given half-rations. Two brick ovens worked around the clock near a tiled gas chamber that appeared to be a working shower. The chamber had sixteen nozzles and a long slit pipe, invisible to prisoners along a wall, feeding Zyklon B from a gas conduit. Nathan knew it as "the killing field."

Mauthausen was one of only two "Class III" punishment camps, an especially severe designation. It was known within the Reich as the "bone-grinder," and many prisoners' files were stamped, "Return Undesirable." Yet the camp was also merely a giant sprocket in the machine. It formed the hub of a system with nearly sixty sub-camps in the region, each feeding on slave labor for secret armaments manufacturing and other industrial pro-duction. Some of the most extreme cruelty in this network was delivered at three camps close to Mauthausen in or around Gusen, a neighboring village. In all, nearly 200,000 prisoners passed through the Mauthausen-Gusen concentration camp system between 1938 and May of 1945. At least 95,000 died in the camps or while working nearby, including more than 14,000 Jews, although those estimates likely underscore the reality.

In contrast to Treblinka or Auschwitz, Mauthausen was not built soley for genocide. First envisioned to contain so-called traitors to the Austrian Nazi Party, the camp system grew chiefly to exploit slave labor for manu-facturing war materials and turning a profit for SS-owned companies. The SS had selected granite quarries in Mauthausen and Gusen to supply stone for the Third Reich's monumental building projects being planned by architect Albert Speer. This use pivoted to armaments production, the apex being a massive underground plant producing the fuselage and wings for the Messerschmitt Me 262, the first jet-powered fighter aircraft that became the Reich's last hope to turn the tide of the war.

Locals had long built beer cellars inside mountains formed by sand deposits from an ancient sea. The stability of these sandstone *kellers* in the Mühlviertel region did not escape SS planners scouting for reinforced spaces to hide their armaments manufacturing. They constructed two main tunnel networks and within one built the Me 262 plant—the largest in the heavily obscured Messerschmitt production system—which had a relentless operational target. Inmates from Gusen and Mauthausen were rushed to build the plant, exacting some of the heaviest casualties among the entire Nazi camp system with an estimated 40,000 deaths.

Ritualized killings of prisoners in Gusen, Mauthausen, and in neighboring village St. Georgen took on even more depraved forms as they dug tunnels and broke rocks in the quarries. Tens of thousands of men were wantonly "exterminated by labor," wrote Rudolf Haunschmied, an Austrian historian who co-authored a book chronicling the complex Nazi armaments system surrounding his hometown of St. Georgen an der Gusen. "Assignments to production jobs were more or less permanent," he wrote. "Once trained, one worked at a job until one died."

The largest underground project began just west of Mauthausen in St. Georgen, about twelve miles from the provincial capital, Linz. Called *Bergkristall*, which means *rock crystal*, or Project B-8, mining began a few months before the Offens' arrival, with plans for some fifty thousand square meters of underground manufacturing space dedicated to jet fighter assembly lines. A second tunnel system close to the Gusen camp called *Kellerbau* was used to manufacture machine gun parts and submachine guns.

Work expanding the tunnels was especially onerous that summer when the Offens arrived. Driven hard by *kapos*—barracks chiefs who were often hardened criminals—SS guards, or by Austrian or German foremen, six thousand men swung picks and hammers, operated compressed air drills, built steel reinforced concrete walls, and pulled lorries loaded with sand. Toiling with a constant barrage of noise and poor ventilation, they drank infected water and faced frequent equipment malfunctions, blackouts, and cave-ins. Prisoners had to smash rocks roughly a foot in diameter into two-inch fragments while unknown to them, a stone crusher operated outside. "We learned to be docile and disciplined, no matter how useless or difficult the work," wrote Martin Lax, a Hungarian who concluded by his second day working that the main objective was "to break us." By the fall of 1944, construction on the jet fighter plant went full bore, bent on meeting an increasingly desperate goal: some ten thousand slave laborers were to produce 1,250 aircraft a month by the next spring.

Yet working in the tunnels was not to be Sam or Nathan's fate. They had already ground it out inside the Wiliezcka mine, and there was plenty enough to contend with above ground.

Everything was closing in, yet the two young men hung on. As they came into the main compound at Mauthausen for the first time, entering the gate under a domineering iron eagle, Sam was struck by how clean the camp appeared. Flowerbeds were planted beside the barracks, and the camp roads were rolled flat. Entering the main square, they passed what was known as the "Wall of Lamentation," so named because many of the newly arrived had to wait there for hours, with some breaking down as they stood. The prisoners were once again categorized by race or nationality, and kept apart from certain political and criminal detainees. A so-called infirmary camp where the sick and injured were actually left to die was scrupulously confined from the main population beside a large SS sports ground with a football pitch. The Jewish block was located next to the ash pits.

Nathan and Sam stripped off their rags and were sent to the barbers. Each was shaved with a new identifying mark, a stripe two or three inches wide from the forehead to the back. They went through disinfection and registration. Assaulted by an unmistakable stinging smell, each formed an idea of what was going on somewhere in the camp, in the chambers close to the south wall.

For Nathan, at least, the confirmation of a gas chamber and crematoria would somehow cease to matter in the months ahead. "It was no secret but we couldn't care less where we died or no matter what," he said, "because overnight they were taking people outside of the barracks and stacking them like bricks." Or cordwood, as the comparison was often made by other prisoners, and ultimately, by American liberators who entered nine months later. Swollen, rat-chewed deadwood, piled eight- to ten-feet high. Unlike anything those young GIs who hailed from the Lower Peninsula and places like Sioux Falls or the Northeast Kingdom had ever seen drying beside their fields and outbuildings. They were unprepared for the scale of this depravity. But that knock to their skulls would come only after a deep and brutal winter.

The brothers' next vision was sustained for the rest of their lives. Despite how difficult one considers it must have been for each to retrieve the broken glances, somehow those remained in tact as if stored in some dry cranny deep in a cavern. Called to assemble for a selection about one week after arriving at the camp, the four Offens heard their names called as registration forms were read. Nathan and Sam were sent one way, their father and younger brother into another line. Nathan remembers seeing them both in a long queue leading to the showers. "I looked and I saw Bernard hanging on to my father in the distance," Nathan said. "I saw them, I don't think they saw me."

It was his last glimpse of his father. Sam had a premonition that he would never see either of the two again.

This time there were actual showers with running water to enter. Afterwards both Bernard and his dad were marched back to the village and on to a train headed to Auschwitz. Once again, Jacob shielded his son in the cattle car, securing a space against the wall to find a little more air with Bernard crouched between his legs. Their thirst grew severe during the three days, although Bernard was allowed to get out once and bring back a bucket of water. More bodies collapsed, and he grew more scared. They had little idea what the separation meant. On August 22, they arrived back in Poland.

Bernard submits to being pulled through another maelstrom. As the freight car pulls in he hears frantic shouts, he sees fires on the horizon with enormous smoke clouds. Without recognition he traces the charred, oily smell. The door opens as people in striped uniforms and more dogs chase them. *Alles raus!* Get out! Wires and barracks on both sides, soldiers beating them. They line up keeping five or so abreast, narrowing down to a single file.

Amidst the blur he still sees his father's final protective act. It is as if the memory is being meted out by a strainer, through which the course remnants of epochal denial have finally squeezed through. It is the day after Christmas in 1981. Bernard is giving his oral history to a university professor in Michigan. Offen had recently returned to Poland for the first time, visiting his native city and some of the camps. Things have been coming back to him in rips, and the tear is evident in his voice, which is one part whispered reluctance, one part acknowledged breakdown in the whirl. Bernard had just recently begun to confront his trauma and enter some of the gaps. He wears blue jeans and a thick dark sweater over a casual buttoned shirt, from time to time glaring at the camera directly, strategically, through large rimmed glasses.

I remember father being there all the time. I mean, you know, I had the connection with my father.

Someone told him to lie about his age again. He doesn't recall understanding why: "I'm trying to remember if I was in front of my father or behind him . . . I think I was behind him. I remember coming up to the SS man and he was just like that," he says, jerking an upright thumb to one side. He believes it was Mengele himself in a neatly pressed tunic and polished boots, the death's head SS cap slightly tilted. "I remember running toward him, pulling myself up, to kind of look tall. That's what my father told me to do."

He is sent walking to his right, seeing his father already on the left. A minute or so later they regard one another; they're pretty far apart, close to fifty yards. He cannot quite recover the exact look. But it is not actually their last. At that moment, he realizes it must be the end, although reason cannot quite grasp this. *There is another glance at one another while being chased, like, "Keep running—over there."*

He winces, trying to hold back the searing prick of a needle piercing the outer side of his left forearm. The tattoo reads "B7815." Later that day, or maybe the next, he goes through processing, waiting in yet another line, still trying to keep moving in some way. Other men guide and push him along. He is sent to the quarantine camp at Birkenau.

Bernard slows down with the interviewer, his voice a trickle. He'd like some water. He asks to take a short break. Reading a prayer during a recent Shabbat service, he says he found himself recalling the sound of his father's voice for the first time.

I didn't understand what it meant. I could almost do it.

Sam and Nathan qualified again for hard labor, joining a transport of 270 prisoners who moved to one of the sub-camps at Gusen. Early each morning they marched to a large quarry called Wiener Graben near Mauthausen. The complex supplied paving stones for the city of Vienna before the war, and after being taken over by an SS company, stone was sent to Linz for construction and roadwork elsewhere. Heinrich Himmler had selected the site himself in 1938 as he plotted the slave economy. The quarry's stone-making sheds were converted to manufacture fuselages for the Messerschmitt Me 109, a standard fighter plane. But there was still plenty of killing to do there.

Wiener Graben had an especially cruel feature called the "Stairs of Death"—186 steps up which prisoners were made to lug heavy rough-hewn rocks. Particularly steep and irregular with varied heights, these were no ordinary steps. Trying not to slip on the ice or in the rain, prisoners carried rocks by hand or filled in hods on their back. Weighing as little as eighty or ninety pounds themselves, they sometimes carried loads amounting to half their body mass. Mocking the weak from watchtowers and the cliff sides, guards and *kapos* had a field day. Sam and Nathan were expected to keep a fast pace.

"All day long, run down, and run up with a big stone on our shoulders," Sam said. "The guards did not even have to waste bullets to kills us. All they had to do was push us from the top of the quarry to our deaths." Some did, while others sprayed straggling workers with a machinegun or their pistol for kicks. Not far from the stairs, the SS coined a name for an accessible ledge beside the road leading back to Mauthausen, calling it "Parachute Jump." The writer Evelyn Le Chêne, whose exhaustive book about the camp included details from her husband, Pierre, a survivor, noted, "No account of the tortures endured there would be adequate and no photograph of this sinister place would remotely convey an idea of the sufferings of the deportees."

Autumn came quickly striking its cold fist in the mountains. The brothers often worked in the open pit breaking up large rocks with pick axes, hammers, and chisels with perhaps a thousand others. There were pneumatic drills for the more fortunate workers to use, and stones were loaded into wagons and pushed to a crusher to make gravel. "It was already September or October and we didn't have any gloves," Nathan recalled. "So imagine how it would feel to pick up a piece of frozen rock. Sometimes our hands froze to the rocks. But if you work, you keep warm. Otherwise you freeze to death. So we kept working."

They were afraid to look up, knowing that catching one look from a guard might twitch his trigger. Their shoes were almost worthless—wooden clogs with leather sides that Nathan called "clunkers." They added insulation by stuffing wrappers from cement bags in the shoes. They lost track of the days smashing and carrying loads. But at least they weren't in the tunnels, where they heard scores of men were dying because of unsecured walls.

All around them, others wore down or were wiped out. At Gusen I, where the two lived for the next several months, roll call sometimes came in the middle of the night. After standing outside for hours in their rags or completely exposed, inmates froze where they fell. Once a week, they had to walk naked in deep snow to the shower barracks, and back without boots or towels, in temperatures often as low as 15 degrees Fahrenheit. The water was usually frigid, with no soap to help keep off the lice, and their skin froze as they returned to quarters. Acute diarrhea, vomiting, and dehydration were the norm. Already so fragile, "the shock of these cold showers weakened them even further," Sam wrote. "Many succumbed to disease."

In the morning, after washing and standing for a head count, the bodies of those who had died overnight needed to be stacked, sometimes piled by the washroom. Breakfast was a bowl of watery black "coffee" made of wheat, perhaps with a slice of bread and some marmalade or butter. The noon meal might be a thin cabbage soup. Returning from the quarry at night, the men were forced to sing and march, carrying more of the wounded and dead before another body count. The evening meal was usually just a slice of bread. One time Nathan saw a block inspector dishing out soup, a man who was a known murderer. "He looked at you and sometimes dipped the ladle a little deeper into the drum, so if you were lucky you could wind up with some nutrients," he said. "Otherwise, you got a bowl of clear broth . . . without any salt, and no matter how starved you were, it was hard to eat it. It was made of some chemicals and looked gray, like wallpaper paste, and was tasteless." His brother scrounged for apple cores the guards threw away while snacking and smoking. He was never caught in the act.

Sam had something else going for him that proved to be fortuitous.

Gusen held some Austrian Quakers who were war objectors, and despite being interned they were relatively well fed and able to receive food packages and mail. Sam was lucky enough to be picked to clean their barracks. One of the Quakers, a carpenter, discovered that he knew how to sew, and asked Sam to mend his uniform. Approving of Sam's work, the carpenter obtained permission to use Sam from time to time stitching others' coats and pants in his barracks. The Austrians shared extra food with him, which he brought back to Nathan, and when there was enough, to another bunkmate. Beside the Quakers, some German prisoners—including Communists and other so-called criminals—occasionally compensated Offen with food scraps. "Sam was always managing," Nathan said. Those extra nutrients sustained the brothers as an especially severe winter slogged along.

Somehow they had to keep moving whenever outside. It is inconceivable working in a quarry without gloves and proper footwear in the foothills of the Alps during winter, but that is what they both did. Thrown into the mix at Gusen relatively late, only Sam was able to find some inside work that season. Nathan was unable to gain a coveted job such as in the stonemasons' command, or making fuselages in sheds beside the quarry, which had wood stoves, and sometimes, more sympathetic civilian masters. Buoyed by his brother, Nat would have to survive on grit alone.

He was aware of his brain slowing down. He couldn't quite think straight, peering through a fog hoping only to last another week. All around Nathan, prisoners slipped beyond wistfulness for food to desperation and resignation. "It became each man for himself," he said.

If he had still been wielding a hammer for the blacksmith in Kraków, surely he would miss the master's mark. Yet even dragging his feet, he stayed in motion at the quarry. He retained a sliver of consciousness that he was on the edge of losing his essence. "If you are tortured, starved and beaten for a long time, you lose your humanity—you become like a wild, disoriented animal," he wrote. "You cannot think rationally since all of your energy goes into your belly, where pain is from starvation. It is very difficult to explain the hunger. Under those conditions, a father can kill a son or vice versa for a piece of bread." He and Sam traded scraps of moldy bread for salt. The bread wasn't doing them any good; they, too, were beginning to slip past hunger. They bundled the grains in a tiny oilcloth, seeking to make the thin soup somewhat eatable. Then someone stole their salt.

Nathan even admired those few prisoners who charged the electric fence, reaching it before the guards could shoot. "They had control over what happened to them," he told me once. "I was too scared to do that."

He and Sam remained inseparable. Born seventeen months apart, they had always been close, their dispositions different and often complementary. Sam was always the more cerebral one, preferring card games—bridge, poker, and sixty-six—with his friends over outside sports. Nathan was more muscular and verbal, lifting weights in preparation of defending himself and his brother. Sometimes they divided crumbs of bread for each other, counting them off to save and share, neither wanting to take it from the other. Caring for one another was unconditional; no earthly force could wrest this from them.

Yet the SS came perilously close. Feeling far too weak to work one morning, Nathan checked himself into the infirmary and later brought himself back to the barracks. Two big guards came in and began kicking him, their boot heels pounding like a horse's hooves. They hung him up from the third bunk tier and continued the beating, but that was not the worst of it. As he faded in and out of consciousness, bleeding from the head and buttocks, a block leader picked Offen up, dragging him into the showers. There the *blockalteste* sexually assaulted him.

Left for dead, the next morning Nathan somehow washed himself up and reported to work. He did not return to the sick bay.

He found out later about friends who had gone to the infirmary and never returned.

Someone guided me. But why? It took decades to get his arms around an explanation.

By then Private First Class Donald Montgomery had seen his share of carnage. A truck driver with the 575th Anti-Aircraft Artillery Battalion, Montgomery's unit had been in Bastogne that winter and crossed the Rhine for the push deep through Bavaria, supporting the Third Army's most extreme probe to the east. It was the last week of April, a season when ice-out had usually cleared highland ponds and the first spring wildflowers emerged. In Berlin, the Soviets were tightening their stranglehold around the city. Hitler would take his own life by the week's end. Still, there was nothing prosaic about what the twenty-two-year-old would experience during the next two weeks.

All his friends back in Pontiac had answered the call to war, and when he reported to Fort Custer, Don looked forward to army life, even if he had no idea what the conflict was all about. He had left a job running a forklift and stocking parts at the GM Truck & Coach Plant and was yet to have a steady gal. More than two years later, the service had already sent him north of Casablanca to guard German POWs, back stateside with a boatload of Krauts, and then attached him to the 11th Armored Division. Battery B's mission was to protect the Thunderbolt tanks from air fire, while also eliminating enemy mortar positions with 50-calibre machine guns. An expert rifle marksman, in moments Montgomery marveled at his unit's luck or veered to complain about weaponry he felt was pitiful. Their guns only seemed to be effective if a large group laid down a barrage at a plane; they had downed only one in about four months of combat.

As they edged closer to the Austrian border outside of Munich, his unit came across the remains of a death march, most likely in or close to Cham, a small city. This was not a column of Jews and other prisoners barely moving. Instead, they found those left behind, marched east apparently in an effort to stay ahead of the American advance, and murdered when they could not keep pace—or just because. "Literally hundreds of them beside the road—men, women, and children," Montgomery said. "Some looked like they died of exhaustion or starvation, some had a bullet hole in their head. We came close to a POW camp. I don't know the name. We had some German officers who were able to ride on the bumper of a car . . . the only prisoners I saw were dead."

It was beyond comprehension. His battery mates were in disbelief as well; they had no preparation for this. Like most of the Americans—or enlisted men, at least—Montgomery knew nothing about extermination camps targeting Jews. Flossenbürg was the closest one in the area, and Dachau was perhaps 150 miles away. While articles had begun to appear in *Stars and Stripes* about soldiers liberating so-called POW camps, those had not yet reached him.

The young GIs had no clue as to their identities or stories, their livelihoods and families lost: the tailor from Bremen, the Czech university gang, the plumbers and shoemakers of Kraków. The victims were nameless, amorphous "displaced persons."

Montgomery drove all day, never losing sight of the bodies, which he estimated at several thousand. He grew angrier at the enemy, but did not discuss it.

Within a week, Montgomery's unit was in Austria along with much of the division, well aware that they were close to Red Army patrols. By May 5, they were perhaps ten miles north of Linz and only about twenty-five miles away from Mauthausen, with no notion of what lay nearby.

Supporting the Thunderbolts column were the engineering companies, and among one of them was a classmate of Donald's from Lake Orion High School named Dick LaLone. A heavy-set crane operator, LaLone's family had a farm until the Depression. He later worked a crane lifting vehicles and heavy materials at another truck and coach plant in Pontiac. His 996th Engineer Treadway Bridge Company erected steel bridges across pontoons for river crossings from France and Belgium to the Rhineland—the longest one crossing the Rhine into Frankfurt. He took part in D-Day as his company boarded an LST and landed at Omaha Beach, where he likely drove an amphibious truck. From there, Sgt. Richard Henry LaLone often blew up large pill boxes or hardened bunkers as a wrecker crewman while his unit was on detached service with various outfits.

By April he and some others from the 996th were attached to Combat Command B, one of the lead units. After returning to his company, on May 5 LaLone went on assignment again. A couple of days later, the call went out for digging equipment. At a massive fort overlooking the Danube, the command needed to bury some five thousand bodies.

They had beaten incredible odds. Yet their time was about up.

Nathan and Sam were brought back from Gusen to Mauthausen in April. Considered unfit to work, they were fortunate not to have been gassed at Gusen I as some nearly seven hundred others were one day that month, or beaten to death along with six hundred sick prisoners the following day because of a shortage of Zyklon B at Gusen II. Instead, they marched back to the barracks in the so-called "sanitary camp" where several thousand spent prisoners were mostly left to die. Among those nearly three hundred inmates sent to Wiener Graben along with the brothers seven months before, less than a handful remained alive. Quarry laborers were rarely expected to survive more than six weeks—three months tops.

Nathan lay on the top tier of their bunk, suffering from diarrhea and a swollen belly, and some kind of infection as well. His feet swelled and he nursed wounds from the guards' and *kapo's* beating, unaware that he was bleeding internally. He and the others had stopped going to work. They could barely move. Once in a while, guards threw them a slice of stale bread. All green. "We were supposed to die," he says.

Sam was a little better off physically. And through his contacts with the Austrian Quakers, he still saw a faint fiber of light. Weeks before, a few had actually read letters to him from their sons fighting on the front. Things weren't going well for the *Wehrmacht*, and the Red Army's advance was no secret. He saw that the objectors anticipated the outcome, and while subdued, they were very happy about it.

In the final few months the overcrowding and killings escalated to even more heinous levels at the Gusen camps, in Mauthausen itself, and the other sub-camps. By March the prisoner population surged to nearly 85,000 after tripling the previous year. Some prisoners decided their own fate after seeing signs of their demise, most notably a large group of Soviet officers who broke out of Mauthausen—but only seven avoided being hunted down. Most others were too weak to choose.

The final act unfolded as the SS pressed its desperate plan for underground destruction. Early that spring, fighter jet manufacturing ramped up inside the *Bergkristall* tunnel. Hydraulic presses and welding equipment were concentrated inside a supposed bomb-proof area, and production increased by more than two-fold—though still falling well short of capacity. Allied reconnaissance flights had identified the armaments production facilities, and on April 16, Soviet fighter planes dropped a dozen bombs on the Bergkristall underground railway station entrance. It was too late for the Me 262 to make a difference.

Around this time, the SS, likely at the direction of Henrich Himmler, scripted its departing scene for the Mauthausen camps. If the Reich was to lose the war, tens of thousands of prisoners and perhaps even local civilians who knew about the armaments plants would go down with it, buried inside the tunnels. They would deny the Russians or Americans the aircraft production and free labor, while eliminating witnesses. At minimum this meant the Gusen camps inmates—as many as 25,000—plus about 16,000 at Mauthausen. The camp commandant, Franz Ziereis, supplemented the twenty-four tons of dynamite placed near the fighter jet plant with more than twenty aircraft bombs. But the bombs were never connected to detonators.

Allied commanders were warned that April of the impending humanitarian disaster at the known camps in the Linz area. Yet they may have known nothing of the mass demolition scheme. Dubbed *Feuerzeug*, or "Lighter," it was held as a top secret among a handful of Nazi officials. The ruse would be to sound air raid alarms to move prisoners inside the tunnel workshops. The date was set for May 5 or 6.

Around this time, Sam noticed a spike in executions. Some of his friends were brought out to the forest and never returned. He and Nathan kept a dead man in their bunk. When a block leader did distribute the dark, sawdust-like bread, they stuck out the man's arm to get an extra piece.

Bernard stayed in Birkenau only a few months, where adults gave him clothing and extra food. They told him where to go, and before inspections and a selection, how to run up smartly, as if he still had strength. Looking only at the shiny black boots.

He slept beside adults in bunks, close and warm. One of the *kapos* picked him out. The man had a green triangle patch on his shirt indicating he was a criminal of uncontrolled venom, and he wanted the fifteen-year-old to perform sex. Bernard tried, and was not up to it; he did not satisfy the man. The criminal did not beat him.

He often tucked a little piece of bread inside his jacket for the next morning. Cloying for something to look forward to and still not wanting to believe what was happening, his mind did something with it. He decided: "I'm going to survive because I am going to tell people about what is happening here."

Bernard moved out of his body. Watching a bird on a barbed wire fence, in his mind he transformed himself into the bird and jumped off. Years later a friend created a painting of this vision, but he lost track of her finished work.

In the fall of 1944, Bernard went by truck to Lansdberg-Kaufering, a sub-camp of Dachau west of Munich. It wasn't just luck; someone had picked him for the transport. From there he worked at a construction site in the blacksmith's shop. Conditions were a little better than in Poland, the barracks were built half underground and retained some heat that winter. A German master in the shop was kind to him, bringing extra food after the scrawny teen started the fire and did errands as shop gopher.

Late in April, as Landsberg was being evacuated he and others were sent on a forced march. They went several days, and their column was strafed by airplanes, likely Americans who mistook them for soldiers. Along the way, "Whoever could not keep up was just shot, blown away by the roadside," he said. But Bernard was one of the stronger ones. They continued south more than forty miles for almost a week. One night they reached a town called Wolfratshausen south of Munich and were loaded into some barracks. By morning the guards had disappeared. It was May 2.

He and some of the men wandered out cautiously. Someone suggested to Bernard that he follow the road from where they came, so he struck out alone. Hearing guns in the distance, he stayed in the woods walking along the edge of a river. He came across bodies, battered armaments, and trees denuded from explosions.

Approaching a village, he hid for perhaps the last time, crouched and watching. Tanks with white stars rumbled through, and "I didn't know what that was but I knew it wasn't the Germans, so I ran, and met some GIs." Approaching them with his arms raised, he tried communicating in Polish and Yiddish, and after a while they found someone who spoke Polish. Two soldiers returned with him carrying as many supplies as they could for the several hundred remaining men. "And that was it," he says.

Decades later he was asked why he thought he got those breaks when others suffered worse. "Call it God, call it anything else, I don't know what to call it," he said. "It was meant for me to survive. I don't know, the mystery of *how come me?*"

Like the others clearing the way for the Thunderbolt tanks of the 11th Armored Division, Charlie Torluccio and his mates would never forget exactly when they learned what they were fighting for.

They remained on high alert even with the war's end just days away. Coming through the foothills near the Danube valley, there could be no letup, not even as some large *Wehrmacht* elements were surrendering. Die-hard Nazis were believed to be holding out to make a final stand, and lead American forces also had to be careful not to penetrate too far and brush up against the Red Army. They had pushed on quickly, spearheading the Third Army's drive at some nineteen miles a day despite physical obstacles and the enemy's delaying tactics—an advance of about 130 miles from Bayreuth in a week. Heavy snow held them up for one day, but that was about it.

Torluccio was in the second platoon, Troop D, of the 41st Cavalry Reconnaissance Squadron, Mechanized. On his nineteenth birthday a week earlier, his unit came across a death march from Flossenbürg. Seeing those walking skeletons in what looked like pajama pants had been unsettling, but he still didn't really know who those people were. He hadn't really had time before to consider them, but Torluccio was about to find out.

An unlikely intermediary whose timing proved prescient arrived in Mauthausen on April 28. Louis Haefliger, a Zürich bank clerk, had agreed to be a delegate for the International Committee of the Red Cross, which for many months had been stonewalled in its attempts to deliver food and medicine. Hoping to save face in its final hours, the SS had only recently given Red Cross authorities assurances to escort food convoys into the camps. Commandant Ziereis at first refused to distribute the food, but Haefliger would not budge, insisting that Ziereis contact his superiors to confirm the order. Returning two days later, the Red Cross delegate met with the chief of Mauthausen's counterintelligence—a first lieutenant named Reiner—and Ziereis, who finally agreed.

Many provisions never reached the inmates, who were drying up as they starved. Officers devoured condensed milk and biscuits, butter, sardines and crackers, chocolate, and other preferred goods, sometimes throwing emptied, leaking cans at prisoners. Yet sharing a room with Reiner at the camp one night, Haefliger found out something more precious.

Reiner, who like Haefliger had been a banker, confided in him the plan to blow up the plane factory with prisoners in the tunnel workshops. Outraged, Haefliger demanded a meeting with the commandant and the Messerschmitt plant chief. In Ziereis's office, Haefliger cringed at the number he heard: 40,000 inmates would be buried in two or three days. He called upon Ziereis to annul the order. The thirty-nine-year-old commandant—nicknamed "baby-face" because of his soft features, yet fully able to drive a "special" gas van that diverted exhaust fumes into a sealed compartment to kill prisoners en route to Gusen—protested that he could not. Haefliger persisted, later claiming he received a verbal promise from Ziereis to counter the order. At one point the two men were left alone. Haefliger described some of their exchange:

> All of a sudden in front of me, another man, feeble and trembling, aged and discouraged. He asked me what he could do. He got up and started to play with his pistols. I followed his movements with more curiosity than fear.

For some reason detonation of the tunnels were never carried out. Different theories and conflicting stories emerged. By one account, some Polish inmates at Gusen heroically thwarted the plot in one tunnel. The plant manager of the quarries claimed to have repeatedly stalled Ziereis's orders by calculating too much explosives and then hiding detonators, including those for the additional aircraft bombs the commandant wanted. Many claims were self-serving, perhaps including Haefliger's contention that civilians were targeted as well—that may have been a defense against charges that he had no authority to interfere in military operations unless civilian lives were in jeopardy. Haefliger said that he initiated contact to bring American soldiers to Gusen and Mauthausen before the explosives could be set off, actions which twice prompted his consideration for a

Nobel Peace Price. Whatever the full story was, the evidence witnessed by the GIs spoke for itself.

Captain Edward Ardery, company commander of the 56th Armored Engineer Battalion, went into Bergkristall a week after liberation. A platoon joined him following the rail line as they eased below a huge camouflage net hanging from some tall buildings at the tunnel entrance. Inside they found the jet fighters, and a lot of explosives with delayed fuses. "We spent a lot of time cutting wires and were making a lot of educated guesses about which wires to cut," Ardery told Haunschmied in 2005. "The explosives were lined up. If they were trying to blow the thing up they would put them at the best places they could to cause the thing to collapse."

On May 5, patrols of the 41st Cavalry Recon fanned out in varied assignments near Linz. Attached to Combat Command B in an area just north of Gusen and Mauthausen, twenty-four members of another platoon in Charlie Torluccio's troop set out to check the bridges at St. Georgen. Staff Sgt. Albert Kosiek, a Polish-American from Chicago, led his First Platoon D Troop squad through a town called Lungitz. A machine gunner with another unit accompanying them came upon about three hundred caged inmates in what was the smallest Gusen sub-camp, and freed them. A lone German soldier then approached Kosiek, telling him that up the road there was an annex to a large concentration camp. Moving toward the village of St. Georgen, Kosiek's platoon stopped with M24 light tanks to clear a roadblock of piled logs. They saw a motorcycle with a white touring car headed their way with the Red Cross emblem on its side and a white flag. Reiner and another SS officer stepped out along with Haefliger.

After some terse exchanges with guns trained on the three German speakers, Haefliger brought them to Gusen I, where the camp commandant remained. Believing Kosiek was an officer, he turned the camp over to the Americans, and the sergeant radioed his CO, gaining permission to move ahead. They barely had time to take in the scene at Gusen—which was about to uncoil into a new catastrophe later that day. The Swiss delegate led them up to the fortress.

The quiet outside unnerved Sam. He had noticed during the past week or so that the SS seemed to be in disarray—roll call had stopped, and some of the *kapos* and block leaders were gone. It was rumored that prisoners from Gusen's crematorium command, who each morning were forced to retrieve the dead from a gas chamber, had been shot in Mauthausen.

He felt a strange void in the early hours. No guards yelling, no dogs loosened; rats ransacked the piles and the stench of bodies hovered close, but the stinging smoke was gone. Ziereis had melted down and fled to his hunting lodge. A few shots rang out in the distance, and then it grew still again. Sam felt too scared to go investigate.

From their second-tier perch, Nathan was able to look out a small window despite the sun shining directly in his eyes. He had been too weak to go out for days and weighed fifty or perhaps sixty pounds. He could barely feel the sores all over his body, and by now a respiratory infection was spreading. There was no food, no contact with guards throughout the day, and it felt as if he was finally being left alone to die. Sometime that afternoon he looked out and heard the rumble of vehicles, some tanks with big white stars and half-tracks approaching the gate. He thought they were Russians.

When the soldiers lifted Nathan from the bunk he clenched a crumb of moldy blue bread. Someone tried to take it away and he refused to let go, clenching it harder. They put him on a stretcher, stripping off his clothes until he was left with just a belt, still holding the stale bread in his right hand. He was driven to a makeshift field hospital where there were white linens, pajamas, and glucose. American nurses washed and dressed him. He wanted to say something, to show them he was alive. He didn't know exactly what or how.

Yet there was one word he knew: the international word for chocolate. He murmured, "Chocolate," using the Spanish inflection of "te." A nurse brought Nathan a Nestlé's bar. He could not yet eat it.

He clutched the candy as an IV flowed into him. Looking up at the vast tent, it seemed as big as a soccer field, and he noticed hundreds of others around him. The chocolate melted in his fingers and falling asleep, Nathan felt his body rise. He recalled in his memoir:

> The nurse smiled and took the chocolate out of my hand and gently washed the palm of my hand. I started getting drowsy and went into a deep sleep and I started to dream. I felt like I was being lifted

upward and getting higher and higher, with no pain and saw a blue sky and a fire with big flames. It was such a wonderful feeling floating in space and being weightless. To this day, I feel that I came back from the dead.

It felt warm and good, a first step toward starting a new life. "My time wasn't up," he said. "It wasn't meant for me to die. I had a story to tell."

Sixty-five years later, facing an audience at a library in Delray Beach, Florida, Nathan capped the narrative by saying, "I would like to be the vessel to tell the world how inhumanely we were treated."

In the morning when he looked around at the empty cots, Offen knew that most of the other patients had not survived the night.

Thousands of inmates went wild as Kosiek's platoon entered Mauthausen.

Peering out of their turrets and walking behind the high granite walls, the burst of pandemonium was a scene the GIs would never forget: people in blankets, others completely naked, many in striped uniforms, others still in winter coats topped by berets and chapeaus. Stepping up into the inner yard, the ovation made Kosiek feel like a celebrity being feted back at Soldier's Field. Spanish prisoners shouted ¡Viva España! as French and Polish prisoners waved their nations' flags. Rounds of the varied national anthems broke out, and Communists sang the "Internationale" anthem. A makeshift camp band played "The Star Spangled Banner"—apparently taught to them the night before by one of the few American POWs—and many cried as the platoon stood at attention presenting arms.

The band also played a rendition of "Roll Out the Barrel" that remained with some of the liberators for the rest of their lives, even when they could not talk about what they'd lived through. In a macabre juxtaposition described by a captain in another unit, a group of German bandsmen on a raised platform were made to play Nazi marches and songs while being beaten and jeered. Late in the day, prisoners tore down the Nazi eagle over the entrance and hung a long banner which read, "The Spanish Anti-Fascists Salute the Liberating Forces."

The Americans tried, but they could not contain the inevitable outburst. Freed prisoners ravaged the kitchens, dipping into soup pots with their hands and fighting over chickens, a fracas Kosiek partly quelled by firing a few rounds into the ceiling. Others looted the commandant's and soldiers' quarters or disabled workshop machines. Some who had sensed the depletion of guards and managed to scale the fences the previous night roamed nearby villages, gathering eggs, pleading for bread, and taking livestock; one group killed a horse and persuaded a local woman to fry its liver with onions. The soldiers were told not to give out their C rations or too much candy, since inmates who gorged themselves got sick, with many perishing, the shock of too much rich food overwhelming their compromised digestive systems. Some GIs soon located potatoes and made a very thin soup; while lacking wheat flour or yeast, they made unleavened bread out of oats. Sam and Nathan—who likely remained in a bunk for the first day or two—were able to abstain from overeating. Soon Sam went out knocking on doors at nearby farms. While most neighbors would not open the door, he returned with a few table scraps.

The purging began in earnest that afternoon. Some days before, inmates pledged to kill many of those remaining guards who had tortured them. The beatings with sand-loaded rubber truncheons, the exposure of being chained to an iron ring just inside the main entrance, struck or spit at by anyone walking by, the massacre of scores of Dutch Jews in the quarry—none of this was forgotten. Some inmates who felt strong enough began the hunt for SS who had fled for nearby cities or the mountains, and others who were hiding on a nearby island.

Returning to his barracks at the sanitary camp after greeting the Americans, a young Jew saw others using a German soldier for target practice with a kitchen knife as he hung naked from the rafters. One GI observed men maul a *kapo* with a bicycle. Mobs of inmates dragged block leaders and room chiefs to the *appelplatz*, exacting revenge with wooden clogs, clubbing and stomping their tormentors until faces became "flattened shapeless masses of flesh," their pulpy intestines spilled over the ground. Still, others resisted the revenge killings and cooperated with calls to return to their quarters that first day. Kosiek's platoon gathered weapons before heading out with more than a thousand guards and the few remaining SS. Other American units began arriving two days later, followed by medics who set up a field hospital.

Meanwhile, the scene at Gusen I and II was even more chaotic. Soon after Kosiek's platoon left for Mauthausen, shooting began as prisoners turned on the guards, and themselves, lynching some five hundred, including the commandant. The unit returned late that day and took on more German guards and local militia members, marching the column to bed in a field that night.

The next day, a Sunday morning, hundreds of former Gusen inmates-turned-refugees descended on the nearby St. Georgen parish church. As villagers came in, they were shocked to see scores of strangers lying on the sanctuary floor, thanking God for having endured. The parish priest remarked in a church bulletin about "the touching scene of thousands of believing Poles." For some, the jolt of being free was overwhelming. "Many died from sheer joy," the historian Le Chêne noted. "They had lived on hope, on fear and on their nerves for so long that the sudden relaxation of tension, when it came, was too much for them."

Meanwhile, a health crisis threatened to implode at Mauthausen and its sub-camps. Typhus raged at least in the Gusen II camp, and tuberculosis became seen as an even larger threat elsewhere. Some three thousand would die from starvation and disease in the weeks ahead. The camps overflowed with feces and garbage, and cleanup crews including the most able former prisoners were formed.

Within a few days Donald Montgomery and Dick LaLone's units made it to Mauthausen. Both men would befriend Sam years later in what felt like another lifetime to each man, but they apparently never met that May. Montgomery's battalion left a village north of Linz and moved closer toward Gusen and St. Georgen on May 5, while his old classmate's engineering battalion completed a bridge outside of Linz. Someone approached LaLone's command and said they needed digging equipment at the camp. Within two days he was excavating trenches there with a dragline, a quarter-yard bucket mounted on a crane.

The first thing LaLone observed coming in on a fairly warm day were men out in the yard in what seemed to be tattered underwear. They looked like the "living dead," he said. "Some were just skin on the bones." He estimated that a thousand bodies were piled alongside one barracks, packed tight and thirty or forty feet long. He dug trenches for two or three days, six feet deep, forty feet by eight feet wide. Locals carried and buried them—shoveling dirt while dressed in their best jackets and ties, and skirts—on Eisenhower's orders. Ultimately, 15,000 bodies were buried in mass graves.

LaLone heard the remarks secondhand from villagers who claimed to know nothing about the camp's operations. He shook his head and his stomach churned. They were instructed to pick up the bodies and lay them gently in the trench one by one, sometimes at gunpoint. Sam observed this as well. Even when the locals had no choice but to confront the dead, he noted a "visible disgust and hatred on their faces." One soldier grabbed a woman's arms, forcing her to train her eyes on exactly what she was burying. Medics began arriving toward the end of LaLone's assignment and he saw them feeding the sick soup with eyedroppers. Soon small portions of a thick, wholesome gruel were dished out in a frequent rotation. Finally walking into one of the barracks on his last day, the staff sergeant was set back: the narrow bunks, more or less wooden boxes, with four or five people pitted together in squalor. It was worse than a chicken house on the farm at home.

Late in the afternoon on May 9, 1945—two days after the Germans surrendered—nurses, doctors, and medics from the 131st Evacuation Hospital arrived close to the Mauthausen camp to set up a field hospital. Their task was massive: victims were dying rapidly from starvation and disease; the Americans found feces and rubbish everywhere; men were lying on "their death beds"; there was a crematorium with human bones in it and a place for hanging and firing squads; a group of prisoners killed a horse and ate it within a short time. "There was nothing about this camp that could be possibly exaggerated," an officer recorded.

Two nights later the tents were up and they contained 1,500 beds with some 1,800 patients. Nine days after liberation, patients' diets were being increased to four meals a day—three for those still considered starving—while those at the Gusen field hospital received bread for the first time. By May 15, the 131st was caring for some 3,496 patients. When they ran out of beds and mattresses, more were made, supplemented by teams from the Army's 130th hospital unit. A six hundred-bed hospital for women was set up, along with a separate unit inside the former SS barracks for 1,180 patients.

Sam never forgot the day he felt reborn. Yet as thankful as he was for the Americans, there was no instant salvation. As euphoria and revenge-seeking consumed others around him, "my thoughts were elsewhere," he recorded. "Free at last and lucky to be alive, but what price did we pay for our freedom?" With Nathan hanging on for dear life, Sam wondered if they were the only ones in the family left alive.

Like Dick LaLone, Montgomery had considered himself a good Catholic. He would be unable to cleanse the sight of those corpses, unable to fully reconcile any of it. It was not in him to make this stuff up, and he would crave for someone at home to believe him. Don snapped shot after shot of the rows and the complex itself—and the only frame that got developed he sent stateside. *Dad, you will never believe what you'll see in this picture.*

He wrote a note on the back:

"I took this picture myself so you will know it is no phony. This is not unusual in the POW camps here. Hang on to this for me, Dad."

Montgomery did not realize there were many Jews there until much later, believing they were all political prisoners. Some others in his unit who had talked with inmates pointed out the granite walls to him. "The prisoners told them that for every stone in that wall there was at least one dead person," he said. Montgomery found evidence for himself, a gas chamber with three bodies nearby and an oven that reminded him of an old furnace you might find in a school. "As soon as I saw that, I knew what they were using it for." Interrogated on his deathbed, Commandant Ziereis supposedly confessed to overseeing the executions of sixty-five thousand people at the main camp.

Don never considered himself a hero. By one measure used by military and Holocaust historians, Montgomery wasn't even technically a liberator, not having arrived at the camp within the first forty-eight hours after contact. "I was drafted, and I sat on the back of a half-track and the driver drove to Mauthausen," he said in 1993. "To me they were people."

By then he could finally express some of it, struggling for the words as he teared up. Taking off his glasses, he looked a bit like an archetypical TV judge, maybe Perry Mason's foil, wiping his strained eyes. Montgomery had been an imperfect, harsh father at best. When he became upset or nervous he bounced his right knee, the remnants of a war wound. A normal guy, a bottled up union guy who didn't stick out too much and who'd been thrown into a terrible situation. Having met Sam Offen just a few weeks earlier, Montgomery now wondered whether he had lost perspective during the intervening years, failing to winnow out those unimportant things from the vital ones.

"I can't do much, and what little I can do, I'd be glad to do," he told an interviewer from the Holocaust Memorial Center in suburban Detroit, his voice crawling on a gravel road. "I believe it could happen again, and it wouldn't take very long, either. People are gullible, and hatred is a lot easier to teach than love."

To Sam, Donald was always one of his liberators. None of the rest was that important, and nothing else mattered more.

21

AMERICAN FISHING

. . . .

S tuck in a refugee camp near Munich after the war's end, Bernard felt
dazed. He had no family around, so for a month or more he hung out
with GIs. The men adopted him as their mascot. They fed and clothed him,
giving him rides on a tank. Although Bernard knew almost no English, he
could interpret their motions and body language, sometimes joining in
as they played basketball or soccer. He had just turned sixteen that April.

One soldier took him for a ride on a motorcycle, a big Harley Davidson
with a hand shift, winding through the countryside until they reached a
partially dried up riverbed. Walking over the washed stones toward the
water, the soldier suddenly instructed Bernard, "Get down," motioning
with his hands to the ground.

He pulled the pins from two grenades, throwing them into the water.

"American fishing," the soldier told him before gathering in the catch.

The camp was run by a United Nations agency in a barracks. Bernard
heard some of the adults talking about trying to get to Palestine, which
meant little to him. Growing itchy to do something, but not knowing
exactly what, one day he saw a man reading a list of survivors. Often
snatched the loose-leafed booklet from his hands. He turned the pages
frantically to reach the "O"s, finding Sam and Nathan's names listed. His
own was missing.

That night he headed to the freight yards and jumped aboard a coal
train headed to Salzburg, where according to the list, his brothers were

last known to have been. Asking around in German and Yiddish, he got directions to a displaced persons' camp. Yet his brothers had already left. Despondent, Bernard sunk into another haze, giving up for a short time until learning that they had gone to Italy. After weeks arranging to get his travel permits, Bernard found himself aboard a truck with other refugees climbing the Alps. Soon he would pick up his brothers' scattered trail.

Weeks after their liberation, Nathan and Sam were unsure of what to do next. Recuperating at a farm in Linz, not far from Mauthausen, Sam considered returning to Kraków. But as word trickled in from survivors who had gone back to Poland, the enormity of what had happened began to seize him. He realized that their apartment, if it even still existed, had probably been taken over. They scoured lists of registered survivors but could not find their relatives. As Nathan recovered, though still weak from an upper respiratory infection, they considered going to Palestine.

It was another long shot. As a teenager Sam had trained for future emigration to the Holy Land, encouraged in part by his Uncle Joel. His uncle was gone, although the brothers met up with some of their mother's distant cousins, the Schiffers. Uprooted Jews all across Europe were trying to get to Palestine in defiance of the British occupation and strict immigration quotas. Someone from a clandestine unit of the Jewish Brigade, which had been allowed to fight with the British in Italy late during the war, approached the brothers to recruit them. Known as the *Bricha*, or "the Escape," the unit's mission was to bring as many Jews to Palestine as possible. They both agreed to try. While still malnourished and healing, the two were smuggled across the Italian Alps with a group of returning POWs. The heights were dizzying to Nathan, and he was speechless looking at the peaks and down at the villages. Like their younger brother, they had no idea what was in store.

They wound up in Ancona, a fishing port on the Adriatic Sea after staying at several camps. Boarding trains and even trucks made them flinch, but the young men were greeted warmly by townspeople on the platforms. Meeting twenty or thirty others hoping to get to Palestine, they pitched tents on an isolated hill looking down to the ocean. Over several weeks a truck occasionally brought canned food and cigarettes, some of which the men bartered for fresh vegetables and fruit during forays into the village. Sam was strong enough to begin exercising and swimming, while Nathan was still barely walking. During the evenings their group gathered around a small beach fire singing and dancing to Yiddish, Polish, and Hebrew songs. They waited for a starless night when a ship might sail into port unseen, but the opportunity never came.

Instead, one day they met a couple of soldiers in British uniforms wearing a Polish eagle on their berets and an insignia on the side of their arms. Speaking Polish, the men introduced them to an officer who suggested the brothers join the Polish Army, which was under command of the British Eighth Army. A train to an induction center in Bologna was expected in a few days. Homeless and still hungry, the decision to enlist was a no-brainer.

In Bologna, an Army captain—a Jewish doctor from another Polish city—befriended Sam and Nathan. Recognizing that neither was fit for duty, he sent them to a convalescent hospital. Even after gaining weight there, weeks later Nathan still had to be lifted on to a truck because he lacked muscle tone. Eventually they were shipped to another seaport for basic training. They received uniforms, plentiful food, money, and light duty assignments. They met Polish veterans who had driven up the Italian peninsula and fought in a pivotal battle for Monte Cassino, where they hoisted their flag in the ruins of a venerable abbey. The soldiers had yet to meet any survivors, and when one officer asked them, "What happened to all the Jews in Poland?" everyone inside the tent went silent.

Moving north up the coast again, the brothers guarded food supplies and a depot, and even German POWs for a few days—which unsettled Sam as he fingered a Tommy gun, worried that he might be overcome with rage. Nathan resumed playing soccer and waded out into the cool water, re-energized as he dunked his head in. "We began to feel like human beings again," he recalled.

Bernard closed in on their trail. He checked at displaced persons camps up and down the coast, by rail, walking, and hitchhiking around. He learned they had joined the Polish Army, and got to where they were stationed—only to find they had gone into town. He finally caught up with Nat and Sam late that summer in Barletta, another port.

Dressed in uniform, the two were on the street headed toward a Jewish soldiers club. They felt a tap on the back of their shoulders.

"Hello brothers!" Bernard cried out.

Sam's heart beat furiously, and he was speechless. Years later, he remembered:

> We looked at each other with disbelieving and tearful eyes, and started hugging in front of the other soldiers. It was if he had come back from the dead. We had never given up hope that we would find our family members, and finally our optimism and hope were well rewarded.

What Bernard witnessed was equally incongruous. While it had been perhaps thirteen months since they were separated, here was Sam beginning to fill out again, an infectious smile spreading across his tanned face. Nathan, while thinner, was still a head taller than his younger brother, looking so grown up in his camel-colored linens, with a beret angled crisply on his head.

They found a quiet spot on a hill, sitting down together on a concrete wall. They began comparing notes of where they had been—the older siblings amazed to figure out that at one point, Bernard had only missed them by a day or two. How their brother, whom they still thought of as a little boy, could find his way through a strange country, not knowing a foreign tongue, and scrounge up food, was shocking. They took photos of one another. Then came the most difficult revelation, as Bernard told them about their father. The three took some moments together. "It was finally sinking in that never again would we see the happy faces of our parents, sister, grandmother, uncles, and aunts," Sam wrote, "not to mention the giggling faces of our countless young cousins . . . Even the consolation of being able to visit their graves was denied us."

Yet Bernard had survived. And unlike many other families, there were three of them left to say Kaddish for lost relatives.

Bernard stayed a few days at a military camp. Since he was too young to serve, they had to find another place for him to live in the interim, so he joined other refugees at a large camp in a fishing village further down the coast. Santa Maria di Bagni was another gathering place for Jews hoping to sail across the Mediterranean, and also a community offering rigorous classes for children and adults, recreation, and training for professions such as tailoring and electrical science. There was a camp theatre group, and its soccer club played matches against local teams. Bernard began attending *yeshiva*, an Orthodox religious school, but only because the food there was delicious. "That was my inducement," he recalled. "I was not into [it], I had a great conflict about God and how could God have [allowed] that thing to happen."

He resumed wandering. Over the next few months, using the camp as his base, Bernard explored the rocky coast on foot and hailed rides to other villages. He went out to sea with local fishermen and basked in the strong sun on beaches and cliff sides. He took in movies, especially Hollywood films, whenever he could.

There was no language yet for what he had been through, and while hiking through the dry scrub to find new vistas, he kept his troubles tucked away. They remained nascent, accessible in the way one senses a subtle stir in the darkness before first light, until one day he realized that his life was *still some kind of survival*.

On weekends Nathan and Sam got a pass to go see him. Bernard also hitchhiked to visit them, staying together in the barracks for a few days beside the ocean. Returning to Santa Maria di Bagni, he was still very much alone.

Before a year had passed, Nathan and Sam remembered they had relatives in America. Their grandmother occasionally had asked Uncle Joel to write letters for her. The envelopes had read "Detroit, Michigan"—that much they knew. Hirschman was the name Nathan retrieved. They composed a letter stating their names and listing relatives, addressing it to "Hirschman" in Detroit.

A few weeks later, they received a letter in English from cousins on their mother's side, Rose and Harry Saltzman, who sent a picture of their parents. Finding someone to translate it, they learned that the Saltzmans wanted to know more about their relatives in Kraków. Following another exchange of letters, their connection was confirmed, and Sam and his brothers were overjoyed. Even in their wildest dreams, they had never thought there might be family waiting for them in the United States. Getting there was another thing.

In the fall of 1946, as the British occupation of Italy was winding down, Sam and Nathan learned that the Polish Army would soon leave for England. Soldiers' family members would also be allowed to go a few months in advance, but they didn't know where Bernard would live. At the camp where he was staying, Nathan and Sam found a teenager who had relatives in England. They asked Hiela Singer if she would change her last name to "Offen" so that Bernard could travel with her, and Singer agreed. The brothers quickly located a man who did calligraphy to falsify documents for her. "Nobody had real documents," Nathan recalled with a throaty laugh. "We made her our sister, and once she got to England, her family changed her name back to Singer." Bernard began living with some of his "sister's" actual relatives in London.

***

"Stop poking at the fire!" Louis Freedman scolded his son.

Young Stephen couldn't help it. He loved the pungent smell of tar and couldn't help playing with the poker. Inside his father's barbershop, most of the fuel for the fireplace came from tar blocks that were plentiful in his neighborhood. As the government continued ripping up Bermondsey, razing the flats and food factories that were bombed during the Blitz, more blocks were unearthed. They'd add a little kindle wood to start it, and occasionally bought some coal too. But tar was the main source. And there were still plenty of craters to dig through.

The shop was on the ground floor of his grandmother's brick house, close to the battered docks in Southeast London. Miriam "Mitch" Freedman shaved men from their working-class neighborhood, often dockers, bus conductors, or laborers. Behind two large barber chairs in the front room, Miriam also ran a salon for women in the back. Her son Lou took up the trade cutting men's hair and giving shaves.

A wartime baby, Stephen was born in the summer of 1944, nearly four years after the city was first besieged. Close to the Freedman's house at 2 Drummond Road, antiaircraft guns at Southwark Park fired in a deafening noise during those fifty-seven consecutive mind-bending nights. A thick wood table set against the wall reverberated from the bashing all around them, and "the walls felt like they were coming in and out," relatives would tell Stephen after the war.

One day when Freedman had turned three or four, his grandmother introduced him to three "boys" who were staying at her house. Sam and Nathan had arrived first, with Bernard leaving his first family hosts to join them a few months later. In Stephen's eyes, they were jolly and animated, kidding and chasing each other around when not at work or school. The brothers instantly took a shine to him, letting Stephen pursue them and attempt a whack on the backside. Sam was the friendliest, while Bernard kept to himself more. Nathan earned the nickname, "Lucky pop," because his face felt wet and slobbery as he grabbed the boy for a kiss on the face, prompting the child to say, "You got me, you lucky pop."

Arriving in England with the Polish Army early in the winter, the oldest two had been sent up to a base along the Scottish border. The first English they learned were lyrics to "My Bonnie Lies Over the Ocean," and marching through Carlisle trying to sing the folk song, they were cheered by bystanders. "Of course, we did not understand the lyrics, but we felt proud anyway," Sam noted. In order to be discharged they needed jobs and proof of housing. They took odd assignments such as guard duty, and one day visiting the town, the brothers stopped at the window of a furrier shop. They headed in armed with an English-Polish dictionary but didn't need to translate. The owner was Polish, and he invited them in for tea. Mr. Kirschner let Sam work in his shop occasionally, another step to procuring his future livelihood.

Still, they needed to find steady work plus a place to live near Bernard in London. They took the night train down to see their brother, who, while living comfortably with a well-off family in Kensington, often skipped school to watch more films. Some days Bernard saw as many as four, mostly comedies and westerns. He imagined being a GI or cowboy—"but never, never, the Indian," he wrote later, confessing that he learned more English at the movies than in class. Nathan applied for a laborer's job at the Payne tea factory near Tower Bridge, and this became his ticket out. With an assist from Mr. Kirschner, Sam also found work with another furrier in the capital.

Like most others in Bermondsey, times had been tight for the Freedmans since just about anyone could remember. Food rationing and restrictions on electrical service and coal extended well after the war, and both housewives and men queued up in long lines for staples like potatoes and onions. They continued to make do. Many of Stephen's friends had never eaten an orange or banana. The Freedmans used an outhouse and like many of their neighbors, went to the public baths once a week. Locals whetted their appetites on the sweet smells of biscuits baking at Peak Freans, or on wafts of shortcake coming from other nearby factories.

Mitch Freedman's husband had abandoned her years before, and she lived nearly alone in a three-bedroom flat above the barbershop. Young Stephen stayed there four nights a week to attend a school his parents had selected, while they lived in the opposite end of the city. After her nephew introduced Mrs. Freedman to the two lads he had met at a social club on the Carlisle base, she made room for them and eventually their brother. She didn't only provide the Offens beds and meals. Able to speak bits of Polish and Yiddish herself, Stephen's grandmother could talk at length with them. Yet as Stephen understood in later years, she apparently gleaned little about what they had been through. Each brother was incapable of expressing it; while struggling to learn English and appreciating a budding new life, this wasn't even a consideration.

Mitch kept a close eye on the trio. Sam and Nathan began dating and sometimes went dancing, but they stayed in on Friday nights. After getting paid for the week—Bernard included, who landed his first job as a furrier's apprentice near Picadilly Circus—they each brought their savings books to the bank, dividing their earnings equally even as Sam's pay topped his brothers', and they helped Mrs. Freedman with expenses. Observant and self-reliant, she kept a kosher home and prepped for Shabbat by killing her own chickens, baking bread, and serving homemade cherry brandy. Soccer matches filled much of the remaining day for the guys.

During winter months on Drummond Street, "the fireplace gleamed, and we roasted chestnuts on the fire," Nathan wrote. "There would be a white tablecloth on the table, and Mrs. Freedman would put the candle into the candelabra and say a prayer." After Sunday dinner she often tuned in to the BBC for Alistair Cooke's *Letters from America* radio broadcast. Mesmerized by Cooke's evenly clipped voice and crisp narratives, the brothers formed early impressions of the States, even when his admonishments about the vagaries of unfettered capitalism or ignoring the nation's true history sailed over their heads.

For the first time in years, the Offens attended a local synagogue that had been partly damaged and rebuilt by the government. Stephen's parents were married there, and the synagogue became a hub for the men as they made new friends at its social club. Sam even played Sherlock Holmes in a play once, giving up cigarettes to smoke a pipe—a habit he would continue for decades. They attended services with the Freedmans and on Sunday often went on rambles, or outings in the countryside together.

Around this time their distant American relatives sent word by a letter that they were flying to England to meet them. Meeting at their hotel, the young men were relieved that the Saltzmans spoke Yiddish. The couple wanted to know whatever they could about their relatives and family life, and stories unfolded as they opened up a feast of food packed in the luggage: a five-pound kosher salami, rye bread, and mustard. Even more astonishing were the three one-way tickets to Detroit they handed out. Yet this was not quite meant to be. Being foreign born, Sam and his brothers could not simply obtain a visa to travel to the States; they needed to register at the US Embassy and get in line. They were told this might take five years. The Saltzmans returned home greatly disappointed, but at this time in 1947, Sam and Nathan were ambivalent about leaving London.

While menial and repetitive, Nathan's job at the tea factory soon led to greater things. His routine consisted of opening large cartons and shoveling tea into a big drum for blending and testing. At lunch he joined other men playing soccer, and one day the trainer of the factory team took notice of Nathan using both legs with equal skill. He came over and said something that Nathan interpreted as, "'You can play,'" and the next day as Offen arrived at work, the coach would not let him punch in. He brought Nathan in his car to the field, where he began practicing with the George Payne & Sons squad. Instead of shoveling, Nathan played inside-left and right-halfback, traveling by bus around the country for matches twice a week against other factory teams, sometimes accompanied by Sam. Suddenly he was a semi-pro player, rediscovering a love for the sport. His wind and endurance surprised him, the rips building on his quadriceps, and a growing core strength. He enjoyed playing in front of small crowds.

Yet something else nagged persistently: Nathan still didn't know English well. Tired of carrying around a piece of paper with cues to ask for directions, he grew weary of being regarded as dumb. After six or eight months, he quit the job and went to night school. There he met Helen Goldberg.

To compensate for a shortage of books, Nathan's English teacher paired students from the same country together. He found himself next to a petite blonde girl, who while quite pretty, was obviously much younger than him, and very shy. At first he tried to ignore her, but they got to talking.

She grew up just east of Kraków in a small city called Dąbrowa Tarnowska. An orphan who was raised by her grandmother, Helen had slipped out of the Dąbrowa ghetto perhaps some months before the liquidation of Kraków's ghetto. It was winter, and lacking good shoes she ran off to some neighboring farms. She went from village to village and no one would shelter her. Fearing for their lives, families chased and pushed Helen away, and others beat her. Freezing and hungry after wandering for several days, she felt ready to give up. Helena crept into a stable one night and fell asleep in some hay. When the farmer came in to check his animals, he found her there, lifting the nine-year-old up and bringing her inside. He sat her on the stove, giving her some warm milk, and told her she could stay. With her hair color, blue eyes and light skin, she could pass for his niece, a refugee from another area who had recently died.

Helen did endless chores to earn her keep: rising early to milk and tend the cattle, clean the house and weed the crops, while also taking care of the farmer's ill wife whose life was fading. A local priest must have acquiesced because she went to church and learned Christmas carols. Occasionally German soldiers visited the farm to have a uniform sewn by the farmer's son, who was a tailor, and Helen stayed hidden there until a year after the war ended. She told Nathan that her mother came to her in a dream, telling her she should return to Dąbrowa. Helen did, and upon finding a cousin, learned that a rabbi from London was taking orphaned children to England. She did not return to the farm.

After class one night Nathan asked her if she'd like to get a cup of tea. They ordered the only item on the menu, toast with beans, along with a fresh pot. He told a little joke, maybe that night, or perhaps *nie:* "We thought we could create a telephone company—we have two Poles already." He was falling in love.

He invited Helen to join the social club at his synagogue. And even though she lived a distance away in North London, they began seeing each other. She met the Freedmans on their weekend outings, and Mitch and her family accepted Helen easily.

Meanwhile, Sam especially began making his way up. He found another job at a fur shop that doubled his wages and he attended evening classes at the Royal College of Fashion and Design. His English improved markedly, and like his father he began a lifelong pursuit of reading the news to stay up on current affairs. He also subscribed to a Polish newspaper, finally learning about the post-war situation in Eastern Europe, which included a retreat of Polish borders to the west and the rise of a new communist regime. As London revived and a sense of normality slowly returned, Sam felt energized. His prospects were good. He saw plays such as *Death of a Salesman* in the fashionable West End, and joined the choir at his shul during the high holidays. When the US Embassy contacted Offen and his brothers early in 1951 with news that their visas would soon be issued, he felt lukewarm at best. The notion of leaving Mrs. Freedman and his new life tossed him about.

Once in a great while, Stephen Freedman pulls out a black and white photo that he has long held on to. In the picture he stands on the right side of his grandmother's living room in a suit and tie, a child of five or six with arms cast straight down, his mother holding his side as if to ensure he won't fidget. The centerpiece is Nathan and Helen holding hands just to the left of Mitch, flanked by sixteen others hemmed in close in their suits and dresses. Among them are Stephen's father, an uncle and aunt, a few cousins and invited friends whose names he's misplaced: someone who owned a sweet shop nearby, and a jeweler. A grinning, be speckled Bernard clasps Sam's right shoulder with his hand, his oldest brother the tallest person in the back row. This was Nathan and Helen's engagement party, a first of firsts.

Nearly cropped from the picture are the decorations on two tables, white linens and a silver menorah, and Mitch's treasured three-pronged candelabra. Nathan looks pleased, yet a hint of lament seeps from the depths of his eyes. Recalling how he felt in that moment would trigger a lacquered feeling beyond bittersweet, the image stuck in gray, washed with glazes of burnt colors and a sepia fringe.

Mrs. Freedman prepared them delicacies, yet he hesitated to bring back the taste. The brothers were enveloped with care and love, yet the branches and roots of their own clan had been usurped. Those four years were a time of grace and desire, and yet unspoken and staring back at them were those who went missing: as the rest of their lives began, his parents and Miriam would forever remain frozen in other scratched portraits.

Stephen, too, remembers whatever he can. "They weren't blood family," he recalled. "But they were so taken in to the hearts of the family, not as lodgers or strangers. I think that was the main thing. They were so happy that they were accepted, not just as three boys from Poland."

Rose and Harry Saltzman met the brothers at the end of a dock in New York on a Sunday morning. Crossing the ocean on an American freighter that carried only a dozen passengers, the trio had dined in the officers' mess hall served by waiters wearing white gloves. They were stunned by the sight of the Statue of Liberty as the ship anchored near it the night before disembarking on the first day of spring in 1951.

Staying for two nights at the Hotel Statler facing Penn Station on Seventh Avenue, the Saltzmans showed them the sights of city. It was a whirlwind week, taking in the skyscrapers and squares, the marquees on Broadway, before driving to Detroit to meet newfound cousins. Along the way Harry pulled over for dinner at a restaurant. Sam, for one, could not believe the size of the portions, noting his plate "would have easily fed two or even three people." They were bowled over by the scope and generosity and wealth. Everything was so big—the buildings, so much food everywhere, so many cars on the highway, endless farms and factory towns. Nathan felt a bit overwhelmed.

As conversation in the car went almost non-stop, they began to piece together the new names among their mother's first and second cousins: Rose, Gertie, and their three sisters and two brothers; Gertie's husband, Jack Fishman, and many others. They learned that their great aunt, Anna Hirschman, who had first emigrated and started the American branch of the family, had died. Meeting more cousins as they arrived in Detroit was a blur. Photo albums showed their grandfather and their parents' wedding.

Sam had to pinch himself from disbelieving how fortunate they were to have relatives who had kept all these mementos. Amidst teasing about their acquired British accents, the three pointed out who was who in other photos. The resemblance among Rochme and her sisters to their first cousins was striking—even her Jewish given name, "Geitel," was the same. The Hirschmans also brought out some letters they had received from the brothers' uncles, including Uncle Joel, written early during the German occupation. While sending his regards about his aunt's health, Joel had pleaded with his American family to send him an old suit and not be embarrassed by his condition. "The holiday is now approaching," he wrote, "and I am so ashamed to go and pray with worn and tattered attire."

The next day they took a break. Harry drove the brothers downtown, introducing them to teeming Woodward Avenue and its mix of theatres and nightclubs set curiously amidst churches and synagogues. They stopped in at Sanders Candy, Detroit's famous confectionary store, which according to legend had invented the ice cream soda when one of the counter guys ran out of fresh cream one day. Harry Saltzman ordered something called a *banana split*. "When the first enormous dish appeared, we thought we were going to share it," Sam recalled. "But to our amazement, three more followed." He downed the whole thing, unsure years later whether he was just being polite.

As Sam began looking for a job and Bernard considered returning to school, the two of them began living with Gertie and Jack Fishman. Nathan stayed with the Saltzmans, knowing that it would not be for too long. Helen would sail over in a few weeks, having an uncle in Jersey City who had obtained a visa for her. After she arrived, Helen and Nathan were married that June—with the Saltzmans driving to New Jersey to give him away. Sam and Bernard also drove down together in a brand new white Chevrolet that Sam had bought.

Walking down the aisle, Nathan felt a flash of guilt and his legs wobbled. He had a vision of watching a hanging and punished himself for not having his parents at his side. As if peering down from above his body again, he regarded "all the people, strangers, that I hardly knew."

Cory Scanlon's girlfriend waited in her car outside Honey Dew Donuts as the three of us took a booth.

We searched his brown eyes, his trembling face, and felt some of the crushing weight. It was four and a half years since the crash that killed our son, and Cory had been out of prison for maybe a year. As part of his probation he was required to speak to high school students about the dangers of drinking and driving. We had heard he was doing this with sincerity, perhaps as a commitment to Mike and P.J.

We needed to verify this.

Denise and I had actually cried with him once before, early that first winter when he got out of the hospital. He and his parents, Dan and Paula, came to our house, where we sat again in the living room, broken and unknowing, while Chris and Amanda retreated upstairs. What the Scanlons did was a decent gesture by good people, and while we later raged at Cory, I don't think we ever hated him.

She listened to Mike first. This became our ground floor, setting the bar: *He wants us to do this,* my wife instructed me. To not turn Cory away, and maybe even show support for what he was doing.

Mike would not want his life ruined, buried in self-hate or pity, or so burned by our wrath that he had to numb himself in order not to feel.

My son had taught me about never giving up, except letting go of perverse conditional love, a warped mirror of wanting him to be more like me. To reach back when you think there's nothing left because surely there is more, if not for yourself, then for those you love. Or for others like my students, who needed scaffolding and hard pushes and people to remind them they were worthy of mounting any struggle. To give a little more.

On my runs I called for Mike and P.J. to send me a little extra. I ran for them, locked in at seven miles as my stride quickened, yelling to him with all I had cherished and learned—he never stopped battling, scrapping, churning and gnawing, in your face rebutting, or holding a baby with such calm sweet acuity that someday we knew it would all come together.

I began running for Cory as well.

He told us about some of his audiences. He felt many teenagers responding. They could relate to him, still so fresh-faced at twenty-three, still like them with his close-cropped black hair, a meaty stump of five foot four inches. At one school he noticed some guys in the back who dressed just like he and Mike had, the wise guys who typically laugh and blow it off. Cory kept eye contact with them and tried directing his talk their way.

Afterwards a bunch of them approached him and said something to the effect of, "You described everything we do," and, "I'm just like you." He'd already spoken to 12,000 students. Of course, some would still fail to fully get it, feeling untouchable like our sons did. That required repeated messages and exposures, and sometimes their own experiences making poor choices. But it sounded like Cory was connecting with many.

Still, we had to pinch ourselves sitting in that booth. At a parole hearing more than a year earlier I had urged the state to keep Cory behind bars. I didn't feel he had taken full ownership; his comments that morning sounded mushy. Denise disagreed but did not say so then. Soon afterwards, she drove up to the prison in Dedham hoping to see him herself, but was turned back because she hadn't submitted paperwork for a background check. He was denied parole.

A month or so later, she was in Boston for an appointment when P.J.'s sister called her. Cory was being released that very day, two years earlier than expected. We had been blindsided again. Perhaps I had failed to read between the lines *encore une fois*, since the attorneys had struck a side deal that no one apparently bothered to run by the victims' kin. When Cory changed his plea back in 2004, an "understanding" was reached that if he wasn't granted parole by 2006, his sentence could be revoked and revised— cutting the four-year total for the motor vehicle homicide convictions in half. The assistant DA who reached the deal with his attorney had since left to do exchange trips on Russian and American law. We were frozen out.

Cory had also cut his prison stay by taking advantage of the state's "good time" sentencing provision, shaving off up to ten days a month by joining programs and being a model prisoner. Unlike many other inmates, he had been earnest and taken advantage of this. Agreeing to speak about drunk driving also played a role in reducing his time, but how much so was never communicated to us by parole authorities.

The lawyers' discussions on revising his plea went on out of our earshot. Two years earlier, they had agreed that if Cory showed "constructive involvement" in DUI prevention education, he might be spared some of the sentence. By the spring of 2006, a new assistant DA, and perhaps his colleagues, seemed impressed with Cory's starring role in a new video that the office had produced about the dangers of driving impaired. In the video "In One Split Second," Scanlon faces the camera in the prison library talking about what he did wrong, and walks the halls in between scenes of teen drinking and wrecked cars. It cuts to a cross alongside the highway in Foxborough—the one Denise and her sister placed for Mike.

Who knew?

Retrieving evidence of this years later in the lawyers' correspondence I had kept in my files, I posted a sticky note: "Did we get played?"

I don't recall either of us overreacting to news of his early release. On one level someone could rationalize him serving the two sentences concurrently. And as the victim's advocate later explained to me, the intention when Cory pled guilty was for him to serve at least one year for each count, with some of the rest cut if he took advantage of the state's good time credit. His sentence for a third charge—manslaughter—had been dropped as part of the plea, a common occurrence in our liberal commonwealth, and a fourth, operating to endanger, was imposed as three years of probation.

The math was still a bit fuzzy to me. Yet by then we had been ground down like the head of a screw stripped by a blunt, oversized tool.

Facing us in the coffee shop, Cory said he wasn't doing the talks for himself, but to honor Mike and P.J. Nothing could be undone, he told a reporter a few weeks later, "but maybe by speaking about it, I can change someone else's future."

We wanted so much to believe again. Maybe that's what we needed to hear. Denise followed her heart, and I her lead. Mike probably sent me signals on this, too, when I was less butt-headed, visiting his grave after work on a Friday, watching the flight of a large heron across the fluid sky. Cory told us he wanted to take community college classes the next fall, and perhaps turn his experience into some sort of career. Where his goal had once been joining the Coast Guard, he was working at a gas station and painting houses.

The conversation felt almost too unforced at points. He attempted to contain words so they didn't spill out too fast. We even laughed at some memories, and he reminded us of the New Bedford game in 2000, Mike's first varsity appearance as a junior, when he came in and changed the pace of the match. He remained in after that. Cory said that while he, Griff, Walsh, Travis, and Mark were on the bench as juniors, Mike represented them each. I glanced back at a different season, a state tournament with

Cory's dad coaching in the spring league, all us parents amazed at our sons playing successive games in the searing heat. Mike suffered a mild concussion going for a head ball, and after a trip to the hospital, returned for the final match. Many of the families stayed in a rundown hotel along the river in Chicopee, the best we could find, checking for bed bugs and laughing at the times. That seemed so long ago.

We put things in motion, arranging for Cory to speak at the high school. His appearance would keynote the fourth year of safe driving and drunk-driving prevention programs our parents group brought to the school district. I set up an interview in *The Boston Globe*, feeling a bit the tactician, since while in the article I conveyed that our recent conversation with Cory was strained, perhaps some of that was a maneuver befitting the angry father. "Reconciliation between us can never happen," I declared, "but we're working together to deliver a message." Maybe I was afraid to admit that it had already begun.

A week later Cory Scanlon stands on his old high school stage, not so far removed from the entire senior class. Denise and I sit to the side, never intending to go up there with him. "We were young, we were invincible, and we thought nothing could touch us," Cory tells the group. They get it—for now, at least. He's almost still one of them.

Except that he served half a sentence, and left us their mangled bodies.

They play the video with Scanlon in his green prison garb and the wooden cross. It extolls students to make better choices. When this ends, as the students sit in silence for several minutes, a retired art teacher who knew both Scanlon and our son consoles Cory with a hug. We slip out.

We must be out of our freaking minds.

Sam Offen made good on a connection to restart his career. One of his cousins was an accountant who worked for the president of the Detroit Master Furriers Guild, and two furriers, Harry and Sol Ceresnie, hired him. Sam began as a fur cutter in the store basement, making tiny diagonal cuts to pelts of the day—grey mink and fox, coyote, sable, and marten, raccoon and beaver—which would be stitched and sometimes dyed for coats, stoles, wraps, and hats. He could sew linings and had a knack for design. Both skilled fur mechanics themselves, the Ceresnies figured they had a keeper in Sam.

He was also a natural salesman. Erudite and never pushy, moving up to the showroom he always offered customers a smile. He bantered genuinely, remembering the names of spouses and their children. They were attracted to this warm, cuddly gentleman who barely concealed his tact and finesse, and this helped build the Ceresnies' largely word-of-mouth clientele. In later years, Sam and Sol spiced up the business by making joke gifts and knick-knacks: babies' fur booties, mink jock straps and bras for bachelorette and bachelor parties, and fur hot pants. They stayed on a roll through many of the business cycles ahead.

Detroit's fur industry was nearing its peak as Offen set down roots. The city's shopping scene included more than one hundred retailers meeting the post-war fashion boom in an era of fur-clad starlets. Marilyn Monroe barely wrapped herself in a large fox stole in *Gentlemen Prefer Blondes*, Zsa Zsa Gabor and Jean Hagen strutted in coats trimmed with white fox collars, and a mobster boyfriend covered a sleeping Cyd Charisse with a silver fox trimmed coat in the 1958 classic, *Party Girl*. The Ceresnies, who also hailed from Poland, were among the many immigrant families running small shops. After working in the industry in Toronto, Harry and younger brother Sol had opened their store on Dexter Avenue in 1946, just themselves and a stitcher or two at a sewing machine. Depending upon the vagaries of mass culture, and well before concerns over the ethical treatment of animals became a bona fide cause, their future was wide open.

Around this time, Sam was introduced to a demure, attractive social worker who happened to be the daughter of a cousin of one the Ceresnie's wives. Hyla Lesser was a University of Michigan graduate whose father had emigrated from Russia, while her mother grew up in Romania. She swept Sam off his feet, and after six weeks of dating—he counted nine dates—he proposed in unconventional fashion. He had taken up fishing as a hobby and realized that a fishing license would be valid for a spouse once it was co-signed. One night he took out the license and offered her a pen, telling Hyla, "You can fish with me forever."

She never became much of an angler, but they married just before the summer solstice in 1952 with both Nathan and Bernard serving as best men. Two children arrived during the next few years and they moved into a three-bedroom apartment not far from the fur shop. Hyla gave up being a caseworker, devoting herself to young Jerry and Gail, while supporting her bubbly, energetic husband. Almost instantly Sam's family doubled in size.

Hyla's family gathered summer weekends at a cabin on a small lake that her parents had built in the twenties, where her father, a milkman, would leave by 2:30 a.m. for work. It was at Horseshoe Lake that Sam became a true Michiganian. In the quiet of the morning he could fish off the dock with worms on a bamboo pole for bluegill or even yellow perch. In the years ahead, he'd get his own boat with better gear and there would be countless trips showing his kids and nephews the little tricks and his favorite lures, and going out with the Lessers and Ceresnies. Whether snagging for salmon out of Ludington on "the big lake," or catching walleye up north or on Lake St. Clair just beyond the city, he eagerly planned the next trip to a new spot. Chartering to remote areas in Canada or idling aboard his father-in-law's twelve-foot aluminum boat on Horsehoe, Sam seemed to carry his good luck with him.

As Jerry Offen grew up, regardless of where they put in, his father insisted that bluegill was the tastiest fresh water fish. He always cleaned and filled his catch, handing it over to Hyla for preparation and cooking.

Within a year of arriving in Detroit, Bernard was drafted into the Army. He was gung-ho about America and willing to go. *These were my liberators,* he thought, *and they saved my ass.* GIs had showed him how to handle a weapon back in Germany, after all. Plus, he wanted to ride with the cavalry, the good guys, fighting bands of outlaws who otherwise came in and took over a town. He reported for a medical exam and trained at Fort Riley in the hot Kansas sun. He had just turned twenty-three.

Once during those first sixteen weeks he passed out on maneuvers and was hospitalized, then completed his training with a different company. He was given leave to attend Sam's wedding, and shipped over to South Korea with a rear quartermaster company. Doing guard duty and working in a warehouse, Bernard did not see any combat. It was mostly a boring routine, patrolling the perimeter of a converted brewery on the outskirts of Seoul.

Yet even from a relative distance, this was still another war, and he felt strongly that he was helping to defend liberty, this time against the communists. "I just wanted to be like other Americans," he said, "whatever the hell that was, or is. I just wanted to be one of the people." By his count, he stayed in Korea seventeen months and ten days, again not knowing what would come next.

Returning to Detroit after his discharge, Bernard needed a career. On occasion he found some work with Sam stitching furs, and he earned a high school diploma. Then came trade school for refrigeration and appliance repair, eventually working for Sears & Roebuck and a few other companies. Along the way he met his future wife, Sybil Weinstein, while rotating to other jobs and learning more about dishwashers, washers, and dryers. In 1957 he and Sybil married, and the brothers had made arrangements for a special guest: Mitch Freedman. By then sixty-eight, she flew to the States for the first time by herself, staying for six months, rotating between Detroit and Nathan's home in New Jersey.

On the surface, the opportunity was ripe for Bernard to "stand on his two feet" like his brothers were doing in their adopted country. The dream felt within reach. As a newspaper declared in a short article about Private Offen returning from military duty, "The 'good life' beckons a new citizen." Living within ten miles of Sam, he and Sybil soon joined his brother and the Lessers out at Horseshoe Lake. Their marriage produced two sons, but it was not meant to last.

Nathan began grinding it out from Jersey City, taking the 99 express bus each workday into New York's garment district. Getting off at the Port Authority terminal, he walked several blocks to Thirty-Seventh or Thirty-Eighth Street, which varied depending on the job at hand. With three daughters by the summer of 1958—Ruth, Gail, and Suzanne—he had joined the shuffling masses.

He worked as a pattern maker, translating a designer's ideas from paper onto fabric. Usually standing at a table close to the height of his chest, Nathan transferred sketches onto a thin cardboard pattern paper, cutting sections to be placed on a dummy before making the fitting. The patterns were for women's clothing, and he was part of a team including tailors and designers, making corrections when a fabric was fitted on a live model.

In a sense he was an interpreter, the vernacular being the transfer of a one-dimensional vision and making quick changes. While a high-pressure environment in an industry teeming with replacements, it easily beat the first job he had found in the States—making uniforms at a rural factory in New Jersey, where wages were miserable even compared to a similar plant in England where he had worked. Securing work in Manhattan, he happily reported to Helen that his pay would nearly double.

"So much money?" she asked.

As he established a livelihood, Nathan felt cut off from his family. He usually saw his brothers around the Christmas holidays. He drove with his family to Michigan, or vice versa, or they met somewhere in the middle, at a hotel in upstate New York or Pennsylvania. Hearing stories of Sam's extended clan at the lake, Nathan felt he was missing out on something greater.

He loved Helen in full. When she had arrived at Ellis Island that spring of 1951, Nathan greeted her with a dozen roses. Since her only family included an aunt and an uncle in Jersey City, he decided to live with her there. That first summer, their fifth-floor apartment was so hot they sometimes slept out on the fire escape. But the view of the Hudson and Statue of Liberty was breathtaking. Together they watched the RMS *Queen Mary* come into port, along with other intrepid ocean-crossing vessels. From so near the rooftop, they felt they had truly arrived; by simply opening the window at twilight, a week's grind began to fade. "It was never lonely if I sat down at night and looked at the view and all the people, all the big ships and all the lights," he said. "And on the west side, the cars and all the lights and everything."

Still, their social interactions were limited. He made friends among co-workers in the city, taking lunch hour together in a cafeteria on Seventh Avenue or at a park near the public library. While Helen's Uncle Harry had been generous at first, helping them furnish their place, he was introverted and wound his life around running a small grocery—up before dawn, closing at 10:00 p.m. Nathan felt he had no one to really talk to.

When their first daughter Ruth arrived, he was afraid to even hold her, wondering if he deserved to even have a child, or a family. Colicky and gassy, she was a handful for her new parents, keeping them up at night in their bedroom. Nathan helped sterilize bottles and boil diapers while Helen tried everything she knew. Some nights they took turns rocking Ruth's crib with their feet, and eventually things settled down.

Her father focused on work to provide enough for food and rent. He never contemplated much beyond the next month or year, not saving money, or preparing for anything else. "And I was always looking for somebody to guide me, for somebody to give me advice," he reflected. During the high holidays, the few friends he and Helen had made went with their own families.

Sam opened his own business after a few years, buying out a fur shop close to the Ceresnies'. About two weeks after taking it over, a thief broke in through a window and stole two minks off the mannequins. Rather than railing about the theft, Sam quickly shook it off. "You know," he remarked to a reporter, "that thief has good taste. Out of all the furriers in this town, he picked our store."

He and the Ceresnies were friendly competitors, and Sam adopted the work cycle that is peculiar to his trade: swamped and often working seven days a week from mid-fall into the early winter as customers take their coats out of storage and buy new ones; hibernating a bit through the quiet winter months; and reviving again in May and June as customers bring their coats back in for storage, repairs, and alterations; followed by a summer respite.

One night exactly eight years after he had arrived in Detroit, Sam planned to go out bowling after work. This was becoming a favorite pastime of his alongside playing poker and gin rummy, or heading out to fish. It was already March, some weeks before the late spring rush, and he stopped to do an errand at his accountant's office. As Offen crossed the street toward his car, a drunk driver slammed into him.

Offen awoke in a hospital a few days later finding Hyla beside him. Sam could barely move, and young Gail and Jerry were not allowed inside the room, though they threw him kisses from the lawn below the window. His wife and a doctor delivered the news in fragments: he had internal injuries, his right arm was in traction, and his pelvis and left shoulder had been crushed. Worse, Sam's left leg had been amputated at the hip. A nurse brought in a copy of the *Detroit News*, which began a report on the car crash with this unsettling lead:

"The Nazis tried their best to kill Sam Offen. They couldn't. But what they failed in has almost been accomplished by an American—a hit-run driver."

22

TATTOO IN THE MIRROR

Hospitalized for months, Sam was fitted with a prosthetic leg and learned to walk again. His progress might have surprised the physical therapist, but as his daughter Gail points out, that's just who he was. "*Everybody* has problems," he intoned to her, locking eyes. She considered how often he had suffered life's snowballs hurled at him. This one, packed with ice, nailed him squarely.

He couldn't just brush this off. He did his exercises diligently, dragged and lifted his left leg around the room, intent on seeing days when he would drive and dance and swim again. There was something about his planning—thinking four or five steps ahead—that had contributed to staying alive in the camps, making sure that his sewing impressed those Quakers enough to secure other jobs, and more food scraps. Doing rehab required some of the same stuff.

Years later, going on fifty-eight herself, his daughter doubled back to this, wanting to know about that side of her dad's perseverance, and the optimism he inexplicably had welded onto it. "I don't know where that came from, I wish I knew," she said, promising to ask when they met again.

Gail was only a toddler that spring, and her brother just five. Their parents were having a house built in the suburbs, a dream home nearly completed. Hearing about the crash, the contractor visited Sam in the hospital. After talking it over at length, Sam and Hyla agreed that the new home wasn't going to work for him in his physical state. The contractor refunded their deposit, and a year later, they found a suitable house in Southfield, northwest of the city.

His employees and friends kept Offen's furrier shop afloat the first year. Strangers and customers alike sent him sympathetic cards; his room at Mt. Carmel Mercy Hospital was bedecked with about three hundred of them. Tickling Sam's fancy, one of those wished him a speedy recovery because "my fur coat needs you." He had already built up a decent clientele, yet sustaining the business would be uphill sledding.

Then the Ceresnies, who had moved their store to Detroit's "Avenue of Fashion," did a remarkable thing. They asked Sam to become a full partner, and he joined them at the new Ceresnie Brothers & Offen Furs in Livernois. Michael Ceresnie was only six at the time, and over the years he grew to appreciate what his father and uncle had done. Certainly taking Sam on was a risk. There was no guarantee that his mobility would not interfere with work. Yet as Michael began helping out during the busy fall season, bringing storage coats from the cold basement vaults, he picked up on something in Offen's makeup. There was a toughness he could not quite identify, more than a physical thing. Ceresnie marveled at how his eventual mentor moved about with an artificial leg and cane.

Offen, meanwhile, refused to rage against the driver who had nearly killed him. A day after the crash a local auto salesman went to the police station, saying he had been drinking heavily the night before and did not know if there had been a man in the other car he had hit. Pieces of glass found at the intersection matched a smashed headlight in Paul O'Niell's blue Rambler, and he pled guilty to leaving the scene of an injury accident.

Remarkably, as Sam learned that the driver had children, he appealed to the judge for leniency. He felt that O'Niell had "suffered enough." What purpose would there be in sending him to jail, and perhaps destroying another family? Writing to the judge, Sam said his experience in the camps had taught him to forgive.

The traffic judge could have imposed a maximum sentence of five years in prison. Instead, he placed the driver on probation and took away his keys for five years.

As Sam recovered his mobility, good times followed as his kids grew and business took off. When things weren't too busy at the store, Sol and Sam would go out back and play cards, usually poker. They were often joined by other furriers who became regulars as they retired—Johnny and Phil, still in their pressed suits, whom to young Gail had that old men smell of cloying cologne and hair jell. If a customer came through to use the bathroom, someone in the gang threw a cover over the table. When one of the Ceresnie sons walked into the showroom noticing their father and Sam engaged in serious conversation, it was usually about cards. The two men also bowled together once a week, and their families occasionally took in sporting events—the vaunted Tigers and Red Wings, or lowly Lions. Sam jumped into the full sports cycle, bringing Gail and Jerry to Tiger Stadium a few times. The kids met Tigers' great Al Kaline, who bought a mink coat at the store. Grabbing some eggs across the street at a deli one morning, Sam introduced Mike Ceresnie to Red Wings' defenseman Red Kelly.

During that era both Sam and Sol relished customizing long coats with wild furs that were in style. Most were made to order, and Sam ably cut long-haired pelts of coyote and fox on a small basement table. Women flocked to him in the showroom, and while a charmer and natural flirt, he posed no real threat. To avoid having to fit a "large" or "extra large" size on a rotund client, he and Sol devised a color-coded sizing tag system—red for extra large, green for large, etc., which continued in use during the next generation.

Their knockoffs and gag gifts made became legendary. Along with kinky party accessories, these included mink car visors to hold mail, dog collars, and bow ties. They occasionally ran short of time, but not ideas, while Sam found the means to make things like favorite fur slippers for himself and his wife. He also donated items to Jewish organizations and other charities: Cossack-style hats made from black Persian lamb, rabbit muffs, and collars. He went out of his way to make items for relatives, who received them as gifts from the heart.

In December of 1964, a short article carried by the Associated Press ran in newspapers all over the country:

Now, of all things, a mink cloak for toes.

That's right, a mink toe piece, and Dr. Morton B. Lesser, a Detroit dentist, has it—thanks to his brother-in-law furrier, Sam Offen.

Dr. Lesser broke his Achilles tendon playing squash. A doctor put a cast on his leg, leaving, as usual, the toes sticking out.

With winter coming on, Offen came to the aid of his brother-in-law, doing him up with a toe cover in Lutetia mink, labels, initials and all. A tie around the cast holds it in place.

Sam's spunk permeated all facets of his life. He took pride in collecting new jokes, even bawdy ones, and didn't flinch from extolling them at a fashion show or another event. In key moments he also deployed subtle showroom diplomacy. During one era, pimps began frequenting the men's coat section. Other times a man would come in one day with his wife and return the next afternoon with his mistress. Sam kept it straight, playing dumb in his banter. He was a true mensch in every way.

Having hidden beside a Catholic cemetery outside of Płaszów and marched from Landsberg, having hitchhiked through the Abruzzo region to Puglia, and having patrolled a warehouse near Seoul to kill time, a recurring dream came to Bernard.

He was Atlas holding up the entire world.

I started to shake the thing, cursing everything else. I would be committing suicide if I kept shaking the world. Because I'm part of the world.

He forced himself to wake, shouting, "Cancel! Cancel that dream!"

By the early seventies, Bernard owned a coin laundry and dry-cleaning business beyond the city on 9 Mile Road, not far from his brick, three-bedroom bungalow. It was more house than a home, since his relationship with Sybil was dissolving. They collided in arguments behind closed doors, wringing some of the spirit and childhood from their two sons.

To his oldest son, Jay, his father often seemed disengaged when he returned from work—there, but not really. It was up to their mother, a school gym teacher, to run the household. The boys went to public schools and sometimes accompanied their father to work on weekends. Jay would recall holding the flashlight while his father repaired someone's dishwasher, proud that he, too, became a "hands-on Jew" adept at fixing things and working on cars. On summer weekends, he and his brother Michael played with their extended cousins out at the lake. They learned to water ski and fished with Uncle Sam, while their dad eventually bought a boat with an outboard motor. Yet the acrimony between their parents could be punishing. When a divorce court judge called the boys into his chambers, he told them he'd handled thousands of cases, and their parents' fighting was amongst the worst he'd seen—not exactly a salve for eleven- and seven-year-old boys. By 1975 the breakup was official.

Bernard felt like an emotional cripple. He was still unable to peer below the surface of his feelings. Equating sex with love, at times he felt rejected by his wife: if they weren't doing it, he thought she must be pushing him away. He started seeing other women, and when Sybil wouldn't let him visit the boys, one night he broke a window banging on the door. Michael, who suffered mild epilepsy and became depressed when his father left, blamed himself. His father's unexpressed emotions, lurking in a slow-leaking cranny, wreaked havoc on the family.

Only once or twice did Bernard confide to his wife about his past. Sybil tape-recorded his recollections, which he tucked away in a safe-deposit box.

Climbing the American ladder like his oldest brother also wasn't working out. Running a business didn't come easy. He didn't have Sam's entrepreneurial zeal, his easy way, and marketing and numbers were not Bernard's bag. How do you build a rapport with customers if you don't yet know yourself? Years into the new millennium, he still didn't feel competent on his PC.

As Bernard's anger at the world festered, he began connecting dots in jagged lines. Anti-nuclear movements were growing in the United States and across Europe, and the threat of nuclear catastrophe tore into him. Activists called for a freeze to end the Cold War-era buildup of strategic warheads. Others opposed nuclear power plants from California to New England, and the partial meltdown at Three Mile Island in 1979 galvanized public outcry. Bernard heeded warnings by nuclear industry critics: "Either we improve, or the future is dismal indeed." This hit close to home as he read an article about what would happen if a warhead reached Detroit. The prospect of covering oneself and stocking food in fallout shelters seemed obscene. To him, the escalating arms race meant humanity was entering "a potential planetary gas chamber."

"Helping my sons go to college and just doing business is insane if I don't do anything with what is going on in the nuclear race."

Connections were forming, but he didn't peer deep inside until shaving one morning. In the mirror he noticed his tattoo from Auschwitz-Birkenau, number B-7815. He had ignored it for what seemed forever.

Hey Bernard, that was you. That was me. For thirty-six years I stuffed down my fears and pains.

Nathan says his fears and memory are located in the back of his head, but I realized my fears and trauma are also located in the whole of the body. I knew if I didn't go back I would get sick.

I needed to go back and confront my fears.

He felt the world had forgotten about the Shoah. "We are not paying attention really to what transpired," he told me. "It's business as usual. Most of the circumstances that were instrumental in creating the Holocaust were business and politics and religion. And two of those things are ongoing."

In 1981, martial law had been declared in Poland. The regime tried to hold back the sweep of history catalyzed by a trade union's demands, led by a shipyard electrician, Lech Walesa. Ready to face his ghosts, Bernard Offen booked a flight to Kraków with a girlfriend.

What if his life ceases to matter?

As much as I tried to avoid it, the question rattled me. Nine years after losing Mike, God, fate, karma, or something else threw another switch, bringing this to the fore again.

Another of his buddies died in a hiking accident. Only twenty-seven, Frank Madeiros was a union electrician taking advantage of a layoff and apparently seeking his own way. Early in 2011 he had begun through-hiking the Appalachian Trail in Georgia, startling friends and relatives with the announcement. While athletic—he had played hockey in high school—few saw this coming in Frank. He survived a fall in Virginia and often wore his favorite Bruins jersey, sometimes hiking by flashlight at night so as not to miss seeing a playoff game somewhere off the trail. After reaching Mount Katahdin in Maine that September, he was soon back climbing again in Alabama with three of his AT friends.

About three weeks before Christmas, he lost his footing while leaping boulders and fell eighty feet—the other guys telling his sister that Frank had a huge smile on his face making that final jump. We didn't hear any of the details, and it wasn't our place to ask. Frank had an infectious personality and many close friends, and he was also incredibly loyal to Mike, scrawling many notes in the journal at our son's grave. We found ourselves briefly caught in the current again along with their mates.

Naturally, the guys' lives had taken off over the intervening years. Travis had become a special education teacher working with autistic kids; Griff joined the same fire department where his dad thrived before cancer claimed his life; and John taught history and continued drumming in a band. Jeff, probably Mike's closest friend, was a graphic artist working at Staples, while Tom, one of the first guys he hung out with to escape our house, honed his craft as a sportswriter at the *Boston Herald*. Kevin was setting up networks and fixing teachers' laptops. Others sometimes still drank too much, and there had been inevitable shifts in friendships. Denise and I wondered how they were doing with this latest upheaval. The surges came and went, and as stoic as a few of them acted, here was another tsunami.

"Frank loved Mike so much," Jeff Walsh told me as we embraced.

They were both mates and antagonists, playing basement poker games, Mike and Frank once crashing through a screen door wrestling. But I really knew nothing about all this and longed to hear their stories. More of the trash talk coming between grins, the occasional fisticuffs, weekends snowboarding with Tommy and the risks they took—maybe he found some boulder-strewn glades like we did a few times, coming down whipping snowballs at his buds. Or the tender side with his girlfriends that we caught glimpses of, helping Tanya and her dad with the wash and cleaning his house.

What if the years drain by and we stop reminiscing, we stop feeling in full as we over-seed the excuses from our busy lives? How do we hold him present? And perhaps what feels even worse: What if others around us forget?

I was driven back to a pivotal point in the criminal case against Cory Scanlon. We actually ran into him at Frank's wake, in the same damn funeral home where Mike had lain. It was the first time we'd seen Cory since the high school program; he had married Lisa, and I went over to speak with him. We knew he had attended one friend's wedding, and while sensing that these guys somehow had moved on to embrace Cory had pained us, we let most of that go.

Still, there was a lingering notion connected to seeing him that almost felt like paranoia. I wondered whether the judge in Cory's case really considered our victim impact statements, those letters from Mike's grandfathers, his aunts and uncles, and both of us. What weight they had, and where they resided.

It was nothing personal against the judge. I didn't even remember his face, nor recall any slight from the bench. One might have argued persuasively that cutting Cory's sentence in half after he killed his two friends was lenient, but that's not where I was going.

I wanted to know who remembered. Where the record existed of our pleas for a commensurate punishment, for Cory to take full responsibility, and for him to fully honor Mike and P.J.'s lives.

It was never about justice, so-called. To me, that had become a mere construct as I watched other victims' families get stretched over years, flattened by the appeals and other mechanistic legal processes—well before even meeting Connie Clery. "Mere drapery on a sandcastle that the tide washes away," I wrote to Judge John Cratsley.

There could be no justice for us.

He was gone forever. Unable to be at those weddings, build a career, or become an uncle. We would always wonder how much we missed while his buds grew old. And began having babies. Buying their first homes. Training a puppy, and dad installing a play set in the backyard.

Until our tears trickled from a deep place where joy had finally begun to thaw.

I needed to read those letters again but did not have copies. Two months after I inquired, the district attorney's office could not locate the statements. The victims' advocate said they often get destroyed in the interests of privacy, although she kept copies of many in her own files. Checking further, she found them at the probation department. While relieved, I still felt chilled by this indiscriminate handling: our voices might have been shredded.

Or not.

A roll of the dice on the conveyor belt.

I read my wife's letter to the judge once more. She asked, "How do I help my children with such an enormous loss?" She envisioned growing old with this sadness, lingering below the surface only to pierce through again and again. Our guts had informed us this would never change during the course of our lives, perhaps not so unlike Bernard and his brothers, reluctant and unrelenting. *Soon I'll hear old winter's song.*

Those last falling leaves. Always the turn of that season, bringing us to our knees.

Since her deepest wish could never come true, Denise wrote, "All I can hope for is that no mother will have to stand in my shoes and no family will have to bury their child, brother, or sister because of a senseless accident." Urging Cory to devote his life to prevention, she offered him forgiveness.

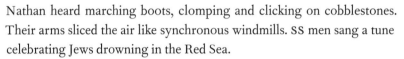

Nathan heard marching boots, clomping and clicking on cobblestones. Their arms sliced the air like synchronous windmills. SS men sang a tune celebrating Jews drowning in the Red Sea.

Knocked on the ground, he bled, looking around—but neither his brothers nor father were there.

> *Die wellen schlagen ʒu*
> *Und die welt hat ruh.*
> The waves close over them
> And the world has peace.

He woke up yelling, quieted by Helen.

As they moved from Jersey City to a house in North Bergen, life progressed in many of the ways one expects. Bright and curious, their three daughters were well tended to by Helen, and both parents made sure one was always around at home to preclude any mischief as they grew older. She drove them to Hebrew school in the afternoons, and on weekends the family frequented a nearby drive-in, savoring treats like French fries and ice cream. They attended synagogue and made seasonal trips to Michigan. Their father's one complaint was his children wasting food. Sometimes they'd taste cereal, and into the sink it would go. He could not always catch himself in those moments, while knowing it was not their fault that they did not know about hunger.

As an adolescent Ruth became rebellious and opinionated, in some ways following her father. She asked many questions. But neither of her parents felt equipped to answer. No information came from Nathan, and the early lives of both adults remained sealed. Ruth began to see through this, in part while taking piano lessons from another survivor's son, whose father, Max Hilfstein, had attended school with Sam in Kraków. Well into his forties, and having learned parenting on the fly, Nathan was incapable of expressing what he'd been through. Like his brothers, he found that other survivors mostly did the same. Who in America really wanted to hear about this? He kept to himself, making sure he caught the bus on time. He tried to move on.

At fourteen, Ruth informed her parents she didn't want to be Jewish any more. Sometime after moving to their new house, she put on a pair of black boots, clicking them and walking up the stairs. Until her mother shouted, "Enough."

Helen went into the interior decorating business a few years later. She had worked extra hard to raise herself up, her education having been interrupted when she was nine. Inspired by her daughters' learning, she finished night school with a high school equivalency degree when the girls were young. Nathan, who lent his support by feeding them and making sure homework got done, helped with the new venture.

They opened a store near a larger new home they bought in Paramus, north of Hackensack. Below the shop there were cutting tables and a sewing machine, and they sold supplies like knitting wool, canvases, threads, and dry goods, while Nathan hung drapes and shades on weekends. It was a continuous affair, and often their youngest daughter, Suzanne, helped Helen at the store after school. They took brief breaks at home, pausing to realize they had reached the middle class, a once unimaginable suburban tableland, spread out with lawn mowing and house painting, and Helen growing flowers and vegetables in a decent-sized yard. They had a basement recreation room and enjoyed grilling with charcoal during the warm months. Nathan took up tennis on outdoor courts nearby, sometimes bringing his daughters to play in the summertime.

The years pushed by. Ruth's battle of wills with her father escalated: she drove his car without permission when her parents went to England, smashing its headlights; she joined protests against Vietnam, dropped drugs with high school longhairs, and left home at eighteen. To her parents, the world was turning upside down. During her high school commencement in 1970, Nathan was disgusted by barefooted graduates and a couple with a baby in their arms. "The parents were losing control over it, and we were the first ones on the firing line," he said. "We didn't know how to handle it." Ruth was carrying baggage she couldn't even see—and it was not hers. Decades later she fired back, "It was them and it wasn't their fault. They were two ill-equipped people to have children."

Three years younger, her sister Gail excelled in school and won early admission to Hofstra University. Helen and Nathan fought over whether she should go before graduating—one of their few battles—with her father worried that being petite, and in his eyes immature, Gail was not ready. In the end he gave in, while youngest Suzanne matriculated through school, vying for early acceptance like her sister. She was interested in marine biology, but changed her mind after working one summer for an optometrist, which became her career path.

During a routine checkup in 1980, Helen's doctor located a lump in her breast. She underwent a mastectomy, followed by radiation and chemotherapy. Naturally, her daughters and husband were deeply shaken. With Ruth only twenty-eight, they felt much too young for any of this. Some months later, the declaration that she was cancer free lifted everyone.

Nathan and Helen celebrated by jetting to Hawaii. Arriving at their hotel in the afternoon after the long flights, they fell asleep in their clothes, waking to find that their suitcases had already been unpacked. They enjoyed a restful vacation on Oahu, taking in the international village and many other sights. Helen returned refreshed and glowing, determined to continue learning about holistic medicines to help keep herself well.

About once a month, Sam's children noticed a thin, mysterious blue letter arriving in the mail for their father. They thought he had a pen pal, but their parents kept it hush-hush.

Sometimes at night they heard noises as he woke from a nightmare. Gail figured out that he had been through something pretty bad, and on occasions she overheard bits of conversation between her parents. He didn't talk about his family in Poland; the subject was taboo. Their mother didn't directly discuss any of this, and neither did Hyla's mom, who lived with them for many years. Both women were devoted to Sam, preparing all the foods he craved and taking care of the kids and house.

The letters contained reparations from Germany. Offen deposited the checks, and his daughter wondered later if he tapped into that account at times to support charities, or people who just needed a hand. Very likely only his accountant knew the scope of this unspoken benevolence. Practicing an ancient ethic that the highest form of humility is anonymity, Sam gradually instilled this in his children, imploring them to give more and count their blessings.

Gail knew little about the Holocaust. Even with a large concentration of survivors in metropolitan Detroit, it wasn't taught at her school during the seventies. "There was this serious Hitler thing that involved my father's family, but that was all I knew," she said. "Sometimes people would ask me questions and I would say, 'I don't know. We don't ever talk about it.'" As an adult, she added this to a list of what she needed to ask him, wondering whether it was just too much for many survivors to bring up.

Her father's passion became traveling the country with his family. They packed the car and took off during the lull in business every summer, with Sam always behind the wheel. Having a fantastic sense of direction—keen with maps, and declining to use a GPS in later years—he drove to every region, staying in small hotels along the way. He had a penchant for taking them to places with big factories, anywhere things were made or grown. They toured a Gerber plant and a Budweiser brewery. On the north shore of Lake Ontario, they stopped in Leamington, Canada's tomato capital, which features a giant tomato in the square, and fished off the pier. They did it all: from the Soo Locks, Wall Drug, South Dakota and Mount Rushmore, to the St. Louis Arch and the Grand Canyon. "My brother, mother and I, posed stiffly or waving, rendered in saturated Ektachrome slides and Super 8 film," Gail recalled. As the miles unfolded her dad smoked a pipe and whistled. Hyla, content to see her husband in his element, tied on a headscarf when the convertible top came down.

During a month-long trip in a burnt orange '68 Pontiac Catalina, the Offens traversed some of the country's great national parks—the Badlands, Grand Tetons, Yellowstone, and Yosemite—before resting a while in San Francisco. Son Jerry was in the eighth grade, and he and his sister each claimed one side of a non-crossable divide in the back seat. Sam had an ulterior motive heading all the way west. He crowed to his son that the best deals for buying a car were found in Michigan, and he planned to unload the Catalina in California and fly home with a profit. But it was rear-ended and he had to drive the Pontiac back—albeit taking a southern route through destinations like Albuquerque. Turning sixteen, Jerry inherited both the car and his dad's love of the open road.

The very notion of being handicapped never found a home in Sam. He began swimming six days a week, he played catch while sitting on a chair, played Ping-Pong, shot pool, you name it. He tried water skiing on one leg, a rare failure. He even took up snowmobiling with Jerry, who caught the enduring winter bug. They started out riding on a local golf course, and when Jerry lived out at the lake as an adult, his father set his crutches in the foot well, and off they'd go into the woods. One time Mike Ceresnie drove with Sam to buy wild furs from a trapper, the ground was iced-over and Offen slipped, catching his foot under the front wheel of Ceresnie's mini van. For a moment, "He was yelling in pain, it was heart-wrenching pain," Mike recalled. Releasing the power steering, he was able to turn the wheel and get Sam out, and he was fine. "Nothing would stop Sam," he said. Later in life he deployed a three-wheel Amigo scooter.

He was not finished battling health issues. In the late seventies Offen was diagnosed with chondrosarcoma in his remaining leg, which had spread through cartilage cells in his femur. After one doctor recommended amputation, horrifying Sam and Hyla, he was able to find an orthopedic surgeon in New York doing experimental treatments such as removing the femur instead. His femur was replaced with a stainless steel rod, but there was a big glitch: the steel rod was two inches short. Sam had no choice but accept it. While noticeably diminished in height, he remained thankful to the surgeon for saving his leg.

By then, the fur shop had relocated to a high-end suburb, Birmingham, and the Ceresnies insisted on adding one accommodation for him. Descending to the basement level—a former bowling alley with large rooms for coat manufacturing, repair, and storage—they added a mechanical lift connected to a black steel rail. When a young child came in with her parents and noticed the chair, Sam sat her on his lap and went for a ride.

Several years later a rabbi approached Sam with an idea that would have been untenable earlier. Bits and pieces of Offen's wartime experience had been trickling out to his relatives and close friends. Driving with Hyla and his cousin, Marilyn Fishman, Sam shocked Fishman and her husband after they bought some granite at a quarry to use as bookends. Turning to them casually, he said, "You know during the war I worked in a quarry . . ." and described surviving the steps of death. The couple had no idea, never having pressed him about that era. Charles Rosenzveig, a rabbi in Port Huron, was looking for survivors like himself to share their stories. He, too, had grown up in Poland, and founded the first freestanding Holocaust museum in the United States not far from Offen's home. Sam demurred on Rosenzveig's request, considering himself an inadequate public speaker, but he acquiesced eventually. "It seemed important to confront a some-times-disbelieving public, if for no other reason than to memorialize those who were lost," he said. By the mid-eighties Sam was a regular presenter at the new Holocaust Memorial Center housed in a Jewish community center.

Offen understood that he needed to go back home. Like Nathan and Helen, Sam and Hyla had already traveled to London for a reunion with the Freedmans. Gail remembers friends throwing them a bon voyage party, one of those fading sixties' conventions that seemed silly, akin to playing Twister at a fondue party and dipping into a sludge-like cheese. Preparing for a return to Poland was an animal of a far different stripe.

Sam might not have admitted it, but it is likely that Bernard paved the way for his return.

Nathan and Sam tried convincing their younger brother not to go.

The three men had opened a savings account anticipating they might return to Poland some day. When Bernard checked it perhaps fifteen years later, only a few hundred dollars had accrued. His brothers and a travel agent warned that moving about would be too risky. Transportation and lodging were not guaranteed given the government's crackdown against the growing Solidarity movement, and the agency canceled a group trip that he had signed up for.

Yet Bernard had experiences his brothers did not, having gone to places where no one thought he could. He felt ready. Returning to what he called "the snake pit" dovetailed with another destination—Israel—where he planned to join a first-ever gathering with thousands of survivors, including Elie Wiesel, complete with a ceremony of remembrance at the Wailing Wall.

He and his girlfriend, Annetta, met some Poles on the plane to Warsaw, open young musicians who invited the couple to stay with them. From there they boarded a train to Kraków. Back in his hometown, Bernard walked to his old apartment at Krakusa 9. Its exterior was gray stucco with splotches of stains, and examining the windows, he conjured the faces of those who had lived inside. At street level there was the one window that had framed his parents' tiny concession stand. The building seemed smaller than he remembered, and once inside, more things surfaced. He recalled where the stove had been, and a cabinet by another window where his father stored a bottle of schnapps for his Shabbat blessing. He re-imagined the smell of chocolate wafting through the complex and playing with friends, checking the view from the courtyard up to balcony railings strafed by peeling paint.

His older brother also returned to the building—during a family trip a few years after Bernard—convincing a stubborn woman preparing dinner to allow them a few minutes inside his old apartment. To Sam, it looked almost the same. There were some new furnishings, a refrigerator and other appliances. He visualized his parents and sister moving about, keeping busy at different tasks, a lump in his throat pulsing. Sam tried to reconstruct his childhood, yet he had not been sure he'd even be able to go in. Still fluent in his native tongue, he confided that he was afraid of being recognized on the streets in Podgórze. That didn't happen. Yet while attending services inside a three-hundred-year-old synagogue with Hyla and his children, he met another survivor. The man helped Sam find various relatives' birth certificates and his parents' marriage license.

Continuing down the street, Bernard picked out where another uncle had lived with two children around the corner. He passed a low building where the ritual baths had been, the bakery. He recognized the synagogue entrance. "The streets were full of life and activity," he remembered. "There were friends and neighbors everywhere."

Like diesel fumes lingering above the chalky streets, remnants of a faint threat hovered in the air. A section of the arched ghetto wall constructed in the shape of a Hebrew tombstone served as a schoolyard border—still *a useful wall*, he considered. The Yiddish theatres and distinguished *yeshivas*, religious schools where future rabbis were educated, were long gone. Bernard discovered a handful of Jewish-style eateries, some with klezmer bands catering to tourists outside. Yet only a few hundred Jews remained in the city.

The tower of Saint Joseph's looming behind the market square made him retreat again. Nearby was a hill where he went sledding as a child, and fields where he watched soccer matches, yet Bernard still did not want to face the church. Perhaps the cobblestones and sidewalk pavers whispered, since he remembered so much—shopping with his parents, the humiliations, hunger and disease, and bartering his family's remaining items for food. The stones would not relent.

He and Annetta drove to Auschwitz. It occurred to him that during his first days there, despite what he breathed in and the rumors circulating, he still had resisted believing. Surely, God did not know of this. He felt an impulse to reach out and touch the barbed wire, shrinking back. He had missed those last chaotic months, the crematorium crew's revolt, and the SS blowing up gas chambers and furnaces before the final Russian offensive. He saw that some of Auschwitz I and Auschwitz II-Birkenau had been preserved.

The couple were greeted by the museum director and a research historian, who offered to help find records such as his family's transport documents. They met a former prisoner named Odi, a man who chose to remain in the camp after being held there four years. He worked for the museum, his window overlooking the lone remaining gas chamber. Stunned by this man's means of resolution, Bernard and Annetta sat in silence for some time. Odi told them that by staying he was able to elude dreams of the past. "On the outside, I would have to pretend and try to be something that I am not," he said.

They met another man, Berndt, who helped teach German teenagers who spent a summer doing volunteer work at the museum. The two men walked to a ramp leading to the ruins of two chambers at Birkenau. Berndt asked Bernard whether the memories came more easily now that he had returned. They certainly did, and Offen felt he was rounding a corner, determined to examine everything.

As official museum guests, he and Annetta stayed in the commandant's former office. It was a long, cathartic night, the scene of what might have been a crushing juxtaposition. Rudolf Höss had overseen the murders of perhaps 1.5 million people. Höss's wife and five children lived in a villa just minutes away. Unconvincingly, he had maintained that, despite his pivotal role, he might be understood differently. The world, Höss seemed to complain, once referring to himself coyly in the third person, "would never be able to understand that he also had a heart and that he was not evil." The couple stayed up late, pacing the room and talking, attempting to sift what Bernard had gone through. "I just stayed with it, I did not block it out," Offen explained. "*That* was the beginning of my healing process."

After ten days in Poland, Bernard went to Jerusalem for the survivors' gathering. Everyone was encouraged to bring a stone inscribed with the names of lost family members, but he did not. He found the ceremonies very moving and met a man whose tattoo number was exactly one hundred less than his. The two were unsure if they had arrived on the same transport to Auschwitz. Bernard never spoke with him again.

He pulled out of Detroit, heading west to pursue his healing. Soon before leaving Bernard put together a slide show about being a survivor, presenting it to Jay's high school when his oldest son was a sophomore or junior. "The other kids were like, 'Hey, your dad's really cool,'" Jay recalled. Yet not much more was said at home. Bernard sold the laundromat as the boys continued living with their mother, and his departure hit Michael especially hard. Both later attended college, but their father was not around much, returning only for short stints.

Landing in northern California, Bernard took courses in video production and journalism at Sonoma State University. He recovered another vision he had in Birkenau: that he would live to teach about what happened. The world would know. Two years after going to Poland, in 1983 he produced a short film about some of his experiences, calling it *The Work*, a reference to both his need for non-clinical therapy, and also to the slave labor that so many succumbed to. Clearly a debut production, his narrator's voice is sometimes stilted in staccato-like segments as if attempting to constrain his emotions, while at other points his flowing lyricism is arresting. Dubbed over an image of a field of wildflowers outside Birkenau, he wonders whether his father's remains were dumped into the river, or "were they part of the ashes that became fertilizer for the revitalization of spring flowers?" In the next sequence, whether we choose to get it or not, Bernard stands inside a crematorium:

I'm looking at each brick that was built and made and put into place,

deliberate, deliberate, deliberate, the bricks of a place of destruction, and the agony that people went through; and here we also
build brick by brick the possibilities of planetary destruction, by
the failure of us to look within and be examining everything that
has preceded us, this *heinous mundi*.

While the film is part documentary stocked with still photos of Bernard
and his family in Kraków and historical snapshots, his hope was that it
would be a catalyst for self-reflection.

Moving around north of Santa Rosa, he continued this inner work while
making broader connections. He also spent a year in Israel, seeking spiritual
guidance from mentors and pondering some of the great intractable questions, including the struggle to sort out our differences and live with each
other peacefully. He became an anti-nuclear activist and marched at rallies,
joining groups like Global Walkers for a Livable World in hopes of educating
people about the parallels between environmental collapse and the Holocaust.
Often trekked more than three months from Ohio to New York, presenting
slide shows ahead of the route. Returning to California, Bernard attended
men's groups and divorcees' groups to talk about his trauma in small circles.

Along the way, he began to realize the limitations of his potential audience. Most people, including the Jewish community, were not very interested in a survivor's experience. Let alone one who suggests to others that
they heal themselves by delving into their trauma—not by medicating
or otherwise avoiding it. Bernard became his own doctor, determining
when and how far to go. Nathan and Sam didn't get this either. They tried
explaining that people didn't want to hear his story. They repeated, "Why
don't you get a job and make some money?" Behind the scenes though,
they continued to help him out, especially Sam.

While striving for a more spiritual life, Bernard rejected organized religion of every stripe. He declared, "I don't believe in God. I look at the orthodoxy in Judaism and the orthodoxy in every religion we've got, and they've
got the direct word from God. It starts wars. So I say, a curse on them."

Bernard warmed in the sun and grew a ponytail. He stopped paying
income taxes. Entering his sixties, and relishing the serenity of drives
through the desert, he began to consider himself a gypsy.

$$23$$

RECLAIMING THE PAST

Nathan needed to make good on a promise. He and Helen had talked about returning to Poland in hopes of finding the farmer's family who had sheltered her during the war. Raising three daughters and starting a business had interceded. Early in 1989 Helen began to feel sick again, gaining weight and losing color. Her doctor told them that her cancer had metastasized and was spreading up her spine, so she resumed chemotherapy and radiation treatments. He knew it was time.

Many years earlier Nathan had joined a group called the New Cracow Friendship Society, which supported Holocaust survivors in Poland and gave scholarships to students in Tel Aviv. He and Helen traveled with the group to Kraków and then set out on their own, unsure of what they might find. Reaching her native Dąbrowa, she located her old neighborhood easily enough. Yet perhaps because she could neither read nor write as a child, Helen didn't recall the last name of the farmer or his wife. Neither did the name of their village where she had hid resurface. Instead, her main clue was recalling that the farmer's son had been a tailor. With that kernel of information, instinct began guiding her search.

Helen had an inkling that something would jar open by walking the streets, and she picked up the direction she had taken fleeing the Dąbrowa ghetto. They headed west in a taxi, eventually toward a village called Olesno. Going door to door, she and Nathan asked residents how long they had lived there, and if anyone knew a tailor. Following their second good lead, the cab passed a church and she suddenly told the driver, "Yes, I know this place," giving directions to the farmer's house.

Driving into the yard, Nathan saw a small woman walking with a cane, her head bowed toward the ground. His wife approached her, bending down, and the woman cried, "Helenka!"

Nathan felt his heart beating fast.

The woman's husband, Ignac Szadowic, was the tailor, the oldest man left in the village. His father, the farmer who had found Helen half-starved in the barn, had passed some years before. Ignac burst out crying, telling Helen, "My family is now complete."

Helen and Nathan followed Ignac and Janina into their house. They were poor, and she was obviously ill. As they spoke of the past Nathan tape-recorded the conversation. After visiting, the Offens left them some money to help with medical expenses.

Some weeks later, Janina wrote Helen a letter, saying, "I remember you as a little girl, the orphan with the sad face. I understood your pain and I treated you like my own daughter . . . I knew the risk we were taking since my husband is a tailor and the Germans were coming all the time to have their uniforms fixed. I was afraid very much, but God gave us strength, and we all survived."

While in Poland the couple visited other places including the Wieliczka salt mine. A tour guide remarked that the Nazis had killed all the Jews who were enslaved there. Without flinching, Nathan raised his hand to interject, "I worked in this mine, and they did not kill this Jew." The guide apologized, promising to correct the record. After stopping in London to see many of the Freedmans, including Mitch, they flew home.

A few months after returning, a local newspaper interviewed Helen and Nathan, running a front-page feature about her reunion with the Polish family. Their phone in Paramus seemed to ring off the hook for days. One call in particular made Nathan stop in his tracks.

A guy named Andy Ferrara told Nathan he had been in one of the tanks that liberated Mauthausen. Ferrara hoped they could get together, and Nathan took down his phone number in disbelief. He had rarely considered meeting one of the GIs who came through the gate. This Ferrara lived maybe twenty minutes away in Hackensack.

By that time, Anthony Ferrara had retired from sales at a steel company and filled some of his days booking trips as a travel agent. Active in a local Knights of Columbus where he had been commander of the color guard, Ferrara relished being around other veterans of the 11th Armored Division. He and his wife Audrey were regular attendees at Thunderbolt reunions held across the country, and at local meetings amongst a large contingent of New Jersey vets. Andy had even been president of the division's national association in 1978.

To Nathan, the six-foot-two-inch man was a gentle giant, and they quickly hit it off. Andy was interested in Judaism, and he began celebrating many of the holidays with the Offens along with his wife. Sometimes gathering with their younger two daughters' families for Passover Seder, Nathan and Helen would be joined by the Ferraras, who were childless. Andy mentioned that his priest at Our Lady of Peace in nearby Maywood wanted to join them someday. While that never transpired, he and Nathan went to local synagogues a few times to speak about their experiences. Ferrara told audiences that entering the camp completely changed his outlook on life.

Nathan's new friend may have embellished his role slightly, but that is largely immaterial. Ferrara served with A Troop of the 41st Cavalry Reconnaissance Squadron, Mechanized, a cousin to the platoon that is widely credited with first coming upon the Gusen and Mauthausen camps. Ferrara's troop certainly was nearby, perhaps as close as seven miles north of Mauthausen the morning of liberation. It is likely that Ferrara's company reached the camp where Nathan lay close to starving a few days later. Trained as a low-speed radio operator, Ferrara told Nathan that he was an officer. Yet he was actually discharged as a private first class after the war.

Regardless of any of that, their connection mattered a lot to Nathan. Ferrara invited him to local 11th Armored Division meetings, casual dinners where he became an honorary member. Besides gathering at a local veterans hall, the men and their wives sometimes met in very modest joints like Joe's Bar in New Brunswick, which was pretty much a dump in the early nineties. They took over a room beside the bar with missing ceiling tiles and storage boxes scattered about. Its owner was a Thunderbolt, and the men caught up over buckets of fried chicken, salad, and pitchers of beer, while someone usually brought Twinkies for dessert. While it was nothing fancy, Nathan and Helen enjoyed being invited and began to relish the camaraderie filling the small room. Doris Torluccio, whose husband, Charlie, was a D Troop veteran of the 41st Cavalry Recon, found Joe's Bar a suitable place as well. "We were right there together and did full membership along with the men," she said, the couples exchanging gifts at holiday parties like extended family.

As president of his state chapter, Ferrara thrived on planning their excursions to national conventions in places such as Spokane and Buffalo. Survivors were often invited, although Nathan never went to one. Some of the couples also traveled to Austria on the big anniversaries, including the fiftieth commemoration of liberation in 1995, and groups such as Andy's chapter raised money to help the men return. Years before that benchmark trip, the Ferraras and Torluccios traveled together, paying their respects at American military cemeteries in Belgium, Luxemburg and Germany before going to Mauthausen. Returning to the camp, some of the men were overcome. One man from Ferrara's group, Arthur Jacobson, a Jewish veteran from New York City, stood with his wife outside the front gate inhaling one cigarette after another, unwilling to step in.

Nathan didn't go overseas on those trips, but he and Helen enjoyed dinners with the Ferraras back home. He became an honorary Thunderbolt brother.

Elizabeth Brandon would have forgiven Sam for not showing up. An early November snowstorm dumped several inches during his two-hour drive north of the city alongside Lake Huron to tiny Lexington, her hometown. Yet Offen steered his Cadillac into the United Methodist Church parking lot to give a talk organized by the high school senior, a presentation on genocide past and present.

As part of a school leadership class, Brandon wanted to make the connection more real to her classmates. Even after a field trip to a Holocaust museum outside Detroit, she noticed that many of her peers didn't seem to grasp a lot. Crises in places like Darfur and Rwanda felt a million miles away, and perhaps for some students, growing up in a village dependent largely on tourism, sugar beets, and canning pickles was just too far removed. That Sam didn't cancel showed how much educating her generation meant to him.

First impressions of Sam Offen were often misleading. He used walking braces to enter a hall, and standing up without them invariably in a well-cut suit, one regarded a broad face topped by an atrocious comb-over. Yet his color was healthy if not ruddy, giving a hint of his fifty-minute swimming routine. Regarding his audience with shining eyes, Sam entreated them to open their hearts and minds.

"I am one of the very lucky ones," he sometimes began. "I lived a simple, normal, middle class life." Sam asked them to consider their own lives as he briefly laid out how his family's was ravaged by the occupation. "Picture yourselves," he continued. "I was about your age. There was no more school, sports, soccer, there was nothing . . . From that day on, for me, life stopped in its tracks."

For more than twenty-five years, he eagerly shared his family's story while imploring middle and high school students to go beyond their study of history. "You are all going to be our future leaders," he said, a hint of overarching optimism revealed in his upturned mouth. "You must know what happened during that period. And not just Jews, many other nationalities were victims of oppression. It could happen to any group. So please, fight for democracy, for justice, and for freedom."

This proclivity brought Sam across Michigan to rural areas with few if any Jews, to suburbs, and cities like Ann Arbor. He went just about anywhere he was asked, traveling with Hyla to Ohio and other states. "I say it facetiously—business is good," he quipped when asked about his speaking schedule, which amounted to once a week during busy stretches at age 90.

On that weekend in Lexington, Elizabeth Brandon and her parents were each struck by how attached Offen was to positive associations and memories. His face lit up recalling how Bernard tracked his brothers across Italy, and the eighteen-year-old found it "really mind blowing" that Sam was able to find happiness with his brothers after all they had endured. Snacking on refreshments with him following the talk, her mother, Karen Brandon, saw how Offen took such joy in small things: the teenagers who gathered nearby, or just savoring a cookie. "He said, 'This is a really great cup of cocoa,'" she remembers. "You just wouldn't expect it, just his constant noting on things." Both she and her husband, Tim, sensed Sam's determination to create a new life. "Once you've lost all of that, you tend to not take things for granted," Karen continued. "I think he focuses to choose what's good and positive perhaps because he's had enough of the negative."

Sam also revealed some of what came later as he and Hyla raised a family: not telling his daughter until she'd begun to ask questions; and the insistence of some his Jewish neighbors that he had a responsibility to let others know. "For a long time he did keep it somewhat hidden, he could not deal with it," Tim Brandon reflected. "And then encouraged by his daughter and his son to share the story. That's an amazing thing."

Inevitably, the question most frequently asked was how he survived.

He answered: "Simply, I hope that Providence had a hand in it, and I was lucky to be in the right place at the right time."

Offen became a beloved presence at the Holocaust Memorial Center, the museum and archives located near his home in West Bloomfield. He took a keen interest in how young people responded to the museum tours and talks—his daughter recalls him waiting below the lecture dais to console muscular, tattooed-covered guys. "My father, like a dinosaur, and *he'd* have to comfort them," Gail says.

Here I am. Pinch me.

When the museum was relocated to a new building in neighboring Farmington Hills—oversized with towers that invoke crematoria chimneys and wrapped cable resembling barbed wire—Sam kept showing up. His reach would soon extend even further.

A year after returning to Poland, Helen and Nathan tried to hang on as her cancer spread.

Helen continued treatments and took alternative medicine, thinking that if she could just leave the hospital, things would improve. She pressed Nathan until he finally signed her out, bringing her home in an ambulance against the doctor's orders. He took a leave of absence from work and became her chief caretaker, dispensing painkillers, administering suppositories, changing her, and cooking. Women from their synagogue often brought lunch and their daughters visited, sometimes with Helen's young grandchildren. Her constant companions were two cats who lay on the bed like "towel guards," one staying if the other got up. Pressures mounted as she became bedridden. Nathan wasn't sleeping, and trying to fight off a worst-case scenario late one night, he briefly considered how he might end the misery for both of them.

The two had a routine in earlier days, taking their cats and a mixed Collie-German Shepherd for a neighborhood walk. One of the cats was named "Pretty," the other was a diabetic that Helen issued daily shots of insulin to, and "Mara," the good-natured dog, never needed a leash. As the couple strolled with their three pets, people stopped on the sidewalk in disbelief.

Helen did not want to give up. A rabbi tried comforting her early that winter of 1991, saying it was okay to let go. "She was so strong, she loved life, so she wouldn't," Nathan said. But he had to make the calls, and as his brothers gathered, Ruth flew east with her husband, while Gail and Suzanne, both married as well, were close by. Helenka, the young girl Nathan had fallen for in his English class, died in her sleep that January. She was fifty-eight.

Late in his life, it gnawed at Nathan that she had never enjoyed the fruits of working so fervently to better herself. "It doesn't work out," he snapped.

In the months ahead he desperately needed to keep busy. Suzanne and Gail gave him babysitting jobs—Suzanne had a toddler, Veronica, while Gail's son Jason was a few years older. Their grandfather had to learn how to change modern diapers, vaguely remembering linen ones with safety clips, and now reversing the front end with the flowers for the back. He taught himself how to cook. He needed a plan for each day, enough to get himself out of bed, which sometimes meant cleaning the garage, repainting, anything that required maintenance. He prayed for his wife and by that spring, joined a Jack LaLanne fitness and swimming club. He began playing more tennis. Sometimes Nathan went away on weekends and "Pretty," his remaining pet, played hard to get when he returned, scratching his shin under the table.

He and Sam flew to Poland, meeting Bernard for their first return trip together, having vowed to go as one to the places where their relatives had perished. They drove five hours in the rain from Kraków through forests and small towns, reaching the former camp outside the village of Bełżec, and learned that both their mother and sister had died there. A caretaker opened the gate, and inside they lit a candle and once again said Kaddish. Shivering in the raw weather, the three left quickly. The return trip brought long stretches of silence. Within his shallow breaths, Sam, at least, felt anger and depression resurfacing.

Later that first year after losing Helen, some guys who Nathan played tennis with introduced him to a divorcee. No pushover herself, Gloria Lack had endured a difficult childhood in the Bronx to become a teacher working with learning-disabled kids. Despite his hardboiled skin, Nathan's makeup and background impressed her, and Gloria became curious about his story. They talked a lot on the phone and began seeing each other mostly on weekends. When Nathan sold his house and found a bachelor's apartment, his daughters were surprised to learn how fast their father was moving on.

After nearly fifty years, Sam tracked down one of his saviors. He came across an address in a commemorative book published by the 11th Armored Division Association, a retired pipefitter who lived only twenty miles away.

Finally, someone in the flesh and local, who had served in a battalion attached to the storied Thunderbolts. Ever generous in the same way he would bait and unhook a fish for his nephews even though he felt a bit squeamish doing it for himself, Sam had long wanted to meet one of these men. He dialed the number.

"Are you Mr. Donald Montgomery?"

"Yes."

"Were you with the 11th Armored Division?"

"Yes."

"Were you with the 575th Battalion that liberated Mauthausen?"

"Yes."

"My name means nothing to you," Sam said, his voice a welcoming lilt of upper Midwest vowels mixed with Polish and Yiddish. "But you were the one who saved my life. I'm one of the living skeletons you liberated."

There was a long pause over the line.

"Well, I'll be darned," Montgomery returned. "I never expected any of you would make it."

Hanging up, he told his wife, Dorothy, "Oh my God."

They met the next day for lunch over a few martinis, initiating a bond that lasted another fifteen years. Their wives became friends, and there were dinners out and shared anniversaries. A few weeks after their first meeting, Sam invited Don to join him at a talk he was giving at the Holocaust museum. Montgomery had rarely spoken about his experiences to anyone, let alone in public. When he had tried to tell relatives he felt that no one was interested.

Hoisting up his burly frame, a half head above Sam's, Donald pulled a photo yellowed with age from his wallet, the one he had sent home to his dad in 1945. He stood before the students, having wiped away some tears, and read a note written on the back:

I took this picture myself so you will know it is no phony.

Classmates in grade school, Montgomery and Dick LaLone had rarely crossed paths when they returned to the Pontiac area after the war. It wasn't until the fall of 1993 when a Detroit newspaper ran an account of Montgomery meeting Offen that LaLone got back in touch with his childhood friend. He, too, had something to say about what he had experienced. Within a week of reading the article, like Montgomery, LaLone gave his story to the museum.

Dick and his wife Betty also met Sam and Hyla, and the three couples enjoyed going out to dinners on occasion. This was chiefly for the men, who mostly bantered about work or fishing. Dutiful to her chatty husband, normally vivacious Hyla demurred and took a back seat in their conversations. Their association helped lift a weight off Don, and his wife Dorothy saw a change.

Before then it had been so hard for him to bring up what he had encountered—and here was Sam in the flesh, cracking one-liners and maybe tearing into a juicy steak. Montgomery's expressions remained limited. One time while trying to present alongside Sam, as Nathan and Bernard sat in a small audience with other Offen relatives, Donald broke down. "He couldn't remember jack," his wife said of the occasion. "It was kind of hard because he would always tear up."

In May of 1995, Sam celebrated a half-century of liberation by throwing a party at a restaurant next to a marina, one of his favorite settings. Don and Dorothy were his guests of honor. Every May 5th, Montgomery sent Sam a card to remind him of his new birthday.

When the Thunderbolts' national association published a fiftieth anniversary commemorative book, among the members' short bios was Donald Montgomery, who by then lived in Auburn Hills and had six grandchildren. An Army photo shows his hat skewed to the right and an ample smile framed by dark eyebrows. "Introduced to airplane strafing Christmas 1944," the text below the photo reads in a precursor to his trademark understatement.

Andy Ferrara asked Nathan and Sam to write the book's introduction. Their full-page account ends with this:

> Even now, there are some fascist organizations claiming that the Holocaust never happened and Jews invented all the horror stories. Thank God, that you were there . . . you are our best eyewitnesses and can refute their claims.
>
> Please accept this letter of thanks from two very fortunate and eternally grateful brothers.
>
> "He who saves one life is as if he would save the entire world."—Talmud, Tractate Sandhedrin

Back in Podgórze in 1999, Bernard stands with a half-dozen people in the market square directly across from Saint Joseph's Church. For eight straight summers he has guided small groups on a tour of his past, returning to face remnants of Jewish life and the former ghetto and Plaszów camp in a new way.

A pile of grey hair sweeps below his beret and over the collar of a blue windbreaker. His voice is assured, a well-practiced momentum rolling in his narrative. From time to time Bernard punctuates his talk in exclamatory riffs, asking group members, *You understand what I'm saying?* This is not a tour for those with short attention spans, nor the superficial visitor. While he continues going back to these places in an attempt to make himself whole, it's become less about him.

Offen tells the tourists bundled similarly in rain gear that as a child he had to be careful walking near this church, especially during the Christian holidays. "Depending on how antisemitic the priest was, the more dangerous it was for us," he says.

One woman doesn't get it. She asks, "Dangerous in what way?" and Bernard briefly explains the twisted Easter fears of the slaughtered lamb and Christ-killing by Jews. He punctuates this by implying that a similar slander continues to trickle below the surface; not from the church any more, but from a society that resists facing its prejudices and history. Students "need to be taught, they need to be challenged," he declares. Walking the same ground even five years earlier, Offen had caught himself feeling too afraid to look up at the church spires again. Yet he made himself go inside. Crossing down the nave, Bernard found a pew from which to finally regard what had felt like the antithesis of a sanctuary.

What had emerged as his great hope—enlightening a new generation of witnesses—felt illusory much of the time. In Poland, where he was beginning to spend half of each year, some schools' fledgling efforts to teach the Holocaust discouraged him. Although celebrations of Jewish culture had been rekindled and a Museum of Judaism had been established in Kraków's Kazimierz district where seven synagogues remained, Bernard's affiliations with local teachers and cultural groups usually fizzled after a brief promise.

Returning from the United States in the spring, he operated largely alone, posting handbills and fliers along the streets, though in later years groups from as far away as Spain would track him down to educate their students. He hungered to share his history, and the lack of interest could be painful. "Sometimes there are no people to tell stories to," he explained, noting that he frequently did not charge for the tour. Their reluctance, and even denial, became understandable. "People don't want to hear something bad," he told me later. "It's not an irrational behavior." It wasn't much different back in the States, where he felt indifference to his message of confronting trauma head-on.

He pressed ahead, befriending other survivors and meeting an array of people committed to peaceful conflict resolution. He met a French Jew, a hidden child during the war who started a nonprofit focused on fostering healthy family relationships, traveling with her family to Kraków. A

Buddhist priest from Santa Fe informed him further about bridging the deep gulf between victims and perpetrators, leading a five-day retreat among clerics of many religious stripes to bear witness at Auschwitz-Birkenau.

While a salve to his soul, these new connections prompted more questions. In order to fully discover their common blood, he wondered whether young people from around the world should visit places like the camps and "touch the roots of suffering," or if that was really the best way to engage a new generation. "In so many ways, our culture is in a situation of undisclosed grief," he wrote. Continuing, Bernard posited:

> "We seem to have made ourselves fundamentally numb because the reality we live in is too much to face. Suffering is relative, each person has his or her own pain, a sustained horror that is something extremely difficult to grasp. Maybe staying too much within the identity of Auschwitz is less than helpful. Maybe that identity has to be transcended in order to be fully healed."

After leading another small group in Kraków, Bernard interviews three people at an outdoor cafe on camera. One woman, an American, tells him that while walking the streets of the former ghetto and the Plaszów camp, she was able to step out of her usual world. Yet, "I still can't understand it," Emily Chapman says, "I can't see how someone could go through that. I can't understand how you feel. But I do feel that people should not forget and appreciate what you're trying to do."

A German woman who took the tour confides that she struggles with her own guilt. Kristine Kulk sees racism and sexism on the rise in her country. "But I got a powerful feeling," she tells Bernard. "What you did to express your resistance and oppression, I was really moved."

A local man perhaps in his late thirties, Robert Kardzi, claims to have been deceived—but not by Offen. Countless times he had passed buildings in Podgórze that were once Jewish bakeries or Hebrew schools, without a trace of recognition of their former identity. "Because nobody has told me about these things, these places, these stories," Kardzi says. "Perhaps if not for you, I wouldn't know that, ever."

In one of Offen's films, members of another group stroll across some gentle hills nearly overgrown with brush and small trees. Bernard tells them about the nearby Julag camp where his uncle sheltered him, and he points to the site of the Plaszów execution pits. They reach a monument to its victims. One plaque begins with something like, "In this place human speech does not have the words to describe . . ." The camera cuts to Bernard walking down a path ahead of the six tourists.

"It's been a little hard on me, I want to end right now," he says, almost out of breath.

I'm complete for right now.

Much of this puzzled his brothers and extended family. Sam and Nathan could not grasp the New Age stuff.

Zen and the art of motorcycle—what? Where are you now? A sweat lodge near Taos? Tucumcari? The hell if I know.

Based north of San Francisco, or sometimes traveling in a Sunrader camper he called "Sun Lover," Bernard might as well have been on grass-fed Mars. Around this time he began living with his Polish girlfriend, Krysia, an affluent, well-educated Krakówian whom another survivor introduced him to. After spending half the year in Poland, the couple traveled the States and Hawaii during the fall and winter, soaking up vistas until Krysia's visa ran out. She paid the bills and encouraged him to continue his internal probing. When Bernard breezed through Detroit for a few days, Sam scolded him, "Why aren't you staying here a month?" He missed out on much of his sons becoming men.

Over time, both Nathan and Sam began to accept Bernard's drive to lead the tours. Teaching people to never forget and put pieces together—that much they got. Not so much his bent toward what their brother calls self-determination in the process of healing, or actively examining his experiences. Once again, they suggested he find a good paying job.

To Sam's daughter, Gail, her uncle's documentary films and later a book about his past and path toward healing are impenetrably dark and difficult. His book does not always flow chronologically as he spades in descriptions of stops on his Kraków walking tour along with anecdotes and history. For many years she couldn't have a conversation with him that didn't involve the

Shoah and how he was feeling. A friend in Poland called him a "professional survivor," perhaps milking it beyond limits. He was obsessed.

Fifty years later, the violinist picked up a faint smell of horses inside the old synagogue. It was as if particles of hay and sweet grains lingered with oiled leather, drifting in dust as he moved through the beige-colored galleries. A taint of ammonia from urine seeped through what had been a lime-covered floor. Herwig Strobl could almost feel their warm breaths.

In one sense Strobl might have been considered an interloper, a voyeur at the Izaak Synagogue, a Baroque-era building in Kazimierz. The Austrian was the son of a Nazi party boss, a child just four years old when the war ended.

He grew up in Linz, and as an adult became uncomfortable with the secrets and denial embedded throughout the hardened Mühlviertel region. An accomplished composer and performer, he came from a family of musicians and teachers, at first following the course that had been set for him.

When Strobl's father returned from an American prison a few years after the war, he started a family orchestra: nine-year-old Herwig was told to learn the fiddle, while his three brothers played other strings and drums, and their mother a harmonium. Their repertoire included songs from popular Viennese operettas whose composers fused waltzes with Hungarian folk songs, including so-called Gypsy folk dances. While he didn't know this as a boy, the sound that Strobl grew to love most closely resembled the instrumental music dear to Eastern Europe's Jews.

This was klezmer, Yiddish folk tunes.

As a man in his forties switching his life onto a new track, Strobl dedicated himself to playing their music. He felt deeply touched by both the sadness and happiness in the tunes, and by a parallel sonorous sweep in his country's history. He began introducing audiences to an enigmatic chunk of a culture that had been threatened with burial. While classically trained and a longtime member of the Linz Chamber Orchestra, Herwig took to the streets, busking on plazas and joining music festivals. He formed his own ensemble with a guitarist and an accordion player, performing his interpretations of songs across the continent. And while first immersing himself in klezmer, Strobl also began telling some of his family's story, and gathering those of other Linzers.

One night in 1994, a thin, bearded hippie with a greying ponytail approached Strobl after his trio gave a concert in Kraków. Herwig found Bernard to be incredibly open; it was as if they had been longtime friends. Bernard suggested he go experience the acoustics at the Izaak Synagogue. Although Offen had never worshipped there as a child, he had seen the recent restoration inside, with scrubbed frescoes of Hebrew prayers and symbols on its walls below soaring vaulted ceilings. Most acutely though, Bernard had heard something extraordinary in the halls, a reverberation of sound that took seven seconds to complete. Showing his first film there to small audiences around that time, to whoever wanted to see it, or sometimes just him and a girlfriend, Offen remarked on the delayed echo effect.

It was as if Bernard had introduced his new friend to a fresh muse, setting him to work. "For me it was an inspiration for poetic remembrance of old Jewish life and worship, and it sparked my imagination," Strobl explained years later. "What I would share in the process of remembrance that Bernard had given to so many people."

Entering the synagogue Strobl was transported to the prolific Krakóvian bard, Mordechai Gebirtig. He considered the people who had once worshipped there. Like Offen, he questioned, *Who were the members? Where did they live? Did they survive?* "This kind of building does not come out of nowhere," Bernard told him.

He thought, *My goodness, I must do his songs.* Strobl went deeper, contacting a collector of Gebirtig's music. He began practicing in a modern church in Linz with acoustics similar to the synagogue. Following a concert in Aachen, Germany, he asked violinist Falk Peters to replicate a custom violin called a Braccioline d'amore, which Peters had made for himself.

With its five strings and an additional sixth resonant one, the Renaissance-era instrument produced an uncanny deep timbre, an elongated voicing that would stretch even further in the synagogue's sound chamber. Notes were suspended and dipped quickly like groups of tiny shore birds hanging and darting in the wind, phrases hummed and crackled along the walls.

After a year Strobl thought he was nearly ready to return to Kraków. But his son, Axl, a sound engineer, said not quite. *Dad, you'd better practice a half-year more.*

Bernard and Herwig were unlikely collaborators only in a superficial sense. While playing hundreds of concerts, Strobl's appreciation of klezmer was infused both by guilt for his nation's sins and a drive to purge his own sense of having been "kept dull" for forty years. Unlike in Germany, which he saw facing its past with determination, attempting to make amends for moral and psychological wounds while educating new generations, he found that many Austrians had ducked their own responsibility. Perpetrators remained almost everywhere, processions of those who had marched well inside the outer ring of indifference. Yet his government's policy had been neglect and denial, as what Strobl called "the Kurt Waldheim syndrome" had revealed, referring to the former United Nations Secretary-General who lied about his role as a *Wehrmacht* intelligence officer. Among his countrymen, the only true victims were the descendants of men like Waldheim and his own father. Herbert Strobl, while a talented cellist and pianist, had been at minimum a witness to the burning of villages in Ukraine.

Herwig had taught secondary school in a district shadowed by the former Gusen and Mauthausen camps. Yet no one, none of his colleagues or the townspeople, seemed to talk about the years of destruction and exclusion. The grey Danube froze over in a vast silence. Around this time his father warned Herwig not to get involved with a young woman who had told his son that she was Jewish, saying she "would never come into our clan." Upon meeting her again sixteen years later, Strobl apologized for having cut off their relationship, and the woman told him she had been joking about her identity. He could not shake off the "joke" as he cut ties to the church, got divorced, and felt cast off by his family. Herwig went further into the folk tunes and traveled to Israel.

Also a writer and a poet, Strobl published a book of stories told by people in his region who finally unburdened themselves. Some of his family's once unutterable paradoxes emerged as well. While his father had completely embraced Hitlerism, the SS at Hartheim Castle euthanized two aunts who suffered mental breakdowns, half an hour from his home, in one of most hideous scenes of mass extermination of both civilians and POWs. The remote former asylum for imbeciles was converted into a killing mill for perhaps thirty thousand handicapped and so-called mentally ill people, in addition to those victims from Mauthausen and its sub-camps. His aunts were gassed in the same chamber where some of Sam and Nathan Offen's workmates died. Herwig spent a night in the former doctor's quarters there, wanting to know what it felt like sleeping where a murderer had lived— around the same time Bernard stayed overnight in the commandant's office at Auschwitz. Later Strobl produced music for a play about the atrocities at Hartheim.

His fiddle told the story, his playing burst open a channel. It brought some audiences to an intersection of melancholy and gay, crossing between each in "a symbolic attempt to right wrongs." Penetrating recesses that language fails to reach, the music ushered in at least a momentary connection with the very traditions, the same oscillating life, that many of their relatives and neighbors had tried to wipe out.

Sometimes tossing a shock of frosted hair as he strummed, Strobl urged his audiences to go further. His bow scratched and plucked high on the frets, he soared in streams and doubled back, he broke into minor keys, casting allusions to Johann Strauss and J.S. Bach, all the masters he had grown up with. Knowing that words have gaps and are easily misinterpreted, he realized that *by just playing, inside the music you can relate and tell it again. Always my idea was, it's necessary to transport the idea of the song and the background of how I got to the song, and the stories people want to know, and the experience.*

At seventy-five years old, he questioned his own reach. "Was I successful in the respect of reaching other people's hearts?" Strobl wrote me in 2015. "Did Austrians change their minds to become more aware and more empathetic?"

It is after midnight in July 1996. Meeting by chance again in Kraków, Strobl and Offen have gone to the synagogue to record. While they had not been in touch for almost two years, this was more than a fortuitous run-in. Herwig returned to Kazimierz with intention, but earlier this night it had been too noisy outside the building to make music. Walking through the quarter with his son afterwards, they met a group of people standing around Bernard.

This is perfect, he thought. He had several of Gebirtig's songs ready. Now we must improvise.

> And you stand around and stare
> While the flames grow higher.
> And you stand around and stare
> While our shtetl burns.

Three blows pound a heavy door.
"*Aufmachen!*"
"Open up!"
"*Aufmachen!*"

Someone enters the synagogue's gallery, and Herwig begins bowing in short bursts, perhaps martellato hammering. He concedes to a furious rhythm from boots striking the floor around him: Bernard.

The steps come closer, menacing footfalls of the night, rounding from a distance. Herwig unleashes early strains of a lament, a taut and screeching melody, trying to build upon it. Then it's cut off. Bernard yelling, "*S'Brent!*" "It burns!"

"*S'Brent!*"

Twice, thrice, away from the bursting light. His cry circles the cavernous hall, twining into one.

Discordant notes pierce the air, shrill and sparking. They fall back into what seems like a reverse scale. Herwig reaches, caressing toward his range. Then he settles back. Bernard's boots clack incessantly. The marching pits one's stomach lining, until you hear it gurgle, emptying.

His stomps threaten to drown out the melody, but Strobl persists. He adds mournful phrases of a German song about two kings' children who, although meant for each other, would never be able to be together. He peels slices of a Bach sonata. His violin-viola aches, and another spiral of notes crash. A flurry like doves flits toward the high ceiling.

Wondering to his friend, he thinks, "How could you creep into German boots?"

You were so weak, but strong the same moment—having overcome all the humiliation, having taken up the task of healing and without accusations showing: I am human, therefore I am witnessing.

Ich bin ein Mensch, deshalb lege ich Zeugnis ab.

The marching fades, and Bernard slams the door shut.

Sam always said he had lived three lives. While born free, he had endured hell. And once in America, he found paradise. If he could taste a scone every day, and forget about washing and waxing his car, that was bliss.

Yet early into his eighties, he was reminded of how paradise is tainted by those who shirk accountability when confronted with the past. Those who declare: Get over it already.

In 2003, the arrest of a tool-and-die maker residing thirty minutes away who had been an SS guard at Mauthausen delivered this crude, backhanded swipe. Johann Leprich had lived in the United States on and off since 1952, only a year after the Offen brothers arrived, lying about his wartime role on his immigration application. Although his identity was later discovered—his US citizenship was revoked in the late eighties, and a Nazi hunter tracked Leprich down a decade later—it took the feds six more years to act.

Agents finally found Leprich cowering in a secret compartment beneath the basement stairs of his brick ranch house. Some of his neighbors in suburban Clinton Township disagreed with making Leprich face the music near the end of his life.

Described as a quiet man, he took evening walks and raised two children with his wife. He tended geraniums among pristine flowerbeds, and kept two ceramic deer and a cottontail bunny statue beside a blue spruce. Plump tomatoes were shared generously with the neighbors, one of whom said Leprich confided that he had worked as a concentration camp guard. "You couldn't have asked for better people," an elderly woman next door commented. A photo taken after his arrest showed a clean-shaven man with jelled silver hair neatly combed back, perhaps a hint of regret showing from his dark eyes and heavily creased mouth.

In 1944, when he was nineteen, Leprich wore the skull-and-crossbones symbol of the Death's Head Battalion on his uniform, among the notorious guards who patrolled the Mauthausen perimeter and oversaw work crews. Perhaps he, too, fired upon or pushed prisoners down into the quarry as Sam and Nathan kept moving. Later, he may have had to take this up with his maker alongside one of the ditches. Perhaps. The house Leprich bought in 1976 had grown in value by twenty-fold. He cashed social security checks and renewed his driver's license without stirring trouble.

Despite that Johann Leprich had fled to Canada after a deportation hearing a decade earlier, once he was located near Detroit again, the government never deported him. Neither Germany, Hungary, nor his native Romania would accept him—a scenario that thwarted attempts by US authorities to deport other suspected death camp guards around this time. By 2009, a Spanish judge issued international arrest warrants for Leprich and several others. Despite Leprich's claim that he had been coerced into becoming a camp guard, Sam Offen's friend Rabbi Rozenzveig would have none of it. "Nobody was forced to be an SS guard," he said. "They volunteered because they didn't have to go to the front lines."

While some of the ex-Nazi's neighbors offered pale excuses—"Do you think that when you take him your people are coming back?" another woman asked a Jewish investigator—Sam was drawn in. It got under his skin, and his daughter once again saw rare flashes of anger.

Unlike those neighbors, he could not just forget. "How can they claim these people are not murderers?" he told a reporter. "If we survivors never get justice, then how can we say anything will change?" He followed the case tirelessly, penning letters to the newspapers, clipping articles, and giving more interviews. Unlike some other camp guards like John Demjanjuk, the retired Ohio autoworker whose deportation received widespread attention, Leprich lived out his life in the States. Sam refused to budge. On many days he wore his Zachor pin, with three Hebrew letters declaring, "Never again."

Sam and Hyla continued their mobile love affair.

Most winters they drove to Florida, staying at hotels for a month or a few more weeks while visiting relatives and friends. Rarely in a hurry to get there, the two took minor routes and back roads whenever possible. Their favorite destinations were old-school Florida attractions like the sponge divers in Tarpon Springs, alligator wrestling, and watching human mermaids from a submerged theatre at the Weeki Wachee hot springs. Besides Sam scouring his beloved maps for new places, they would spot things on a billboard and go check them out. He could scarcely resist a "Souvenir" sign and didn't mind stopping for directions, since that was a way to meet the locals. When the couple returned home, inevitably, sacks of grapefruits and bagged chocolate coconut patties were distributed to all.

As part of his new routes back and forth, Sam sometimes found a school or library with a fresh audience to stop at. Hyla never failed to accompany him, whether close to home or hundreds of miles away. Her daughter, for one, didn't quite know how she was able to endure his talk over and over again. "I could only manage once or twice a year because it was too depressing," Gail says. Although she sat off to the side as he embraced the spotlight, it was obvious to most in the way Sam carried himself with Hyla that she always remained the apple of his eye. As the years rolled by and her bob cut greyed, their mutual devotion strengthened.

The couple dropped by Whitwell, Tennessee, a former coal-mining town on the edge of Appalachia. He had read about the world's first children's Holocaust memorial taking shape there, in the perhaps unlikely form of a massive paper clip collection. The school initiated the project as a way to teach students about tolerance and diversity, setting a goal to collect six million paper clips in remembrance of every Jewish victim. With eighth-graders doing most of the work, they surpassed eleven million to include the total number of estimated victims of all creeds, nearly tripling that amount later. The drive inspired a book and a documentary film while lighting a flame among other enterprising educators and students.

Sam got hold of David Smith, an assistant principal and teacher at the local middle school who had helped launch a voluntary after-school class for eighth-graders and their parents. One student came up with the idea of collecting paper clips after reading how Norwegians had worn them on their lapels during the war to protest the deportations of their neighbors. The group set out scavenging through drawers at home and getting donations from local businesses, thinking they could make a clip sculpture for victims, while someone set up an online form on the school's web site. By the end of the first year they collected 100,000, and things really took off when two German journalists found the page while researching survivors. The couple, both longtime White House correspondents, was intrigued. They interviewed school administrators, a social studies teacher leading the class and some of the kids. When their stories were published in a group of European newspapers, tens of thousands of more paper clips began flooding in from overseas.

Peter Schroeder and Dagmar Schroeder-Hildebrand knew they needed to experience Whitwell. Nestled in a valley not far from Chattanooga, the small town had only a handful of black and Latino families, and Fundamentalist Protestant churches were its bedrock. Few residents had ever met a Jew, let alone anyone from Deutschland.

Not knowing what to expect, the Schroeders found displays outside a classroom, a wall with pasted faces behind real barbed wire. Continuing on Wednesday afternoons, a new batch of students sorted letters and counted all sorts of clips: traditional silver-tone, plastic and artsy, heart-shaped red ones, sent by other kids, celebrities, even presidents. Some German middle school students sent a suitcase with notes of apology to Anne Frank, and more than 30,000 letters eventually arrived, which the teens saved along with the attached art work. Having reached out to broaden their view of the world, the world responded.

The couple were so taken they wrote a book about this. Reading some letters with paper clips that were sent to themselves, they understood that each one had its own story. "We are the last generation who will know this," Dagmar told a magazine writer. "We have a certain responsibility as Germans."

Not long before Sam contacted David Smith, the assistant principal, the Schroeders had an idea to help solve a storage problem at the middle school: finding one of the cattle cars used to deport victims. They approached a German railroad company, among those that had once profited from a "cargo of death" while workers wore earplugs to shut out the assault on humanity. The firm's president wished them well but claimed there were no boxcars left. The couple kept looking, locating one in a museum close to Berlin, which was shipped to Whitwell just a few weeks after the 2001 terrorist attacks.

On their way to Florida the next winter, Sam and Hyla stopped at the school. Smith had already met scores of survivors during the project. Intrigued to catch glimpses of their lives and their feelings toward perpetrators, he wondered what had pulled them through. Speaking with Sam at length, he was struck by something very different than he felt from most of the others.

Smith asked Offen how he could remain so upbeat and trusting in people. Offen explained that this sprang from "his faith, his hope, his love of his people and his love of his family, and what had been instilled in him from birth by his family, his hope for a better day." Smith continued, "He basically said he was raised a certain way and still believed that way, and even the events of his life didn't change his beliefs, or who he was."

He always had that hope of a broader day, and a better day.

Much of their conversation continued alongside the cattle car, which the kids decorated with butterflies to signal new life. Offen was interested in how the school nurtured tolerance, and Smith shared tidbits of the curriculum. He stressed that while collecting paper clips was student-driven, the key understanding teachers sought was acceptance, as students moved up the critical thinking ladder from knowledge and application to synthesis and beyond. "We always taught our kids, tolerance is not enough," he told me, "because if you say you're going to tolerate someone, that's not always an acceptable thing."

Sam regarded the car with its two fixed axles and four wheels set on fifty feet of rail. By then it housed more than eleven million clips that students had decided to place in glass partitions, brought in one wheelbarrow full at a time—six million in one end of the car, five million at the other. Another 1,600 clips were kept aside in a box to represent the number of townspeople, some of whom had planted a garden around it.

Walking up a ramp, Sam took a moment with his wife as Smith asked his kids to give them a little time. They may not have noticed or recalled its number: 011–993. But the car was similar to others used in the transports. He went inside.

Sam asked someone where it came from, and the answer was striking: the car had been abandoned in Sobibor, the site of a death camp in eastern Poland along the border with Ukraine. In his mind, at least, it may have passed through Kraków.

Not long afterwards, he sent Smith a note thanking the kids and adults for "awakening the world."

Whitwell's children's memorial continued to open for Friday tours, conducted by students who tell its story and show the artifacts. A plaque there reads: "Never doubt that a group of thoughtful, committed students can change the world—one class at a time."

Long encouraged by Hyla to put his life's story down in words, Sam bought packets of yellow legal pads and began writing. Well into her seventies by then, Hyla's memory was beginning to fail, and she was diagnosed with Alzheimer's. As she became sicker, it drove him to write faster. He so wanted her to read it, and she did.

They celebrated a golden wedding anniversary in June 2002 with a brunch at The Whitney, an iconic mansion in Detroit built by a lumber baron. Close to fifty family members including Nathan and Bernard joined them for champagne toasts and eggs Benedict as they sat beside Tiffany-stained glass windows and polished jasper columns. Amidst this ornate setting, the speeches given by Sam and the others were largely homespun, and he retold how he asked Hyla's permission to apply for their joint fishing license.

As the disease progressed her husband assumed full care for her. He brought Hyla to a nearby adult memory care center for activities on many weekdays, while he could go do his own thing, sometimes stopping by the fur store in his role as emeritus salesman and mentor. He hired caretakers for home and eventually, after putting it off as long as he could, had to move her into a nursing home. It was one of the worst days of his adult life and he visited at least once a day. Gradually, while her mother no longer seemed to recall the three of them by name, Gail knew she remained connected in some visceral way—"a sound, a smell, a visual . . . she always knew we were someone she loved."

Gail continued typing her father's longhand for his book, and in it he touched upon other highlights as well, cracking a few closed doors. Early in 2005, the Offen brothers and their partners attended a banquet in Miami Beach where Steven Spielberg was honoring the New Cracow Friendship Society at the luxurious Fontainebleau Hotel. While they didn't meet the filmmaker, they each caught up with some former neighbors and regaled in the moment.

One bid to recover a key piece of the past was stymied. Seeking to find their mother's needlepoint picture of Moses, the Offens finally tracked down the Ciesliks from Kraków. But the father, who had moved to Chicago after the war, was dead, his wife had dementia, and the children still in Poland said they knew nothing about the heirloom.

Eventually Gail added a daughter's tribute to the manuscript. She might have included how her dad learned to convince himself into thinking he was actually not being tickled, an act of suppression that otherwise might have been hilarious, or perhaps still was. "I think that was part of his Jedi mind trip, where he somehow could disassociate himself from the pain," she said. "Or it was just mind over matter for him."

After his memoir was published in 2005, Hyla could no longer accompany him to presentations and book signings. He sat with her every day, and in July 2008, Sam lost his bride of fifty-six years.

Nathan's daughters could not hide their bitterness. Yes, he had taken good care of their mother; there was no doubting that. He had certainly provided for them. But many times their father was an uncompromising hard ass, straining to express his love when they were little.

His seventy-fifth birthday was meant to be a celebration. He and Gloria, his partner of six years, invited their new friends from Long Island and members of the Kraków friends group, and all of his family. Ruth stood before the room with her son, and told them, "Well, I hardly know my father, I hardly know him." Gail came up with her son to give Nathan a watch, smiling. She said, "I am presenting my dad a watch, so that he will know when he comes to me, he will know to be at the right time."

Their father took up painting a year or two after their mother died. Sudden bursts of floral colors and still lifes emerged in a studio at Gloria's house, which seemed discordant to them. Where did this energy come from, this eye for beauty? Begonias, now? He was buying a condo overlooking a golf course in Florida, and she'd be there too. Meanwhile, Nathan kept improving at tennis, even mashing down younger men. He became a champ rather than one of the downtrodden. Ruth, at least, gradually became aware that playing the sport allowed him to see both sides.

His oldest daughter began to accept why both her parents had shielded their identities. Yet reaching this awareness had scarred her. Ruth left home soon after high school and never returned for more than short junctures, joining the counterculture that stumbled through the seventies, moving around frequently, marrying and divorcing. Eventually she settled in the San Juan Islands near Seattle, where she operated an art gallery for more than twenty-five years.

Ruth came to know her father's duality, perhaps some of the ambivalence embodied by many survivors. Condemning evil in the world and also believing in the goodness of individuals; feeling an irretrievable loss of self and family while restarting and bringing forth new life; and being vulnerable, yet also stronger. Her father, Ruth told me, "is sensitive and he's not; there's some concept of understanding missing. I think in some respects living through what he did took away his heart and soul. My parents gave me the gift of survival. My job now is to live my life, which is a totally different story."

A few years after that caustic birthday gathering, Nathan was out in California attending a wedding with Sam and Hyla. They decided to visit Ruth up in Friday Harbor. Taking a ferry across Puget Sound, something else began to open in him as Nathan finally glimpsed her life on the lush, rugged island. He felt truly welcomed and enjoyed the week with her and his grandson, Zachary. Four years later, in 2008 Ruth convinced her dad to travel to Poland together. She may have needed it more than he did—reaching her mid-fifties, finally able to reconcile her parents' flaws after counseling and an awakening, what she called "the end of the growth for me." Their trip was a mutual gift.

They stayed in Kraków, even meeting her uncle for a difficult but unforgettable reunion. Nathan and Bernard stood in Plac Zgody where her grandmother and aunt were last seen alive, arguing over different accounts of what happened. She played referee; of course, her father was the one who had been right there. Seeing the camps was brutal, but it reinforced an appreciation of her father's sporadic witnessing. "I think it's something that really excited him to share his life and his story," she said later. "I'm hopeful he can still continue." From time to time, Ruth would still admonish him to no longer drive at night, or not to go out without having a nap. In moments, she said, it was "like having a two-year-old."

In the foreword to her father's book, Ruth Offen wrote: "As one ages, one rediscovers one's own story and the need to share it with family members and, perhaps, with the world."

She ended with: "It is now the time of sharing and forgiveness of others."

24

HOPE FOR A BROADER DAY

. . . .

Nathan chose not to answer this question from seventeen-year-old Elvis Batiz.

"Did you ever stop believing in God?"

Offen had just finished a forty-five minute talk to about three hundred students at my high school, his voice echoing off the brick auditorium walls. Elvis remained seated a few rows from the stage as the presenter prepared to leave. Visibly depleted, Nathan began moving slowly up the aisle when the lanky junior spoke up.

Nathan paused, telling a teacher accompanying him that he could not answer the question since he assumed the young man was Christian. "I don't want to confuse him," he snarled. It was his second talk on this warm spring day. In the morning he'd been out to Deerfield Academy, a prep school in western Massachusetts stocked with the privileged, including his grandson, Jason. Now he was at the former "Dot High" beside Dorchester's Codman Square, thick in an inner city neighborhood throbbing with families trying to make it. He continued toward the exit.

So Elvis wanted to know if Nathan Offen had lost his faith. What a great question, I said aloud a moment later, squatting down to speak eye level with him.

This polite young man—whose family came from Honduras and now lived close to the scenes of several recent shootings in Forest Hills; Elvis, who had reported feeling sick during second period a day earlier and by the afternoon said the nurse told him to eat more breakfast; who struggled with past tense verbs and pronouns and his spelling—he stone got it, listening with intention and noting both Nathan's literal and body language, informed by his own understanding of faith. Elvis peeled back layers of our human condition in a three-point swish. All net.

What a great question.

Nathan told our students he never gave up hope. This was before I had met him or his brothers, or any other Holocaust survivor I could recall. Yet as he spoke, the words seemed musty and stale, like a room where the drapes have been closed for some time.

What he mostly conveyed was that he actually had survived on hate. His audience, mainly black and Latino students, most of whom had read *Night* and studied aspects of the Shoah, waited attentively during short pauses as he gathered himself before recalling brief grim details of the roundups and killings. Just one student asked annoyingly whether Offen had met Hitler, and others hissed at the query. Someone else asked why Jews did not resist. Nathan cringed at that, offering a tart rebuttal. No one interrupted him.

A day after the talk, Elvis and I discussed why Nathan did not directly respond to him. Writing about it in his English class journal, details of Offen's suffering gripped him: "Also I learn that the reason why he goes around and talk [*sic*] about the Holocaust is because he feels as that he still is alive to tell the story that some people think did not happen—this shows that millions was effect [*sic*] also the bad things they did to kids, shooting them, using them as [targets], and throwing them out of the train."

One reason he posed that question, Elvis wrote, was "that growing up my parents also taught me that God is real and that's what gave them hope during all their bad times."

"Maybe that was the question that would break him," I offered. Elvis looked at me with dark, unflinching eyes. We didn't need to say much more.

I put that conversation aside, but his question lingered below the surface. Later I realized how off track I had been.

Shoes crunching gravel augment a conversation I'm taping with Ellery Kirkconnell as we trudge past the ruins of prisoners' barracks at Dachau. He is among the seniors who've been studying genocide in a class taught by two of my colleagues, a freckle-faced guy I've known since he was a freshman. Ellery is inspirational to many of his teachers. Self-driven and articulate, he plays squash and attends summer programs at Harvard and will soon receive a full scholarship to Oberlin College. Eye-popping two-tone shoes and an occasional Cardigan sweater punctuate his style. He is passionate about combating intolerance, especially discrimination against one's race and sexual orientation, having experienced both of these firsthand.

The Dachau Concentration Camp is our first jarring stop at on this eleven-day trip, which Denise and I have joined as chaperones. We arrived in Munich the previous morning in a hazy onset of jet lag, setting out on a walking tour of the Nazi party's rise in the Bavarian capital. Brendan Malanga, a history teacher who, while affable, won't hesitate to tell a student he's being a shithead, guides us to places such as the party headquarters at the Braune Hause. We go to a square beside a nineteenth-century war memorial where the Nazis' premature push to take over the regional government came to an end. Later that night, after most everyone has eaten kabobs standing beside a kiosk and students return to the crammed hostel, a few of us walk to the famous Hofbrauhaus for a beer. The cavernous hall feels oddly inscrutable to me, as if something lurks behind a veneer of relaxed conversation. I catch myself looking for symbols or clues to the past as we walk through to the biergarten, rather than to a second floor hall where Hitler made some famous speeches.

The next day, a short distance from the city, Ellery and his classmates creep through Dachau's replica barracks and a museum chronicling Nazi atrocities and the sprawling network of camps. Built to initially imprison communists and other political opponents, this was the party's first regular concentration camp and held at least 188,000 people during the next dozen years. More than 28,000 people perished here or at one of Dachau's thirty-plus sub-camps after 1940.

When American forces reached Dachau they found more than thirty coal cars filled with decomposing bodies, and more than 30,000 prisoners still alive. The students have been introduced to facts like these during their yearlong Facing History and Ourselves course, but seeing this up close is quite another thing. As they view photos of prisoners used as experimental lab rats, exposed to stuff like malaria and hypothermia, I notice a few seniors freeze as if their few remaining shreds of disbelief have been overrun.

Walking outside together just minutes later, Ellery asks, "Why target a group of people, why them? Why must one group of people feel that they are superior to others? Why must they sacrifice the lives of others in order to satisfy their self-esteem? Why must you feel it's okay to annihilate a race just to satisfy your greediness? And that question may not be answered today or tomorrow or next year, or who knows? But it's a question that we find ourselves even today contemplating and stumbling across.

"You must realize that selfishness and greed can really take a toll on people."

I wonder about his generation's grasp of this—and the depth of my own. Even if we get it, do we ever apply this knowledge to new scenarios? Hell, have I ever put myself on the line? I pose to him, "Where do we find an answer to that, where do we turn, because as you said, we have not yet?"

"As corny and cliché as it may sound, treat others as you may want to be treated?" Ellery responds, the hint of another query lingering for just a moment.

I'm also interested in how he first felt walking into this place.

"A lot of emotions definitely came in . . . all I can say is I've been classified and put into different minority groups. So maybe that's why I've been so accepting toward others [who] are different."

Ellery also feels some kind of presence of the victims and survivors. "On this land, many people were starving and people were dying and many were being abused," he tells me. "And that to me brought fears, because it's weird but I almost felt like a presence still at the camp. As if, yeah, they were liberated [that] year but their souls still remain in this camp, and the reason why I say that is because till this day this world still continues to go on with apathy, and many people say they will never continue to allow this to happen again, but you see it coming back on so many different levels."

I turn off the tape recorder as we approach a brick building housing the gas chamber.

Two days later, following a welcome break of sightseeing one afternoon at Neuschwanstein Castle—apparently the source of Walt Disney's fairyland creation—and visiting sites in Prague, our bus brings us to Kraków.

Staying on the outskirts of Kazimierz, once the main Jewish district, nearly everyone has some free time to roam inside the nearby medieval Old Town as tourists. We regard its large market square that was laid out in 1257, where a bugler plays every hour from a tower at Saint Mary's Basilica, and Denise and I will check out a cafe or two during the evenings. While not yet fully aware that the Offens and other Jews were forbidden from entering this same area of the city by 1940, we are not quite typical visitors, and neither are the students. Inquisitive and often boisterous, there's a mix of black and white kids, a clutch of girls with Dominican and Puerto Rican roots, and others born in Albania and China. They are well prepared, and fully tuned into the empathy that Ellery Kirkconnell carries.

It's been nearly a year since Nathan Offen spoke to our students. And while I still know very little about his coming of age in this city, some key gaps are about to be filled in.

First we must go to Auschwitz, where one's senses are attacked in the ways you might expect, and some that cannot be anticipated. Near the parking area, the presence of a hotel and an Internet café ticks off at least one of our charges, who resents what he views as a bald attempt to cash in on the visitors. We halt at the front entrance, struck by the infamous, insidious words above the gate: *Arbeit Macht Frei* (work makes one free). Shuffling through the museum itself is unnerving. We wind through narrow halls into rooms filled with shoes, suitcases and purses, glasses, and hair, all stored behind Plexiglas dividers. Feeling the need to get some fresh air, I find myself focusing outside on things that were not here six decades ago, like a cluster of birch trees near the commandant's villa that appear bowed by an unseen weight.

Samaria Austin, bright and obstinate, sporting long black braids, walks alongside the old rail bed with Denise and I near the end of the tour. She asks me whether I think any of the guards ever vomited, knowing what they did. I'm not sure I ever answer her fully, watching as Samaria suddenly remarks on some blue wildflowers growing between the creosote ties, as she stoops down reaching for this unexpected, shimmering sign.

Returning to Kraków that afternoon, about half our group takes off on a bicycle tour from the Old Town's main square. The sun is strong and everyone seems a bit lighter moseying through the side streets of Kazimierz in the open air. Our bearded guide, an American transplant, offers some facts about the former Jewish community here, and we stop to take pictures looking into a Hebrew cemetery. Making our way into Podgórze, the Offens' old neighborhood, he points out at least one ghetto gate and sections of the remaining wall. Suddenly we come upon a small square that is devoid of people. Instead, Plac Zgody is populated by seventy large metal chairs, sculptures spaced well apart and daring us to identify what the distance means. We fall silent again without even fully knowing.

Renamed as "Ghetto Heroes Square," this is from where Nathan's mother and sister and more than ten thousand others were sent to Bełżec. For decades after the war, the staging area was left as a mangy parking lot. The chairs, our guide explains, are meant to represent both departure and absence in a tribute to ghetto victims. There is a place for candles and reflection, but I notice trash cluttering the ground, and before long we're moving again.

He leads us through the park to a small hill—one of Kraków's ancient mounds, this one likely the resting place of a legendary prince—which we bound up on foot to take in a grand view of the city. One of the girls challenges me to run straight up the grass as she did rather than take the path, and I oblige her. Lingering at the peak, there's a sense of relief as we resume being tourists, huddling together for rounds of photos. On the way back we stop outside of Oskar Schindler's factory and cruise beside the Vistula River, where Krakovians stretch out taking advantage of the spring warmth.

Two days later, Ellery and I talk again on tape as the chartered bus crosses Poland. The emotional intensity and fast pace of the trip is having an effect, as a few snits bubble up among the crankier students. We adults are certainly not immune either, as a whispering, tight clique among some of the lead teachers makes others feel like outcasts. Long stretches of the bus trip east to Majdanek and then back toward Germany are bleak. At a rest stop we notice a prostitute climbing down from a tractor-trailer. Healthy food seems non-existent, and it's hard to make sense of the zloty on the fly. Denise and I continue reading on the drive, and in between I take a few exploratory morning runs with some of the guys.

Despite all of this, Ellery's spirit is intact. On the bus he announces his college selection—Oberlin—delighting his teachers, especially one who hails from Cleveland, prompting a welcome wash of kudos.

I return to an earlier topic: "Do you think people will ever learn, will tolerance ever reign?"

"That's a question that many people will just jump right out and just say 'No,'" Ellery responds. "The people who say no—I like to be a person who's optimistic about the world and the human race. We will find a way to abolish other hate in this world. It's definitely going to take lots of time. I'm a person who believes we'll find solutions to hatred crimes.

"For those who say, 'no, I don't believe anything, I don't believe the human race will progress,' they're just adding more to the negative of it. It's just one at a time. If you start showing your true colors and start living the way that you should be, the world will be a better place for every single one of us. Even on a small scale, other people will notice that."

On the flight home I start writing a poem about our travels. Although we're both a bit tapped, the moral lessons are obvious, and my emotive lens is clear. Many of these young people's questions will reverberate with me during upcoming seasons of teaching, and then as I leave the classroom to begin another trek. It's only when digging further into survivors' testimonies and other perspectives of a post-Auschwitz world that I begin to see how complicated sorting this out really is.

A few months after the Europe trip I meet Sam with Nathan for the first time. Hyla died the previous year, and he is on Long Island for a midsummer visit dovetailing with his eighty-eighth birthday. Both men welcome me warmly inside Nathan and Gloria's ground floor condo, where Sam's Amigo scooter is parked by the door. After I introduce my goals, they quickly urge me to ask questions. Setting a handheld tape recorder on a living room table, some of my queries seem rusty, and others perhaps a tad naive. But these will sharpen soon.

Nathan has no trouble recalling the exchange with Elvis at my school the year before. "I lost faith in God, I was saying to myself, 'Where was God?'" he says. "But my personal belief I did not want to impose on my children. I had no right. Let them develop their own." The same with this earnest stranger in Boston. "I didn't want to answer the question because

I didn't want to mislead him. If he has a strong belief, why would I say my own belief, I'm not a believer or something like that? He's in high school, he's maturing, he's learning, so why would I confuse him?"

He begins explaining why he tried to keep the past from his daughters for so long. "After the war I hated everything so much," he says. "My first born I couldn't even touch her, I felt I didn't deserve it . . . Later on I learned that hate is self-destructive from life experience, my street smarts, fixing things for myself. My nature is to fix things. There is a limit to hate; you have to go on with your life."

As Nathan speaks, his native intonation asserting its dominance, I look into his eyes. Behind thick glasses I sense a swirling acidic storm, strained but not quite bloodshot, determined but not so hard. A survivor's eyes. Gloria tells him that he woke her up screaming the previous night. He remembers this, the clicking steps to that song which celebrates drowning. His recurring nightmare.

It took him longer than his brothers to work these things out, which had its own cost. At this time, Gail and Suzanne rarely speak with their father. He raises the subject as we sit, complaining bitterly that he only sees their busy families once a year, even though they live relatively close. Gloria gives a knowing look, and pleads, "But when they do come . . ." and he abruptly shifts the conversation. A few minutes later she offers the three of us cantaloupe slices and ice water.

He is a bit more pugnacious than cantankerous, eager to rib a waitress he knows about her hair style—"You didn't get any sleep last night, I can tell"—yet his life has its joys. There is tennis three or four times a week—doubles only, at this point. He's still got the thick forearms of a man who has long worked with his hands, and maintains good muscle tone. Nathan clearly relishes his continued vigor; the high cheekbones so prominent in photos of him as a mature adult remain sharp, as if hinting at nascent nobility that refuses to fade. Dozens of his bright floral paintings decorate their apartment. On one hand he's proud of his hobby, recalling occasional art shows he's participated in and how one of his grandchildren once introduced him to someone as a painter. Then he tells me he's given it up because there is no more room to display them.

I ask if he feels he has fulfilled his purpose. "I feel confused," he snarls, though later he becomes more sanguine. He points to hatred of Israel and jealousy over the myriad accomplishments of Jewish scientists. "Education, education of the people," he says in what begins to feel like a rant, though it's not unmerited. "I think the Holocaust will repeat itself, people forget, and there is something about the Jewish people. We are blamed for things."

Sam listens quietly and does not interrupt. Yet he disagrees with some of this. He remains buoyant as he grieves for his wife; few can know fully the toll Alzheimer's took on them both. In contrast to his brother, Sam continues to believe in humanity's beneficent potential. "I'm optimistic the Holocaust will not reoccur, in part by keeping the memories of loved ones alive, and also through teaching," he says when Nathan has finished. "I feel we have good support groups. I'm hopeful future generations will take good care." If you could plant a thousand hearts like his, bulbs tucked a few inches into the soil, what a spring eruption that would bring.

Even Sam's body language is upbeat. He tilts his head back playfully while telling a story, folds his arms as if to caress himself, his soft voice nearly a lisp. Unlike many other survivors, he didn't feel guilty that he made it, and he says that the Shoah does not dominate his life. He tells me a little about the furrier business, and his passion speaking to young audiences. Thousands of students send him letters, some declaring how meeting Offen has changed their life. When he gives talks, "I'm able to speak and then it's over. I don't dwell on my experiences."

It's only when he speaks of Hyla's passing that Sam's eyes and voice drop.

Nearly a quarter century after he began gathering the experiences of the Offens and other survivors, Sid Bolkosky doubted he was actually doing them a service.

Bolkosky sat beside one of his graduate students in a ruffled gray plaid shirt that agreed with the somber tone of his slacks. With his thin face, slightly unkempt white hair and gentle manner, he seemed to fit the part of a self-deprecating history professor. Having done well over one hundred interviews with survivors, he was being a bit hard on himself, while perhaps trying to contain his pessimism. Rubbing his folded hands together, he tilted his head sharply to regard the young woman introducing him on camera, an angle that suggested Bolkosky had spent a lot of time wading through pretty incongruous stuff. This once, he was the one being interviewed.

Their voices counted the most. Ambivalent, at times contradictory in emphasis. Yielding to moral schisms. Not heroic, and rarely triumphant. Broken voices.

"It's been very gratifying, but very difficult," he said a few minutes into the interview. "They're always thinking about it, and talking about it takes it to a different level." Countless times survivors told him they hadn't slept the past few nights and suffered migraines before speaking with him. When Bolkosky's own children were young, he found himself checking on them in bed after waking from his own cattle car nightmares. Years later he realized how his preoccupation had affected his kids, his daughter confiding to a rabbi at her wedding—attended by many survivors—how much those stories dominated her life.

He might have just washed out as a cynic who refilled his glass. But Bolkosky was among only a handful of American scholars who interpreted successive interviews with survivors, gathering their splintered memories amidst the narratives. He was prolific, ultimately interviewing about 150 people and often becoming friends as he followed up with them. He helped build and direct the Voice/Vision Holocaust Survivor Oral History Archive at the University of Michigan-Dearborn, a significant collection that contributes to larger ones at Yale, the United States Holocaust Memorial Museum, and at the Holocaust Memorial Center where Sam Offen spoke regularly.

As classes resumed on the Dearborn campus in 2005, the historian couldn't help signal feeling a bit down. As his colleague Jamie Wraight said later, "I don't think he saw anything good at the end of the day. He saw a lot of loss."

Like many survivors themselves, Sid had long been skeptical of interpreters who sought sweeping lessons and generalized meaning from the Holocaust. He even quit Steven Spielberg's project—which filmed 52,000 people—in the nineties when, according to Wraight, Bolkosky found interviews being framed "trying to find the happy ending." To him, survivors were often contorted, confused, and even contaminated by layers of guilt. Yet their authenticity—a bare inconclusiveness, sometimes coupled with maintaining a moral identity "by holding some inward space of the self untouchable," as he wrote in 2002—had increasingly taken hold.

There was a messiness to many testimonies that he came to appreciate. Their torrents defied written language's serialization of events: fragmented anecdotes, overflowing streams of consciousness, a backpedaling, splintered disorder; halting attempts to construct stories for what cannot be told, and to "translate the language of after into the language of before"; silences between words gnashing as much as words themselves; memories leaching into the present; simultaneous infusions of "external descriptions and internal rumination," with survivors' associations altering what the sight of a chimney, a landfill, or what a loaf of bread meant. "The sheer weight of testimony," Bolkosky offered, "supersedes more controlled texts."

From what they were able to extract and express, many of those he met found shame to be the overriding meaning; silence and darkness and shame forming a pyramid that rose like a miasma of fear from the drained swamps of Płaszów.

Some professed ambivalence about God: Could there be divine responsibility for the Shoah? Was it punishment for having gone astray?

Others such as Abe, a longtime friend of Sid's who grew up in a village in Transylvania, had continued to pray at Auschwitz. Abe's former life had been strictly scripted by secular and religious study. At the camp he cleaned himself of lice, not wanting to die and fearing God for that very reason. Ultimately, was the search for meaning a self-deluding quest? The answer to that pained well-known survivors like Primo Levi, who, unlike Nathan Offen, considered his fate to have been more than blind luck. Levi thought that many of the saved were "preferably the worst: the selfish, violent, insensitive, the collaborators." Surviving to bear testimony was yet another broken construct, he wrote, since, "We, the survivors, are not the true witnesses."

After forty years living in shadows, another survivor named Meilech who grew up in a devout Hasidic family broke his silence during twenty-five hours of interviews with Sid. He was fourteen when Hungarian police sent him and his family to Auschwitz. Like others, he asked later, "What happened to my childhood? Why?" Yet unlike the Offens, following liberation he was unable to summon his former life. Buried was the one patched suit each son wore, Friday nights singing, and his mother's lullabies. He told the professor:

> The question is that a Jew who knows that his wife and children were killed, on Yom Kippur, in the camp, he goes, [*beats breast in ritual penance*] "I sinned; I stole; I cheated." He lost everything, and yet he tells God *he* sinned . . . and you asked me why I don't go back to that way of life again.

With a background in European intellectual history and the development of psychoanalysis, Bolkosky's forte was digging further into how memory works and intersects with the history of literature. He knew his way around the experimental techniques of modernists like Joyce, while his dissertation was on German Jews between the world wars. After arriving in Dearborn, Sid was asked to join a university committee on Holocaust education. This led to the first modest tape recordings in people's homes, and by the end of 1981 Bolkosky started videoing the exchanges—one with Bernard Offen among his first.

As a lecturer, he sometimes helped students make personal connections to otherwise dry stuff, such as analyzing the Nazi-era railroad bureaucracy across Europe, where hundreds of thousands went about their work in what he called "the ultimate in rationality." A manager at Ford attended one of those classes, invariably arriving in a white shirt and tie. After finishing a unit on the rail system one evening, Bolkosky found the man unable to rise from his seat.

It turned out he had been part of the engineering team that worked on the Pinto. He was in the room the day a decision was made to use only one bolt to attach the muffler, a calculation meant to save fifty cents on each car. The man believed this was among the design flaws that had contributed to deaths when Pintos were rear-ended and the gas tank exploded—though certainly not as crucial as placing the tank behind the rear axle. The student told Bolkosky that engineers knew some cars would explode on impact, "and he didn't object," Sid recalled. "He had tears in his eyes and he identified with the railroad bureaucrats."

Bolkosky sat down with each of the Offens for a taped session in the fall of 1987. Some of this interview is confounding and careening, with hints of both Sam and Nathan vying to have the authoritative last word. They give some altered versions of events, while in other moments the revelations and reflections are startling, and flowing. A few times Bernard strains to keep up with his brothers, and there are long pauses over remnants that he continued to sort out.

While Nathan announces he has just become a grandfather, Bernard tells Bolkosky he only recently discovered his true birth date. Entering Auschwitz in 1944, he somehow got away with declaring he was twenty years old—when he was actually just fifteen. He is fifty-eight, not fifty-six as he'd thought.

"Okay, I think we'll begin," Bolkosky opens. "Could you—starting with Sam—just tell me your names and where you were born, please."

"Okay, my name is Sam Offen. I was born in Kraków, Poland, August 7th, 1921, which makes me sixty-six years old."

"I am Nathan Offen. I was born in Kraków, December the 15th, 1922. This makes me, next December, [I'll] be sixty-five."

Bernard says, "I was born the same place because these guys are my brothers. So up to a month ago, I thought I was born on March 7th, 1931. But a month, two months ago I found out that I was born on April 17th, 1929. So I'm two years older than I was two months ago . . ."

"This makes us closer," Sam comments.

"That's true," says Bernard.

"Um, now this . . ." Sid intervenes, attempting to move on.

"Not only in age," Sam shoehorns in the last word.

When I spoke with Bolkosky the same summer that Nathan and Sam first met with me, he was polite and open, never condescending toward a newbie dabbling in his life's work. I wondered how survivors of genocide could heal. How is that possible when, as in Rwanda, you've seen neighbors butcher your mother with machetes?

"That continues to amaze me," Bolkosky told me. "What survivors teach is primarily about loss, irreparable loss, loss you never recover from. Losing not just someone in your family but everyone in your family, all your life and culture. That's virtually impossible to overcome, but what they've made after that speaks of resilience and hope, and only the best they can get out of life.

"Even though there is a great deal of cynicism in a lot of them, there is another side to them as well, it's not even their core nature," he continued. "They feel that, but they've gone on to make lives for themselves, have children, they did what everybody else does, and became real Americans. When you hear their stories it's like two different planets, how they acted so remarkably different."

Even as their days dwindled, easing the load of hatred was not an issue he saw survivors addressing regularly. "Very few express anger. There's nobody left to be angry about, I suppose," he said. "Very few express forgiveness unless you ask; they won't forgive direct perpetrators. I don't think there's any general feeling of wanting to release themselves of this burden."

It had been more than twenty years since their interviews—though he referenced having stayed in sporadic contact with the brothers—and he recalled the Offens vividly. Like others, Bolkosky had been astonished by how upbeat Sam was. Other men could be forgiven for being bitter about losing one leg to a drunk and having cancer in the other. Asking Offen about these two post-war events, Sam had told him, "Well, I just don't dance as much as I used to."

Sid found Nathan probably the most candid interview that he would ever do. Nathan did not duck the toughest stuff, boring straight into the most private, humiliating scenes. Though not necessarily depressed, he seemed particularly sad that he had been unable to build a career he really loved as Sam did. "He said not a day goes by when something doesn't come up in his mind to make him think of it," Bolkosky observed. Nate was able to turn things around, and after his brothers pressured him into giving his story, "a few years later he said this was the thing that opened his life up."

Bernard was clearly on a different plane, though perhaps not so unlike other survivors who began sorting things out late in their lives. When Bernard became obsessed with facing his trauma, "they were worried about him," Sid said. "But he, too, has found something, something to salvage his own life."

Bolkosky noted the world had largely sat on the sidelines during eighteen bona fide genocides from the Second World War through the next fifty years. Despite this, and withstanding the personal load doing these interviews, he felt a tad better about the future.

He was less worried than the survivors themselves about what will happen when they are gone.

Before cancer claimed his life in 2013, Bolkosky suggested that the collective web of narratives were making a difference, perhaps more than the teaching of history itself. The empathy that new generations gained in Whitwell and Dorchester and elsewhere after meeting people like the Offens could be a profound force for change. "Both they and I know that giving an interview won't prevent it," he said, referring to survivors' fears once more in that filmed interview. "But something's going to be different, because they [the interviews] are so connected to some intellectual rigor . . . I think we're going to rescue the history and the memory of the experience."

Still, at least one of his acerbic questions continued to hover: Why would ordinary people kill with such enthusiasm and sadistic cruelty?

Confusion seemed more probable than clarity. Within survivors, and outside their world, stony grit continued to mix with blood and saliva.

Other stringed instruments played dirges with mournful notes downshifting in trembling, rapid strokes. Chunks of dried joint compound and plaster lay scattered on the floor, whorls of graywater sluiced through rubble. What arose was a thin ersatz bile, and low leaden clouds, sullen, undefined, bewildering, the wind buffeting snarled scarfs and snapping dogs.

Denise and I are rushing across Long Island in her Camry on Halloween, trying not to be late for Nathan's speech. Passing farm stands and navigating the parkways, the early afternoon sun is bright and it feels unduly warm. He is going to keynote an event in Long Beach commemorating Kristallnacht, the night of the broken glass. We arrive just in time to greet him and Gloria outside city hall.

Inside the council chambers, the mood among a predominantly elderly Jewish audience is terse and caustic. Old scars were rubbed raw two days earlier by the discovery of bombs concealed inside desktop printers bound for a Jewish community center in Chicago, and early evidence pointed to Al Qaeda. We begin to observe how marking the start of the Holocaust in November 1939 still packs a punch. An older couple next to us introduces themselves, and it turns out she fled Vienna with her family shortly after the invasion of Austria. Color guards from four veterans group open the program, and noticing a few Jewish War Veterans with shaking arms, I'm unsure whether it's mostly their advanced age showing, or a combination of something else.

Nathan sits behind the dais waiting his turn as the opening speakers condemn anyone who opposes taking a hard line against Muslim extremists. They also excoriate US complicity—both then, and now. The master of ceremonies, a round-faced, cheerful man who identifies himself as an Italian-American, warns against accommodating Islamic hate speech with so-called free speech protections. He mentions the Evian Conference of 1938, when attendees from thirty nations led by the United States failed to increase immigration quotas for Jewish refugees. We dare not send that signal again, he warns, recounting how we telegraphed to German leaders that the world did not care. A city councilor goes further, declaring that with "fanaticism on the loose, peace-loving Muslims have been made irrelevant by their silence." Just as in Nazi Germany, in Serbia, and in other places where genocide has taken hold, the passive "majority is too busy to care" until it's too late, she declares. Following her, a rabbi makes a connection between how Jews felt that God hid from them to the absence of vigorous prosecutions of today's fanatics. These warnings, issued a few years before the rise of Islamic State of Iraq and Syria, ring in a clamor of undissipated deja vu.

Nathan sits with his arms crossed during much of this and frowns. "Politicians," he scoffs later, and then smirks revealing that it was actually okay, he couldn't hear all the words anyway. He's also irritated that no one had told him he'd have to sit for so long. Still, during the invocation I catch him singing or at least mouthing a prayer. By the time he unfolds his notes and places his tape recorder in front of him, the audience seems already drained, perhaps ready to rush home and draw the shades on sunlight that's beating into the chamber.

He stands stiffly at first, left arm balanced on his hip. Complaining that the emcee preempted his thoughts on Kristallnacht, he removes that page of his notes and shifts on the fly into some of his life story, halting erratically as he warms up. Nathan looks tired, but who can blame him? It's his third speech in a month, following ones to community college students and at a local temple's men's club.

This time he expands on some details and withholds others. He'd been a happy child growing up, and although his family was poor, he tells the audience, "We didn't care, we didn't know better because everyone was poor." There's taking up boxing to defend himself, and he tells them, "I never gave up" during those confrontations. As he reaches the most difficult parts, I look again at the few family photos displayed on a table facing us—two of Nathan and his brothers, and one of their parents. And there is Miriam, forever suspended as a teenager, angelic. His voice cracks describing that last moment seeing his sister and mother alive, his eyes moisten, and Denise shifts beside me. "She kept screaming at me, 'Run away, run away,' but I didn't." He describes the soldier breaking his teeth, and we each try to hold back tears.

The audience stirs just once when he offers the anecdote of surviving that first night after liberation, somehow asking the nurse for the one thing he could pronounce in English: chocolate. His accent stresses "la-te," provoking a rustle of relieved laughter. This lightens him briefly, but Nathan rushes through the closing, saying once again that he'd survived when others did not in order to tell the world. He seems to have reached his limit.

When the program ends, as Nathan sells some books we talk more with a tiny, hardy-looking woman sitting beside us. Hedy Pagremanski, whose family got out of Austria just in time, is a sidewalk landscape artist known for painting buildings that are about to be torn down in Manhattan. On this day she, too, has a title to sell, on a far more personal subject than historic preservation. She and her husband, Eric, wrote and illustrated a book describing supports for Long Islanders with a range of disabilities, portraying services for autism to cerebral palsy, and improving the lives for homebound developmentally disabled adults. In the text, Eric Pagremanski explains how he was inspired by his mother, Anna's, legacy. She was a generous woman who celebrated the worth of those "who so often have been relegated to the fringes of society." He last saw her across a fence at a concentration camp near Gdansk. We quickly purchase the paperback, and Hedy signs ours, adding, "Thank you for understanding."

Nathan rejuvenates as we sit in a diner for an early supper along the boardwalk, which feels like a fitting place to dial back some of the afternoon's heaviness. He and Gloria are eager to leave for Florida the following week, though he has cut back on tennis because of a sciatica nerve in his back. This returns with colder weather, and "it's probably because of the beatings I took," he confides over the phone another time. In what I'm appreciating as his contrarian nature, on one hand Nathan calls it "a little problem." Then minutes later he notes the pain shooting from his back to his foot. He's also got another speaking gig booked for the following spring when they return. He hasn't mentioned whether he's finally arranged to speak at Andy Ferraro's church, and I neglect to follow up on that.

He tears through a steak salad, craving a protein infusion, while the three of us fork through tilapia. Denise asks if speaking to groups like this helps him heal, and Nathan responds that it just makes him feel better. Especially when young adults and teens are in the audience, which unfortunately was not the case today. I wonder if perhaps he's not so unlike Bernard after all, who purposefully heals himself leading the confessional tours.

Then Nathan's face, slightly sunken under both cheekbones, lights up and gleams for a few minutes. These days, he explains, he feels joy seeing a baby at his synagogue, which he attends mostly on holidays. "Hitler didn't get rid of us, because we're still here," he perks. "He didn't succeed." That gives him the greatest satisfaction: his bulging-vein defiance, the next generation affirming his struggle. Perhaps also the possibility of reaching them.

I nod and say something that feels very ordinary. Yet I sense something different emanating from Nathan than when I first heard him present at my school two years earlier. It's as if he now restocks his own cache of hope and draws from it once in a while. He's certainly a long way from 1952, when he felt so guilty for being alive. These days he'll probably even ask to hold a newborn.

Returning home the following day, I open an email from Bernard in Poland. He's sent me something transcendent once again. He links to the trailer for a new documentary film—not his, this time—*Alice Dancing Under the Gallows*. It's about the world's oldest Holocaust survivor, Alice Herz-Sommer, who turned 107 that November. A concert pianist in Prague before the war, she was fortunate to land with her son at Theresienstadt in the Czech Republic, the sham camp the Reich created to show the world. Jews played concerts and performed plays there while children lived with their parents, forcing smiles for the international press.

As Herz-Sommer kept playing, performing more than one hundred concerts at Theresienstadt, music sustained her. Interviewed in her East London apartment, the camera zoomed in on her brown eyes, still soft, almost unworldly so, and yet so grounded. "Music is God," she declared. "In difficult times you feel it; it helps your suffering."

Then this, which immediately reinforced my belief in Nathan. Herz-Sommer recalled that German journalists who came for interviews at the concentration camp paused at her door, asking, "Do you mind if we come in? Don't you hate us?"

"My answer was, 'I never hate. Hatred brings only hatred.'"

As always, Bernard signs off with, "Love Light and Courage."

Weeks later in December, shortly before his eighty-eighth birthday, Nathan goes to an emergency room in Delray Beach. There's blood in his urine and he's been in terrible pain. He undergoes tests for a possible cystectomy and they give him catheter for a couple of days. Gloria calls with the news and says the doctors have ruled out bladder cancer. She emails an update when the catheter is removed and he begins to recover.

He tells her that he knows tomorrow "is going to be better." And she conveys to me, "I was so impressed with this remark. I have a tendency to think of the worst possibilities of a situation and I realize that Nathan uses such positive thinking in his life. I imagine that as bad as things were in his Holocaust experiences, he may have thought 'tomorrow is going to be better.' I just questioned him about this and he said that he always said to himself, 'I had to live through the night because tomorrow is going to be better.' Nathan just told me that he never gave up.

"I think that this is amazing," Gloria writes.

For years, Sam had a side deal going with a certain bookshop in the nation's capital.

Unbeknownst to Bernard and Nathan, he arranged with the United States Holocaust Memorial Museum to sell his memoir. He drove by stealth several times a year for book signings, not just an annual trip as he had disclosed. Nathan felt a bit stung by this when he found out. His brother, a guy who sold several thousand books compared to his hundreds, had promoted his business tirelessly throughout Detroit. "He made himself famous," frequently using his jovial mug in the store's advertising, Nathan huffed, but not without pride. Early in 2012 Bernard interceded, convincing his siblings to sell their books together in Washington, D.C.

Sitting beside his brothers on the museum's second floor one spring day, Sam is clearly at ease, authorial-casual in a blue blazer and designer jeans. He appears both docile and keenly alert, eyeing groups of students from as far away as Wisconsin who approach their tables. Lined up in order of their respective ages, Nathan is distinguished in a warm beige jacket with a thatched pattern and camel-colored khakis. He looks uncomfortable, angling his face in a silent glare as if wanting this to be over already. Farthest to the right, Bernard dons a dark blue jacket covering suspenders, his dark trousers riding a little high. He's the one most likely to rise and chat with anyone who stops by, a bit more like a shopkeeper discussing his wares than a Zen-like conveyor of peace and understanding. From across the hallway the museum shop director comes by intermittently to check on the trio. When a cluster of students asks them to sign museum ID cards instead of books, the men oblige half-grudgingly.

Sam smiles thinly, leaning in as a teenage boy maintains a short distance and asks a question. He beams at the occasional insightful query, while remaining patient with others. At ninety, he and his daughter Gail recently traveled to a school outside of Dayton—about two hundred miles from home—to give a talk. Meeting someone at the museum during another book signing sparked the trip. He's also brought along his new companion, Ellen, who is straw-haired and seems a decade or two younger. They apparently met at the pool. His brothers' partners are also here, staying mostly off to the side, while several of the adult cousins including Ruth and Jerry will be in town for several days as well.

As these things go, some of the school groups are better prepared than others for this field trip on the cusp of Memorial Day weekend. One chaperone from a local high school tells me outside that while her ninth graders have read Anne Frank, many know little more about what happened. While Sam is more forgiving about this sort of gap, Nathan can barely conceal his scowl.

Three students from an orthodox high school in New Jersey wearing skullcaps approach him and Bernard. "Were you separated? How did you reunite after the war?" one asks. "When?"

"Do you have an hour and a half?" Bernard cracks, leaving the table for a moment.

"Read the book if you want to know," Nathan intones.

"Yeah we're three brothers, we all have different stories," Bernard responds to another question that arrives like a slow-pitch softball. Then to the mercurial follow-up: "A little bit the same but mostly different."

As they round a corner and realize who the brothers are, some of the adults are speechless as well. "It's as if they went through the Natural History Museum and came out seeing living dinosaurs," Gail cracks. Her father seems to understand some of the students' body language. "Going through and experiencing the horror of it is one thing," he tells me. "Then seeing a survivor, they think, how could there be any survivors after that?"

He will sell a few dozen books this afternoon, but that's far from the point. When a twelve-year-old girl begins sobbing, Sam takes her hand and says, "Honey, don't cry. Look at me. I'm here. I'm alive. And maybe the reason I survived . . . is that some day I would meet you."

I'm meeting Bernard here in person for the first time, and we're able to grab a few minutes aside. He and his partner, Krysia Lapczynska-Ryba, will soon leave for another season in Poland, where he also has citizenship. He has a tour booked in early June with twenty people from Michigan, and others following. During those months the pair live in an apartment building she owns.

Krysia's late husband was a surgeon, and when Bernard met her one hot August day, she was depressed in grief refusing to eat. As they each moved forward she supported his inward treks, eventually writing a book that compares Offen's experiences to another survivor's. Meanwhile, Krysia encouraged Bernard to go further examining the relationships that sustained him. As he tells me about continuing to lead his walking tours of the ghetto and Auschwitz—he may be the only person in the world who passed through those gates and returns to conduct tours—I get a sense that while fresh triggers still arise, those visits have become slightly less emotionally laden for him.

Still, while leading those groups, "I cry, I react, and then I explain what happened," he says.

Bright and direct, Krysia wears plum-colored lipstick and tells me a bit about their recent travels, from driving into the desert from San Diego to camping at national parks in Utah. She keeps a BMW in San Francisco and comes across as someone you usually defer to. Their main gig this winter was staying on four of the Hawaiian Islands. His favorite is Molokai, which is less frequently traveled, and where "the paper comes three days late, and that's just what we like," Bernard says. "The town hasn't changed in about one hundred years." When I ask how that helps him recharge, he points to his stack of books, saying, "I need to not think about this."

Before their books-signing concludes, and not wanting to intrude further on the family gathering, I head to the airport.

Gail Offen hears her father joking from heaven.

"Oh, *now* you're going to synagogue. Oh, now you like it."

She pictures him nibbling Kit Kats with a Dunkin' Donuts coffee, perusing the latest issue of *Time*. Or pickled trout and babka at the Stage, warmed up just so.

Sam died of a fast-moving brain tumor late in 2012. Just a few weeks earlier he had attended a gala dinner for a cousin who was being honored by a children's leukemia foundation. The next day Gail could not talk to her father, his cognition suddenly decimated.

Unlike her mother's illness, which became a long goodbye, they had no time to prepare. He underwent radiation treatments and fell down at home, breaking some ribs. He was unable to communicate during the final few weeks. Nathan flew out twice and they could not have a last conversation, though Sam expressed himself with his eyes or a touch of his fingers. His brother felt they had some unfinished business. "We were going to do a movie or something," Nathan told me a few weeks later. "When the big guy calls us, it's like *The Gambler*, and you have to go."

Sam's service was a love-in, and few people could resist smiling. Eulogizing her dad, Gail highlighted how he never gave up on anyone, sometimes intervening with family members to say, *you should be more forgiving; this is wrong, you should speak to them.* She mentioned his fondness for bad jokes. "He called his two canes 'Cane and Able,'" she said. "And anyone who dined with him knew he always insisted on picking up the check with the strength of ten men."

With his daughter, at least, Sam always ended their conversations with, "To be continued."

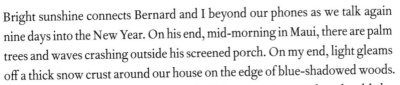

Bright sunshine connects Bernard and I beyond our phones as we talk again nine days into the New Year. On his end, mid-morning in Maui, there are palm trees and waves crashing outside his screened porch. On my end, light gleams off a thick snow crust around our house on the edge of blue-shadowed woods.

I struggle a bit asking him my finishing questions: What should the world remember? In the end, is he hopeful?

His answers flicker back and forth. "I wanted to save the world I thought, which I still do, but I realized it's impossible, it's impossible," he says. "But the best way I can do that is by telling my story."

Then I hear Krysia speaking Polish to him in the background. He pauses to listen closely. They enjoy taking drives together, and he tells me about one.

Two days earlier they went up to Maui's Haleakala volcano, some 10,000 feet above the Pacific. *Haleakala* means "House of the Sun." Fully awake now after two cups of coffee, Bernard becomes wistful describing it: "The site is so fantastic, that if people could see the starkness and beauty that is there, in actuality we are so small as human beings, maybe we could see the unity and work for peace from such a beautiful, beautiful view and sight. When we look out over it and there are clouds coming in over one side of the extinct volcano—the caldera, the side that collapsed—it looks like a blanket that you can cover yourself with. She and I both started crying from the beauty of it.

"And from there across we can see the big island, and see snow. People are caught up in just our daily surviving, just keeping the body together, like in the camps. We cannot get out of going against others and hurting. People are suffering, people are suffering, because of stupid behaviors."

"Why did I survive?" Nathan asks again. "To tell the world."

His expression is unprompted; I certainly did not ask. It feels scripted only in the sense that he's used the same words before. Yet something feels different.

We're seated inside a Turkish restaurant in Port Washington on Long Island's north shore. The summer is nearing its end, and Nathan and Gloria are in the midst of several transitions, each one grueling in its own way.

They've decided to give up the warm weather months here and live year-round in Delray Beach; these snowbirds will pretty much be grounded. Their unit, actually Gloria's, has already sold. For weeks they've been packing and sorting what to give away, which appears to be plenty to accomplish in and of itself. They gave half of their dinner service to some local veterans. Boxes are strewn about, and he insists I take some books lingering on a shelf. I grab Rachel Carson, a Jewish High Holiday prayer book, and one of Gloria's academic texts on family therapy—she counseled families for a few years after her teaching career.

Maybe it's the sheen left from an afternoon rain that had just moved on, but as I came down Main Street beside boutiques and a movie theatre, and around a millpond that looks out to the bobbing harbor, Port Washington felt clean and comfy. They'd lived here eight years, amassing new friends along with older ones nearby. The move will be a major shift for Nathan, who spent decades of his adult winters schlepping through grimy snow, and for Gloria, who grew up in the Bronx.

Gloria, who is a few years younger than Nathan, also feels it's time to join an assisted living community. They've found one not far from his condo, a place that will provide both a vibrant social life and medical facilities as needed. But some bad luck has forced their hand. After they flew north in April, mold spread through the condo in Delray Beach. Either the AC failed or something burst. It was a washout: their clothing, the kitchen, wallpaper, rugs—ruined. The unit was condemned, and they had to go back down to deal with the cleanup and estimates and insurance. Nathan was not a happy camper, snarling about it over the phone several times. And now they must consolidate their stuff from two condos into one that's some nine hundred square feet.

Still, there's an openness about him this afternoon I've never felt before. When we've visited or just spoken together, usually Nathan's reflectiveness has clear limits. Even when he does share something personal, he cranks open the skylight only for a moment. His phrases are hammered in short bursts, as if he's working at the table again making patterns. Then he shuts the window abruptly with, "But that's life." Foot on the brake, ball over the baseline. Done.

He tells me this: At that birthday party a few years after losing Helen, the new partner on his arm told Nathan not to place photos of his wife with the other family pictures. He capitulated, and his eyes reveal his mistake. He conveys this when Gloria goes into another room; perhaps this contributes to the distance with two of his daughters.

I do not know what to say, it is not my place. Who am I perhaps to even note this, or consider how one clamps such a seal so tight?

Yet there's a shift in Nathan. Surely I should understand why without it being said. Before we go to eat, he tells me how much he misses Sam, volunteering this before I can ask.

They used to call one another every day or two. He didn't relinquish being Sam's protector. They competed over things, not yet fully resolved.

"A good life," he muses. There are very few men left who he feels close enough to talk with. Bernard had recently mentioned to me that Nathan told him, "'We used to be the three Musketeers. There's two, then there's none.' And he's right." Nathan has one close friend in New Jersey, a guy who grew up in Kraków and fixed cars for a living.

He is lonely, but not down and out. I sense his spirit arcing in an indelible way, even lifting. While sadness over losing Sam and other laments of his life are closer to the surface, there's also a stubborn resolve. He may only crank open the window for glimpses, but those feelings are not shuttered entirely.

Now he sits with arms folded across his chest, those handsome strong forearms, a workingman's arms. He's never known riches, and never hides this. Nathan used to retrieve tennis balls for rich kids in Poland, and he's back playing a bit more now—there's two hours of doubles tomorrow over in New Hyde Park. His rotator cuff hasn't bothered him much lately, though it's a recurring pain, forcing him at times to stay off the court and do physical therapy again. The sciatica nerve in his back seems to be less of an issue. As he wolfs down a garden salad and bread, I realize that while he may have shrunk a few hairs in the four or five years I've known him, his gait is steady. Maneuvering Gloria's Camry into a parking lot, he deploys the same zing I felt when he picked me up at the train station some years ago.

"I'm not going anywhere," he tells me later, looking straight ahead. "I'm taking names to throw myself a one hundredth birthday party. We're going to fly into space."

There's at least one thing that he rarely talks about, which didn't make it far into his book or his occasional public talks. It was the evening after Nathan had checked himself into the infirmary at Mauthausen, when systemic starvation was about run its course. He recalls the hallway, the dead and dying lying close by. He lay down nearby and received another beating. Bleeding from the head, and elsewhere, they left him, fading out.

Sometime that night one of the *kapos* assaulted him in the showers. He says the words, the act.

"He what?" Gloria interrupts. Her fork scrapes a plate as if slamming the brakes. She's undoubtedly heard this part before during the twenty-one years they've been together. Yet she throws him a look, surprised that he's offering this now. We're early birds for supper, the first to be seated, and a few other diners have since come in. The wait staff is also within earshot. He's mentioned some of this to me before, but there's something different in how it comes out.

"He raped me," Nathan says, unblinking. "A German *kapo*." Always a straight shooter. "The next morning, I was able to clean myself off. And I went back to work."

He's not done. Here comes the conundrum, the real twist of fate that Nathan apparently wants to deliver. Years later, he found out about ambulances meant to deliver sick prisoners to a nearby hospital that actually were mini-death chambers themselves. The SS sealed them up and piped in exhaust fumes; the commandant of Mauthausen drove one. Nathan didn't know about ambulances, he was in a dying fog. "What are you going to do, pick up a rock? You can't do that, you can hardly think," he says. He might have been loaded on to an ambulance from the infirmary.

Instead he was beaten badly. Somehow, it wasn't meant to be. "Why did I survive?" he ponders again.

Gloria breaks in with a question, which she relays from a friend. "What was it that gave you the determination to live?"

"Hatred," he says. "Hatred. Hatred." He pauses. "The opposite of love." The same message he gave our students in Boston. Later he adds: "And blind luck."

I still wonder about him and Sam at that camp, how they sustained each other. I'm also curious about his fondest memories of Sam. Driving to New York that day I sought to center myself before asking. I turned the radio off for long stretches to sort out what my core questions really were.

For Nathan, it is not, "What have we learned from the Holocaust?" It is also not, "How did you get up each morning and go to work?" I tried drilling down further. I resolved: "What comes next?"

"How do you make sense of this? What is your sweetest memory of him—as boys, and as mature men?" I'm not sure I get each of these out directly. Yet the responses are already there.

Nathan reminds us there is always room left for love. This space is mashed up, we threaten to tear into it again, seizing up, and it conflicts with what we believe we're looking at. His face may be parched and blotched in a few spots. One of his knees soon will be down to bone on bone. He'll try a new platelet-rich plasma treatment, but must stop when he becomes anemic. Nothing can extinguish the prospect of summer's return.

A year later, watching the protests in Ferguson overheat into a rampage, and then a cynical backlash building, Nathan sympathizes with those he says have nothing. His daughter Suzanne, once estranged, will go to Austria with her husband on a business trip and see the death steps. Traveling also to Israel, she will visit Yad Vashem, finding that her father is listed among the dead in the archives. Nathan will vow to fix this. He opts out of returning to Poland again with Ruth and his grandson, telling me that it would bring back too much for him. He opens and closes the valve, noticing the threads on the fitting are nearly stripped again.

Nathan asks if I would like to hear what he said to Sam at the memorial service. Our supper, a $12.95 surf and turf coupon special for each, hasn't yet arrived. At the table he sings softly, recalling:

> We'll meet again.
> Don't know where.
> Don't know when.
> But we'll meet again
> Some sunny day—
> And we'll go fishing.

PART FIVE

THE COST

He tried to do his best but he could not.
—Neil Young

25

WHEELS OFF

The challenge that Denise's doctor issued that first winter lingered. She had urged us to recognize the signs of how we each grieve differently. Not to take symptoms like blowouts from unmitigated stress or self-medicating for granted. Beware of widening divisions such as our feelings about memorializing Mike versus letting go, or reconciling Cory's mistake. Or me plunging into the mire of underage drinking in Providence. Find a way to step back and support one another.

Most of all, in order to help others heal she needed to take care of herself. Doing so was not a luxury.

I often missed the signs.

She shouldered so much starting a nonprofit, despite the people finding comfort who thanked her for creating this place, amidst the efforts of others helping to run support groups, her terrific counselors, spirited yoga teachers, and other practitioners. A few years later, Hope Floats Healing and Wellness Center received an influx of new energy from volunteers helping to plan our major fundraiser—a community memory walk.

Other inputs came from a variety of sources. Employees at a nearby medical office gave an afternoon cleaning windows or gardening and painting. One of our son's closest friends, who teaches autistic students and oversees a program helping them gain work skills and transition into young adulthood, brought his charges over to rake leaves, vacuum, and do more windows. Friends who had recently lost a husband or nephew organized treasure and trash for our fall barn sale.

Still, the dishes stacked in a perilous load for my wife. Taking calls from those fresh in their loss was enough in and of itself. Yet there was also co-facilitating two support groups and planning for others; scheduling workshops; being a wellness networker and fundraising thank-you writer; tamping down her anxieties to present at Kiwanis and conduct our board meetings; paying bills, e-newsletter editor, toilet cleaner, visionary. Vetting proposals from self-interested practitioners and slick presenters. A broken heat cooling pump, mice skittering behind the wall, rain leaking into a counselor's room every nor'easter.

Hackers took down her website. The Internet provider sucked. Meetings with our bookkeeper, the accountant, and changing our 501(c)(3) status with the IRS. Off goes the fire alarm, and someone forgets to turn down the heat again. Weeds engulf the main garden while the labyrinth needs fresh stone dust.

By the way, where did you put those stands for the peonies?

She needed to follow her gut. Relearning to trust intuition: turning away people who do not feel like a good fit; referring mom to a certain counselor; inviting a couple into the right group; and identifying those sources that drain her energy while shifting to ones that nurture her work. Resuming a weekly oil painting class, Denise loosened her technique while exploring dappled light on a forest floor. Canvasses re-emerged in the studio space near our woodstove, studies of Amanda walking in the woods or lying in the snow.

Doing this kind of work involves monitoring one's personal cistern. Self-sustaining water drains as you strive to help others through their trials, dropping more rapidly than you realize. So where do you go to refill? Committing to a life of service would require replenishing this source frequently, while acting on those things you need to let go of. She simply could not always be there for everyone else.

On another winter morning I asked what was wrong. The creases in her face reflected more than a pale slate of February blahs.

"What's going on?" As if I didn't know. Conflict avoidance redux.

"I'm broken."

I held on to her, just trying to transfer something good.

We needed to keep Hope Floats on course. The core work, her passion, was the free support groups. Demand for them kept growing as more people learned of us by word of mouth, from their doctors, through her e-newsletter, and the like. They came from well beyond our region of the state, enduring gridlock on manic highways.

Some days she took two or three anguished calls from parents desperate to find help.

Staying focused meant cutting back on accessory stuff. She planned fewer workshops and said no to new therapeutic massage therapists and yoga teachers seeking to join us. She declined offers to set up a booth at generic healthy living fairs. We were not an aspiring spa, nor purveyors of New Age product lines. After a couple of years, even our mission statement felt cluttered and vague. Clarifying it was like power washing mold off the siding, or scouring the front porch until it faintly gleamed again.

We took intermittent breaks for self-care and to clear space for our grief. Joining a small couple's group in the old parlor of the house, a therapist guided a reflective afternoon of remembrance and dialogue about how our responses to Mike's death sometimes diverged. We lit a candle for him and I journaled about my regrets and best memories, both refreshed by the opportunity to do this together—the focus, especially for her, rotating from taking care of others' needs. On occasion Denise's Reiki practitioners and massage therapists recharged us at mini-clinics they held for the public. There were also escapes traveling to Germany to be with her mom's welcoming family, discovering Wilhelmshaven and Cologne, and a romantic stretch for the two of us returning to St. John, where a sea turtle surprised us kayaking and our rental was a quick hop to Skinny Legs, a bar and burger joint where you could pull up a stool or dance forever.

Otherwise I continued my part at Hope Floats, a cycle of outside cleanup, mowing, and landscaping, plus minor indoor maintenance. I tended lavender beds, pruned trees, raked, and cleaned gutters until the snow fell. All good things—until those last rain-slogged leaf piles. Not really work, but just to keep moving and loosen my knotted brain. I did a lot of this for Mike and to assure a comforting place for those families.

And for myself, an implicit therapy to sustain some of that forward-moving reciprocity.

Most often we worked together in tandem. Preparing the budget at the kitchen table, conversations over to-dos in the bathroom, check-ins on her groups or meetings with practitioners while preparing supper. I wrote copy for donors' letters and press releases. We checked the profit and loss statements as I analyzed trends, preparing financial snapshots for the board. We wrestled with the nonprofit paying rent to the corporate entity that we had been advised to set up to hold the property. Agonized over our sustainability, woken again to grant-writing deadlines and the press to forge partnerships. Eventually we tried setting boundaries like a work-free zone at dinner. Which doesn't always work, since sometimes things just need to be said.

One day I got fed up mowing amidst the dust and pollen of a dry spring, muttering as I cleared my nose of unfiltered crud. Putting the tractor away I heard a young girl outside in the drive. She was perhaps seven years old and struggled to express herself, asking questions of an elderly caretaker as they left a counselor's office. She had dark hair and an oval face that was set on the brick walk. Halting, I wondered what she was going through, what had brought her here. That we could provide a space for her to query and perhaps regain some control of events, and even feel more normal— because these things are—that's all that truly mattered. I retreated for another minute into the shed.

Another night she cried out: *I want a normal life again.* I can't take this: all this grief, this healing. I just want him back. Our life. I come home and sometimes I still expect to see him in the kitchen.

Sleep was often interrupted, sometimes till four, five—way past the hour that had ripped life apart. How do we keep this going? Feeling guilt about giving up teaching, the pension she'd be accumulating. Denise was on the outskirts beyond what I acknowledged or perhaps could bear to see. Downplayed it for a husband who hits the pillow and out. Who takes longer walks and bike rides alone, Nordic skiing around the bogs out back. Always taking care of himself.

Aren't I allowed to grieve as well?

A normal life again.

Of course, the catastrophe that had severed my family struck somebody else.

It was bound to. An agonizing déjà vu: teens who feel invincible, trashed after drinking in a sleazy joint that looks the other way.

I didn't really have time for this load. I only followed Rhode Island news in sporadic outbursts. When I did, this meant racing down lists of archived articles, consuming parents' laments and official attributions, aware of the sleaze glaring my way from online fringes. Scouring databases of the clubs' principals and their business interests, I heard the staccato gunfire of clicks, copy and saves until an afternoon had seeped away.

For what?

As if chasing every lead would make any difference. That was my crutch, my avoidance, ratcheting up the instinctive measures I took those first few months by the woodstove after Mike's death. Making calls and gathering information on a legal pad. Maybe there was a familiar comfort in doing this, but it always led to a headache, an urge for an adult beverage. A desire to attack cordwood with my splitting maul.

There was a wretchedly similar crash a day before Mike's birthday in 2009. Five Massachusetts teens hurtled down a highway toward Providence. They had been drinking a "jungle juice" concoction of beer, fruit juice, and hard stuff at two of the guys' apartments. They went to a bar called Mug Shots, where police said the group bought more drinks without being questioned by the staff. Upon arrival several of them were already wasted; by midnight they pretty much carried the intended driver out as he flipped his keys to a friend.

Two of the nineteen-year-olds didn't make it out of the Ocean State. The driver lost control and struck a rock ledge. He was paralyzed from the waist down, but his buddies were gone. The bar's license was revoked. The victims' parents went after the owner, a slug who was later involved in a suspicious fatality when a woman not half his age jumped out of his car and died on I-95.

I reached the mom of one of the deceased guys. She was a mess. She had a medical-legal background and basically stayed in bed the first four months. She had held up many of her son's friends, but seemed unable to help herself. It was as if her shaking hand came through the landline, pawing for my arm, my throat. But I kept taking notes.

Her son had planned to attend college and study business. He had loved playing hockey since he was four. "He was getting his life together," his mother told me. "He wanted to own a business."

I'm in a very bad place.

"He had a future."

He yelled at his friend to slow down.

I mentioned an inkling I had to try and advocate for banning under-twenty-ones from bars. But this was far too early for her; the woman's despair felt like a deep-sea canyon of uncharted depths. Unknowingly, it was exactly a year after the driver had been sentenced. He "served ten months after killing two kids," she told me.

Why did I call? What the hell did I have to offer her?

What in God's name was I doing to myself?

Resolved to take a stand, I closed my pad. My head squeezing through a rabbit hole of my own making.

The night. All the wheels. Finally. Came off.

Mike came through the door with his buddy Griffin and two girls in tow, freshmen over-applied with makeup for two senior dudes. Obviously buzzed—no, hammered. We didn't react at first, as they went into his room. Then our son announced that he was driving them home.

Denise confronted him.

No. Absolutely not. Whaddaya mean? No fuckin' way. Don't talk to your mother like that. No way.

He went after her first. This was not like him, not at all.

Wrestling around the breakfast bar. Grabbing shoulders, her hands clawing at anything, fists hitting his chest. Oak cabinets absorbing hits. Flying fruit, and papers scatter to the floor.

Hades bust open: we've had enough.

Too much arguing and slamming doors. Worried about him failing a class. Senior on thin ice. The bitch chemistry teacher. Always someone else's fault. Study. Get a tutor. Get over it. This ain't nothing, I'm fine.

You planning to graduate? Yeah right.

It's a few weeks after the holidays, a goddamned weeknight. I jump in, no longer able to just to lock his flailing arms. We're about the same size; I'm strong enough, he's all poison and tendons. Three of us banging against the boards.

Don't you talk to her like that. Sick of you, sick of you tearing apart this family. Something breaks. Sick of you.

He and I in the hallway by the door. Don't you do it, you can't drive— sucker punch. Suck-Er-Punch. Furious speed. Nails me a couple. I try to cover, not a fighter, never. Well, maybe once in fifth grade after Tommy Ruiz clocked me in the ear on the playground. Don't land one; don't need to. This is payback: Why did you take so long?

So many mistakes. Yet here for you. Always me. Kicking a ball in the apartment hallway. Long passes together in the backyard, ricochet bullets off the tie wall I built. Coaching: outdoor, indoor, since kindergarten. Truck broke down on the way camping when we both needed that time together. Rotten. Contorted. So gentle with everyone else. Honest Iago.

Your Achilles heel, my mother warned.

Always me.

My eye is closing.

Chris and Amanda must be upstairs, awakened again. My daughter actually has two friends over, which I've forgotten for thirteen years.

This is unbelief, wheels off. The end of family itself. Rotted putrid squash in the compost.

He barely spoke to us after a long weekend in the county lockup. Approaching him in the courthouse hallway, he looked ready to start up again, until his mother told him what he had called her.

There was no doubt. We absolutely did the right thing.

Three weeks later we took a long-planned family vacation to St. John, our first time there, together with close friends and their three kids. We rented a house on the east end of the island, the farthest point from town. Looking out to a passage where whales sometimes come through, we inhaled the lushness of afternoon rains, and four-wheeled to beaches with our coolers and snorkeling gear.

Mike seemed to be on the phone with Tanya half the time, but there were also football games in the sand, water Frisbee and hikes through the dry scrub. One night the power goes out when the adults are naked in a hot tub. Bubbles down, periscopes up. Dad gets out to replenish the wine and Coco Lopez.

We're back in Cruz Bay one afternoon so the kids can do something different with organized activities. At the Westin there's a pool the size of the Gulf of Maine, plus a float in the swimming area for bouncing around. We sign up for paragliding, but Mike doesn't want to go. He seems to be telling us to stuff it, content to sit on a beach chair.

We leave him be, and I get to go with Amanda. It is amazing, the rush upward and then the view, this unspoiled aqua blue sea and parched mountain tops you can almost touch. I'm with my eleven-year-old baby girl. Never need to do this again because this is the moment.

We come back over to the beach where Mike remains. I grab a chair beside him, and we talk a bit. We're heading home in a couple of days and I want to encourage him. It will be a tough winter's end with his classes, but he can do it. *I know you can do it.*

A waitress comes by and I order two Coronas. I'm not supposed to do this, since a judge ordered him to stay drug free. But I do it anyway. We're in the friggin' Caribbean, we've summoned our best Johnny Depp. He must by dying.

Mike thanks me, and we enjoy ours slowly, watching the kids play out on the floats. I will have no regrets.

We're out with friends at a local burger and ribs joint one night, a scruffy place with too many TVs. After eating, on the spur of the moment we go to a pub across the street, a narrow room almost like a crawl space with a wrought-iron swivel staircase leading to the second floor. There's often a Bruins crowd stirring inside The British Beer Company, and they seem to play just the right Zeppelin at opportune times.

Walking in Denise spots Mike's good friend Jeff Walsh, whose face lights up. Jeff is with his younger brother Sean and a small group. We're not regulars and he's surprised to see us, although we've brought my in-laws here before to crank up a boisterous night—Denise's mom cradling a Jägermeister, Chris and I enjoying smoky Scottish ale. Soon Mike's other buddy Travis Dupuis arrives. Jeff's fiancée Brittany is about to get off work.

Travis, who is loquacious and emits his feelings in the way a fast-rotating lighthouse makes its rounds, gives Denise a big hug. He's the special education teacher who works with teens and young adults who are on the autism spectrum. His passion is unmistakable. Travis goes full out, saying how deserving these young people are—so much that we feel he must be in the right place. He's one of those people born to teach, and you just know, damn, those students are lucky to have him, and he them. And following Jeff, Trav is next in line among Mike's friends to get engaged—his girlfriend teaches English at the esteemed Boston Latin Academy. Taking a moment with Denise at the bar, he unveils his stealth strategy to propose to Kristy: He's got a ring and is waiting to select the perfect moment. They've been together a long time; surely she expects this. I hear my wife offer a mild cautionary note, adroitly intimating that he not to wait too long. Remember, Travis, not everything goes as planned.

Beside them Jeff and I strike up a conversation. And this will be among a handful since 2002 that matter the most to me.

We've known Jeff and his family for years, having met alongside the soccer fields when they were kids. It would have been impossible not to run into his mother, Janet, a big-time hockey mom who has yet to find a referee who does not require an immediate visit to the ophthalmologist. I'm talking two decades of catcalls during any of her four sons' games, sirens that weren't exactly luring Greek sailors.

If you hadn't yet seen her in the stands or sidelines, the flare of Janet's nasal Southie accent across the field was an inevitable acetylene torch. Jeff, while more reserved and perhaps cautious than Mike (and his mother), was also another terrific, speedy player. When Mike clashed with us and pushed to get out during high school, the Walshes were often his second home. Janet, who became a stalwart friend helping out at our soccer tournament—which all of her other sons played in—had stopped in to see Denise at Hope

Floats a day before what should have been Mike's twenty-seventh birthday. She delivered the breathless news that Jeff and Brittany wanted to have their ceremony on the grounds.

This was one of those things both of us needed to blink back while retreating to that couch again. In the way that cold, dense lake water changes places with warmer water, an unfiltered mixing of our sadness and profound joy would not abate.

Around this time I had asked Jeff about gathering a group of their friends together to hear stories and catch up over a few beers. He brings this up and offers to pull it together. The one thing you're going to hear from all of us, he tells me, is how much we've grown from losing Mike.

How much we've grown.

Although we think we do, Denise and I don't even know the full trials these guys faced. "I got through that, I can get through anything in life," he says. "Nothing can get to me. Nothing can compare to that. You know, right? You survived it, you know, right?" His questions pepper me for emphasis; that is just Jeff's way, and the ale is flowing. He adds, "It gave me this piece of armor, so I could deal with anything."

He spins a story: One Friday night maybe their junior year, Mike slips two freshman girls into our house through his window. This astounds me, since typically his mother can hear an owl fart or anything else moving outside. How did we miss this? Apparently they spend the night, and sneak out the next morning with him to the high school field for a practice. There's something extra in his game that day; he's nailing everything. Of course Mike's bragging about it too—and the girls are actually inside Cory's car in the parking lot watching the team. "And these girls were really, really hot," he says. "We're dying. I decided right then, this is the guy I want to hang out with."

Brittany arrives and we each hug her. Tomorrow morning she and Jeff will begin some wedding shopping—picking out items for their registry, from the sounds of it. He seems bemused by it all, nodding that she'll know what to do. But tonight Brittany gives the two of us some space as she sits with friends. I order shots for him and Travis and myself; I'm not a big whiskey drinker, but Jeff's is Jameson. They slide it down immediately while I double clutch.

We continue, and there's an elevated moment when everything else becomes suspended around me, as if I've found a makeshift raft amidst the flotsam.

Jeff Walsh is relaying what Mike gave him. He carries this always; I hear layered heartbeats more than words. Voices drift through the bar: I meet Mike for the first time, helping him fiddle with a stereo dial at his aunt's. It's almost as if we both anticipate it coming. Denise's parents and sister watch, I see a smile curling from a little determined face, our lives intertwining with the snaking stereo cords. Jeff and I lock in and it's not about the drinks. "I feel so lucky," he says, "to have been Mike's friend. If I never have another, I had this."

He always has his best friend. Wee Dude brought something, a crazy light that needed to be trained and made complete. Maybe he was meant to prepare them. And they all felt it.

My greatest fear, that his life did not matter, falls below the deepest aquifer.

One day as we spruced up his grave, I checked a little basket we kept under his bench with mementos like a favorite visor and a wrinkled teddy bear. I cracked open a dusty CD cover of Bob Marley's greatest hits that someone had left. Inside was a faded note I'd never read, in barely legible runny blue: "Brack, I could write on forever about the good times. We miss you more than words can say."

It was signed "Carey." Brendan, the friend who crawled out of the crash with cuts and bruises. And I've often wondered with what else.

The rain held off for Jeff's wedding at Hope Floats with an assist from our son. It had drizzled or poured much of the week prior to Columbus Day weekend, postponing my final lawn duties until Friday, a warm Indian summer day. Everything was cut and raked, we planted some eye-popping mums, and I scrubbed the deck and back stairs of the house where the bridal party would gather.

Jeff had purchased a wood arbor and varnished it for the ceremony, setting it up with his brother below a small tree. Some of the bridesmaids along with their moms trimmed the arbor with seasonal flowers, rust orange and a red with the same vibrancy as bittersweet berries. They laid store-sized straw bales and pumpkins on the trimmed grass; the guys hung globes from tree branches. The wedding cake came from Wal-Mart, and the connection on a little PA box Janet bought would falter.

They did not choose a priest or religious text for their sacrament. Instead, the town clerk married them, a mom from up the street whose son had struggled since returning from a second tour of duty in Iraq. A justice of the peace, she held our hands in a private moment just before the ceremony as Denise and I spoke of Mike and Jeff's bond.

There was one surprise: they invited Cory Scanlon and his wife. Somehow it had slipped by to inform us. Spotting Cory outside the main house, I didn't quite know what to say, but went over to greet him and Lisa. It had been just ten months since we saw him at Frank Madeiros's wake. I'd never imagined he would come on the very grounds where we poured so much into making something lasting because of Mike. At first this energy had been singularly attached to his memory, but our connections were expanding. A few years earlier, our son Chris had reacted to seeing his brother's image on television during an interview with his mother. That along with the portrait of Mike framed in the Hope Floats' entryway, flashing his seemingly perfect white teeth, sparked a rare rebuke from Buds. "I don't want to see Mike on TV ever again," he shot back. He worried about his parents' preoccupation with grief.

But his brother's presence did not feel overwhelming to us most of the time. In the winter I went down by the river to a granite bench we had placed among the silver beech trees, listening to the flowing water, thinking of him and all we were doing. From her office up the hill in a corner of the wellness barn, on occasion Denise took notice of a red-tailed hawk scouting the lawn and woods in stealth. Signs of him were all around.

Just as Brittany reached the ceremonial arbor, a large hawk whirled above the trees, cruising to survey us all. Many of us took note.

Jeff and Britt's reception at a former mill just across the little river rolled deep into the night. The anticipated frolic delivered on its promise, building with each new hit served up by a DJ. Techno and hip-hop gyrations shuffled with ageless stalwarts; from "Brick House" struts to attempted slides on "Billie Jean," even Johnny Cash's throaty "Ring of Fire." The wedding party took over the floor's center, eight ushers in black suspenders and white shirts, the bridesmaids in underscored elegance, their dresses like a warm cocoa fudge swirl. Sean, the youngest Walsh brother, emerged as a floor star, at first prancing low and lean, a college junior puffing his feathers.

We caught up with several of Mike's old friends and parents we'd once met beside the playing fields. Back on the dance floor, the wedding party surged again with the forceful strumming of an acoustic guitar. The Lumineers' "Ho Hey" commenced to roar, an anthem of mates not immune to bleeding together. The guys hoisted Jeff up and bodysurfed him, still clutching his beer. A chair was brought over to lift him higher.

Denise and I smiled to each other standing off to the side. This was their music and their time, fluid and studded with tradition and still all their own. As one of Mike's friends had said a few months earlier, these guys needed something positive. They deserved this. Yet with a short look we both recognized a drop-off few others could see forming, as if the floor of the old tack factory gave way under the shadows. Mike was among the missing. In a flash I couldn't help feeling left behind again, raking those trampled leaves in the November gloom. Yet Mike signaled to me later that Jeff had been right.

The groom asked Denise to dance with him. As Jeff Walsh took Denise in his arms, she felt herself dancing with our son again across the plaited floor.

26

WARPED

....

Reading those files about Bar One, the club where my son and his friends partied in Providence, was a barrage of bad energy, a sour-mouth whiskey hangover.

I should not have made space for this shit. The demands of teaching were more than enough. There was nightly preparation updating PowerPoint slides with "Do Now" exercises and tweaking lesson plans, correcting homework and trying new approaches to reach English-language learners. Hustling to keep my head just above water.

As much as SumpPumpville stoned me, I returned for more.

By the time Mike and his buddies drove there, Bar One already had a nasty track record. A year earlier, in 2001, seven other teens were caught drinking, none found with fake IDs. Wristbands supposed to be issued to those of legal age were not used. One sergeant concluded the bar "had no system of differentiating" between the two.

Police repeatedly warned that the bar was out of line and little was done. The year our son was killed, there were fights and an alleged stabbing, and a shooting just outside. On occasions, the bar would be fined and closed a few days, once on a Wednesday night in mid-August when few students were around.

Bartenders were occasionally arrested for flaunting the law. Club employees yelled out a warning for under twenty-ones to "put your drinks down" as cops entered. During weekend hip-hop and dance party nights, what might have been dubbed the Ludacris Saloon was stuffed to double capacity as the doorman stopped using a counter.

Cops working details were disgusted. They broke up fights, ducked their heads to gunfire shortly before the 2:00 a.m. closing, and were showered with bottles. After his first detail there in 2004, one patrolman reported his concern about potential violence, writing, "I was appalled at how this club runs its nightly operation." Veterans like Detective Sergeant John St. Lawrence saw oversight deteriorate even further, commenting a year later, "It is still a place of concern for us, especially on the weekend nights. When we go in there, we seem to find violations of underage drinking, just about every time we go in."

Checking beyond the police reports and excuses made by the club owner and his managers, it got even worse. Other melees percolated in depositions and case files of lawsuits brought by patrons claiming injuries after being knocked unconscious by bouncers or struck by bottles. One man claimed he was beat up by three bouncers because they didn't like a person of color talking with a white girl.

The guano finally hit the fan in February 2007. Police arrested four clearly underage girls including a seventeen-year-old, three of them seated at the bar with mixed drinks. The bartender, another loser who was the brother of Rhode Island's secretary of state, was charged for the second time with serving minors. The young women said no one checked their IDs. Two nights later, another underage drinker was arrested.

Owner Alex Tomasso must have reached for his Advil that week. In between the two busts, cops broke up an illegal after-hours party at another joint of his called Therapy, which held after-hours dances from 1:00–4:00 a.m. It was Cape Verdean night and a cop was assaulted while the assistant manager wrangled with another officer. Therapy didn't have a license to serve booze or an entertainment license for that evening. He fought a two-day closure and lost.

Tomasso shuttered Bar One that winter and still the license was not revoked. He applied for a license transfer and his attorney blamed past problems on a college crowd, yet during the licensing hearings no one apparently addressed the club's long record of serving minors. A new plan was hatched to reinvent the "college bar" as an upscale club. Tomasso told the board he hoped to add a "neighborhood feel, maybe a baby grand piano, where I might perform one night a week."

The club's makeover sailed through.

There was something warped about the thrill of this chase.

I perused civil complaints filed against the owner in Providence Superior Court and while the personal injury claims caught my attention, others seemed stale or spurious. On the flip side, he had initiated half a dozen complaints himself, and I didn't bother much with those. I came across our own lawsuit, based on the state's Liquor Liability Act, with the Bracks and Shaughnessys demanding a trial by jury. Tomasso's attorney had refused to respond to most of our requests to produce certain records, chiefly, the evidence of insurance. We had been stonewalled. Examining the case file felt surreal, as if half of me was interviewing the other part of myself on tape.

Something else jumped out at me in a file of one of the lawsuits. There was evidence that Bar One had general liability insurance at least through 2000. Here was the policy, tucked inside the case of a guy claiming he'd been whacked with a pool cue by a bouncer. The underwriter was Lloyd's of London. The aggregate coverage was up to $2 million, and while there were exclusions such as covering the assault and battery of patrons by employees, I didn't find a specific exclusion related to serving alcohol. For this policy, the owner paid a $2,425 premium. I rushed to the copy machine in an adjunct building where court records were stored.

Certainly this did not prove the bar owner had the applicable liability insurance in November 2002. Yet if I had been able to stumble upon this, what else lay buried?

While off on this tangent, from time to time I tried to connect what I was doing in Providence with my students. As a high school teacher, one of my overarching goals was helping each one articulate his or her voice. Especially to sharpen one's tools to do this in writing, and apply some of the crafts writers use for storytelling and persuasion. While recognizing that there's more than just one learning style, I tried to honor and support their expressions of voice. *Your voice matters.* This wasn't always explicitly connected to any of the educational frameworks we were expected to build our lessons from. Yet following my gut, and being a bit of a contrarian, I tried it anyway with my eleventh and twelfth grade classes, or while facilitating the school newspaper.

Perhaps I was in tune with this to a fault. Yet some of our urban students arrived with narratives that could rock the world, poems and college essays zooming in on a crucible moment, and then what came next. Among my favorites was a young man's resolve after a house fire destroyed nearly everything he and his siblings and his mom had; Aaron's will to be the man of his house, which along with his strengths in math and his business acumen helped propel him to Bentley College. Argumentative Maki, often late to class and yet expressing desire, committing himself to school rather than a gang. Sashel, an introvert in my writing class, reeling from the losses of a close cousin and other relatives, who shared her belief in our newspaper that forgiveness is stronger than hate.

One year I taught Julia Alvarez's *In the Time of the Butterflies.* It wasn't in the curriculum, and my department head didn't acknowledge my request to buy books, so I got my own on the cheap. Exploring her novel and the ruthless Trujillo regime turned into one of the best units I ever taught. In one particularly unruly class, I began to successfully differentiate the instruction with small groups examining specific parts of the book, group members taking on roles matching their strengths to track characters, themes, literary devices and history, and reporting back to the whole. But what stood out the most were the voices of the four Mirabal sisters conveyed by Alvarez. *Las Miraposas.* The butterflies. Through them we glimpsed life in the Dominican Republic, while some of my Dominican and other Latino students shed new understandings for the rest of us.

Their voices.

As I thought of Mike and P.J. again, and the interminable mass of crap leaching from Bar One, I wondered who was left accountable. By withdrawing our lawsuit against the club owners, in a sense our sons' testimony had been lost. Who would ever know? In the middle of the night, the questions got even worse.

There had to be other ways to hear their voices and recognize that their gifts still mattered. Perhaps I had no right to extend this to P.J., or to assume anything on his family's behalf. For Denise and I, we needed to know somehow that Mike was still around.

I felt a nagging itch as we geared up for Mike's tenth anniversary in 2012. Lingering with the fear about his life that Jeff Walsh had helped me resolve, I wanted to know more about Providence. Had anyone clamped down on underage drinking in the clubs? How many more families had been put through the wringer?

Did the voices of victims' families pleading for sanity—if not just to hold people accountable to the law—make any difference?

I found that little had changed.

It's not worth going too far into this, but that spring I went up the chain of authority to ask about implementing an under-twenty-one ban. The previous summer, Rhode Island's legislature had empowered municipalities to ban minors from entering clubs with repeat violations of underage drinking. Under its charter, the Providence licensing board could have imposed this restriction on repeat offenders.

It had not. I was told there had been no discussion of this, and such a recommendation would have come from the city solicitor's office. That had not happened.

I pursue the hell out of it. I meet with the board's administrator and chairman, its attorney, the city solicitor, police commissioner, and a detective who investigates license complaints. The solicitor says he and the commissioner—who is on record determined to change the city's reputation and make its nightlife safer—have begun drafting tougher policies for nightclub licenses, including under-twenty-one sanctions. They want to give city regulators sharper tools. "What everybody tells me is if you come down like a load of bricks on one, others will listen," Solicitor Jeff Padwa says. Great.

Meanwhile, there's been a crush of nightclub violence in the so-called "Creative Capital" this spring: melees that began in another club's VIP lounge and spilled outside; testimony of metal detectors not working and locked club doors; bouncers sneaking people in through a back entrance after 1:00 p.m.; police describing a riot in the streets. Entering the snake pit, a small corner room where the Providence Licensing Board conducts its business in city hall, I observe a hearing for Level II, a joint where five people were stabbed Easter morning.

It was pretty much a slaughterhouse, Patrolman Kenneth DeMarco says.

Chaos. Fights all over the place. "Blood on the floor," testifies Patrolman Edward Leste.

They were fighting all the way down the stairs, adds Patrolman Gregory Daniels. *They were rolling down the stairs.*

Local business owners and anyone else paying attention have long recognized this as one of the worst managed, most dangerous downtown dance clubs. One morning the previous November, cops counted 848 patrons, more than double its capacity—so much that police and a fire inspector couldn't even move through the crowd. There's also been under-age drinking, yet the board declined to revoke its license and declare it a "disorderly house."

It's outrageous: same crap, different decade. A brick firetrap waiting to happen. One of its owners is a new state representative who has hired another lawmaker for counsel. The pump still reeks. I wonder how many cities put up with such garbage.

Yet, why wear these two hats again? Is it a reporter's urge to uncover this sludge, more about inserting himself into the mix, or a father's responsibility to do something for his son? Perhaps this is misplaced, like mixing water and oil. Is this ego or salvation? My stomach churns. The meter maid nabs me before I can dash out to refill quarters.

Another co-owner sits with his attorney, who will soon try to trip up a firefighter and squelch a detective's testimony. With a five-o'clock shadow, he looks cast out of the Flintstones, a co-worker of Fred's at the quarry, except for his fine threads. He pouts, dog-faced. The writing is on the wall.

"These things don't happen overnight," Detective Joe Amoroso tells me during a break. "It's part of a culture."

That July, Rhode Island MADD took an unusual step of teaming up with a popular downtown nightclub to amplify its message. One of the owners of Club Colleseum, a Roman and Greek-themed mega club—not one of the clubs under scrutiny at the time—offered to gather his servers, bartenders, and door people for a close-up look at how serving practices can put patrons and those who come into contact with them at risk. The mayor and the head of the state police came along with other city officials. I accepted an invitation from the MADD director to tell some of our story as a featured speaker.

Entering the bowels of one of Providence's entertainment areas, Denise and I realized we were only two blocks from Chris's freshman dorm at Johnson & Wales University. One of the Colleseum's owners welcomed us as we stepped in, eyeing the busts of emperors alongside seating nooks and faux columns. I greeted the state police colonel and Public Safety Commissioner Steven Paré, who had recently penned a column in the *Providence Journal* warning club owners to quell late-night violence and underage drinking. To me, the presentation would highlight prevention, remembrance, and accountability—with me focusing on remembrance. We placed some photos of Mike in front of the audience.

Twenty or so of the club's employees sat facing us. Although being a teacher had meant performing daily in front of students and occasionally presenting to colleagues, I felt uncomfortable catching the eyes of these young adults as I scanned the room. Yes, they were here, and they might benefit from heightened awareness. But perhaps they were not the ones who most needed to be reached. And likely none of them had served my son. When it was my turn, I told them about Mike and some of what we missed. Bubaloo and his restless spirit. Sensing Mike's impatience, his uncle Clay once told him that life is about the trek, not the destination.

I addressed the matter of Bar One directly, letting them see that I knew *exactly* where it was, and how shoddy its record had been. I shared the impact on our family, the floor giving way beneath us, connecting that to their responsibilities around serving alcohol.

"Mike doesn't get to see his sister blossoming into an artist," I told them. "He doesn't get to see his brother, a young entrepreneur, doing things."

I was not aware of this, but part of my message echoed what Cory Scanlon had continued telling high school seniors over the years. On one occasion, he told students in a large school near Boston that all he remembered about the crash was waking up in a hospital room in a neck brace, with cuts all over his body and tubes in his arm and nose. Finally able to focus, he saw his parents crying. He looked at his mother and asked what had happened. He could see in her eyes that there was something she did not want to tell him. "I killed two of my best friends," Scanlon warned the students. "I took them away from their families."

He had used his fake ID at Bar One. The Jeep rolled over three times before landing on its roof. Brendan Carey recalled going eighty-five miles per hour. State police estimated their speed at twenty mph above that.

I tried scanning the faces of the club staff again. Denise was somewhere in the back supporting me, even though I had dragged her through yet another ordeal. I emphasized how their decisions resound. I flew off the handle once, referencing the virulent mix of club violence and underage drinking that still maligned the city. "It doesn't matter whether they are white, black, or brown," I recall saying. "The fucking color of their blood is the same."

The MADD director must have gulped; from the corner of my eye I think I saw Mayor Tavares twitch. Afterwards, a young woman on the club staff came up to my wife expressing her condolences and thanks.

As we drove home I became faintly aware of having turned a corner, like a hint of fall beckoning on a crisp late summer night. I could give this up, this singular rant, a twisted, toxic coping mechanism. Friends withheld comment changing the subject when I brought it up. My wife deserved better.

There was scant media coverage of the MADD event—one article buried inside the newspaper—but we had tried. A few weeks later, one of the club owners sent Denise and I a card, saying that he, his partners, and employees "will be forever changed for the better."

No one wanted me to do this.

Denise repeatedly admonished, "We need to talk about this first." But I had promised myself to get my arms fully around it, returning to Providence at least one last time.

I never saw a counselor during those years. I didn't fall in the gutter, though I recognize its knife-edged traverse well enough. It might have been different given another lurch backwards or coming upon some other evidence. There were long walks at dusk railing at myself. Or trying to be still and listen: please, shut up, just listen. Be there for your kids, and for her. Clear this infernal chatter. Come across peals of peepers rising from the swamp on an early warm-throated night. Stop by Mike's grave on the way home at last light, trying to work something out, telling him what his mom and sister and brother were up to, and how they love him so.

I dealt with it by taking runs and calling for his strength. Returning on a long flat stretch beside some stubble fields, I called to him and P.J. to help me make a half-sprint final push. They would never give up, and we would never surrender their memories.

And the occasional sail alone. A few times I beat down Buzzards Bay in *Cinnamon Girl* as the rollers built into a dark green froth, heading into twenty or twenty-five knots flying only the genoa. Other boats were returning home, and I figured the bay would broil out past Cleveland's Ledge.

Our girl still looks a bit beamy to me when she sits, as if big boned with wide hips. Yet she sails true, personifying our brief sojourns to rebalance and navigate joy again. Releasing from land I motored out past the sandbar, surveying the waves as we headed into the wind with the diesel humming. Reaching the open bay I unfurled the sail and we instantly heeled up on a starboard tack. Shutting off the engine, I braced a leg against the seat, back pressed on a stanchion as we lit out at a keen angle.

I knew her feel, when she'd begin to point up, and just when to ease off leeward. Even without the mainsail the boat balanced well enough. Plenty of sheet driving forward in the gusts, fast. Adjustments at the wheel came by themselves, the trick being letting go: Just us and the rollers, scanning for the odd lobster pot in the pitch.

Her bow nosing through each swell, crossing the approach to the canal in a freshening chop, slicing toward Wings Neck. Come about with unspoken timing, bring her around, crank in the Harken winch, four wraps, get that finger out—*Think!*—cleat it quickly, shift sides, braced and ready. Off on a new tack I hear Mike's laugh in the other room as he cracks up with everyone, cocky in a hoodie and then supple like a meandering toddler again.

Where would you be now? Becoming a better man. A career, a good partner. Treating her right.

Appreciating him alone, just for himself. Not for me this time.

For whatever reason, heading toward a green bell I start imagining that night at the club. Surely this has been foretold: barely half-informed, be forewarned. Taut dew rags, low-hung jeans and oversized, long white tees.

Brothers' caps in colors signifying territory signifies nothin' in the end 'cept your cousin dead whose button you wearin'. G's down for an away game, a bottle of Hennessey; youse with me? Steroid-brawn white dudes and beef jerky trash borrow the talk, most can't do the walk, alt-right crackers whisperin', vesperers off the block; lock jaw, sliced raw, never actually been on the seesaw. That's phat.

Lemme break it down for you: Damn Nelly it's Hot in Here, Dre and Eminem reveal a Guilty Conscience, We Thuggin', Aaliyah I Care 4 You. Forcin' it now? Nas and Damien Marley a burning justice spear; Akon, one fierce look. Jay Z, Busta Rhymes Break Ya Neck, Faith Evans, U Don't Have to Call, Usher, 50 Cent, Biggie Smalls, Diddy, prowl. Tupac long since gunned down but unlike Huey he never left, actually releasing more music since they all bereft. Mixing beats = samples = tossing allusions =

Don't let 'em say you ain't beautiful, oh
They can all get fucked
Just stay true to you

Whaddup, B?
That was one of Mike's.
Word.

The boat is barreling like a fuselage toward Woods Hole. We appear to be alone, outcasts banked against the spin and spit of the world. Sunshine glints in and out against the whitecaps and the islands stretch out like an unclaimed necklace. Four- and five-foot rollers funnel up the bay in a classic sou'wester, each chop of the hull its own arc, rising and slashing ahead. Spray kisses the deck with a flirtatious smirk, rushes along the gunnel, seething. She rears again into the next one.

Inside outside, leave me alone.

A second oil can
Held so tight
Hard a lee
Serves you right

Damned if I care
Strafed by lament

Another length forward
the further we're set.

Belief streams far ahead of knowing, cackling and clutching, free and wrought-up coiled, passively imposing, gathering in those I adore and pushing them away. Sanguine, observant, then flippant, yelling, never lose the can; in you go but don't let go, pleading with her to understand.

I'm flowing under bridges
Then flying through the sky.

It begins to move behind me, or perhaps finally I'm laying it down. How Denise held everyone up and continued to teach and run the house. How she snuggled under blankets with our kids to watch Syfy flicks on weekend afternoons as if to extend short breaths into deeper ones, finally taking moments for herself, stretched full to exhale, and feeling Mike close by, only to be tortured that he was never coming up the front steps again. What I believed was how we held together, torn and unyielding, defying those splintered odds after all we had been through, sharing things read on the couch in recovered fragments with long embraces in the shower and bedroom scrapes, alarming the dogs with suitcase threats and attached abandon, yet still as one, a light in your eyes remains since that first time you walked into the room. And how he loves you. He will always love you and knows that he is fully loved.

By staying open, our hearts broken wide to his presence.

Beyond the helm a battalion of grey clouds is lowering and the gusts keep picking up. I am shouting, ragged, hoarse. Regrets alight like sparks against the incredible sky, declared to the ravenous sea, asking her forgiveness, calling on him again, calling,

Please take my advice
Please take my advice
Please take my ad—

A rogue wave crashes over the bow, cresting in wayward oblivion, soaking me clean through.

Roaring *Arrrgghh Mike, you got me.*

PART SIX

UNSPEAKABLE GIFTS

Now I will you to be a bold swimmer,
To jump off in the midst of the sea, rise again, nod to me,
shout, and laughingly dash with your hair.
—Walt Whitman, "Song of Myself"

27

SAY HIS NAME

Amidst what remains for Dolly and Jim Sullivan is a hero star stone cut from odd-shaped granite, standing like a sentry in their side yard. It is not too far from a large sugar maple that their son struggled to climb as a kid. Chris chafed while watching one of his older sisters scale it, trying again and again to do it himself. He finally made it when he was about ten.

There are mementos the Sullivans hold on to, a blend of intense pride and equally sharp lament. A customized riding helmet has the blazing "Big Red One" insignia of the army's 1st Infantry Division, in which Chris and his father and grandfather all served. One picture in their den shows Chris on leave with his parents, relaxed in a blue polo shirt checking out the Tall Ships gathered in Boston Harbor. Within another frame is the program for a two-day concert that a group in his hometown performed to raise money for a memorial scholarship.

Both parents wear wristbands bearing Chris's name on their left arms. His mom, a retired postmaster with deep lines that descend from the sides of her mouth, sometimes fingers dog tags bearing her son's image that hang from her neck as she talks. What they have are letters he wrote from Kosovo and Iraq, and his many uniforms—Eagle Scout, Civil Air Patrol cadet leader, and a scout platoon commander—and childhood stuff like a footlocker full of his toys.

What they do not have, besides their only son, is access to his blonde-haired child, who turned fourteen in 2017. The boy's mom, Christopher's widow, returned to her native Germany after Sullivan died and severed ties with his parents, denying them contact with a grandson.

Beyond this, their worst fear is that people will forget Christopher James Sullivan.

He was killed in Baghdad on January 18, 2005, when an improvised explosive device went off near his parked vehicle. By then a captain in the 2nd Battalion, 12th Cavalry Regiment, 1st Cavalry Division, he had taken a call to check out a disturbance. His father says that as a company commander he didn't really need to go investigate this himself. But that was not Chris's way. He lived largely for the men who served with him, once promising their wives and girlfriends at Fort Hood, Texas, that he would take care of them. "It would have bothered him more to have one of his men under him get killed," his dad says. Long-legged at six feet tall, Chris had warm blue eyes and his mother's broad smile. He was twenty-nine.

A piece of the makeshift bomb entered his hip just below his flak jacket and came out through his neck. Before he died Sullivan mouthed to his mates, "What happened? What happened?"

His mother was at work when the news came, and his dad was home sick. As word spread across Princeton, a small town in central Massachusetts, Dolly and Jim felt an outpouring of support, with some gestures continuing well into the years ahead. It snowed heavily before Christopher's memorial service, and a neighbor saw to it that this didn't complicate things further for the family. Jim, a Vietnam veteran who comes across as reserved and strained, and whose cloudy blue eyes sometimes appear fixed in the distance, recalls, "Bob Mason up in town plowed a lot. He went in with a front-end loader and took every bit of snow out of the cemetery. Things like that get to you."

The town dedicated a memorial to Sullivan at a park on Veterans Day the next fall. It's above a soccer field behind the town highway barn, looking up to Mount Wachusetts, a small peak with a ski area. Some surprise guests flew in from Fort Hood, including a major who had been close to Chris, and General Peter Chiarelli, who had led the 1st Cavalry in Iraq. After giving the town manager Chiarelli's email, the Sullivans had no clue that anyone was coming. That the general and Chris's colleagues made it meant so much to them, among the many things they would never take for granted. Like jumper cables set in the back of Jim's Ford pickup, they stored those gestures away to retrieve in lean times, turning to them deep in the winter to restart, or to reach someone who was similarly stranded.

Across from his monument, Chris's grandmother later donated a granite bench that has "Freedom is not free" engraved on its front face and the emblems of the five armed services on the back. That expression became their mantra, and sometimes a loaded trigger especially for Dolly, who wished more young people would be taught to appreciate this logic. In the years ahead, administrators and teachers at the local school made sure their students learned about Chris and his sacrifice.

After Sullivan's remains were interred at Arlington National Cemetery, which had been his request, eighth graders from his hometown began visiting his grave during their annual trips to Washington, D.C., actually stopping there before his parents did. Classes at the Thomas Prince School sent calendars, hand sanitizer, and other items to troops overseas. The principal stayed in touch with the couple.

When Sullivan was leading a tank platoon in Kosovo a few years earlier, he wrote to one of his sisters that his soldiers' duties included guarding children on their way to school each morning and helping villagers get firewood. He would approach local leaders asking what was needed that day, working out security so people could cut logs for their fuel. Known among his college friends for opening his wallet for homeless people, Chris was thrust into places where generosity and tolerance appeared to be irreconcilable with ethnic hatred and retaliation.

His parents' ordeal multiplied during the next few years. Chris's widow, Sandra, took her toddler to Germany and cut off contact, not even allowing the Sullivans to send David a Christmas card or gifts. Chris barely had enough time to know his son. He was home only twice from the time David was born until he was killed. He did see David William stand up for the first time during an early holidays celebration at his parent's house.

Jim and Dolly thought miscommunication and cultural differences had played a role in the rift. Five months after Chris died, Sandra had brought David east from Fort Hood and stayed with them for a month before moving to New Hampshire. The couple does not believe they were being overbearing, yet perhaps a separation was inevitable. "After that happened, we don't know," Jim says. "We told her you must find a place to live, and offered to help her. We were not trying to take control of her life. She thought we wanted to take David away from her, and we don't."

Their split, however, did not indicate that Chris's wife did not continue to hold him close. Signing in as Sandra Sullivan, she gave an online tribute four years later.

"You are still the best man I ever met because you had an inner beauty and such a good heart which I never found since I lost you," she wrote. "I always knew what I had in you and if there will be another man in my life one day then just one whose heart is in the right place and whose inner beauty and love will give David and myself a home again. If this should ever happen again then I know that it was you who sent him and I also know that you watch over us to make sure that we will find the right one."

The toll from this accumulated along with other family tensions, such as the parents' insistence that the proceeds from Chris's memorial concert—some seventeen thousand dollars—be used to establish a scholarship rather than go to his wife and son, as one of their daughters wanted. The Sullivans thought their son's army pension and death benefits would see Sandra through, and they wanted to help graduates interested in mechanical engineering, which was Chris's major.

Jim continued to work as a meter reader with a local utility. He had friends at the nearby American Legion hall, and upkeep to do on their vinyl-sided home. Over long stretches his wife felt unable to do anything, even as she made quilts with a group of friends, worked part time, and got together with moms from other military families. The second time we met, several weeks before the sixth anniversary of her son's death, she said she had suffered a nervous breakdown. "It just got to me at some point," Dolly acknowledged.

Adding to this was the fear that others would stop remembering, not unlike my own cringing thoughts about Mike.

A few people moved away from them. While as inevitable as the crusted pockmarked snowbanks on his street, this nagged at Jim too. Despite the other mementos they stored—a rubbing of his name from the Fort Hood memorial, Chris's framed fraternity T-shirt, a patriotic quilt given to Dolly, and even the thought of flags being flown at half-mast in town for a week—despite all these things, he wondered who would know. "I think that's the worst thing," he told me, "feeling that people forgot about your son, that it didn't mean anything. It's just kind of unbelievable."

Captain Sullivan's remains are interred in Section 60, gravesite 8545 at Arlington, which his parents visit several times a year. They usually go during the spring, on Veterans Day, and always in December for wreath laying.

Near his grave, but not only there, the Sullivans began connecting with other parents. They haven't shirked from making new friends or attempting to comfort them.

A holly tree grows behind Sullivan's plot, and each year another family decorates their own son's grave on the other side of it, sometimes stringing lights while children hang ornaments provided by service members on the tree. Nearby, some years ago Jim met another dad whose son had just been buried a month or so before. "I went over and got talking to him," Jim says. "He was a nice guy and you talk about his son and you tell him about yours, and it helps, I think, in the long run, because not everybody wants to hear, or you think they want to hear but they don't know how to ask you."

It wasn't too much for them to hook up with others back home. They helped out at fundraisers such as runs for wounded warriors or a pancake breakfast at Legion Post 172 in Orange. They met other adults walking a similar road through the Tragedy Assistance Program for Survivors, or TAPS, which provides grief supports to military families, and later the Sullivans became mentors themselves. Dolly joined Gold Star Mothers, eventually becoming president of its Massachusetts-Rhode Island chapter.

Chris was a go-getter, destined to live life to the fullest. As a teenager at Wachusett Regional High School, Sullivan seemed bored with his classes and got by largely by being a skilled test-taker. He'd tell his friends and parents, "Just get over it. Get over it and move on." His grades were strong enough to get into a demanding program at UMass Lowell. He golfed and enjoyed skiing, and like both of his sisters worked at the ski area nearby.

His family was steeped in military service, and from an early age Chris set his sights on doing the same. Books about tanks, planes, and battles filled much of his shelf. He took uniforms seriously as a Cub Scout up through the Civil Air Patrol, where he was taught search and rescue techniques, good manners, and patriotism. He was his unit's cadet leader as it moved from Fitchburg to Worcester. He dreamed of becoming a fighter pilot but did not have the requisite perfect eyesight.

His father didn't talk much about Vietnam, where he had been assigned to a transportation outfit, yet the desire to serve was an undiminished force on both sides of the family. Dolly's brothers had also served during the war, including one who was Chris's godfather, a career man in the infantry who had married a German woman as well. When Christopher Sullivan was commissioned, Sergeant Major Luther Davidson stuffed himself into his dress uniform and was there to give his nephew his first salute. Following protocol, Chris then slipped Luther a silver dollar as they shook hands.

The family tradition went back at least another generation as Chris's maternal grandfather, William Davidson, was captured in Algiers during the Second World War. Some months later, Davidson escaped from a box-car with other POWs in Italy and was among less than a handful of about eighty men to survive the ensuing hunt. They were eventually picked up by British forces and returned to the States. After the war, he joined the Teamsters driving trucks and was a heavy machinery operator. Davidson became the head of a local POW/MIA chapter, yet his adult children knew very little about their father's past until decades later. They pained to learn what had happened to him and why he had been so harsh, and sometimes abusive, to their mother.

Somewhere down the line the Sullivans began giving themselves an early Christmas present. Jim has roots in eastern Maine, where his dad owns a house amidst the blueberry barrens in Washington County. He and Dolly don't go up there to rake berries though.

A few times they've actually joined truckers and other veterans' families in the Wreaths Across America tour, a massive holiday delivery of goodwill and tribute initiated by a Maine couple in 1992. Each year, scores of trailer trucks bring fresh balsam wreaths with signature hand-tied red bows to Arlington and other military cemeteries, a drive that has expanded to more than 150 locations. Jim and Dolly spent a week on the tour with its escorts in December 2014, catching up with people they'd met during previous years and meeting new arrivals.

It began with laying wreaths during a sunrise service at Quoddy Head, and stopping at the international border at Calais and Saint Stephen. After a dinner that night in Columbia Falls, not far from drive founder Morrill Worcester's wreath-making factory and tree farm, the Sullivans were aboard a coach bus with other Gold Star parents and relatives, near a film crew and even some Revolutionary War re-enactors. They reunited with a Mainer named Alan who suffers from PTSD and had been in both Afghanistan and Iraq. The previous year, a service dog accompanied him to help with his limited vision. Alan's dog Basil had since died, but he opened up a bit more about what he had experienced his last time overseas, knowing the couple would not judge him.

Winding through New England and making stops further down the coast was an epiphany to them. Dolly especially found herself warmed by events hosted by schools, the color returning to her face. Kids surrounded them cheering in Wells, Maine, sword-carrying Knights of Columbus members passed by outside Portland, they stopped at veterans homes, and were on their feet for an assembly at the Ponnagansett Middle School in North Scituate, Rhode Island. She was later moved by cadets marching at the Valley Forge Military Academy, and met an artist who pays tribute to the fallen by drawing their portraits—including a sketch of Chris beaming—at a Remembrance Wall at the Topsfield Fairgrounds. Further along, their group delivered a thirty-foot wreath to the Statue of Liberty, and they stopped in Annapolis and at the Pentagon.

Those they met along the way meant the most, further helping the couple heal themselves. Dolly rode in a Mack truck with a volunteer driver from New Mexico named Ralph Garcia. She consoled the mom of an Army Ranger from South Carolina who was making her first trip, and they met an older man riding for his grandson. They found another woman who was less withdrawn than the previous year. Sometimes they shared common issues like splits within the family; at other times the weight someone carried had an unexpected source. "It's not something you want to dwell on all the time, but when you can share that with someone, that's good," Dolly said. "On my low days she can lift me, and vice versa."

They met a longtime friend at their son's plot, laying out the fresh dark greens.

Ten years had nearly drained by with the cycles of spring melt rushing off the mountain and a trickle of summer streams. Retired and in his early seventies, skin hung loosely under Jim's chin. He wore a light blue vest over a long-sleeve shirt, among the inexorable, utilitarian habits of a New Englander who rarely leaves home for long.

I had met the couple a few years earlier at a 9/11 service event in Boston, approaching them as they scarfed pizza slices on a break from filling soldiers' care packs. They wore their emotions openly along with buttons of their son, drawing me in with unspoken solidarity. During my second visit to their home we sat in the den by a gas-fired stove flanked by stuffed birds and wooden duck decoys along the windows. Jim perked up talking about Maine again, and the places we both knew up in God's country.

Before the Wreaths Across America bus trip, Jim and a few guys from the Sterling Legion hall had stood outside a Wal-Mart in the chill collecting for local veterans. With about six hundred dollars in bills and change from shoppers, they bought gifts for men including two-piece fleece sets and extra material that someone at one of the assisted living homes offered to stitch together. He and Dolly also stayed active in more formal ways, following legislation that affects veterans and occasionally showing their support at State House hearings. They attended selectmen's meetings in other towns, advocating that officials purchase POW/MIA chairs of honor.

His wife had let some things go, while a few others still needed to be arranged. Going on three years without receiving a picture or hearing a word about their grandson, Dolly tried not to be judgmental. "I've put it in God's hands, there's nothing I can do," she told me over the phone before we met at their home again. "It took a long, long time to get there."

Her mother had also passed more than two years earlier at age ninety, when she was still able to enjoy an occasional lobster roll and had lived a few good years after many hard ones. As Dolly sorted through her parents' belongings, she came across her dad's old army records. Scattered details emerged, and it is likely her mother picked out some shards to show her children near the end of her life.

Prudence Davidson had been loyal to William, even to a fault. During his escape as a POW, he dug holes to hide in by day, moving at night. He witnessed others being caught and killed. The British didn't believe the few survivors' stories; they had no dog tags, IDs, or uniforms, and there were suspicions they had actually been collaborators. He suffered from battle fatigue and one news article claimed he was the last American POW to return from North Africa. Growing up, Dolly's father could be brutal, Jekyll and Hyde on the bottle, treating her the best of anyone in the family. His daughter still searched for the full chronology, she and her brother, Luther, each wanting to know.

That fall Dolly had been invited to a POW/MIA commemorative event in Georgia with escorts by Rolling Thunder riders, and she visited the National POW Museum at Andersonville Prison. While still torn about her father's legacy, the trip was a salve. "I loved my dad dearly but sometimes I hated the man he was," she said, her voice cracking. "The ride was very healing. A lot of good came from it."

Sitting at their kitchen table, Dolly brought out a partial trove of her father's recovered records—army telegrams and citations, clippings and letters. There were blanks yet to be filled in. She looked hard at me, almost piercing through, as if pleading for someone new on the scene to help make sense of it.

She and Jim were trying to make peace with all these things. They each had to believe that Chris continued to watch over his son, and each of them.

"We do whatever we can when we can. Anything that has to do with veterans or veterans services is what we've made our mission in life," she said. "You just don't wallow in self-pity."

Jim Sullivan noted again how his son was more interested in taking care of others. He offered, "So we're carrying that on."

Emerging from chaos and heartbreak, we created community.

By 2016 our nonprofit, Hope Floats Healing and Wellness Center, met a variety of needs that neither of us could have foreseen when Denise opened shop eight years earlier. We provided free support groups meeting every other week for parents who've lost a child, adults grieving the loss of a spouse or partner, for families struggling with the brutal stigma of suicide, and others whose lives had been strafed by addiction and overdose. Most of these were peer-led, while others were co-facilitated or led by licensed counselors in what felt like a symbiosis of life and professional experience. Her early core group of three counselors renting space in the rear of the house and upstairs had grown to six women meeting clients a few days a week.

We tried to offer supports tailored to specific circumstances while proactively addressing some of the crises that brought on others' grief. Facing one of these, a dad whose son lost a long battle with opioids spoke to parents about interventions and the systemic causes of an epidemic. Denise made room for expressive arts and writing workshops, evenings of sound healing in the barn and a popular pet loss group. Physicians and mental health practitioners increasingly referred patients to us. Months and even years following tragedies that made us flinch watching the evening news, some of those families passed Mike's portrait in the entry way.

Hope Floats was getting out there.

Making connections with others traveling a similar road continued to be the anchor. Active remembrance, doing things to honor a loved one and hold her close, continued to be a salve. Despite its double-edged poignancy. If we ever lost our grounding, new families coming in asserted this vitality, like resetting a mooring below a fast-moving channel.

I want others to say his name.

"Who are *you* walking for?"

A week before Mother's Day, the morning brings spotless sunshine and low sixties as the lawn behind the main house fills in. The following week will be damp and chilly nearly each day, and we don't take this shift in our favor for granted. Yet she didn't need a forecast to know.

"If you haven't already, head over to our raffle tables to bid on some cool stuff!"

An earnest guy in a black hockey jersey with a dragonfly on the front wields a mic under one of the big maples, crooning like a maniacal play-by-play announcer.

Nearly five hundred people walk a three-mile route through the town center down to its snug little harbor and back. Many understandably would rather be anywhere else than strolling in the brisk absence of a friend or relative. This is more than double the participants from a year ago, and I am blown away. It's just impossible to thank everyone.

We're also lifted by the show of local support: a young police patrolman leapfrogs in his cruiser to secure the busiest intersections, and three churches provide overflow parking. Parents of one of our son Chris's close friends walk again, winning a coveted raffle to dine in the North End.

Team B-Roons, a group of twenty-eight or so in purple T-shirts, raise their arms for a photo, honoring a young woman they love. Her dad stretches on the grass in front, his smiling face propped up with an elbow, giving a thumbs up.

Taking off her director's hat, Denise speaks to the crowd as Mike's mom. She dreads this. She's practiced in the living room, to herself in the car. I tell her that people *yearn* to hear her words; she is fluent teaching a universal language. Far beyond what she realizes.

"We know this day is about more than being a fundraiser," she says. "It's about loved ones who can't physically be here with us. Today is about opening our hearts and making space for our grief, our sorrow, and our joyful memories. It's a day to make connections with family and friends, and people we've never met before.

"Most importantly, we are reminded today that they will never be forgotten. We will never let that happen."

One of our new counselors, who has endured child losses of her own, welcomes guests and supporters to pin dragonflies with a name or message for a loved one on a board. Our daughter and her friend Nate face paint a steady line of children, their second time helping us out this month.

Another mom who lost her only son several years ago, one of our board members, sits and holds a baby off to the side, reuniting with a couple who were his high school friends.

Spying Jeff Walsh with Kevin, Tommy, Travis, and several of Mike's other friends and their partners, I get to sit down with them. I ask Brittany and Jeff to pick out a tree that I can plant on the spot where they married, not twenty feet from us.

Before heading out, we name those we miss in unison.

He is not just a name, you know.

My aunt sends Denise a congratulatory card a few days later. I walk with her and my uncle, my brother, Bill, and our dad, a string of good conversations we don't always get to. "And I think most people are in need," Bev writes Denise. "Not necessarily because of a death in the immediate family, but because of so many issues that touch us in painful ways."

Who are you walking for?

In mid-July Hope Floats' lawn is transformed into a carnival.

Little kids are getting their faces painted under a tent and someone spins wands of cotton candy beside a machine churning out snow cones in deep blue raspberry heaps. A tangy aroma of pizza mixes with sugary wafts as a woman strums her guitar, singing folk songs and classics for two young girls in wheelchairs.

Nearby, a parachute with a multi-colored sunburst design is spread on the grass in partial shade. A half-dozen children in wheelchairs with power seating and other adaptive gear gather around its periphery, tended by their parents, home health aides, and care assistants, plus a few grandparents relaxing under a tree. This is the fifth time we've hosted "Fragile Footprints," a half-day camp for kids who are in palliative care or have a sick sibling, along with children who have lost a parent or brother or sister. The camp runs for a week and is an extension of Denise's collaboration with a local hospice. For these youths, it amounts to a brief stretch of camaraderie while offering their caregivers a breath of fresh air.

From across the lawn comes a cacophony of blocks, drums, and bells. Tony, a percussionist who thrives on playing West African and Cape Verdean rhythms, encourages children to join him as he ambles around with a drum strapped to his waist. He's back for the fourth time, guiding his charges under a smaller tent. "Red, blue, green, blue, red," he sings to help one boy locate the different heads and tones of several drums.

Many of the children have also been expressing themselves with paint, plaster, and other means this week. One arts therapist led a group sculpting lumpy rock monsters as well as a project that began as pressing stamps on large canvases under the tent. Someone suggested painting "Julia" in memory of a young girl who had attended the camp before and died that spring, opening the floodgates to a torrent of other names. Soon the kids were adding the names of someone they were thinking of, not just the

deceased. The children, thought Kathleen McAleer, one of the camp leaders, were leading the way once again. Rather than creating memory boards,
she thought the next time they might make "somebody special boards."

McAleer is a veteran of creating safe spaces where families make connections. She is the bereavement coordinator at Cranberry Hospice and
Palliative Care, an agency that has been doing this work since the late 1980s.
Foremost, she is a terrific partner for Denise, and the two built a compelling
synergy to expand services for local families. They complement and feed
off each other, bouncing ideas for new groups and developing training and
check-ins for group facilitators.

A licensed social worker, McAleer has an arts background and can vac-
illate between being supremely organized to a bit goofy. She chuckles at
spotting a "bacon-infused" burger on a menu when we attend a conference in Indianapolis—and orders it, with regrets. While Denise wears her
parent's hat, relating to adults through shared experience—and reaching
into her teacher-nurturer tool belt—Kathleen is the seasoned clinician.
While Denise often hugs other moms after group, McAleer maintains a
slight outward reserve. She can be no-nonsense setting boundaries, staring an unruly teen down, or informing a new dad that he seems too angry
and would upset a group's balance. But that doesn't mean she is any less
compassionate.

Both women also coordinate occasional "Grief 101"-style seminars for
parents and adult siblings, including dealing with loss around the holidays. Kathleen even has shared musical tastes and led a teen group dubbed
"Three Little Birds" after the iconic Bob Marley song in our art room, a
converted kitchenette overlooking the backyard.

As McAleer well knows, two things these families crave most is a little
normalcy and having fun. While the latter comes in sporadic bursts, finding
community can be like sighting an even rarer species. Which makes their
intersection so empowering.

A while back, she watched a widow who had been in one of her groups
for a while take a newcomer under her wing. The second woman had
recently lost her husband. Dana looked at Kim and said, "I was you a year
ago."

During the holidays, Kim was unable to put up her tree. Dana came over, pulling ornament boxes from the attic and banishing Kim to her sister's while she decorated the house. "Now they are best friends," McAleer says.

The first year of Fragile Footprints, a mom accompanying her ill daughter confided to Kathleen that she had been advised to start a feeding tube. Mom resisted taking this step with every fiber. Then she met two parents who demonstrated how a tube works, bringing her into our barn with their kids. "Low and behold," says McAleer, "afterwards the mom decided to start one."

Throughout the week of camp, parents sample a smorgasbord of self-care provided by Denise's wellness practitioners: discovering a half hour of calm with a back massage, trying Reiki, or relaxing with healing touch, a therapy that taps into energy fields around the body. On the second day, two friends of ours provide sound healing in the great room. Gently playing gongs and Tibetan bowls, Paul and Sharon produce frequencies that open you up, clearing stress as you lie still on a yoga mat or take a nap. A little girl in a wheelchair responds in her own way, her heart rate calming noticeably amidst the expanse of vibrations. Offering these treatments and modalities to complement the support groups is part of what makes Hope Floats unique. Early on my wife recognized an ebb and flow in these things that provide comfort and healing, as supple as the shifting tide in the nearby river.

So used to juggling their kids' appointments and their other coverage duties, some of these moms and dads let a volunteer or nurse take over as they seek a few deep breaths. Closing their eyes, if only for a brief respite.

Outside the barn more activities are in motion. There's pickle Frisbee, Hula-Hoops, and a puppet show, while older kids make mosaic glass art inside the house. Others wave loopy three-foot-wide bubbles that wobble over the grass. It's a pure release for some. "A big mash-up," McAleer says.

That Wednesday, a skinny six-year-old boy and his older brother climb aboard a fire truck with a handful of other guys, which Denise arranged with the local fire department to show campers. They check the view from the driver's seat and younger Tim practices his hold on a railing on the back step before jumping off. Sitting beside a buddy, offering a precious facsimile of a Boston accent, he croaks, "We've got a two-alahmah." When it's his turn, older Zack straps on a pack with an oxygen tank and mask to try out breathing as one fireman gives assurances and instructions. The pump truck stays for perhaps forty-five minutes, the two men patiently introducing their gear and answering questions.

The boys had lost their dad about a year earlier. Their mom, who lives almost an hour away, contacted Denise eager to find supports for her sons. She also sought out other parents attempting to navigate the same ground. Denise was able to connect her to McAleer's children's group, then held at a nearby boys and girls club.

As we clean up after the truck leaves, Tim and Zack's mother stops me on the grass. She had already found Denise in her office for a few moments. We had never met, and their mom tells me that getting connected with Hope Floats has been a lifesaver. "Being around people who know what we're going through" is the key, she says. "People who help make my loss more bearable, not easier."

Her older son, who had been cloying beside her early in the week, is still running around with new friends. She gives me a long hug, and I wish them the best for the summer.

While I am mainly a visitor at camp, stopping by to observe and thank people, much of what goes on here coincides with a shared goal we have to expand Hope Floats' reach. We'd like to help more children.

It's well established how grieving kids benefit by interacting with others going through similar tough stuff. They have their own ways of communicating and melting barriers. We've both visited bereavement centers that focus foremost on children and families rather than adult services as our nonprofit joined networks with other providers. We learned that there is no single template, but successful programs seem to share a lot in common. Kids are encouraged to express themselves creatively and construct narratives of what happened while remembering loved ones in authentic ways. They find that they are not so alone.

To do this, some outdated so-called truisms must be turned on their head. Instead of being afraid to talk about the deceased person, adults are advised to do so—and be truthful. Rather than setting a time limit for grieving, parents learn ways to help kids deal with emotional surges that come with birthdays, graduations, and other milestones. Each child's response is different, and those may be wildly inconsistent.

Rather than shuttering a son's room or squelching anecdotes about him, adults find ways to help their other children stay connected. If a little girl repeatedly draws a picture of her daddy in the place where he died, it's likely all right. She's trying to figure it out.

The tools for what's known as peer-based children's bereavement begin with the basics: bean bag chairs and other comfy seating, stickies on construction paper, scissors and sand trays, iPods and scratched boom boxes. Little ones wiggle with pillows or smack plastic bats against pads, passing around a stuffed duck as they begin circle time. Rules are set to not interrupt or judge and say mean things. Older kids build memory boxes and dream catchers, perhaps naming that person before devouring the Snickers bar dad could never quite resist. Teens film each other remembering their loved one, or do skits to show others the things that are hurtful for them to hear, and what helps.

The essence of these groups is providing a place where kids process and vent among others who are equipped to understand. "You find your own form of expression—art, music, the punching bag," says Donna Schuurman, longtime executive director of The Dougy Center in Portland, Oregon, a pioneer in the field. "And just because we don't have a $5 million university study doesn't mean it's not working."

Although Hope Floats had yet to take the full plunge into this, we both had a good sense of why these approaches matter so much to families. In some environments, kids' interactions with one another are more meaningful than any information or advice coming from the adults. They also benefit most by gathering with children roughly their same age, rather than in large, noisy settings with competing factions. Rather than feeling like an outcast in class, they can speak the same language. And whenever practical, encouraging adults to gather under the same roof during those evenings helps a family unit to step forward together, rather than being "treated" or supported in silos. Often without even realizing it, the families help one another.

In 2015–16, Denise and Kathleen committed to starting age-appropriate groups at Hope Floats. This meant taking another leap. It necessitated transforming the main house and a shift in our thinking.

Teens flooded into an upstairs room, adding their own decorative touches, "Middles" took over the art room, while younger ones in wee-sized chairs filled space off a former master bedroom. McAleer stocked props and more tools: question boxes, weekly themes, acrylic paint and sets of "feeling faces" meant to be stuck on popsicle sticks and cans to prompt discussion. The pizza delivery guy made multiple trips to his car every other Monday night.

They called it, "Mike's Club."

Hearing the name for the first time nearly stopped me in my tracks. The name took on even more meaning because of a connection with one of Denise's closest colleagues and friends. Teresa Lally lost her son, Michael, in a motorcycle crash in 2014. She and her husband, Scott, both longtime bikers, donated to help start the club after a fundraising ride with hundreds of others for their son's foundation. A few weeks before the kids groups began, the four of us painted the teen room, spreading drop cloths over the ruddy pumpkin pine floor. It is dedicated to Michael Patrick Lally.

Around this time, Denise and I received an affirmation of this new direction, like a freshening wind that boosts one's heading on the water. We were attending a conference alongside providers of children's bereavement supports from all over the country, the one where Kathleen ordered the bacon-infused cheeseburger. Stepping away for even two days was an eye opener as we met others with a similar passion. One of the keynote speakers, another architect in the field who had taken her own risks to help children, extolled the courage it takes to do this work. A kind of dialectic that's in play resolving contradictions, the movement out of darkness and back into light.

"The willingness and ability to hold, to cradle really, both crushing grief and abundant joy," Mary Ann Emswiler told us. "One of the great gifts of doing grief work, I think, is that it grows kindness in us as we recognize our common brokenness."

Emswiler urged both the mom-and-pop nonprofits like ours and the larger ones to continue stretching. Keep birthing new ideas. Keep listening to those kids, to their parents. And to this close-knit community of volunteers. She quoted verse from Rumi and Mary Oliver, two of our favorite poets. She offered a telling anecdote of having to explain to someone on a plane what she does for a living.

Believing I heard her say "reverent joy," I put down my pen. I no longer needed that crutch, and Emswiler's phrasing deserved hearing her melody unfiltered.

She spoke directly to us.

Our common brokenness.

I looked over at Denise seated behind me in the hotel ballroom. Emswiler's message would continue to resonate in the months ahead.

Upstairs, the old house on Elm Street rocked as kids and teens clamored in. One night I showed them the labyrinth, with "Littles" and "Middles" winding along its circular path to place rocks they had painted. Someone donated a basketball hoop to help channel some of their energies and the head of a medical center offered to buy a rug. We dreamed of expanding our capacity, perhaps retrofitting the garage as an activities' room, and adding a second night just for children who've lost a sibling.

I met a pre-adolescent girl who had lost a parent and made fantastical sketches on a notepad. I told her about my daughter, who started sketching at about her age, now a professional illustrator.

We kept on stretching. And Mike gave us his nod.

Sandy White brightened as another mom shared her story for the first time in the old house. For too long, nightmares had hemmed in her brooding, clouded blue eyes. The rivulets etched in her broad face relaxed.

An older woman served up a comical tale involving her children. Nearly a dozen women and two men encircled her on folding chairs, a sofa, and two low-seated, burgundy velvet parlor chairs perched like ostentatious wings beside the marble fireplace. Sandy cracked up in her seat. She noticed a few guffaws and a lightening around her. Surely, some of the kids were elbowing each other, thrilled to see their parents easing back.

It's okay to laugh.

You don't have to feel guilty about it.

White is a veteran of parents' support groups who offers herself to others. Having attended several groups for a couple of years, including one led by Denise in the same room, Sandy then joined Denise as a co-facilitator to help other adults find common ground in their grief. Although she dislikes highway driving, during much of the year Sandy comes off Cape Cod in her SUV every other Monday afternoon to help.

A drunk driver killed her son, Paul Rudeen Jr., in 2006. P.J. was twenty-one, a towheaded boy born to be an entertainer. He was heading to his apartment after taking his father out to for a birthday dinner when a drunk in a pickup truck smashed into the car. Loving, independent, and non-judgmental, Sandy's light went out. He was her only child. Long since divorced, she had plans and investments to help P.J. start a family. She considered herself his fixer. Their joke was that when he had kids, she was going to spoil them rotten—and then send them home.

"You're not going to be able to see them," he retorted.

After his death she retreated. The only place that felt safe to White was home; going to the grocery store became her limit. A native of the Florida Panhandle, she had grown up surrounded by bayous, a tomboy outside all day climbing trees and getting into jellyfish fights with her neighbors. She worked for an insurance company and came north with her husband, finishing a degree in elementary education with a minor in psychology. When P.J. was four or five they did homework together at the dining room table, her son working on his letters and numbers. *Are you almost done mom?*

"Yeah, go ahead and play."

White found a summer theatre camp when Paul was in middle school, the first in a line of camps and productions. He fell in love with acting, continuing on and joining an adult improvisation group as a teen. He hurdled enough Elizabethan English to play the fairy king Oberon in *A Midsummer Night's Dream* at Grafton High School. Some friends asked Paul to model tuxes one prom season, "and he came out strutting his stuff," his mother recalled, rotating her shoulders suavely and striking a regal pose.

He had a steady girlfriend and was working in a call center at Lifeline, the emergency medical alert provider. During his last summer, when Paul got tickets to a Hot Chili Peppers concert for Jenny and himself, White briefly fumed, really wanting to go with them. He was on his way, never asking her for a dime. "It was like watching a door open," she said. "It was exactly a year after he moved that he was killed."

The call came around one in the morning. Sandy and her partner Ed were at a hotel near the Pensacola airport, where they had a flight home a few hours later. A state trooper told White there had been a fatality; she acted as if the words had bounced off her. *Excuse me?* Ed saw the phone launch as she began vomiting.

On the flight back she could not contain her tears but resolved to not utter a sound, believing she would erupt. One of the flight attendants assumed it had something to do with Ed. The woman glared at White's mate: *You piece of shit. You are the worst.*

"It's funny now," Sandy told me some years later between sips of iced tea, the flushness receding from her face. "I was visibly upset, and knew I couldn't say anything."

I asked her how we do this. How do we reassemble hard memories into something new?

"I don't know," she said after pausing. "Is there something inside us that searches not only for meaning, but for relief for the most horrible day of your life? Maybe."

He's not just a name, you know.

Her nightmares often came in pairs, even three times a night. Sandy stands in the middle of I-495. P.J. is driving her Saturn. A pickup weaves in and out of traffic. *You see it coming and there's not a damn thing you can do about it.* She wakes up hysterical.

A month or two after his death, lying in bed she felt a hand cup her jaw. *Sleep mom.* Sleep.

She came down into the kitchen another night, and just for a split second, saw Paul against the counter, leaning sideways like he always did. Chill.

Terrified of stepping into a car, White didn't drive for a few years. She associates sudden loud noises with the crash. If she's on a highway and sees a truck approaching she'll fight off an urge to pull over. "A freezing panic," she tells me.

Finding affirmation at our center helped her turn things around. Looking across the room, she met others seeking answers. She saw a couple whose young son died in a fluke accident. Saw another whose daughter got hooked on painkillers following a sports injury. Over time, she glimpsed the legions of victims to lethal prescriptions and opioid overdoses. Heard people racked by stigmas as if pressed in a basement workshop vice, their muffled cries inaccessible to neighbors. Heard a mom's despair that her son was not a bad person but had made terrible mistakes. Met another who told her, *I haven't laughed yet.* Each with a desire that goes uncontested here. Each vying to break through, regardless of how they name isolation. Many concurring with her that, "People just don't understand." Wanting them to return to "normal"—whatever that means.

"How can someone say that when you've lost a child?" my wife agreed, consoling Sandy and the others. "They want you to be the same person you were before, and you're not going to be. It's not possible."

Some of the group members became friends. Some only for a season in their need, occasionally meeting elsewhere for coffee or lunch. Some able to open up only after a few months; a few expressing themselves right away; and the occasional parent who cannot return, unable to make the time work, or clamped shut because sharing is not his way.

To White, someone always seemed to have the right thing to say. She caught eyes with another mom who had also lost an only child, their unspoken dialect cutting through the vacuous din of the masses. She felt uplifted hearing someone's story of receiving a signal from a son, or getting away for a weekend of self-care. She saw parents struggling with the fallout to their other children—one crying, "What about me?" and another trying to protect mom and dad. Saw partners beginning to feel themselves growing apart. Met another who, much like her, had to know all the details. Despite being warned not to, Sandy had viewed the crime scene photos.

"I don't know why," she pauses, "but the feeling was very strong. I just had to know how he died."

She felt a call to step up. Her group, after all, had helped deliver her from a dank, dark place. Not so unlike Laura Dunn or Cindy McGinty, White wanted to give again. A new purpose stirred and she trained to become a facilitator.

Opening each session alongside Denise or a volunteer like herself, Sandy stresses that, this time, she is not fixing anything. "We're *still* in your shoes, and we come together in a common cause," she says.

Many years before Paul died, Sandy learned something that was worth sharing with her peers later. An old friend of hers from Florida was killed in a car crash, a guy recovering from drugs who had met a wonderful girl and told Sandy that they planned to marry. The day of the crash, Sam told Sandy he wanted her to meet his fiancée. Writing a letter to his mom, Sandy expressed how that touched her, not having known how close a friend Sam had considered her.

His mother had difficulty finding White's phone number, but she finally called giving thanks for her kind words. Loaded with guilt about her son's past troubles, she needed to hear how thoughtful and selfless Sam was. He took pride in telling Sandy that he was off everything. White attributed his decency to his mom and their family.

Sandy took stock of how much her reaching out had meant to Sam's mother. Like most people, she had always assumed that the least said, the better. "I just really wanted her to know that his life counted for something," she says. "That he had a positive influence on someone despite his issues."

The dream on the highway revisits her, but it's no longer the same. It has softened like waves spread over time, less intense, though still rolling out. In moments the *wooshh* of swells breaking on a distant ledge is irrefutable.

Her priority in that phone conversation was letting Sam's mother know that she would miss him for the rest of her life. She has not forgotten, and even named her German Shepherd after him. *Somewhere inside I think he knows this.*

"And that," Sandy says, "means everything to me."

28

THEIR GIFTS

. . . .

By keeping our hearts open, even in darkness we embrace invincible summer.

My wife and I must be natural optimists. She is less the illusory kind than myself, being more practical and having endured a harder life. While I was named "sunniest personality" in eighth grade and hoofed around in leather moccasins, she worked as a housekeeper at a hotel in order to buy herself fashionable jeans rather than wear hand-me-downs. I fiddled about in college and drove to Grateful Dead shows while she did her Air Force training in San Antonio and Biloxi. Our shared hope for the future and in the best sides of people bubbles up in subtle ways.

It stirs in the patter of wind chimes at the camp in Maine, finally retrieved from an antique ice chest after we had searched and searched to no avail. The chimes hang by a deck overlooking the bay in the very place my mother was drawn to, where we lean in to feel her soul most keenly, and where our children are drawn back to replenish their energies. An osprey passing by with a fish similarly impresses us, its wings undulating with purpose, as does a second one clutching its prey the next day when we're out on the water. We interpret them as a sign of renewal and sustenance.

And the visits from another seal—or could he be the same one?—who follows us kayaking on another August day. Approaching within a few yards, his dark eyes observing in wonder, he follows us for an hour in a dance of effortless dives and snorting surfaces.

Equally curious, we ponder him. We believe, halting our paddles, adrift. Whispering, we love you.

Is Mike with us? Yes.

His presence as if to say: All bodes well. Balance is within reach. You are still with me, and I with you.

The way forward hinges upon not closing ourselves up. It is the efficacy of being emotionally responsive. Seeking. Sharing. Stumbling and reconvening. Being both vulnerable and resilient in our yearning.

Our friend Sandy White has this, as do so many others we are fortunate to have met through Hope Floats. With or without us in the years ahead, some of them will continue to provide a beacon for those searching in their grief, conveying that, yes, summer will eventually return. Undiminished and brilliant, altered in the shifting light of memory and time.

Even for you. Especially for you.

Adding their own signatures, Sandy, or others doing this work, will undoubtedly pass along something distinctive.

Holocaust survivor Viktor Frankl found that reaffirming love during the winter solstice of one's life is the inviolable triumph of the human condition. As camp guards shouted at the men to dig ditches in the pre-dawn cold, Frankl looked at the fading stars and emerging pink light. His mind clung to his wife's image, and the ultimate wisdom transfixed him. That was not so long ago, after all—we forget at our peril—and perhaps it is our job to help spur others toward embracing this essence.

Keep on keeping on. It sounds so pure and simple, yet is so difficult to achieve.

For the two of us, developing Hope Floats has meant discovering and working out our dharma, or a sacred duty and passion. Doing so requires the equivalent of bringing one's car in regularly for a front-end alignment to prevent uneven tire wear. We bumped through many potholes on back roads, more than once as I veered to the wrong side. Perhaps our purpose to help others lift each other up will span the rest of our lives. Or maybe our dharma will extend into new directions. Either way, our commitment to one another, and our everyday routines, must first be properly aligned. Before we've relinquished managing Hope Floats—hopefully continuing in perpetuity as a public charity—someone else will have stepped in. Other Sandy Whites will heed the call.

I consider this to be an unspeakable gift. It is unutterable in the sense that I would not wish the circumstances that brought us here upon my worst enemy—and I have none.

No one would condemn us for clamming up and never expressing or trying any of this. Yet we did. We do. It's here in these pages, resounding in the many hundreds of conversations I've had. It is embedded in Denise's eyes when she introduces new members to a group, and when she meets a grieving parent for the first time. Surely these are gifts, secured in a similar way to how Frankl held on to the vision of his wife, moving through each us from God.

What was Mike's gift to us? At times we both want to be sure, but do we even need to be? Maybe that's a big leg of the odyssey: to try it on, strike a note, and hear how it expands and sustains.

Like a musician who suspends thinking to express himself in full, belief resurfaces again in the way notes pour out with gut-honed fingering. You just feel it, suspecting it's been there all along. A resonance plying across the room, re-conjured along the channels your life has traversed. Early morning joys raising your children you can never take for granted, opening again to your mom's voice and your dad's presence, much of their lives given for others, and a deep, fierce love for your partner. The music plays itself; the road beckons us forward. Food of love, play on.

For his mom, part of Mike's gift is his energy and laughter. I see him snuggling with her in their tiny apartment after another long, stressful day. Hustling him to day care at the air base, grinding out work at the armory, and finally back to pick him up in her arms—he's bouncing to get out of the car seat in her Ford Escort, jabbering, try not to look into the rear mirror too long—home safe, whisk him upstairs, cook supper. And finally, sitting down to play. Those minutes on the rug with belly smooches and reading stories. Goodnight stars.

His light continues, and from his loss Denise figured out that she wanted a life of service. "How did I survive this?" she asks me late on another summer's day.

We're sitting beside a fire outside the camp in Maine. Dusk is approaching above fields stoked with goldenrod and Queen Anne lace. The air has stilled save for a slight rustle of a bamboo thicket behind us. A thin line of clouds shifts almost imperceptibly, unthreading to reveal deep blue mussel flakes, as if offering a glimpse into another world—even if only for a few minutes. The capacity was already within her, but she learned from Mike how she might reach others. She followed her heart. "I listened, I listened to what I needed to do at this part in my life," she continues. "It may change, but I just listened." At another stage she sees herself as a hospice volunteer to accompany the dying.

Someone might posit to us, and to you in your loss, was it his time? Was Michael's life meant to be cut short so that we could support other families?

Was it meant to be?

I have a hard time swallowing this notion. I reject that he was destined to die young so that we would travel this route. As she reminds me, free will was involved on all sides, beginning with the choices he made that night. Wrestling to make some sense of our grief, we located a trailhead and lit out. We took chances and successive leaps of faith—without always considering them as such—starting the drunk driving prevention group and changing careers.

Still, we're also receptive to an alternative view of expanded consciousness, the ancient idea that our souls have an ongoing purpose and that we're supposed to learn lessons during a lifespan. Even emerging reincarnated in a new body seems possible. Both of us dipped our toes into these waters, reading and listening to psychotherapists who describe past-life and progression therapies, as well as a few so-called New Age visionaries. And for me, at least, gravitating toward mystics. I guess we'll see what turns up.

Denise offers that Mike may have accomplished what he was supposed to. "It's not him coming here so mom and dad have this purpose," she says, "but he had a soul purpose being here eighteen years and touched many people in that time, and we've chosen this path to help people in response to their loss." While there may not be a linear connection between these things, we can both raise our eyes attempting to catch sight of the flow at dusk.

An early spring weekend tradition where we live is lighting a burn pile after cleaning up the yard and gardens. Relaxing on a log well back from the blaze later one afternoon beside stacks of fallen branches and overgrowth pruned back, an iron rake and shovel at the ready, I felt that minor accomplishment of resting worn arms and legs. Denise came over eager to ask me something. Her eyes reflected the fire's glare with an inquisitive shine. She wanted to create this unnamed place that would become Hope Floats. The idea had been sparking for some time, and she told me the call to get started was strong.

I replied that she should go for it. My thought was immediate and unequivocal. We talked over a beer watching the pile turn to embers, continuing to warm us in the gathering chill. This would mean giving up her first graders, shortcutting a career and contacts with her colleagues. Also shedding the demands of teaching an inclusion class and force-feeding preparation for standardized tests. Her ear was set in place.

In the years ahead she felt the divine working through her. She caught herself finding the appropriate words to help one of her groups make a transition, or give an expression of comfort to someone struggling to hold it together. On the occasional Monday or Tuesday evening, upon returning home after a group session, Denise became effusive. Her eyes lit up again, and as her auburn hair brushed against her lean, coffee-tinged face, I felt that she had never seemed more at peace. Marveling at how the parents had jelled that night, holding each other up, she knew they would not find that bond anywhere else. They often told her so. Alternately, my wife sometimes doubted whether she was actually helping. After expressing this to me at supper, or during our evening routine of reading good fiction side-by-side in bed, I tried to drop whatever I was thinking. *You're reaching them more than you even know.*

Meeting with a new mom, or planning with a colleague to address an emerging need, she recognized there was a higher source in play. And she wished the same for me.

Pouring everything into it became the work of our lives. More often than not, this was neither grudging toil nor self-congratulating backslaps. When we facilitated our first couples' retreat together one Saturday, listening to their stories and seeing others nudged toward even a momentary pause made me again realize that I was in the right place. So elevated from the self-inflicted rabbit hole I had gone down in Providence. She coordinated regular retreats for grieving moms that became a cherished day of repose, the women doing body treatments after meditation, spread around lunch and being able to talk freely as a mom and spouse. When clients and visitors remarked about the amazing work Hope Floats does, Denise gently stepped them back. It was much bigger than the two of us.

I kept returning to the reciprocity of giving that Reverend Lyndon Harris had articulated inside Saint Paul's Chapel months after 9/11. Reinventing itself at our little nonprofit, and emanating throughout the world. The notion hit me again as I crouched on one knee weeding a walkway in the baking sun.

All good things, I hope.

Some years ago I was driven to learn about how South Africans had attempted to reconcile the tortuous legacy of apartheid. Archbishop Desmond Tutu, who helped lead his country's healing, reflected on this reciprocity and renewal in way that spoke directly to me.

Tutu wrote, "What we are, what we have, even our salvation, all is gift, all is grace, not to be achieved but to be received as a gift freely given."

I'm often intrigued by a sepia-tinged portrait of a man that hangs by the staircase in the house that became host to our bereavement center. The original occupant, Edward Holmes, has a serene expression. His lips are set together and his warm eyes emit a trace of sadness. While Holmes became a successful shipbuilder and owner in the mid-nineteenth century—his largest, the bark *Solomon*, weighing six hundred tons—he also suffered along the way. His wife died at thirty-one soon after giving birth. Later one of his sons drowned, a loss that his oldest boy, who became a heavy drinker and an unfit parent, apparently never recovered from. Echoes of an unforgiving time lay embedded in the nooks and horsehair plaster and lath walls of the old house.

Sunshine washes through the oversized windows into the dining room as Teresa Lally opens up a fold-up wooden pedestal table one summer morning. Dark and oval shaped, the table has three legs and needs a minor repair. A hardware fitting is worn so a slat that locks in the legs won't quite glide into place. I go to fetch a flat-edged screwdriver from the basement, and stepping into the granite foundation, it briefly occurs to me what spirits might still be lurking around. After bending the fitting back into place we're ready to experience table tipping, the first time for me. In this form of physical mediumship, Teresa's table will become the channel through which a spirit sends its energy, reaching those who surround it. While I've researched some of the Holmes family history, we have little idea of who may come through from the house and beyond—although Denise expects Mike will want to burst in.

Five women sit in folding chairs around the table along with Denise and myself. Lally, who is also a practitioner in healing modalities such as Reiki and acupuncture, is taking notes from the side of the room, guiding us as she leads a spirit investigation of the 1844 house. I've never experienced it, but there's been a bunch of activity during the two years we've been here. A contractor fixing some holes in the front door heard someone breathing behind him, thinking it was his boss, but found no one there. Several people reported seeing the figure of a woman staring out of an upstairs window; an electrician working alone heard thumps and loud noises upstairs; a psychic claimed to see a man in a sea captain's hat smoking a pipe. Another believes Mike likes to play in the attic.

Several of the women with us are also mediums or use pendulums and dowsing rods to connect with and clear paranormal energies. Earlier this morning our group checked each room, sensing varied spirits throughout the house. There is Liz, a girl with long brunette hair in a dress who is Edward's daughter. A younger girl, Isabelle, informs us she is the child in an undated photo hanging on the wall. There is also the presence of an older female who remains in the bedroom where she died, who apparently feels that something is unfinished, and has yet to cross over. Little kids laugh in the twin bedroom. And others, bitter and wanting revenge, linger in a newer wing and outside the house.

As we begin, a few of our companions sense a very clear energy in the dining room. A candle is lit on a large, brooding dark set piece that has stayed with the house. One medium says she feels the presence of two deceased women whose portraits sit on a nearby bureau. There may be a slight irony to this, or even logic, since one of them, Pat, was the co-facilitator of Denise's first support group. Both women passed within the past year, and they seem to be protective of this space.

We place our hands palms down on the table, lightly so as to not obstruct its motion. Our guide, Mel, sets our intentions for the session, invoking spirits of the "highest good" or white light to come through. She will first contact a spirit table guide, who acts as kind of a traffic cop to keep things moving smoothly among those spirits who want to come in. Mel stresses that we only want to communicate with them, which comes off as an abbreviated, tempered prayer. Another woman records the exchange with a digital camera.

Someone says she feels several spirits present and willing. Mel asks if someone wants to speak. The table leans sharply toward Denise and I, rising a few inches at the end opposite us, and bringing the edge a little closer to us, its legs skirting across the rug. No one around the table seems to be doing this. Someone announces that it's Mike, which Denise already knows.

He is so excited that I am here. He presses the edge of the table up against my knees in an embrace that lasts maybe ten seconds. This may sound absolutely bizarre, yet it's a kind of hug; I feel both physically embraced and enveloped by something ethereal. It's like he's been waiting and waiting for this chance. He does it again less intensely minutes later when I ask if he's with me when I go running. Mike does the same for Denise a couple of times, and even bobs the table around showing off his approval of the others in our group.

This first sequence takes only several minutes, and I'm unable to put my finger on why I'm not in denial or disbelief. This is a rip tide through uncharted waters. Perhaps I've been conditioned a bit since my wife has done this a few times to connect with our son. We've both seen other mediums, both privately and sometimes in raucous, moving displays with large audiences. A few years later, a niece of the nationally-known medium, Maureen Hancock, an expectant mom of twins who has a gift similar to her aunt's, will lead us contacting Mike in our living room. Among the messages in that extraordinary reunion, she conveys Mike's excitement about our idea to ride in a bike-a-thon for cancer research in memory of his grandmother. We had not yet shared word of this to anyone.

Still, I had stayed somewhat detached from digesting all this. I was aware that for a long time séances, channeling, or so-called spiritualism were derided as hucksters who took advantage of the bereaved and naive were exposed. Yet the table in front of me takes on Mike's very personality. Surely this is the real thing.

Communication with spirit seems to come in two ways—by asking direct questions, and by sounding out answers letter by letter. One tip of a side or a tap means yes, the absence of one or no movement indicates no. Words are sounded out by watching the table's movement as we spell out the alphabet. If it stops moving at "S," that is the appropriate letter. At times one of the mediums will receive or interpret a message more directly. Mel asks, "What would you like to tell us?" After a few letters we estimate the reply and declare it. If correct, the table tips once, or in a more enthusiastic response, rocks back and forth. We spell out "I love you," Mike's first message for Denise. He's very polite, someone at the table says, usually beginning with "please."

"Please play," he tells us.

To his mother: "Please stop crying." That seems to be in response to the recent engagements of his pals Jeff and Griffin. Wonderful news, yet still triggers. She mentions this to the group in tears as I rub her shoulder.

Mike is not quite done, as there's something about a rock. Sitting beside Denise, Kate, who is a medium and also lost her daughter, interprets for us. Kate says Mike loves the labyrinth we created on the grounds last spring. A friend who works as a lighthouse keeper laid out the spiraling pattern for us. One takes a path toward the center as an intentional journey, perhaps to work something out or pause in the middle, and then follow it back out. We've placed distinctive rocks hauled back from Maine to augment its healing energy and meditative purpose.

Kate asks if I've noticed the rock that Mike moved. Everyone looks at me, chief groundskeeper and bottle washer. I'm a little flustered, since no, I had not noticed, and look down. I just weeded there a couple of days ago. Was I unmindful? Which rock? I tell him I'll look for it. I mention we're going to Maine in two weeks and we'll get him a really nice one. The table tips toward me again.

Next come spirits from the house and some from outside. Liz, one of the girls, says she stays here because it's comfortable, and she likes Mike. Her brother comes in, and we spell out his name: "L," "E," "M." I know it is Lemuel, Edward's son who drowned going to sea on one of his grandfather's ships. Unless the women in the room are familiar with the Holmes' genealogy, I am the only one around who would know this. Responding to my questions, he says it was an accident. Someone tried to save him, and his body was never found. He indicates feeling a connection with me and is glad to be remembered. The following day I will go visit the family burial plots, sensing how much Lemuel was loved and missed. Engraved near the base of his six-foot-tall monument is a three-masted ship, heading for the safety of a lighthouse.

Edward enters next. He still visits the house, and says he likes what we are doing with it. He led Denise here because he knew we would do good work. There is something else. He spells out: "Help men." Do something for the dads and brothers. Which makes me shudder, because in the back of my mind I feel that is where I am headed. I thank him and say I will try to do that.

When it's over I go out to the labyrinth. Right in the center of it there's a heart-shaped concrete planter. Missing from this is one large crazy rock, a glaciated gull-gray hunk with bulging white quartz veins. I found it on the beach where Mike would bat rocks endlessly as a child. I had placed this in the planter just because—it is so distinctive, and seemed to fit. But someone has moved it a few feet away, placed in the middle of one path.

It's time to find another centerpiece.

One of the kids answered the phone as we gathered around our kitchen table with visiting family.

"Mom, it's Mike's friend Brenda."

Recognizing the name, Denise stepped into another room. Brenda Cormier grew up in the other end of our town, and many years back we had picked Mike up at a birthday party at her house. Brenda sounded nervous and apologetic, yet determined to get through.

"I hope it's okay that I called you," she told my wife.

"Of course it is."

A few weeks earlier, Cormier had rushed out the back door of The Station nightclub with her brother and father to escape an inferno. One hundred people died in the fire, nearly a third of those crammed inside for a concert. The Cormiers weren't near the entrance or back exits when the band's pyrotechnics—sparklers adorning the stage—ignited soundproofing foam on the walls and ceiling.

I have to tell you this, she repeated.

Mike had guided them out.

Somehow he showed them the way. She felt his presence as they muscled to the back past bouncers and security guards, who tried turning the trio toward the front door. Her father told the guards to get out of the way. "Are you an idiot?" he yelled, pushing through. Mike helped create a path.

Brenda was sure it was him. She didn't know how Denise would react. From where they had been standing, they probably should not have survived. She had always been intuitive; she had to share this.

The fire was two months after our son's death.

Denise came back into the room in tears.

We both had to sit down to absorb this. I could hardly connect with the tragedy in West Warwick, just outside of Providence. It was too immense and way too close.

At first I couldn't wrap my head around what Brenda was telling us. A chill ran up my spine and down my arms, my neck tightening. Another breakthrough.

Barely eighteen, Nicholas O'Neill was in the front row stage right, close to Great White's rhythm guitarist. A musician himself with a mop of blonde hair, Nicky was also an actor and upcoming playwright, a raconteur who mimicked his older siblings and parents. He loved going to Disney World, especially to the old time Hoop-Dee-Doo Musical Revue, and had a thing for the Rodgers and Hammerstein musical *Carousel*. His brother Chris considered him to be their family's "beating, glowing heart." Nicky wrote songs on the guitar, and his band Shryne was to open the next night before the same eighties hair band at the roadhouse that had once been a popular Italian restaurant.

As flames shot up the back wall and much of the audience surged into a bottleneck near The Station's main entrance, Nicky helped the guitarist off the stage. He then went over to aid a panicked woman who had thrown herself to the floor.

O'Neill never got out. He was the fire's youngest victim, whose last words to his father were, "The show must go on."

Years later, Nicky's dad Dave Kane contacted Denise at her office. Kane is a veteran radio talk show host in southern New England, once a wise-cracking know-it-all who isn't shy about going out on a limb. He is also a comedian known for a one-man show that features the character of a priest he calls Father Misgivings. He approached us with a purpose that was at once serious and playful, converging like disparate rays of sunlight through a convex lens. Having heard about our bereavement center, Kane offered to come and speak while promoting a book he had written, *41 Signs of Hope*. It is about Nicky, and he offers a singular message for grieving families: "They're not gone."

Informed by his son, Kane testifies to the ongoing connections with loved ones that are real if we remain open to that possibility. He suggests that we can recognize their signs rather than prolonging what he calls self-centered grief, such as believing "I'll never have . . .", "or get to see . . ." a loved one again. He suggests that death as we often perceive it is a misnomer. "Because these people are not dead," he says. "They are heart and soul. They are love and joy. They are yours . . . still here, right now."

In the years following the fire, as Kane and his wife, Joanne, and their three adult sons stayed open, Nicky kept checking in with them. Forty-one, his favorite number since childhood, showed up everywhere: on clocks during pivotal moments, on hymn lists, tickets, spare change and addresses, a key-wound music box given on Mother's Day that began playing itself at 9:41 p.m. The nightclub's geographic coordinates are latitude 41:41; (41 degrees 41 minutes north); the number of the call box outside was 4414; and do the math adding the eighteen years and twenty-three days of his life.

Other signs arrived in flurries. Driving one day and consumed by her greatest fear that he had suffered in the fire, Joanne noticed the license plate of an oncoming car. It read, "NOPAIN." Some of these signals, like the windshield wipers in Dave's car that turn on by themselves, seem to defy logic. The family accepted "synchronicities that stand far outside suspicion of coincidence, and miracles that have extinguished our fear of death," Christian O'Neill wrote. His family rolled on, producing a documentary film about Nicky's legacy, while Kane continued to offer his message.

It is not for everyone. When he has spoken to small groups of families at Hope Floats, I've wondered if Kane's advice comes off as too rehearsed and jarring for some, especially those who are raw from a recent loss. "He's tap dancing around, trying to get your attention," Dave says, suggesting that it's our problem if we block ourselves from this. He's used to occasional pushback and understands it. People are afraid of taking the plunge, afraid of believing in their desperation and then being crushed by charlatans. He tries to set the table and invite them into the room.

Despite our initial caution about some of this, there's another element that Denise and I fully embraced. Dave knows that Nicky is helping other souls connect with their loved ones. He offers examples, with some of the kids coming through via mediums, and at other times simply leaving unmistakable tidbits for their parents or cousins and siblings to pick up. When my wife relays Brenda's vision about Mike, Kane suggests that his son and ours have brought us together.

"This is what they're doing. They're banning together," Kane reminds me one day over the phone. "This is one of the things that is helping us, this is when he was supposed to pass. Now we know this was his job to do stuff, like moving me to go out there and encourage people to be open. This is a whole big thing here, and it never stops . . . there's a reason the kids are doing this."

Nicky was also prescient in a number of ways. About a year before the fire, he wrote a one-act play about three guardian angels who are recently deceased and wander around New York, reminiscing and ruminating about God's seeming inaction in a wretched world. One of the spirits, Cyrus, is the playwright himself. They deliver a message to an anguished young man, and the play ends with the line: "Do not fear to hope." Directed by his brother, the play was first performed in a church with Nicky's friends in the cast. Called *They Walk Among Us*, Christian and his father later turned the debut into a movie.

Brenda Cormier counted her many blessings. She got married and gave birth to a son almost eight years after the fire, which broke out at 11:11 p.m. Her child arrived on January 11, 2011.

I have to tell you this.

Joe Mlynarczyk, the former New York firefighter who lost so many brothers during 9/11, helped steer me straight during one of our conversations. I told him how Mike died in that horrible crash. Perhaps being overly deferential, I added, "But that's not comparable to what you've been through."

He corrected me right away. Yes it is, Mlynarczyk said. Actually it's worse. He was your son. And when he confessed that he doesn't have answers, he asked if I had any.

At times I must admit I'm still staggering, or at least close to careening into another ditch.

We had come so far, married for nearly thirty years, defying uncertain odds with the prospect of a full life remaining together. Our young adult children were making their way ahead. They worked hard to start their careers, self-reliant and just thoroughly decent kids in ways that made us profoundly happy.

Despite the work at Hope Floats and the connections we felt with Mike, a warped force undercut the positive growth in our lives. Paradoxes and ironies piled up around and between us, colliding in treacherous places. Compulsion and solace. Denial rutted in impaired thinking drowned within carelessness seeping from something I had yet to get to. Neither of us had considered how compartmentalizing our emotions—bundling them up out of reach—at times complicated the work to support others' healing. This had its own cost. That winter's song resumed playing as a shroud of fallen leaves formed. Darkness obscuring the light.

I suppose many of us go through a similar vortex at some point. For those whose lives have been compounded by sudden loss or life-limiting illness, the path forward is pockmarked with contradictions. Resolving them amounts to more than easing a tension of opposites. People far wiser than myself attempt to negotiate these forces through meditative practice and even by integrating them into their lives. Someone once advised me to beware of the place where these things collide. Yet the very confluence of opposing currents felt like the most vital ground one must attempt to hold. It became the very place drawing me in, and I turned to face it again and again.

Denise initiated one of those sturdying conversations one morning close to his anniversary. She had slept in a little late and her head poked out from the comforter facing the window. Those brooding eyes, tiny bowls of guacamole awaiting only a pinch of fresh cilantro for perfection, looked far away. The rip was strong, coursing through both of us this week.

It hurt her that a few people who should be closest had again failed to acknowledge that Mike was gone, and how our wounds would never close completely. Plus the accumulation of others who want you to be the same person you were before, their eyes indicating months and years later, *Why aren't you over this yet?*

While we'd both tried to suspend judgments, we felt the undertow of resentment. How do they stay so mired in their puny orbits, forgetting the potency of remembrance and reaching out? She grew to dread Thanksgiving, and we usually withdrew at home with Amanda and Chris.

A few gestures arrived as well, reinvigorating our gratitude like the reach of a full moon tide. A friend texted her: "I'm thinking of you and Mike." A pal of his posted on Facebook how the best of both Mike and P.J. continued to resonate among many of the guys taking flight.

I sat on the bed as Denise vented. Then she looked into me and said, "I think one of the things we've both done is keep our hearts open, open to grief, when others shut close."

Her words washed into me, and from time to time I must remember to retrieve that wisdom. This felt natural, despite the emotive fracking we injected into ourselves. Ideally, when not veering back and forth, perhaps we could approach a mindfulness to settle ourselves and look more deeply within. Attempting, as Buddhist monks and laypeople do, to be "radically open," or to be present and observing without reacting to stuff, practicing this by walking or sitting to touch stillness, even while bike riding or sailing. Reaching stillness. Overcoming negative energies by recognizing and addressing them, seeing their impermanence as a gust that blows through and goes.

Setting out each day to do one small act of kindness. Which must start with caring for each other.

Like the Clerys and Winuks, the Offens, and other families I had met over the years, my wife and I knew that maintaining all this would not always be possible. We kept churning over the same questions beside new burn piles. I failed to clear the weeds that threatened to choke us, crying one day out beside my blistered, deer-nibbled squash and tomato plants: It's over. We gathered more shards amidst the charcoal and ash, trying to piece some together.

Surely there would be other seasons.

Early one August morning I set out alone on a sea kayak across Machias Bay. The placid water mirrored the world's rooftop at first light, the only sound an intermittent gargle of a few distant workboats. A cluster of eiders and other ducks edged over the surface, their destination as impenetrable to me as their straggled line.

Heading toward the rear of the group I stilled the paddle, gliding and trying not to disturb them. Their leaders took off in flight anyway, followed by the horde. I hoped to make it to an outer island before the wind rose, stirring the sea from her bed. In the channel two lobstermen caught up on a break as their boats drifted a short distance apart, their smoky banter rolling along above the idling engines. I slipped past, moving without seeking, rounding another island with a grassy nub facing the open water.

On the way back time slowed as the sky and bay fused further into one. I focused on taking light breaths and strokes, dipping each side in an easy rhythm while extending my peripheral vision. The bow skirted the water as long, mellow swells nudged us forward. The current shifted slightly ahead, opening a fresh rippling lane and we entered, further letting go. A sighing wash over a ledge drew us closer, and I spied a rock on a spit of beach where Denise and I had seen an eagle perched the previous year. Everything was aligned, and another harbor seal scoped me out, poking his head up.

> This is a day of moment,
> each breath from the sky
> a riser to a step
> in an oozing rite, slowly dispersed.
>
> A day to wash in cold water,
> not a day for action
> or putting new ideas into play.
> An afternoon for a hummingbird
> twisting
> and dipping by the porch.
> A day to read your daughter's story in full
> and lie on the ledge with your partner.
> Do not comment, nor augur further,
> open your eyes and give thanks.

I don't know if that addresses Joe's question, but it feels like a start.

Cory Scanlon wanted to drive again and move on. Approaching thirteen years after Mike and P.J.'s deaths, he appealed his license suspension, which had been mistakenly increased to fifteen years rather than ten years after his conviction. Under Massachusetts law, it was also possible that his license could be revoked indefinitely because a few months prior to the fatal crash, Cory had been charged as a minor in possession of alcohol.

Seated what felt uncomfortably close to him in a small courthouse conference room, P.J.'s sister, Mary MacKinnon, thought she heard Cory shifting from taking full responsibility. On one hand he said all the right things. He was subdued and choked up. "I know I can't take that night back," Cory told the three-member Board of Appeal panel. "I should have listened to my friends, I love my friends. I put them in danger. There is no way I should have been behind the wheel that night when I had been drinking." At nineteen, he didn't know how fragile life was.

He appreciated this now. Having a two year-old son, and having just bought a house in Mary's hometown.

In her eyes, Cory appeared to consider his license revocation as a concession he had agreed to. While he didn't say that verbatim, she sensed it. Asked when he had last used alcohol, Scanlon paused, saying he had a glass of champagne at his wedding. Then he was asked about drinking more recently. Pausing again, he said, yes, he had had a drink—without saying when. "I am trying my hardest not to be around alcohol," he said. "If this is a factor (in restoring the license), I don't want to be around alcohol."

A victim's advocate from the district attorney's office looked at Mary. *Did you just hear what I did?* Was he bargaining with the board?

During a probation hearing a decade earlier, Cory said he would never drink again.

Granted, things change. But the advocate, who stood with us back in 2003 and 2004, noticed other backpedaling along with P.J.'s sister. The pledge was gone, and she wondered if Cory had since dropped that from his talks to students.

To his credit, Scanlon had continued speaking to middle and high school students way beyond the conditions of his parole. He estimated having reached 75,000 teens in nearly one hundred presentations during nine years, including four at our high school. I checked the list twice.

Neither Denise nor I wanted to attend the license hearing, although she had a late urge to go. I pleaded with her not to do that to herself and she deferred, missing a grueling replay of details. We didn't oppose his license being restored some day, continuing to interpret what Mike would want: that Cory be able to live a full life.

Yet despite his indicating that the right to drive is a relatively minor consequence, listening to a recorded transcript of the hearing I, too, felt an undercurrent in Cory's expressions. As if he had suffered long enough, the one with the hardship. He still worked as a painter, a co-worker giving him rides each day. He had earned a degree in sociology and psychology going to night school. In that confounding meeting on our property before Jeff's wedding, he'd told me that his goal was to work with high school students as an adjustment counselor. "I want to continue to help influence people's decisions," he told the board.

Mary MacKinnon felt forever broken; nothing could be the same for her scattered family. Her sons had been robbed of an uncle. Restoring Scanlon's driving privileges made no sense to her since P.J. could never reclaim his. She feared crossing Cory's path while driving through town.

"Isn't that enough?" she asked. "It seems that our system ignores the rights of victims in favor of the convicted." She told the panel that as soon as the hearing ended, she would drive over to P.J.'s grave.

The DA's office recommended that Cory's request be denied. The RMV did the same, suggesting a review in another five years. But a week later the board reinstated his license for two years anyway, mandating that he use an ignition interlock device to prevent any possible drinking and driving. The panel noted that the suspension had been incorrectly tied to his release date in 2006, rather than his conviction in 2004. They failed to notify Mary and the rest of P.J.'s family of the decision.

We applauded Cory for wanting to help teens avoid the mistakes he made. Deep inside, I wanted to accept that he might stay true to his own sacred duty. He said that having his license might help him do more positive work. In his application to the state Division of Insurance, among the testimonials was a disarming email from a celebrated athlete in a nearby town. While destined to play soccer at UCLA, she told Cory about her own repeated risk-taking, and how his message had spurred her to change. A classmate of hers had asked Scanlon how he coped with the pain of killing his two friends. Rather than counseling or church, he told them it was coming before groups like theirs. "I'm sharing what happened that night, and try[ing] to keep Mike's and P.J.'s memories alive by doing so," he later told the board.

Yet I couldn't help noticing something else. To my ears, those words sputtered out a bit like regurgitated stage lines.

Other things bore under our skin—mine and Mary's, at least.

At the Shaughnessy's house that November night, they sang happy birthday to P.J., and Cory made the promise to Sharon, his friend's mother. The guys went outside, and standing in the driveway, Cory knew he had a full tank of gas. He offered to drive his Jeep. *We never thought about the ride home.*

People knew where we were going that night. We were going to a bar to underage drink. But I'm not putting the blame on anybody else, because I did it myself.

As if the only reason he was driving was because he had gassed up.

As if twelve years were enough.

As if life just picks up where it left off.

As if we hadn't already had enough.

While Cory's license appeal was in motion, I reached the state trooper who had led the crash scene investigation. Shayne Suarez told me he has four children of his own. "I don't want to imagine it," he offered.

He suggested that perhaps it was not a bad idea for me to look at this one more time, to find a place to manage it before finally putting it to rest. Suarez knew there were no winners that night. "Is one to blame more than the other?" he asked. "By the grace of God it didn't happen to them that night."

He may have had a point. Yet, did he know that Brendan and P.J. yelled at Cory to slow down?

That same evening in our kitchen, my wife saw my face sag, sucked into the whirl again.

"You've got to let this go," she said. I thought I already had.

In Providence, too, a load of crap still hadn't passed under the bridge.

My conscience—and perhaps some other compulsive twitch—made me check again in 2015. It was three years since I had renewed digging into the underage drinking scene, and we had not set foot in the city since.

When I left off, the city solicitor and police commissioner told me they were drafting new rules to sanction bars and clubs that repeatedly served minors. A load of bricks burying those bad apples. The city also had the authority to ban under-twenty-ones outright.

Neither of those things happened. And while Providence had not tried to prevent more roadside carnage in these ways, another attempt in the legislature to ban under-twenty-ones outright from drinking establishments across the state gathered dust, held in a House committee for further study. Meanwhile, a juicy corruption scandal involving one of the Bar One owner's old business partners held everyone's attention. Former Rhode Island House Speaker Gordon Fox was heading to federal prison for his crimes, including accepting $52,200 from a sushi bar in exchange for helping the owners get a license when he was also on the city's licensing board.

To its credit, I suppose, the board had closed down a few trouble spots. A year earlier, it finally held another club fully accountable after a double shooting; I noted with sadness that one of the young men injured appeared to be a former student of mine from Mattapan who dropped out of school. At least two bars that blatantly served underage students around Providence College had been shuttered. But coinciding with the latest trend of trouble at hookah bars and new gang hangouts was a resurgence of violence in the Washington Park neighborhood.

The simplest excuse for not preventing underage drinking with a broader brush, the most base, and obvious, is there's just too much money to be made. Paré, the public safety commissioner, observed, "They continue to squeeze money and continue to turn a blind eye to under-twenty-ones."

By then, most of the players I met earlier had rotated off or up: the licensing board chairman's term expired; the board attorney was elevated to a magistrate; there was a new mayor and new solicitor. Even MADD's executive director flew the coop; Paré and the board's administrator were the main familiar faces left. When I asked what happened to sanctioning repeat violators, it felt like the runaround again. This far out there was no sense in taking it personally.

The former city solitor had assured me in 2012 that under-twenty-one sanctions would be proposed for the licensing board to consider. Yet no one had a record of anything about this. Instead, the board adopted rules to better document their procedures, blah, blah, blah. Nothing came forward on under-twenty-one sanctions, new Solicitor Mario Martone told me. I filed a public records request for any notes, drafts, or meeting minutes concerning this. The response was that no documents existed.

When I asked the former solicitor—hired as a deputy state treasurer—who had called it off, he chafed at the question, saying no pressure had been applied. Then he stopped returning my phone calls.

Let it go, she reminded me.

I still wondered about other victims, their voices, the muffled cries of their parents and siblings. How do I do that again?

Jeff Doyle recalls the guys stretching out beside the track, freshmen with quaking nerves and some with long faces knowing they would not make it. And select dudes strolling in with their headphones on.

Mike immediately stripped off his shirt. "He'd enjoy that, even without any girls around," Doyle was telling me. "He had that six pack, that jacked body," those ripped abs. "And telling people he had his shirt off." *He just had that body.*

Jeff laughs gazing back for a moment. We're in the kitchen at Hope Floats, the guts of the old house. Maybe Edward and his daughters are listening in; one of the girls enjoys flirting with Mike's spirit, after all, the kid in Adidas flip-flops. Doyle says he doesn't distinguish among most of his former players. Matches and records and other stats kind of glaze into one, even some of the names.

But not the morning of The Deuce.

Doyle was a talented player himself, a member of Silver Lake's state championship team in 1988, and then a captain on the Southern New Hampshire University squad, which won an NCAA Division II National Championship the following year. In college he had to pass the "Cooper test," running two miles in twelve minutes, his best time coming as a freshman at 11:25. When he became head coach at Silver Lake Regional High School in the late nineties, Doyle introduced the same training standard to all of those vying for a spot.

Someone had dubbed it "The Deuce" by the time Mike arrived for double sessions late one summer.

It was usually a Thursday morning, and just after checking the boys' paperwork, Doyle began assigning them to line up for the heats. There was no prescribed training for it other than an outline he issued during the spring meeting. Coach Doyle advised them to alternate their running, perhaps doing three, then five, to seven miles, rather than going out just doing two miles faster and faster. "I always told the kids, it's a measure of fitness. It's a measure of what you've got." They needed a goal for the summer.

Failure to pass did not mean they were ineligible or off the team, despite the popular fear that careened through kitchens and dens like our own. They might not start, or play a full game. Doyle often made them repeat. He applied the benchmark unevenly, sometimes retaining starters like big, slower backs whom he just wanted on the field. Mike was cool in front of his friends, a bit snappy at home with us. He didn't want to have to run it again.

The guys psyched each other up body smacking with light punches and trash-talk. A few savvy ones grouped with older guys who'd already been successful and knew what pace to set. Others tried talking themselves into it. Coming into the eighth lap, those on the sidelines roared, with some running alongside the track urging a teammate to finish. *You can do this.* Balls to the wall.

Mike just took his shirt off and flew.

He unleashed that Tasmanian devil energy. He had something of his mom's gazelle legs and track-running stock, and probably some of my bent to get lost in the run and go harder.

Coming into his junior year, he passed at 11:44, among the top four.

He tied with Harrison Walters, whom Doyle called the "H-bomb," having devised as a non-strategy that if the game were in doubt, they'd kick the ball as far as possible hoping speedy Harrison would get to it first.

During senior year Mike finished in the top three with his best buds. He came in at 11:34, behind Jeff at 11:30. Travis, despite puking on the track, was first at 11:27.

"Some guys would do the best they ever did with all the support and camaraderie," Doyle says before chuckling again. "It was great. Still, and then they had to go out and practice after that."

She decided to make our kids quilts using cutouts of their brother's clothes.

Denise told me her plan a few months before his tenth anniversary. A big vanilla Singer sewing machine had been sitting in Mike's room, which we had left pretty much untouched. Most of his clothes were still there, along with bins of T-shirts with "Brack 3" printed on the back, extra team shirts from the soccer tournament we held in those torrential years.

Mike's seventh tournament in 2009 was the last. It had been a good run and we felt ready to let it go while pursuing new things. His memorial scholarship continued, and while we both missed seeing his friends and the reunions occurring in between the games, most of the planning had fallen on Denise. The same handful of volunteers met at our house dividing up who would get which raffle items, and cases of water and food. She brought out plastic jars and rolls of tickets from his room.

It was time.

The sun broke through again that June day after a long stretch of rain. I framed the seven years saluting the participants who had helped us blend a "good cry and party put together." I noted how many of us missed Mike's determination battling for a loose ball, or his cackle. When we could pause from our busy lives, we detected signs from him, and his presence was surely felt by many. "Mostly though, he marvels at all of us being here," I ventured, "stepping outside our routines for a few hours, gathering again, laughing in between matches, and kicking the ball." I heard myself recall some John Lennon lyrics that had taken me decades to fully appreciate: *Life is what happens to you while you are busy making other plans.*

The support we felt from these young people and those who had stood beside us during the years was another unspeakable gift.

My favorite part was lying on the grass with Denise taking in the afternoon's final match. Usually her sister and mine were close by, with most of our family splayed out nursing bottled water and stretching sore muscles. We marveled at the players' energies and skills, their touches, charged and drained and suddenly renewed again. I could not help recalling how Mike gave everything.

We called out encouragement, we watched in silence. Spent and complete, we both owned all of it.

Finally at rest, our tears still, the sweat dries; he is extant.

Other than storing those tournament shirts and repainting his walls an azure blue, nothing had changed in Mike's room. Yet neither could it remain the same.

I occasionally opened his bedroom door in an attempt to air out the mustiness. We kept a single advent candle plugged in by the window, and pinned to his walls were ticket stubs to Red Sox and Celtics games, and a boarding pass to St. Thomas on our last family vacation. Posters of BMX bikes and Kobe and Renaldo had lost their sheen, and a framed World Cup USA '94 collage looked down at a rug blotched with stubborn stains. A poster of a guitar-picking skeleton seemed to acknowledge his dad's musical influences. Our sweet dog Nikki sometimes curled up on a hand-me-down mattress and box spring, as if waiting for his return.

Quilts for the kids. The idea came from my sister, Jinny, who early on had offered to make them with some of Mike's clothes. But Denise realized that if anyone was going to do this down the road, it should be herself. She didn't know how to yet, but would figure it out. She went through his drawers and closet, reopening those bins. The smell made her wonder if his stuff wasn't rotting away. "I felt like I was going to be able to give each of us a part of him in a different way," she told me as we sat by the wood stove on another late afternoon. "As difficult as it was doing that knowing it's his, then it became something else."

She turned to a colleague who counsels children and adults once a week at our center for an assist starting the project. Maureen Walsh guides kids through their grief, helping them to express their feelings and understand how normal those are. Sometimes they make memory quilts together, perhaps using a collection of a dad's favorite shirts. Denise had a pattern in mind, and Maureen gave her tips such as which end to start sewing if she wanted to center her design with an object such an image from one of Mike's T-shirts.

When she asked our kids, a few iconic figures quickly came to mind. One that Chris liked was emblematic of growing up in the nineties: a "Butt Marley" Beavis-esque reggae player splashed in full Jamaican colors. Then Amanda suggested another, which neither of us had remembered. A shirt Mike wore the last time she saw him, a cartoon satire of a Pillsbury-like donut shop cop: "Doughboy—Coffee and Cuffs." Thankfully, we still had both.

The first fabric she chose was a pair of his brown corduroy pants, and Denise hesitated making the inaugural cut with her scissors. This was the hardest step. She selected a gray T-shirt and blue tournament shirt to go with the pants, and began cutting each into five inch-long strips. She went to work with the Singer at our kitchen table, stitching the strips together in a right-angle pattern. This took some time, stints of several hours on weekends or in the evening, and I mostly left her alone with bursts of the clacking machine. She made the edging and attached synthetic batting to fill in between the felt backside. This first one was for both of us, subdued and cozy with its brown, gray, and blue. "It became more of a process for me than just making this quilt," she observed. "It's part of my process." It resides on our living room couch, often spread out as she curls up to read or watch a movie on Sunday afternoon.

It took another year to finish quilts for Chris and Amanda. His embodies a pair of his brother's blue jeans, a green shirt and red tournament shirt, while hers combines a brown tournament shirt, a blue one, and yellow from another favorite shirt of Mike's with a hula dancer on it. By the next holiday season, we had to mail his to Oregon where Chris had moved, while Amanda came home for Christmas from her apartment in the city. Our son told us in a card that he was very happy his mom was able to put Mike's clothes to good use.

They became ours.

ACKNOWLEDGMENTS

B ringing this book to fruition required periodic gut checks along with the support and grounded feedback of many people.

Foremost, this would have been impossible without Denise Fonseca Brack, my wife and soul partner. Her patience and fortitude is an embedded untold story. Collaborating with my daughter, Amanda Brack, whose cover illustration and interior design elements populate the book, also means the world to me. The support of our son, Chris Brack, and other family members who didn't mind broaching the subject of the book's status was also vital.

Thanks to my early readers, Sandie Bernstein, John Cavanaugh, Judith Bradshaw Brown, John Cowan, Mary Donellan, Beverly Droz, Tom Layman, and my dad and sister, Robert Brack and Jinny Brack. Author Ellen Cassedy's advice to keep zeroing in on moments rather than form composites has stuck with me, even though I'm sure my execution was imperfect. Editor Bob Haskell taught me a ton while weeding much clutter, and thanks also to Joe Tessitore at Significance Press for his insights.

Michael Charney, formerly of Riddle Brook Publishing, helped drive the work forward with his exacting input on structure and retaining focus. In addition, my gratitude to Kirsty Walker at Hobblebush Design for her precise editing, skilled layout, and guidance producing this book. My heartfelt thanks also to Karen Alves for her eye-popping cover design, and for her embrace of what this this journey has meant.

A shout out goes to my Bridgewater Talespinners writing group: Adelene Ellenberg, Kathryn Golden, Nancy Gay, Christine Muratore, Georgeann Votruba, Phyllis Goldfeder, Marcia Orcutt, and T.J. Herlihy. Keep writing, ladies! Appreciation also to Stephanie Blackman of Riverhaven Books for her ongoing authorial support, and Boston's GrubStreet, whose writing conferences and workshops continue to enlighten. Judah Leblang's memoir class stands out as a pivotal touchstone.

Especially helpful in my Clery family research were Ellen Wendruff at the Robbins Library in Arlington, Massachusetts, and Joan Barney at the New Bedford Free Public Library. Jack and Dodie Boyle deserve much thanks, as do the Clerys' longtime friends who filled in much of the family's backstory. Many thanks to Laura Dunn, founder of SurvJustice, a national nonprofit helping sexual assault survivors obtain justice, whose story informed this book beyond measure; and Angela Rose, founder of Promoting Awareness, Victim Empowerment, for her encouragement and sharing her own response as a survivor.

Several contacts at Marsh Inc. and Marsh & McLennan Companies documented the scale of the firm's response to 9/11 and the damage done. They include Laurie Ledford, Sally Rogers, Kathryn Komsa, Reginald McQuay, Jacqueline Ferreira, Ellen Clarke, Glenn Hille, and Lora Cora. My thanks also to Cathy Williams of the Bellevue Public Schools in Bellevue, Nebraska, for digging out Mike McGinty's academic record.

I also appreciate the openness of several people at Manhasset, New York-based Tuesday's Children, helping me meet families while chaperoning two teens during a memorable job-shadowing day at the New York Stock Exchange on April 28, 2011. Thanks especially to Kathy Murphy, director of teen programs, and Sara Wingerath, family programming director. Voices of September 11th co-founder Mary Fetchet and Susan Dahill, the group's communications director, were also supportive. My appreciation extends to Sally Siller and the Stephen Siller Tunnel to Towers Foundation, and condolences and best regards go to Jane Pollicino's family.

Thanks also to Feiga Weiss among a terrific staff at the Holocaust Memorial Center Zekelman Family Campus in Farmington Hills, Michigan, and to Robert Pfieffer, former secretary of the 11th Armored Division Association, for his generous assistance. Geoff Gentilini at Golden Arrow Military Research compiled the company movements and records of several servicemen who became connected to Nathan and Sam Offen. Brent Truscott was very accommodating with remembrances of his grandfather Donald L. Montgomery's wartime service.

My deep gratitude goes to the surviving Offens and members of their families. Denise and I treasure our visits with Nathan and his partner, Gloria Lack.

A major thread of this book is how children, teens, and their parents cope successfully with loss. Several people were instrumental introducing us to the work of peer-based children's bereavement centers both for my research and for our planning at Hope Floats Healing and Wellness Center. My gratitude begins with Deborah Rivlin at The Children's Room in Arlington, Massachusetts, and Jennifer Kaplan Schreiber, founder of Jeff's Place in Framingham, Massachusetts, along with her former sidekick, Ryan Loiselle, program director at Friends Way, Warwick, Rhode Island— also founded by Schreiber. An enduring thanks for a morning spent with Beverly Chappell, co-founder of The Dougy Center in Portland, Oregon; to Dougy's longtime executive director, Donna Schuurman; and to Peggy and Lee Bohme, founders, and the welcoming staff at The WARM Place in Fort Worth, Texas. Megan Lopez and others at the National Alliance for Grieving Children are champions of this cause.

A poignant, lasting embrace goes to Mary MacKinnon and all of the Shaughnessy family. May their memories of Peter, Jr. resonate as strongly as our own in the years ahead.

Finally, a nod to two places that occasionally served as my "writing residences": the house in Mattapoisett harbor, where I anticipate my mother having a lunchtime Colt 45 with a sandwich on the porch, and Little Respite in Machiasport, where Mike and I could just be ourselves.

Ken Brack
April 2017

NOTES

PART I: INTO THE RIP

Chapter 1: What Now?

9   *Psychologists call this posttraumatic growth*: This describes how many
     people who struggle with loss undergo positive change. While transfor-
     mation from extreme suffering is an ancient theme embraced by many
     religious traditions, the term was coined in the early 1980s by two practic-
     ing psychologists, Lawrence Calhoun, Ph.D., and Richard Tedeschi, Ph.D.,
     who lead the Posttraumatic Growth Research Group at the University of
     North Carolina, Charlotte. Their research helped flesh out how this growth
     is manifested among people who experience a variety of loss and other
     trauma. New understandings continue to be offered on how this plays out,
     whether for child survivors of hurricanes, soldiers recovering from trau-
     matic stress, or for grieving parents and children who've lost a loved one
     to suicide or addiction. "The growth experienced tends to fall into three
     broad domains" or common responses: "a changed sense of self, changed
     relationships, and changed philosophy of life," including existential and
     spiritual growth, Calhoun and Tedeschi wrote in *Meaning Reconstruction
     and the Experience of Loss*, Robert A. Neimeyer, ed, (Washington, D.C.:
     American Psychological Association, 2010), 158. For example, survivors of
     loss often feel an increased connectedness with others and greater empa-
     thy. To resolve their grief in a healthy way, many people also maintain
     emotional bonds with a loved one, creating places for the deceased in their
     lives rather than "moving on." *See also* Dennis Klass, Phyllis R. Silverman,
     Steven L. Nickman, eds, *Continuing Bonds* (Washington, D.C.: Taylor &
     Francis, 1996).

10   *She advised other families*: Sandy Phillips, "Mother of Mass Shooting
     Victim Becomes Gun-Control Advocate," *Morning Edition*, National Public
     Radio, September 19, 2013, http://www.npr.org/2013/09/19/223965801/
     mother-of-colo-mass-shooting-victim-becomes-gun-control-advocate.

12   *"I credit the families . . ."*: Janice Lloyd, "Cantor Fitzgerald Family Creates Fund to Help 9/11 Families," *USA Today*, August 22, 2011.

13   *"There are days I am sad . . ."*: Gail Minger, interview with author, April 12, 2013.

Chapter 2: The Crash

20   *But Cory kept turning around*: Shayne A. Suarez, Massachusetts State Police, Collision Reconstruction Report, Speed Analysis by Trooper Deborah A. Ryan. In author's possession.

20   *They "became nervous . . ."*: Suarez, Massachusetts State Police, Incident Report, Incident No. 2002-OH3-1873, November 15, 2002. In author's possession.

PART II: WRENCHED OPEN

Chapter 3: The Best Qualities of Both

31   *She didn't have an enemy*: Joseph Shapiro, "Campus Rape Victims: A Struggle for Justice," *Morning Edition*, National Public Radio, February 24, 2010, http://www.npr.org/templates/story/story.php?storyId=124001493.

34   *"Have you forgotten to . . ."*: Dan Fricker, "Slain Lehigh Student is Lain to Rest," *The Morning Call* (Allentown, PA), April 10, 1986.

39   *Chock full of self-hatred*: Many details in this narrative of Josoph Henry's outbursts while a student at Lehigh University, his family history, romantic failures, and his actions on April 4 and in the early morning hours of April 5, 1986, are compiled from a manuscript written by the Clerys' attorney, Joseph Fioravanti, in 1992. Fioravanti, of Media, Pennsylvania, completed a 351-page manuscript authorized by the family, which was provided to the author by Mrs. Clery with Fioravanti's permission. While never published, it offers a complete, direct account of the family's ordeal from 1986 through the early 1990s, including accounts of the Clerys' family life and Jeanne's murder, highlights of Henry's criminal trial and sentencing, Howard and Connie Clery's lawsuit against Lehigh University, and their early advocacy to improve college campus security.

    A former First Assistant US Attorney for the Eastern District of Pennsylvania, Fioravanti was in private practice in May of 1986 when his partner, former US Attorney Robert Curran, asked him to advise the Clerys at a preliminary hearing for then-murder suspect Henry. Fioravanti continued advising the Clerys during Henry's trial, and then represented the family in its civil complaint against Lehigh filed in 1987. His account relies on first-hand observations, numerous interviews and other primary sources. It also includes extensive details provided by Henry's trial lawyer, J. Michael Farrell of Philadelphia. Farrell gave Fioravanti unfettered access to accounts of Henry's life, including medical records, the defendant's own statements about his state of mind and his past troubles, including his sexual dysfunction and aggressive behavior, along with correspondence Henry had with Farrell in prison. Henry agreed to waive attorney-client privilege and granted Farrell permission to share those details and documents.

To reconstruct events the author also integrated select details about Jeanne's murder and the prosecution's case from trial testimony reported in newspapers, from Fioravanti's first-person account of a preliminary hearing held in Northampton County Courthouse, Easton, Pennsylvania, on May 20, 1986, and from a court transcript of Henry's sentencing hearing on April 28, 1987. Fioravanti reviewed portions of his manuscript with the author and provided additional details and context during four interviews in 2011–2013. Farrell provided further details during interviews in 2012 and 2014 including Henry's behavior, Farrell's unsuccessful attempts to introduce pathological intoxication as an insanity defense during the trial, and as a mitigating factor during the penalty phase, and his critique of Lehigh's affirmative action program. Select details of the Clerys' family life as chronicled by Fioravanti are also integrated into the narrative.

40   *Marie Henry held a job*: Michel Marriott, "Jo-Jo Makes the Papers. Lehigh Murder Suspect's Neighbors Expected Likable 'Brainiac' to Outrun Newark's Odds," *The Philadelphia Daily News*, April 14, 1986.

40   *"We were just trying . . ."*: Testimony of Marie Henry, Sentencing Proceedings, Commonwealth of Pennsylvania vs. Josoph Henry. Court of Common Pleas, Northampton County, Pennsylvania, April 28, 1987.

42   *After a student-alumni*: Gay Elwell, "Trial Ordered in Lehigh U Slaying, Classmate Says Henry 'Told Me That He Killed Somebody,'" *The Morning Call*, May 21, 1986.

42   *He picked up*: Ibid.

44   *After returning from Jeanne's dorm*: Joseph Fioravanti, Untitled (unpublished manuscript, September 1992), Word document, 55–56.

44   *Despite staying: at* Ibid., 64.

46   *"May you take some comfort . . ."*: Fricker, ibid.

Chapter 4: Compelled to Act

49   *His presence in and of itself*: Elwell, ibid.

50   *Connie's whole body shook*: Fioravanti, ibid., 113.

50   *Ken Copeland also recalled*: Elwell, ibid.

50 *The Clerys left the room*: Gay Elwell, "Henry Guilty of Murder—Death Penalty Sought in Killing of Lehigh University Freshman," *The Morning Call*, April 26, 1987.

52 *Farrell, who a year earlier*: Josoph Henry's trial attorney, J. Michael Farrell of Philadelphia, had represented James Terry Roach, who was executed by South Carolina in January 1986 for the brutal killings of two teens, including a fourteen-year-old girl he had raped and shot. An appeal for clemency was rejected despite Farrell's argument that since Roach was seventeen at the time of the murders, the death penalty violated the Eighth Amendment. As part of Henry's defense, the trial judge granted Farrell permission to conduct a test called a sleep deprived alcohol provocative brain scan. It was meant to simulate the conditions in Henry's brain leading to his entering Jeanne's room. Farrell sought to demonstrate the biochemistry of pathological intoxication, or what some derided as an "intoxication blackout defense": that after drinking, Henry's decision-making abilities shut down, and "he only had the reptilian brain," the primitive limbic system structures related to survival, eating, and sexual urges. After spending a night with Henry in his jail cell, early that morning Henry was videotaped as he drank beer. As a neurologist monitored the brain scan, Henry's consumed about half the level considered to be legal intoxication in Pennsylvania—a 0.05 blood alcohol content. According to Farrell, Henry drifted into a stream of consciousness rant. The court barred showing the videotape at the trial on the basis that it didn't accurately simulate the circumstances of that night. In 2014, Farrell offered to look for the video among his files but was unable to find it.

54 *Clery's face reddened*: Fioravanti, ibid., 191.

54 *Rejecting the alcohol-related insanity*: Ibid., 204.

55 *Marie Henry then tried*: Ibid.

55 *Henry's mother and two friends*: Sentencing Proceedings, Commonwealth of Pennsylvania vs. Josoph Henry. Court of Common Pleas, Northampton County, Pa., April 28, 1987, 20–23.

55 *Farrell used every means*: Elwell, "Henry Guilty of Murder," ibid.

55 *Finally, her son stood*: Ibid., 34.

59 *"No fifteen-year-old should . . ."*: Jeff Wright, "Family Holds Informative Dinner," *Kingston Reporter* (MA), May 2004.

61 *Howard was astonished*: Fioravanti, ibid., 131–134.

62 *Scouring through the report*: Ibid., 136.

63 *He also could not have known*: Rhonda Bell, "Tulane Murder Trial Nears," *The Times-Picayune* (New Orleans, LA), September 5, 1999.

64 *"We are not the type . . ."*: Patrick Thornton, "Murder Sparked Battle Against Campus Crime,'" *The Brown and White* (Lehigh University), April 4, 2006.

Chapter 5: No More

68   *The movement's roots were deep* : "History of the Crime Victims' Movement in the United States," California Department of Corrections and Rehabilitation, Office of Victim and Survivor Rights and Services, accessed September 30, 2012, http://www.cdcr.ca.gov/victim_services/historical_landmarks.html.

68   *Lightner's thirteen-year-old daughter*: David J. Hanson, "Candy Lightner," Alcohol Problems and Solutions. State University of New York, Potsdam, Dec. 1, 2015, accessed July 13, 2015, https://www.alcoholproblemsandsolutions.org/drinking-and-driving/.

68   *Among the highlights*: "History of the Crime Victims' Movement in the United States," ibid.

70   *Determined, as her son Alex*: Beverly Beyette, "Von Bulow Stepchildren Speak Out: They Open Victim Advocacy Center in Mother's Name," *Los Angeles Times*, March 30, 1986.

71   *He wrote books and law*: 102 Cong. Rec. H32–33. (daily ed. Jan. 22, 1992) (statement of Rep. Ramstad).

72   *"The numbers are just astronomical . . .":* Frank Carrington, "The Campus Sexual Assault Victims' Bill of Rights, 1991," https://www.youtube.com/watch?v=E3N1FbnynSI

72   *Carrington offered to help*: Fioravanti, ibid., 142.

74   *Connie told a reporter*: Brian Cooke, "Clerys Explain Lawsuit against Lehigh," *The Brown and White*, September 11, 1987.

78   *Connie figured that since schools*: Brian Cooke, "Clerys Distribute Questionnaire on College Security," *The Brown and White*, September 15, 1987.

79   *As classes resumed at Lehigh*: "Noble but Futile," editorial, *The Brown and White*, September 15, 1997.

79   *Others assailed the family's motives*: Peter Harter, John Amorison, letter to the editor, *The Brown and White*, September 22, 1997.

79   *"If one student is spared . . .":* Ibid.

80   *"It will not be effective unless . . .":* "What Jeanne Didn't Know: Part 2," Clery Center, 1990, https://www.youtube.com/user/CleryCenter/WhatJeanneDidn'tKnow/.

80   *Originally she and Howard*: Cheryl Wenner, "2 Years After Clery Slaying, Panel Passes Security Bill," *The Morning Call*, April 6, 1988.

83   *By 1985, Rapidforms*: Jack Farber, "Rapidforms, Inc.," (unpublished manuscript, October 2012), printed Word file, 85–95.

83   *Clery made out very well*: Ibid., 92.

83   *Clery's former laser-like business focus*: Ibid., 95

83   *Too often, he said*: Fioravanti, ibid 99.

83   *This involved placing electronically*: "Lehigh to Pay in Suit Filed Over Slaying," *The New York Times*, July 27, 1988.

84   *"But there has to be . . . ."*: Denise Brack, sentencing hearing, Commonwealth vs. Scanlon, Norfolk County Superior Court, Dedham, Ma., June 18, 2004.

85   *"They would have done . . ."*: Nadine Hoffman, "Defendant Forgiven by All But the Judge: Four Years," *The Patriot Ledger*, June 19, 2004.

86   *The president said the couple*: Pete Leffler, "President Bush Cites Clerys For Fighting Campus Crime," *The Morning Call*, April 26, 1990.

87   *Even the Clerys' housekeeper*: Fioravanti, ibid., 287.

88   *Howard had told the priest*: David O'Reilly, "Redeeming a Daughter's Death," *The Philadelphia Inquirer*, October 18, 1990.

88   *"We have our martyrs . . ."*: Ibid.

91   *In the midst of appealing*: Attorney Joseph Fioravanti's manuscript about the Clerys' ordeal and Josoph Henry's trial includes transcripts and excerpts from six letters Henry wrote to his attorney in prison between September 14, 1988, and July 30, 1991. Five of them are addressed to counselor J. Michael Farrell. A sixth dated April 16, 1990, was addressed to the Clerys. Knowing it was inappropriate for Henry to initiate direct contact with the victim's family, and realizing this might be construed as an attempt at intimidation during a future appeal, Farrell never passed along the letter to the family. He provided copies of the letters to Fioravanti after he no longer represented Henry, and Fioravanti gave the Clerys the one addressed to them.

Chapter 6: Grinder

93   *Three starters had been held*: *Arlington Advocate*, September 27, 1945.

94   *Later on during that infamous*: Howard B. Winkler, "Menotomy Minuteman Historical Trail, A Walking Tour of Arlington's Past," Arlington Historical Society, September, 2007.

94   *Howard squinted upwards*: Fioravanti, ibid., 8.

95   *"Only Two Infantile Paralysis Cases . . . ."*: *Arlington Advocate*, September 20, 1945.

95   *The iron lung was used*: Siddhartha Mukherjee, *The Emperor of All Maladies* (New York: Scribner, 2010), 94.

95   *While dreaded, and making*: Meg Haskell, "Bangor Man Living with Effects of Polio Still Using Iron Lung," *Bangor Daily News*, September 30, 2011.

96   *The spa was already*: Roosevelt Warm Springs Institute for Rehabilitation, The New Georgia Encyclopedia.org, accessed September 13, 2012, http://www.georgiaencyclopedia.org/nge/Article.jsp?id=h-1101.

96   *Roosevelt visited do̧ens of times*: "Franklin D. Roosevelt in Georgia," ibid., accessed September 13, 2012, http://www.georgiaencyclopedia.org/nge/Article.jsp?id=h-2727.

96   *He exercised in the pool*: Doris Kearns Goodwin, *No Ordinary Time:*

Franklin and Eleanor Roosevelt: The Home Front in World War II (New York: Simon & Schuster, 1994), 116.

96 *Roosevelt created an advocacy group*: Mukherjee, ibid., 98.

99 *Raised in a two-family*: Steve Bailey, "The Invisible Hand of Jack," *The Boston Globe*, June 3, 2007.

101 *They joined requisite collections*: Arlington Advocate, Index of Articles, Robbins Library, Arlington, Ma.

101 *It also ran special children's*: "*I Remember Arlington When . . .*": *A Collection of Reminiscences*. Meontomy Celebrates Its 350th, 1985, 19. Courtesy of Robbins Library Historical Collection. Arlington, Ma.

Chapter 7: More to Do

113 *Baer's murder drew national attention*: The response of Margaret and Dr. Thomas Baer, the stabbing victim's parents, paralleled the Clerys in key respects as they became allies. Refusing to be muzzled by the University of Tennessee, the Baers did a television interview on *20/20* in which Mr. Baer said campus police committed "a comedy of errors." The university had failed to even inform him immediately of his son's death, and Baer said when he called Knoxville police, they hadn't been told about it, either. The university wouldn't turn over the police report for two months until the family's lawyer forced their hand. The couple continued advocating for improved campus security protocols in Tennessee and nationally during the next two decades, including a landmark federal law advancing campus sexual assault survivors' rights. An especially dogged campaigner, Margaret Baer often teamed up with Connie Clery. *See* Maria M. Cornelius, "Father of Slain Student Rips UT Probe on National TV," *The Knoxville News-Sentinel*, December 4, 1990; Marti Davis, "UT Becoming Safer," *The Knoxville News-Sentinel*, August 23, 1993; Rebecca Ferrar, "Bill Requires Tracking Off-Campus Crime," *The Knoxville News-Sentinel*, February 3, 1993.

116 *He was able to open*: Mike Stanton, "R.I. House Majority Leader Has Been on Providence Licensing Board and Bar Owner in Warwick," *The Providence Journal*, January 31, 2010.

116 *The mayor almost survived*: Associated Press, "Bye-Bye Buddy: Era Ends with Rogue Mayor," *The Westerly Sun* (Westerly, RI), June 29, 2002.

116 *Then came "Operation Plunder Dome"*: Mike Stanton, *The Prince of Providence* (New York: Random House, 2003), 263.

119 *At least one in five experiences*: Robin Hattersley Gray, "Sexual Assault Statistics and Myths," *Campus Safety*, March 6, 2012, accessed January 7, 2013, http://www.campussafetymagazine.com/Channel/Public-Safety/Articles/2012/03/Sexual-Assault-Statistics-and-Myths.aspx.

119   *More likely it is one*: Matt Rochelau, "Nearly a Quarter of College Women Say They Were Assaulted, Survey Finds," *The Boston Globe*, September 21, 2015.

120   *The vast majority of these attacks*: K.B. Wolitzsky-Taylor, H.S. Resnick, A.B. Amstadter, J.L. McCauley, K.J. Ruggiero, and D.G. Kilpatrick, "Reporting Rape in a National Sample of College Women," *Journal of American College Health* 59, no. 7 (2011): 582–587.

120   *As few as 7 percent*: Rochelau. Ibid.

120   *In addition, research suggests*: Devin Thorpe, "Victim-Turned-Victims Rights Attorney Builds National Organization," *Forbes*, September 6, 2016, http://www.forbes.com/sites/devinthorpe/2016/09/06/victim-turned-victims-rights-attorney-builds-national-organization/print/.

120   *"Victims in these cases . . ."*: Mary Lou Leary, "Keeping Students Safe on Campus," US Department of Justice, Office of Violence Against Women, October 9, 2013, http://blogs.justice.gov/main/archives/2516.

120   *Sexual assault is widely considered*: M. Planty, L. Langton, C. Krebs, M. Berzofsky, H. Smiley-McDonald, "Female Victims of Sexual Violence, 1994–2010," US Department of Justice, Bureau of Justice Statistics, March 2013.

121   *A variety of factors on*: B.S. Fisher, L.E. Daigle, F.T. Cullen, M.G. Turner, "Acknowledging Sexual Victimization as Rape: Results From a National-Level Study," *Justice Quarterly* 20, no. 3 (2000): 401–440. *See also* Robin Hattersley Gray, ibid.

121   *"Alcohol use is never an excuse . . ."*: Alison Kiss, "Investigation, Evaluation, and Adjudication of Sexual Misconduct: Practical Implementation of Title IX and Dear Colleague Letter," Ballard Spahr/Clery Center for Campus Security webinar, Sept. 20, 2012.

121   *Nearly three-quarters*: Meichen Mohler-Kuo, George W. Dowdall, Mary P. Koss, Henry Wechsler, "Correlates of Rape while Intoxicated in a National Sample of College Women," *Journal of Studies on Alcohol*, 65 (2004): 37–45. This study analyzed data from 119 schools participating in three Harvard School of Public Health College Alcohol Surveys. Random surveys were conducted of 8,567 women during 1997, 8,425 females in 1999, and 6,988 in 2001. Roughly one in twenty (4.7 percent) reported being raped. Seventy-two percent of the victims said they were raped while intoxicated. Other studies, perhaps most prominently those conducted by the National Institute of Justice as recently as 2010, report the percentage of completed or attempted rape victimization among college women as 20 to 25 percent. A 2012 survey from the CDC also found that 19 percent of undergraduate women have experienced an attempted or completed sexual assault since entering college.

122   *Critics argued that universities*: John Lauerman, "College Men Accused of Sexual Assault Say Their Rights Violated," Bloomberg News, December 16, 2013.

123   *King media misogynist*: Justin Berrier, "Limbaugh: Violence Against
Women Act Signed 'Under The Guise That Women Are Being Beat To
A Pulp In This Country,'" Media Matters for America, March 7, 2013,
accessed April 30 13, https://www.mediamatters.org/blog/2013/03/07/
limbaugh-violence-against-women-act-signed-unde/192954.

123   *Then came Angie Epifano*: Angie Epifano, "An Account of Sexual Assault at
Amherst College," *The Amherst Student*, October 17, 2012, accessed February
20, 2014, http://amherststudent.amherst.edu/?q=article/2012/10/17/
account-sexual-assault-amherst-college.

123   *Sophomore Andrea Pino suffered*: Andrea Pino, "Rape, Betrayal, and
Reclaiming Title IX," *The Huffington Post*, April 29, 2013, accessed
February 21, 2014, http://www.huffingtonpost.com/andrea-pino/more-
that-a-teal-ribbon_b_3165293.html. A Title IX complaint brought against
the University of North Carolina, Chapel Hill, by Pino and three other
students was a catalyst expanding public awareness of colleges' failure to
handle assault complaints properly. Asserting they represented sixty-three
women who endured a climate of sexual harassment and re-victimization,
the complainants alleged that UNC failed to impartially investigate assault
claims and provide appropriate grievance procedures, while giving school
staff inappropriate training. Pino discovered that in her hall of thirty-six
women, seventeen had been sexually assaulted by the time they finished their
sophomore years. The women also filed a complaint against UNC under
the Clery Act. This focused largely on how survivors were treated after
reporting assaults and stalking. During the university's adjudicatory process,
accommodations should have been given to them—including options to
change dorms and classes, and written notice of the hearing procedures and
dispositions. Pino and Annie Clark, another complainant, helped form the
nonprofit End Rape On Campus, guiding others to bring Title IX and Clery
Act complaints, along with the "IX Network" for survivors.

124   *At the University of Connecticut*: Tyler Kingkade, "UConn Failed To
Investigate Sexual Assault Reports And Protect Victims, Complaint
Claims," *The Huffington Post*, October 2, 2013, accessed February 20, 2014,
http://www.huffingtonpost.com/2013/10/21/uconn-sexual-assault
complaint_n_4133713.html?utm_hp_ref=college.

124   *Reviewing ten years of complaints*: Kristen Lombardi, "A lack of consequences for sexual assault," The Center for Public Integrity, February 24,
2010, accessed February 17, 2014, http://www.publicintegrity.org/2010/
02/24/4360/lack-consequences-sexual-assault-0.

124   *For example, by one*: A 2016 review of 23,000 student responses, "New
document: Understanding Crime Statistics," Clery Center for Campus

Security, September 2016, http://clerycenter.org/sites/default/files/
Geography_1-pager_PRINT.pdf.

124 *However, of about 11,000*: "91 Percent of Colleges Reported Zero Incidents
of Rape in 2014," American Association of University Women, Nov. 23,
2015, http://www.aauw.org/article/clery-act-data-analysis/.

Chapter 8: An Abundance of Caution

128 *The voice on the other end*: Fioravanti, ibid., 296.

131 *She ruled that a trial*: Memorandum and Order, Josoph Henry v. Martin
Horn, et al. 98-CV-2187. US District Court for the Eastern District of
Pennsylvania. Justice Anita B. Brody, Jr., May 16, 2002.

131 *Henry's lawyers, who had appealed*: Elliot Grossman, Tom Coombe,
"Death Sentence Overturned," *The Morning Call*, May 23, 2002.

132 *"If the bereaved family . . ."*: Tyra Braden, "Henry Trades Appeal Rights
for Life in Prison," *The Morning Call*, August 31, 2002.

132 *Jack Farber had seen*: Farber, Howard Clery's business partner at
Rapidforms Inc., a business forms company in Bellmawr, New Jersey,
described the firm's growth and a narrative of his relationship with Clery
in an unpublished memoir spanning his own entrepreneurial career.
Farber shared a portion of the manuscript with the author with permission to use in 2012.

135 *To Carter, the scene outside*: "Knoxville Man in the Middle of the Virginia
Tech Aftermath," *Knoxville News Sentinel* website, Knoxnews.com, April
17, 2007. Courtesy of S. Daniel Carter.

135 *"How do you think . . ."*: Katie Couric, "Massacre at Virginia Tech," *CBS
Evening News With Katie Couric*, April 16, 2007, http://www.youtube.com/
watch?v=hEQ2VfqokHc.

136 *Investigators would discover*: Hollis Stambaugh, remarks during presentation on campus emergency notification systems at the Massachusetts
Institute of Technology, Cambridge, Massachusetts, November 29, 2011.
Director of the Center for Public Protection, Stambaugh served as deputy
director on a panel formed by Virginia Governor Tim Kaine to investigate
the Virginia Tech massacre.

136 *Hollis Stambaugh, a security consultant*: Ibid.

137 *The shooter, who wore a T-shirt*: Matt Williams, "NIU Report Reveals
Different Sides of Shooter," *Rockford* (IL) *Register Star*, March 19, 2010.

137 *Local law enforcement officials*: Benji Feldheim, "NIU Police Comments
Draw Criticism," *The Daily Chronicle* (DeKalb, IL), April 18, 2008.

138 *My skin turns black*: Job 30: 30–31.

140 *EMU's cover-up and complacency*: "Expensive Mistakes," editorial, *The
Grand Rapids Press* (MI), December 26, 2007.

140 *"How could they never have . . ."*: Rich Keenan, "On-Campus Murder Shouldn't Be Kept a Secret," *The Detroit News*, June 28, 2007.

140 *He did not go ballistic*: Nate Reens, "EMU Apology is 90 Miles Short," *The Grand Rapids Press*, June 20, 2007.

140 *To her mother, Laura was*: Dave Gershman, "'You Took Away the Gift God Gave Us,' Killer Told," *Grand Rapids Press News Service*, May 8, 2008.

141 *"EMU made mistakes . . ."*: Reens, ibid.

141 *Allison Campbell fell*: Julia Lynn Kauffmann, "In Memory of Allison Ann Campbell," Glenbrook South High School, Class of 1973, September 14, 2008, http://www.classcreator.com/Glenview-IL-Glenbrook-South 1973/ class_profile.cfm?member_id=414002.

143 *The change was reflected*: In 2017, thirty years after Jeanne Clery's murder, the nonprofit again refocused its mission with a shortened name, the Clery Center. "Our audience will be our country's colleges and universities," it declared, "and we will affect change by guiding those institutions to create truly safer campus communities."

Chapter 9: If Not for Themselves

149 *Smeaton had long since commended*: John Smeaton, email to author, July 8, 2013.

152 *After a graduate assistant*: "Time Line of the Scandal," *The New York Times*, July 13, 2012.

152 *Before the case blew open*: Richard Pérez-Peña, "In Report, Failures at Every Level of Hierarchy," *The New York Times*, July 13, 2012. *See also* Sara Lipka, "Ignorance and Low Priority of Clery Act Obligations May Extend Beyond Penn State," *The Chronicle of Higher Education*, July 12, 2012.

152 *As Louis Freeh*: Ken Belson, "Abuse Scandal Inquiry Damns Paterno and Penn State," *The New York Times*, July 13, 2012.

155 *Once she was able*: Kristin Jones, "Lax Enforcement of Title IX in Campus Sexual Assault Cases," Center for Public Integrity, February 25, 2010, http://www.publicintegrity.org/2010/02/25/4374/ lax-enforcement-title-ix-campus-sexual-assault-cases-0.

155 *An assistant dean said*: Ibid. *Also* Steven Elbow, "Student Slams UW Handling of Rape Charge; D.A. Investigating," *The Capital Times* (Madison, WI), May 6, 2006.

155 *Over time, Dunn vowed*: Dunn shared some of her narrative in a series of interviews and email exchanges with the author between 2011 and 2014, focusing on her commitment to help other student assault survivors. In addition to the breakthrough reports by the Center for Public Integrity and NPR, select details of her ordeal were also confirmed from these public sources: Karen Rivedal. "When the Booze Flows, Watch Out, Women

Urged," *Wisconsin State Journal*. June 25, 2006; Steven Elbow, "UM Senior Seeks to Change Handling of Rape Cases," *The Capital Times*, June 25, 2006; Shapiro, ibid.

155 *Resolving, as she said*: Denise Restauri, "This Law Grad Gets Justice For Survivors Of Campus Sexual Violence," *Forbes*, September 1, 2016.

155 *She was among a group*: Tyler Kingkade, "Ending Campus Rape Won't Be Easy, But These Activists Aren't Going Anywhere," *The Huffington Post*, May 6, 2015.

155 *Taking a cue from some*: Restauri, ibid.

156 *While the outcome was still*: Gwen Moore, "Democratic Leader and Advocates VAWA Press Conference," YouTube video, March 1, 2013, http://www.youtube.com/watch?v=mfhK8GHJCis.

156 *"I am humbled . . ."*: Laura Dunn, "Democratic Leader and Advocates VAWA Press Conference," ibid.

156 *The new law, contended*: Wendy Murphy, "Campus 'Safety' Bill Endangers Rape Prosecutions," Womens enews.org, May 16, 2012, accessed February, 2015, http://womensenews.org/story/rape/120516/campus-safety-bill-endangers-rape-prosecutions.

156 *This standard of proof*: Wendy Murphy, "Campus 'SaVE' Law Does Exact Opposite," Womens enews.org, January 22, 2014, accessed February, 2015, http://womensenews.org/story/education/140121/campus-save-law-does-exact-opposite?utm_source=email&utm_medium=email&utm_campaign=email.

157 *"That one-to-one . . ."*: S. Daniel Carter, "Combating Campus Sexual Violence: Complying with the Final VAWA Rules," CampusAnswers.com webinar, November 13, 2014, http://www.campusanswers.com/vawa-final-regs/.

160 *Most keenly, before graduating*: Ally Bogard, Allie Hoffman, "On Resilience: How Laura Dunn Went From Campus Assault Survivor To Groundbreaking Legal Advocate," *Forbes*, January 23, 2017.

161 *"There's no final result yet . . ."*: Ken Brack, "Campus Sexual Assault Survivor Pushing Harder for Awareness," *The Huffington Post*, February 6, 2014, http://www.huffingtonpost.com/ken-brack/despite-awareness-campus-_b_4737806.html?utm_hp_ref=tw.

161 *Dunn, for one, rebutted*: Laura Dunn, Letters, *The Wall Street Journal*, December 12, 2013.

161 *Not three years after starting*: Tyler Kingkade, "Making Her Case," *BuzzFeed*, February 7, 2017, https://www.buzzfeed.com/tylerkingkade/laura-dunns-campus-rape-fight?utm_term=.smRJVX8O2#.iiow4D3z6. Also see Bogard, Hoffman, ibid.

161 *Her goal was*: Bogard, Hoffman, ibid.

161   *Too often in sexual assault cases*: Laura Dunn, "Dear Prudence: Stop Victim Blaming," *The Huffington Post*, October 20, 2013, http://www.huffingtonpost.com/laura-l-dunn/victim-blaming_b_4132630.html.

162   *She offered advice and resources*: Kingkade, "Making Her Case," ibid.

162   *"Sometimes they just need . . ."*: Laura Dunn, interview with author, April 9, 2014.

PART III: A WAY FORWARD

Chapter 10: Into Harm's Way

171   *He borrowed a first response*: Dennis Smith, "Jay Winuk," *A Decade of Hope* (New York: Viking, 2011), 272.

172   *As each floor crashed*: Smith, ibid., 2.

172   *The priority needs were triage*: Thomas Von Essen, Affidavit, Hearing Officer Claim Determination, PSOB Case Number 01-911-0421, Glenn J. Winuk, Jericho, NY, Fire Department, September 10, 2005.

173   *"And to have that glimmer . . ."*: Smith, ibid., 274.

176   *Lieutenant George Orzech*: Hawke Fracassa, "Death is More Real Now," *The Detroit News*, September 11, 2002.

176   *"There was nothing . . ."*: Ibid.

178   *The* Daily News *began*: Dave Saltonstall, "Triple Attacks Rock Nation," *New York Daily News*, September 12, 2001.

178   *A city employee emerging*: Ibid.

178   *In a suburb near*: Avis Thomas-Lester, Hamil R. Harris, Nancy Trejos, "Toll Weighs on Families, Community," *The Washington Post*, September 12, 2002.

178   *A poet began writing*: Nedra Weinreich, "Remembering Amy O'Doherty—Five Years Later," Weinreich Communications (blog), September 10, 2006, http://blog.social-marketing.com/2006/09/remembering-amy-odoherty-5-years-later.html.

179   *A couple from Idaho*: Mary Perez, interview with author, May 3, 2011.

179   *Four golden dogs*: "Smile Retrievers," Voices of September 11th Newsletter, accessed April 4, 2011, http://www.voicesofseptember11.org/dev/Newsletters/newsletterarchive/eNewsletter_special_edition.htm.

182   *Cantor, the international brokerage firm*: Tom Barbash, *On Top of the World*, (New York: HarperCollins, 2003), 7.

182   *A fifth-grade teacher*: Gay Storms, "Fifth-Graders Give on 9/11," *Graham Leader* (Graham, TX), September 18, 2003.

182   *"I mean, you know . . ."*: Kathleen Hays, "One Day's Pay: Creative Charitable Giving in Wake of 9/11." *The Flipside*, CNN, September 11, 2003.

183   *In one accounting,*: Brett J. Blackledge, David B. Caruso, "Some 9/11 charities failed miserably," Associated Press, August 25, 2011. *See also*

David Campbell, "The Lessons of 9/11 Philanthropy, a Decade Later," *The Chronicle of Philanthropy*, September 6, 2011.

184 *Although many charities*: James Barron, "Behind Relief to 9/11, a Man's Flaws," *The New York Times*, April 3, 2006.

184 *Two parents in Vermont*: Charles M. Sennott, "A Mother's Mission—Her Son's Death on 9/11 Spurred Sally Goodrich To Do the One Thing She Knows Best: Educate," *Boston Globe Magazine*, May 13, 2007.

184 *Americans contributed*: Aaron Smith, "How Sept. 11 Changed Charity in America," CNN Money, September 6, 2011, http://money.cnn.com/2011/09/06/news/economy/katrina_donations_911/. See also Brett J. Blackledge, David B. Caruso, ibid., David Campbell, ibid.

185 *Later on, someone reported*: William Honan, Affidavit, Hearing Officer Claim Determination, PSOB Case Number 01-911-0421, Glenn J. Winuk, Jericho, NY, Fire Department, September 10, 2005.

Chapter 11: Affirmation

197 *"I have been chasing . . ."*: Carrie Melago, "A Moment in Time for 9/11 Family," *New York Daily News*, February 4, 2006.

202 *As Von Essen testified,*: Thomas Von Essen, ibid.

204 *"We're sorry . . ."*: Susan Enriquez, "Sept. 11 Hero Finally Recognized," *Newsday*, September 8, 2009.

204 *A year before, Andrew Maloney*: Amy Katz, "Real Heroes," *Super Lawyers*, New York, September, 2011.

207 *When it was dedicated*: Denise D'Alessandro, "Park Renamed to Honor September 11 Victim." *Syosset-Jericho* (NY) *Tribune*, June 28, 2002.

209 *It can be summed up*: Martha M. Driver, "Ice Transformed to Bronze," FDNY Memorial Wall, FDNY10, July, 2006, http://www.fdnytenhouse.com/fdnywall/about.htm.

212 *Experiencing all this*: David W. Dunlap, "A Hands-On Tribute to the Pain and Valor of 9/11," *The New York Times*, June 11, 2006.

212 *Tom Geraghty lost his*: St. Paul's Chapel and 9/11, Trinity Church Wall Street, accessed December 30, 2010, https://www.trinitywallstreet.org/about/stpaulschapel/911.

212 *George Washington prayed there*: "St. Paul's Chapel: Lower Manhattan's Living Hope." *iStopOver Magazine*, accessed December 31, 2010, http://magazine.istopover.com/2010/01/08/st-pauls-chapel-lower-manhattans-living-hope/.

213 *The chapel was transformed*: R. William Franklin, Mary Sudman Donovan, *Will The Dust Praise You?* (New York: Church Publishing, Inc., 2003), 76–81.

213 *"The place so eerie . . ."*: Ibid., 74.

213 *Reverend Harris noted*: Rev. Lyndon Harris, "Celebrating the Relief Ministry at St. Paul's Chapel," *Trinity News*, (Trinity Church, New York, NY), June 6,

2002, accessed December 31, 2010, http://www.trinitywallstreet.org/news/articles/celebrating-the-relief-ministry-at-saint-pauls-chapel.

215 *On a June morning*: Jay Winuk. Remarks at FDNY Memorial Wall Dedication, June 10, 2006. Courtesy of Jay Winuk.

Chapter 12: Best Man McGinty

228 *On that morning*: Laurie Ledford, Sally Rogers, emails to author March 11, 2011 and December 6, 2011, respectively.

228 *While many were killed instantly*: National Commission on Terrorist Attacks Against the United States, *The 9/11 Commission Report* (New York: W.W. Norton & Company, 2004), 286.

228 *Hundreds of civilians trapped*: Ibid., 286.

230 *With its four operating*: Glenn J Hille, email to author, March 2011.

230 *The immediate challenge*: Dave Thomas, "9/11 Impact on Marsh & McLennan Cos. Nothing Short of Devastation," *Insurance Journal*, September 10, 2004.

231 *While dwarfed by*: Tom Barbash, ibid.

233 *Niven and his wife*: "John Ballantine Niven, An Oyster Bay Getaway," *The New York Times*, October 2, 2001, accessed July 25, 2011 on Legacy.com, http://www.legacy.com/sept11/Story.aspx?PersonID=96842&location=1.

237 *New York City did*: Charles Dimaggio, Paula Madrid, "The Terrorist Attacks of Sept. 11, 2001 in New York City," *Mental Health and Disasters*, ed. Yuval Neria, Sandra Galea, Fran H. Norris (Cambridge: Cambridge University Press, 2009), 522–536.

238 *If anything, author*: Rebecca Solnit, *A Paradise Built in Hell* (New York: Penguin, 2009), 219.

238 *Difede and some colleagues*: S. Evans, I. Patt, C. Giosan, L. Spielman, J. Difede, "Disability and Posttraumatic Stress Disorder in Disaster Relief Workers Responding to September 11, 2001 World Trade Center Disaster," *Journal of Clinical Psychology*, 65, no. 7 (2009): 1–11.

238 *"Resilience may be related . . ."*: Ibid.

238 *"What is perhaps most intriguing . . ."*: George Bonanno, *The Other Side of Sadness* (New York: Basic Books, 2009), 47.

240 *Meanwhile, Marsh paid*: Jeffrey W. Greenberg, "September 11, 2001: A CEO's Story," *Harvard Business Review*, October 2002.

241 *Towards the end*: David Barstow, Diana Henriques, "Charity Payments Criticized," *The Times Union* (Albany, NY), December 26, 2001.

241 *One woman whose husband*: William Sherman, "Big Bucks and Big Problems—Problems Persist in Doling Out 9/11 Cash," *New York Daily News*, September 1, 2002.

245 *"Now I feel like . . ."*: Dave Wedge, "9/11: One Year Later—Healing Now Begins for Foxborough Widow and Her Sons," *Boston Herald*, September 12, 2002.

Chapter 13: Finding Her Voice

250 *While Kennedy's personal touch*: Senator Edward M. Kennedy's tenacious support for 9/11 victims' families in Massachusetts is a largely untold story, documented in small part here by former Kennedy aides Steve Kerrigan, Tom Crohan, and Scott Fay. *Also see* Alison King, "9/11 Widow Reflects on Relationship With Sen. Kennedy," New England Cable News, June 16, 2009, http://www.necn.com/Boston/Politics/2009/06/16/911-widow-reflects-on/1245158107.html, viewed Oct. 22, 2010; Sharyn Alfonsi, "Ted Kennedy and the Attacks on Sept. 11th," ABC News, August 27, 2009, http://abcnews.go.com/WN/story?id=8430287, viewed Oct. 22, 2010; Andrea Stone, "Kennedy Took Public's Battles to Heart," *USA Today*, August 28, 2009.

251 *Both women and several*: Stephen J. Kerrigan, "Kerrigan: Find Time This Weekend to Remember Heroes," *MetroWest Daily News* (Framingham, MA), May 27, 2010.

252 *They held on to*: Seth Jacobson, "Abington Resident Instrumental in Instituting New Military Fund," *Abington Mariner*, June 4, 2009.

256 *While she's still*: Michele Morgan Bolton, "Bad Day, Good Deeds," *The Boston Globe*, July 8, 2010.

266 *Many years later,*: Morris D. Davis, "Guantánamo's Charade of Justice," *The New York Times*, March 27, 2015.

270 *He wrote an op-ed piece*: Jay Winuk, "9/11 Day of Service to Honor a Brother," CNN, May 11, 2011, http://www.cnn.com/2011/OPINION/05/11/winuk.brother.9.11/.

Chapter 14: 9/12

274 *The LA-based media*: Andrew Adam Neiman, "Good/Corps Aims to Help Business Meet Social Goals," *The New York Times*, May 12, 2011.

282 *What do you want me*: Grateful Dead. "Box of Rain," Robert Hunter. *American Beauty*. 1970. Ice Nine Publishing. © Copyright 2017 Hal Leonard.

283 *Siller had worked*: "Stephen's Story," Stephen Siller Tunnel To Towers Foundation, http://tunnel2towers.org/stephens-story/.

288 *A former firefighter*: Nicole Neroulias, "Quietly, Another Mosque Operates in the Shadow of Ground Zero," *Houston Chronicle*, July 29, 2010. *See also* "Landmarks Hosts Three-Hour Hearing on Mosque," *The New York Observer*, July 14, 2010, accessed July 23, 2011, http://www.observer.com/2010/real-estate/landmark-hosts-three-hour-hearing-mosque.

289 *One responded by blogging*: Jennifer Peltz, "The Painful, Public Journey of the 9/11 Families," Associated Press, September 7, 2011.

291 *One of their critics*: Pamela Geller, "Obama calls on Americans to service on September 11—9/11 is a day of mourning, not service," AtlasShrugs .com, August 28, 2011, http://atlasshrugs2000.typepad.com/atlas_ shrugs/2011/08/obama-calls-on-americans-to-service-on-september- 11–911-is-a-day-of-mourning-not-service.html.

292 *Like other schools*: Joie Tyrrell, "9/11 A Decade Later: Teaching 9/11, Educators See Anniversary As Time to Address It," *Newsday*, July 12, 2011.

292 *The previous June,*: Jordan Lauterbach, "9/11 Education Discussed at Jericho HS Town Hall Meeting," *Syosset-Jericho* (NY) *Times*, June 10, 2011.

Chapter 15: A Place of Service

305 *Elementary-aged kids*: Rainey Coffin, "Project Helps Kids Mark 9/11," *The Spokesman-Review* (Spokane, WA), September 22, 2011.

305 *In St. Louis,*: Mikal J. Harris, "Students at Bayless Elementary Mark Sept. 11 by Helping Others," *St. Louis-Post Dispatch*, September 12, 2011.

306 *David and Jay dipped*: "9/11 Day Observance: Preliminary Program Impact and Results," 9/11 Day. Courtesy of Jay Winuk.

310 *A few days earlier*: Cindy McGinty, "Cindy McGinty: Remembering and Paying Tribute on 9/11," *The Huffington Post*, September 7, 2011.

310 *Saturday begins with*: Catherine Krug, "Day to Pause." *The Sun Chronicle*, (Attleborough, MA), September 12, 2010, Heather McCarron, "Never to be Forgotten." *The Country Gazette* (Bellingham, MA), September 9, 2011.

310 *"From the ashes . . ."*: Patrick Mitchell, "Foxborough 9/11 Memorial Dedication Highlights," Foxboro Cable Access, September 11, 2011, https://www.youtube.com/watch?v=JkD4GHgle30.

311 *He walks up*: Chris Mitchell, ibid.

311 *"It doesn't really matter . . ."*: Cindy McGinty, ibid.

Chapter 16: Heart Work

319 *Jane sat down and wrote*: Courtesy of Jane Pollicino.

323 *In a review*: Lloyd, ibid.

324 *Edie offers this advice*: Laura Dunn, "Women in Business Q&A: Edie Lutnick, Co-Founder and President, The Cantor Fitzgerald Relief Fund," *The Huffington Post*, September 10, 2015.

331 *Hillary O'Neill*: Stav Ziv, "Turning 9/11 Into a Day of Service and Remembrance," Newsweek.com, Sept. 11, 2015, http://www.newsweek .com/turning-911-day-service-and-remembrance-371004. *Also see* "Hope Was Born on 9/11," 9/11 Day, August 18, 2015, https://www.youtube. com/watch?v=gHc90Iz_w40.

PART IV: THE DEPTHS OF HEALING

Chapter 18: Podgórze

347 *Many people kept cows*: Halina Nelken, *And Yet, I Am Here!* (Amherst: University of Massachusetts Press, 1999), 35.

348 *Diverse strains of Judaism*: "Krakow," Holocaust Encyclopedia, US Holocaust Memorial Museum, accessed November, 2013, http://www.ushmm.org/wlc/en/article.php?ModuleId=10005169.

352 React*ing to a pogrom*: Mordechai Gebirtig, "S'Brent" ("It Burns"), *The Song That Never Died: The Poetry of Mordecai Gebirtig*, trans. Simcha Simchovitch, (Oakville, Ontario: Mosaic Press, 2001).

354 *Listeners were asked*: Malvina Graf, *The Kraków Ghetto and the Plaszów Camp Remembered* (Tallahassee: Florida State University Press, 1989), 7.

355 *By early 1941,*: "Krakow Timeline," Holocaust Encyclopedia, United States Holocaust Memorial Museum, accessed October 14, 2012, http://www.ushmm.org/wlc/en/article.php?ModuleId=10007458#seealso.

355 *A fifty-acre area*: Tadeusz Pankiewicz, *The Cracow Ghetto Pharmacy* (New York: Holocaust Library, 1987), 3. *See also* Graf, ibid., 36.

355 *By horse, farm wagons*: Pankiewicz, ibid., 2.

Chapter 19: Sounds in the Stones

357 *The breaking day*: Select details of the *aktion* or deportations of October 28, 1942 come from first-person accounts including Nathan Offen and Sam Offen; Pankiewicz, ibid.; Graf, ibid.; and Gusta Davidson Draenger, *Justyna's Narrative*, (Amherst: University of Massachusetts Press, 1996). *See also* "Kraków Timeline," ibid.

358 *Sam and his brothers*: Reuben Ainsztein, *Jewish Resistance in Nazi-Occupied Europe: With a Historical Survey of the Jews as Fighter and Soldier in the Diaspora* (London: Elek, 1974), 826. Other estimates differ on the numbers of Jews massacred in Kraków during Aktion Reinhard on June 1 and June 3–4, 1942. Drawing from primary sources, Ainsztein wrote that "several hundred who resisted in one way or another were shot on the spot" June 1, while another "several hundred were mown down by machine guns to terrorise the others" on June 4.

358 *For a time, Jacob*: "Rescue Story, Julius Madritsch," The Righteous Among The Nations. Yad Vashem, accessed November, 2013, http://db.yadvashem.org/righteous/family.html?language=en&itemId=4016227.

358 *They were not among*: Ibid.

359 *"Standing was forbidden"*: Pankiewicz, ibid., 74.

359 *That afternoon, work crews*: Nathan Nothman, interview by Donna Miller,

June 9, 1984, video recording, Holocaust Memorial Center Zekelman
Family Campus Library Archive, Farmington Hills, Michigan.

360 *Kraków was to be cleansed*: Ainsztein, ibid., 825.

362 *A digging machine unearthed*: Bernard Offen, *My Hometown Concentration
Camp* (Portland, Oreg.: Valentine Mitchell, 2008), 51.

362 *The estimates of inmates*: Estimates of the numbers of prisoners at Płaszów
and how many were killed there vary greatly—from 35,000 to 150,000
inmates, and from 8,000 to 80,000 murdered. In *Schindler's Ark*, Thomas
Kenneally noted that Polish publications, drawing from the work of its Main
Commission for the Investigation of Nazi Crimes in Poland and other sources,
believe upwards of 150,000 people went through the camp and its sub-camps,
and that 80,000 died, mainly in mass executions on a hill overlooking the
complex, and during epidemics. Many others were shipped to other concentration camps. In his 2008 book, *My Hometown Concentration Camp*, Bernard
Offen references other sources reporting Polish Supreme Court estimates
that as few as 35,000 prisoners came through the camp, with 8,000 killed there.
Kenneally wrote, "The distance between the two estimates looks narrower
when it is remembered that executions of Poles, Gypsies, and Jews would
continue at Chujowa Górka (or "Chuy's Hill") and at other points around
Płaszów throughout most of that year (1943), and that the SS themselves took
up the practice of burning bodies immediately after mass killings." Kenneally,
Schindler's Ark (New York: Scribner, 1982), 254.

To compile select details of the Płaszów camp and prisoners' experiences,
the author also drew from other oral histories and survivors' books. These
include: Fred Ferber, interview by Sidney Bolkosky, September 11 and 25,
2001, audiotape, The Voice/Vision Holocaust Survivor Oral History Archive,
Mardigan Library, the University of Michigan-Dearborn, http://holocaust
.umd.umich.edu/ferberf/; Nothman, ibid; George Topas, *The Iron Furnace*
(Lexington: The University Press of Kentucky, 1990), 180–188; Joseph Bau,
Dear God, Have You Ever Gone Hungry? (New York: Arcade, 1998), 139.

363 *The ghetto was further*: Graf, ibid., 70.

363 *Those deemed fit to work*: Ainsztein, ibid., 826.

363 *The pharmacist Pankiewicz again*: Pankiewicz, ibid., 114.

363 *Amon Goeth, tall*: Graf, ibid., 72–73.

364 *A doctor, a beautiful woman*: Pankiewicz, ibid., 115–116, Graf, ibid., 75.

364 *Yet not all*: "Rescue Story—Julius Madritsch," The Righteous Among the
Nations, Yad Vashem, accessed, Nov. 4, 2012, http://db.yadvashem.org/
righteous/family.html?language=en&itemId=4016227, *see also* Graf, ibid., 61.

364 *Nine thousand Jews*: Ainsztein, ibid., 827.

364 *The next day,*: Ibid.

364 *"To weep for them . . ."*: Graf, ibid., 78.

366 *Cooperatives making army uniforms*: "Płaszów-Kraków Forced Labour Camp," Holocaust Education & Archive Research Team, accessed November 3, 2012, http://www.holocaustresearchproject.net/othercamps/Płaszów/Płaszów.html.

368 *His heart pounding*: Sam Offen's first recorded account of surviving his encounter with Amon Goeth came on December 27, 1981 in an oral history interview conducted by Sidney Bolkosky, a professor of history at the University of Michigan-Dearborn. As part of the university's Voice/Vision Holocaust Survivor Oral History Archive project, Bolkosky conducted hundreds of interviews with about 150 survivors, including several with each of the Offen brothers, and one with all three. It should be noted that Thomas Kenneally's *Schindler's Ark*, (later retitled *Schindler's List* and the inspiration for Steven Spielberg's film, which depicts Goeth at Płaszów), was published in 1982, while the Academy-award winning film was released in 1993. The author is in possession of each of the Offens' interviews with Bolkosky, copies of which were provided by the university. Transcripts of selected histories are available at http://holocaust.umd.umich.edu/offens/. Sam Offen also described facing Goeth in his 2005 memoir, *When Hope Prevails*.

   Each of the Offens also gave their testimonies to the USC Shoah Foundation Institute in 1996–97. The archive, which contains testimonies of nearly 52,000 survivors and other witnesses, includes two interviews with Nathan, http://sfi.usc.edu/content/nathan-offen-recalls-separation-his-family; http://collections.ushmm.org/search/catalog/vha20084 ; one with Sam, http://collections.ushmm.org/search/catalog/vha17401; and one with Bernard, http://collections.ushmm.org/search/catalog/vha27135.

368 *Legend had it that*: Fay Cashman Greer, "Kraków's Wieliczka Mine is Fascinating Evidence of Man's Initiative and Ingenuity," *The Jerusalem Post*, January 12, 2008.

369 *While the Nazis exterminated*: "Wieliczka History," Virtual Shtetl, accessed November 2012, http://www.sztetl.org.pl/en/article/wieliczka/5,history/?print=1.

369 *Covered by a wooden*: Greer, ibid.

370 *Before he was killed*: Nelken, ibid., 213.

371 *"Gute Nacht Mutti . . ."*: Ibid., 212.

371 *"Nad kolyska matka czuwa . . ."*: "The Trial of Amon Goeth—Part 3, Selected Extracts from the Testimony," Holocaust Education & Archive Research Team, accessed November 19, 2012, http://www.holocaustresearchproject.org/trials/goeth3.html.

371 *The graves behind*: Bau, ibid., 151.

371 *Lit pyres spread*: Ibid., 151

371   *Another young boy*: Ferber, ibid.

371   *This final desecration*: Nelken, ibid., 213.

372   *In the infirmary*: Topas, ibid., 185.

372   *Old men blackened greying*: Bau, ibid., 111.

372   *Mrs. Webber, scalding hot*: Ferber, ibid.

372   *Dr. Max Blanke emerged*: Topas, ibid., 192, 195.

372   *One in particular*: Graf, ibid., 130.

373   *A prisoner discovered*: Topas, ibid., 199.

373   *To where the shades were covered*: Dante, *The Inferno of Dante: A New Verse Translation*, Canto XXXIV (14–15), trans. Robert Pinsky (New York: Farar, Straus and Giroux, 1994), 295.

373   *Picking one up*: Bau, ibid., 114, 135.

Chapter 20: Liberation

376   *Near where the door closed*: Ferber, ibid.

377   *"Even then, we had no . . ."*: Sam Offen, *When Hope Prevails* (Livonia, Mich: First Page Publications, 2005), 51.

377   *"Sort of, not exactly . . ."*: Sam Offen, interview by Sidney Bolkosky, December 27, 1981, audiotape, VVA, Mardigan Library, the University of Michigan-Dearborn, http://holocaust.umd.umich.edu/offens/.

377   *Three miles ahead*: Michael Hirsh, *The Liberators: America's Witness to the Holocaust* (New York: Bantam Books, 2010), 265.

378   *Two brick ovens worked*: "The Gas Chamber," Mauthausen Memorial, (KZ-Gedenkstätte Mauthausen), accessed June 3, 2013, http://en .mauthausen-memorial.at/db/admin/de/show_article.php?carticle=375& topopup=1&topopup=1.

378   *Mauthausen was one of only*: Wendy Holden, *Born Survivors* (New York: HarperCollins, 2015), 246.

378   *In all, nearly 200,000*: "Mauthausen: Forced Labor and Sub-camps," Holocaust Encyclopedia, United States Holocaust Memorial Museum, accessed June 5, 2013, https://ushmm.org/wlc/en/article.php?ModuleId=10007730.

378   *First envisioned to contain*: Tom Hundley, "Facing a Grim Reality in Austrian Town," *The Chicago Tribune*, June 10, 2007.

379   *They constructed two main*: Rudolf Haunschmied, Jan-Ruth Mills, Siegi Witzany-Durda, *St. Georgen-Gusen-Mauthausen. Concentration Camp Mauthausen Reconsidered* (Norderstedt. St. Georgen an der Gusen, Austria: Books on Demand GmbH, 2004), 168.

379   *Tens of thousands of men*: Published in 2004, *St. Georgen-Gusen-Mauthausen* is a comprehensive study of the Mauthausen Concentration Camp system's integration with key armaments installations in the neighboring villages of Gusen and St. Georgen. Rudolf Haunschmied—who as a child in the 1970s played

in one of the underground complexes—and two co-authors went further than existing survivors' memoirs and histories to document the perfidious role that slave labor from the network of roughly sixty sub-camps played in industrial production for the SS. Their research includes interviews with twenty survivors and Austrian civilian witnesses; materials from the private collections of a dozen survivors and academic researchers; and more than 2,300 other primary sources. While Haunschmied did not interview any of the Offens among the camp survivors, he combines partial accounts from several American liberators, including the narratives of men who served in units connected to those of three servicemen whom Sam and Nathan befriended in later years.

379 *"Assignments to production . . ."*: Haunschmied, Mills, Witzany-Durda, ibid., 174.

379 *Called "Bergkristall . . ."*: Ibid., 37, 135–137.

379 *Prisoners had to smash*: Ibid., 87, 95, Martin Lax, Michael B. Lax, *Caraseu: A Holocaust Remembrance* (Cleveland: The Pilgrim Press, 1996), 87.

379 *By the fall of 1944*: Haunschmied, Mills, Witzany-Durda, ibid., 165.

380 *Entering the main square*: Evelyn Le Chêne. *Mauthausen: History of a Death Camp* (Bath, U.K.: Chivers Press, 1971), 61.

382 *"I'm trying to remember if . . ."*: Bernard Offen, interview by Sid Bolkosky, December 26, 1981, video recording, VVA, Mardigan Library, the University of Michigan-Dearborn, http://holocaust.umd.umich.edu/interview.php?D=offen&section=14.

383 *The complex supplied paving*: Haunschmied, Mills, Witzany-Durda, ibid., 177.

383 *Heinrich Himmler had*: Le Chêne, ibid., 22.

383 *"All day long, run down . . ."*: Sam Offen, ibid., 52.

383 *The writer Evelyn Le Chêne,*: Published in 1971, Le Chêne's *Mauthausen: The History of a Death Camp*, culminated twelve years of research including gathering extensive accounts of the major sub-camps at Gusen, Ebensee, and Melk; details of medical experimentation, euthanasia, and means of torture; the camp system administration; statistics on inmates and deaths; and liberation. The author's husband, Pierre Le Chêne, an Englishman who served in the French Resistance, was captured late in 1942 and spent ten months in solitary confinement in the Fresnes prison before being transferred to Mauthausen. He survived starvation and working in the infamous Wiener Graben quarry. Evelyn Le Chêne concluded that a range of 120,000 to 200,000 deaths in the Mauthausen-Gusen system "may be a fairly accurate assessment," above other estimates of 95,000-plus noted by researchers at the US Holocaust Memorial Museum, and others.

384 *Already so fragile,*: Sam Offen, ibid., 53.

384 *"He looked at you . . ."*: Nathan Offen. *To Life!* (Bloomington, Indiana: Xlibris. 2009), 40.

385 *One of the Quakers*: Sam Offen, ibid., 54.

385 *"If you are tortured . . ."*: Nathan Offen, ibid., 41.

387 *An expert rifle marksman,*: Donald L. Montgomery, interview by Donna Sklar, October 13, 1993, video recording, Holocaust Memorial Center Zekelman Family Campus Library Archive, Farmington Hills, Michigan.

387 *As they edged closer*: Hal Steward, "Hungarian Force Surrenders," *Thunderbolts* (Washington, D.C.: 11th Armored Division Association, 1948), 120. This official division history includes detailed daily unit reports. On April 23, 1945, a column of Combat Command B came across some 16,000 "starved slave workers from Flossenbürg and Buchenwald near Cham." Division artillery including Montgomery's unit were in that area supporting CCB. The history further notes a nearby road "between Stamsried and Posing and the adjacent fields, were dug with shallow, improvised graves containing the bodies of at least 100 shot down in cold blood."

387 *"Literally hundreds of them . . ."*: Montgomery, ibid.

387 *While articles had begun*: Hirsh, ibid., 261.

388 *By May 5, they were perhaps*: US Army Morning Report, Battery B, 575th Anti Aircraft Artillery Battalion, May 5, 1945.

388 *A heavy-set crane operator*: Richard LaLone, "Liberator—Mauthausen," interview by Hans R. Weinmann, October 27, 1993, audiotape, Holocaust Memorial Center Zekelman Family Campus Library Archive, Farmington Hills, Michigan.

388 *Considered unfit to work*: "Gassings at KZ Gusen Camps," Gusen Memorial Committee, accessed April 17, 2017, http://www.gusen.org, "Cruelties at KZ Gusen Camps," Ibid.

389 *Quarry laborers were rarely*: Le Chêne, ibid., 68.

389 *Some prisoners decided their*: Le Chêne, ibid., 154.

389 *Early that spring, fighter jet*: Haunschmied, Mills, Witzany-Durda, ibid., 105, 150–155, 168–177.

390 *If the Reich was*: Ibid., 219–220.

390 *Allied commanders were warned*: Ibid., 207–208, 219–220.

392 *They had pushed on*: Steward, "Infantry Welcomed by Populace," ibid., 124.

392 *Louis Haefliger, a Zurich bank*: Le Chêne, ibid., 156, Haunschmied, Mills, Witzany-Durda, ibid., 219–221.

393 *Many provisions never reached*: Le Chêne, ibid., 158.

393 *Reiner, who like Haefliger*: Gusen Memorial Committee, "Louis Haefliger," accessed June, 2013, http://www.gusen.org/life-and-death-in-the-kz-gusen-camps/outstanding-personalities/al-kosiek-lous-haefliger/. *See also* Le Chene, ibid., 158–159, Christian Bernadac, *The 186 Steps*, trans. S. and L. Van Vliet White (Geneva: Ferni Publishing House, 1978), excerpted in "Gusen sub-camps of Mauthausen," Scrapbookpages.com, accessed June,

2013, http://www.scrapbookpages.com/Mauthausen/KZMauthausen/Subcamps/Guseno1.html

393 *The thirty-nine-year-old commandant*: Le Chêne, ibid., 34, *See also* KZ Gusen Memorial Committee, http://www.gusen.org.

393 *"All of a sudden in . . ."*: Le Chêne, ibid., 159.

393 *The plant manager*: Haunschmied, Mills, Witzany-Durda, ibid., 220.

393 *Many claims were*: Ibid., 222.

394 *"We spent a lot . . ."*: Ibid., 221–222.

394 *Staff Sgt. Albert Kosiek*: Albert J. Kosiek, "Liberation of Mauthausen (and KZ Gusen I, II & III)," *Thunderbolt*, 11th Armored Division Association, Vol. 8, No. 7, May/June 1955, accessed from Gusen Memorial Committee, June 4, 2013, http://www.gusen.org/kosiek1x.htm. The author's abbreviated account of the liberation of the Gusen camps and Mauthausen on May 5, 1945 draws primarily from Kosiek's narrative, which is also on the 11th Armored Division Assn.'s website, from Haunschmied and other Mauthausen researchers, along with select details from other liberators' narratives. Hirsh's *The Liberators* offers an exhaustive account chronicling the experiences and impressions of several Americans whose units arrived later that day and shortly thereafter.

394 *A machine gunner with*: Martha Gammer, email to author, August 16, 2013. *See also* Kosiek, ibid. Gammer was president and a founding member along with Haunschmied of the Gusen Memorial Committee, a research center and archive for the Gusen concentration camps. The "machine gunner" she identified as Thomas Nicolla of Loudonville, NY, whom the author interviewed June 6 and July 7, 2013.

395 *He recalled in his memoir*: Nathan Offen, ibid., 44.

396 *In a macabre juxtaposition*: Alexander Gotz, MD., "Recollections of Mauthausen, May 1945," The 11th Armored Division Legacy Group, accessed August 9, 2013, http://www.11tharmoreddivision.com/history/recollections_of_mauthausen.htm. Gotz was a captain in a medical detachment of the 41st Armored Cavalry Reconnaissance Squadron, Mechanized.

396 *Freed prisoners ravaged*: Kosiek, ibid.

397 *Some who had sensed the*: Haunschmied, Mills, Witzany-Durda, ibid., 224.

397 *Mobs of inmates dragged*: Bernadac, ibid., excerpted in "The Liberation of Mauthausen, May 5, 1945," Scrapbookpages.com, May 7, 2010, accessed August, 2013, http://furtherglory.wordpress.com/tag/albert-j-kosiek/.

398 *Soon after Kosiek's platoon*: Haunschmied, Mills, Witzany-Durda, ibid., 227.

398 *The parish priest remarked*: Ibid., 224.

398 *"Many died from sheer . . ."*: Le Chêne, ibid., 171.

398 *Typhus raged at least*: Ibid., 171.

398 *The first thing LaLone observed*: LaLone, ibid.

399 *Even when the locals*: Sam Offen, ibid., 57.

399 *One soldier grabbed*: Hundley, ibid.

399 *Their task was massive*: Unit History 131st Evacuation Hospital, MDEH-131–0.1, US Army, April 12-June 27 1945, 81–83. In author's possession.

399 *Two nights later*: Ibid., 82–85, Haunschmied, Mills, Witzany-Durda, ibid., 238–240. *See also* Unit History 130th Evacuation Hospital, MDEH-130–0.1 20301, US Army, 1–2, May 31, 1945. In author's possession.

400 *He wrote a note*: Montgomery, ibid.

400 *Interrogated on his deathbed*: "The Confession of Franz Ziereis, Commandant of the Mauthausen Concentration Camp," Scrapbookpages. com, last updated August 10, 2012, accessed August, 2013, http://www. scrapbookpages.com/Mauthausen/KZMauthausen/ZiereisDeath.html.

400 *"I was drafted . . ."*: Montgomery, ibid.

401 *"I can't do much . . ."*: Ibid.

Chapter 21: American Fishing

404 *Known as the Bricha*: Rochelle Caviness, Review of *The Brigade* by Howard Blum, The Jewish Eye website, November 10, 2003, accessed January 17, 2013, http://www.thejewisheye.com/hblum.html.

405 *They met Polish veterans*: Kennedy Hickman, "World War II: Battle of Monte Cassino," About.com Military History, accessed January 16, 2013, http://militaryhistory.about.com/od/WWIIEurope/p/World-War-Ii-Battle-Of-Monte-Cassino.htm.

405 *"We began to feel . . ."*: Nathan Offen, ibid., 47.

405 *He finally caught up*: Over the years the three Offens offered different stories of their reunion in Italy, which is not surprising given their reconstructed memories. In his first oral history interview in 1981, Bernard said he found his brothers in a synagogue in Bari—just down the coast from Barletta—on Yom Kippur, September 17, 1945. Sam recalled that they were walking on the streets in Bari late in July, while Nathan insisted they were actually in Barletta when Bernard found them on a street corner that August. It is likely that some of conflicting details are also a result of the Offens' reunion some weeks later with a cousin, Ignac Traubman, who had joined the Polish Army before occupation—the only close relative they found after the war. Sam and Nathan recalled finding their cousin in Bari early in the fall of 1945, and Nathan remained adamant through 2014 that his brothers had confused that reunion with their own. The author's account attempts to composite and reconcile the three versions, relying primarily on Nathan's with excerpts from Sam's memoir.

406 *Years later, he remembered*: Sam Offen, ibid., 67.

406 *It was finally sinking . . .*": Ibid., 68.

406 *Santa Maria di Bagni*: "Santa Maria di Bagni," United States Holocaust Memorial Museum, accessed January 17, 2013, http://www.ushmm.org/exhibition/displaced-persons/camp7b.htm.

409 *"Of course, we did not . . ."*: Sam Offen, ibid., 68.

410 *Food rationing and restrictions*: Lynne Olson, *Citizens of London* (New York: Random House, 2010), 227–228.

410 *During winter months*: Nathan Offen, ibid., 56.

414 *Sam, for one*: Sam Offen, ibid., 79.

415 *While sending his regards*: Ibid., 82.

415 *They stopped in*: "Sanders," Encyclopedia of Detroit, Detroit Historical Society, accessed February 10, 2013, http://detroithistorical.org/learn/encyclopedia-of-detroit/sanders.

415 *"When the first enormous . . ."*: Sam Offen, ibid., 81.

417 *When Cory changed his plea*: Dennis C. Mahoney, Letter to The Honorable Justice John C. Cratsley, Norfolk Superior Court. Re: Commonwealth v. Cory Scanlon. April 10, 2006. Letter in author's possession.

418 *Nothing could be undone*: Christine Wallgren, "Facing a Painful Past," *The Boston Globe*, South Edition. April 26, 2007.

419 *"Reconciliation between us . . ."*: Ibid.

419 *"We were young, we . . ."*: Kristen Walsh, "This Return Difficult For Silver Lake Graduate," *The Enterprise* (Brockton, MA), May 3, 2007.

420 *Detroit's fur industry*: Josie Schneider, "A Passion for Pelts," *Hour Detroit*, September 2014, accessed February 15, 2013, http://www.hourdetroit.com/Hour-Detroit/September-2014/A-Passion-for-Pelts/#.VCHG4yi3DRA.

422 *As a newspaper declared*: "The 'good life' beckons a new citizen," *The Detroit News*, undated article. Courtesy of Gail Offen.

424 *"'You know,' he remarked . . ."*: "Offen Brothers Celebrate Second Reunion in 10 Years," *The Detroit News*, undated article, 1954. Courtesy of Gail Offen.

424 *"The Nazis tried their best . . ."*: "The Nazis Failed to Kill Sam, But Now," *The Detroit News*, March 25, 1959.

Chapter 22: Tattoo in the Mirror

426 *Tickling Sam's fancy,*: Sam Offen, ibid., 88.

426 *A day after the crash*: "Ex-Nazi Prisoner Helps Save Driver from Jail," *The Detroit News*, undated article, 1959. Courtesy of Gail Offen.

427 *In December of 1964*: Associated Press, *Detroit Free Press* archives, December 1, 1964.

429 *Bernard heeded warnings*: John W. Gofman, Foreword to the 1979 printing, *Poisoned Power* (Emmaus, Pa.: Rodale Press, 1979).

430 *Early in 2011 he had*: Rich Harbert, "Last Trail: Friends, Family Mourn

Loss of Hiker Frank Madeiros," *Old Colony Memorial* (Plymouth, MA), December 17, 2011.

430   *About three weeks before*: Ibid.

432   *She asked, "How do I . . ."*: Denise Brack, Victim's impact statement, Norfolk County Probation Department, May, 2004. In author's possession.

433   *Soon I'll hear old winter's song*: "Autumn Leaves," Giorgio Canali, Francesco Magnelli, Gianni Maroccolo, Massimo Zamboni, Giovanni Lindo Ferretti. Lyrics © Universal Music Publishing Group. Lyrics Licensed & Provided by LyricFind. The recorded version alluded to was sung by Eva Cassidy on *Live at Blues Alley*, 1997.

433   *Die wellen schlagen zu*: Nathan Offen, ibid., 105.

438   *"It seemed important to confront . . ."*: Sam Offen, ibid., 89.

439   *To Sam, it looked almost*: Ibid., 93.

439   *"The streets were full . . ."*: Bernard Offen, *The Work*, directed and produced by Bernard Offen, 1983. In his first documentary film, Offen described his 1981 return to Poland and his healing process.

440   *The world, Höss seemed to*: "Frankfurt Trial," United States Holocaust Memorial Museum, accessed May 5, 2014, http://www.ushmm.org/information/exhibitions/online-features/collections-highlights/auschwitz-ssalbum/frankfurt-trial.

441   *"I'm looking at each . . ."*: Bernard Offen, ibid.

Chapter 23: Reclaiming the Past

444   *The woman's husband, Ignac Szadowic*: Janet DeStefano, "A Journey of the Heart: Couple Finds WWII Saviors," *The Record* (Bergen, NJ), October 4, 1989.

444   *Some weeks later, Janina wrote*: Ibid.

445   *It is likely that*: To verify the movements of Anthony N. Ferrara's troop, the author hired Golden Arrow Military Research of Columbia, Missouri to check surviving military records at the National Archives & Records Administration. A partial narrative of the unit's movements and actions may be constructed by compiling Army company morning reports, which includes details of reassignments, and during days of conflict, counts of casualties taken and given, prisoners taken, and other details. Morning reports for A Troop show that in the final weeks of the war, Ferrara's unit saw heavy action in Bavaria northeast of Munich before heading into Austria, including apparently liberating a POW camp holding 2,000 British soldiers and 175 Americans on April 25, 1945. However, similar reports are missing between April 26 and May 4, and then again from May 6–9, and the location in the May 5 notation is illegible. An official history of the 11th Armored Division, *Thunderbolts*, also provides a detailed

chronology of many units' movements, including A Troop of the 41st Cavalry Reconnaissance Squadron, Mechanized. Those are integrated into the abridged accounts of both Ferrara's company and those of two veterans whom Sam Offen befriended, Donald R. Montgomery, and Richard H. LaLone. Golden Arrow also located Montgomery and LaLone's military records and some of their units' movements during April–May of 1945, which appear in Chapter 20. Most of the documents—morning reports, rosters, and personnel files—are held at the NARA archives in St Louis. Records of payment vouchers and other Veterans Administration documents also helped confirm aspects of each man's service.

446 *One man from Ferrara's*: Alice Marie Jacobson, interview with author, August 19. 2013.

447 *"I am one of the very . . ."*: Sam Offen, videotaped presentation with Donald Montgomery at Holocaust Memorial Center, West Bloomfield, Michigan, October 5, 1993. Resides at Holocaust Memorial Center, Zekelman Family Campus Library, Farmington Hills, Michigan.

447 *"You are all going to . . ."*: Ibid.

448 *When the museum was relocated*: Jeffrey Zaslow, "Should a Museum Look as Disturbing as What it Portrays?" *The Wall Street Journal*, October 8, 2003.

452 *Their full-page account*: Introduction, *11th Armored Division, Thunderbolt* (New York: Turner Publishing, 1988).

453 *"Depending on how antisemitic . . ."*: Bernard Offen, *Process B-7815*, directed and produced by Bernard Offen, 1999.

453 *He met a French Jew*: Zillah Bahar, "Petaluma Filmmaker Treads History in Walks for Peace," *The Northern California Jewish Bulletin*, October 23, 1992.

453 *A Buddhist priest*: "November 2014 Bearing Witness Retreat at Auschwitz/ Birkenau," Zen Peacemakers.org, accessed May 10, 2014, http:// zenpeacemakers.org/events/bearing-witness-retreat-at-auschwitzbirkenau/. *See also* "Buddhism, Reconciliation And Auschwitz: An Interview With Zen Master Bernie Glassman," *The Huffington Post*, July 16, 2010.

454 *"We seem to have made . . ."*: Bernard Offen, *My Hometown Concentration Camp*, ibid., 111–112.

454 *"I still can't understand . . ."*: Bernard Offen, *My Hometown Concentration Camp*, produced and directed by Bernard Offen, 1997.

455 *"It's been a little hard . . ."*: Ibid.

458 *Perpetrators remained almost everywhere*: Sidney M. Bolkosky, *Searching for Meaning in the Holocaust* (Westport, Conn.: Greenwood Press, 2002), 111–112. *See* Bolkosky's indictment of the scale and primacy of bureaucratization across Europe.

459 *The remote former asylum*: Le Chêne, ibid., 105.

460 *And you stand around and stare*: Gebirtig, ibid.

461 *You were so weak*: Herwig Strobl, "Aufmachen" liner notes, *Herwig Strobl, Braccioline d'amore solo. Music in the Izaak Synagogue Cracow. Bayit Chadash,* 1996.

461 *He tended geraniums*: Tony Manolatos, Edward L. Cardenas, "SS Guard's Capture Ends Secret Life in Metro Suburb," *The Detroit News,* July 9, 2003.

462 *In 1944, when he was*: Ibid.

462 *By 2009, a Spanish judge*: Robin Jennings, "Spain Indicts Michigan Man Accused as ex-Nazi," MLive Media Group, September 17, 2009, accessed July 23, 2013, http://www.mlive.com/news/detroit/index.ssf/2009/09/spain_indicts_michigan_man_acc.html.

462 *"Nobody was forced to . . ."*: Manolatos, Cardenas, ibid.

462 *While some of the ex-Nazi's*: Charlie LeDuff, "Ex-Death Camp Guard Avoids Deportation," *The Detroit News,* Sept. 3, 2009.

462 *"How can they claim . . ."*: Ibid.

463 *The drive inspired*: Dita Smith, "A Measure of Hope: The Whitwell, Tenn., Holocaust Project Has Spread Far Beyond the Classroom," *The Washington Post,* April 7, 2001.

463 *One student came up*: Peter W. Schroeder, Dagmar Schroeder-Hildebrand, *Six Million Paper Clips: The Making of A Children's Holocaust Memorial* (Minneapolis: Kar-Ben Publishing, 2004).

464 *Nestled in a valley*: Leslie Milk. "Can You Feel The Souls?" *Washington Magazine,* October 1, 2003, http://www.washingtonian.com/articles/people/can-you-feel-the-souls/.

464 *Continuing on Wednesday*: Dita Smith, ibid.

464 *Reading some letters with*: Carolyn Park, "School's Holocaust Project Reaches Far," *Chattanooga Times Free Press,* December 15, 2000.

464 *"We are the last generation . . ."*: Milk, ibid.

464 *They approached a German*: Schroeder, Schroeder-Hildebrand, ibid.

465 *Another one thousand six hundred*: Theresa Ast, "Children's Holocaust Memorial: Six Million Paper Clips," The Reinhardt History Blog, September 16, 2014, accessed November, 2014, http://blogs.reinhardt.edu/history/childrens-holocaust-memorial-six-million-paper-clips/.

465 *Sam asked someone*: Schroeder, Schroeder-Hildebrand, ibid.

Chapter 24: Hope for a Broader Day

473 *Built to initially imprison*: "Dachau," Holocaust Encyclopedia, United States Holocaust Memorial Museum, accessed August 22, 2009, http://www.ushmm.org/wlc/en/article.php?ModuleId=10005214.

480 *"It's been very gratifying . . ."*: Sidney M. Bolkosky, interview by Marlise Beaudoen, videotape, The Voice/Vision Archive, September 20, 2005, http://youtu.be/ekZgkeby2Co.

480 *Yet their authenticity*: Bolkosky, *Searching for Meaning in the Holocaust*, ibid., 103.

481 *Their torrents defied*: Elie Wiesel, "A Plea for Survivors," *A Jew Today*, trans. Marion Wiesel (New York: Random House 1978), 198–200. For a full discussion on the limits and forms of recounting, *see also* Henry Greenspan, *On Listening to Holocaust Survivors Beyond Testimony* (St. Paul, Minn.: Paragon House, 2010). Greenspan, a longtime colleague and friend of Bolkosky, interviewed many of the same survivors.

481 *Simultaneous infusions of "external descriptions . . ."*: Bolkosky, "And in the Distance You Hear Music, A Band Playing: Reflections on Chaos and Order in Literature and Testimony," eds. R. Clifton Spargo, Robert Ehrenreich, *After Representation? The Holocaust in Literature and Culture*, (Brunswick, N.J.: Rutgers University Press, 2010). Copy of the article manuscript courtesy of Jamie Wraight, Voice/Vision Survivor Holocaust Oral History Project, University of Michigan-Dearborn.

481 *"The sheer weight . . ."*: Bolkosky, ibid.

481 *Others such as Abe,*: Bolkosky. *Searching for Meaning in the Holocaust*, ibid., 67.

481 *Levi thought that*: Primo Levi, *The Drowned and The Saved* (New York: First Vintage International, 1989), 82–83.

481 *After forty years living*: Bolkosky, ibid., 74.

482 *"The question is that a Jew . . ."*: Ibid., 80–81.

482 *The man believed this*: Christopher Leggett, "The Ford Pinto Case: The Valuation of Life as it Applies to the Negligence-Efficiency Argument," Law & Valuation, Wake Forest University, 1999, accessed August 15, 2014, http://users.wfu.edu/palmitar/Law&Valuation/Papers/1999/Leggett-pinto.html.

483 *"Okay, I think we'll begin . . ."*: Bernard, Nathan, and Samuel Offen, interview by Sidney M. Bolkosky, audiotape, September 3, 1987. VVA. Mardigian Library, the University of Michigan-Dearborn, Dearborn, Mich.

487 *In the text,*: Eric Pagremanski. Hedy Pagremanski, *The Beauty of Our Special Children* (Long Beach, NY: Harvey Weisenberg, 2008), 41.

491 *When a twelve-year-old girl*: Gail Offen, eulogy for her father, Sam Offen, 2012. Courtesy of Gail Offen.

PART V: THE COST

Chapter 25: Wheels Off

505 *They had been drinking*: Krista Perry, "Bar May Lose License After Fatal Crash," *The Milford* (MA) *Daily News*, December 3, 2009. *See also* Joyce Kelly, "Mother of Driver in Fatal Crash Speaks Out," *The Milford Daily News*, June 13, 2009, Gregory Smith, "Board Denies License Request for Restaurant," *The Providence Journal*, May 31, 2012.

Chapter 26: Warped

515   *One sergeant concluded*: Sgt. Michael J. Figueiredo, Show Cause Hearing transcript, Providence Board of Licenses, Tomasso Bar & Grill, Inc., Providence, Rhode Island, February 17, 2002. Each of the hearing transcripts and police reports cited are in the author's possession.

515   *Club employees yelled*: Show Cause Hearing transcript, Providence Board of Licenses, Tomasso Bar & Grill, Inc., December 8, 2006.

516   *After his first detail there*: William O'Donnell, report to License Bureau, Providence Police Department, December 11, 2004.

516   *Veterans like Detective Sergeant*: John St. Lawrence, Show Cause Hearing transcript, Providence Board of Licenses, Tomasso Bar & Grill, Inc., December 2, 2005.

516   *One man claimed he was*: Dennis Fernandes vs. Tomasso Bar & Grill, C.A. No. PC02-4785, Providence Superior Court.|

516   *Police arrested four*: Providence Board of Licenses, letter to Alexander Tomasso, Show Case Hearing continuance, May 23, 2007.

516   *It was Cape Verdean*: Ibid., *See also The Providence Journal*, February 26, 2007.

516   *Tomasso told the board*: Show Cause Hearing transcript, Providence Board of Licenses, Tomasso Bar & Grill, Inc., January 31, 2008.

517   *I came across our*: John Shaughnessy et al vs. Tomasso Bar & Grill, C.A. No. 04-6821, Providence Superior Court.

520   *It was pretty much*: Gregory Smith, *The Providence Journal*, April 11, 2012.

521   *"Mike doesn't get to see . . ."*: Michael McKinney, "Learning the Lessons From Fatal Night Out," *The Providence Journal*, July 26, 2012.

521   *On one occasion, he told*: Ed Baker, "WHS Seniors Get a Sobering Message," Wicked Local Weymouth, GateHouse News Service, May 15, 2008.

522   *"I killed two of my . . ."*: Baker, ibid.

524   *"Don't let 'em say you ain't beautiful . . ."*: Eminem. "Beautiful," Marshall Mathers, Jeffrey Bass, Luis Resto, Don Black, Andy Hill. *Relapse*. 2009. © Copyright: Eight Mile Style LLC, Sony/ATV Harmony.

524   *"Inside outside, leave me alone . . ."*: The Who. "5:15," Pete Townsend. *Quadrophenia*. 1972. Published by Lyrics © Universal Music Publishing Group, ABKCO Music, Inc., Pete Townsend Catalog, Fabulous Music Ltd., Spirit Music Group.

525   *"I'm flowing under bridges . . ."*: Pete Townsend, "Drowned," ibid. Published by Lyrics © Universal Music Publishing Group, ABKCO Music, Inc., Pete Townsend Catalog, Fabulous Music Ltd., Spirit Music Group.

525   *"Please take my advice . . ."*: Neil Young, "Tired Eyes," *Tonight's the Night*. 1975. Silver Fiddle Music. © Copyright 2017 Hal Leonard.

PART VI: UNSPEAKABLE GIFTS

Chapter 27: Say His Name

532   *"You are still the best...."*: Sandra Sullivan, Guest Book, Christopher J. Sullivan, Legacy.com. January 18, 2009.

Chapter 28: Their Gifts

556   *Tutu wrote, "What we are . . ."*: Desmond Tutu, *No Future Without Forgiveness* (New York: Doubleday, 1999), 85.

558   *She will first contact*: Teresa Lally, *Table Tipping for Beginners* (Woodbury, Minn.: Llewellyn Publications, 2012), 53.

561   *She felt his presence*: Franci Richardson, "Nightclub Nightmare: Bouncers Initially Blocked Exit, Patrons Say Confusion Delayed Escape," *Boston Herald*, February 28, 2003.

562   *"Because these people are not . . ."*: Dave Kane, *41 Signs of Hope* (Woonsocket, R.I.: New River Press, 2006), 106.

562   *The family accepted "synchronicities . . ."*: Christian O'Neill, "Nicky, the Boy Who Would Not Grow Up," "The Song of Nick" (master's thesis, Emerson College, 2004). Courtesy of Christian O'Neill.

565   *Attempting, as Buddhist monks*: Thich Nhat Hanh, *One Buddha Is Not Enough* (Berkeley, Calif.: Parallax Press, 2010), 87.

567   *"I know I can't take . . ."*: Cory Scanlon, Hearing transcript, Cory Scanlon vs. Registrar of Motor Vehicles, Commonwealth of Massachusetts Division of Insurance, Board of Appeal, July 7, 2015.

567   *"I am trying my hardest . . ."*: Scanlon, ibid.

569   *"People knew where we . . ."*: Ibid.

570   *"Former Rhode Island House . . ."*: John Hill, "Court Receiver Appointed in Shark Bar Case," *The Providence Journal*, March 30, 2015.

573   *Life is what happens to you*: John Lennon, "Beautiful Boy," *Double Fantasy*. 1980. Sony/ATV Music Publishing LLC, Universal Music Publishing Group, Downtown Music Publishing. Lyrics licensed and provided by LyricFind.

PERMISSIONS ACKNOWLEDGMENTS

Grateful acknowledgment is made to the following for permission to reprint previously published material:

ALFRED MUSIC. "Keep On Keeping On." Words and music by Curtis Mayfield, copyright © 1971 (renewed) by Warner-Tamerlane Publishing Corp. All rights reserved. Used by permission of Alfred Music.

BEACON PRESS. An excerpt from *Man's Search for Meaning* by Viktor E. Frankl, copyright © 1959, 1962, 1984, 1992 by Viktor E. Frankl. Reprinted by permission of Beacon Press, Boston.

"BEAUTIFUL." Words and music by Andy Hill, Don Black, Jeffrey Bass, Luis Resto and Marshall Mathers. Copyright © 2009 Sony/ATV Music Publishing (UK) Limited, Songs Of Universal, Inc., Shroom Shady Music, Jeff Bass Music LLC, 8 Mile Style and Resto World Music. All rights on behalf of Sony/ATV Music Publishing (UK) Limited administered by Sony/ATV Music Publishing LLC, 424 Church Street, Suite 1200, Nashville, TN 37219. All rights on behalf of Shroom Shady Music administered by Songs Of Universal, Inc. All rights on behalf of 8 Mile Style and Resto World Music administered by Kobalt Songs Music Publishing International. Copyright secured. All rights reserved. Reprinted by permission of Hal Leonard LLC.

"BOX OF RAIN." Words by Robert Hunter, music by Phil Lesh, copyright © 1970 Ice Nine Publishing Co., Inc. Copyright renewed. All rights administered by Universal Music Corp. All rights reserved. Used by permission. Reprinted by permission of Hal Leonard LLC 2.

ABOUT THE AUTHOR

KEN BRACK is a narrative nonfiction author moved by how people grow through catastrophic ordeals. His first book, *Closer By The Mile*, is the story of the country's leading single-event athletic fundraiser, the Pan-Mass Challenge bike-a-thon for cancer research. A native of Natick, Massachusetts, he blogs for *Psychology Today's* website and other publications, and in 2008 co-founded a nonprofit bereavement center, Hope Floats Healing and Wellness Center, in Kingston, Massachusetts. A longtime journalist in New England, Brack has a M.Ed. from Northeastern University and taught high school English in Boston.

Proceeds from this book will support Hope Floats' outreach to grieving families.

WWW.HOPEFLOATSWELLNESS.ORG